MW00779138

Asia and Postwar Japan

HARVARD EAST ASIAN MONOGRAPHS 451

Asia and Postwar Japan

Deimperialization, Civic Activism,
and National Identity

Simon Avenell

Published by the Harvard University Asia Center
Distributed by Harvard University Press
Cambridge (Massachusetts) and London 2022

© 2022 by The President and Fellows of Harvard College
Printed in the United States of America

The Harvard University Asia Center publishes a monograph series and, in coordination with the Fairbank Center for Chinese Studies, the Korea Institute, the Reischauer Institute of Japanese Studies, and other facilities and institutes, administers research projects designed to further scholarly understanding of China, Japan, Korea, Vietnam, and other Asian countries. The Center also sponsors projects addressing multidisciplinary, transnational, and regional issues in Asia.

Cataloging-in-Publication Data is on file at the Library of Congress.

ISBN 9780674270978 (cloth)

Index by the author

♾ Printed on acid-free paper

Last figure below indicates year of this printing
31 30 29 28 27 26 25 24 23 22

Contents

    in a Time of Change   298
    The Asia Boom in Post-Bubble Japan: Building an East
    Asian Community   302
    The Return of the Past: Movements for Compensation
    and Reconciliation   309
    The New Asianism: Resistance, Revival, or a New Common House?   316
        Hard-Line Asianists and Civilizational Warriors   317
        Moderate Instrumentalists and Fusionists   326
        Progressive Visionaries   334
    Conclusion   354

    Conclusion: Japan's Postwar Odyssey with Asia   357
    Rethinking Postwar Japan in, through, and with Asia   361
    Mapping Asia onto Postwar Japan   366
        Asia and Responsibility   368
        Asia and Civil Society   370
        Asia and National Identity   374

    Bibliography   379

    Index   411

Figures

Acknowledgments

A great many individuals and institutions helped me complete this book. I am extremely grateful to the Hakuho Foundation for its generous funding, which enabled me to collect the primary source materials necessary for completion of the book. While I was in Japan, Philip Seaton graciously hosted me at the Tokyo University of Foreign Studies. I thank the staff members at the National Diet Library of Japan, who diligently accessed hundreds of journals, books, and other source materials for me. Similarly, the Fujisawa Municipal Library proved to be a gold mine for material on policies for foreign residents in Kanagawa Prefecture and the role of nongovernmental organizations (NGOs). The project also benefited greatly from materials collected over many years at the Rikkyo Research Center for Cooperative Civil Societies, particularly primary sources for civic movements of the 1970s. In Australia, my work was greatly advanced by the extensive collections held at the National Library of Australia and the Menzies Library at the Australian National University. I thank Miyuki Matthews of the Menzies Library for acquiring a whole range of rare source materials for me. Yonjae Paik and Shuge Wei provided expert help in deciphering the pronunciations of many Korean and Chinese names used in the book.

Numerous people read and provided valuable comments on sections of the manuscript as it evolved, including Tim Amos, Reto Hofmann, Nick Kapur, Tessa Morris-Suzuki, and Naoko Shimazu. I thank you all sincerely for helping me clarify my ideas. I also express my deepest appreciation to Laura Hein and the other reviewer for engaging so rigorously with the manuscript and providing such rich feedback. I am indebted to Bob Graham of the Harvard Asia Center for skillfully shepherding the project from submission through to publication, as well as the center's publication committee for supporting this endeavor. I also sincerely thank Angela Piliouras of Westchester Publishing Services for expertly guiding the production process and Jeanne Ferris for her meticulous and thoughtful copyediting work. Finally, I thank my family for always being there.

Abbreviations

AAR	Association for Aid and Relief in Japan
AEC	Asian Economic Community
AFC	Asian Financial Crisis
AJKK	Ajia Josei Kōryū Shi Kenkyūkai
AMF	Asian Monetary Fund
ARI	Asian Rural Institute
ASEAN	Association of Southeast Asian Nations
ASSK	Ajia ni taisuru Sengo Sekinin o Kangaeru Kai
AWA	Asian Women's Association
AWF	Asian Women's Fund
CCP	Chinese Communist Party
CYR	Caring for Young Refugees
EAC	East Asian Community
FDI	Foreign direct investment
GNP	Gross national product
JANIC	Japan NGO Center for International Cooperation
JATAN	Japan Rainforest Action Network
JCNC	Japan Committee for Negros Campaign
JCP	Japanese Communist Party
JCWO	Japan Christian Women's Organization
JOCS	Japan Overseas Christian Medical Service
JSP	Japan Socialist Party
JVC	Japan Volunteer Center

KCIA	Korean Central Intelligence Agency
KSTI	Kakyō Seinen Tōsō Iinkai
LDP	Liberal Democratic Party
LSTS	landing ship, tanks
MOF	Ministry of Finance
NCK	Nihon Chōsen Kenkyūjo
NGO	Nongovernmental organization
NHK	Nippon Hōsō Kyōkai
NICCO	Nippon International Cooperation for Community Development
NIES	Newly Industrialized Economies
NIRA	National Institute for Research Advancement
ODA	Official development assistance
OISCA	The Organization for Industrial, Spiritual, and Cultural Advancement
PARC	Pacific-Asia Resources Center
PHD	Peace, Health, and Human Development Association
SSAFK	Shinryaku = Sabetsu to Tatakau Ajia Fujin Kaigi
SVA	Shanti Volunteer Association
VA WW— NET JAPAN	Violence Against Women in War—Network Japan
WCNCC	Women's Committee of the National Christian Council in Japan

INTRODUCTION

> If decolonization is mainly active work carried out on the terrain
> of the colonized, then deimperialization, which is no less painful
> and reflexive, is work that must be performed by the colonizer
> first, and then on the colonizer's relation with its former colonies.
>
> —Kuan-Hsing Chen, *Asia as Method: Toward Deimperialization*

The Asia Problem in Postwar Japan

In 1945 the Japanese empire collapsed and along with it the country's
grand ambitions for a New East Asian Order and a Greater East Asia Co-
Prosperity Sphere. Stripped of its territories, all that remained was a
"small Japan," now a dotted ruin of fire-bombed rubble and atomic de-
bris.[1] Compounding the agony, the dissolution of empire heralded a hu-
miliating loss of sovereignty as the victorious Allied powers, led and controlled by the United States of America, systematically "liberated" former
colonies and countries of the defunct Co-Prosperity Sphere and began a
full-scale occupation of the homeland. The defeat could not have been
more absolute or more spiritually devastating. For close to a century the
Japanese had striven to build a nation capable of warding off colonization, defending sovereignty, and—as time progressed—rivaling the great
imperial powers of the world through external conquest. But now all of
this was gone.

The collapse of empire and capitulation to the United States affected
every aspect of Japan's postwar reconstruction, profoundly shaping
how the Japanese would imagine and forge a national identity in the

---

1. The idea of a "small Japan" is Ishibashi Tanzan's. See Wakamiya, *Sengo 70-nen*,
142–51.

postcolonial, Cold War world and, moreover, how they would reengage with the countries of Asia in the wake of a tainted past in the region. While *Amerika* would function as both an aspirational benchmark and lightning rod of dissent for Japanese of all political persuasions, *Ajia* (Asia) occupied a far more ambiguous intellectual space, making it all the more difficult to grasp and highly susceptible to derogatory ideologies and kaleidoscopic idealisms. Historically speaking, such veneration of the West and ambivalence toward Asia was by no means new, but defeat in war brought with it a new layer of complexity. For some Japanese the country's historical involvement in Asia slowly emerged as damning evidence of the fundamental bankruptcy of modernity and humanity in Japan—a realization that, in certain respects, was even more traumatic than the moral weight of so-called war responsibility scrutinized so earnestly in the early postwar era. Indeed, if *Amerika* encapsulated a vision of cataclysmic national destruction followed by postapocalyptic regenesis, then *Ajia* confronted those Japanese who cared to look with the horror of unatoned "original sin" and the weight of an "ethnic responsibility" of historic proportions. This was the heart of an Asia problem that would continue to confound and complicate the spiritual rehabilitation of postwar Japan.

Historians and political scientists have rightly sought to deemphasize the notion of an absolute rupture in Japan in 1945, pointing to the many transwar continuities in institutions, practices, ideas, and personnel.[2] This book too is partly a story of the tyranny of continuity. Yet by any account, defeat in war and the loss of empire also marked a genuinely momentous historical disjuncture. By severing a mode of engagement with Asia some eighty years in the making, defeat laid the roots of a challenging new set of issues for the postwar generation, and particularly for people of a progressive persuasion. Most significant was the conundrum of how to reengage with Asia in the wake of empire and coprosperity. How were Japanese to make amends for the transgressions of earlier generations? How could new solidarities be constructed on the ruins of domination and aggression? Questions of war responsibility

2. See, for example, Gordon, "Society and Politics"; Dower, "Useful War"; Yamanouchi, "Total War and System Integration"; Garon, *State and Labor*; Johnson, *MITI and the Japanese Miracle*.

loomed large here, but the problem went much deeper, connecting to prejudices, insecurities, and mentalities stretching back to the mid-nineteenth century. The relatively soft landing of decolonization facilitated by the Allied Occupation only served to delay genuine engagement with these problems of postcoloniality or, more pertinently, with the problems of postimperiality. In fact, by effectively de-Asianizing Japan, the Occupation exacerbated the problem. As the country was drawn further and further into the embrace of Pax Americana after 1945, these postimperial residues remained, receding for a time only to reemerge around the late 1950s, when Asia as a problem slowly began to force its way back into the consciousness of some leftist intellectuals and activists.

This book traces the history of what I call Japan's Asia problem and the accompanying self-reflexive project for deimperialization among progressives after the demise of the country's empire and the reckless duplicity of co-prosperity.[3] Charting six historical phases of transformation from 1945 through the early decades of the twenty-first century, the book focuses on the mentalities and activism of leftist intellectuals and civic activists, tracing their slow reconnection of "Asia" to empire, their internal and external struggles to overcome deeply engrained biases toward the region, and their sustained efforts to forge productive new solidarities and regional imaginaries in the wake of empire and in the shadow of a bamboo curtain stretching across Cold War Asia.[4]

In the chapters that follow I reveal the critical importance of Asia in Japan's postwar intellectual history, civic activism, and national identity formation—Asia as a symbolic geography, a site of transgression, a space of activism, and ultimately an aporia of identity and the source of a new politics of hope. While much change (and continuity) in Japan's postwar period can be attributed to the embrace of America, I argue that there have been significant transformations in the ways Japanese people think, how they engage in political activity, and how they imagine their national community that are directly attributable to, and indeed inexplicable

3. I define and discuss the concept of deimperialization below.
4. I put "Asia" in quotations here simply to flag the obvious fact that it is a contested and slippery idea. As I show, contestations over the meaning of Asia offer a useful ideational window into the ways Japanese have dealt with (or not dealt with) the legacies of empire.

without, considering the impact of Asia. In the context of ideas, the slow reconceptualization of and reconnection to Asia among progressives profoundly influenced wider understandings of, and debates over, responsibility for empire and war. In the sphere of political activism, Japanese activists' involvement with fellow Asians—especially in transnational grassroots alliances beginning in the 1970s—fundamentally influenced the development of civil society in Japan through processes of grassroots regionalization and grassroots globalization. Moreover, in terms of identity, progressives' growing attention to Asian imaginaries and regional economic entanglements throughout the postwar era deeply informed struggles over how to imagine the nation, which reached a kind of crescendo by the turn of the century. In short, progressives' involvement with Asia as both an idea and a regional geography deeply shaped critical spheres of activity in postwar Japan and, hence, demands attention in any attempt to comprehensively understand the dynamics of this era.

It is worth clarifying up front who I mean by "progressives" because they are at the core of this study and, moreover, because the changing and expanding composition of this group over time tells us much about the way the Asia problem was evolving in postwar Japan and the wider transformations that resulted. In the first two postwar decades so-called progressive intellectuals (*shinpoteki chishikijin*) or progressive men of culture (*shinpoteki bunkajin*) dominated discourse on and attention to Asia. Politically, most supported, were members of, or shared an affinity with the Japan Socialist Party (JSP) and the Japanese Communist Party (JCP). They adopted a pacifist and/or neutralist stance internationally and were wary or critical of American influence over their country. Domestically, they opposed rule by the conservative Liberal Democratic Party (LDP) and advocated strongly for the protection of democracy and maintenance of Japan's war-renouncing postwar constitution. All were sensitive to questions of individual and state responsibility for the war although, critically, Asia and empire remained missing elements of this consciousness for some years. University professors were prominent among progressives, but writers, journalists, and artists also played significant roles. They found their voice in influential leftist and centrist monthlies and weeklies such as *Sekai*, *Shisō no kagaku*, *Ushio*, *Chūō kōron*, and *Shisō*, as well as large-circulation newspapers like the *Asahi shinbun* and *Mainichi shinbun* and books produced by publishers such as Iwanami Shoten.

Into the 1960s and 1970s, the early postwar progressives were joined by new groups such as students, leaders of prefectural governments, antiwar protesters, environmental advocates, women activists, and nongovernmental organizations (NGOs)—all of whose members began to awake to Asia through their programs for social, economic, and political change. These groups shared many of the political values of the earlier progressives—opposing the LDP, supporting international neutralism, and so on. However, their increasing focus on nonelite forms of political activism and growing hostility toward existing leftist parties and organizations made it possible for them to approach Asia in new ways. Indeed, because of their sustained activism over time, whether in state institutions (that is, local governments) or civic movements, these individuals and groups were able to cultivate deep and substantive transnational linkages with activists throughout Asia and minority groups within Japan, paving the way for the infiltration of a regional consciousness into Japanese civil society more broadly.

As the nation's anticipated first responders in terms of empathy, understanding, and remorse—in this case toward Asian victims—such progressives embodied the limits of deimperialization at any given moment and hence, historically speaking, become for us a barometer of how much the Japanese nation had (or had not) come to terms with its Asia problem. In terms of the evolution of national historical consciousness and repentance, the difficulties they faced in deimperializing themselves and reimagining the Japan-Asia nexus through the recent past underscores just how challenging the process would be for Japanese society more generally. After all, if expunging imperial mentalities so challenged and traumatized the most empathetic and remorseful elements in society, then how much more difficult would eliminating those mentalities be for Japanese of a less progressive persuasion?

Rather than a history of denunciation—something that would be all too easy to write from the perspective of our moral universe of the present—this book is above all an inquiry into the historical dynamics of transformation in thought and activism. It is about the capacity of individuals, groups, and organizations to undergo fundamental intellectual change as they react to external circumstances and engage with their own mentalities and predispositions. In this connection, I address a number of specific questions. What were the reasons behind Japanese progressives' slow engagement with earlier empire and war in Asia, what factors stimulated their awakening to such issues around the late 1950s, and what were the subsequent transformative outcomes of this process in progressive thought and activism? Furthermore, how does this history of incorporating ideas and interactions with Asia enrich our understanding of the broader intellectual trajectory of postwar Japan? While exogenous factors such as US clientelism during the Cold War profoundly shaped postwar progressive thought and activism in Japan, I argue that deeply entrenched attitudes toward Asia in progressive circles also hindered and delayed deimperialization. But I also show how the gradual collapse of established intellectual frameworks in the 1950s and 1960s facilitated the emergence of new intellectual trends and civic movements intent on a thorough and genuine investigation of the past and the construction of new and authentic inter-Asian solidarities.

Extant research on the history of thought and activism in postwar Japan has revealed the important ways in which intellectuals dealt with defeat and their sense of complicity and remorse, as well as their efforts to nurture democratic subjectivities in the new Japan under the shadow of the United States.[5] Research on civic activism has shown how ordinary Japanese citizens and students, drawing on such intellectual energies, began to carve out activist spaces from which to contest the political and economic frameworks being erected by a resurgent conservative camp under the so-called 1955 System.[6] While such histories of ideas and activism in postwar Japan have certainly been very sensitive to the problems of Asia and the historical legacies of empire and war in the region, to date we have almost no studies that systematically trace the development of postwar intellectual and activist history in Japan through the lens of Asia and deimperialization.[7] We might say that although these factors have been implicit (and occasionally explicit) in earlier works, to date they

5. See Barshay, "Postwar Social and Political Thought"; Koschmann, *Revolution and Subjectivity*; Oguma, *Minshu to aikoku*; Bronson, *One Hundred Million Philosophers*; Gayle, *Marxist History*.

6. See, for instance, Sasaki-Uemura, *Organizing the Spontaneous*; Michiba, *Senryō to heiwa*; Oguma, *1968 <jō>* and *1968 <ge>*; Avenell, *Making Japanese Citizens*; Andō Takemasa, *Nyūrefuto undō*; Kapur, *Japan at the Crossroads*.

7. Exceptions include Oguma's works on 1968, Andō's *Nyūrefuto undō*, and, in English, Seraphim, *War Memory*. Yoon Keun-Cha, a second-generation resident Korean

have not been foregrounded in the historical narrative. But it is precisely through such foregrounding of Asia, I suggest, that we can better understand fundamental transformations in ideas, activism, and identity during the postwar era. Moreover, we can also better approach the underlying causes of Japan's ongoing challenges in coming to terms with its past.[8] As Barak Kushner asks, "what Japanese history seems to be missing is empathy; it remains stuck in a self-reflexive mood. Why is Japan only concerned with itself or unable to see itself from the outside?"[9] Part of the answer, I suggest, is to be found in the history I trace herein.

On a broader level, this study attempts to expand our spatial comprehension of Japan's postwar history by positioning it within a wider East Asian narrative. Here I draw on the insights of Nakanishi Shintarō and others who have stressed the necessity of rethinking the internal problem of Japan's postwar period in the context of the global and regional. As Nakanishi asserts, "we need to consciously reconsider the ways Japanese society's 'postwar' as an internal problem has connected to the world-historical postwar. The problems of the Korean Peninsula, relations with East Asia, and the war responsibility problem are the same. The formation of a national image of the postwar disconnected from these is problematic."[10] Indeed, I argue that shifting the analytical focus of postwar Japanese intellectual and activist history to Asia in this way offers some illuminating new perspectives for imagining the postwar period itself.

Certain dates, moments, and events loom large in the extant narrative of the postwar era: August 1945, of course, but also 1951–52 with the signing of the San Francisco Peace Treaty and US-Japan Security Treaty and the end of the Occupation, 1955 as the birth of postwar conservative rule, 1960 as the zenith of popular protest, the 1973 oil shock, the Plaza

---

and political scientist, was among the earliest to explore this slow uptake of the Asia problem among progressives. See Yoon, "Sengo shisō."

8. There is a large literature in English and Japanese on Japan's war memory and its history problem. Recent works in English include Iokibe, Komiya, and Hosoya, *History, Memory, and Politics*; Koyama Hitomi, *On the Persistence*; Saito, *History Problem*; Akiko Takenaka, *Yasukuni Shrine*; Hashimoto, *Long Defeat*.

9. Kushner, *Men to Devils*, 307.

10. Nakano Toshio, et al., "Tettei tōron," 21. All translations from the Japanese are mine unless otherwise indicated.

Accord of 1985, the death of Emperor Hirohito in 1989, the bursting of
the economic bubble in the early 1990s, and the triple disaster of March 11,
2011, to list but a few. Recentering on Asia and deimperialization, however, shifts our attention to other moments such as the Chinese Communist Revolution of 1949, the Korean War of 1950–53, Asian nationalism and the Asian-African Conference in Bandung in the 1950s, the mass
exodus of resident Koreans to North Korea beginning in 1959, the signing of the Japan–South Korea normalization treaty and commencement
of the Vietnam War in 1965, the struggle against Japanese immigration
control in 1969–70, the establishment of diplomatic relations between
Japan and the People's Republic of China in 1972, the Fukuda Doctrine
on Southeast Asia in 1977, and the New Asianism of the 1990s and
beyond—again, to list but a few. While there is certainly a great deal of
crossover, reemplotting the postwar era around these latter hot spots arguably opens up a more regionally embedded and regionally interconnected narrative of postwar Japanese history—in other words, a history
of postwar Japan in Asia and a history of Asia in postwar Japan. Thus,
while at the micro level this book traces the Asia problem in postwar
Japanese thought, activism, and identity, at the macro level, it is also an
attempt to regionalize the extant narrative of postwar Japanese history
that is increasingly evident in recent scholarship on this era.[11]

The Mentality of Abandoning Asia and
the Politics of De-Asianization

We can identify the contours of Japan's Asia problem almost immediately
at war's end. In late 1945 progressive Japanese intellectuals and activists,
at last liberated from wartime oppression, leaped headlong into the project of national repentance, redemption, and spiritual reconstruction. They
began to search for the domestic causes of the war and to identify the
complex loci of responsibility. The American-educated philosopher

11.   For example, see Esselstrom, *That Distant Country*; Hoppens, *China Problem*;
Kushner and Muminov, *Dismantling of Japan's Empire*; Morris-Suzuki, *Borderline Japan* and *Exodus to North Korea*; Seraphim, *War Memory*.

Tsurumi Shunsuke, who had served as a civilian official in Japanese-occupied Indonesia, vented his pent-up fury at Emperor Hirohito—a "rogue," in his telling—in whose name the war had been fought but who had outrageously called on the Japanese people to "endure the unendurable" in his surrender broadcast to the nation of August 15, 1945.[12] In a spirit of remorse, Tsurumi and others like the economist Ōkuma Nobuyuki turned the public spotlight on their own wartime shortcomings as well as the broader problem of intellectuals who had recanted their political beliefs and given in to the wartime regime, often wholeheartedly.[13] Such was the soul-searching of this moment that Japan's leading political thinker, Maruyama Masao, later characterized these progressives (himself included) as a "community of contrition" united in a rare historical process of self-critique and remorse.[14] Even Prince Higashikuni Naruhiko, who was prime minister just after Japan's defeat, told his fellow Japanese that the "first step toward national reconstruction" would be nothing less than a "collective national repentance."[15]

The prime minister's entreaty may have appeared straightforward at the time, but his assigning of a kind of collective national responsibility for the outcome of the war prefigured later controversies over just who was responsible and for what.[16] Moreover, directed as it was at the Japanese people, Higashikuni's entreaty presaged an even thornier question that haunts the Japanese to this day: responsibility to whom? Telling in this respect was the prime minister's speech to the Imperial Diet on September 5, 1945, in which he attributed Japan's defeat to the overwhelming superiority of American military power. No reference was made to Japan's invasion of China or colonial empire in Korea, Taiwan, Southeast Asia, and the Pacific—there was simply no recognition of defeat or sense of Japanese transgressions in these countries and regions.[17] The

12. Tsurumi, Ueno, and Oguma, *Sensō ga nokoshita*, 125.
13. See Tsurumi Shunsuke, *Tsurumi Shunsuke shū*; Ōkuma, *Kokkaaku*.
14. Maruyama, "Kindai Nihon," 254. Also see Barshay, "Postwar Social and Political Thought," 282.
15. Higashikuni made the statement at his first postwar press conference on August 28. See "Gokajō goseimon o tai shi," *Asahi shinbun*, August 30, 1945, morning edition, 1.
16. James Orr makes a similar point. See Orr, *Victim as Hero*, 2.
17. Wakamiya, *Sengo 70-nen*, 152.

empire had simply vanished. The same can be said of progressive intellectuals' expressions of remorse at the time, which like Higashikuni's remarks did not overtly acknowledge what the Japanese people had done to others, especially Asian Others.

Of course, the Japanese were hardly exceptional here: forgetting or otherwise suppressing regrettable misdeeds of the past, whether on an individual or societal level, is the norm and not the exception.[18] In this, the national histories of most if not all nations are complicit, especially those of former imperialist nations. Writing of Britain, Jodi Burkett notes how the "forgetting" of empire is "crucial" to "understanding post-imperial British culture."[19] As Ian Hall observes, in the "immediate postwar years," historical writing on empire in Britain tended to tell a "whiggish story about the building of institutions that culminated in the creation of a Commonwealth of free and equal nations," and not until the 1960s did the "radical argument" that empire was "above all a system for the economic exploitation of the colonies" make "great inroads in the British academic and public spheres."[20] Indeed, for a great many years the British Left found it very difficult to speak about empire, meaning that "they were often outwardly anti-imperial while relying unthinkingly on the 'realities' of British superiority to articulate the world around them and their place within it."[21] Britain's European neighbors struggled similarly. Elizabeth Buettner identifies a time lag "between the formal endings of empires and the process of reckoning with their implications and legacies" among former European imperial powers.[22] She says that we must distinguish between a postcolonial Europe in the "literal, temporal sense" and one that "has examined this past in depth and 'undo[ne] the ideological heritage of colonialism.'"[23] Historians of France, for example, have characterized the two decades after the end of "Algérie française" as an era of "orchestrated *oubli* (forgetting)" as France looked toward a "new

18. As scholars of Germany's memory discourse note, that country's debate has been "relentlessly polarized" and marked by "tortured memory debates." See Moses, *German Intellectuals*, 2 and 32.
19. Burkett, *Constructing Post-Imperial Britain*, 12.
20. Hall, *Dilemmas of Decline*, 147.
21. Burkett, *Constructing Post-Imperial Britain*, 12.
22. Buettner, *Europe after Empire*, 5.
23. Buettner, *Europe after Empire*, 5–6.

future and revisited only selective facets of its recent past."[24] In the intellectual sphere, nowhere was this "postcolonial amnesia" more evident than in the "structuring absence in French intellectual discourse" of postcolonial theory. As Robert Stam and Ella Shohat point out, "only in the twenty-first century" did French intellectuals begin to visibly engage with postcolonial theory, critique, and studies—an ironic situation, given that postcolonial discourse draws so heavily on the French poststructuralist theories of Jacques Derrida, Michel Foucault, Gilles Deleuze, Jean-François Lyotard, and others.[25] Stam and Shohat remind us that, "with the possible exception of Derrida," prominent poststructuralist intellectuals "rarely showed any systemic interest in colonialism."[26] Other scholarship reveals similar processes of forgetting and selective memory in other former imperialist nations like the Netherlands, Portugal, Italy, and Belgium.[27] And finally, although not pertaining to colonial empire but to conduct during World War II, historians such as Alon Confino describe how a "basic moral unwillingness to face up to genocide" in early postwar West Germany "commingled with the urgent need to construct, from the total bankruptcy of German nationhood, a somewhat viable post-'45 collective identity."[28] By situating themselves as "doubly victimized" by the Nazi regime and then by the communists, West Germans were able in the 1950s to construct a narrative of victimization claiming that "Jews and Germans had experienced the same forms of persecution."[29] According to Confino, this discourse produced a "dissonance between Germans who started the Second World War in which they exterminated the Jews, while blaming the war on the Jews," but it also used "this same suffering as a model to construct their own post-1945 sense of victimhood."[30] Such histories remind us that Japan's fitful process of deimperialization is hardly unique and is instead part of a wider postcolonial and postwar global history that is still unfolding.

24. Buettner, *Europe after Empire*, 431.
25. Stam and Shohat, "French Intellectuals," 84 and 86.
26. Stam and Shohat, "French Intellectuals," 86.
27. See Rothermund, *Memories of Post-Imperial Nations*; Nicolaïdis, Sebe, and Maas, *Echoes of Empire*.
28. Confino, "Remembering the Second World War," 53.
29. Confino, "Remembering the Second World War," 54.
30. Confino, "Remembering the Second World War," 54.

As I show in the case of Japan, remorse about and recognition of the interconnection of Asia, empire, and war responsibility took a great many years to emerge and mature among progressives. The legacy of empire and militarism in Asia was not a pressing or obvious task for Japanese progressives at war's end and, in fact, did not really become overtly so until around the 1960s, over a decade after the war. Extirpating empire—so-called deimperialization—would be a far more complex process than expressing war remorse, important though this was. The problem went deeper and was so tightly woven into the intellectual fabric of the progressive mind that the pre-1945 imagination of Asia managed to survive the disjunctive trauma of defeat largely intact. The critical fusion of American overlordship with the swift dissolution of empire helped sustain attitudinal and intellectual continuities across the transwar years in the form of unconscious prejudices and stereotypes about Asia and Japan's relation to the region. In turn, such intellectual predispositions deeply shaped the subsequent trajectory of progressives' attention and responses to the transgressions of Japan's colonial empire and military expansionism. To give an example, in the mid-1960s the historian Hatada Takashi observed that many progressives still felt not the slightest unease with fields of study such as "Korean and Manchurian History" (*Mansen shi*), which owed their existence and legitimacy to the now-defunct Japanese empire.[31] Hatada's point was that even the most genuine and remorseful of progressives could remain blissfully ignorant of the vestiges of imperialism they harbored within themselves. In his famous 1960 speech "Hōhō toshite no Ajia" (Asia as method), the sinologist Takeuchi Yoshimi hinted at the way attitudes with deeper historical lineages were shaping understandings of the war and what Carol Gluck has called the "amnesia of empire."[32] As Takeuchi observed, "the Japanese lack any sense of having been defeated by China. . . . Certain complex reasons have been put forth in order to explain this phenomenon, most pointing to the presence of the American Occupation. Yet we can also see here the *Japanese contempt for China*."[33] In other words, for Takeuchi the facts that "mighty" Japan had lost to "backward" Asia and that it had "surrendered" to China were

31. Hatada, *Nihonjin no Chōsenkan*, 198.
32. Gluck, "Operations of Memory," 51.
33. Takeuchi, "Asia as Method," 162 (emphasis added).

simply unimaginable for most Japanese—including progressives—who could more easily comprehend having lost to "superior" America.[34] So inattention to empire and co-prosperity was about more than circumvented or repressed memories. It also overlay an ongoing dissonance between Japan's self-identity and the country's identification (or lack thereof) with its regional neighbors and the symbolic geography of Asia. This is what Takeuchi meant by Japanese "contempt" for China. Some argue that this "imperialist mentality" or "postcolonial superiority complex" continues to impede Japanese understanding of its neighbors in East Asia to this day.[35] As Dietmar Rothermund explains, "post-imperial nations have been imbued with their cultural superiority for such a long time that they are not amenable to . . . a metanoia" or "change of mind." Although these nations have adjusted their memories to "live with the loss of empire," it has been far more difficult for them "to overcome ingrained prejudices of cultural and racial superiority."[36] "Habits of thought" ranging from "inconsequential practices of daily life" to "formalized systems of philosophical abstraction" continue to "reproduce inherited and often unseen colonial mentalities."[37]

Naoki Sakai has called this phenomenon the "paradox of Japanese nationalism," in which the Japanese "insist on the separation from and even indifference towards people of neighboring countries in East and Southeast Asia," while "they perversely welcome United States' domination and tend to find their own desires within the scenario of Pax Americana."[38] This paradox is not new. There is a great deal of scholarship on Japan's ambivalence vis-à-vis embracing or abandoning Asia from the earliest days of industrialization and nation building. A famous 1885 essay titled "Datsu A ron" (On abandoning Asia) by Fukuzawa Yukichi, a nineteenth-century intellectual and founder of Keio University, is often cited as the earliest expression of this tendency.[39] In contrast to Fukuzawa's call for abandonment, almost simultaneously we see opposing calls for

34. Japan did in fact surrender to China, as one of the signatories of the Potsdam Declaration.
35. Sakai, "From Area Studies," 268.
36. Rothermund, "Memories of Post-imperial Nations," 67.
37. Schwarz, "Actually Existing Postcolonialism," 16.
38. Sakai, "Trans-Pacific Studies," 306–7.
39. Saaler, "Pan-Asianism," 4. See also Fukuzawa, "Datsu A ron."

uniting or joining with Asia. In 1893, for instance, the former samurai
activist and Meiji politician Tarui Tōkichi published a book calling for a
"Great Eastern Federation," while in 1903 the scholar of fine arts
Okakura Kakuzō (aka Tenshin) proclaimed that "Asia is One" in his
English-language book *The Ideals of the East with Special Reference to the
Art of Japan.*[40] Carol Gluck conceptualizes Fukuzawa's perspective as a
"triangulation of the West, Japan, and Asia," in which America and Europe were "superior to Japan" and, "by the same Western standard of civilization, Asia became inferior to Japan"—thus constituting an ideal "orientalist grammar of the idiom of civilization and power."[41] This dissonance
born of self-liminalization was resolved politically through the creation
of a Japanese colonial empire and later brutal military expansion throughout East and Southeast Asia. The resolution involved a replication of
Western imperialism in Asia while proclaiming Japan's leadership in a
purported struggle for Asian liberation.[42] Admittedly, some Japanese Pan
Asianists detested the dénouement of co-prosperity, but even among the
most genuinely pro-Asian advocates like Okakura, there was always a
sense that Japan was somehow the natural leader of Asia, whether due to
its developmental prowess or to its ability to synthesize the very best of
the region—Japan as a kind of final and most pure repository of all things
Asian.[43] Japanese Pan-Asianist thought, as Sebastian Conrad and Prasenjit Duara note, was quite capable of combining seemingly contradictory
impulses as two sides of the one coin: "an ecumenical, non-hierarchical"
vision that was "essentially egalitarian and harmonious," on the one hand,
and a belief in "the special role reserved for Japan in bringing about Asia's
unity," on the other.[44]

40. Tarui, *Daitō gappō ron*; Okakura, *Ideals of the East*, 1.
41. Gluck, "Call for a New Asian," 3.
42. Morris-Suzuki, "Invisible Countries," 7.
43. There is a very rich scholarly literature on Pan Asianism in English and Japanese. Key works on Pan Asianism in Japan include Saaler and Szpilman, *Pan Asianism*,
vols. 1 and 2; Eri Hotta, *Pan-Asianism*; Saaler and Koschmann, *Pan-Asianism*; Aydin,
Politics of Anti-Westernism; Weber, *Embracing "Asia"*; Uemura Kunihiko, *Ajia wa "Ajiateki"*; Duara, "Discourse of Civilization"; Hiraishi, "Kindai Nihon no Ajiashugi";
Takeuchi, *Gendai Nihon shisō*.
44. Conrad and Duara, *Viewing Regionalisms*, 13. See also Duara, "Asia Redux,"
969.

Defeat in war offered no quick solution to the so-called resolution that had been the Greater East Asia Co-Prosperity Sphere other than simply sweeping it under the historical carpet. In fact, the sense of "derived cultural superiority" endured and was reproduced within progressive thought.[45] The sphere certainly "collapsed in form," but since it was a collapse driven from the outside, there was no proactive internal reconstruction of the understanding of Asia, and hence the "old framework" survived almost intact.[46] Japan thus began the postwar period with a challenging intellectual quandary: on the one hand, the empire had been "eradicated as an object of attention," yet on the other hand, "inertia from the prewar" era maintained the old sense of Japanese superiority over backward Asia.[47] For both Marxists and modernists, Asia remained a "trope of backwardness" and "stagnation" in the early postwar years, only contributing to the disappearance of the problem of empire.[48]

A constellation of both exogenous and endogenous factors exacerbated this condition. Most significant geopolitically was the onset of the Cold War and the accompanying incorporation of all noncommunist states in Northeast Asia into the US "hub-and-spokes" security configuration.[49] By erecting a bamboo curtain between Japan and its former colonies and by drawing all of them into the US orbit, this arrangement insulated Japan from sustained interrogation by neighboring countries into its recent indiscretions in the region.[50] It also contributed to the solidification of a nationalist mythology of victimization and monoethnicity within Japan that was dismissive of both the troubled past as well as the existence of diversity within the nation.[51] Against the backdrop of internal struggles in China, Chiang Kai-shek's realist "let bygones be bygones"

45. Iwabuchi, *Recentering Globalization*, 9.
46. Ishida, *Shakai kagaku*, 50.
47. Ishida, *Shakai kagaku*, 50.
48. Nagahara, "Sengo Nihon," 8.
49. Kang, "Nihon no Ajiakan," 99.
50. Seraphim, *War Memory*, 19. Robert Moeller notes a similar dynamic at work in West German memory of the Holocaust, noting that the Americans "did little to encourage postwar Germans . . . to dwell on German crimes against Jews and other civilians as they rushed to draw a clear distinction between a handful of evil Nazis and the overwhelming majority of good Germans who could be rapidly integrated into postwar military alliances" ("Response," 66).
51. On this issue, see Oguma, *Genealogy of Japanese*; Lie, *Zainichi*.

approach to Japan helped dampen the sense of Japanese defeat by, and guilt toward, China. The later peace treaty between Japan and Chiang's Republic of China only reinforced this impression, as the Taiwanese side abandoned any further claims for reparations.[52] Furthermore, the US recasting of the earlier conflict as a Pacific war that started in 1941 with the Japanese attack on Pearl Harbor (rather than with the China Incident of 1937–38 or even the Manchurian Incident of 1931) helped fundamentally reconfigure the "mental map of the war," literally writing Asia out of that history and opening the way for Japan's postwar cult of victimization—a "victim fantasy" inscribed in a "postcolonial rhetoric of the wounded nation," as some have characterized it.[53] As Kang Sang-jung argues, it was almost "inevitable" that "this historical narrative, which highlighted parts of the past while obscuring others in the background, would bring about a 'striking amnesia of the (colonial) empire.'"[54] This internalist rendering of the past was further reinforced by the emergence of a Cold War intellectual configuration for the production and diffusion of knowledge about Asian countries, known as area studies.[55] Radiating outward from universities and think tanks located within the heart of the US knowledge imperium, this configuration contributed, intentionally or not, to the moderation of deimperializing processes, historical amnesia in Japan, and the resurgence of "local ethnic nationalisms" that "served as an integral component of American colonial governmentality."[56] The United States was little interested in any "exploration of colonialism" by Japan or its former colonies, lest this destabilize its construction of a "democratic alliance" against communism in Asia.[57] Moreover, the fact that the "old network of the Japanese Empire survived in the American collective security system" only added to this lack of interest.[58] Geographically and in certain ways structurally, "the Cold War mediated old colonialism and new imperialism"—"imperialism without colonies," as Yonetani

52. Wakamiya, *Sengo 70-nen*, 154–55.

53. Conrad, *Quest for the Lost Nation*, 108; Sakai and Yoo, "Introduction," 9 and 15. On the politics of victimization in postwar Japan, see Orr, *Victim as Hero*.

54. Kang, "Imaginary Geography," 77.

55. See Harootunian, "Postcoloniality's Unconscious."

56. Sakai and Yoo, "Introduction," 5.

57. Chen, *Asia as Method*, 8.

58. Sakai, "From Area Studies," 268; Yonetani, *Ajia/Nihon*, 153–54.

Masafumi terms it—making any genuine exploration of the past all the more unwelcome in Washington.[59] In the case of Japan, in the immediate postwar period it convinced many Japanese, including most progressives, that their predicament was more "colonial" than "postimperial," and by the early 1960s it was underwriting a stunning rehabilitation of the country's modern history.[60]

Deimperialization and the Late 1960s and Early 1970s as a Turning Point

Although this larger geopolitical backdrop can help explain why the Japanese government managed to skirt its responsibilities to Asia; why war crimes remained largely unexamined in Japan for many years (some until the 1990s); and why many ordinary Japanese remembered the war naïvely, seeing themselves as victims, I argue that it only partially explains why progressives—many of whom loudly criticized Japan's incorporation into the American security framework—began to pay intensive attention to the Asia problem only in the late 1950s. The sense of Asia being forbidden territory certainly played a role. Some scholars have observed that progressives avoided the question of Japanese responsibility to Asia because they were "still haunted by echoes of the Greater East Asia Co-Prosperity Sphere" and its "unpleasant historical memories."[61] Sonoda Shigeto describes how Japanese sociologists were reluctant, or at best cautious, about studying Asia in the early postwar era because of their discipline's earlier complicity in Japanese empire building and militarism in the region.[62] Yet if a simple aversion to facing traumatic memories was the cause, how do we explain intellectuals' early and extensive attention to the war

59. Yonetani, *Ajia/Nihon*, 154; Chen, *Asia as Method*, 8. On the link between Japanese control over sovereign Manchukuo and postwar American clientelism in Asia, see Duara, *Sovereignty and Authenticity*, 78 and 247; Sakai, "Trans-Pacific Studies," 282 and 293.

60. Gluck, "Operations of Memory," 51. On the latter role of American modernization theory, see Conrad, "The Colonial Ties."

61. Sun, "How Does Asia Mean?," 24.

62. Sonoda, "Fīrudo toshite," 23.

responsibility of their own kind?[63] Clearly a more complex constellation of factors was at work.

To unravel this perplexing problem, I argue that we need to reposition the issue of Japanese war responsibility and memory in the longer history of Japanese progressive thinking about, and engagement with, Asia. From this perspective, the notion of forgetting and later remembering—while accurate in broad strokes—begins to look a little more complicated. It is important to recognize that progressives did not simply forget about Asia after defeat. On the contrary, as I show in chapter 1, discussions about Asia, Japan in Asia, and Japan's Asiaticness flourished from the war's end, only to intensify in the 1950s in the wake of the Chinese Communist Revolution, the Comintern criticism of the JCP, the Korean War, and the rise of Asian nationalism around the time of the Bandung conference in 1955. What was almost wholly lacking in these debates, however, was any attempt to connect Asia to earlier Japanese imperialism and military expansionism in the region. Instead, most progressives (but, importantly, not all) reverted to a time-honored tradition of either disparaging Japanese identity for its affliction of Asiatic backwardness or, later, positioning this identity within an idealized Asian nationalism. So Asia, variously imagined, was certainly present in progressive consciousness from the early postwar years, but it was, for want of a better characterization, an un-deimperialized imagination thereof. The historical questions thus become how and why the process of deimperialization began when it did, and what eventuated.

The most prominent exponent of the idea of "deimperialization" is the theorist Kuan-Hsing Chen, notably in his 2010 *Asia as Method: Toward Deimperialization*. There Chen defines deimperialization as follows:

If decolonization is mainly active work carried out on the terrain of the colonized, then deimperialization, which is no less painful and reflexive, is work that must be performed by the colonizer first, and then on the colonizer's relation with its former colonies. The task is for the colonizing or imperializing population to examine the conduct, motives, desires, and consequences of the imperialist history that has formed its own subjectivity. These two movements—decolonization and deimperialization—

63. See Ōkuma, *Sensō sekinin*; Tsurumi Shunsuke, "Chishikijin."

intersect and interact, though very unevenly. To put it simply, deimperialization is a more encompassing category and a powerful tool with which we can critically examine the larger historical impact of imperialism. There can be no compromise in these exercises if the world is to move ahead peacefully.[64]

Chen's basic opinion about Japan is that, thanks to the Cold War, the country's deimperialization was regrettably interrupted, only to be resuscitated with the easing of this bipolar division in the 1990s. "Almost overnight," Chen explains, "Japan went from being a colonizing power to being a U.S. colony, from victimizer to victimized. This mutually negating shift dissolved any momentum Japanese society had had to reflect on its relations with its former colonies and colonial subjects. The arrival of the cold war [*sic*] soon after further diminished the possibility of deimperialization."[65] The Occupation and subsequent security arrangement prevented Japan "from doing the reflexive work of deimperialization within its own territory and from grappling with its historical relations with its former colonies (Korea, Taiwan, and others) or its protectorate (Manchukuo)."[66] Chen is not alone here. The political scientist Ishida Takeshi has forcefully argued that the Cold War ensured that the "problem of war responsibility toward Asia" went more or less "unrecognized for almost half a century."[67] The historian Mitani Taichirō agrees, characterizing the deimperialization process as "frozen" by the United States and its Cold War strategy.[68] Importantly, Mitani identifies a troubling mutation in Japanese consciousness under the weight of the Occupation, wherein the "the specific problem of decolonization" was subsumed (and thereby obscured) by the "general problem of demilitarization."[69] For the Japanese, the impact of this mutation was relatively consolatory, facilitating the Pacific war perspective on history and a victim consciousness of the war.[70] But in terms of Japan's future relations with its neighbors,

64. Chen, *Asia as Method*, 4.
65. Chen, *Asia as Method*, 193.
66. Chen, *Asia as Method*, 8.
67. Ishida, *Shakai kagaku*, 4.
68. Mitani, *Kindai Nihon*, 76.
69. Mitani, *Kindai Nihon*, 76.
70. Mitani, *Kindai Nihon*, 76.

this mutation could not have been more tragic and damaging. As subsequent chapters reveal, some would later describe this as a wound or original sin.

The weight of this scholarship suggests, then, a situation in which Japan was stripped of its colonial possessions but managed to avoid the difficult deimperialization work—what we might call the responsibility work—necessary for forging a new relationship with its former colonies and sites of its military aggression. Critically, most accounts of this process identify the thawing of the Cold War in the 1990s as a significant turning point. Mitani, for example, says that only with this thawing did the "unresolved process of decolonization (the so-called second stage of decolonization) begin."[71] Ishida similarly identifies this as the moment when the "moratorium" on Japan's war responsibility to Asia ended, "war victims in Asian countries finally begin to raise their voices," and the Japanese were "pressured to recognize 'Asia' once again."[72] Gluck likewise identifies 1989 and the 1990s as critical moments of transition, although for her it is not only the thawing Cold War but also the death of Emperor Hirohito and "the return of Asia to Japan's geopolitical agenda" that caused the "unfreezing" and "eruption" of war memory.[73]

This book corroborates the significance of the 1990s in the history of deimperialization. That decade was indeed a time when new visions of Asian community began to emerge, along with promising discursive and activist initiatives for the promotion of multicultural coexistence with Japan's so-called internal Asia. Nevertheless, the notion of a half-century deep freeze of deimperialization tends to overlook the important changes happening in progressive circles in Japan before then. The empirical data suggest that the developments of the 1990s are better understood as the culmination and maturation of various streams of earlier deimperialization processes than as an abrupt thawing. The roots of change are evident in the 1950s, but the period from the 1960s to the early 1970s marks a significant paradigmatic shift in the intellectual and activist history of modern Japan. Progressives finally began to break away from two bugbears

71. Mitani, *Kindai Nihon*, 77.
72. Ishida, *Shakai Kagaku*, 4 and 14.
73. Gluck, "Operations of Memory," 64, and "*Sekinin*," 96.

that had haunted their predecessors since at least the mid-nineteenth century: an attitude of superiority toward their regional neighbors, on the one hand, and a concomitant inferiority complex toward the West, on the other hand.[74] This syndrome—evident not only among progressives—expressed itself in ongoing tensions and stunning reversals over whether Japan was part of Asia, should abandon Asia, should lead Asia, or should be some kind of hybrid. It was a problem that neither of the two major streams of progressive thought—Marxism and modernism—were able to solve. Indeed, they were complicit in it. Only with the rise of Asian nationalism in the 1950s do we begin to see cracks in this cognitive dissonance on Asia. Moreover, from around the mid-1960s we witness the start of its collapse and the emergence of a new vision of the region and a challenge to national identity.

As I show in this book, processes of deimperialization and grassroots solidarity movements in the 1970s opened the way to productive new thinking about and involvements in the Asian region. As the practice of embracing or abandoning Asia slowly began to recede, Asia as an abstract ideal gave way to more substantive visions and involvements. I suggest that in the 1970s and 1980s, we begin to witness nothing short of a combined grassroots regionalization and grassroots globalization of Japanese progressive thought and activism, as intellectuals and activists began to more proactively deal with the unresolved past and forge new border-crossing solidarities.[75] It is no coincidence that this transformation coincided with the global spread of ideas about human rights, gender, minorities, refugees, developmental assistance, and the environment during the 1970s. Japanese progressive intellectuals and activists were deeply influenced by these trends—which collectively have been referred to as "shock of the global"—as they engaged with Asian countries and reimagined Japan in its region.[76] Moreover, since deimperialization necessarily inculpated the

74. Sakai, "Trans-Pacific Studies," 304; Stefan Tanaka, *Japan's Orient*, 12–13 and 20.
75. I should note that other scholars, although still a minority, have also shown an appreciation of the 1970s as a moment of reconnection and reflection. See Hanasaki, "Decolonization," 180; Morris-Suzuki, "Japan and Its Region," 123; Michiba, "Posuto-Betonamu"; Lee, "*Nikkan rentai*"; Seraphim, *War Memory*, 207; Avenell, "Asia and the Development of Civic Activism" and *Transnational Japan*.
76. Ferguson et al., *Shock of the Global*.

nation, it simultaneously sabotaged postwar progressive ethnic nationalism, opening the way for an exploration of the Asia within. These processes reached a crescendo in the 1990s, when progressives broached the
topic of Asian community that had long been taboo among those on
the Left.

Given this trajectory into and beyond deimperialization, the history
we need to explore is one that reveals the process by which progressives
slowly became sensitive to the cognitive dissonance surrounding understandings of Asia; how they subsequently embraced the project of deimperialization; and the ways this sensitization played out thereafter, both
intellectually and in the realm of progressive civic activism. This history
will reveal the centrality of Asia in the transformation of progressive
thought and activism in postwar Japan.

Organization of the Book

I begin my exploration of the Asia problem in chapter 1 by tracing the
early postwar processes through which intellectuals and activists started
to address the Asia bias in Marxist and modernist thought. After analyzing the role of the Occupation and security arrangement in fumigating
the memory of Japan's geographical empire in Asia and its remnants
within the country, I look briefly at the intellectual climate in the early
postwar era, followed by a discussion of the key turning points of this
period: the rise of Asian nationalism and the impact of new articulations
of Asia by Takeuchi, the historian Uehara Senroku, and other leading intellectuals. The triumphant return of Marxism, with its so-called "theory of
history" based on "stages of historical development," required a concept of
"Asian stagnation" theoretically and in the realm of praxis.[77] Modernism
was hardly different. As Victor Koschmann notes, in the early postwar period, thinkers like the economic historian Ōtsuka Hisao, deeply influenced
by Max Weber, "perpetuated" an Orientalist view of Asia as both "stagnant"

---

77. Nagai Kazu, "Sengo Marukusushugi," 643, 652, and 667–70. See also Ishida,
Shakai kagaku, 68.

and "devoid of the inner subjectivity" characteristic of the modern human type.[78]

But by the late 1950s the idea of Asiatic stagnation so entrenched in earlier views of Asia was under attack (although not entirely in retreat)—thanks to Asian nationalism and thinkers like Takeuchi, who proclaimed that in order to attain genuine ethnic liberation the Japanese needed to discard their "slave nature," which pursued transformation by shallowly mimicking and "chas[ing] after Europe."[79] In a similar vein, Uehara published a flurry of essays around the same time, calling on social scientists to expel deeply engrained biases toward Asia and "Eurocentric" assumptions in historical thinking.[80] Still lacking in these reimaginations of Asia, however, was any attention to the problem of empire. For the most part, Asia remained confined to the realms of revolutionary ideology and nationalistic romanticism. However, from around the late 1950s some scholars, like the anthropologists Umesao Tadao and Nakane Chie, began to call for a more informed approach to the region.

It was in the late 1950s and 1960s that a new generation of grassroots activists and intellectuals began the task of deimperialization. Discrimination against resident Asians (especially Koreans and Chinese) in Japan and international developments such as the mass exodus of Koreans to North Korea starting in 1959 and negotiations for the Japan–South Korea normalization treaty of 1965 mattered deeply in this process. In chapter 2, I trace deimperialization processes in the rising discourse on ethnic responsibility (*minzokuteki sekinin*) that challenged and supplemented—if not replaced—the earlier discourse on ethnic nationalism (*minzokushugi*) inspired by the nonaligned movement and Asian nationalism. One of the key innovations of this ethnic responsibility discourse was the recuperation of an internal Asia or Asia within—most notably in the 1958 Komatsugawa Incident and the interventions of the writer Pak Sunam. Such perspectives were not only different from earlier calls for Asian liberation and neutralism that bolstered Japanese left nationalism, but they also

78. Koschmann, *Revolution and Subjectivity*, 165–66. Also see Conrad, *Quest for the Lost Nation*, 174.

79. Takeuchi, "What is Modernity?," 72. See also Nagahara, "Sengo Nihon," 39.

80. Uehara, "Sekai shi ni okeru," 150.

represented a critical break with Marxist and modernist biases toward Asia and, hence, the first systematic steps toward deimperialization.

Chapter 3 extends this discussion to the interventions of Oda Makoto, Honda Katsuichi, and others involved in the anti–Vietnam War movement, along with the rise of a consciousness of war responsibility among historians and student activists in the late 1960s and early 1970s. Anti–Vietnam War activists, for instance, began to excavate Japan's neglected imperial past via their criticism of the American war in Indochina, in turn articulating a vision of Asian community based on genuine repentance as citizens of a so-called perpetrator nation. By presenting Japan as an aggressor in the past and present, activists and intellectuals in these initiatives and movements opened the way to new investigations into the complex historical entanglements of Japan in its region as well as the recuperation of an internal Asia that the Occupation reforms and conservative resurgence had effectively eradicated from popular consciousness. Student and anti–Vietnam War activists were alerted to problems of discrimination against Asians in Japan in the late 1960s when they began to oppose proposed changes to Japan's immigration control system, following the dramatic protest suicide of Li Zhicheng, a Chinese medical student. Thereafter a number of highly influential works dealing with discrimination were published, including Tsumura Takashi's *Warera no uchinaru sabetsu* (The discrimination within us) and Mihashi Osamu's *Sabetsu ron nōto* (Notes on discrimination). Yet for all their empathy and sense of guilt toward Asia, it was only in the later stages of the anti–Vietnam War movement that activists began to recognize their lack of knowledge about, and substantive connections with, Asian nations and people. As the activists came to appreciate, knowing the past did not amount to knowing Asia or the people living there. Student activists too, through their struggles against Japan's draconian immigration control system and in the face of denunciations from minority student groups, began to recognize the Asian blind spot in their struggle against Japanese neo-imperialism.

Chapter 4 examines the transformative moment of the 1970s, when civic activists began to address the problem of not knowing Asia in a range of transnational solidarity movements. Japanese industry's triumphant return to the region was accompanied by a range of troubling issues such as industrial pollution, political collusion, and sex tourism. Students, civic activists, journalists, and intellectuals from the region like the Filipino historian Renato Constantino responded with angry accusations of a second Japanese invasion and the rise of Japan as the Yellow Yankee of postwar Asia. In response, individuals who had cut their activist teeth in the anti–Vietnam War movement and student protesters dove headlong into a new wave of solidarity movements—not only for fellow Asians, as in earlier movements, but importantly with other Asian activists, such as South Korean dissidents like the poet Kim Chi-ha and the academic Chi Myong-kwan. This new generation of transnationally active movements marked an important evolution in postwar civic activism, stimulating a kind of grassroots regionalization in Japanese activist circles with the result that by the end of the 1970s, Asia, Japan in Asia, and the rights of people across the region had captured the attention of more Japanese activists than ever before.

Chapter 5 traces the Asia problem from the late 1970s into the 1980s—a period distinguished by its unabashed celebration of internationalization in the newly minted economic superpower Japan. Against the backdrop of this haughty, nationalistic discourse, however, another alternative internationalization was unfolding as a type of grassroots inter-people diplomacy with Asia. It was led by progressive intellectuals, local governments, and activists in concert with activists and groups from the region who called on the Japanese to reconsider the country's complex entanglements with Asia through the lenses of human rights and social justice. Discussions of postwar responsibility (*sengo sekinin*), projects to critique Japan through the lens of the mangrove swamplands and banana plantations of Southeast Asia, and a new generation of Asia-focused international NGOs offered a vision of Asia beyond existing notions of perpetration and victimization. As intellectuals and activists came to comprehend the realities in Asia more deeply, the region also began to function for them as a space for self-reflexivity and action aimed at refashioning postwar Japanese identity, democracy, and external relations. Asia, to use the words of one activist, came to be seen as a "teacher": to know the region was also to know and transform the self as a consumer, citizen, Asian, and individual responsible for protecting the human rights of others.[81] In this sense, Asia served as a conduit for Japanese progressives

81.   Ikezumi, Sugimoto, and Nakamura, *Banana kara jinken e,* 175.

to begin internalizing the norms of an emerging global civil society in a process of grassroots globalization starkly at odds with mainstream internationalization.

Such trends only became stronger into the 1990s, when a chorus of so-called New Asianists from across the political spectrum advocating for East Asian community and a wave of movements seeking apologies and redress for wartime transgressions forced their way into the public consciousness. As I show in chapter 6, some of these New Asianist voices invoked the region in ways that were starkly at odds with the postwar intellectual and activist trajectories of progressives, largely dismissing the existence of an Asia problem in favor of utilitarian and often chauvinistic blueprints of Asia as recessionary Japan's solution. Attracting most attention were right-wing nationalists like the politician Ishihara Shintarō who, agitated by Japan's domestic decline and its subservience to the United States, stridently trumpeted Asian values and demanded a regional resistance to the United States. These nationalists were joined by a hodgepodge of civilizational warriors, who prophesized a coming clash in which the symbiotic and disciplined East would resuscitate and revitalize a world ravaged by the decadence and destruction of Western modernity. Others who still clung to the fantasy of Japanese leadership in Asia offered self-delusional narratives of Japan as Asia's sacrificial lamb, martyred for the region both militarily and economically on the altar of Western subjugation. In a more moderate tone, a larger group of instrumentalists turned to Asia as the solution to Japan's economic woes, some envisioning an Asia-Pacific fusion in which Japan could draw on the economic dynamism of the region to recalibrate its skewed relations with America.[82] Whether extremist or moderate, however, most of these New Asianist ideas led back to Japan, essentially replicating earlier notions of Japanese superiority and the utility of Asia for the country's economic and/or geopolitical strengthening vis-à-vis the West.

As I show in chapter 6, the New Asianism of the 1990s presented progressives with both challenges and opportunities. Most troublingly, there was a danger that crude yet alluring discourses on Asian values and civilizational confrontation might obscure and even obliterate Japan's still unresolved past in the region, in a sense replacing the Asia problem with

---

82. Funabashi, *Ajia Taiheiyō fyūjon*.

an assortment of Asian solutions. Yet at the same time, the New Asianism—precisely because it stepped into the taboo territory of Asian community—also ironically served as the catalyst for a significant progressive breakthrough. Faced with these nationalist and utilitarian incursions into the territory of Asian community, for the first time some progressives dared to imagine and articulate blueprints for Japan's future within the symbolic geography of Asia—in effect stepping out from beneath the long shadow of co-prosperity. Intellectual activists like Wada Haruki and Kang led a chorus of progressives calling for East Asian community and the formation of a common house of Northeast Asia. Others, like the historian Hamashita Takeshi, began to challenge internalist national histories by reembedding the Japanese archipelago in entangled and fluid regional narratives. Unlike the hard-liners or moderate instrumentalists who downplayed or discarded the past in their regional visions, progressives positioned remorse and redress as the first (and critical) steps on the path to community. Drawing on years of activism with and for fellow Asians, advocates of Asian community like Wada and Kang argued that if Japan was to be genuinely integrated into Asia, the Japanese needed to recognize the depth of the scars their country had left on its neighbors and the ways such traumas were knit into the core of those peoples' collective identities. At some stage, Japan's leaders needed to be courageous and magnanimous enough to offer an apology acceptable as genuine by the country's former victims. This would aid in healing, to be sure. But more significantly, the advocates believed that it could facilitate the construction of a robust and legitimate East Asian community capable of transcending the vulgar and catastrophic error of Japan's earlier misadventure in co-prosperity.

To be sure, the Asia problem was hardly solved by these progressive pronouncements, nor was deimperialization finally realized. But as I show in the following chapters, the awakening to Asia and Japan's unresolved past in the region had important implications in terms of how war responsibility and postcolonial culpability were understood and debated in Japan; how the broader sphere of civic activism evolved over time; and, finally, the ways in which national identity could be imagined and reimagined. Indeed, the fact that progressives could, by the 1990s, broach the taboo topic of Asian community within their lengthy project of remorse and responsibility marked an important breakthrough. It was made all the more significant thanks to the growing presence of internal

Others—including resident Koreans like Kang—who now joined the ranks of Japanese progressives as vocal and influential voices. This rediscovery and embrace of Japan in Asia alongside the emergence of Asians in Japan raised important self-reflexive questions about identity as the country entered the new millennium, feeding into debates about multiculturalism. Would it be possible to imagine Japan as a porous, hybrid, diverse, and multiethnic construct, or would the logics of exclusion, separation, superiority, and distinctiveness maintain their stranglehold over self-recognition?

Historians have long debated when and even if Japan's postwar era ended. Officially, at least, 1956 was when government documents declared its conclusion, but some suggest that the end came with the return of Okinawa to Japanese control in 1972 or with the death of Emperor Hirohito and the collapse of the Japanese bubble economy (1989–90)—or even that the long postwar period has never really ended.[83] A key consideration in such debates is whether or not Japan has come to terms with its past—in other words, the extent to which Japan has been deimperialized. As the following chapters attest, deimperialization as a self-conscious intellectual process among progressive intellectuals and activists did not really begin until around the 1960s. Only thereafter, and slowly, did voices of the former colonized become audible in this discussion, and even today those voices are muted and sporadic in the face of nationalist vitriol. Given this path to deimperialization and the continuing struggle to deimperialize, I am inclined to conclude that while Japan may be postwar (being demilitarized, institutionally democratized, and post-Hirohito) and postcolonial (having lost its colonies), it is not yet postimperial in the sense of having resolved its past transgressions with former colonial subjects and deimperialized itself. Postimperial Japan is still very much a work in progress, but as this book attempts to show, significant progress has been made nonetheless.

83. The Economic Planning Agency declared the postwar era over in 1956. See the section titled "Ketsugo" in Keizai Kikakuchō, *Shōwa 31nen*. Oguma Eiji argues there have been three postwar periods, and only the first two have ended thus far: 1945–55, 1955–90, and the third 1990 and beyond (*Minshu to aikoku*, 12 and 811). Handō Kazutoshi argues that the postwar era ended with the reversion of Okinawa to Japan in 1972 (*Shōwashi*, 531). In 1993, Andrew Gordon tentatively proposed the end of the 1980s as the end of the postwar period (conclusion, 463). Gluck also discusses various endings for the postwar era ("Past in the Present," especially 92–95).

CHAPTER I

The Early Postwar Period

Asia as Ideology and Ideal

The bus to Asia is departing today. If Japan fails to board, we must realize that Japan will become the orphan of Asia.
— Matsumoto Jiichirō, "Ajiajin no Ajia ni," 1953

Who are the Japanese? The Japanese are Asians.
— Shimizu Ikutarō, "Nihonjin," 1951

Japan's empire may have vanished in 1945, but Asia did not recede from the Japanese progressive imagination. In fact, it is difficult to comprehend the intellectual atmosphere in Japan during the late 1940s and 1950s without considering the prominence of Asia as an ideological and idealized category of analysis and debate. For most progressives, the urgent task in this early postwar moment was to tackle individual responsibility for having supported (or, at least, not actively opposed) a catastrophic war that had resulted in untold suffering and millions of needless deaths. Critical investigation here tended to focus on a search for the social, psychological, and ethical flaws that could explain the ruinous degeneration of progressives and, more generally, the Japanese nation. "Asia" as an ideal type proved extremely useful for both Marxists and modernists whose investigations drew on developmental trajectories that in one way or another explained the recent past based on some form of stunted or distorted national-historical development. Herein "Asia" served as the symbolic expression of the backwardness and stagnation within Japanese institutions and individual consciousness. Japan's Asiaticness, it was argued, lay at the heart of a variety of deficiencies, including an incomplete revolution in the mid-nineteenth century, the psychology of Japanese ultranationalism beginning in the 1930s, and the very structure of modern

Japanese society. Only through a concerted fumigation of this Asiaticness, whether through social revolution or the attainment of modern individual subjectivity, would progress be possible. In this way, the discourse on Asia fell squarely into the intellectual and political lineage of
abandoning Asia and joining the West or, for some, joining the Marxian
communal utopia. I will call this the ideological view of Asia in the early
postwar period.

But although such notions of Japan's Asiatic stagnation dominated
progressive discourse in the late 1940s, they were quickly supplemented
by a remarkably different view of Asia among progressives in the following decade. The successful Chinese Communist Revolution of 1949, rising Asian nationalism starting in the early 1950s, and the lengthening
shadow of American domination over Japan began to foster an idealistic
image of Asia as liberation, autonomy, and even peace—which had fascinating commonalities with prewar Pan-Asianist thought. Many progressives who had initially latched onto notions of Asian stagnation and
backwardness to explain Japan's past now began to qualify (if not repudiate) such viewpoints, embedding their desires for national independence
from America within the new language of Asian nationalism and revolution. This Asian idealism became dominant in the 1950s and stayed so
until at least the early 1960s. It was an idealism with solid (if sometimes
troubling) historical roots dating back to the Meiji activist Tarui Tōkichi,
Okakura Tenshin, the Pan-Asianist movement, and the wartime Greater
East Asia Co-Prosperity Sphere. However, it differed fundamentally from
these forebears in not ascribing to Japan any leadership role in Asia and,
on the contrary, in looking to Asian leaders such as Jawaharlal Nehru,
Sukarno, Mao Zedong, and Zhou Enlai for guidance and inspiration.
Most emblematic of this vision was Takeuchi Yoshimi (1910–77), the
sinologist who led the resurgence of thinking about Asia in postwar
Japan by launching a fierce frontal attack on the assumption that Asia
(primarily China) was hopelessly stagnant and incapable of modernizing.
I call this the idealistic view of Asia in the early postwar period.

While these two approaches to Asia differed profoundly—the one
being negative and the other positive—they had two important similari-
ties. First, neither vision of Asia incorporated a thorough consideration
of Japan's colonial empire. Most progressives attracted to the decolonial-
izing imperative underlying Asian nationalism utterly failed to connect

this attraction to any analysis of Japan's colonial past. We see very little evidence of any deimperializing impulse until around the late 1950s, and even then, that impulse appeared only sporadically and tentatively. Second, neither approach was based on a grounded and nuanced understanding of everyday realities and transformations in countries of the region after Japan's colonial retreat. This understanding and related activism did not arise until the late 1960s and early 1970s. Thus, while progressives' image of Asia was leaning in a positive direction by the end of the 1950s, away from the stagnation perspective, it tended to conflate discussions of Asia with those about Japanese independence (or lack thereof) from the United States under the rubric of ethnic nationalism (*minzokushugi*). As I suggested in the introduction, this had to do with progressives' innate attitudes toward Asia that were born of their theoretical worldviews and postwar aspirations, but it was also a function of the historical situation in which they found themselves. The disappearance of empire from early postwar views and understandings of Asia also had much to do with processes of de-Asianization during the Occupation, US Cold War strategy in Japan, and the resurgence of Japanese conservatives.

But while highlighting the shortfalls, in this chapter I also want to show how this period of ideology and especially idealism in progressive approaches to Asia yielded some positive intellectual outcomes in the direction of deimperialization by the late 1950s. The progressive embrace of Asian nationalism, while not entirely eradicating the notion of Asian stagnation, had the effect of greatly diminishing its prominence. Asian idealism reconfigured the region as a space of transformation, possibility, creativity, and community. As Asia emerged on the world scene in the 1950s as a sphere of liberation and positive political change, some Japanese progressives even began to shed the abstract idealism of Asian nationalism, focusing instead on a more grounded approach to the region based on actual field observation and empirical research. Lionizing the region without really knowing it, they argued, was unscientific if not utterly irresponsible and myopic. Albeit unintentionally, then, Asian idealism played a dual role in undermining the idea of Asian stagnation on the one hand and, on the other hand, opening a way to rudimentary calls for deimperialization and reengagement with the region thanks to growing dissatisfaction with the idealistic view's detachment from Asian realities. But before exploring this intellectual process, we need to begin with the objective circumstances that progressives found themselves immersed in after Japan's defeat, especially the unfolding process of de-Asianization under American hegemony.

The Occupation as De-Asianization

For all its positive legacies, the Occupation of Japan tended to suppress memories of empire while contributing to a mythology of monoethnicity that detached Japan from its regional neighbors historically, politically, and psychologically. Although the defunct Japanese empire had been constructed on a racialized hierarchy with Japan as the leading nation and colonized subjects ranked below as lesser and outer, for practical and operational reasons the empire had had to incorporate the dual notions of Japan in Asia and Asia in Japan as ethnic Japanese moved out into the colonies, intermarried with colonized peoples, and colonial subjects flowed into Japan. In the 1930s and beyond, discourse on the Greater Japanese Empire (*Dai Nihon teikoku*) stressed multiethnicity and, with considerable intellectual acrobatics, a history of the Japanese nation based on the "fusion" and "assimilation" of numerous ethnic lineages all tied together under the unbroken imperial line.[1] As Oguma Eiji explains, the existence of "non-Japanese Japanese" in the form of Taiwanese, Korean, and other colonial subjects demanded a broader, multiethnic vision that was not possible in monoethnic mythologies of the nation. The "mixed nation theory" popular at the time "lent itself to the claim that the Japanese nation embodied the unification of Asia, and that the peoples of neighboring regions could be assimilated into the Japanese nation and their lands annexed by the Great Japanese Empire."[2] We must take care, of course, not to mistake crude political instrumentalism for genuine commitment to regional community in the operations of the Japanese empire. The reality is that the notion of a multiethnic Japanese empire was both discriminatory and brittle, and in large part it was a servant to Japan's economic and geopolitical objectives in the region. Nevertheless,

1. Yoon, *Nihon kokumin*, 259.
2. Oguma, *Genealogy of Japanese*, xxiii–iv.

as Takeuchi would not unproblematically argue in 1964, "at the time, the Japanese had a strong awareness of Asia. As they would learn through defeat in war, that awareness of Asia was mistaken, but even if it was, at least they possessed their own independent stance. . . . With defeat in war [the process] of civilization and enlightenment began again, and in this atmosphere the Greater East Asian War was utterly rejected. [. . .] [T]his was probably unavoidable, but the result was the loss of something important."[3] That "something important," of course, was a sense of connection to the region: a perception that Japan's fate was inextricably bound to that of its regional neighbors.

The Occupation played no small part in this process of simultaneously impeding deimperialization and de-Asianizing Japan. To begin with, from 1945 through 1952 the Japanese government, with the blessing of the Occupation authorities, methodically excluded former colonial subjects from rights and recognition as citizens in the new postwar order. The experience of Koreans who remained in Japan at the war's end is most telling in this respect. In December 1945, resident Koreans with Korean family registers were stripped of voting rights under the Shūgiin giin senkyo hō (the House of Representatives' election law) by replacing the existing citizenship qualification with a Japanese household register prerequisite. In May 1947, on the day before the new postwar constitution came into effect, the government passed the Gaikokujin tōroku hō (the alien registration law), which classified all former colonial subjects as foreigners. This law was supplemented in 1955 by a requirement for all registered aliens to be fingerprinted like criminals. Combined with the 1947 Gaikokujin tōroku hō, the Kokuseki hō (the law for nationality) promulgated in 1950 exacerbated de-Asianization and monoethnic bias by requiring naturalizing citizens to choose Japanese names and excluding noncitizen residents from fundamental state services such as the national health insurance program, the pension system, rights of entry and departure, military pensions, and public-sector employment. When Japanese sovereignty was finally restored with the implementation of the San Francisco Peace Treaty in 1952, resident Koreans and members of other colonial-era minority groups lost their Japanese citizenship rights once and for all.[4] Occupation

3. Takeuchi, "Nihonjin no Ajiakan," 95.
4. Lie, *Zainichi*, x.

authorities contributed to the destabilization of resident Koreans' status in Japan by classifying Koreans in 1945 as potentially "liberated peoples," "enemy nationals," or both and then, in 1947, as individuals from a "Special Status Nation."[5] Such equivocation only exacerbated discrimination and prejudice against Koreans, who were scapegoated for profiteering from "victimized" Japanese in the booming black markets of the immediate postwar period.[6]

Elite Japanese politicians like Prime Minister Yoshida Shigeru desired the immediate repatriation of all Koreans and former colonial subjects, and Yoshida expressed these views unreservedly in a 1949 letter to General Douglas MacArthur.[7] Yoshida was one of the principal Japanese advocates of a de-Asianized Japan, believing strongly that the country's political, social, and economic development made it more Western than Asian. Since Japan had a certain cultural and geographic proximity to Asia, Yoshida conceded that the country could contribute to the spread of liberal values and economic growth in the region, but under no circumstances should Japan be lumped together with the backward nations of Asia and Africa, where cultural standards remained undeveloped.[8] Even leftist organizations such as the JCP and resident-Korean support groups contributed—if inadvertently—to the idea that Japan was now a monoethnic state only for Japanese nationals. These groups strongly advocated repatriation and showed no interest in any project to "formulate a new vision of coexistence within Japan."[9] John Lie explains how until the 1970s ethnic Korean leaders were convinced that it was the "destiny" of resident Koreans to eventually repatriate, and many of them did—most notably in a tragic exodus of some 90,000 people to North Korea beginning in 1959.[10] Despite the close connections between resident Koreans and the JCP, Japanese communists showed little sensitivity to the situation

5. Joint Chiefs of Staff, "Basic Directive for Post-Surrender," Part 1.8. Prisoners of War, United Nations Nationals, and Other Persons, d.; General Headquarters Supreme Commander, "Definition of United, Neutral, Enemy," clause 5.

6. Ishida, *Shakai kagaku*, 55.

7. For this letter see Sodei, *Yoshida = Makkāsā*, 448–50.

8. Yoshida Shigeru, *Kaisō jūnen*, 36–38.

9. Oguma, *Genealogy of Japanese*, 298.

10. Lie, *Zainichi*, 33. On this mass repatriation, see Morris-Suzuki, *Exodus to North Korea*.

of Koreans, simplistically positioning them within the wider struggle to topple Japan's emperor system. This focus on domestic reform made it difficult for the JCP to grasp the complex situation of Koreans in Japan and more or less forestalled any possibility of the JCP's relaunching itself on the basis of responsibility and remorse for Japanese colonial rule and the wider war of aggression in East Asia.[11]

As the internal Asia was systematically extirpated in these years, other processes acted to suppress any systematic consideration of Japan's wartime transgressions in Asia. Most influential here was the International Military Tribunal for the Far East, or the Tokyo Tribunal, which was convened in April 1946 and tasked with dispensing justice on the architects of Japan's war. In terms of deimperialization, the root of the problem lay in the tribunal's production of what has been called a "Pacific War view of history," according to which the scope of the war was essentially limited to locations of conflict between America and Japan in the years from 1941 to 1945.[12] A clique of military leaders was held to have highjacked political control of Japan, thereafter waging an unjust and unprovoked war against the United States—which, thanks to its overwhelming military and technical prowess, thoroughly defeated Japan and liberated the victimized Japanese people. In this view, Japan's prolonged war against, and defeat in, China receded into the background, as did war crimes like the massacre at Nanjing, the horrific experimentations on Chinese people by the infamous Unit 731, and wartime sexual violence and military prostitution.[13]

The assigning of culpability also shadowed this logic. Members of the political elite who had supported militarism in East Asia but nevertheless opposed the war with America received light treatment or were not charged with any crime. Wakamiya Yoshibumi gives the example of Yoshida who, despite having helped "lay the groundwork" for the invasion of China, avoided indictment thanks to his opposition to the war against America. Similarly, General Ishiwara Kanji, one architect of the notorious

11. Yoon, "Sengo shisō," 147.

12. He, *National Mythmaking*, 72.

13. On the Nanjing massacre, see Takashi Yoshida, *Making of the "Rape of Nanking"*; Fogel, *Nanjing Massacre*. On Unit 731, see Tsuneishi, "Unit 731." On the so-called comfort women, see Yoshimi Yoshiaki, *Comfort Women*; Kumagai, *Comfort Women*.

Manchurian Incident of 1931 that resulted in the escalation of Japanese militarism on the Chinese mainland, likewise avoided charges thanks to his opposition to Japan's wartime leaders and their policies.[14] In this way, issues of culpability for war crimes in Asia never received any sustained scrutiny during the tribunal: they were secondary to the crimes committed against the United States.

But the effects of the Pacific War view of history were even more profound when considered in the context of deimperialization. The tribunal was not tasked with scrutinizing or passing judgment on Japan's colonial empire. Indeed, this was not even politically possible because most of the prosecuting nations were themselves unapologetic imperial powers that, after Japan's retreat, shamefully returned to reclaim what they saw as their Asian possessions. Telling in this respect is the way military tribunals against Japanese in European colonies of Asia were often controlled by former suzerain states, effectively denying Asian peoples their right to pass judgment on Japanese war crimes against them.[15] Ironically enough, as Sebastian Conrad notes, one of the key motivations fueling the Pacific War view was the American occupiers' desire to eradicate the notion of a "Greater East Asian War" (Daitō A Sensō), which they correctly saw as symbolic of Japan's wartime propaganda.[16] But banning this terminology had unintended consequences since "it implied a fundamental shift in the mental map of the war," leading away from China, East Asia, and any association with Japan's colonial empire.[17] Even progressive historians deeply sensitive to the history of empire and war in Asia subsequently adopted the Pacific War nomenclature in their publications. It was not until the philosopher Tsurumi Shunsuke's proposal of the "Fifteen-Year War" idea in 1956 that the vocabulary of the war came into question again—but even this term was limited by its temporal origin of 1931, which tended to obscure the more fundamental problem of Japan's colonial empire in Asia.[18]

14. Wakamiya, *Sengo 70-nen*, 156.
15. Ishida, *Shakai kagaku*, 52.
16. Conrad, *Quest for the Lost Nation*, 108.
17. Conrad, *Quest for the Lost Nation*, 108.
18. Tsurumi Shunsuke, "Chishikijin no sensō sekinin," 9.

The San Francisco Peace Treaty signed by forty-eight nations in 1951 further intensified de-Asianization and the delay of deimperialization in Japan. Importantly, this settlement did not include the People's Republic of China or North or South Korea—arguably the greatest victims of the Japanese empire and militarism. Progressive discussions in influential magazines and journals leading up to the treaty reveal an eye-opening lack of sensitivity to the link between genuine peace and resolving the legacies of empire and war. For instance, the famous December 1950 third statement by the influential intellectual group Heiwa Mondai Danwakai (Peace Problems Discussion Group) in the progressive magazine *Sekai* spoke of the "momentous" "collapse of colonial rule" and "sudden rise of ethnic movements" in Asia, but it made no mention of Japan's very recent history of colonial rule and military aggression.[19] In keeping with the narrow Pacific War narrative, the statement noted that it would be "necessary to solve the problem" by facing not "outwards" but "within": "We can say that past warmongering by Japan had institutional origins. In other words, the problems needed to be solved institutionally."[20] To be fair, this was a forward-looking document, primarily concerned with how the unfolding Cold War would affect world peace and, more directly, the nature of Japan's postwar peace settlement. Even so, the almost complete lack of attention to Japan's earlier military expansionism and its effects on contemporary Asia is quite striking.

Among the many discussions of the peace settlement around this time, the most direct reference to Japanese militarism I could uncover is in a 1951 article in the JCP mouthpiece *Zen'ei*, titled "Ajia no jinmin wa naze tandoku kōwa ni hantai shiteiruka" (Why Asian peoples are opposing one-sided peace). Akimoto Yukio, the author, pointed out that the largest countries in Asia and the ones most victimized by Japanese aggression during the war were not involved or refused to be involved in peace negotiations in San Francisco. Of the one billion Asians, Akimoto said, 800 million were excluded.[21] He also noted that from the Manchurian Incident of 1931 to the war's end, the Chinese people had lost fifty

19. Heiwa Mondai Danwakai, "Mitatabi heiwa," 23.
20. Heiwa Mondai Danwakai, "Mitatabi heiwa," 50.
21. Akimoto Yukio, "Ajia no jinmin," 19.

billion US dollars in material resources and ten million lives.[22] Observations such as this, however, were the exception.

Compounding the problem, the various reparations agreements signed by Japan with Asian nations after the 1951 treaty generally included a clause stipulating that all claims to rights and reparations were thereby "completely and finally settled." Although such agreements were primarily about material compensation, they also strongly implied that issues of war responsibility had been resolved when, in reality, they had not. This process was repeated again and again, in agreements with Burma (1954), the Philippines (1958), Indonesia (1959), South Korea (1965), Malaysia (1967), and China (1978). Moreover, Japanese businesses and the country's government viewed reparations as much as a tool to regain an industrial and commercial foothold in Asia—to revitalize plant and equipment exports and build a sense of familiarity with Japanese products—as they were expressions of apology. As Ishida Takeshi suggests, the conflation of "reparations" with "investment" or "ODA" (official developmental assistance) had a dual effect: on the one hand, it pushed the issue of war responsibility into the background, while on the other hand, it tended to reinforce prewar notions of Japanese superiority and leadership in Asian modernization.[23]

The Ideology of Asiatic Stagnation

Given these far-reaching processes of de-Asianization, Japanese progressives can hardly be blamed for their inattention to the need for deimperialization and reconciliation in the early postwar years. Yet by the same token, it would be wrong to conclude that their inattention stemmed wholly from a meek internalization of the ideology and priorities of the Occupation or governmental elites. The reality is that progressives had their own aspirations, objectives, and theoretical proclivities in this period, which strongly affected how they understood the trajectory of modern Japanese history and how they deployed the idea of Asia. We know

22.   Akimoto, "Ajia no jinmin," 20.
23.   Ishida, *Shakai kagaku,* 59.

this empirically because at the same time that empire, Asia, and Asians were receding as visible social realities in everyday life, progressives were actually reinvoking a view of Asia with prewar origins in their efforts to understand what had gone so wrong in Japan. To an extent, these two seemingly contradictory processes of extirpation (that is, de-Asianization) and reinvocation were complementary and consonant. The Pacific War view of history was, in essence, a modernist narrative about Japan's derailment midway along the progressive track from backwardness (Asiaticness) to Western civilization. Progressives' attention to Japan's Asiatic stagnation offered a similar explanation of derailed or, more accurately, stunted progress inasmuch as it assumed that the persistence of primitive Asiatic aspects could help explain Japan's modern catastrophe. Both were premised on West-centric modernist hierarchies that explicitly or implicitly demarcated Asia as something backward and to be expunged.

The early postwar ideological view of Asia, then, unfolded around an ardent desire to understand what had gone wrong. Where were the roots of the problem located? Was it the mentality of the people, Japan's institutional structures, the configuration of socioeconomic relationships, or some combination of all these? Opinions varied. Some stressed Asiatic social relations and other forms of Asian stagnation in their historical analysis of the pathogenesis of Japan, while others proposed hybrid explanations that presented Japan as an amalgam of the very worst of Asia (backwardness) and modernity (fascism), thus explaining how the country had avoided colonization while remaining incompletely modern. Nevertheless, in terms of the image or view of Asia, these perspectives differed very little, if at all. The focus on national history (*kokushi*) meant that, other than as an abstract geography of stagnation, Asia was rarely if ever imagined as a living, interconnected region with a distinct, entangled history, including Japan's recent imperialism and militarism.[24] On the contrary, as Kang Sang-jung, Yoon Keun-Cha, and others have noted, through the lens of an internalist national framework, Asia served principally as a tool for understanding Japan. It helped explain the backwardness inhibiting and distorting Japanese society and consciousness and, together with the West, provided a developmental reference point that

24. Yoon, *Nihon kokumin*, 182.

positioned Japan as slightly more "advanced than other Asian countries."[25] But whether as a developmental stage in a universalist theory of world history or as a geographically ambiguous non-Western cultural sphere, Asia always signified everything backward, stagnant, and deplorable. Marxist and modernist progressives trying to understand the recent past disagreed about much, but on the debilitating consequences of Japan's Asiaticness, they were in almost complete agreement.

Consider first Marxist discourse on Asia. The notions of Asian stagnation and despotism, as well as the Asiatic mode of production, had an esteemed intellectual lineage among Japanese Marxists stretching back to the 1920s and 1930s, when the ideas entered Japan in the writings of Karl Marx and other European theorists. In the preface to his 1859 *A Contribution to the Critique of Political Economy* (translated into Japanese in 1923), Marx had famously observed that "in broad outline, the Asiatic, ancient, feudal and modern bourgeois modes of production may be designated as epochs marking progress in the economic development of society."[26] Such ideas were deployed in Japan to "explain Japanese and Chinese backwardness," inasmuch as some "Asian societies" apparently "did not pass through the classic stages of development but instead formed an Asiatic mode of production characterized by societal stagnation and a lack of class antagonisms."[27] Important to recognize is the way Japanese Marxists tended to treat the notion of Asian stagnation both as a developmental stage that all nations should pass through and as a mode of production and social and political organization unique to a geographical region or a group of countries understood as Asia. Asia could thus be usefully deployed temporally to explain backward vestiges within Japan as well as spatially in terms of differences between Japan and China or Korea. Many prominent Japanese Marxists adopted this latter interpretation in the face of national historical differences and, more significantly, to help solve the puzzle of why prewar Japan had secured independence while most other Asian nations had become colonies or semicolonies. This Marxist perspective that distinguished Japan from China, Korea, and elsewhere was quite easily subsumed into the pre-1945 rhetoric of Japan's

25. Kang, "Nihon no Ajiakan," 71.
26. Marx, "Preface," 211–12.
27. Conrad, *Quest for the Lost Nation*, 212–13.

leadership over the rest of Asia and, moreover, resonated seamlessly with the de-Asianization processes of the immediate postwar years. To borrow from Conrad, it was a "temporalization of space" in which Asia became "an essentialized Other" that could be usefully deployed to differentiate Japan from both its regional neighbors and the West.[28]

The tendency to deride Asia and Asiaticness persisted in Marxist discourse after Japan's defeat. A 1948 essay by the Marxist scholar Okamoto Saburō titled "Ajiateki seisan yōshiki ni tsuite" (On the Asian mode of production) more or less replicated earlier depictions of Asia. Okamoto explained how "consolidated unified states had formed in Asia under the conditions of irrigative agriculture": "Tribal and clan leaders and powerful families became despots and ruling classes on the basis of new social functions. They wielded absolute dictatorial power and reigned over the various communities as the highest consolidated formations" of power.[29] The Asian mode of production was a "permanently stagnant" formation, "historically produced through the maintenance of tribal and clannish relationships." It was an "undeveloped slavery type of production unique to Asia."[30] Similar to other treatments of Asian stagnation at the time, Okamoto's references in the essay to India, Persia, and Egypt reinforced the implication that Asiaticness was not only a state of development but was also identifiable in a regional geography of stagnation.

The notion of Japan's developmental superiority over stagnant Asia also persisted as a central theme in early postwar Marxist historiography, best exemplified in the writings of the prominent medieval historian Ishimoda Shō (1912–86). In an important 1946 essay "Chūsei seiritsu shi no nisan no mondai" (A number of problems concerning the formation of the medieval world) Ishimoda asked why Japan, unlike India and China, had avoided semi- or complete colonization. Ignoring the possibility that exogenous international circumstances might have played a role, Ishimoda looked backward, tracing the divergence to Japan's alone having "almost completely overcome the decrepit ancient state system" and successfully constructed a new medieval world.[31] In China, however, the

28. Conrad, *Quest for the Lost Nation*, 12.
29. Okamoto, "Ajiateki seisan yōshiki," 317.
30. Okamoto, "Ajiateki seisan yōshiki," 319.
31. Ishimoda, "Chūsei seiritsu," 36–37.

story was remarkably different—and grimmer. For Ishimoda, class division and conflict between the feudal lords and the producing class of farmers in China failed to develop in a "sharply defined" way, instead remaining "submerged" within primitive "communal" relations and various other historical strictures. In contrast to their dynamic Japanese counterparts, Chinese feudal lords embodied everything "stagnant, languid, and depraved."[32] The contrast between Japan and China could not have been starker.

The image of Asia fared no better in modernist discourse of the time, which focused not on class antagonisms (or their absence) but on questions of mentality and consciousness. In 1947 the legal sociologist Kawashima Takeyoshi (1909–92) offered a detailed analysis of the "Asiatic social structure" in Japan, manifested for him in slave-like relations masked as familial loyalty. Kawashima pointed to the ways "relations of domination and appropriation" were "misrepresented" as "relations of familial allegiance" within Japan's "Asiatic" social structure—for instance, between landowners and tenants or between store owners and clerks.[33] The aspect of coercion gave such relations their Asiatic character. Important to keep in mind is the fact that Kawashima's discussion of Asiatic feudalism in Japan was as much about the present and future as it was about the past. Overcoming Asiaticness was the key to attaining a modern mentality in the wake of individual and national failure.

The thought of the economic historian Ōtsuka Hisao (1907–96) exemplified this reformative perspective. For Ōtsuka, Japan had almost "completely lacked the capacity to autonomously transform into a democratic society," and only with "force from the outside" in the form of "defeat and forced occupation" did the country finally have the opportunity to "free itself" from its "Asiatic destiny."[34] Deeply influenced by the German sociologist Max Weber, Ōtsuka focused on the emergence of the "modern human type" in the West and the conditions and mentality required for its realization in Japan. Asia proved extremely useful as an antithetical identifier of the stagnant and shallow Japanese psyche, bereft of any inner subjectivity. As Ōtsuka explained in a 1946 essay, "the

32. Ishimoda, "Chūsei seiritsu," 40.
33. Kawashima, "Nihon hōkensei," 18.
34. Quoted in Tōyama, *Sengo no rekishigaku*, 52.

human type evident in our populace cannot simply be called feudal, as I believe it contains more complex, so-called Asiatic aspects."[35] He compared the internalized ethics of the Western psyche with the shallow, external ethics of Asians, in much the same way as the American anthropologist Ruth Benedict distinguished between "guilt culture" in the West and "shame culture" in Japan in her classic study of the same year, *The Chrysanthemum and the Sword*.[36] Ōtsuka's writings of the time thus reveal his overwhelming desire to reform a fallen Japan not only through a thorough Westernization but also a comprehensive de-Asianization.

Maruyama Masao (1914–96), arguably Japan's leading postwar intellectual, contributed to this early postwar derision of Asia through his landmark studies of Japanese nationalism, ultranationalism, and intellectual history. A striking example is the introductory essay, "The Formation of Tokugawa Confucianism," in Maruyama's *Nihon seiji shisō kenkyū* (translated as *Studies in the Intellectual History of Tokugawa Japan*). The essay was first published in 1940 and incorporated into this book after the war. In the essay, Maruyama left readers in no doubt as to the juxtaposition he wished to draw. The first in a list of key terms below the essay's title was "the static character of Chinese history and Confucianism." In the opening paragraphs, Maruyama noted that "the characteristics Hegel ascribed to the Chinese, or Oriental, stage can also be discerned at some point in the historical development of practically any nation. But what is significant is the fact that in China these characteristics did not constitute only one phase; they are constantly reproduced. This is what is called the static nature of Chinese history."[37] Referring to the "closed family society under the absolute authority of the patriarch," Maruyama suggested that "because this social structure was very firmly established in imperial China, the subject (the individual) failed to attain his own rights and, not giving birth to any internal opposition, remained an unmediated unity. In consequence, China remained an 'empire of duration.'"[38] Moreover, Maruyama saw absolutely no capacity for autochthonous transformation: "Chinese history remained 'unhistorical' despite frequent dynastic

35. Ōtsuka, "Kindaiteki ningen," 94–95.
36. Benedict, *Chrysanthemum and the Sword*, 222–23.
37. Maruyama, *Studies in the Intellectual History*, 4.
38. Maruyama, *Studies in the Intellectual History*, 4.

changes, not because of internal dissension but because it lacked such dissension."[39] As we will see, Maruyama partially abandoned this view of China in the early 1950s, but at this early stage China served as a useful juxtaposition for him to show the process of internal intellectual transformation in Japanese Confucian thought toward so-called modern consciousness. Here again we see a modernist inflection of Ishimoda's Asian version of Asian stagnation, with Japan as dynamic and changeable and Asia (China) as inferior and static.

Others have also taken Maruyama to task for the lack of attention to empire and Asian aggression in his writings on Japanese nationalism, specifically in the landmark 1946 essay "Chō-kokkashugi no ronri to shinri" (translated as "Theory and Psychology of Ultra-Nationalism"). Here Maruyama explored the political, social, and psychological forces that had driven Japanese modernization off course into expansionism and war. For Maruyama, the pre-1945 emperor system had been organized in such a way that notions of truth and morality remained in the hands of the state, while individuals found themselves trapped in a coercive system of control in which relations of oppression were transferred downward.[40] From the perspective of responsibility to Asia and deimperialization, this depiction left itself open to the criticism of freeing all but the highest of wartime leaders of responsibility. After all, if the majority of Japanese had no free choice due to oppression from above, how could they be held responsible for individual war crimes against Asians? When discussing the "atrocities committed by Japanese forces in China and the Philippines," Maruyama suggested that "given the nature of Japanese society, it is no wonder that the masses, who in ordinary civilian or military life have no object to which they can transfer oppression, should, when they find themselves in this position, be driven by an explosive impulse to free themselves at a stroke from the pressure that has been hanging over them. Their acts of brutality are a sad testimony to the Japanese system of psychological compensation."[41] To be fair, Maruyama was in no way an apologist in search of excuses: on the contrary, he was sincerely attempting to identify a social malaise so that it could be repaired. But in

39. Maruyama, *Studies in the Intellectual History*, 5.
40. Maruyama, "Theory and Psychology."
41. Maruyama, "Theory and Psychology," 19.

terms of the consciousness and view of Asia and empire, there were a number of problems here. First, by removing or downplaying individual responsibility, the notion of downward psychological coercion tended to obviate the need for individual or societal deimperialization through an exploration of specific acts and instances of aggression in Asia on an individual level. It was enough for Japan to become modern like the West through a shedding of psychological coercion. Second, since Maruyama's depiction implicitly presented the Japanese psyche as not modern in the Western sense, it tended to reinforce notions of Asiatic backwardness and despotism as the root of the problem.

Beyond Stagnation: Idealizing Asia in the 1950s

As the 1940s drew to a close, then, a pejorative view of Asia dominated the progressive imagination in Japan, resonating quite seamlessly with the processes of de-Asianization that were proceeding apace under the Occupation. In this atmosphere there was essentially no intellectual imperative for considering (or even recognizing) the need for deimperialization. After all, the empire was gone, and Japan was in tatters. Nonetheless, the dominance of this pejorative perspective on Asia in Marxist and modernist thought proved to be surprisingly short-lived, as a number of domestic and international developments that began late in the decade facilitated the emergence of a remarkably different view of Asia as a space of dynamism, creativity, transformation, and hope. The Chinese Communist Revolution of 1949 was the first and strongest stimulus behind this new image of Asia, but the outbreak of the Korean War (1950–53) and the surge of Asian nationalism and decolonization movements throughout the 1950s also played a critical role. Against this international backdrop, Japanese progressives could only lament the sorry course of developments within Japan. Beginning with its banning of the general strike of 1947, MacArthur and his Occupation officials appeared to be moving away from their initial reformist agenda toward a more conservative, anticommunist line strongly shaped by American strategic priorities given the escalating tensions of the Cold War. This trend was only further reinforced in mid-1950 when US Occupation authorities orchestrated the so-called

Red Purge of members of the JCP's Central Committee, followed by subsequent purges of communist elements in the media, government agencies, educational institutions, and radical labor unions. At the same time, individuals previously purged for their involvement in the wartime regime were depurged, and some even resurrected their careers in the highest echelons of political power. In the face of this apparent course reversal, many progressives began to fear that Japan was heading toward a situation of permanent US subservience greatly at odds with their vision of a neutral, independent, and genuinely sovereign Japan. In 1951, Iizuka Kenji, a geographer and director of the Institute for Advanced Studies on Asia at the University of Tokyo, worried out loud about the "psychological subservience" to the "political conditions" of the Occupation, which seemed to be becoming stronger "by the day and by the month."[42] The incomplete San Francisco peace settlement and the US-Japan Security Treaty of 1952 underscored such trends.[43] To make matters worse, in 1950 the Cominform (Communist Information Bureau) had published a report authored by Joseph Stalin that criticized the JCP for its cooperative stance toward the Occupation—its so-called lovable JCP approach—and that called for more confrontational tactics.[44]

In addition to driving the JCP into a period of reckless and sometimes violent radicalism, one upshot of these international and domestic developments was a heightened attention among progressives to issues of the nation (*minzoku*), ethnic self-determination, and ethnic nationalism. The Marxist historian Tōyama Shigeki, who was in his mid-thirties at the time, observed how this sense of a "crisis of ethnic independence" stimulated progressives to ask questions such as "what is the Japanese ethnic nation" and "what are the ethnic nations of Asia."[45] As Curtis Anderson Gayle observes, invigorated by rising Asian nationalism and fearful of American control, Marxist historians now "set their sights upon promoting a 'national awakening' (*minzoku jikaku*) of the people" in

---

42. Iizuka, "Ajia no kakumei," 11.

43. The formal name of the treaty is the Treaty of Mutual Cooperation and Security between the United States and Japan (in Japanese, Nihonkoku to Amerika Gasshūkoku to no aida no sōgo kyōryoku oyobi anzen hoshō jōyaku).

44. On the Cominform criticism and JCP response see Stockwin, *Collected Writings*, 106.

45. Tōyama, *Sengo no rekishigaku*, 314.

which "the nation (*minzoku*) and ethnic national culture (*minzoku bunka*)" could become tools to reveal "the American presence and its policies in East Asia" and, more importantly, "to push forward the goal of a socialist revolution in Japan."[46] In 1951 and 1952, for example, the annual meetings of the Rekishigaku Kenkyūkai (Historical Science Society of Japan, or Rekiken) had the respective themes of "the problem of the nation in history" (*rekishi ni okeru minzoku no mondai*) and "on national culture" (*minzoku no bunka ni tsuite*), while in 1952 Ishimoda brilliantly encapsulated the tenor of this ethnic nationalist awakening with his landmark study, *Rekishi to minzoku no hakken* (The discovery of history and nation).[47]

In terms of the view of Asia and attention to Japan's imperialist past, the *minzoku* discourse contained a number of problems. Observers of the *minzoku* phenomenon in 1950s Japan routinely note that this discourse essentially neglected prewar Japanese imperialism and war responsibility (that is, it contained no deimperializing moment) and instead positioned Japan as another "victimized nation" alongside the other colonized nations of Asia. For instance, a 1956 article titled "Ajia no minzokushugi undō to Nihon" (Asian ethnic national movements and Japan) suggested that although Japan did "not find itself under the same circumstances as these countries" (that is, it was not colonized), it was substantially dealing with the same situation given the presence of American military bases scattered across the archipelago.[48] The author argued that "the solution to the impasse between Japan and Asia is to heroically discard the illusions and vestiges of the past buried within ourselves. We must begin by clarifying our attitude of opposing all forms of colonialism." The path for Japan was to "comprehensively settle the excessive dependency on America," "overcome our existence as an Asian outsider," and commit to "mutual support."[49]

In hindsight such assertions of solidarity betray a shocking historical amnesia, given that a number of the Asian nations Japanese progressives claimed to share an ethnic allegiance with had been Japanese colonies and brutalized victims just a few years earlier. The only attempt to

46. Gayle, *Marxist History*, 1.
47. Ishimoda, *Rekishi to minzoku no hakken.*
48. Hamanishi, "Ajia no minzokushugi," 21.
49. Hamanishi, "Ajia no minzokushugi," 21.

bridge this problematic gap was via simplistic assertions that Japan, previously an imperialist aggressor, was now an "oppressed nation" and that the warmongers had been fumigated.[50]

Nevertheless, the advent and symbolism of anticolonial ethnic nationalism and revolutionary movements in Asia did not fall on barren ground in Japanese progressive circles. Attention to Asian nationalism greatly undermined notions of Asian stagnation, opening the way for progressives to fundamentally reconceptualize their view of Asia. This certainly did not culminate in any significant deimperialization work during the 1950s—that would have to wait until the 1960s and beyond for fuller expression. But releasing Asia from the shackles of stagnation made it something worth knowing about, initially in the abstract realm of ideals but slowly thereafter as a complex geographical, political, and economic configuration with which Japan was deeply intertwined. In this way, developments in Asia directly influenced the evolution of progressive thought and activism within Japan during the decade.

The positive reappraisal of China and Chinese history among influential Japanese progressives is quite telling in this respect. As we saw above, the leading historian Ishimoda initially posited two very different trajectories for China and Japan, the former stagnant and the latter evolutionary. By the eve of the Chinese Revolution, however, Ishimoda was having second thoughts and had begun to question his earlier simplistic comparisons between two very different national historical experiences. In a 1948 article titled "Chūsei shi kenkyū no kiten" (The starting point of medieval historical research), Ishimoda announced that he was making some "revisions" to his earlier "one-sided" perspective on the medieval world.[51] He admitted that he had been wrong to assert that only Japan had experienced a great jump in agricultural productivity in the transition from ancient to medieval society and, concurrently, to claim that productivity in medieval China was "stagnant" when it was not.[52] Moreover, empirical facts aside, he said that it had been a "methodological error" to determine the "direction of historical development" or "differences

50.   Yoon, *Nihon kokumin*, 187.
51.   Ishimoda, "Chūsei shi," 400.
52.   Ishimoda, "Chūsei shi," 403.

in historical formations" simply by "comparing productivity."[53] While he remained faithful to his earlier assertion that, in contrast to the situation in Japan, the strength of communal and village ties in China had reinforced traditional communal relations between feudal lords and peasant farmers, he felt that his earlier work had failed to clarify the "*historical substance*" of "direct class relations between these two groups."[54] It was simply not satisfactory to consider "communal aspects" in China in isolation: future research needed to understand these in a comparative way as one "concrete manifestation of class relations."[55] Indeed, he said, "we have reached a stage where we must think specifically about the diverse pathways to the formation of feudalism" in each nation.[56] Rather than a history of cyclical stagnation, Ishimoda now envisioned medieval Chinese society as a complex fusion of "ancient," "feudal," and "early modern" elements.[57] With the "grand victory of the Chinese revolution" now likely, he predicted that such issues would be of major concern to Chinese historians in the post-revolutionary period of reconstruction: "We too must greatly elevate our scholarship through cooperation with this Chinese historiography."[58] Although his ideas were still somewhat nebulous, we can see how Ishimoda was starting to break away from rigid universal laws of history premised on linear, Euro-normative historical development. What he had previously characterized as "stagnant" was now reconceptualized as merely different. China had certainly not developed like Japan, but an investigation into Chinese history revealed that China had its own unique processes of change—which, for Ishimoda and other adherents of Chinese communism looking through rose-colored glasses, helped explain the revolutionary present.

The critical point for this discussion is the way revolutionary upheaval in China fueled historical reinterpretations that, in turn, transformed the view of China among Japanese Marxists almost overnight. By 1953 Ishimoda was triumphantly announcing that "democracy, socialism, and

53. Ishimoda, "Chūsei shi," 405.
54. Ishimoda, "Chūsei shi," 407.
55. Ishimoda, "Chūsei shi," 410.
56. Ishimoda, "Chūsei shi," 431.
57. Ishimoda, "Chūsei shi," 433.
58. Ishimoda, "Chūsei shi," 433.

communism . . . no longer belong solely to Europe. The Chinese Revolution has born witness to the arrival of an age in which the Asian
masses—long thought to be governed by different principles from
Europeans—are creating these systems through their own efforts."[59]
Others like Uehara Senroku (1899–1975), a historian of Europe, soon
jumped onto the celebratory bandwagon. In a 1955 essay Uehara emphat-
ically rejected the notion of Chinese stagnation. On the contrary, he argued that the development of Confucianism in China actually facilitated
a dynamic "new Sui-Tang culture" that absorbed "the newly imported
Buddhism and the newly reformed Daoism."[60]

Even prominent modernists, who were somewhat less enamored of
the Chinese Revolution than their Marxist counterparts, were engaged
in a revision of their assumptions about Chinese stagnation at this time.
In an essay on Japanese nationalism written for the eleventh conference
of the Institute of Pacific Relations in Lucknow, India, in late 1950,
Maruyama Masao offered a fascinating reevaluation of China. He accepted mainstream interpretations that China's semicolonial status
stemmed from its leaders' inability "to adapt to the new circumstances."
But instead of linking this to a discourse of perpetual Chinese stagnation, Maruyama now suggested that it was precisely thanks to this humiliation by the West that the Chinese had "accomplished the task of
fundamentally transforming their society and political system through
a nationalist movement opposing imperialist rule." Although Chinese revolutionary leaders had their own unique styles and approaches, Maruyama
identified a clear historical tradition combining anti-imperialism
and social reform in the thought and action of Sun Yat-sen, Chiang Kai-
shek, and Mao Zedong.[61] Japan, in contrast, managed to resist colonization only thanks to government support for industry, which promoted
the development of monopoly capitalism. In Japan, "feudal remnants"
remained in "the mode of agricultural production and the relations of
land ownership." This systemic inequity, Maruyama said, "impeded the
smooth development of democratic forces," and the "endless reproduction of patriarchal labor relations and low wages" meant that Japan's

59. Quoted in Oguma, "Postwar Intellectuals," 203–4.
60. Uehara, "Ajia no unmei," 133.
61. Maruyama, "Sengo Nihon no nashonarizumu," 170.

leaders had no choice but to engage in imperialistic and militaristic expansion.[62] In other words, Japan turned to expansionism because of both its backwardness and its relatively more advanced state of modernity. China, conversely, experienced a more fundamental process of internal transformation.

Maruyama reiterated this perspective in the afterword to his classic 1952 *Nihon seiji shisō kenkyū*.[63] In reference to his comments on China in the book's introductory essay (initially published in 1940), Maruyama confessed that "in terms of a general self-critique, the most striking deficiency" in the essay was "the perspective at the outset of Japan's relatively advanced condition compared to China's stagnation. While this perspective is accurate on a certain level, as is widely accepted in academic circles today, it also runs the risk of incorrectly oversimplifying the situation."[64] In fact, "from the perspective of modernization at the foundation of the masses," Maruyama admitted that "Japan's experience of a parenthesized 'modernization' and China's lack of success" was "now giving birth to a reversed contrast. It is within this complicated historical dialectic that we need to reconsider the issue of 'why Japan was the first to create a modern state in the East.'"[65] As I explain below, Maruyama's reappraisal of China here drew heavily on the thought of Takeuchi.

Other liberals joined Maruyama in lionizing the new China. As Kamachi Noriko notes, from the late 1940s, the liberal monthly *Sekai* "carried more reports and discussions of China than any other monthly magazine," paying significant attention to the revolutionary developments on the mainland.[66] Notably, on the eve of the establishment of the People's Republic of China in 1949, *Sekai* ran a special issue on China containing a discussion among leading Japanese historians and social scientists of China.[67] Although there were then very few such scholars, some even traveled to China at this time. In early 1949 Takeda Kiyoko (1917–2018), a historian and member of the modernist group Shisō no Kagaku Kenkyū

62. Maruyama, "Sengo Nihon no nashonarizumu," 170.
63. Maruyama, *Nihon seiji shisō*.
64. Maruyama, "'Nihon seiji shisō kenkyū' atogaki," 289.
65. Maruyama, "'Nihon seiji shisō kenkyū' atogaki," 289–90.
66. Kamachi Noriko, "Japanese Writings," 54.
67. See *Sekai* 44 (1949), 12–40.

Kai (Institute for the Science of Thought), documented her recent visit
to China and India as secretary-general of the Japanese Young Women's
Christian Association in an article for the magazine *Asahi hyōron* titled
"Atarashiki Ajia no sedai" (The new Asian generation). Takeda was
clearly taken aback by the revolutionary sentiment in China and sensed
that the country might actually have progressed further than Japan. She
described a memorable encounter with a young customs officer on her
arrival at Shanghai's airport. The young man had said: "Are the Japanese
people satisfied with being ruled over? We must make Asia into an Asia
for Asians. Young Chinese all think this way. The Japanese are planning
to threaten China again in the future, right? Japanese are so stupid: why
do they threaten fellow Asians when we really should be comrades cooperating for the independence of Asia?"[68] Takeda could only be impressed
by this sense of autonomy and pride, concluding that "the Chinese,
whether students, leaders, or [members of] the CCP [Chinese Communist Party], advocate a communism different to [that of] the Soviets. The
Chinese have a curious pride: what might be called a kind of Chinese
spirit or Chinese honor. There is somehow a feeling that it is shameful to
simply copy the ideas of another country or reconstruct a replica of another society."[69] In the midst of the Occupation, Takeda was sending a
subtly coded message to Japanese readers about the state of their country
under US domination. In terms of the changing view of Asia, it is noteworthy that she did so through a lionization of China.

   However, the definitive exaltation of China at this time came not
from a Marxist or a modernist, but from the mercurial sinologist Takeuchi Yoshimi. Much has been written about Takeuchi, including his problematic support for the Pacific War and his postwar resurrection of
Asianism, and I deal with some of these issues below. Takeuchi's important rehabilitation of the view of China came in the provocative 1948
essay titled "Chūgoku no kindai to Nihon no kindai" (Chinese modernity and Japanese modernity) and the 1949 article titled "Nihonjin no
Chūgokukan" (The Japanese view of China). Compared to Ishimoda's
and Maruyama's somewhat measured, scholarly reappraisals of China,
Takeuchi's iconoclastic essays were lessons in clarity: China was genuinely

---

68. Quoted in Takeda, "Atarashiki Ajia," 59.
69. Takeda, "Atarashiki Ajia," 59–60.

modern, and Japan was a deplorable, malfunctioning imitator. By modern, Takeuchi primarily meant, first, the ability of an ethnic nation to resist domination from without (specifically, the ability of the colonized nations of Asia to resist the West) and, second, the ability of those nations to subsequently reform themselves on a spiritual or psychological level. For Takeuchi, Japan's incessant desire and actions to replicate the West by abandoning its own traditions and adopting everything European were proof of its slave-like nature—born of a shallow desire to be an honor student, always at the top of the class yet with no internal substance. He identified this condition in the phenomenon of "*tenkō*" (meaning ideological recantation or about-facing) in modern Japan: "*Tenkō* invariably takes place when honor students act conscientiously. If they do not commit *tenkō*, they can no longer be honor students since they lose their ability to incorporate new things. Conscientious behavior consists in abandoning communism for totalitarianism when the latter appears newer. If democracy comes, the progressive attitude most befitting the honor student is to follow democracy."[70] And precisely because Japan was constantly changing on a superficial level, it "never underwent the historical discontinuity of revolution; it never experienced new birth and the revival of the old by severing itself from the past"—hence "its history was never rewritten."[71] Japanese modernity contained no "moment of resistance," and for Takeuchi, this absence meant that Japan was not only not Asian but also "not European," because it lacked any "wish for self-preservation." He could only conclude that, in "the absence of the self," Japan was "nothing": the culture was "structurally unproductive," proceeding "from life to death, never from death to rebirth."[72]

As others have shown, Takeuchi's grim diagnosis of Japan's condition strongly informed his subsequent civic activism.[73] But these late 1940s essays were just as important in thoroughly refurbishing the image of China from one of stagnation and nondevelopment to being the very "paradigm for postwar reform."[74] This was no accident: Takeuchi made

70.　Takeuchi, "What Is Modernity?," 74–75.
71.　Takeuchi, "What Is Modernity?," 75.
72.　Takeuchi, "What Is Modernity?," 75. See also Nagahara, "Sengo Nihon," 26.
73.　See Oguma, *Minshu to aikoku*, 513–15 and 518–21.
74.　Gayle, *Marxist History*, 57.

it clear that his target was the Japanese "sense of contempt toward China," especially among intellectuals. It was a contempt that had intensified after the first Sino-Japanese war (1894–95) and had "not changed" either "intellectually" or "emotionally" thereafter.[75] He singled out Marxism for provoking this contempt by focusing on "productive power" as the "only way of explaining history." Because Marxist scholars were able to "prove 'scientifically' how China's modernization lagged behind Japan's," they established a "scientific contempt" to replace the earlier "naïve contempt" of Fukuzawa Yukichi and other advocates of "abandon[ing] Asia."[76] Conversely, Takeuchi commended Maruyama for breaking with such "formulaic historical materialists" by "clearly distinguishing the modernization process in backward countries from Europe." But he believed that even Maruyama had failed to recognize the "qualitative difference" between the "forms of backwardness in Japan and China." Accordingly, Takeuchi could not help feeling that "even a scholar such as Maruyama" remained under the influence of this "contempt for China," which "clouded correct understanding" of the country.[77]

What then was Takeuchi's view of China? Unlike Japanese culture which constantly mimicked the West, Takeuchi depicted Chinese culture as one of rebirth in the sense that it constantly involved self-renewal through resistance. Takeuchi concentrated on the history of ethnic resistance in modern China, based on a fusion of revolution and nationalism forged in the process of resisting colonial rule. As Yoon observes, here he identified a dynamic "history of self-formation."[78] According to Takeuchi, "due to the intense resistance of tradition, Chinese modernization was delayed," but this also meant that the "transformation," when it did come, was all the more "thorough." He saw in China nothing short of a "renewal" of the "national mentality."[79] "In China, the force of reactionism was so great that it stifled even those dissident activities within the bureaucracy. This drove the revolution lower and lower, allowing it to spread its roots among the people at the bottom. In Japan, however, even

75. Takeuchi, "Nihonjin no Chūgokukan," 63–65.
76. Takeuchi, "Nihonjin no Chūgokukan," 65.
77. Takeuchi, "Nihonjin no Chūgokukan," 68–69.
78. Yoon, "Sengo Shisō," 149.
79. Takeuchi, "Nihonjin no Chūgokukan," 69.

the people's movement was sucked upward by an open conduit, beyond the military academies and imperial universities, where it withered and died."[80] Conversely, the 1911 revolution in China was one in which "the force of internal negation constantly sprang forth. For Sun Yat-sen, revolution was always to be conceived of as 'failure.' The 1911 revolution negated the warlordism . . . after which it negated the bureaucratization of the revolutionary party itself. In other words, this was a productive, and hence a true, revolution."[81] As Takeuchi reiterated some years later, "Chinese modernization . . . was forged on the basis of its own ethnic-national characteristics, and this is what allowed China to modernize more purely."[82]

While Takeuchi and others were busy rehabilitating the image of China in this way, another critically important challenge to the Asian stagnation thesis appeared at the 1953 meeting of Rekiken, whose appropriate name was "Sekai shi ni okeru Ajia" (Asia in world history).[83] Instead of lionizing aspects of Chinese and Asian modernity, this approach advanced a novel explanation of Asian stagnation based on exogenous international factors. The architect of this approach at the 1953 meeting was the Marxist historian Inoue Kiyoshi (1913–2001), who delivered an address titled "Nihon teikokushugi to Ajia" (Japanese imperialism and Asia). Inoue's title alone was provocative and pioneering, given that almost no progressive scholars were drawing links between Asia and Japan's imperialist past at this time. But the thrust of Inoue's argument was just as innovative. His analysis began with one of the central issues of concern to Japanese students of modern Asian history: why was it that their country had managed to avoid colonization and modernize while other nations, like China, had failed? As we have seen, most explanations revolved around Japan's capacity to change internally through class conflict and productivity improvements, versus China's and India's failure due to the grip of Asiatic social relations. In contrast, Inoue explained the difference—quite simply—on the basis of luck and timing in world

80. Takeuchi, "What Is Modernity?," 78.
81. Takeuchi, "What Is Modernity?," 76.
82. Takeuchi, "Asia as Method," 164.
83. I discuss the conference further below. For its full report, see Rekishigaku Kenkyūkai, *Sekai shi ni okeru Ajia.*

politics. Japanese independence, he said, was greatly facilitated by the general state of conflict in Europe and troubles within the United States from the late 1850s onward, stretching from the Crimean conflict to the American Civil War. Such unrest in the West literally "tied the hands" of Britain, France, Russia, and the United States with respect to Japan.[84] This was an "exogenous situation" that proved to be a "beneficial condition" for the Japanese and, importantly, was not a benefit that either the Chinese or the Indians enjoyed.[85] Moreover, Inoue highlighted how Japan had benefited greatly from the Western powers' troubles with Asian resistance movements at the time, such as the Indian Rebellion of 1857, the Taiping Rebellion in China in 1850–64, as well as the French campaign against Korea in 1866—which arguably fashioned a more conciliatory, or at least careful, approach to opening up Japan.[86] These differences, argued Inoue, helped explain the subsequent historical trajectories of Asian nations.[87] Japan benefited because "by the time the European capitalist powers arrived . . . they had no choice but to greatly moderate their Asian policies."[88] At the same time, Inoue also stressed that while Japan may have avoided direct colonization, the unequal treaties, the loss of tariff autonomy, and extraterritoriality made it subservient to the European powers in a kind of "semicolonial" way.[89] So broad generalizations that Japan had won independence while allegedly stagnant China and India had lost everything were, at best, exaggerations. Japan responded to its relatively advantageous position by, on the one hand, accepting its subservience to Western imperialism (notably in the 1902 alliance with the British) and, on the other hand, becoming an imperialist power in East Asia: "So, while Japan's was a second- or third-rate subservient imperialism, in Asia at least it was the only country capable of threatening" other nations.[90]

As Tōyama observed, Inoue's interpretation was a critical breakthrough inasmuch as it recognized the need to "emphasize the relative

84. Inoue Kiyoshi, "Nihon teikokushugi," 121.
85. Inoue Kiyoshi, "Nihon teikokushugi," 121.
86. Inoue Kiyoshi, "Nihon teikokushugi," 121.
87. Inoue Kiyoshi, "Nihon teikokushugi," 121.
88. Inoue Kiyoshi, "Nihon teikokushugi," 122.
89. Inoue Kiyoshi, "Nihon teikokushugi," 123.
90. Inoue Kiyoshi, "Nihon teikokushugi," 126.

importance" of global capitalism in the eighteenth and nineteenth centuries, as well as that of global imperialism in the late nineteenth and twentieth centuries, in "restraining and distorting Asian development."[91] As the historian Eguchi Bokurō put it in a 1953 article for the monthly magazine *Chūō kōron*, "so-called Asian backwardness, then, is not simply [because Asia] is backward. It must also be recognized that it is also deeply tied to European capitalistic development. It might be possible to say that Europe's modern development would not have been possible without the sacrifice of Asia."[92] While debates over the different historical trajectories of Japan, China, and other Asian nations were hardly resolved by Inoue's thesis, undoubtedly it—together with modernist and Marxist reappraisals of China—was a crucial intellectual intervention, transcending earlier cultural and civilizational explanations of Asian stagnation that bordered on tautology: in other words, that Asia was backward primarily because it was Asiatic.

The Fervor of Asian Nationalism

Together with the Chinese Revolution, the emergence of movements for decolonization and Asian nationalism fueled the rise of Asian idealism in 1950s Japan. The sense of expectation, excitement, and optimism in the voluminous Japanese writings on the phenomenon is palpable—all the more so thanks to the unambiguously negative image of Asia that had been dominant up to that point. But progressives were not only enamored of the momentous events in Asia; most fervently believed and advocated that Japan must join with and learn from this historic wave. The historian Uehara, for example, resolutely concluded that "the urgent task for the Japanese today" was "to transcend their old view of Asia and to not only think and feel as Asians but also to live as Asians for the good of the Japanese themselves, for other Asians, and for all of humanity."[93] For Uehara, the historical significance of "contemporary Asia" was about

91. Tōyama, *Sengo no rekishigaku*, 308.
92. Eguchi, "Joron," 264.
93. Uehara, "Gendai Ajia," 81.

much more than independence: rather, it was in the ways "the various nations and ethnic groups of Asia" were "uniting toward 'One Asia,'" based on their consciousness of collectively "shouldering the tasks of political and economic independence." Uehara singled out the 1955 Asian-African Conference in Bandung, Indonesia (discussed below), as "powerful evidence" of this process.[94] It represented for him a historic recuperation of "subjectivity and self-autonomy" from Europe, both "politically and economically."[95] Takeuchi expressed similar sentiments, noting that a "new factor" had emerged that could not be explained by "ideological discourse or fixed notions of opposition between two [the communist and the noncommunist] worlds."[96] He said that Asian nationalism, under the influence of Mao, had "proceeded from the stage of resistance and acceptance of the West to the stage of inheriting the system of values born in Western modernity such as liberty and freedom."[97] For him, this was nothing less than a new "humanism."[98]

Jawaharlal Nehru (1889–1964), India's first prime minister, appears again and again in Japanese writing on Asia in the 1950s as the embodiment of and spokesperson for this new Asia. He encapsulated the sense that Asians (including Japanese) were at the forefront of a world-historical process—a "new humanism" emanating from the region. The geographer Iizuka, for instance, suggested that Nehru had located "the demands of Asian nationalism and today's Asia in the context of world history." And according to Iizuka, Nehru was "not only speaking as an 'Indian' or even as an 'Asian' but on behalf of 'humanity.'"[99] Uehara identified in Nehru's words a "qualitative transformation in the Indian thought process" that shattered the general belief that there was "no possibility" of Indians' comprehending historical phenomena or thinking about the "overall structure" of the world in an "interconnected" way, as "Europeans do."[100] Nehru's "political principles" and his "thought process when considering

94. Uehara, "Gendai Ajia," 86.
95. Uehara, "Gendai Ajia," 83.
96. Takeuchi, "Ajia no nashonarizumu ni tsuite," 112.
97. Takeuchi, "Ajia no nashonarizumu," 126.
98. Takeuchi, "Ajia no nashonarizumu," 128.
99. Iizuka, "Ajia no kakumei," 12.
100. Uehara, "Ajia wa hitotsu ka," 67.

political problems" were always attentive to the "flow of world history" and the place of Indians "within" that history.[101]

An important statement informing such opinions was Nehru's opening address at the Institute of Pacific Relations' conference on Asian nationalism in Lucknow, India, in October 1950. It reverberated powerfully with Japanese progressives, who repeatedly referred to and quoted from the speech. Two sections were particularly captivating for them: Nehru's discussion of an "Asian sentiment" and his appeal to the "torment" of Asia. On the former, Nehru observed that "Asia is a huge continent and when we talk about an Asian feeling I do not quite know what it means, because we differ so much amongst ourselves. Great countries like China, Japan, India, Indonesia, Burma or the countries of the Middle East have ancient traditions and cultures, with a tremendous background of history and past experience and it is difficult to jumble them together and just call it Asia, because geographically they happen to be in that area." Yet Nehru agreed that "in the present context of things there is such a thing as an Asian sentiment, although there may be large differences between the countries. Possibly it is merely a reaction to the past 200 or 300 years of Europe in Asia."[102] Much in the same way that Takeuchi understood Asia as a symbol of resistance to the West, Nehru located the empathy of Asians in their shared "torment" born of this history: "In the final analysis if you seek to understand us you will understand little of us by discussing our economic . . . social . . . and . . . political problems . . . you have to look a little deeper to understand this torment in the mind and spirit of Asia. It takes different shapes in different countries, of course, and it is a problem ultimately for us also to understand and to solve with the help of others . . . but the burden is ours. Nobody else can solve it except us; others can help, as others can hinder; they cannot solve it for us."[103] Nehru's blending in the speech of Asia's historicity, victimization, suffering, and historic rebirth proved irresistibly intoxicating for many Japanese progressives with similar aspirations for their country.

Moreover, the fact that Asian statesmen like Nehru, Zhou, and Sukarno now presented themselves as advocates of world peace also

101. Uehara, "Ajia wa hitotsu ka," 66.
102. Nehru, "Opening Address," 2.
103. Nehru, "Opening Address," 2.

resonated with the growing pacifist sentiment in Japan, faced now with the escalating Cold War (especially on the Korean peninsula) and the incomplete peace settlement in San Francisco. Pacifists were deeply inspired by Zhou's and Nehru's five principles of peace, announced in 1954, and the subsequent "Final Communique of the Asian-African Conference" issued by participating nations at the Bandung conference in 1955.[104] As one Japanese observer put it, "Asian nationalist movements forged in opposition to imperialism and colonialism" were "not only refusing to become involved in international conflicts," they were "also solidifying their independent stance as a third force, a force for peace," and thus "leading world politics in the direction of peace."[105] Uehara similarly observed that not only did the character of contemporary Asia lie in its "attainment of agency and autonomy" but that also an "independent Asia" was at the "forefront" in addressing the "problem of world peace," "more than any other region in the world."[106] The novelist and commentator Hotta Yoshie, who traveled extensively throughout India in late 1956 and early 1957, confidently concluded that "looking at the countries of Asia, I think that the 'principle of peace' is a central axis. The West may fight wars but we [Asians] do not."[107] Asians "have the confidence and idealism that they can make world peace despite their *backwardness* and *underdevelopment*."[108] Interestingly, Hotta used the Japanized English of these italicized words—"*bakkuwādonessu*" and "*andādeberopumento*"— presumably to emphasize how they were as much Euro-normative value judgments as they were material realities. Of course, one wonders how Hotta understood the Korean War in light of his claims about Asians not fighting wars. Perhaps he saw this as a war of the great powers played out by hapless Asian puppets on an Asian stage? Regardless, his observations reveal just how quickly and comprehensively the idealistic view of Asia had overtaken the earlier view of stagnation—to the extent that

104.   For the five principles of peace see "Agreement between the Republic of India and the People's Republic of China," and for the communique see "Final Communique of Asian-African Conference," 102.

105.   Hamanishi, "Ajia no minzokushugi," 16–17.

106.   Uehara, "Gendai Ajia," 87.

107.   Takeuchi et al., "Zadankai," 180.

108.   Takeuchi et al., "Zadankai," 181.

"backwardness" and "underdevelopment" were now being treated as the language of Western imperialists.

The Asian-African Conference further fortified the progressive image of a newly autonomous and proactive Asia. It is worth noting the slippage between Japanese involvement in Bandung on the ground and the way progressives interpreted the conference. As observers have pointed out, other than two JSP members, the Japanese delegation consisted primarily of individuals affiliated with the conservatives, and their aims at the conference were related to economics rather than peace or human rights.[109] That said, the Japanese agenda did resonate with the spirit of independence in Bandung. Wakamiya suggests that Prime Minister Hatoyama Ichirō and his cabinet ministers saw the conference as an opportunity to create some distance between the United States and Japan, despite the country's already deep entanglement with America.[110] Takasaki Tatsunosuke, one of the Japanese representatives, even had an impromptu meeting with Premier Zhou, although it proved stillborn given the tightening US grip on Japanese conservatives in the 1950s.[111] Not privy to any of these motives and developments, Japanese progressives could only assess the Bandung conference from afar through extremely rose-colored lenses. Once again, progressives like Tōyama stressed "the pacifist, anti-imperialist features of this new kind of Pan-Asianism" and the fact that this was the first large-scale international conference "held by the various countries of colored people," excluding the "white races."[112] Uehara best summed up progressive sentiment, writing in 1955 that "this conference captured world attention for revealing the transformation of Asia and Africa in world history from objects to subjects. In the old-world order with Europeans as the standard, Asia and Africa were the targets of European colonialism, nothing more than objects. But this conference has proven that Asia and Africa are now attempting to become the protagonists of their own destinies and the agents of history."[113]

109. Dennehy, "Overcoming Colonialism," 214.
110. Wakamiya, *Sengo 70-nen*, 167.
111. Wakamiya, *Sengo 70-nen*, 168.
112. Dennehy, "Overcoming Colonialism," 216; Akiyama, "Shokuminchishugi," 30.
113. Uehara, "Sekai shi no kōzō," 47.

One further phenomenon deserves discussion in the context of the emergence of an idealistic view of Asia in 1950s Japan: namely, the link between Asian idealism and progressive ethnic nationalism. We have already seen this dynamic in Takeuchi's late 1940s essays on China. He clarified this link in dramatic language in 1951, saying that "the perspective of 'Asian nationalism'" represented the "final opportunity" for "saving the Japanese ethnic nation from self-destruction."[114] But it was the controversial sociologist and writer Shimizu Ikutarō (1907–88) who most forcefully articulated this sentiment. Shimizu, of course, is famous for his criticism of the 1960 movement against the renewal and revision of the US-Japan Security Treaty (the so-called Anpo struggle) and his later advocacy of Japanese possession of nuclear weapons. In the context of early postwar views of Asia, however, Shimizu's important contribution came in a 1951 special edition on Asian nationalism in *Chūō kōron*, where he presented a melodramatic juxtaposition of Japanese failure and Asian success. Shimizu suggested that one possible "new method" for the transformation of the Japanese nation would be a "restoration of unity with the countries of Asia sharing the same destiny." Despite the fact that the "traditional relations Japan shared with these countries" had been "completely severed," he saw no future for a Japan permanently isolated from the countries of Asia. In fact, should Japan "turn its back on Asia, peeling away its skin like an onion," Shimizu warned—in chilling terms—that there would be no way for Japan to survive "other than with the assistance of war."[115] The reality now was that Asia had changed dramatically: "The Asia we are trying to restore connections with is being newly reborn around the central demands of nationalism. Its rebirth in this way and its unwavering confidence is one of the major developments of the twentieth century and perhaps all of modernity. These swarming millions who have been walking on the underside of history have emerged on its main stage."[116] Drawing on Nehru's opening address at the Asian-African Conference, Shimizu said that the "torment in the spirit of Asia" manifested in Asian nationalism represented a third force in the world, after the first force of the United States and the second force of the Soviet Union: "In

114. Takeuchi, "Ajia no nashonarizumu ni tsuite," 113.
115. Shimizu, "Nihonjin," 12–13.
116. Shimizu, "Nihonjin," 13.

other words, the intense unconsciousness lying in one part of the globe has surfaced as a similarly intense consciousness."[117] But unfortunately, the Japanese had yet to extirpate their Western inferiority complex: among the "eight hundred million" in Asia, "eighty million" called themselves "Japanese," but they could think about things only in terms of "America, Britain, and Japan" or "Japan, Germany, and Italy."[118] Indeed, now the tables had turned completely. According to Shimizu, Japan found itself on the scrap heap of nations, below the West for sure but now also below an Asia resplendent in its independence and unity.[119]

Toward a Rediscovery of the Region

Shimizu's ideas exemplify the process by which an early progressive view of Asian stagnation and backwardness was slowly supplemented, although not entirely replaced, by an idealistic view of Asia that drew energy from the revolutionary developments in China and the various decolonization movements throughout South and Southeast Asia. Before concluding the chapter I want to explore some of the outcomes and new intellectual directions opened up by this process. In general terms, it is possible to say that, thanks to the emergence of the idealistic view of Asia, by the late 1950s progressives were in a position to begin thinking about the region in ways not possible when Asia simply signified backwardness. This is not to say that all progressive treatments of Asia were suddenly favorable. In 1953, for example, at the height of the China and Asia boom, Minobe Ryōkichi (1904–84), a young Marxist economist who would later serve as the progressive governor of Tokyo from 1967 to 1979 and become a pro-Asia advocate, wrote a scathing critique of Asian reality after visiting cities in India, Myanmar, and elsewhere in Asia. "My greatest impression of Asia," Minobe wrote, "was the miserable daily lives of the general populace."[120] He commented that "in Rangoon filthy barrack-style food

---

117. Shimizu, "Nihonjin," 14.
118. Shimizu, "Nihonjin," 14.
119. Shimizu, "Nihonjin," 7.
120. Minobe, "Ajia to Nihon," 34.

stalls were lined up on both sides of the road. The foul smell of rotten
cooking oil filled the air."[121] To make matters worse, Asians who had "the
worst daily lives in the world" were "the most populous people in the
world."[122] Asian economic growth, moreover, was not only "extremely delayed," it was also "absolutely stagnant."[123] Minobe contrasted these
Asian conditions with his delightful experience in the West: "When visiting America and Europe I could only stare astounded at the people's
high standard of living. . . . [L]ooking at the beautiful peaks of the Alps
while bathing in the autumn sun with a bountiful breakfast of jam, but-
ter, and honey on the table in front of me, I felt as though I had gone to
heaven."[124] Moreover, even Japan seemed like a wonderfully developed
place compared to Asia. Having been in Rangoon and the cities of India, Minobe declared that he was "glad to have been born in Japan and
to be living in Tokyo": "Arriving at Haneda Airport I was filled with the
sensation of having returned to a wonderfully clean city."[125] Minobe's observations remind us that we need to take care when tracing transitions
in mentality. Old views are not necessarily replaced but tend to remain,
often submerged, and reemerge in unexpected places. As I show in subsequent chapters, Japanese progressives continued to struggle with ways
to understand and describe the reality of poverty in Asian countries while
remaining sensitive to the need to transcend essentialized portrayals of a
so-called Asiatic Asia.

Nonetheless, several developments warrant mention in relation to the
positive new directions opened up by Asian idealism in 1950s Japan.
Among the first to reconsider their earlier negativity toward Asia were
Japanese historians. The 1953 annual meeting of Rekiken, "Asia in World
History," at which Inoue delivered his address on Japanese imperialism
and Asia, appears to have been a particularly important moment. Organizers saw the gathering as an opportunity for historians to think seriously for the first time about the origins of the political and socioeconomic transformations happening in Asia. Referring to the "liberation"

121. Minobe, "Ajia to Nihon," 34.
122. Minobe, "Ajia to Nihon," 35.
123. Minobe, "Ajia to Nihon," 36.
124. Minobe, "Ajia to Nihon," 36.
125. Minobe, "Ajia to Nihon," 37.

of China and India, Doi Masaoki, a historian of the ancient world, declared that historians' "first matter of concern must be to understand just how this power—this kind of transformative energy—came into being."[126] Tōyama called on participants to think about "the concrete historical connections between Japan, located in Asia, and other Asian nations."[127] Subsequent discussions in subcommittees at the meeting focused on the limitations of "one-nation history" and the necessity to consider "regional history" and "world history" when trying to identify the "subjectivity of the people."[128] The 1953 meeting certainly drew heavily on the energy of Asian nationalism and the attention to *minzoku* among historians at Rekiken's annual meetings in 1951 and 1952, but it also tapped into a new initiative for "world history" (*sekai shi*). Tōyama understood this initiative as a methodology for transcending earlier Marxist approaches based on uncovering "laws of social development primarily through comparative investigation." Instead, the emphasis in the new world history would be on the "unique characteristics of each civilizational sphere" and their "unique modes of development." In particular, Tōyama (along with his colleagues) pointed out that historical materialism offered no "adequate theory" for understanding the "development of the People's Republic of China" or the "energy" of "ethnic liberation movements" in "Asia, Africa, and Latin America." Existing approaches to world history were trapped in rigid notions of "stagnation" in "backward nations" and could explain recent Chinese history only on the basis of, for example, the "preeminent leadership of the Chinese Communist Party" or, in the case of "other colonized peoples," only on the basis of changed international conditions after World War II. In other words, there was no way of seeing the capacity for change within Asia itself. According to Tōyama, frustration with this position led the new generation of world history advocates to focus on modes of development and transformation different from those in Europe and developed within each of the respective civilizational spheres—especially Asia.[129]

The eight-volume series *Sekai shi kōza* (Lectures on world history) published in 1955–56 was an early manifestation of this reconsideration

126. Doi, "Iwai no hanran," 3.
127. Tōyama, "'Kindai' mondai," 118.
128. Tōyama, *Sengo no rekishigaku*, 141–42.
129. Tōyama, *Sengo no rekishigaku*, 203.

of Asia.[130] The series brought together twenty-four historians of Western and Eastern history who were united by a common desire to transcend philosophies and methodologies of history based on the West as the model and objective of modernity. Instead of a linear, stage-theory approach to history, they advocated an approach that recognized diversity among civilizations, ethnic groups, and social development. The series editors called on the Japanese to overcome their consciousness of world history as something "passive" and shaped from without: "Although we Japanese are rooted in Asia and until very recently faced the same political predicament as other Asians, our consciousness and conceptualization of the world is above all European, and most Japanese people cannot genuinely empathize with other Asians or conceive of themselves as Asians." For this reason, the Japanese people's "construction of world history" adopted a similarly "passive approach." But the appearance of Asian leaders like India's Nehru and Egypt's Gamal Abdel Nasser demanded a change. "In the process of self-liberation through internal ethnic desire," people in these countries "had no choice but to aspire to a world history autonomously and actively from within themselves" and, in turn, "to construct this view of world history."[131] For Japanese historians involved in the series, this endogenous Asian transformation demanded a fundamental rethinking of Asia in world history.

Perhaps more than any other historian at the time, Uehara Senroku led the way in rethinking and repositioning Asia in this new world history. His work is emblematic of just how deeply Asian idealism had penetrated progressive views of Asia by the mid- to late 1950s. As we have seen, apart from Uehara's exploits as a historian, throughout the 1950s he published countless essays praising the advent of Asian nationalism. His key contribution in the context of historiography was the 1960 coauthored volume *Nihon kokumin no sekai shi* (A world history of the Japanese people).[132] Informing Uehara and his coauthor's approach in the work was

130. Onabe et al., *Sekai shi kōza.*
131. Quoted in Tōyama, *Sengo no rekishigaku*, 201.
132. The book was initially completed in 1957 as a high school world history textbook but failed the government certification process in 1958—prompting Uehara and coauthors to publish the book for a general readership. Uehara et al., *Nihon kokumin no sekai shi*, iii.

a deep dissatisfaction with Euro-centricity and Euro-normativity in history writing. As Uehara wrote in a 1955 essay, in the great German historian Leopold von Ranke's multivolume work on world history, only four chapters of the first volume were devoted to the "ancient Orient," with the remainder on Europe—there was no mention of Japan, China, or India.[133] He could only conclude from this that the "greatest flaw" of world history delineated by Europeans was its "Euro-centricity" which allowed "no independent position" for "the Asian world" or the "Islamic world" in the history of humanity: "In other words, when Europeans look at the Chinese, Indian, or Islamic worlds, they merely treat them as peripheries." Furthermore, "history is imagined on the basis of one-dimensional European values and not on the basis of a diversity of values."[134] As Nagahara explains, Uehara thus called on Japanese historians to overcome this Eurocentric perspective, proposing instead the imagination of a "new world history" in which former colonized nations in Asia, Africa, and Latin America were "properly positioned" as the "subjects of world history."[135] This new comprehension of world history would emphasize the "historical significance of contemporary Asia" beyond the "framework of world history constructed by Europeans and Americans," who merely "appended" Asia to their own worldview. On the contrary, the new approach would challenge the "total structure of their view of world history" at its very "core."[136] From this perspective Uehara and coauthors in the 1960 volume asserted the necessity of establishing a concept of the Japanese people or nation (*Nihon kokumin*) that was fundamentally different from earlier national subjectivities based on the West as standard. As Yoon notes, to this extent, the book made great strides in undermining the authority of the Asian stagnation theory and pushing Japanese historians in the direction of studying Japanese history as East Asian regional history.[137] To this end, *Nihon kokumin no sekai shi*'s contributors conceived of "civilization" not as the antithesis of "underdevelopment" or "barbarianism," nor as the "product of human intellect"—as was common in eighteenth-century

133. Uehara, "Sekai shi ni okeru," 149.
134. Uehara, "Sekai shi ni okeru," 150.
135. Nagahara, "Sengo Nihon," 17.
136. Uehara, "Sekai shi ni okeru," 151.
137. Yoon, *Nihon kokumin*, 194.

European Enlightenment thought. On the contrary, "civilization" denoted the totality of "politics, economy, society, and cultural organization" produced by an ethnic group with its own "distinctive historical characteristics."[138] Since Japanese history was "none other than a history within the Eastern Civilizational Sphere," Uehara and coauthors felt that "the Japanese people's attainment of a historical consciousness must start with recognition of these fundamental facts."[139]

Overall, then, the volume was a testament to the positive rethinking of Asia among historians that developed throughout the 1950s. Nevertheless, for all its criticism of national history and calls to reposition Japan in its region, Uehara and coauthors showed little sensitivity toward the Japanese people's responsibility as an ethnic nation for recent transgressions in Asia. Sections on Japan's aggression in and invasion of China in the 1930s and 1940s were brief and descriptive, making no reference to the atrocities committed there by Japanese. The country's colonial exploits were almost entirely absent. Moreover, a problem confounding not only Uehara's book but progressive historians' view of Asia more generally at the time was the tendency to treat the Japanese nation (indeed, all ethnic nations) as "ontologically inviolable" and largely homogeneous, while mounting an attack on the Japanese state.[140] The result was that historians' positive view of Asia left almost no room to consider internal diversity, especially within Japan. Here, unfortunately, progressive Asian idealism resonated with and effectively reinforced the contemporaneous process of de-Asianization occurring in Japan.

More positively, the rise of Asian idealism also stimulated some progressives to begin advocating for a move beyond idealism and toward an understanding of the reality—or realities—in Asian countries. In a fascinating article titled "Ajia no ninshiki to Ajia no kenkyū" (Asian awareness and Asian studies) in *Sekai* in 1961, Ara Matsuo, a scholar of Indian and South Asian history, criticized so-called understandings of Asia for their utter lack of empirical knowledge about the region. Instead of disparaging a stagnant Asia or projecting Asian resistance and solidarity onto "rose-colored idealism and slogans," Ara called for "a thorough

138.   Uehara et al., *Nihon kokumin no sekai shi*, 8–9.
139.   Uehara et al., *Nihon kokumin no sekai shi*, 10–11.
140.   Gayle, "Progressive Representations," 14.

understanding of the reality" in Asian countries.[141] Invoking the words of Asian leaders from "conference reports and speeches" was "not all that difficult." Truly challenging was understanding "why" they said "such things" and the "basis of their leadership"—knowledge attainable only through comprehensive field research.[142]

Ara was not alone in his calls for Japanese to truly "know" Asia. He was joined by two influential scholars whose work, quite ironically, would subsequently attempt to differentiate—if not divorce—Japan from its region based on the country's supposed civilizational uniqueness. I refer here to the anthropologists Umesao Tadao and Nakane Chie. Umesao (1920–2010) leaped to prominence in 1957 with his essay "Bunmei no seitai shikan josetsu" (Introduction to an eco-historical view of civilization).[143] Umesao divided the world into "first tier" and "second tier" regions, with the first tier consisting of "wet, forested regions" and including "Western Europe and Japan, both of which had passed through feudalism and subsequently built modern civilizations."[144] Second-tier regions such as China and India, "although geographically belonging to the same Asia" as Japan, "exhibited striking differences."[145] In contrast to Asian countries like India and similar to Western Europe, Japan created colonies, it experienced multiple revolutions (on each occasion transcending the earlier system and making a "great developmental leap"), and its historical change was primarily driven by "internal energies." Conversely, India experienced no revolution, and its history was "primarily shaped by energies from the outside."[146] As Umesao observed, "although of late it is often said that Japan is Asia's orphan, my sense is that this is not something of recent origin. I think this has been the case for hundreds of years."[147] He commented: "I am extremely skeptical about the actual substance behind claims such as we are 'all Asians together.' Asia is only homogeneous in a

141. Ara, "Ajia no ninshiki," 190.
142. Ara, "Ajia no ninshiki," 190.
143. Umesao's thesis has been extensively discussed elsewhere, so here I will limit myself to its core arguments. See Umesao, "Bunmei no seitai"; Barshay, "Postwar Social and Political Thought," 317–18; Conrad, *Quest for the Lost Nation*, 208–9.
144. Umesao, "Tōnan Ajia no tabi," 36–37.
145. Umesao, "Tōnan Ajia no tabi," 37.
146. Umesao, "Nihon wa Ajia no koji," 188.
147. Umesao, "Nihon wa Ajia no koji," 188.

sensory or idealistic way. In a logical or substantial sense it cannot be said to be homogeneous. This is especially true for Japan. The history it has trod is different; its current physiology is different."[148]

As others have noted, Umesao's thesis helped define a potent discourse on Japanese uniqueness (or non-Asianness) which shared close affinity with the older discourse of abandoning Asia and joining Europe. It was a discourse that resonated with de-Asianization, not to mention providing a sophisticated intellectual foundation for the emerging postwar Japanese economic miracle.[149] But, ironic as it may seem now, Umesao's eco-historical extirpation of Japan from Asia made him all the more attuned to the necessity for Japan to know and to connect with its Asian neighbors—not the opposite. Indeed, precisely because Japan was so different from nearby countries, Umesao argued that the Japanese had even more responsibility to comprehensively know their region. Like Ara, for Umesao "knowing Asia" involved something more concrete than the ubiquitous Asian idealism among progressives. He was particularly riled by unempirical claims of Japan's Asianness. As he wrote in *Chūō kōron* after a trip to Southeast Asia in 1958, "I simply cannot understand the notion that Japan belongs to the same Orient as Lebanon." He commented: "We Japanese possess a really strong concept of 'the Orient' and use it thoughtlessly without restraint. Once again, this error stems from ignorance. Originally, we had no viewpoint of a single homogeneous [region] stretching from the Islamic sphere to Japan. The concept of the Orient, after all, was a European import."[150] In addition, "genuinely believing that Asia is one both culturally and historically reveals an astonishing disinterest and unsophisticated thinking about Asia."[151] Historically it had had disastrous effects, such as the wartime idea of "same script, same race" (*dōbun dōshu*) with China, which essentially underwrote invasion and became the "intellectual foundation of the 'Greater East Asia Co-Prosperity Sphere.'"[152]

148. Umesao, "Tōnan Ajia no tabi," 48.

149. On Umesao's thought and Japan's economic miracle see Conrad, "Colonial Ties," 197–98; and Barshay, "Postwar Social and Political Thought," 318.

150. Umesao, "Tōnan Ajia no tabi," 35.

151. Umesao, "Tōnan Ajia no tabi," 36.

152. Umesao, "Tōnan Ajia no tabi," 48.

Instead, Umesao proposed to "analytically rethink Asia" not as something "homogeneous" and beyond "nonsensical" approaches "separating the Orient and the Occident."[153] He believed that "necessary is unsentimental, composed observation and research. Voices for Asia have swelled in our country in the postwar era, but they seem to be going around in circles."[154] The key lay in understanding and embracing diversity and heterogeneity: "The idea that we are all Asians is a kind of diplomatic fiction. I do accept that this sort of diplomatic fiction is on occasion useful, hence I do not think it is unconditionally worthless. But a fiction is a fiction. In order to think about how to construct a new relationship between Japan and Southeast Asia in reality, we must begin by discarding fictions. We must think about how we can fuse together heterogeneity based on a mutual recognition that we are heterogeneous."[155] After his trip to Southeast Asia, Umesao posed the following question: "Honestly speaking . . . what do we know about Southeast Asia? We know almost nothing. I am ashamed to admit that until I visited I only had a paltry knowledge."[156] He noted that although there had been numerous important developments in Southeast Asia of late, Japanese intellectuals were still showing more interest in "Hungary" and "Algeria"—in other words, a tendency to focus on the Western countries and their predicaments.[157] But the idea that developments in Thailand or Indonesia were somehow "regional" was simply "ridiculous."[158] Umesao wrote: "Many so-called men of culture visit foreign countries, but most go to America or Europe. The only knowledge they have of Southeast Asia is that Bangkok Airport is absurdly hot. If Southeast Asia is so important for Japan, then why don't more [intellectuals] go there?"[159] He lamented the fact that none of Japan's major newspapers had a full-time correspondent stationed in Bangkok: "I simply cannot comprehend this."[160] Indeed, "because we do not have

153.   Umesao, "Tōnan Ajia no tabi," 36.
154.   Umesao, "Nihon wa Ajia no koji," 189.
155.   Umesao, "Tōnan Ajia no tabi," 48.
156.   Umesao, "Tōnan Ajia no tabi," 32.
157.   Umesao, "Tōnan Ajia no tabi," 33.
158.   Umesao, "Tōnan Ajia no tabi," 33.
159.   Umesao, "Tōnan Ajia no tabi," 34.
160.   Umesao, "Tōnan Ajia no tabi," 34. By 1961 there was at least one full-time Japanese newspaper correspondent in Bangkok. See Takeuchi and Umesao, "Ajia no rinen," 28.

correct knowledge about the various regions, the discourse tends to be abstract and generalized. This is a deplorable situation."[161]

Not all pro-Asia progressives were satisfied with Umesao's method of denying Japan's Asianness while energetically advocating for greater attention to the region. Takeuchi, for example, took issue with Umesao's denial of an Asian civilization. In a fascinating dialogue between the two in 1961, Takeuchi attempted to sidestep the issue of diversity in the region, arguing that Asia is "the configuration of that internal movement which occurs as countries colonized by Western Europe or imperialism attempt ethnic liberation or the formation of a modern state"—in response to which Umesao asked whether Takeuchi's definition of Asia might not also logically include South America. Trapped by his own definition, Takeuchi could only answer in the affirmative.[162] But on the issue of Japan not knowing (or even trying to know) about its neighbors, Takeuchi and Umesao spoke with one voice. In another 1961 essay Takeuchi lamented that the Korean language had been taught at the University of Tokyo before 1945 but not thereafter: "We Japanese really don't know anything about Korea, even though it is geographically closest to us. Indeed, we don't even try to know it, as evidenced by the fact that there are no universities here that teach Korean. How strange this is! In fact, I would suspect that Japan is the only nation in the world whose universities do not teach the language of that country which is closest to it."[163]

Nakane Chie (b. 1926), another rising star in 1950s Japanese anthropology circles, echoed Umesao's calls to better know the region because Japan was different. Unlike Umesao, however, Nakane argued for Japan's absolute uniqueness among all cultures of the world, even compared to the West: "Looking back over 100 years of history is there any time that Japan was not an orphan?"[164] Nakane could only conclude that Japan belonged "essentially to no one but itself and that what it need[ed] today" was "not theories of cultural affinity but more facts about other countries

161.   Umesao, "Tōnan Ajia no tabi," 34.
162.   Takeuchi and Umesao, "Ajia no rinen," 23.
163.   Takeuchi, "Asia as Method," 157.
164.   Nakane, "Koji Nihon," 32. A large portion of this essay is translated and reproduced in Olson, *Dimensions of Japan*, 285–89. I use Olson's translations here.

to serve as a guide for autonomous thinking and acting.[165] In fact, "Japanese intellectuals should spend less time constructing elaborate theories about the 'Asian' or 'European' character of Japan's cultural development and give more attention to learning the facts about societies other than their own." As she explained, "it is essential first of all to know each country well. How many Japanese who sympathize with the utterances of Nehru and Nasser really understand India or Egypt? The important thing is why Nehru speaks as he does, not the contents of his speech. And why he speaks as he does is conditioned by India's place in the international arena, by various internal conditions, and by tradition. While listening to Nasser's words last summer, how many Japanese were able to call to mind the burning desert heat; the flowing of the mother Nile, which brings fertility and gives to man the happiness of endless life . . . ?"[166] The sorry reality was that Japanese knew "no more about Asia" than they did "about Europe." Moreover, "the inclination of the Japanese to look toward Europe, resulting from many years of contact with European culture," was proving to be a great obstacle to . . . [the] understanding of Asia today."[167] She asked, "Why is it that the Japanese, who value Christian culture highly, cannot do the same for Hindu culture?"[168]

Of course, as with contemporary historians, the glaring problem with both Umesao and Nakane was that both, albeit in good faith, conflated ethnicity and nationality, which automatically reified the national space into something purely Japanese. This no doubt explains their utter ignorance of the historical problem of Japanese colonialism and aggression in Asia. Moreover, although both certainly spoke about understanding the complexity of Asia, by either triangulating Asia, Japan, and Europe (Nakane) or juxtaposing Japan and Europe with other stretches of Asia (Umesao), they tended to replicate earlier paradigms of Asian stagnation without Japan. Nevertheless, in terms of the evolving postwar progressive view of Asia, together with individuals such as Uehara and Ara, the value of their late-1950s interventions lay in the identification of a regional knowledge gap in Japan that was sorely in need of attention. It is certainly

165.   Olson, *Dimensions of Japan*, 284.
166.   Olson, *Dimensions of Japan*, 284
167.   Olson, *Dimensions of Japan*, 286.
168.   Olson, *Dimensions of Japan*, 287.

one of the great ironies of postwar Japanese intellectual history that the two intellectuals who most forcefully called for attention to Asia in the late 1950s would also be the architects of an ideology that celebrated Japan's fundamental separation from the region.

Conclusion: Embracing Asia and the Imperial Blind Spot

The Allied Occupation of Japan, the escalation of the Cold War, and the resurgence of Japanese conservatives underwrote a thorough process of de-Asianization in early postwar Japan. Marxist and modernist intellectuals were not immune to these political trends and in their own ways contributed to the suppression of certain aspects of World War II and the process of de-Asianization. But as we have seen in this chapter, progressives did not completely abandon the idea of Asia. In the early postwar years Asia and Asiaticness served as useful symbols of backwardness and stagnation for intellectuals in their investigations into Japan's failed modernity. I called this the ideological view of Asia. Some intellectuals subscribing to that view made the simplistic diagnosis that Japan's Asiatic aspects could explain its descent into militarism. Still others identified significant developmental disparities between Japan and other Asian countries such as China and India—disparities that, they argued, explained Japan's unique capacity to resist colonization in the nineteenth century. Common, however, was the assumption that Asia was hopelessly stagnant. But the Chinese Communist Revolution, the Korean War, and the rise of Asian ethnic nationalism in the 1950s challenged this view of Asia, stimulating new positive visions of the region among Marxist historians and intellectuals such as Takeuchi. Even prominent modernists began to revise their negative views of Asia and its so-called Asiaticness. I called this positive vision the idealistic view of Asia. It was dominant throughout the 1950s.

Despite their antithetical stances, both views of Asia had an almost complete lack of attention to Japan's recent colonial empire and militarism in East Asia. Even when Asia advocates spoke about breaking free from the chains of the past, it was as though they had erased all memory of troubling unsolved issues from the very recent past. Moreover, as I have emphasized, another limitation of the idealistic view of Asia was its premise of self-determination by nations assumed to be monoethnic in composition. This assumption did not lend itself to a sensitivity toward diversity within the nation—in other words, Japan's internal Asia. This blind spot in the discourse on *minzoku* and Asian nationalism directly contributed to de-Asianization, and as we will see in subsequent chapters, progressives would begin to address it in a systematic way only thereafter.

Nevertheless, the period from 1945 to the late 1950s was not without its advances in the progressive view of Asia. Attention to Asian nationalism did more than undermine notions of Asian stagnation: it opened the way to new calls from Umesao, Ara, Nakane, and others to move beyond idealism toward a substantive understanding of the countries in Asia. Few took up the challenge and actually visited the region at this time of limited international travel by Japanese, but the idea had been planted and would be embraced by Oda Makoto, Tsurumi Yoshiyuki, and other activists in the coming decades.

Moreover, although the Asia problem and progressive deimperialization remained in a state of relative suspension, throughout the 1950s we begin to see at least hints of change. In 1956, for example, Tsurumi Shunsuke published his landmark essay on the "Fifteen-Year War," effectively directing attention away from the Pacific War view of history and toward Japan's war in Asia. Admittedly, this view was still limited by its inattention to the longer history of colonial empire, but it was an important reframing nonetheless. Other progressives also began to make connections between Asia and the war. In a 1958 discussion titled "Ajia no naka no Nihon" (Japan in Asia) in *Sekai*, Ishida called on the Japanese to "deal with problems of war responsibility" that had not been "resolved after defeat." Although the postwar era had supposedly ended (according to a declaration by the Economic Planning Agency in 1956), Ishida argued that the "Pacific War had not been finally resolved" and, moreover, that there would be "no progress on Asian issues until the problem of war responsibility" was "settled." The issue, as Ishida saw it, was that the war experience survived only as a "victim consciousness" and any sense of Japan's "guilt as an aggressor tended to be forgotten."[169] Takeuchi echoed these

169.   Takeuchi et al., "Zadankai," 175–76.

sentiments, remarking in 1961 that the fundamental problem between Japan and Asia was "one of atonement." This was "true in regard to Japan's sense of atonement for crimes committed against China, but even more so in the case of Korea. It might well be that Japan's poor diplomatic relations with Korea are due to President Syngman Rhee's intransigence, but let us not forget the terrible oppression that Koreans suffered under Japanese rule."[170]

By the early 1960s, Ishimoda was also focusing a critical spotlight on Japanese historians. In 1963, he admitted that both Japanese and Oriental history from the Meiji period (1868–1912) onward were characterized by a "nationalism of domineering ethnic consciousness" produced by "the modern Japanese state's development into an imperial state."[171] He called on historians to "forcefully resist" the tendency to forget this aspect of Japan's past and to "construct a new historical consciousness and historiography" built on "solidarity among the peoples of Japan, China, and Korea."[172] Ishimoda praised historians for exposing the destructive effects of the emperor system on history—the ways it had "suppressed" and "degenerated" the discipline.[173] To an extent, postwar historians had been successful in liberating themselves from that ideology. But this liberation was primarily through a reflection on the emperor system as a "domestic system of domination." The emperor system was primarily understood in terms of "ultra-nationalism," and this unwittingly contributed to "the oversight of not seeing it as imperialistic power"—in other words, as the principle of "rule over other peoples" and "colonized territories."[174]

To be sure, such observations were hardly mainstream, but the fact that they were being articulated at all by leading intellectuals of the day suggests the naissance of an embryonic deimperializing mentality among progressives by this time. Building on this foundation, an expanding cadre of activists and intellectuals would begin to tackle the question of ethnic responsibility thereafter.

170. Takeuchi, "Asia as Method," 164.
171. Ishimoda, "Rekishikan ni tsuite," 223.
172. Ishimoda, "Rekishikan ni tsuite," 224.
173. Ishimoda, "Kindai shigaku," 232.
174. Ishimoda, "Kindai shigaku," 232.

CHAPTER 2

From Ethnic Nationalism to
Ethnic Responsibility

If the late 1940s and early 1950s witnessed the triumph of a resplendent Asian idealism over earlier ideologies of Asian stagnation, then the late 1950s and early 1960s marked the first embryonic attempts by some Japanese progressives to rethink Asia in the context of colonial empire, militarism, and war responsibility. This was a slow and subdued recognition, and it took over a decade for even a handful of intellectuals and activists to finally stand on the starting line of deimperialization. The small scale and muted nature of this undertaking when it did begin is a sobering reminder of just how inconsequential the legacies of empire and militarism in Asia had been in the early postwar years in the consciousness of most Japanese—including most progressives. Nonetheless, by the end of the decade, the Asia problem was something almost no progressive intellectual or activist of conscience could ignore, in much the same way that the celebrated peace and democracy (*heiwa to minshushugi*) of the early postwar era was coming under increased scrutiny and sometimes attack from militant students and other grassroots activists of the time. In this chapter I look closely at the period from 1958 to the mid- to late 1960s, tracing the historical causes of this important reorientation and the ways it unfolded in the thought and activism of that time.

A number of brutal murders involving resident Asians in 1958 and 1968, the repatriation of thousands of resident Koreans to North Korea starting in 1959, and tensions surrounding negotiations for the Treaty on Basic Relations between Japan and the Republic of Korea (signed in 1965) fueled this reorientation in the 1960s, propelling the Asia within (*uchi-naru Ajia*) to the forefront of progressive consciousness as both an unresolved past demanding ethnic responsibility and a present deeply disfigured by ingrained prejudice and discrimination against Asian minorities. This reorientation was small in scale to be sure, but it was important nonetheless, especially given what had come before. Recall how in the early postwar era, progressives had understood the Asia within primarily as a marker of Japanese backwardness and stagnation, while in the 1950s it had underwritten their idealized struggle for ethnic national independence from the United States. By the late 1960s the Asia within had been transformed again, becoming an unsettling manifestation of the original sin (*genzai*) thwarting the spiritual rehabilitation of postwar Japan. Moreover, because it was an original sin that some progressives recognized as their own, they tackled the problem with the intensity of battling a life-threatening ailment.

We can trace the origins of this intellectual reorientation most directly to the late 1950s, when a small number of academics, journalists, and writers concerned about the state of Korea-Japan relations and ongoing discrimination against minorities—especially resident Koreans and Chinese—began to address the problem of Japanese ethnic responsibility (*minzokuteki sekinin*). This perspective broke sharply with earlier Asianist-inspired ethnic nationalism (*minzokushugi*), unfolding instead as a self-reflexive dissection of the Japanese Left's unproblematized sense of solidarity with fellow Asians and its myopic comprehension of war responsibility (*sensō sekinin*). These progressives began to realize that the combination of those factors (or self-delusions) had severely impeded, if not absolutely extinguished, their attentiveness to the unresolved past of empire. And they began to see that, even more worryingly, lurking beneath the veneer of solidarity and war remorse lay stubbornly entrenched and unreconstructed imperial mentalities that continued to implicate the Left in a history of discrimination, prejudice, and racism against fellow Asians stretching back to the beginning of Japan's drive for modernization in the mid-nineteenth century. This compounding sense of guilt intensified throughout the 1960s, intersecting with similar awakenings in the anti–Vietnam War and student movements of the late 1960s and early 1970s and pushing Asia to the forefront of progressives' consciousness.

The Komatsugawa Incident and Ethnic Responsibility

The massive protests against the revision and renewal of the US-Japan Security Treaty in 1959 and 1960 have dominated histories of Japan in these years.[1] This is understandable: the protests were among the largest in modern Japanese history, they resulted in the downfall of Prime Minister Kishi Nobusuke, and they exposed the limits of popular energies in the face of recalcitrant conservative rule bolstered by US patronage. From the perspective of the Asia problem, however, it is also clear that the Anpo protests largely ignored unresolved historical issues in East Asia, with the struggle unfolding mostly as a resistance to old-guard conservatives who threatened to embroil Japan in another war—this time against the communist nations. To be sure, as Michiba Chikanobu observes, Asia-savvy intellectuals like Takeuchi Yoshimi saw the struggle as a chance for the Japanese to face the problem of war responsibility toward Asia, and throughout the crisis he lambasted the treaty for positioning the Chinese Communist Party as the "hypothetical" enemy, despite Japan's unresolved transgressions on the Asian mainland.[2] But Takeuchi's was very much a voice in the wilderness, and perspectives like his gained little if any traction among the Anpo protesters. The Anpo struggle essentially conformed to the blinkered "one-country pacifism" (*ikkoku heiwashugi*) that dominated peace and antiwar movements in Japan until well into the 1960s.[3]

Nevertheless, although issues of Asian reengagement and deimperialization figured very little in the Anpo struggle, this does not mean there were no developments in this area in the late 1950s and early 1960s. In fact, it is possible to excavate other histories of this unsettled time by shifting our attention away from the furor of Anpo in the

---

1. On the US-Japan Security Treaty, see Kapur, *Japan at the Crossroads*; Sasaki-Uemura, *Organizing the Spontaneous*; Avenell, *Making Japanese Citizens*; Oguma, *Minshu to aikoku*.
2. Michiba, "Posuto-Betonamu," 99.
3. Michiba, "Posuto-Betonamu," 99.

direction of movements and initiatives relating to Asia, both internally and abroad. On the conservative side of politics, for example, Kishi—remembered mainly as the great villain of the Anpo uproar—made a point of visiting Asian countries before (as well as after) traveling to the United States for his first official meeting with President Dwight D. Eisenhower in mid-1957. One of Kishi's primary diplomatic principles (concretized in official governmental publications) was that Japan become a full member of Asia and, more provocatively, the international representative of the region in the postwar era. To support this principle, on assuming the prime ministership in 1957, Kishi visited Myanmar, India, Pakistan, Sri Lanka, Thailand, and Taiwan. Significantly, he did not go to South Korea or Communist China—which, for good historical reasons, viewed Kishi with great suspicion. In his autobiography, Kishi recounted how he had wanted to send a clear message to the United States that Japan was the "center of Asia," thereby strengthening his position in subsequent negotiations with the Americans.[4] Kishi also viewed his Asian tour as an opportunity to finally settle the issue of reparations and launch Japan's triumphant postwar return to the region. He later wrote proudly of the red-carpet treatment he received in South and Southeast Asia (although not in the Philippines). In India, for instance, Prime Minister Jawaharlal Nehru told Kishi that the Japanese victory over Russia in the early twentieth century was the inspiration behind the Indian independence movement. Likewise, in Indonesia, President Sukarno effused that his country had gained independence thanks to Japan's "driving out the British and Dutch."[5] Even though Kishi recognized the diplomatic need to express remorse for the war, such accolades coming from the mouths of Asian leaders emboldened him to conclude that there was "no need to be pointlessly abject" about the past.[6] On the contrary, Kishi stated unequivocally that his postwar objective of having Japan assist postcolonial countries in restoring their strength and independence after the intrusion of Western imperialism in no way conflicted with his prewar support for

4. Quoted in Wakamiya, *Sengo 70-nen*, 40.
5. Quoted in Wakamiya, *Sengo 70-nen*, 41
6. Quoted in Wakamiya, *Sengo 70-nen*, 41.

the Greater East Asia Co-Prosperity Sphere and Pan Asianism. As he commented to his biographer, these were "perfectly aligned."[7]

Kishi and Japanese conservatives' reembracing of compliant Asian nations and their haughty claims to Asian leadership were greatly facilitated by a cocktail of American Cold War machinations in Asia combined with Japanese governmental and industrial bankrolling of investment, technology, and trade in the region—in other words, a recipe of guns and money. By contrast, the process of Asian reengagement for progressives in the 1960s was considerably more fraught, as they struggled to transition from the idealistic ethnic nationalism dominant in the 1950s to the heavy lifting of deimperialization. As we saw in chapter 1, the de-Asianization policies and intellectual processes of the early postwar period had resulted in resident Asians' essentially slipping off the radar screen for most progressives at that time. This blind spot made their conversion to 1950s Asian nationalism all the easier because the about-face involved only a rejection of the erroneous Asian stagnation thesis without any thorough investigation of the self as victimizer and colonizer. But things began to change, albeit slowly, around the late 1950s, as a constellation of domestic and international factors essentially forced the problems of these former colonial subjects into the consciousness of certain perceptive progressives. This was a grueling reorientation, but as the 1960s wore on, it became almost a moral imperative for a wide array of activists and intellectuals.

The first provocation—known as the Komatsugawa Incident—came in 1958 with the savage rape and murder of two Japanese women in April and August of that year. Acting on a tip from the perpetrator, on August 21, police discovered the lifeless body of a sixteen-year-old female pupil on the roof of the Komatsugawa High School in Tokyo's Edogawa Ward.[8] Around the same time, certain of the victim's personal effects began to arrive by mail at her home and the local police station. Soon thereafter an individual claiming to be the perpetrator began to make telephone calls to the *Yomiuri shinbun* newspaper and the police, during which he provided specific details about the crime and his motives. The

7. Quoted in Wakamiya, *Sengo 70-nen*, 170.

8. On the Komatsugawa Incident, see Nozawa, *Ri Chin'u nōto*; Ogasawara, *Ri Chin'u no nazo*; Pak Sunam, *Tsumi to shi*; Tsukiyama, *Mujitsu!*.

police managed to trace one of these calls to a public telephone booth, but a suspect was not apprehended until September—when a listener happened to recognize a voice recording of the assailant that was broadcast on the radio news.

The apprehended man was twenty-year-old Lee Jin-wu (Ri Chin'u, using Japanese pronunciation), a resident Korean factory worker who was completing part-time studies at the Komatsugawa High School. After his arrest, Lee—who used the Japanese name Kaneko Shizuo—also admitted to the rape and murder of a twenty-three-year-old woman in April. It also came to light that Lee had documented this crime and his motives in a novella, *Warui yatsu* (Bad guy), which he submitted to a writing competition at the *Yomiuri shinbun*. Despite being born into a poor Korean family and suffering persistent discrimination in Japan, in the novella and his court testimony Lee refused to blame either poverty or ethnicity for his crimes, describing these quite prosaically as acts of premeditated evil. Nonetheless, Lee's Japanese supporters pointed precisely to his Korean ethnicity as the causative factor and, controversially, a mitigating circumstance. As I show below, Lee became for them an embodiment of Japanese ethnic responsibility and a way to interrogate their original sin toward Asia and Asians.

As John Lie notes, although the Japanese public "was not ready to read the Komatsugawa Incident as a consequence of disrecognition"—in other words, as a display of "the accumulated anger against disrespect and discrimination"—it became an important point of entry for some Japanese progressives into the thorny issue of ethnic responsibility.[9] In August 1960, as the Anpo protests were waning, a group including the novelists Ōoka Shōhei and Yoshikawa Eiji, the playwright Kinoshita Junji, and the historians Uehara Senroku and Hatada Takashi formed the Ri Shōnen o Tasukeru Kai (Association to Support the Youth Lee) to pursue legal clemency for Lee, who faced execution for his crimes.[10] The group's September 1960 signature campaign appeal, "Ri Shōnen o tasukeru tame no onegai" (Appeal for support for the youth Lee), noted that Lee had been "prepared to accept the court's decision but, thanks to

9. The concept of disrecognition is John Lie's. See Lie, *Zainichi*, 92–93, for a discussion of this incident from the perspective of resident Koreans.
10. Kim Tal-su, "Komatsugawa jiken," 144.

the concern of supporters, was currently appealing to the Supreme Court." The appeal said that Lee was "deeply regretful" and had been "completely reborn" in jail, thanks to his conversion to Christianity.[11] Although the second appellant court had resolutely stated that Lee would be judged based on his "heavy responsibility as a human being without reference to his ethnicity," Lee's supporters argued that "as Japanese we cannot cover our eyes to the regrettable history between Korea and Japan. Through this incident we want to comprehend the depth of the wound between the Japanese and Korean peoples and think about our responsibility as Japanese."[12] In an appeal against the death sentence lodged with the Supreme Court on Lee's behalf just one day before the deadline (and subsequently read out in court), Hatada declared that "knowing the agonizing condition of Koreans in Japan and thinking through the heartbreaking facts," he could not accept the sentence "based on the facts of the case and the young man's attitude."[13] Lee's crimes, according to Hatada, were "one microcosm of the fate of resident Koreans" who found themselves in an "overtly discriminatory atmosphere."[14] In such an environment it was not possible for Lee and other resident Koreans "to have confidence" in or a sense of themselves as "Koreans," and thus not only was it "clearly difficult for [Lee] to develop normally," but also there was "a great chance he would become a distorted human being."[15] In the 1960s Hatada and others would characterize this condition as the ethnic "obliteration" of Asia by the Japanese throughout their modern history— the absolute disrecognition by the Japanese of Asians as legitimate Others.[16]

The activism of Hatada and his colleagues was ultimately in vain, as both the Tokyo High Court and the Supreme Court rejected Lee's appeals, facilitating his execution in November 1962. But Lee's story did not end with his untimely death. He became a kind of "proverbial floating signifier" for "writers and intellectuals" of all hues, while simultaneously

11.   The appeal is reproduced in Kim Tal-su, "Komatsugawa jiken," 152–5.

12.   Reproduced in Kim Tal-su, "Komatsugawa jiken," 154.

13.   Hatada's appeal to the court is reproduced in Kim Tal-su, "Komatsugawa jiken," 205–9.

14.   Reproduced in Kim Tal-su, "Komatsugawa jiken," 207.

15.   Reproduced in Kim Tal-su, "Komatsugawa jiken," 208.

16.   Hatada, "Nihonjin no chōsenjinkan," 71.

feeding pervasive ethnic stereotypes in Japan about Korean criminality.[17] Indeed, the Komatsugawa Incident was in many respects the first trigger for some Japanese progressives to begin their reorientation from war responsibility in the direction of ethnic responsibility. As early as 1962, for instance, the novelist Ōe Kenzaburō used Lee as the model for a Korean character in his novel *Sakebigoe* (Outcries).[18] And in 1963 the sociologist Arase Yutaka examined the link between discrimination and Lee's crimes in an essay titled "Minshū to sekinin no mondai" (The people and the problem of responsibility). Notably, this was among the first postwar essays to explicitly connect the Japanese people (*minshū*), responsibility, and resident Koreans.[19] In a 1966 essay (discussed below), Suzuki Michihiko (b. 1929), a scholar of French literature, likened Lee to a Japanese incarnation of the French writer and activist Jean Genet, whose life was marred by criminality before he was rescued by Jean-Paul Sartre, Pablo Picasso, and others impressed by his literary skills.[20] But the most influential treatment of the Lee incident was a 1963 work by the resident Korean writer and activist Pak Sunam, titled *Tsumi to shi to ai to* (Crimes, death, and love)—which contained reproductions of letters she had exchanged with Lee during his short time on death row.[21] This book captivated readers, who were astonished by the "murderer" Lee's intellectual sophistication and deep knowledge of world literature.[22] Suzuki later recounted how reading Pak's book forced him to painfully recognize the ethnic responsibility of the Japanese, compelling him to pen the 1966 essay that would so deeply shape his ideas and activism thereafter.[23] In fact, in the 1960s, numerous reading groups were formed to discuss Pak's book, while publications such as *Tenbō* and the *Asahi jānaru* began to run articles and special issues on discrimination against minorities in Japan, slowly exposing what one contemporary observer referred to as the "blind spot" and "shame" of the Japanese people.[24]

17. Lie, *Zainichi*, 93.
18. Ōe, *Sakebigoe.*
19. Arase, "Minshū to sekinin."
20. Suzuki, "Aku no sentaku." On Genet, see also Barber, *Jean Genet.*
21. Pak Sunam, *Tsumi to shi.*
22. Watanabe Kazutami, <*Tasha*> *toshite no Chōsen*, 191.
23. Suzuki, *Ekkyō no toki*, 134.
24. Tamaki, "Atarashii sedai," 244.

Although written some years after the incident, Suzuki's 1966 essay "Aku no sentaku" (The choice of evil)—a response to both the incident and Pak's book—provides an eye-opening insight into the logic informing progressives' support for Lee at the time.[25] Suzuki, then a thirty-seven-year-old literature professor at Hitotsubashi University in Tokyo, was involved in the civic movement for Lee, signing the appeal circulated by Ōoka, Uehara, Kinoshita, and others in September 1960 and thereafter contributing significantly to the discussion on ethnic responsibility. He also took up the treatment of resident Koreans in his seminar with students at Hitotsubashi University, eventually publishing a small-circulation journal on minority issues. Rather than accepting Lee's acts as the "motiveless crimes" of a criminally disposed resident Korean, as the media and authorities had done, in the essay Suzuki presented Lee's choice of evil as the outcome of his challenging circumstances.[26] By pointing a finger in this direction Suzuki broached the disconcerting question of just what (or, more troublingly, who) was responsible for creating and sustaining such circumstances.

For Suzuki, the problem was far more complicated than one of interethnic discrimination: "We must not overlook [the fact] that Lee was a Japanized Korean who took the name Kaneko Shizuo and could speak only Japanese. Lee performed the role of a Japanese person. He probably [would have] even desired to become a complete Japanese had he been given the chance. The fact is that not one of his friends knew that Kaneko Shizuo was ethnically Korean."[27] But the "façade of Kaneko Shizuo was the mask of a Japanese person produced through the denial of the autonomous reality of Lee; it was something alien to himself—indeed, it was the 'Other.'"[28] Yet to Lee's discontent, try as he might, he could never completely become that Japanese Other due to entrenched discrimination. During his trial Lee recounted how after middle school he had secured employment at the Hitachi Corporation, only to have this revoked when his Korean ethnicity came to light.[29] And herein lay the grim reality

25. Suzuki, "Aku no sentaku."
26. Suzuki, "Aku no sentaku," 79.
27. Suzuki, "Aku no sentaku," 80.
28. Suzuki, "Aku no sentaku," 81.
29. Suzuki, "Aku no sentaku," 81.

for Lee because, according to Suzuki, he was forced to accept once and for all that his Koreanness—inclusive of "everything from garlic to poverty"—was an "object of disdain," something of "little value," and "a synonym for wickedness" among the Japanese. That was Lee's destiny.[30]

Yet Lee could not be satisfied with this fate, so he decided to regain his agency and subjectivity by committing evil. "If [the label of] Korean— that synonym for wickedness—was to be forced on him by Japanese society . . . then Lee would conversely pursue a wickedness from within, transforming that wickedness into his own personal objective."[31] Indeed, "it was . . . a way of glaring back in disdain at those who had produced such conditions. It was a declaration [by Lee] that, even though the Japanese had produced the conditions of half-Japanized Koreans, it was pointless pursuing their responsibility. Rather, he would take matters into his own hands."[32] By refusing to attribute his crimes to ethnic discrimination, Suzuki said that Lee had subjected the Japanese, his "main enemies," to the "disdain of 'being ignored' and trampled underfoot," just as he and other resident Koreans had been. "How are we to deal with this disdain?" Suzuki asked. "This is a challenge we must now face."[33]

The provocation of Suzuki's essay, of course, lay in its reassignment of guilt (that is, responsibility) from the criminal to his environment and, by extension, to the Japanese people: "What rises to the surface when discussing the 'offensive' character of this 'atrocious' murderer is the existence of we Japanese who demanded this [offensiveness] in the molding of Lee's character. In other words, it was actually the crime of the Japanese people that was exposed through Lee's crimes."[34] As Watanabe Kazutami observes, Suzuki's important contribution lay in the way his exploration of Lee's inner psychology served as a "denunciation" and expression of "deep remorse" for the Japanese having "forgotten" the "colonial empire" responsible for Lee's crimes—and, moreover, for the psychological temperament of Japanese society that remained shamelessly "unchanged from the

30. Suzuki, "Aku no sentaku," 82.
31. Suzuki, "Aku no sentaku," 87.
32. Suzuki, "Aku no sentaku," 96.
33. Suzuki, "Aku no sentaku," 96.
34. Suzuki, "Aku no sentaku," 96. See also Watanabe Kazutami, <*Tasha*> *toshite no Chōsen*, 194.

prewar" period.[35] In this sense, the crime was not only or even primarily a "full disclosure of the criminal," it was a confrontational exposition of the sullied underbelly of modern Japan and the Japanese.[36]

In terms of intellectual reorientation in the early 1960s, the Komatsugawa Incident prompted Suzuki to ask unsettling questions about Japanese progressives' supposedly natural bond with the alliance between Asia and Africa discussed in chapter 1. In a 1963 essay fittingly titled "Minzokuteki sekinin ni tsuite" (On ethnic responsibility) in the journal *Ajia Afurika tsūshin*, Suzuki criticized Japanese progressives for conveniently "overlooking the responsibility of the Japanese people" when discussing Asia and Africa.[37] Spellbound by the "energy" of the new nations of Asia and Africa, many progressives fell under the "illusion" that Japan had attained full membership in the alliance and was now a full combatant in the "heroic struggle" for "ethnic national liberation."[38] But things looked very different when one shifted one's attention from ethnic nationalism to ethnic responsibility—that is, when the aspirational discourse on Asian nationalism was considered alongside the reprehensible condition of resident Asians in Japan. As Suzuki incisively noted in connection to the Komatsugawa Incident, "we Japanese cannot forget that the world Lee Jin-wu repudiated through his crime was created by us. It is there that our Asia-Africa problem grimly resides."[39]

The recasting of the Komatsugawa Incident through the lens of Japanese ethnic responsibility by Suzuki, Pak, Hatada, and others was a groundbreaking and deeply provocative intervention, especially given that even resident Korean associations such as the North Korean–aligned General Association of Korean Residents in Japan (Chōsen Sōren, abbreviated as Sōren) stridently condemned Lee in line with public opinion. Pak eventually found herself expelled from Sōren in 1962 because she "persisted in communicating with" the imprisoned Lee.[40] Even progressives

35. Watanabe Kazutami, <*Tasha*> *toshite no Chōsen*, 195.
36. Suzuki, "Aku no sentaku," 79.
37. Suzuki, "Minzokuteki sekinin," 1.
38. Suzuki, "Minzokuteki sekinin," 1.
39. Suzuki, "Hitei no minzokushugi," 5.
40. Lie, *Zainichi*, 93. Pak was an activist in her own right, becoming involved in Korean "hibakusha" (atomic bomb victims') movements, the problem of the so-called comfort women, and Okinawan issues.

who would later champion the cause of ethnic responsibility were initially perplexed and even suspicious of the advocacy of Ōoka, Hatada, and others for Lee. Tamaki Motoi, a scholar of Korea and a reporter for various periodicals, is a case in point. As I show below, in the mid-1960s Tamaki made important theoretical inroads into the unresolved legacies of empire, but at the time of the Komatsugawa Incident he felt "somewhat skeptical" toward the support movement, which he viewed as a kind of shallow ethnic noblesse oblige on the part of Japanese intellectuals toward a "pitiful" resident Korean.[41] With regard to Hatada's letter to the court expressing his strong desire to help Lee "in whatever way," Tamaki wondered just what "qualified" this Japanese intellectual to offer Lee assistance, as though he were "looking down" on a "pitiful human" from "on high." Moreover, what gave Hatada the right to offer his "condolences" to the victims' families "as though he were Lee's delegate"?[42] After all, in a letter written in May 1961, Lee stated categorically that he "felt absolutely no regret for having killed people."[43] Nevertheless, appeals issued by his self-appointed Japanese support group claimed that he now felt "deep regret" and was a "completely transformed person."[44]

Here was the crux of the problem for Tamaki: these intellectuals seemed to be forcing their own interpretation and motives onto the incident.[45] It was thanks to "these strong reservations" that Tamaki felt he could be no more than an "onlooker" at the time.[46] Only with the appearance of writings by Pak, Arase, and Suzuki did Tamaki feel compelled to reconsider his initial skepticism and, more importantly, become aware of the "significance of the problem."[47] As Tamaki's skepticism and hesitancy reveals, the provocation of the movement supporting Lee lay in its demand for a self-reflexivity among progressives where there had essentially been none before. It was about understanding the evil of another through the glass darkly of one's inner discrimination and ethnic responsibility—a demand that required strenuous emotional and

41. Tamaki, "Gendai ni okeru Chōsenjin," 112.
42. Tamaki, "Gendai ni okeru Chōsenjin," 112.
43. Quoted in Tamaki, "Gendai ni okeru Chōsenjin," 112.
44. Tamaki, "Gendai ni okeru Chōsenjin," 112–13.
45. Tamaki, "Gendai ni okeru Chōsenjin," 113.
46. Tamaki, "Gendai ni okeru Chōsenjin," 112.
47. Tamaki, "Gendai ni okeru Chōsenjin," 112.

intellectual effort indeed, even among those who saw themselves as the progressive moral conscience of postwar Japan.

The Early 1960s Discussion on Prejudice and Discrimination

The poet, art critic, and journalist Fujishima Udai (1924–97) was among the first to answer this demand for self-reflexivity in the late 1950s, initiating what by 1965 would develop into a sophisticated discussion on ethnic discrimination and prejudice. A graduate of the elite Keio University in 1950, in the 1940s and early 1950s Fujishima focused on publishing poetry in literary magazines such as *Kindai bungaku*. But in the late 1950s he began to diversify, producing lengthy investigative pieces for mainstream monthly magazines like *Chūō kōron*, in which he examined minority issues and social problems relating to Okinawa, Buraku communities that were discriminated against, the labor movement, the Anpo protests, and, ultimately, resident Koreans and Japan-Korea relations. In December 1958, for example, together with coauthors Maruyama Kunio and Murakami Hyōe, Fujishima published an influential article titled "Zainichi Chōsenjin rokujūmannin no genjitsu" (The current situation of the six hundred thousand Koreans [in Japan]) in *Chūō kōron*, advocating strongly in favor of the so-called repatriation project to North Korea. As Tessa Morris-Suzuki and others have documented, this project— initiated by resident Korean groups and supported by Kim Il-sung, the North Korean leader—involved the exodus of tens of thousands of resident Koreans from Japan to North Korea beginning in December 1959.[48] Fujishima and his coauthors based their advocacy for the project on persistent discrimination against resident Koreans (in work, housing, marriage, basic human rights, and so on), coupled with the promise of a better life in North Korea, where the Kim regime was apparently making spectacular progress.[49] To be sure, this discussion was not without its problems. The common refrain in such empathetic tracts that resident

48. See Morris-Suzuki, *Exodus to North Korea*.
49. Fujishima, Maruyama, and Murakami, "Chōsenjin rokujūmannin," 196.

Koreans would be happier and better off in Korea betrayed not only rose-colored visions of North Korea within the Japanese Left, but also deeply monoethnic assumptions about membership in the postwar Japanese nation. This difficulty in imagining Japanese nationality and community beyond ethnicity would be a major obstacle to progressive deimperialization thereafter. Nonetheless, because advocacy for the repatriation project was almost always justified through explicit reference to discrimination and prejudice against resident Koreans, together with the Komatsugawa Incident, it had a catalytic effect on Fujishima and others who were awakening to their own unexamined ethnic responsibility in the early 1960s.

Indeed, Fujishima's writings on and activism for resident Koreans and Korean issues increased dramatically thereafter.[50] His seminal 1960 book, *Nihon no minzoku undō* (Ethnic movements in Japan), represents the first comprehensive treatment of ethnic responsibility in postwar Japan and, to a great extent, can be credited with igniting the discussion of this responsibility at a time when many progressives were wedded to what Suzuki characterizes as a "simple progressive nationalism" built on "anti-American" patriotism (or "one-country pacifism") and, for some, non-aligned Asianism.[51] Fujishima's book used the repatriation project as a launch-pad to probe the deficiencies of war memory and the persistence of ethnic discrimination in Japan.[52] He pointed to official documents leaked from the Japanese Kōan Chōsachō (Public Security Intelligence Agency) in 1958 that characterized the repatriation project as nothing but a furtive strategy by resident Koreans to undermine dialogues on normalization between the governments of South Korea and Japan. The documents asserted that few resident Koreans genuinely wished to "return" to the North and that the repatriation movement was no more than a clandestine ploy to extract higher social security benefits for resident Koreans. According to Fujishima, such cynicism betrayed a deeper prejudice stemming from "a lack of consciousness among the Japanese" about

50. See Fujishima, "Tonari no kuni," "Chōsenjin kikoku," and "Kankoku no taishū."
51. Suzuki, *Ekkyō no toki*, 23. Michiba also notes the importance of this work ("Posuto-Betonamu," 102).
52. Fujishima discusses the repatriation movement in detail in chapter 3 of the book (*Nihon no minzoku*, 276–300).

"Japan's responsibility for the colonization of Korea and destruction of [the Korean] people's daily lives."[53] Because Japanese aggression in Korea had not taken the "form of war" and despite the fact that Korean colonization formed the "basis for aggression on the [Asian] mainland," most Japanese had no consciousness of Korea when talking about their country's "war responsibility."[54] In the postwar period this pervasive mentality had nourished "disinterest and contempt toward resident Koreans" and even led to "mistakes" in movements supporting them.[55] Fujishima identified this mentality in the "surprisingly flaccid cooperation" of Japanese progressives in the repatriation project.[56] This, he said, also explained the ignorance and lack of reflection over how the Japanese economy had recovered thanks to the "thorough sacrifice of Korea" during the Korean War, when America drew heavily on Japanese resources and used Japan as a military staging ground: "In short, even in the postwar era" the Japanese government and people had not abandoned the "mentality of perpetrator toward Asia."[57] Fujishima thus characterized the situation of resident Koreans as one of Japan's three "original sins," together with the treatment of Okinawans and Buraku communities.[58] Fujishima and other progressives would continue to draw heavily on this biblical imagery of original sin in discussing ethnic responsibility, although few of them were Christians. Its metaphorical utility lay in the ways it connected historical transgressions to seemingly unrelated phenomena in the present—for instance, how the postwar generation might bear responsibility for the situation of former colonial subjects and their descendants, despite not having played any role in the Japanese empire or militarism.

Building on the publication of this book, in 1961 Fujishima became a leading figure in the Nihon Chōsen Kenkyūjo (NCK; Japan Center for Korean Studies), established by a group of thirty-four journalists, progressive national and local politicians, lawyers, historians, China and

53. Fujishima, *Nihon no minzoku*, 283.
54. Fujishima, *Nihon no minzoku*, 6.
55. Fujishima, *Nihon no minzoku*, 6.
56. Fujishima, *Nihon no minzoku*, 6–7.
57. Fujishima, *Nihon no minzoku*, 283.
58. Fujishima, *Nihon no minzoku*, 28.

Korea specialists, and others.[59] Founding members included prominent intellectuals like Odagiri Hideo, Uehara, Takeuchi, and Hatada, with Fujishima and the lawyer Terao Gorō serving as prime movers in the organization.[60] A political prisoner during the war, Terao came to the movement with a background as managing director at the JCP's headquarters, while Fujishima brought his extensive experience in reporting on minority issues. Although both sympathized with the JCP and supported the North Korean experiment (including the repatriation project), they appear to have run the NCK as a largely independent organization, which is evident most clearly in the center's perspicuous linking of the proposed normalization treaty between Japan and Korea to Japanese colonial responsibility—a position that contrasted sharply with the JCP's focus on US imperialism and Japanese monopoly capital.[61] In fact, the NCK's articles of association positioned Japanese guilt and responsibility front and center, stipulating that the organization was intended to foster the "study of Korea by Japanese from the perspective of Japan."[62] While some members understandably expressed reservations about limiting membership to Japanese, the prevailing opinion—as codified in the articles of association—was that "right now" it was "necessary to bring an end to the prejudices originating in the erroneous colonial policies of the past, and to organize Korean studies from the perspective of the Japanese people."[63] In other words, Korean studies in Japan needed to be reoriented through the lens of Japanese responsibility for colonial empire, and this was something the Japanese had to accomplish unassisted—almost as a display of progressives' sincerity and genuine spirit of atonement.

From its formation in 1961 until the release of its influential antitreaty publications in 1963 (discussed below), the NCK mainly focused on the contemporary military and economic implications of the treaty, as did the JCP, JSP, and labor organizations.[64] But thanks to the writings and activism of Fujishima, the issue of ethnic responsibility never completely

---

59.   Higuchi, "Kaisetsu 1," 412 and 413.

60.   For the full list of founding members, see Nihon Chōsen Kenkyūjo, "Setsuritsu shuisho," 8–11.

61.   See Higuchi, "Kaisetsu 1," 415.

62.   Nihon Chōsen Kenkyūjo, "Setsuritsu shuisho," 5.

63.   Nihon Chōsen Kenkyūjo, "Setsuritsu shuisho," 13.

64.   Yoshizawa, *Sengo Nikkan kankei*, 310.

disappeared from the organizational agenda of the NCK, and it actually became more important over time. Notably, in a December 1963 article in the high-circulation weekly magazine *Ekonomisuto* titled "Nihon no naka no Chōsenjin: Sabetsu no jittai to haikei" (Koreans in Japan: The background and current state of discrimination), Fujishima catalogued a litany of Japanese historical transgressions against Korea.[65] The land reform policies of the Japanese colonial government, he said, had basically stolen Korean land, the Japanese had "massacred" (*gyakusatsu*) Koreans after the Great Kantō Earthquake in 1923, and in the 1930s the Japanese had forced Koreans to move to Japan to work in coal mines and at construction sites that became "soaked with the blood and sweat of Koreans." As he explained in the article, even Japanese government records disclosed that at least half of the twenty thousand conscripted Korean workers had perished.[66] The fact that a weekly magazine devoted to economics and targeted primarily at Japanese businessmen would run such an article is intriguing, especially given Fujishima's provocative language and no-nonsense presentation of a confronting history of racial prejudice and violence by the Japanese.

Furthermore, in 1963 and 1964 Fujishima and his colleagues in the NCK authored a series of fifty-five articles for the progressive *Nihon dokusho shinbun* newspaper, subsequently published as a 1965 volume titled *Dokyumento Chōsenjin: Nihon gendai shi no kurai kage* (Documenting the Koreans: The dark shadow of Japan's contemporary history). The series was intentionally timed to coincide with the fortieth anniversary of the 1923 massacre and, far more extensively than the writings discussed above, exposed a disturbing historical pattern of Japanese prejudice and discrimination against Koreans. Topics in the series included forced Korean relocation and labor during the Pacific War; "forgotten" Korean soldiers in the Japanese Imperial Army; commemorations of the Great Kantō Earthquake massacres; and contemporary discrimination against resident Koreans such as the foreigner registration system, restricted welfare assistance, insurance ineligibility, and nonrecognition of ethnic schools.[67] As Fujishima explained in the preface to the 1965 compilation, Japan's

65. Fujishima, "Nihon no naka no Chōsenjin."
66. Fujishima, "Nihon no naka no Chōsenjin," 41.
67. Fujishima et al., *Dokyumento Chōsenjin.*

"aggression toward Korea" had deeply shaped Korean history, but—
somewhat paradoxically—the "depth of the relationship" with Korea had
produced a "deplorable blind spot" in the consciousness of the Japanese,
so that Korea had become "invisible" to them.[68] Once again invoking
the biblical imagery he had used in 1960, Fujishima concluded that "original sin is original sin precisely because it is so difficult to see with one's
own eyes, and it is from here that the decay of Japanese thought has
advanced."[69]

The fortieth anniversary of the Great Kantō Earthquake in 1963 also
prompted historians and others to begin tackling the reality of deeply
rooted ethnic and racial discrimination in early 1960s Japan. In September 1963, the leading history journal *Rekishi hyōron* published a special
issue titled "Tokushū Nihon to Chōsen: Daishinsai Chōsenjin junan 40
shūnen no yosete" (Japan and Korea: On the fortieth anniversary of the
suffering of Koreans after the Great Earthquake), which investigated
the 1923 earthquake and subsequent massacre of thousands of resident
Koreans, Chinese, and other targeted groups. Together with eyewitness
accounts by Koreans, the issue contained articles by Hani Gorō and other
historians on the postearthquake massacre, the groundless rumors pre-
cipitating the slaughter, new collaborative research between Korean and
Japanese scholars, and connections (or disconnections) to the ongoing
normalization dialogues.[70] Hani's committed involvement illustrates the
extent of the progressives' reorientation vis-à-vis Asia at the time. In the
1930s Hani had spearheaded the discourse on Asian stagnation and backwardness, but by 1963 he was championing efforts to excavate horrifying
historical instances of Japanese racial prejudice and violence toward other
Asians.

Publications like the progressive mouthpiece *Sekai*, a periodical that
had become ensconced in the insular war responsibility discourse of the
early postwar era, also began to carry articles connecting responsibility
to both Japan's past in Asia and contemporary problems of ethnic prejudice and discrimination in the country. In March 1963, for instance, *Sekai*

68. Fujishima, "Jo," 2–3.
69. Fujishima, "Jo," 3.
70. "Tokushū Nihon to Chōsen."

ran a fascinating article by the cultural anthropologist Izumi Seiichi (1915–70)—himself a scion of empire, having grown up and worked as an academic in colonial Korea—titled "Nihonjin no jinshuteki henken" (Japanese racial prejudice). The article discussed the results of a survey Izumi had conducted on Tokyoites' attitudes toward foreigners in the days before the signing of the San Francisco Peace Treaty in 1951.[71] Interestingly, although Izumi had discussed the survey's results with his academic colleagues in the 1950s, it was only in 1963 that he felt conditions were ripe to discuss this material more widely in a publication like *Sekai*.[72] The bottom line of what Izumi described as his "dreadful findings" was that the Japanese people reserved their strongest prejudice, contempt, and racial discrimination for the members of those nations and ethnic groups most geographically proximate to Japan.[73] Hence, Koreans, Filipinos, and Chinese—"the peoples Japan formerly ruled over"—were "the least liked" among the Japanese who expressed "no goodwill" toward them.[74] Izumi visualized this condition in terms of a series of concentric circles drawn around Japan. The outermost circles contained the Western countries, which evoked a strong "sense of inferiority" in the Japanese; conversely, countries located in the inner circle—in other words, East Asia—engendered a "perspective of superiority."[75] The rather "strange character" of the Japanese mentality, then, was that the most intensely negative sentiment was directed at the most similar, not the most different, cultures.[76] Within this framework, Izumi highlighted how the Japanese reserved their strongest racial prejudice for the nearby Koreans.[77] Echoing the NCK discourse, as a first step toward internalizing their ethnic responsibility for colonial rule, Izumi called on the Japanese people to engage in an even more intensive and sustained effort to "flush out" this "racial prejudice" that was entrenched in the very "foundation" of their "national consciousness."[78]

71. Izumi, "Nihonjin no jinshuteki henken," 82.
72. Izumi, "Nihonjin no jinshuteki henken," 82.
73. Izumi, "Nihonjin no jinshuteki henken," 83.
74. Izumi, "Nihonjin no jinshuteki henken," 83.
75. Izumi, "Nihonjin no jinshuteki henken," 86.
76. Izumi, "Nihonjin no jinshuteki henken," 86.
77. Izumi, "Nihonjin no jinshuteki henken," 87.
78. Izumi, "Nihonjin no jinshuteki henken," 89.

Izumi was not alone. The historian Tōyama Shigeki (1914–2011) made a similar argument soon afterward in a 1963 article titled "Chōsen ni taisuru minzokuteki henken ni tsuite" (On ethnic prejudice toward Korea) in *Rekishi hyōron*. Tōyama identified "ethnic prejudice" (*minzokuteki henken*) as the "common factor" obstructing relations both between Japan and China and between Japan and Korea, and hence it was an obstacle that must be overcome in the pursuit of genuine solidarity.[79] Mirroring Izumi's concentric circle theory, Tōyama detected a more intense Japanese prejudice toward Korea than China. Unlike the latter country, for which many Japanese—including right-wing extremists—felt great affection, Korea seemed to evoke no fondness.[80] Tōyama pointed to the vigorous Japanese support for Sun Yat-sen's republican struggle in China versus the rather tepid support for the March First Uprising in Korea.[81] While it was true that discriminatory attitudes toward China originated in the first Sino-Japanese war of 1894–95, and those toward Korea intensified over a decade later in the wake of the Russo-Japanese War and subsequent annexation of Korea, Tōyama pointed to much earlier instances of prejudice against Korea that were evident, for example, in the furor over Korean invasion (*seikanron*) soon after the Meiji Restoration.[82] This earlier origin of discriminatory sentiment was important because it informed Tōyama's conviction about the very deep historical roots of Japanese prejudice toward Asia, especially Korea. Moreover, precisely because of this historical depth, it was a prejudice with especially profound implications in the present.

In keeping with the emerging mantra of Izumi, the NCK, and other groups, Tōyama called on the normalization treaty protest movement to simultaneously pursue a "self-transformation" in "national consciousness."[83] As long as the Japanese people lacked the "resolve" to genuinely tackle the "difficult" and "painful" reality of their "imperialist" past, the frictions between Korea and Japan would persist. Rather than "assuming" that the postwar period was "over," Tōyama called for an immediate reconsideration

79. Tōyama, "Chōsen ni taisuru," 1.
80. Tōyama, "Chōsen ni taisuru," 2.
81. Tōyama, "Chōsen ni taisuru," 2.
82. Tōyama, "Chōsen ni taisuru," 3.
83. Tōyama, "Chōsen ni taisuru," 4.

of the so-called Pacific War. The Japanese needed to understand the normalization dialogues and other "problems between Korea and Japan" in the context of the "100 years" of "Japanese modern history," and this involved a fundamentally different understanding of the "history of the war."[84] As I discuss in chapter 3, Ienaga Saburō and others (including some nationalists) subsequently spearheaded a reconsideration of the Pacific War with the approach of the hundredth anniversary of the Meiji Restoration in 1968. But as the above discussion reveals, moves to rethink Japanese modern history in Asia were already underway in the early 1960s, thanks to this embryonic discussion on prejudice and discrimination. What resulted was a gradual, yet significant, reorientation from the Asian idealism of the 1950s encapsulated in the progressive embrace of ethnic nationalism to a more somber and self-reflexive sense of ethnic responsibility attentive to Japanese aggression and prejudice toward Asia in the past and the present.

The Japan–South Korea Normalization Dialogues and the 1965 Treaty

The April 1960 student revolution in South Korea, Park Chung-hee's coup d'état in May 1961, and the signing of the normalization treaty in June 1965 (approved by the Japanese Diet on December 11 and ratified on December 18) were of even greater significance in stimulating attention to ethnic responsibility among some progressives. The dialogues between the two countries had continued intermittently since 1951, but it was only with the Park coup and the aligning of interests among Japan, South Korea, and the United States in the face of an impending war in Vietnam that momentum toward the treaty increased—especially from January 1962, when dialogues between President Park and Prime Minister Ikeda Hayato recommenced. In response, treaty opposition movements mobilized in both countries, although they displayed significant differences in intensity and focus. Opposition on the Japanese side was nowhere near as

---

84. Tōyama, "Chōsen ni taisuru," 4.

extensive as in South Korea, and apart from the examples outlined below, for the most part it focused primarily on the present implications of
the treaty. Moreover, the Japanese public was largely uninterested in the
normalization dialogues, and around half of those questioned in opinion polls indicated that they had no opinion on the issue at all.[85]

Groups opposing the dialogues zeroed in on American imperialism,
conservative rule, and monopoly capitalism and thus replicated many of
the grievances raised during the Anpo crisis. Although adopting subtly
different stances, organizations such as the JSP, JCP, and the labor organization Sōhyō all emphasized that a Japanese–South Korean treaty would
solidify the US-dominated military alliance in Northeast Asia, impede
the reunification of Korea, and facilitate the penetration of Japanese industry into South Korea and beyond.[86] The troubled history of Japan-Korea
relations figured only as an appendage. Oguma Eiji identifies a similar fixation on "monopoly capital" and "Japanese imperialism" among student
groups that paid "little attention" to "the ways zainichi Koreans were
shortchanged by the treaty."[87] Indeed, the final ratified instrument "contained not a hint of remorse on the Japanese side," and in return for a massive outlay of "economic assistance," the Park regime—hungry for Japanese investment—agreed to not define this support as compensation for
past Japanese colonialism and wartime transgressions.[88]

Writing in the wake of the protests in 1966, Hatada observed that
this "tendency to forget the past" among Japanese activists was "remarkably out of sync" with both North and South Korean opponents to the
treaty, whose opposition "stemmed fundamentally from their great anger toward Japanese . . . colonial rule," coupled with their "anxieties"
about its "revival." The fact that conservative elements encouraging the
dialogues expressed "positive views of Japan's rule over Korea was to be
expected," but Hatada could only lament the "wholly inadequate" attention to this issue among treaty opponents.[89]

85. Yoshizawa, *Sengo Nikkan kankei*, 278.
86. Yoshizawa, *Sengo Nikkan kankei*, 314.
87. Oguma, *1968 <ge>*, 226.
88. Seraphim, *War Memory*, 204; Babicz, "Japan–Korea, France–Algeria," 207.
89. Hatada, "Nikkan mondai," 123.

As Wada Haruki and others later observed, by failing to foreground the issue of Japan's historical responsibility toward Korea, Japanese civic groups apparently squandered a golden opportunity to forge a new relationship with Koreans at that time.[90] No doubt this is true, but at least for some progressives like Hatada, Fujishima, and Suzuki, the normalization dialogues in the years leading up to the 1965 signing and ratification of the treaty provided a critical opportunity to face discrimination, prejudice, ethnic responsibility, and the unresolved legacies of empire head-on. Precisely in its expression of disappointment toward the treaty opposition's blind spots, Hatada's 1966 lament is clear evidence of this reorientation that was underway for some progressives. And contrary to Wada's depiction of total failure, by the mid-1960s the discourse on ethnic responsibility would reach new levels of sophistication—thanks in large part to the aggravation of the normalization process and the opposition movement, in spite of its failure.

The evolution of the NCK is a case in point. Members participated vigorously in the antitreaty protests leading up to ratification in 1965, delivering lectures on the issue nationwide and releasing numerous influential publications that increasingly focused on ethnic responsibility. In 1962 and 1963 the NCK published two pamphlets, "Watashitachi no seikatsu to Nikkan kaidan" (Our daily lives and the Japan–South Korea dialogues) and "Nihon no shōrai to Nikkan kaidan" (Japan's future and the Japan–South Korea dialogues), which had healthy sales of 70,000 and 10,000 copies, respectively.[91] Under the guiding hand of Fujishima, these pamphlets reveal a novel (for the time) fusion of historical sensitivity with contemporary concern, addressing issues such as "aggression in Korea since the Meiji era," "[Japanese] colonial rule," "the Japan–South Korea dialogues and economic invasion," and "the American-orchestrated Japan–South Korea dialogues." The 1963 pamphlet contained a section titled "the past of Japan-Korea relations: thirty-six years of colonial rule," which stated unequivocally that Japan was a "perpetrator (*kagaisha*)

90. Wada, "Kankoku no minshū," 62.

91. Terao, Noguchi, and Hatada, *Watashitachi no seikatsu*; Terao, Kawagoe, and Hatada, *Nihon no shōrai*. See also Wada and Takasaki, *Kenshō*, 58.

against Korea and China in the past" and was "once again becoming a perpetrator today."[92]

The NCK's exhaustive 1964 book *Nichi-Chō-Chū sangoku jinmin rentai no rekishi to rentai* (The history and theory of solidarity among the three peoples of Japan, Korea, and China) sold some 13,000 copies and best encapsulates the center's innovative fusing of the past and the present. This book also served as an ideal companion to the center's 1963–64 series on the history of Japan-Korea relations in the *Nihon dokusho shinbun* mentioned above.[93] The first chapter of the book, titled "Nihon no Chōsen shinryakushi" (The history of Japanese aggression in Korea), covered transgressions as diverse as the colonial Japanese appropriation of land in Korea, massacres of foreigners in Japan after the Great Kantō Earthquake, forced migration and labor, and the so-called wartime comfort women, of whom it noted that at least 80 percent were forced participants.[94] Echoing Fujishima's landmark 1960 work, the chapter concluded that "in sum, during the long thirty-six years [of colonial rule] Japan stole the Korean nation, stole its farmland and crops, stole Korean culture, stole the language, stole [people's] names, and ultimately, stole their lives."[95] For this the Japanese had to "offer some form of apology and some form of compensation."[96] Furthermore, the continuation of "prejudice" and "contempt" toward Koreans from the prewar period into the postwar era was about far more than simple "everyday experience." There was something in the core of "Japanese society itself" that "perpetually gave birth to prejudice and contempt toward Korea."[97] This explained why youth who knew nothing of the prewar system of "authority" and "order" and who had grown up in a so-called peaceful and democratic Japan could harbor discriminatory attitudes, and why even high school students could commit acts of unmitigated violence against resident Koreans in the present.[98] Overcoming this "prejudice," "contempt," "hostility," and "the poison of imperialism within ourselves,"

92. Quoted in Yoshizawa, *Sengo Nikkan kankei*, 310.
93. Higuchi, "Kaisetsu 1," 415.
94. Andō et al., "Nichi-Chō-Chū," 192–93.
95. Andō et al., "Nichi-Chō-Chū," 198–99.
96. Andō et al., "Nichi-Chō-Chū," 204–5.
97. Andō et al., "Nichi-Chō-Chū," 154.
98. Andō et al., "Nichi-Chō-Chū," 153.

the book concluded, required an "intellectual struggle" without which the Japanese would neither "nurture nor strengthen" the ability to resist the United States and a "resurgent Japanese imperialism."[99] Significantly, the book also emphasized that "ignorance" and "lack of awareness" about Korea was not only a problem for "ordinary citizens" but also for those in the "democratic camp" and even within so-called Japan-Korea friendship movements.[100]

Other groups followed in the NCK's footsteps. In September 1965 prominent historians including Tōyama, Hatada, and Hani formed the Nikkan Jōyaku ni Hantai suru Rekishika no Tsudoi (Group of Historians Opposed to the Japan–South Korea Treaty), which also took aim at the lack of Japanese historical remorse in the normalization dialogues and protests. As the group's 1965 statement pointed out, not only was the treaty unfavorable to Korea, "it was not signed in a spirit of condemnation" of Japanese rule over the country.[101] On the contrary, some Japanese political elites were opportunistically using the treaty to "affirm" the history of Japanese colonial rule in Korea.[102] As early as 1953, for example, Kubota Kan'ichirō, the diplomat in charge of the normalization dialogues on the Japanese side, had commented that "the thirty-six years of Japanese rule over Korea was beneficial for the Koreans."[103] In 1965, Takasugi Shin'ichi, the Japanese representative to the treaty negotiations, reiterated this perspective, saying:

There are some people who claim that the thirty-six years of Japanese rule in Korea was a mistake. But I cannot apologize. . . . Japan ruled over Korea. But our country did good things. People may raise various objections, but Japan did its best to do good for Korea. . . . Japan left all of its industry, buildings, and forests in Korea. The forced change to Japanese names was a good thing. It assimilated the Koreans and was a measure implemented to ensure that Koreans would be treated the same as Japanese, and not for the purpose of exploitation and suppression. Koreans will certainly have complaints about the past, but we have even greater complaints. Hence it

99. Andō et al., "Nichi-Chō-Chū," 333.
100. Andō et al., "Nichi-Chō-Chū," 150.
101. "'Nikkan jōyaku no hantai," 59.
102. "'Nikkan jōyaku no hantai," 59.
103. Quoted in Komatsu, "Watashi no taiken," 14.

doesn't make sense to rehash the past. In particular, Japan believes that the best approach is to discuss things as though we are family.[104]

For Tōyama and his fellow historians, such attitudes revealed that despite the collapse of Japanese colonial rule in Korea twenty years earlier, as a "problem of the Japanese mentality," colonialism had "not ended." Indeed, until the Japanese people "strongly condemn[ed] Japan's previous imperialistic rule over Korea" and "purge[d] the ethnic prejudice within themselves," they would not realize a genuine solidarity with "the Korean people, who desire independence."[105]

Around a month after these historians mobilized in opposition to the treaty, seventy civic groups and prominent intellectuals including the sociologist Hidaka Rokurō, the translator and commentator Matsuoka Yōko, and the literary critic Kurahara Korehito formed the Nikkan Jōyaku Hijun Soshi Bunkajin Kondankai (Colloquium of Literati to Stop Ratification of the Japan–South Korea Treaty, or Colloquium of Literati). Similar to the historians, in a statement of October 20, 1965, this group called on other Japanese to "reflect on the thirty-six years of Japanese colonial rule over Korea and never repeat the same mistake."[106] At a 1966 symposium hosted by the Colloquium of Literati in the wake of ratification, Hidaka—who had played a major role in the Anpo struggle of 1960—admitted that in terms of the "mentality of the Japanese people" and as an "intellectual problem," the Japan–South Korea Treaty was of even "greater significance" for Japan than the US-Japan Security Treaty, due to the "special relationship between Japan and Korea in the past." To Hidaka's disappointment, however, not even members of the "Japanese intelligentsia" were sufficiently aware of this.[107] Suzuki echoed Hidaka's comments at the symposium, noting that the "war responsibility" debate among Japanese intellectuals in the postwar era had not sufficiently dealt with the legacies of colonial empire. While it was acceptable to direct criticism at conservative political leaders for their lionization of empire, the so-called progressive forces also needed

104. Quoted in Wada, "Kankoku no minshū," 59.
105. "'Nikkan jōyaku no hantai," 59.
106. Quoted in Yoshizawa, *Sengo Nikkan kankei*, 313.
107. Hidaka et al., "Kokumin bunka kaigi," 44.

to explore worrying lacunae in their own comprehension of "war responsibility."[108]

From War Responsibility to Ethnic Responsibility

It should be emphasized, of course, that at the time such perspectives were still the concern of only a minority of Japanese progressive groups (not to mention of the Japanese public more generally)—hence Wada's characterization of the treaty opposition movement as a largely squandered opportunity for postwar reconciliation.[109] Nevertheless, it is also clear that the Komatsugawa Incident, the repatriation project, and the Japan–South Korea Treaty were catalysts in the fermentation of a transformative reorientation that would continue to flower and diversify among progressive intellectuals and civic activists thereafter.

We can trace the process of intellectual reorientation in these years most distinctly in the juxtaposition of war responsibility and ethnic responsibility by intellectuals like Hatada, Tamaki, Suzuki, and Nakahara Hiroshi, all of whom had become increasingly frustrated with the lack of self-critique in extant leftist protest and ideology surrounding the normalization treaty as well as in earlier Asian nationalism. At the core of their frustration was an intensifying anxiety—an unnerving sense of original sin, we might say—about the complicity of Japanese like themselves who had been unproblematically rendered as victims in postwar narratives of the Pacific War and subsequent allocations of war responsibility. More and more intensely they felt that the established Left's obsession with American imperialism and Japanese monopoly capitalism and its accompanying veneration of proletarian internationalism, while necessary, was obfuscating the more profound problem of ethnic responsibility that every Japanese person needed to face. Within progressive ideology (socialist or not), American imperialism was connected all to easily to earlier Japanese imperialism, allowing for indulgent assumptions about an unbroken chain of victimization that had the Japanese people suffering

---

108. Suzuki, *Ekkyō no toki*, 137–38.
109. Wada, "Kankoku no minshū," 61–62.

under Japanese imperial fascism in the past and continuing to labor under the weight of Pax Americana in the present.

Behind all of this, such intellectuals realized, lay an unresolved Asia problem evident in endemic prejudice toward resident Asians and the neglect of the history of ethnic obliteration inherent in Japan's colonial empire and military aggression. Hence, reconciliation and healing would require much more than a commitment to either proletarian or Asianist internationalism. Those on the Left needed to examine their deepest prejudices toward Asia: their sense of superiority and their shocking lack of recognition that Japan had lost the war not only to the United States but also to Asia. While Westerners were easily positioned as foreign Others thanks to this narrative, Asians were somehow never completely viewed as foreign even by progressives, yet neither were they genuinely accepted as part of the self, as Japanese—which explained the persistence of derogatory colloquialisms like *sangokujin* and *daisangokujin*, literally meaning "people from a third country" but referring more narrowly to Asians who, being neither Western nor Japanese, were somehow lesser human beings. There was clearly a troubling gap here between the romance of Asian nationalism on the one hand and the actual treatment of Asian minorities and the history behind this on the other hand.

What needs to be emphasized, of course, is that the simple act of recognizing their complicity in this mentality was, in fact, the core of the radical reorientation unfolding in progressive consciousness in the mid-1960s. As I have noted, although it was on a small scale, in the realm of deimperialization and the evolution of postwar civic thought and activism in Japan, it was an important breakthrough indeed. For perhaps the first time in modern Japanese history, some progressive intellectuals were moving beyond the polarity of either Asia as stagnation or Asia as one and toward a genuine encounter with the Asia in Japan and, thereafter, the Japan in Asia. This, I argue, was the nativity of progressive deimperialization.

As early as his 1963 essay on ethnic responsibility discussed above, Suzuki Michihiko had highlighted what he felt to be lacunae in leftist criticisms of the normalization dialogues and, more broadly, in progressive attitudes and approaches to Asia. While opponents (the JSP, JCP, and so on) were quick to condemn the Japan–South Korea dialogues as but "one link" in America's "Anti-Communist military system," Suzuki felt that they often failed to "touch on Japan's own responsibility" and at times even presented themselves as "innocent victims of American imperialism."[110] While Suzuki shared the Left's "resolute opposition" to the normalization dialogues, he could not help feeling that "the most important issue" had "fallen by the wayside" for most Japanese opponents.[111] The leftist commentator Nakahara Hiroshi amplified this perspective at the 1966 Colloquium of Literati symposium in Tokyo, again expressing his frustration with the tendency of the Left to fixate on the task of resisting "anticommunist imperialism."[112] He argued that opponents' excessive attention to these "objective conditions" blinded them to the more fundamental problem of "ethnic agency" and that if left unattended, "this weakness" would be "reproduced" and "enlarged" within the protest movement, "eventually causing its downfall."[113] By "objective conditions," Nakahara meant assumptions about the treaty being "one link in the American imperialist strategy of Chinese containment" and part of the "Japanese–South Korean–Taiwanese anticommunist military alliance."[114] Although he was certainly no "ethnic nationalist" (*minzokushugisha*) and perhaps was even more committed to "proletarian internationalism" than even the "established Left," Nakahara could not, for example, support "the prevailing approach of seamlessly fusing opposition to the Vietnam War and opposition to the Japan–South Korea Treaty," since this approach tended to lose sight of the necessity for the Japanese "to engage in the Japan-Korea problem from a genuinely independent standpoint."[115] Indeed, what "confronted" every person engaged in the "Japan-Korea problem" was "the blackened image" of a "mountain of countless Korean corpses massacred" by Japanese in the past. For Nakahara the "departure point" simply had to be "positioned within [this] history," "within the space" of "subjective responsibility" toward the Korean people." This involved recognizing "the fact of colonial aggression toward the Korean people from the Meiji [era] until defeat in war," as

110.   Suzuki, "Minzokuteki sekinin," 2.
111.   Suzuki, "Minzokuteki sekinin," 2.
112.   Hidaka et al., "Kokumin bunka kaigi," 57.
113.   Hidaka et al., "Kokumin bunka kaigi," 57–58.
114.   Hidaka et al., "Kokumin bunka kaigi," 58.
115.   Hidaka et al., "Kokumin bunka kaigi," 58.

well as the "fact that Japanese imperialism" was "shamelessly embarking on a new form of colonialism."[116] "The Japanese Left must learn more from such historical facts," he said. "Simply identifying American imperialism as the lone villain while characterizing we Japanese, our Korean neighbors, and the Vietnamese as 'victims in common' is excessively self-serving. Whether on the Left or the Right, I believe that the Japanese people must become more sensitive to the pang of ethnic conscience (*minzokuteki ryōshin*)."[117]

Nakahara was not alone in his critique of the Japanese Left's lack of attention to former empire and the plight of resident Asians. Tamaki Motoi (1926–2008), who as we saw above had felt uneasy about Japanese progressives' support for the convicted Lee Jin-wu in 1958, was among the earliest to censure the JCP for its utilitarian treatment of resident Asians. In his late twenties Tamaki had been a member of the JCP, actually dropping out of university to take up full-time activism in 1947. In reaction to the Red Purge begun under the Allied Occupation in 1949–50, Tamaki joined one of the radical mountain village guerrilla units (*sanson kōsakutai*) consisting of groups of workers and students sent to the countryside to create bases for armed revolutionary struggle in the mode of Maoism. As Victor Koschmann notes, this strategy "proved to be woefully inadequate to postwar Japanese conditions" and would be demonized as "far-left adventurism" by the JCP in 1955.[118] A demoralized Tamaki also abandoned the party in that year, having lost "trust" in it thanks to the lack of self-criticism and politicization of leadership within the party.[119] But his frustrations went much deeper than dissatisfaction with the party's abortive and misguided strategy of armed struggle. Tamaki also accused the JCP of ignoring the legitimate ethnic concerns of its Korean members by simply absorbing issues of ethnic and racial discrimination into the broader struggle for revolution. Before the resident Korean movement was even given a chance to pursue its "ethnic demands," the JCP had demanded that Korean party members mobilize their fellow Koreans into the "Japanese

116. Hidaka et al., "Kokumin bunka kaigi," 58.
117. Hidaka et al., "Kokumin bunka kaigi," 59.
118. Koschmann, *Revolution and Subjectivity*, 223–24.
119. Tamaki, "Gendai ni okeru Chōsenjin," 99.

revolutionary struggle."[120] "Intellectually," Tamaki believed that this forced absorption of resident Koreans by the JCP ironically replicated state-led wartime processes of "Japanization" (*kōminka*; literally, "imperial subjectification") and the mobilization of Koreans and other Asians into the military.[121] But just as important as Tamaki's scathing critique of the JCP here was the way he turned the critical spotlight on himself, admitting his own shortcomings while involved in the JCP:

> Around 1947 when I was a member of the Communist Party in a regional city, I became involved in the student and youth movement in that prefecture. One day while walking I got to talking with a Korean youth organizer who had come down from Tokyo. We were getting along well so, quite innocently, I blurted out the criticism that "Korean activism is a bit too radical and tended toward left extremism." With this, his expression darkened and he responded as if to strike me. "You may well say so. But what about the bones of my fellow Koreans buried under the sleepers of railway tracks all over Japan? You have absolutely no idea about the violent rage we Koreans have carried within. The radicalism of our activism comes from that rage. It's something you Japanese cannot comprehend!!"[122]

Tamaki recalled how he had been left with "no words to reply," reduced to merely "walking, speechless, head hung low, not out of frustration at having been outdebated but, above all, out of a sense of shame."[123] "Looking back, I don't think my criticism was 100 percent wrong," he concluded, "but the Japanese must realize that they cannot make half-baked criticisms of Koreans so long as they remain unaware of what the Japanese people did to the Korean people in the thirty-five years after annexation, and indeed, in the eighty years following the debate on the invasion of Korea straight after the Meiji Restoration. This is even more relevant if we recognize Japan's partial responsibility for the tragic fate of Korea in the postwar era."[124]

120. Tamaki, "Nihon kyōsantō," 132–33.
121. Tamaki, "Gendai ni okeru Chōsenjin," 104.
122. Tamaki, "Nihon kyōsantō," 127.
123. Tamaki, "Nihon kyōsantō," 127.
124. Tamaki, "Nihon kyōsantō," 128.

Usami Shō (1924–2003), a journalist for the *Asahi shinbun* newspaper and a nonfiction writer, went further than perhaps any other intellectual of the time in laying bare his internalized prejudice toward Asians—similar in many ways to the confessions intellectuals like Ōkuma Nobuyuki made in the very early postwar years about their wartime collaboration and recantation (*tenkō*). Usami documented his personal struggle with ethnic prejudice in the influential 1966 edited volume *Nihon no naka no Chōsen* (The Korea in Japan). Like other similar works of the time, this volume contained essays on the discriminatory policies in colonial Korea, forced Korean relocation and labor, the Korean atomic bomb victims, and the Komatsugawa Incident.[125] With respect to the title of the volume, the publisher's afterword emphasized that the phrase "the Korea in Japan" did not refer to Koreans' somehow possessing a "concession" or "colony" within Japan: "Rather it speaks to a massive wound (*kizu*) the Japanese inflicted on themselves through the 'original sins' (*shukuzai*) committed by modern Japan. And this 'wound' will remain forever so long as modern Japan fails to take action to remove it. . . . The original sins of modern Japan are profoundly severe. But the tragedy is that the Japanese do not recognize the depth of this 'wound' and have made it a 'blind spot' that is out of bounds."[126]

Usami's personal confession in the book was in part sparked by the normalization treaty, but it also grew out of a series of interviews he conducted in Korean communities in the Ikaino area of Osaka in 1965, at the height of the turbulence over the treaty. This experience evoked traumatic childhood memories of prejudice and fear within him. A graduate of the elite University of Tokyo, Usami recalled how during his youth he had had almost no contact with Koreans, despite living near a Korean community. As he put it, "the ruling ethnic group and the subordinate ethnic group, the middle class and the poor, [represented] solid walls separating Koreans from me. My living environment and the Kimchi town were unrelated. Or rather, to put it diplomatically, I actually possessed a deep-rooted suspicion of Koreans in my heart of hearts. That was, first and foremost, implanted in me by prewar schooling but it was also intensified by the actual realities of Koreans I saw and heard about from

125. Usami et al., *Nihon no naka no Chōsen*.
126. Taihei Shuppansha, "Atogaki," 283.

my youth onward. The Koreans that young boy saw were poor, dirty, rude, and stupid. They were people from a totally different world to the 'healthy middle class' in which I was raised."[127] The "storm of postwar democratization," however, provoked a "deep sense of guilt" in Usami, forcing him to recognize how the apparent "shortcomings of the Koreans" whom he had been "conditioned to treat as a deplorable ethnic group" were "nothing more than the product of Japan's misguided rule." He realized—albeit slowly—that "the bulk of responsibility for the poverty, crimes, and ignorance of resident Koreans lay in Japanese politics, and that Koreans should be relieved of responsibility for most of this."[128] Yet even as he began to accept his ethnic responsibility toward Koreans and other Asians, Usami could not let go of very deep-seated prejudices. As he explained, the many Koreans he saw after defeat had "obstructed the triumph" of his "ideals." For instance, he could not help feeling frustration at seeing "how the Japanese police could do nothing about Koreans selling illegal products at black markets under the railway tracks" or how "simply being a Korean during the war had meant you could not buy a train ticket, but now you could ride the train for free for the very same reason."[129] Although he "understood a hundred times over that only a handful of Koreans engaged in such activity and that the actions of that handful were the product of terrible treatment by the Japanese, there was still something within" that he "could not get over": "I just could not eradicate the suspicion that Koreans were an inferior ethnic group."[130]

Usami admitted that this was the mentality with which he approached his assignment of interviewing resident Koreans in Ikaino in 1965. To be sure, the 1965 treaty, coming "twenty years after the war," was also a moment of "transformation" in his "awareness of Korea" and an attempted "shedding" of his "prejudice." But this was "essentially in the realm of ideals and theory," and "there was nothing such ideals and theory could do about the visceral sentiment toward Koreans cultivated" from his childhood. Usami explained that the fear he had felt passing by Korean bunkhouses as a youngster still made him "hesitate"

127.   Usami, "Ikaino no Chōsen shōnen," 250–51.
128.   Usami, "Ikaino no Chōsen shōnen," 251.
129.   Usami, "Ikaino no Chōsen shōnen," 252.
130.   Usami, "Ikaino no Chōsen shōnen," 252.

at the thought of going into the "kimchi town" of Ikaino to conduct interviews in 1965.[131]

His decisive awakening—like Tamaki's 1947 experience in the countryside—happened only during that week of interviews. One day his guide in Ikaino, a resident Korean named Park, politely asked Usami to stop using the phrase "Korean person" (*Chōsen no hito*) when referring to Koreans (*Chōsenjin*). As Usami explained, "it was as though I had been doused in ice-cold water. Why had I been saying 'Korean person' instead of simply 'Korean?'" "During that week I had been conceitedly acting as though I understood Koreans and had discarded my prejudice, but it was all a façade. 'Korean' (*Chōsenjin*) should have been no more than a simple word, but in Japan it had taken on a strange undertone of contempt. Yet if I had really overcome my prejudice, I should have been able to uninhibitedly use that word. My thoughtless use of 'Korean person' exposed how I was still very much a prisoner of prejudice. The seemingly refined term 'Korean person' was actually my way of shrouding the prejudice I retained within."[132] So "from that day on," Usami "resolved" to use the term "Korean," and despite still harboring "a degree of unease," he now felt capable of uttering the word "'Korean' in front of a Korean." And this, he admitted, was nothing short of a personal "revolution."[133]

Usami, Tamaki, and others' sense of personal shame, then, was important not only in stimulating a critique of the established Left but also, and perhaps more significantly, in facilitating a self-reflexive reconsideration of the past as their own. Indeed, personal shame lay at the core of the important questions Tamaki posed in 1966: What was it that had so "weakened" and "delayed" the Japanese people's attention to the problem of their "ethnic responsibility" toward Koreans and other Asians in the postwar era?[134] Why were empire and its consequences so easily forgotten despite the seemingly endless agony over war responsibility? According to Tamaki, part of the explanation related to the historical situation in Japan just after defeat, especially the relatively painless process of liberating Korea from Japan: "Put simply, the liberation of Korea from the Japanese

131. Usami, "Ikaino no Chōsen shōnen," 251.
132. Usami, "Ikaino no Chōsen shōnen," 260.
133. Usami, "Ikaino no Chōsen shōnen," 260.
134. Tamaki, "Minzokuteki sekinin no shozai," 41.

Empire" was not based on "the independent reasoning and energies of either the Korean or Japanese people," hence the resulting "irresponsibility" in Japan.[135] Tamaki observed that the international relations of both countries had come to be "strangely distorted," thanks to the "external influence exerted by the victorious superpowers." Developments under the Occupation only exacerbated this situation in Japan: "Simultaneous with the emperor avoiding war responsibility in the postwar era, the Japanese were able to discard the Korean problem in the hazy oblivion of the far off Genkai Sea [that is, the waters separating Japan and Korea]. The more the emperor became a popular depoliticized figure, the more Japanese citizens—now the protagonists of 'democratic politics'—could submerge the Korean problem in the political illusion of the Democratic People's Republic of Korea versus the Republic of Korea."[136]

But like Suzuki and others, Tamaki could no longer be satisfied with attributing the Left's sluggish response to "objective conditions" like the weight of American influence. It also had "intellectual causes" that "lay concealed" beneath the surface. First, of course, was the "politicized perspective"—similar to the "Pacific War view of history"—that attributed "responsibility for imperial rule over Korea to Japan's ruling strata" and the "narrow social strata of Japanese who had been in direct contact with Koreans."[137] Another cause had to do with the very act of "taking responsibility." Thanks to the fact that most members of the ruling strata from the emperor down were not really forced to take any clear form of responsibility, no "distinct image of the act of 'taking responsibility' ever developed."[138] Tamaki also pointed to the persistence of a kind of "paternalism" and a sense of superiority among the Japanese people (including intellectuals), who believed that they somehow occupied the "status of elites" in Asia. This was evident, for instance, in displays of benevolence for a "troubled neighboring country" or in "petitions to save the life of the pitiful youth, Lee Jin-wu."[139]

All of this, Tamaki believed, must be abandoned in pursuit of a genuine ethnic responsibility that transcended simplistic war responsibility.

135. Tamaki, "Minzokuteki sekinin no shozai," 41.
136. Tamaki, "Chōsen mondai," 23.
137. Tamaki, "Minzokuteki sekinin no shozai," 41.
138. Tamaki, "Minzokuteki sekinin no shozai," 42.
139. Tamaki, "Minzokuteki sekinin no shozai," 42.

The Japanese had to "begin by accepting the agony" they had inflicted on the Korean people as their "own internal wound" and, from this perspective, build a "new interethnic solidarity" based on an "intellectual self-transformation."[140] This approach had to be "clearly distinguished" from that of building ethnic solidarity simply by attributing "political responsibility" to the "imperialist ruling strata" whose members had led Japan's "aggressive behavior" and, based on this, effortlessly constructing an alternative "political solidarity movement."[141] Ethnic "aggression," "suppression," "domination," "abuse," and "contempt" toward China and Korea, said Tamaki, were about more than "short-lived moments such as war": they had "accumulated" over time within the "humdrum of daily life." Moreover, aggression, prejudice, and the like were perpetrated not only by "state institutions" like the "military" and police but also on a "massive national scale."[142] Rejecting the leftist ethnic nationalism of the 1950s built around comfortable mythologies of victimization as Asians in common, Tamaki thus proposed a new form of solidarity to be constructed through a process of atonement for the original sin—the wound carved into the heart of the Japanese ethnic nation.

Indeed, knowing and accepting that the Asian Other had never been genuinely recognized as a legitimate Other—that it had even been purposely obliterated—was undoubtedly one of the critical intellectual breakthroughs of this early 1960s discourse on ethnic responsibility because it explained for these progressives the continuity of an original sin staining the spirit of every Japanese. Regardless of their disconnection to the past, the members of the postwar generation shouldered this sin of obliteration and disrecognition and would do so until they made this history their own. Nowhere would this be an easy process.

As Nakahara argued at the 1966 symposium, "first and foremost, we Japanese must genuinely recognize the Koreans as 'Others'—in other words, recognizing them as distinct, independent foreigners" and not "third-country people."[143] He envisaged a Sartrean process in which recognition of Korean "Others" as subjects might open a pathway

140. Tamaki, "Minzokuteki sekinin no shozai," 37.
141. Tamaki, "Minzokuteki sekinin no shozai," 36.
142. Tamaki, "Minzokuteki sekinin no shozai," 36.
143. Hidaka et al., "Kokumin bunka kaigi," 61.

to objectification of the self.[144] Although most Japanese had no direct individual responsibility for the horrific treatment of Koreans before or during the war, the postwar generation still bore a "collective responsibility" (*shūdanteki na sekinin*) as Japanese. However, this would become visible only through the grueling process of self-objectification and genuine recognition of the other as legitimate Other.[145]

This notion of self-objectification represents a crucial high point in the reorientation toward ethnic responsibility in the mid-1960s, especially in the way it opened up a frontal attack on the then-dominant notion of war responsibility. As we have seen, this reorientation unfolded mainly among a small group of intellectuals and activists interested in Korea in these years, but from around the mid-1960s it began to gain traction in other movements such as anti–Vietnam War mobilizations and university student activism. For such groups too, attention to Asia and responsibility would also serve as a self-reflexive method of deimperialization through self-objectification, while also providing a convenient new perspective by which to dissect their ostensibly pristine revolutionary ideologies. It would also open a way to productive new solidarities with grassroots movements throughout East Asia. But before we turn to antiwar activists and student radicals, there is one final episode in this early phase of deimperialization that warrants discussion because it is illustrative both of the nascent progressive reorientation to Asia and empire underway by the late 1960s and of the stubborn persistence of prejudice and discrimination toward the Asia within among the Japanese more generally.

The Gwon Hui-ro Incident of 1968

Exactly ten years after the Komatsugawa Incident, the Gwon Hui-ro Incident of 1968 shocked the nation, fueled now by the almost ubiquitous spread of television. Gwon Hui-ro (1928–2010), a second-generation Korean from Shizuoka Prefecture, became headline news in February of that tumultuous year after he shot two Yakuza gangsters dead in a loan

144. Hidaka et al., "Kokumin bunka kaigi," 61.
145. Hidaka et al., "Kokumin bunka kaigi," 81.

dispute at a Shizuoka City cabaret bar named Minkusu and fled to the Sumatakyō hot spring region, where he took eighteen Japanese people hostage at the Fujimiya Inn.[146] After barricading himself and the hostages in on the second floor of the inn, Gwon contacted the local police, threatening to detonate dynamite if they approached. He also demanded a public apology from two police officers who had used racial slurs against him in the previous year, along with full public disclosure of the criminal backgrounds of the two organized crime members he had shot dead.[147] Although one of the officers did subsequently apologize, Gwon was dissatisfied with the official response, and some four days into the standoff he called an impromptu press conference to present his side of the story. During the conference he was arrested by police officers disguised as journalists.

The thirty-nine-year-old Gwon, using the Japanese name Kaneoka Yasuhiro, had a history of crime, and like Lee Jin-wu was the product of a life in Japan encumbered by relentless prejudice and discrimination that had prevented him from securing stable employment, thus provoking his criminal recidivism. But unlike Lee, who had steadfastly refused to attribute his crimes to ethnic prejudice, when addressing the media Gwon incessantly referred to the "ethnic discrimination" he and other resident Koreans faced. He asked reporters to consider the emotional damage of verbal abuse by the police like "you Korean bastards, stop coming to Japan and causing trouble!"[148] Nonetheless, Gwon's pleas (like those for Lee ten years earlier) were ultimately in vain, as he was found guilty of his crimes and sentenced to life in prison in 1973, in spite of strong support from a team of lawyers and progressive intellectuals including Hidaka, Ōsawa Shin'ichirō, Ara Masato, Hatada, Suzuki, Kinoshita, Mihashi Osamu, and others—many of whom had been involved in the support movement for Lee.

Far more than was the case with Lee earlier, Gwon became a cause célèbre for progressives concerned about ethnic responsibility in the late 1960s, as is evident in the civic movement they rallied in his support and

146. For more on the Gwon case, see Mihashi, *Sabetsu ron nōto*, 215–66; Kim Talsu, "Kin Hi-ro"; Lie, *Zainichi*, 92–93.
147. Mihashi, *Sabetsu ron nōto*, 218.
148. Quoted in Mihashi, *Sabetsu ron nōto*, 218.

the numerous articles and books they published on the incident. Mihashi's influential 1973 *Sabetsu ron nōto* (Notes on the theory of discrimination), for example, devoted an entire chapter to the Gwon case. Based on his scathing analysis of the media, police, and judicial treatment of Gwon, Mihashi warned that "unless we transform the totality of relationships mutually binding us together, we will continue to be the perpetrators of discrimination."[149] The racism of journalists, police, and judges was not born of their professions, Mihashi observed. Rather, it connected at the very deepest level to the "choices" and "mentality" of ordinary Japanese people like himself and his book's readers.[150]

At the height of the hostage crisis, Hidaka, Suzuki, and their colleagues hastily gathered at a hotel in Tokyo's Ginza area, where Suzuki penned an appeal titled "Kin-san e" (To Mr. Gwon), calling on Gwon to abandon his mountain siege in favor of a legal struggle against discrimination in the courts that they promised to support.[151] "Your recent actions served as a harsh denunciation of our ethnic biases," the appeal noted, and "your actions roused our ethnic responsibility (*minzoku no sekinin*)." It added, "We want to accept your appeal candidly for the good of the Japanese nation."[152] According to Kim Tal-su, a resident Korean author who had also joined the meeting, after some debate the group reached a rough consensus that Gwon had "staked his life by barricading [himself] in the mountains of Sumatakyō" and that this "desperate plea" against the "problem of ethnic discrimination" was "nothing other than a problem caused by we Japanese" who "must recognize" it as "our own."[153] Equipped with a voice recording of the appeal, representatives of the group—including five lawyers—subsequently visited Gwon at his mountain stronghold where, according to Kim, they were greeted with a "peaceful" and "otherworldly scene." Once they were inside, Gwon leaned his rifle against the wall and in the politest of terms said, "I am extremely grateful that you have all come to support someone like me." He then proceeded to recount the details of his harsh life in Japan, which had been

149. Mihashi, *Sabetsu ron nōto*, 264.
150. Mihashi, *Sabetsu ron nōto*, 264.
151. Kim Tal-su, "Kin Hi-ro to wa nanika," 324.
152. Quoted in Suzuki, *Ekkyō no toki*, 156.
153. Kim Tal-su, "Kin Hi-ro," 324.

haunted by incessant derision and discrimination.[154] Keeping their word, after Gwon's arrest the group of intellectuals and lawyers established the Kin Hi-rō Kōhan Taisaku Iinkai (Gwon Hui-ro Trial Countermeasures Committee), which continued to advocate publicly for Gwon and the plight of resident Koreans throughout the three years of the case.[155]

In a 1969 article for *Chūō kōron*, Kim Tal-su attempted to offer some public justification for Gwon's radical acts by embedding them in a lengthy discussion of Japanese colonization in Korea and the ramifications for resident Koreans, who were often forced to become invisible in Japan. Kim explained that he could not overlook the ironic symbolism of the Gwon incident, coinciding as it did with the hundredth anniversary of the Meiji Restoration of 1868. Gwon's wretched treatment in Japan laid bare the shallow deceit of popular revisionist histories by conservatives like Hayashi Fusao and others who celebrated Japan's so-called one-hundred-year struggle against the West for Asian liberation. Right at the moment Japanese were "singing praises" of the Meiji "heroes," Kim observed, Gwon appeared to challenge them.[156] As with the Komatsu-gawa Incident of 1958, this was precisely the postimperial context in which advocates wanted the incident to be understood. As Kim explained, to a great extent, Gwon had become "too" Japanese. He had become such a "concealed person" (*kakusareta ningen*) that he could no longer tolerate slurs such as "you damn Koreans!"[157] It was this self-demonization of ethnicity that resulted in the "explosion" of this "concealed person." As Gwon put it, "constantly being ridiculed as 'Korean, Korean,' made me who I am today."[158] Only through an excavation of the "full history" of "so-called resident Koreans," said Kim, would it be possible for Japanese to understand the submerged rage that fueled Gwon's explosion.[159]

For Gwon's cadre of Japanese supporters, there was no longer any doubt about their personal culpability and the complicity of modern Japanese history. As Suzuki explained, his group's support for Gwon during

154. Kim Tal-su, "Kin Hi-ro," 325–26.
155. Watanabe Kazutami, <*Tasha*> *toshite no Chōsen*, 198.
156. Kim Tal-su, "Kin Hi-ro," 327.
157. Kim Tal-su, "Kin Hi-ro," 326.
158. Quoted in Kim Tal-su, "Kin Hi-ro," 329.
159. Kim Tal-su, "Kin Hi-ro," 329.

the legal proceedings was not only a way to protect Gwon but was also a strategy of "using the courts to clarify the problems of zainichi Koreans and the responsibility of Japanese."[160] On a personal level, thanks to this case and "through the difficult relationship with Gwon," Suzuki had finally realized the limitations of viewing "ethnic responsibility" through the dualities of "perpetration and victimization," "oppression and oppressed," and "discrimination and discriminated" against. Along with these dualities, "it was also necessary to make an effort to face the Other."[161]

Writing in the *Mainichi shinbun* newspaper five days after Gwon's arrest in February 1968, another member of the support group, Kinoshita Junji (1914–2006), admitted that based on "common sense," Gwon was certainly a "crook" (*warui yatsu*), but the "unjust 'racial discrimination' by Japanese toward Koreans that existed from before he was born undoubtedly damaged one aspect, or even many aspects, of his life."[162] Nevertheless, Kinoshita asked readers to acknowledge that one "outcome" of that "bad act" was the "good" that came of Gwon's being able to "raise the injustice of racial discrimination before society."[163] In yet another invocation of biblical imagery, Kinoshita confessed to his readers that "to the extent I can remember, I personally have never discriminated against Korean, Okinawan, or Burakumin people. Nevertheless, although we have no direct connection, we cannot escape from the crimes committed by our fathers, our grandfathers, and even earlier generations against our own ethnic group and other ethnic groups. We must shoulder this original sin. It is not about sentimentality (*kanshō*). It has to do with the fact that, to the extent we do not accept this [original sin]—to the extent we do not have this 'sense of guilt' (*tsumi no ishiki*) within ourselves—the irrationality of discrimination will not disappear from this world."[164]

Drawing an explicit link between Lee Jin-wu and Gwon Hui-ro, in a 1968 article for the monthly magazine *Gunzō,* the novelist Ōe Kenzaburō struck a rather positive tone as he identified signs of intellectual awakening and reorientation in the tragedy. Although Ōe lamented

---

160. Suzuki, *Ekkyō no toki,* 169.
161. Suzuki, *Ekkyō no toki,* 213.
162. Kinoshita, "Aru bungakuteki jiken," 320.
163. Kinoshita, "Aru bungakuteki jiken," 320.
164. Kinoshita, "Aru Bungakuteki jiken," 319.

the conditions that forced these Koreans to commit terrible acts, he also saw the possibility of a new age opening up. Throughout the piece, Ōe referred to attempts by both individuals to "transcend" (using the French *se dépasser*) themselves in the face of "living with multilayered discrimination" as "zainichi Koreans at the very bottom strata" of Japanese society.[165] Lee's request to the *Yomiuri shinbun* newspaper to publish his short novella, according to Ōe, had been an attempt to communicate with the Japanese who were his "oppressors" and "enemies" from the time of his birth. "The imagination" he had marshaled for this work represented an opportunity to experience the fleeting "pleasure" of "transcending himself."[166] In addition, "speaking from the perspective of his short life, Lee was born into a poor family of resident Koreans and grew up experiencing discrimination. He was left with no choice but to repudiate that totality of continued oppression which forced him to bend and yield."[167] Nevertheless, Ōe could only be positive, believing that "through the frustrated and hopeless actions of the young Lee and Gwon Hui-ro," some (admittedly few) Japanese might have attained a "new imagination": "Turning off the loathsome switches of their television sets with a sense of hatred and shame for being Japanese, on their empty screens I believe they can see a second and third Lee or Gwon rising unexpectedly out of the darkness." Indeed, for Ōe, Lee, and Gwon—in their very acts of rising up—had given a "power" to the "imagination" of some Japanese, who may well have grasped their "most realistic and perceptive political imagination."[168]

The philosopher and citizen activist Tsurumi Shunsuke's (1922–2015) speech about Gwon to the Wadatsumi-kai (Memorial Society for the Soldiers Killed in the War) in 1968 evocatively tied together the themes of ethnic responsibility, memory of empire and war, ethnic prejudice, and original sin. In the speech Tsurumi characterized massacres during the Fifteen-Year War with China and following the 1923 earthquake as "original crimes" (*genhanzai*).[169] Although Korean, Chinese, and Taiwanese

165.   Ōe, "Seijiteki Sōzōryoku," 160.
166.   Ōe, "Seijiteki Sōzōryoku," 163.
167.   Ōe, "Seijiteki Sōzōryoku," 165.
168.   Ōe, "Seijiteki Sōzōryoku," 169.
169.   Tsurumi Shunsuke, "Sensō to Nihonjin," 136.

victims were living proof of these "original crimes," there was a striking lack of recognition of "culpability" or "criminality" (*hanzaisei*) among Japanese, thanks to their tendency to "take refuge" behind the state as a way to "overlook" their complicity.[170] But now Tsurumi called on the Japanese people to "reconstitute" their memory of "war experience" to include an "interrogation of their own criminality."[171] Tsurumi argued that the Gwon Hui-ro Incident was extremely important for comprehending the mental condition of the Japanese. He likened the incident to another recent crime involving a resident Korean who had dismembered the female owner of a night club after an altercation over a loan. The Korean involved had apparently snapped when the owner blurted out racial slurs toward him.[172] In trying to understand the origin of these crimes, Tsurumi turned again to the longer history of Japanese exploitation of Korea and the Korean people. Repeating a history we have seen many others recount in this chapter, Tsurumi explained that Japan had seized Korea and acquired land for next to nothing. The Koreans who had lost their property could not find work in Korea, so many were left with no choice but to come to Japan. For the Japanese who had stolen Korea there was always a sense of "guilt" and fear that the Koreans might take "revenge" at some stage—which explained the believability of the false rumors about Koreans after the Great Kantō Earthquake.[173] Given this history of exploitation, Tsurumi suggested that the crimes of the enraged Gwon, Lee, and others might be understood as "counter crimes" against the "original crimes" of the Japanese state.[174] "As members of this state [and] as citizens, the Japanese people" also shared in this original crime, just as all Americans shared in the "original crime" of the atomic bombings of Japan and the war in Vietnam.[175] According to Tsurumi, "to the extent we are living as Japanese nationals and not just as a conglomeration of people, we are accomplices to that original crime. It is necessary that we properly understand just what this original crime is that we are

170. Tsurumi Shunsuke, "Sensō to Nihonjin," 135, 139, 140.
171. Tsurumi Shunsuke, "Sensō to Nihonjin," 140. See also Oguma, *1968* <ge>, 232.
172. Tsurumi Shunsuke, "Sensō to Nihonjin," 135.
173. Tsurumi Shunsuke, "Sensō to Nihonjin," 135.
174. Tsurumi Shunsuke, "Sensō to Nihonjin," 136.
175. Tsurumi Shunsuke, "Sensō to Nihonjin," 136.

contributing to." The Gwon Hui-ro Incident offered a perfect "opportunity for such awareness."[176]

But nurturing this awareness or sense of ethnic responsibility would not be easy, because "counter crimes" inevitably "obscured" the "original crimes." Hence it would be necessary for Japanese people to accept a kind of "proactive culpability" for the counter crimes of resident Asians like Gwon and Lee.[177] As Fujishima had observed in 1960, the great difficulty of the Japanese people's original sin—indeed, its essence—lay precisely in their difficulty in seeing that sin with their own eyes, and herein lay the fundamental pathology of the postwar mentality.

Fujishima was no doubt correct, but recognition of the Asia problem and ethnic responsibility among some progressive intellectuals and literati in the late 1950s and 1960s marked a significant reorientation and the first important step toward their deimperialization and genuine reengagement with Asia. As chapter 3 shows, the Vietnam War and controversy over Japan's immigration control system would draw antiwar and student activists into this process.

176. Tsurumi Shunsuke, "Sensō to Nihonjin," 138.
177. Tsurumi Shunsuke, "Sensō to Nihonjin," 138.

CHAPTER 3

The Vietnam War, Immigration Control, and Original Sin

The average Japanese feels superior in some way to the other people of Asia. When they see photographs of celebrations in the People's Republic of China, for example, pictures of young women parading in the streets, many Japanese must clench their teeth against a giggle, as though they were being tickled. This sort of defiant pride in Japan's isolation from the rest of Asia goes a long way toward explaining the difficulties . . . which constantly beset Japan-Asia relations. The Japanese tendency to submit to mastery by the Westerner with smiles and shouts of *hallo* while he maliciously snubs his Oriental brothers, this somewhat effeminate tendency, is poisoning not only the Japanese economy but all of Japanese culture as well.

—Ōe Kenzaburō, "Portrait of the Postwar Generation"

When citizen activists and students began opposing the Vietnam War in 1965, few of them imagined that they would be drawn into a gut-wrenching encounter with Japan's sullied history in Asia, nor did they anticipate the implications for their own deimperialization and self-reflexive struggle with postwar responsibility. Although early opposition to the Vietnam War drew heavily on the same insular one-nation pacifism as the Anpo protests of 1960 did (many activists were involved in both movements), the critical interventions of figures like the writer and activist Oda Makoto forced activists to face their individual responsibility as Japanese citizens over and above their denunciations of the United States or the Japanese government. As I have discussed elsewhere, one result of this reorientation was a frontal assault on Japan's ebullient affluence of the late 1960s and a related interrogation of the complicity found in the interstices of

everyday life.[1] But the examination of Japanese complicity in the Vietnam War also had implications in the realm of progressive deimperialization and attitudes toward Asia. Similar to Fujishima Udai, Hatada
Takashi, and others—who were demanding that the Japanese face their
ethnic responsibility for the wretched situation of resident Koreans and
Japan-Korea relations—prominent antiwar activists like the reporter
Honda Katsuichi and Tsurumi Yoshiyuki began projecting notions of
Japanese complicity in the Vietnam War backward onto the country's
modern history in an effort to expose a gruesome and largely unexamined
past of aggression in Asia.

Academic historians and other research groups joined this project
through their systematic investigations into the history of Japanese colonialism and militarism in Asia and, particularly, the devastating effects
for victims of those projects. These historical excavations received a shot
in the arm from contemporaneous conservative maneuvers to rehabilitate and even glorify the recent past, whether through a shrill historical
revisionism affirming Japan's "one-hundred-year war" of liberation for fellow Asians or within the warm embrace of American modernization
theory.[2] As conservative politicians and intellectuals prepared to celebrate
the centennial of the Meiji Restoration in 1968, Honda, Tsurumi, and
historians like Ienaga Saburō and Irokawa Daikichi—goaded by the self-
congratulatory mood—began asking probing questions about the continuities between Japanese aggression toward Asia in the past and the
Vietnam conflict in the present. Similarly, students like Tsumura Takashi,
a radical attending Waseda University, drew attention to Japan's historical transgressions in China, particularly the infamous Marco Polo Bridge
Incident of 1937. From such perspectives Japan's one hundred years of war
in Asia emerged as anything but liberational and affirmative. Through
essays, publications, and speeches, these individuals delved into Japan's
colonial and military exploits in Asia far more methodically and controversially than anyone had before. Moreover, by expanding their purview
beyond the largely Korean focus of the ethnic responsibility movement,
they set the stage for a veritable explosion of Japanese activism in, and
attention to, Asia in the 1970s.

1. Avenell, *Making Japanese Citizens*, chapter 3.
2. On this "hundred-year war" see the discussion of Hayashi Fusao below.

At the same time, the issue of Japan's Asia within by no means receded from consciousness as activists began to widen their vision geographically and historically from the mid-1960s. Discriminatory practices in Japan's immigration control system meant that the problems of Asians in Japan would always be at the forefront of activists' attention. The treatment of Asians at detention facilities, like that of Gwon Hui-ro and Lee Jin-wu, served as proof for their Japanese advocates of the unbroken chain of discrimination stretching from the dawn of Japanese modernization to the present. It was evidence of the penetration of the mentality of abandoning Asia into the viscera of Japanese consciousness and institutions.

University student activists' belated entry into the rough waters of deimperialization at this time was largely thanks to controversy over Japan's immigration control system and detention facilities for foreigners. Students' seeming obliviousness to their inherited responsibility for Japan's past actions, along with their rather tepid response to immigration control issues, provoked caustic denunciations from resident Chinese and Korean students who demanded ethnic responsibility from their Japanese counterparts. Such denunciations came as a rude awakening for Japanese students. In the midst of their supposedly historic struggles for the dismantling of conservative rule, American imperialism, and Japan's imperialistic universities, some student activists recognized—or, rather, were forced to recognize—what Tsumura provocatively labeled the "Hitler within" (*uchinaru Hitorā*).[3] By this Tsumura meant the ignorance among most student activists about their responsibility for crimes committed against Asians by contemporary Japan through its immigration control system, as well as the original sins committed by earlier generations against colonial subjects and their descendants. The "Hitler within" was about the stubborn persistence of an imperialist and fascist mentality among students, ironically concealed in the ornamentation of self-righteous internationalism and proletarian revolution. As Tsumura and others probingly asked, how could students call for solidarity with the people of Vietnam or for an international proletarian revolution when they had not even recognized (let alone shouldered) their own war responsibility? Tsumura and others demanded that before putting on the mantle of

3. Tsumura, *Warera no uchinaru*, 38.

internationalist revolutionaries, students first face their ethnic responsibility to Asians as Japanese.

The Vietnam War and the Self as Perpetrator

The anti–Vietnam War movement, Beheiren (1965–74), was an important stepping-stone on the path to Japanese progressives' reengagement with Asia in the 1960s, greatly expanding the number of activists and intellectuals sensitive to the Asia problem.[4] But contrary to the standard narrative, Beheiren activists were not the first to protest in Japan against the Vietnam War, and until the 1970s they were more concerned with the United States and Japan than with Vietnam or Asia. In fact, in February 1965—some two months before Beheiren's founding rally in April—Vietnamese exchange students staged in Tokyo's Hibiya Park what appears to have been the first rally opposing the Vietnam War in Japan.[5] The Japanese authorities were not impressed and quickly moved to revise immigration regulations to prohibit political activities by exchange students. By contrast, Japanese activists were relatively slow to react to the war, and when the first Beheiren group did eventually form months later, its leaders refused to draw connections to the ongoing uproar about the Japan–South Korea normalization treaty, arguing that theirs was a single-issue movement.[6] At an August 1965 symposium, for example, Oda stated unequivocally that people only needed to oppose the Vietnam War, and he said that in fact he was "against" "lumping together" Japan–South Korea issues and the Vietnam War.[7]

There were certainly valid strategic reasons for focusing movement resources on a single issue, but this approach also reveals that many Beheiren activists understood the Vietnam problem mainly as one between America and Japan, as opposed to a problem of Japan and its relations

4. Beheiren is an acronym for "Betonamu ni Heiwa o! Shimin Rengō," whose name in English is "The Citizens' Alliance for Peace in Vietnam."
5. Utsumi et al., *Sengo sekinin*, 120.
6. Noh, "Beheiren," 60.
7. Quoted in Oguma, *1968 <ge>*, 318.

with Asia. The fact that the victims of the war were Asian only gradually emerged as a critical issue in the movement. As late as 1972—seven years after Beheiren began—Oda was just beginning to decry his and other activists' lack of knowledge about Asia and their weak connections with the region. So, like the early 1960s movement for ethnic responsibility, Beheiren is best viewed as a transitional vehicle in the process of progressive deimperialization in 1960s Japan. Only while opposing the US and Japanese governments did movement activists start to think about the problem of Japan in Asia and the challenge of building a grassroots movement with other Asians based on the recognition of a bloodstained past. Quite telling in this respect is the relative absence of Asian voices in the plethora of Beheiren leaflets and newsletters. The ideas and activities of prominent American activists such as Joan Baez, Howard Zinn, and Stokely Carmichael appear frequently in this material, but only occasionally and only in the latter years of the movement do we see contributions from Vietnamese, South Koreans, and other East Asians.

So how and why did a sensitivity to the Asia problem develop in Beheiren? We can find answers in the intellectual trajectory of the movement's leaders—especially that of Oda (1932–2007), given his overarching influence. Oda was certainly aware of the problematic past between Japan and its neighbors before the Vietnam War, but only gradually did he reconceive of this past as a problem that he and his fellow activists had a responsibility to address in the present. Before the founding of Beheiren Oda had traveled quite extensively in Asia (and elsewhere), something exceedingly rare for young Japanese (in fact, for most Japanese) at the time. Thanks to a Fulbright scholarship in 1959, Oda was able to embark on a world tour after his studies in the United States. On his trip back to Japan, he visited Europe, the Middle East, and Asia, surviving on a shoestring budget and the goodwill of people along the way. He documented his experiences in the best-selling 1961 travelogue, *Nandemo mite yarō* (I'm gonna see everything), which I have discussed in great depth elsewhere.[8] Of interest here is Oda's perspective on Asia in that work. Largely echoing the rhetoric of 1950s Asian nationalism, Oda observed that it was not culture but a shared postcolonial predicament that united Asians (including the Japanese). The sheer "ghostliness" of India, for instance, had left

8. Avenell, *Making Japanese Citizens*, 125–34. See also Oda, *Nandemo mite yarō*.

Oda "dumbfounded" and convinced that Asia was not "one" at all in a cultural sense.[9] Asian unity for Oda was apparent in the way the "West" had "to its heart's content" "extracted" and "half-murdered" "us" (*ware-ware*), the "subservient nations, the colonized nations, the backward nations, the poor." "It is here perhaps that Asia becomes one," he said, adding that this definition of "Asia" would also include the Middle East and Africa: "At the very least, the solidarity born of the fact that we were the playthings of the West is something with far greater authenticity for me than superficial things like skin color or hair color."[10] Oda's use of "us" when discussing Asians and his seeming insensitivity to Japan's having been a colonizer in Asia is quite striking in this 1961 work, although his viewpoint is hardly surprising given the potency of Third Worldism and Asian nationalism even in the late 1950s, ideas of which he was clearly enamored. At the same time, the other aspect of Asia that struck Oda was its poverty—which, he said, the Japanese had no choice but to face head-on as fellow Asians.[11] Hence, at least in 1961, Oda's Asia encompassed an intriguing amalgam of 1940s and 1950s perspectives, combining notions of both Asia as resistance and Asia as stagnation. But there is no sense of Japan's being alienated from the region or having a complicated past there.

The next insight we have into Oda's view of Asia before the founding of Beheiren is a fascinating 1963 article he penned for the monthly magazine *Chūō kōron* after a visit to South Korea paid for by the Park Chung-hee regime. Oda explained that he had accepted the invitation to visit the country because he knew very little about Korea and was troubled by the persistent Japanese prejudice toward its closest neighbor. For instance, when he told two young friends about the invitation, they said with one voice, "Chōsen, Chōsen, *omochiroina*," mocking the accent of Koreans.[12] Oda noted that "if I had been invited by the American government they probably would have been envious of me." He was forced to admit that up to that point even he had "forced Korea out" of his

9. Oda, *Nandemo mite yarō*, 183.
10. Oda, *Nandemo mite yarō*, 184.
11. Oda, *Nandemo mite yarō*, 226.
12. The correct pronunciation is "*omoshiroina*" (the phrase means "Korea, Korea, how interesting").

"consciousness": "Honestly speaking, when I spoke of the countries of Asia and Africa, I meant India, the Arab union, and China, but not Korea."[13] As he would repeat in the late 1960s, he began to feel ashamed that he could not speak a word of Korean.[14]

Oda's awareness of ingrained Japanese prejudices aside, the article is interesting for its revelation of his apparent insensitivity to the weight of history on Japan-Korea relations, not to mention his bewilderment (bordering on frustration) at Koreans' seeming fixation on this history. He recounted a particularly jolting instance of this gap in historical consciousness on his arrival in Seoul. Looking at the Seoul Capitol Building quite absentmindedly from the bus, he thought to himself that this was the kind of garish white building one might see in any capital city around the world. But he was "dragged" from his "dream to reality" and "from the present to the past" when one of his traveling companions identified the structure as the former Japanese Government General Building: "In other words, I was not looking at South Korea through the lens of [its being] 'Japan's former colony' but as one of the new nations of Asia."[15] Oda described how he and most other Japanese harbored a sense of ambivalence about the colonization of Korea. On the one hand, there was a tendency to "sink" into a "sense of guilt" that sometimes bordered on "self-deception" and "intoxication," while on the other hand, there was the perspective that Japan had done "good things" for Korea in the past. Most Japanese, he suggested, tended to weigh up the pros and cons of both perspectives.[16] For Koreans too, Japan was "suspended" in "consciousness," sometimes provoking a sense of sentimentality and affinity and even "admiration," but at other times representing nothing less than a "nightmare." But even worse, Oda felt that Koreans' fetish about "Japan" appeared to be "preventing" them from reaching out laterally to the new nations of Asia and Africa. This debilitating fixation on the past meant that they had yet to establish their position among these nations, even twenty-eight years after colonization.[17]

13. Oda, "Sore o sakete," 224.
14. Oda, "Sore o sakete," 223–24.
15. Oda, "Sore o sakete," 225.
16. Oda, "Sore o sakete," 226.
17. Oda, "Sore o sakete," 227.

A typical example of this fixation for Oda was an elderly man on Jeju Island who had asked him why the Japanese were so enthusiastic about remilitarizing—a question that Oda interpreted as an insinuation that Japan had not shed its aggressive, militaristic character. "One reason this question was difficult to answer stemmed from Koreans' lack of knowledge about postwar Japan," he lamented. In terms of "superficial knowledge," the Koreans knew far more about Japan than any other country in Asia or Africa, but when it came to the substantive postwar period (the psychological transformation of the Japanese people), they were simply drawing "analogies" based on a "thoughtless accumulation of past experiences."[18] Oda was left in no doubt as to the depth of Koreans' animosity toward Japan: One evening after he had dined with a Korean acquaintance in Seoul, two young men approached him, asking if he was "Japanese." When Oda responded affirmatively, they handed him a paper bag, saying it was a "gift." Inside he discovered human excrement.[19] But rather than such experiences provoking Oda to turn his critical gaze inward, they seem to have struck him at the time as evidence of Koreans' inability to simply let go of an unchangeable past.

Indeed, surveying the rocky bilateral relationship, Oda admonished both sides for ceaselessly acting like estranged siblings or a "divorced couple" caught in a "slimy entanglement of love and hate." He demanded that the two instead adopt a less encumbered attitude, something akin to being "just friends."[20] "Solving the problem" required a mutual reconception of the other as an "absolute stranger," the discarding of tedious refrains that "Korea was Japan's former [colony]," and the embrace of "the perspective of the new nations of Asia and Africa." "Nothing," Oda declared, would emerge from "a simple sense of guilt" on the part of Japanese.[21]

So at least at this moment in 1963, the past was the past for Oda, and since nothing could be done to alter it, Japanese and Koreans were best advised to abandon needless historical encumbrances and embrace the bright new solidarity and mentality of a rising Asia. However, the "gift"

18. Oda, "Sore o sakete," 230.
19. Oda, "Sore o sakete," 231.
20. Oda, "Sore o sakete," 231.
21. Oda, "Sore o sakete," 231.

Oda received in Seoul remained an unsettling reminder that discarding history like a pair of worn-out shoes was not something even young Koreans could or would easily do.

Although before the Vietnam War Oda basically adhered to a "let bygones be bygones" approach to the past, he was not completely insensitive to the perspectives of Japan's former colonial subjects and military victims, and on occasion he expressed a vague uneasiness about this history. In another 1963 essay, which recounted his time in Boston as a Fulbright scholar, Oda admitted that he always found it "easier speaking to Americans" about World War II because he could "rely on the sense that America was the aggressor and Japan the victim," even so much that on occasions he could "back them into a corner."[22] "But the tables turned completely when the other person was Chinese," when Oda became "lost for words" because "Japan was unquestionably the aggressor and China was unquestionably the victim." But when a Chinese student whom Oda was teaching Japanese confronted him this way, Oda's immediate reaction was that such criticism of him personally from another Asian was unfair. After all, it was an earlier generation that committed the crimes, and he had "no connection" to "that" Japan because he had been "still a child" at the time. If he had been part of an earlier generation, he probably would have felt a "sense of guilt" (*tsumi no ishiki*). Yet after some reflection, Oda began to suspect that his attitude might actually be an "indulgent justification"— that his generation might share some responsibility for the actions of their forebears.[23]

What we witness in Oda of the early 1960s, then, is an ambiguous and ambivalent view of Asia, a view that was very much in transition. On the one hand, Oda's view of Asia remained very much under the sway of both the stagnation and liberation perspectives of the 1940s and 1950s, while on the other hand, his experiences in South Korea and elsewhere raised troubling questions about his perception of Japanese and Asians as a collective we, not to mention his hesitancy to accept postwar responsibility.

How and why did Oda shed his "let bygones be bygones" mentality of the early 1960s, and what role did he subsequently play in drawing the

22. Oda, "Kanbi na nigekōjō," 264.
23. Oda, "Kanbi na nigekōjō," 264.

attention of anti–Vietnam War activists to the Asia problem as their own? Three factors seem to have mattered immensely: first, the awareness among Beheiren activists of Japan's deep—if indirect—involvement in the Vietnam War; second, Oda's view that all Japanese were complicit in this involvement; and third, the conceptual linking of this complicity in the war to Japan's past transgressions in Asia.

In relation to the first factor, in May 1966, the Beheiren activist Tsurumi Yoshiyuki offered one of the first detailed accounts of Japanese collusion in Vietnam in an article for the official movement mouthpiece, *Beheiren nyūsu*. While US military bases in Japan were clear for all to see, Tsurumi's article described in minute detail the depth of Japanese involvement through military "special procurements" and mammoth corporations like Mitsubishi Heavy Industries, which were supplying armaments and maintenance services for the US Air Force.[24] Military bases in Japan certainly provided a critical staging ground for US bombing raids on North Vietnam, but Tsurumi also noted that Japanese industries were producing up to 90 percent of the napalm the Americans were using in the conflict. Similar exposés flowed back to Japan from Indochina. In a highly influential series of articles for the *Asahi shinbun* newspaper in 1966 and 1967, Honda described the important role of Japanese overseas procurements, especially in the provisioning of South Korean forces involved in the conflict. One South Korean officer told Honda to visit the base at Qui Nhơn in central Vietnam because the place was "crawling with Japanese LSTs [landing ship, tanks]."[25] Honda later reported that Japanese LSTs were the most commonly used in Vietnam and, moreover, that a plethora of Japanese-made tankers and tugboats were also supporting military operations. Even the Japanese printing industry was implicated: US propaganda leaflets dropped on North Vietnam were printed in Japan.[26] As Honda put it, "to the attentive, things 'smell of Japan' on the battlefields of Vietnam. I cannot easily find the precise words to characterize the role of Japan in the Vietnam War. . . . Though I abhor writing them, I'm afraid those words must be 'the merchant of death.'"[27] As a

24.   Tsurumi Yoshiyuki, "Betonamu sensō to Nihon," 16.
25.   Honda, *Senjō no mura*, 222.
26.   Honda, *Senjō no mura*, 222–23.
27.   Honda, *Vietnam War*, 249.

frontline reporter in Vietnam for the left-of-center *Asahi shinbun* news-paper, Honda contributed perhaps more than any other journalist to shap-ing Japanese public opinion on the war and stimulating dissent. Thanks to his unsanitized and at times heart-wrenching reportage from both sides of the conflict, Honda attained a kind of cult status in the activist com-munity that, as I explain below, he adroitly used to heighten progressives' sensitivity to the Asia problem. Honda's battlefield reports of 1966 and 1967 were published in 1968 as *Senjō no mura* (The villages of war), which was an immediate best seller in Japan. Fifty thousand copies of the En-glish translation (1968) were also sold worldwide.[28]

The revelation of this Japanese complicity in Vietnam facilitated some important intellectual breakthroughs within Beheiren—most evident in the interventions of Oda, whose earlier perspective underwent a striking transformation. After accepting the invitation of Tsurumi Shunsuke and Takabatake Michitoshi (both stalwarts from the Anpo 1960 protests) to lead the movement in April 1965, Oda quickly emerged as the intellec-tual dynamo of Beheiren through his public speeches and writings. Most influential was his characterization of ordinary Japanese people as both victims and perpetrators in the context of the Vietnam War. In a land-mark 1966 speech titled "Heiwa e no gutaitekina teigen" (Concrete pro-posals for peace) delivered to Japanese and foreign antiwar activists in Tokyo, Oda explained that "photographs of the brutal acts in the Vietnam War" had aroused his sympathy for the "unfortunate victims," whose ag-onized expressions transported him back to the horrific American fire-bombing he had experienced in Osaka in 1945. But his reaction was more complicated. Also visible in the ghastly images from Vietnam were "the hands responsible for those brutal acts" and, more distressingly, the chilling reality that "those hands" were his "very own": "In reality we are complicit in the Vietnam War. We must recognize our position as perpetrators."[29] As Oda explained, "in the context of the relationship between state and indi-vidual within Japan," ordinary Japanese were "in the position of victims," "but in ways both direct and indirect" they were "being herded into coop-eration with the state and, because of this," became "perpetrators against

28. Lie, introduction, 16.
29. Oda, "Heiwa e no gutaiteki teigen," 108.

the Vietnamese people."[30] As he elaborated in a seminal essay published in 1966, "Heiwa o tsukuru" (Making peace), Japanese citizens were certainly victims in that they had suffered in the latter stages of the Pacific War and afterward as inhabitants of a quasi–US colony. But to the extent that Japanese people benefited from and prospered as citizens and consumers in this system, they also became accomplices and individual perpetrators against the Vietnamese people, albeit indirectly.[31]

The importance of Oda's intellectual breakthrough here cannot be emphasized enough. It is analogous to the reorientation from ethnic nationalism to ethnic responsibility that we saw in chapter 2. As Michiba Chikanobu observes, it was a "discovery that brought about a significant paradigmatic shift in the post–World War II history of social movements in Japan."[32] Before the Vietnam War, Japanese antiwar pacifism was characterized by a strong sense of popular victimization by the wartime Japanese state, the American atomic and fire bombings at the end of World War II, and the continued US military presence in the country starting in 1945. This mentality carried over into Beheiren to the extent that activists superimposed their past experience as Pacific War victims onto the current plight of the Vietnamese people. But seeing the multidimensional involvement of the Japanese economy and government in the Vietnam War prompted Oda to smash such one-dimensional logic.

The impact on Beheiren was profound. Activists now turned their critical gaze to the complicity of the Japanese economy and government, as well as their own affluent daily lives. As Tsurumi Yoshiyuki reflected in 1969, in contrast to the 1960 Anpo struggle when "everyday civic lives" were "to be protected," now they were "things to be rejected." Through the various activities of Beheiren groups such as opposition to special procurements, movements against US bases in Japan, and support for US military deserters, Tsurumi said that activists had finally become attentive to the "fundamental political structure in Asia centered on Japan and the USA," in turn giving birth to their consciousness of the "Vietnam

30.   Oda, "Heiwa e no gutaiteki teigen," 110.
31.   Oda, "Heiwa o tsukuru."
32.   Michiba, "Posuto-Betonamu," 104.

within us" (*waga uchinaru Betonamu*).[33] Beheiren groups responded with creative initiatives like the "single-share movement" against Mitsubishi Heavy Industries, with its provocative slogan "Death to the Merchant of Death." As shareholders, activists could attend the company's annual general meeting, where they posed uncomfortable questions to executives about Mitsubishi's involvement in the Vietnam War.[34] Similarly, the historian Wada Haruki and his Ōizumi Association in northern Tokyo established the Haena Kigyō Shimin Shinsa Iinkai (Citizens' Committee to Investigate Hyena Corporations). This group produced a provocative *Directory of Hyena Corporations* that officially "certified" Japanese corporate heavyweights like Mitsui Trading, Marubeni, Toyota, and Sony as war "profiteers."[35] To overcome individual complicity in the war, Oda proposed—somewhat tongue in cheek—that activists refuse to pay the portion of their income tax slated for "defense expenditure" in the national budget.[36]

But Oda's presentation of Japan and the Japanese people as both victims and perpetrators also had an enormous impact on antiwar activists' response to the Asia problem and the intellectual work of deimperialization. In earlier antiwar pacifism that was dominated by the discourse of national victimization, Asia was essentially rendered invisible, but when Oda connected the Vietnam War to individual complicity, perceptive antiwar advocates immediately realized that the problem went far deeper than the immediate conflict in Southeast Asia. Recognition of individual complicity and of the self as perpetrator served to destabilize any sense of a shared predicament with Asians in either the present or the past. By presenting even sympathetic Japanese people as the unwitting enemies of the Vietnamese, Oda's logic pointed directly to the continuity of a much larger rupture in the modern history of Japan in Asia. It was a logic that undermined his own earlier approach of letting bygones be bygones. In terms of opening a way to progressive deimperialization, it was

33. Tsurumi Yoshiyuki, "1970-nen to Beheiren," 158.
34. Beheiren, "Saidai no 'kōgai,'" 363.
35. Wada, "Betonamu kaihō," 510; Beheiren, "Haena kigyō."
36. Tsurumi Shunsuke et al., "Hansen e no ronri to kōdō (tōron)," 228.

undoubtedly one of the most important conceptual breakthroughs in Japan's postwar era.

The Challenge of Revisionist History

Oda's notion of the self as perpetrator resonated deeply with earlier demands for ethnic responsibility, and by the late 1960s, both streams of thought and activism were rapidly converging in the movements of students, antiwar activists, and resident Asians opposing the treatment of South Korean military deserters interned in Japanese government detention facilities. But progressive attention to the Asia problem and Japanese as perpetrators also developed in response to processes of conservative historical revisionism unfolding within the buoyant optimism of income-doubling 1960s Japan. Of course, by the mid-1960s Hatada and others were already denouncing the history of ethnic obliteration inherent in Japan's colonial projects in Korea and Taiwan, while as early as 1963 others like Hani Gorō had probed the horrific massacres of resident Asians in the wake of the Great Kantō Earthquake. But with the centennial of the Meiji Restoration approaching in 1968 and moves from various quarters to present a positive Japanese past, the need to address historical transgressions began to seem more urgent. In fact, although it may not have appeared so at the time, the tussle over modern Japanese history provoked by this conservative revisionism ironically served as a blessing in disguise for activists like Oda because it forced them to clarify their stance on the Asia problem once and for all, without resorting to insular narratives of state manipulation or grandiose appeals to "we Asians."

Although stratagems to put a positive spin on a repudiated past had provoked fierce responses from progressives throughout the postwar era, in the context of the Vietnam War and concurrent discourses of the self as perpetrator and ethnic responsibility, affirmations of the past could not be countered (either ethically or logically) through appeals to national victimization. Only through an honest engagement with the blood-soaked litany of obliteration, massacre, and original crime would the deceits of revisionism be exposed. As astute progressives were well aware, repudiating revisionism through the lens of complicity entailed a concomitant denuding of the self—a brave acquiescence, as it were, to the lancet of de-imperialization. Armed with Oda's perpetrator logic, anti–Vietnam War activists like Tsurumi, Honda, and Oda himself found common voice with progressive historians and groups committed to uncovering histories of transgression and determined to resist what they correctly saw as an attempt by Japanese conservatives—perhaps in collusion with American Japan hands—to repackage notions of Japanese leadership in Asia in a celebratory narrative of the country's distinctive yet replicable achievement as the only non-Western nation to have attained the holy grail of capitalist modernity. Thanks to this revisionism, by the mid-1960s the historical field was ripe for an abundant self-reflexive harvest, if only within progressive circles. Indeed, along with the Vietnam War, conservative revisionism provides another clue as to how activists like Oda moved from letting bygones be bygones to viewing the self as perpetrator against Asia.

In this connection, in September 1965, just eight months before his landmark speech on the Japanese as perpetrators, Oda published a fascinating opinion piece in *Chūō kōron* titled "Rekishi ni chokushi suru" (Directly facing history) that denounced not the escalating conflict in Indochina but a revisionist history of modern Japan penned by the divisive nationalist writer Hayashi Fusao (1903–75). Once a devout Marxist and exponent of proletarian literature, Hayashi had performed a remarkable ideological recantation (*tenkō*) in the 1930s, renouncing his leftist beliefs for ultranationalism. His provocative postwar intervention came in the form of a sixteen-part series published in *Chūō kōron* from 1963 to 1965 (and later issued in book form) titled "Dai Tōa sensō kōtei ron" (In affirmation of the Greater East Asian war).[37] Basically rehashing the rhetoric of 1930s and 1940s Japanese ultranationalism, Hayashi characterized Japan's one hundred years of war, beginning with the British bombardment of the Satsuma domain in 1863, as essentially an Asian liberation struggle led by Japan against the invading Western nations. Although Hayashi lamented Japanese transgressions against fellow Asians, overall he challenged negative interpretations of the past like the Pacific War view of history, instead presenting a narrative in which the ends justified the means. As Ienaga—one of Hayashi's most vehement antagonists—observed in his authoritative 1968 rejoinder, *Taiheiyō sensō* (The Pacific

37. Hayashi, *Dai Tōa sensō.*

war; published in English as *Japan's Last War*), "Hayashi gave another boost to the name 'Greater East Asian War' and to more favorable interpretations of the conflict," and "although the book [could] be dismissed as stupid and unscholarly, a ghost from the militarist 1930s and 1940s, [its] appearing in Japan's bookstores in the 1960s was significant."[38] In fact, Hayashi's thesis was just part of a wider historical revisionism unfolding in Japan in the 1960s that, I argue, was critical in both focusing and accelerating progressives' attention to the need for deimperialization against the backdrop of escalating involvement in Vietnam.

Although operating from a remarkably different perspective than that of Hayashi, American-made modernization theory that was injected into 1960s Japanese intellectual circles also resonated with and in ways reinforced Hayashi's positive rehabilitation of Japanese history, even while rejecting its fundamental premise of Japan as an Asian liberator. As Sebastian Conrad notes—and as we have seen in chapter 1—modernization theory had indigenous intellectual roots in the early postwar enlightenment and was deeply implicated in propagating notions of Asian stagnation. The great difference between this earlier modernization theory and the 1960s American version was the latter's largely positive take on modern Japanese history, buoyed now by the country's impressive recovery and economic reemergence. While the early postwar modernization theory of Ōtsuka Hisao and others emerged from their "conscience" and "anguish," the modernization theory of the 1960s affirmed the past and was supported by US Cold War policy and ideology.[39]

The critical intellectual event in this connection was the 1960 Conference on Modern Japan, which was held in the resort region of Hakone near Mount Fuji and attended by a who's who of eminent intellectuals like Maruyama Masao, Kawashima Takeyoshi, and Tōyama Shigeki on the Japanese side and Edwin Reischauer, John Whitney Hall, Marius Jansen, and Henry Rosovsky on the foreign (mostly American) side. Summing up the overall perspective of the conference, the historian John Whitney Hall stated that modernization had "occurred in the last several hundred years and brought with it changes" that followed "the same

38. Ienaga, *Japan's Last War*, 253.
39. Nagahara, "Sengo Nihon," 25.

general direction all over the world," including Japan.[40] As another participant, Katō Shūichi, observed, Japanese scholars like Umesao Tadao had actually shown that Japanese modernization had unfolded with no "significant difference" to that experienced in the West—in fact, as we saw above, according to Umesao, Japan was more Western than Asian.[41] In this context, then, Japan emerged as an exceptional and exemplary model of modernization as the first and only non-Western nation to have successfully industrialized.

Reischauer, a historian and the newly appointed US ambassador to Japan, played a pivotal role in promoting this upbeat modernist revisionism. In a fascinating 1961 dialogue with the economic historian Nakayama Ichirō in *Chūō kōron*, Reischauer argued that from a broad perspective, Japan had succeeded and hence represented a kind of textbook for developing nations.[42] As Nagahara observes, Reischauer echoed the US Cold War perspective that "economic backwardness" caused social and political instability—which in turn opened the door to communism and even revolution. The surest prevention was "development" and "industrialization," which Japan had achieved and could be duly proud of, despite some mishaps along the way.[43]

To be fair, modernization scholars did advance the understanding of Japanese history, unchaining it in ways from rigid structuralist approaches. But the problem, according to Nagahara, was the "political conditions" under which 1960s modernization theory unfolded, along with the kinds of "political aspirations" that motivated its proponents.[44] Optimistically reinterpreting Japanese modernization through "industrial success" based on the emergence of important prerequisites in feudal society like proto-industrialization and widespread education had the effect of "making ambiguous" the historical significance of the "social transformations" of the Meiji Restoration and "ultimately" "open[ed] a way" to, if not justify, then at the very least "rationalize" Japanese responsibility for an imperialist

40.   Quoted in Gayle, *Marxist History*, 153.
41.   Gayle, *Marxist History*, 153.
42.   Reischauer and Nakayama, "Nihon no kindaika."
43.   Nagahara, "Sengo Nihon," 25.
44.   Nagahara, "Sengo Nihon," 26.

war.[45] Nowhere was this celebratory revisionism more evident than in the staging of the 1968 centennial of the Meiji Restoration, which Nick Kapur describes as "one of the first attempts by the Japanese government to revive the type of nationalism and patriotism that its aging conservative architects remembered through rose-colored glasses from their youths."[46] Progressive activists and intellectuals, of course, viewed such initiatives as part of a conservative ploy to craft a "legitimating ideology" for the expansion of Japanese capital into Asia—what Tsumura disparaged as a new "Economic Greater East Asia Co-prosperity Sphere" (*keizaiteki Dai Tōa Kyōeiken*).[47]

The Progressive Response: August 15 as Camouflage

Hayashi's revisionism, American modernization theory, and the Meiji centennial coalesced to refract a seductively upbeat narrative of modern Japanese history, seemingly tailor-made for the resplendent economic miracle unfurling before the nation. But their appearance at a moment of heightened tensions over the Japan–South Korea normalization treaty and the Vietnam War also proved to be extremely opportune—albeit unintentionally—in piquing progressives' attention to the linkages between contemporary controversies and Japanese behavior in the past. Attempts to put a positive spin on a repudiated history were like waving a red rag in front of a bull in terms of provoking denunciation from progressive quarters. But as I have noted above, in the context of Japan's complicity in the Vietnam War, it became more and more difficult to counter revisionism with previous narratives of national victimization. Recognition of the self as perpetrator demanded a new response that directly confronted affirmations of the past with the horrifying inventory of Japan's original sins in Asia. The responses of Oda and others to Hayashi need to be understood in the context of this increasingly self-condemnatory progressive milieu.

45. Nagahara, "Sengo Nihon," 26.
46. Kapur, "Empire Strikes Back?," 325.
47. Tsumura, *Warera no uchinaru*, 24–25.

By the mid-1960s activists and intellectuals were also confronted with a small yet growing reservoir of articles, reports, biographies, and academic studies offering detailed accounts of and even statistics on the human costs of Japanese imperialism and militarism. As I have explained above, as early as 1956, Tsurumi Shunsuke was challenging the Pacific War appellation with his provocative "Fifteen-Year War" concept, although at the time he did not delve into Japan's militarism or colonial empire and, correctly speaking, the period he referred to (September 18, 1931, to August 15, 1945) was only around thirteen years and eleven months long.[48] Nevertheless, Tsurumi's was a move in the right direction. Into the early 1960s a few historians began to reconsider modern Japanese history through the lens of Asia. As part of a special April 1962 issue of *Chūō kōron* that reconsidered the Meiji Restoration, the historian Shibahara Takuji published a fascinating article titled "Meiji ishin to Ajia no henkaku" (The Meiji restoration and Asia's transformation) in which he made the then-novel argument that any reevaluation of the restoration had to consider Japan's post-1868 activities in Asia—specifically, how the formation of "Greater Japan" had "suppressed the people" of the region."[49] Shibahara's perspective was quite prophetic, coming as it did before Hayashi's one-hundred-year war thesis and years before the progressive historiography of Ienaga and his colleagues. Other historians focused on the entrenched prejudice against Asia within their profession at this time. In a 1963 article for *Shisō*, the historian Masubuchi Tatsuo took aim at Tsuda Sōkichi, another historian—who, despite experiencing suppression during the war and having resolutely rejected nationalist emperor-centered history in the postwar period, had nevertheless played a leading role in propagating a discriminatory approach to China in Japanese historiography in the wake of the first Sino-Japanese war.[50] Similarly, as we have seen, by 1963 the medievalist Ishimoda Shō was pointing to the "defects contained within the historiography of imperialistically dominant nations" like Japan and calling for a "historical examination of history" in the country.[51] As Nagahara recollected in the late 1970s, Masubuchi's

---

48. Tsurumi Shunsuke, "Chishikijin no sensō sekinin."
49. Shibahara, "Meiji ishin," 270.
50. Masubuchi, "Rekishi ishiki," 173.
51. Quoted in Nagahara, "Sengo Nihon," 42–43.

and Ishimoda's exposition of this "shameful Japanese attitude to China and Korea casting a dark shadow over modern Japanese historiography" had a "profound impact" on him and other historians because it highlighted a problem deeply connected to their "research stance and the subjectivity of researchers themselves."[52] It is no coincidence that Tōyama, Hani, and others were at this very moment busy analyzing Japan's tarnished modern history of discrimination against Korea. Significant also is the novel attention to the defects within progressive historiography, a deimperializing impulse that Wada would later amplify in the context of the Vietnam War.

The previously obscured faces of Japan's Asian victims also became conspicuously more visible in the years leading up to 1965. One of the earliest instances of this arose in 1958—by coincidence, the same year that Lee Jin-wu and the Komatsugawa homicides were capturing headlines. The incident involved Liu Lianren (1913–2000), a Chinese national from Shandong Province who was discovered by a hunting party in the Hokkaido wilderness. Japanese troops had unlawfully detained Liu in China in 1944, forcibly sending him to work in a mine on Hokkaido from which he and fellow prisoners made a daring escape into the mountains. Although the other escapees were quickly apprehended, Liu managed to evade capture and, unaware of the war's end, endured a grueling twelve years in the snowy Hokkaido wilderness before his discovery in 1958. Quite outrageously, after Liu's discovery, Japanese officials seriously debated whether or not he should be indicted for illegal residency, prompting Liu to retort that they should contact Prime Minister Kishi Nobusuke, who was more than qualified to explain why he was in Japan (Kishi had been intimately involved in affairs on the Asian mainland during the war).[53] Much later Liu would unsuccessfully seek compensation in the Japanese courts, but it is the more immediate effect of the incident on progressives' war memory that concerns us here. The publication in Japan in 1959 of the Chinese journalist Wenbin Ouyang's account of Liu's ordeal, titled *Ana ni kakurete 14-nen: Chūgokujin furyo Ryū Renjin no kiroku* (Fourteen years hiding in a burrow: An account of the Chinese prisoner of war Liu

52. Nagahara, "Sengo Nihon," 43.
53. Utsumi et al., *Sengo sekinin*, 15.

Lianren), sparked a new attention to the unresolved legacy of forced wartime relocation and labor under the Japanese empire, giving birth to a genre of publications on the issue.[54] In May 1960, for instance, the progressive monthly magazine *Sekai* ran a lengthy report titled "Senjichū ni okeru Chūgokujin kyōsei renkō no kiroku" (Record of Chinese forced migration during the war), which included details on both Liu's case and the infamous Hanaoka massacre of Chinese laborers in Akita Prefecture in the summer of 1945.[55] Coming at the height of the Anpo struggle, the article naturally began with an extensive discussion on the impact of the revised security treaty on Japanese relations with the Soviets and China before turning to historical issues. Noticeably at odds with the insular antiwar pacifism of the Anpo protests, the article suggested that "we still cannot consign to history the atrocities the Japanese people inflicted on the people of China. We have not resolved our wartime responsibility and nor have we completely atoned. . . . This is the essential point of departure for all modifications to diplomatic relations with China. If we ignore this precondition and point of departure, we will not be able to properly comprehend China's reaction to the new security treaty, and before we realize it very deep misunderstandings will have taken root." Indeed, "regardless of how traumatic, we simply must directly face the unresolved accountabilities of the past [and] the reality of those atrocities."[56] The article noted that countless instances of barbarism toward Chinese who had forcibly been brought to work in Japan, such as the Hanaoka massacre, remained unexamined.

Numerous reports containing graphic statistics on forced labor appeared in the following years. Building on years of activism by groups associated with the Nihon Chūgoku Yūkō Kyōkai (Japan-China Friendship Association) and the Chūgokujin Horyo Junansha Irei Jikkō Iinkai (Executive Committee to Memorialize Chinese Prisoner of War Victims), in 1960 and 1961 the Chūgokujin Junansha Meibo Kyōdō Sakusei Jikkō Iinkai (Executive Committee to Collectively Produce a Register of Chinese Victims'

---

54. Ouyang, *Ana ni kakurete.* Liu was actually in hiding for around twelve years and seven months (July 30, 1945–February 8, 1958).
55. "Senjichū ni okeru Chūgokujin."
56. "Senjichū ni okeru Chūgokujin," 135.

Names) published its three-volume *Chūgokujin kyōsei renkō jiken ni kansuru hōkokusho* (Report on Chinese forced migration incidents), followed in 1961 by *Yonmannin Chūgokujin kyōsei renkō no kiroku* (Record of the forced migration of forty thousand Chinese).[57] In 1964 the Chūgokujin Kyōsei Renkō Jiken Shiryō Hensan Iinkai (Editorial Committee for the Compilation of Resources on Incidents of Chinese Forced Migration) published *Kusa no bohyō: Chūgokujin kyōsei renkō jiken no kiroku* (Tombstones of grass: Record of incidents of Chinese forced migration), while in 1965 Pak Kyong-sik published his *Chōsenjin kyōsei renkō no kiroku* (Record of Korean forced migration).[58] Although these publications hardly constituted a deluge, by offering concrete statistics and putting a human face on the suffering of Asian victims under the Japanese empire, they helped stimulate activists' and academics' attention to Japan's past against the backdrop of growing complicity in Vietnam, on the one hand, and the rise of revisionist celebrations of history, on the other hand.

Pak's publication came at a particularly important historical juncture in mid-1965. The leftist commentator and translator Ōta Masakuni (b. 1943)—then a twenty-two-year-old student radical—recalls that before they read this book, most students had not considered the history of Japan-Korea relations from the perspective of ethnicity and colonialism: "I had thought that analyzing social and political contradictions on the scale of Japan alone was sufficient. I welcomed the liberation and revolutionary struggles of that time in Asia, Africa, and Latin America as 'anticolonial struggles,' but my way of understanding did not lead toward any analysis of colonial rule in modern Japan or self-reflection."[59] Pak's book, Ōta explains, was the "first wedge" that was "hammered into" students' "existence." It "played a decisive role" in their discovery of the "details of crimes committed under imperial rule": for instance, the ways "Koreans with actual names were 'drafted' from specific villages in Korea, 'forcibly removed,' 'mobilized through official mediation,' or 'hunted out.'"[60] With a map of Korea, Japan, and Asia beside him as he

---

57. Chūgokujin Junansha, *Chūgokujin kyōsei renkō* and *Yonmannin*. See Seraphim, *War Memory*, 129–34, for an excellent discussion of this people's diplomacy.
58. Chūgokujin Kyōsei Renkō, *Kusa no bohyō*; Pak, *Chōsenjin*.
59. Ōta, "Minzoku," 185.
60. Ōta, "Minzoku," 185.

read Pak's book, Ōta had his first detailed insight into Japan's "imperialist colonial rule and war of aggression."[61]

Pak's book left nothing to readers' imaginations, providing graphic descriptions of forced migrations, stolen homelands, massacres in the Japanese countryside, mobilization and death in the Japanese military, and the remains of forced laborers littering mines in Kyūshū. Even more shocking were the horrific images inside the book's cover, which showed slaughtered Korean laborers, corpses of 1923 earthquake massacre victims, stacked boxes of Korean human remains, severed heads, and naked cadavers dumped in ditches like so much waste. Here was the hideous corporeality of responsibility and victimization.

As Pak observed in the book's introduction, "only a small amount" was "known in Japan about the era of colonial rule over Korea," with some Japanese even believing that this rule had been "benevolent."[62] While Pak recognized that "to move forward" both sides "should not remain fixated on the past," he felt that Japanese progressives' lack of concrete knowledge about Japan's empire was "obstructing genuinely equal international solidarity and friendship between the Korean and Japanese people."[63] He lamented the almost "complete absence" of "research" on or "attention" to the "historical background of Japanese-speaking Koreans" and their "ethnic sentiment," arguing that "without understanding the feelings of Koreans as an ethnic group oppressed by Japanese imperialism in the past," advocating for Korean issues would remain a "hollow exercise bereft of substance."[64] Simply invoking "Japan, Africa, and Latin America" as though they were part of some shared historical project of oppressed peoples made it impossible for Japanese to "rethink ethnic national consciousness through the lens of Japan's colonial empire."[65] "The more the problem of Korea and . . . China are avoided," he observed, "the further away we move from the crux of the problem." The Japanese people had to comprehend their ethnicity and their colonizer history as "two sides of the same coin."[66]

61. Ōta, "Minzoku," 186.
62. Pak Kyong-sik, *Chōsenjin*, 1.
63. Pak Kyong-sik, *Chōsenjin*, 3.
64. Pak Kyong-sik, *Chōsenjin*, 10.
65. Pak Kyongsik, *Chōsenjin*, 14 and 17.
66. Pak Kyongsik, *Chōsenjin*, 18.

Such confronting works by Pak and others became the empirical and inspirational foundation for progressive counteroffensives to the revisionism of Hayashi and others beginning around the mid-1960s. Among the earliest such work was Oda's September 1965 essay on "facing history," mentioned above. As Oda explained to his readers, while he could agree with Hayashi's assertion that the Pacific War had facilitated the liberation of certain Asian and African countries, it was duplicitous to project that outcome onto Japan's motives for waging the war.[67] Japanese transgressions could not be whitewashed, as Hayashi tried to do, simply by circumventing them or arguing that Japanese motives were based on goodwill, despite the outcomes in practice. For instance, in relation to the annexation of Korea, Hayashi preposterously asserted that an "aspiration for Asian liberation" had motivated Japanese actions.[68] The historical reality, as Pak's book showed, was that annexation was nothing but a self-serving contrivance that functioned as ideological camouflage for imperialist domination. The whole project was always only about Japan—a chauvinistic hypocrisy that Hayashi had reproduced with immaculate fidelity.

As Oda observed, the victimized "Asia" that Hayashi claimed Japan had so wanted to liberate was the very same "backward Asia" it so desperately wanted to abandon.[69] And precisely because this hypocrisy was built on Japan's own self-loathing as an Asian nation, when the country arrogantly assumed the mantle of Asia's "chosen people" with a historic "duty," Asia became the site where Japan vented its conflicted self-loathing through aggression. It was not surprising, then, that Hayashi could never see history from the "perspective of the annexed Koreans," because the self-reflexive vision afforded by the Asian Other exposed not goodwill but sheer aggression and self-loathing. Hayashi's history could thus only be "one-sided," "from the perspective of Japan."[70]

Oda's critique of Hayashi here marks an important transition in his attentiveness to the Asia problem and his internal journey to deimperialization. Faced with Japanese complicity in Vietnam and exposés by Pak

67. Oda, "Rekishi ni chokushi," 260.
68. Oda, "Rekishi ni chokushi," 261.
69. Oda, "Rekishi ni chokushi," 260.
70. Oda, "Rekishi ni chokushi," 261.

and others, Oda's "let bygones be bygones" stance of a few years earlier was no longer sustainable. Oda realized that the only answer to Hayashi and the only solution to the Asia problem was to boldly face the aggression within—a solution he would articulate soon thereafter in his paradigm-shifting concept of ordinary Japanese as perpetrators in Vietnam.

Importantly, Oda was not traveling alone on this intellectual and ethical journey. Historians and fellow anti–Vietnam War activists pushed Oda's line of thought leading to self-reflexivity much further than even he could do at the time. Wada Haruki's (b. 1938) scathing critiques in the 1960s and early 1970s of progressive postwar historians were significant interventions, particularly given his later role in Beheiren and the Asian solidarity movements of the 1970s. In a 1966 essay for *Rekishigaku kenkyū*, for example, Wada took aim at the supposedly "progressive" historiography of leading scholars and groups such as Inoue Kiyoshi, Yanaihara Tadao, Nobuo Seizaburō, and the Rekishigaku Kenkyūkai (Historical Research Association), complaining that their pioneering works failed to emphasize that the Japanese defeat in war represented the "collapse of some thirty years of colonial rule in Korea and the liberation of the Korean people": "How are we to understand this? How is it that the 'end of Japanese rule over Korea on August 15' has not been narrated in Japanese historiography as the 'liberation of the Korean people'? What is the cause of this astonishing oversight?"[71] Here Wada identified the limitation of Japan's postwar reforms based on the blinkered schematic of "democracy" replacing the "emperor system" and "pacifism" supplanting "militarism." Missing from this schematic was any "moment of anti-imperialism," nor was there any expression of remorse for Japan's "imperial oppression" of "the Korean people," and nowhere was there a desire to "cooperate with the Korean people" to "construct a peaceful East Asia."[72]

In a follow-up 1971 essay fittingly titled "Sengo no Nihonjin no hansei to rekishika" (Historians and the remorse of postwar Japanese people), Wada singled out the historian of colonial policy, Yanaihara (who had famously been ousted from academia for his views in 1937), along with other intellectuals such as Ōuchi Hyōe (b. 1938), Kawai Eijirō (b. 1939), and Tsuda (b. 1940). Far from writing hagiography, Wada condemned

71. Wada, "Dainiji Taisengo," 75.
72. Wada, "Dainiji Taisengo," 79.

Yanaihara's tepid postwar criticism of Japanese colonialism, despite the latter's claims to be a Christian and a pacifist. For instance, in a December 1945 speech, "Heiwa kokka ron" (On the peaceful state), Yanaihara had identified "assimilationism" (*dōkashugi*) as the central evil of Japan's colonization of Korea and Taiwan, while suggesting that Japan had contributed to improving living standards in these colonies.[73] For Wada the implication of Yanaihara's logic was that if Japan had operated a British-style empire based on a degree of autonomy (or at least separation), then the colonial project would have been acceptable: "So in the end, Yanaihara's reconsideration was the reconsideration of an imperialist, and not a reconsideration of imperialism. One must conclude that this raises serious questions for us—as a problem for Japanese social science and Christianity."[74] "The Japanese people have not rigorously reflected on their own responsibility as perpetrators," said Wada, and their "scrutiny of the way they were made into perpetrators and, moreover, [how this] caused terrible injury, has been half-baked."[75] He identified the Tokyo Tribunal as a key cause here, given its failure to consider the "oppression, abuse, and murder" of the people of Taiwan and Korea.[76]

As Wada wrote in the magazine *Tenbō* in 1974, "'August 15' is conceived of as the anniversary of war defeat and war's end by the Japanese people. But for South and North Koreans this day is celebrated as the anniversary of 'liberation' and 'independence.' . . . One of the fundamental tasks for the Japanese at the outset of the postwar was to squarely face this reality and to engage in a solemn reflection on the history of imperialism. But the Japanese did not accomplish this task and, hence, squandered this opportunity."[77] "Japanese remorse in the postwar" era was mostly "for militarism and aggression" and did not involve regret and penitence for "imperialism and colonial rule." In this way, Wada explained, the Japanese not only "squandered their first opportunity" for reconciliation with former colonies but also laid the foundations for "new

73. Quoted in Wada, "Sengo no Nihonjin," 100.
74. Wada, "Sengo no Nihonjin," 101.
75. Wada, "Sengo no Nihonjin," 101.
76. Wada, "Sengo no Nihonjin," 103.
77. Wada, "Kankoku no minshū," 53.

crimes of oppression and discrimination" against "the six hundred thousand resident Koreans who remained" in Japan.[78]

Like Wada, Irokawa Daikichi (b. 1925), later a champion of so-called people's history (*minshū shi*), brought Japan's victimization of Asia to the forefront of his retaliation to Hayashi in a 1967 essay titled "Kindai Nihon to Ajia kaihō" (Modern Japan and Asian liberation) in the pacifist-leaning monthly magazine *Ushio* affiliated with the lay Buddhist sect Sōka Gakkai.[79] Of Japan's fourteen major overseas troop deployments in the modern period, Irokawa noted that only four were directed against the West, while the other ten were assaults on Asian nations.[80] In contrast to Hayashi's unctuous hundred-year narrative of Japan in Asia, Irokawa saw only disjuncture, duplicity, and betrayal. Although the Japanese initially shared a desire for independence with fellow Asians in the mid-nineteenth century, they betrayed Asia in the first Sino-Japanese war, thereafter struggling with the West for regional supremacy. And with victory in the Russo-Japanese War (1904–5), the goal of absolute regional dominion took hold, as Japan attempted to throw off Western influence and subjugate Asian nations.[81] Like Oda, Irokawa believed that the major flaw in Hayashi's argument was its chauvinistic "Japanese perspective," which lacked any sensitivity to the standpoint of other Asian nations and peoples.[82] What about the victims and the dead, he asked—along with the Japanese victims, what about the thirty million Chinese and Filipinos or the one million Koreans who had been forced into various forms of slavery? According to Irokawa, "Hayashi Fusao has a responsibility to these dead. Along with Tōjō Hideki he was a leading intellectual at the time who helped force Japan's holy war on Asian people. Today he has not changed his ideas and nor has he stopped advocating them."[83] Furthermore, "he displays a very peculiar mental condition which has no sensitivity whatsoever for the feelings of other peoples." And "there is something similar here to the psychological disposition of

78. Wada, "Kankoku no minshū," 59.
79. Irokawa, "Kindai Nihon."
80. Irokawa, "Kindai Nihon," 117.
81. Irokawa, "Kindai Nihon," 117–18.
82. Irokawa, "Kindai Nihon," 120.
83. Irokawa, "Kindai Nihon," 121.

the Nazi leaders who professed that 'Jews are not humans' and subsequently ordered the genocide at Auschwitz. The fact that many Germans supported the Nazis at this time deeply penetrates our hearts as Japanese." As Irokawa concluded, a "people that continuously fails to question a history of evil leadership and the oppression of other peoples" faces "spiritual collapse."[84]

Ienaga Saburō (1913–2002) pushed Irokawa's critique of Hayashi even further in his landmark 1968 *Taiheiyō sensō* (The Pacific war). Although still attached to the Pacific War nomenclature, Ienaga's book had almost nothing in common with the Pacific War view of history and in many ways represents the emblematic statement of progressive reorientation to the Asia problem at this time. Even though this book did not include Asia in its title, its detailed discussion of colonies and invasion marked an enormous step forward in attention to Japan's war in Asia.[85] Ienaga's was one of the earliest and most important narrative histories to trace Japan's war of aggression (*shinryaku sensō*) in China from the Manchurian Incident of 1931 to the end of the war, providing specific details of the countless atrocities committed against other Asians. As Shōji notes, while Ienaga denounced the pre-1945 Japanese state for stifling society through draconian laws like the Chian iji hō (the peace preservation law), his book broke ground by criticizing the Japanese people's lack of "remorse" (*hansei*) for "aggression against Asia" (*Ajia e no kagai*), and their ignorance about the "victory" of Chinese and other Asians over this aggression (that is, Japan's defeat by Asia).[86] The book also drew explicit connections to the Vietnam War, arguing that thanks to the security alliance with America, Japan was once again contributing to an "invasion of Asia." Ienaga's interpretation of the Pacific War through the lens of invasion and transgression here bore the indelible imprint of Oda's "self as perpetrator" concept. That concept underwrote Ienaga's unsettling conclusion that the Japanese who had died for their nation represented not heroism but "meaningless deaths" (*inujini*)— lives "discarded" in a war of aggression.[87]

84. Irokawa, "Kindai Nihon," 121.
85. Ienaga, *Taiheiyō sensō*. See also Ishida, *Shakai kagaku*, 77.
86. Shōji, "Sengo Nihon," 103.
87. Shōji, "Sengo Nihon," 103.

Ienaga's study is far too rich for a thorough analysis here, but a few aspects of it that relate to Asia warrant comment. First and foremost, Ienaga identified base prejudice and discrimination against Asians as a fundamental cause of World War II. "An understanding of the reasons for this abject slide into aggression must start with the Japanese view of China formed in the decades before the 1930s and with Japan's policies toward China," he explained. Although the Japanese had generally expressed "deep respect" toward China "as a great center of classical culture" and "a powerful nation," this quickly degenerated into "contempt" in the wake of the first Sino-Japanese war, and that contempt thereafter supported the Japanese "advance onto the continent."[88] Korea, conversely, was never "given the respect afforded China," which explained even earlier instances of Japanese aggression toward that country in the Meiji period.[89] Ienaga pointed his finger directly at the state for fomenting this racism and intolerance toward Koreans and Chinese, but he also criticized ordinary Japanese for their inability to critically analyze "imperialist policies" and the resultant wars. The cause, he said, lay "in the state's manipulation of information and values to produce mass conformity and unquestioning obedience."[90] On this point Ienaga echoed earlier interpretations built on the notion of the victimization or, at the very least, deception of the Japanese people by their state.

But Ienaga's book went much further than merely repeating the internalist victim narrative of the war: it drew attention to the most victimized of all, other Asians. In responding to the glossy rehabilitations of Japan's recent past by Hayashi and others, *Taiheiyō sensō* presented readers with page after shocking page of horrific details of Japanese transgressions and depravity, very much in the same spirit as Pak's 1965 book on forced Korean labor. In chapter four of Ienaga's book, for instance, he presented Japan's invasion of Korea as an indisputable refutation of Hayashi's "Asian war of liberation": "If Japan really intended to liberate the peoples of Asia from imperialism, independence for Korea should have been the first step. Anticolonialism should have begun at home. On the contrary, however, the planners of the Manchurian Incident testified that one motive . . . was to

88. Ienaga, *Japan's Last War*, 3, 6, and 11.
89. Ienaga, *Japan's Last War*, 4.
90. Ienaga, *Japan's Last War*, 12.

ensure Japanese control over Korea."[91] "Discrimination," Ienaga observed, was pervasive across the wide expanse of Japan's Asian empire, whether in Korea, colonial Taiwan, the Kwantung leased territory on the Liaodong peninsula, or in the "Japanese army's systematic violation of domestic and international law in Manchuria."[92] According to Ienaga, "the worst single incident was the notorious 'rape of Nanking' immediately after that city's capture" in 1937, but the violations were woven into the operational and institutional fabric of Japan's Asian empire in such a way that they could be normalized and rationalized under the duplicitous veil of liberation.[93] Here Ienaga singled out "the Imperial army with its 'comfort stations'" and the infamous Unit 731, "a bacteriological warfare research unit located in the suburbs of Harbin, Manchuria, under the cover name of Epidemic Prevention and Potable Water Supply Unit." Unit 731 "truly did the devil's work," he observed, but the "U.S. occupation was extremely lenient with Dr. Ishii," the unit's director, who "was not arrested or charged with war crimes" and whose "discoveries and technique" were allegedly used by the Americans "during the Korean War."[94] While Hayashi simply ignored inconvenient facts, Ienaga boldly thrust them into the foreground, compelling readers to face Japan's unatoned original sins in Asia.

Honda Katsuichi (b. 1932) took this historical excavation to an even wider audience in the 1970s, adapting his trademark graphic reportage from the battlefields of Vietnam to Japanese military misdeeds in China in the 1930s and 1940s. The evolution of his critical focus from Vietnam to America and then to Japan and Asia was common among activists and intellectuals at the time, as we have seen with Oda and will see below with Tsurumi Yoshiyuki. After publishing *Senjō no mura* on the Vietnam War, Honda turned his attention to racism and civil rights in America in the 1970 *Amerika Gasshūkoku* (The United States of America), followed by books on Japanese historical aggression in Asia (discussed below) and, ultimately, a critique of contemporary Japan in the 1976 *Soshite waga sokoku—Nihon* (And now my homeland—Japan). Even more than Ienaga's

91.　Ienaga, *Japan's Last War*, 156.
92.　Ienaga, *Japan's Last War*, 157–60.
93.　Ienaga, *Japan's Last War*, 186.
94.　Ienaga, *Japan's Last War*, 187–89.

work, Honda's writings on Japanese militarism were imbued with Oda's self-as-perpetrator perspective, which was evident for example in provocative essays titled "the Japanese people massacred by the atomic bombs and the Chinese people massacred by the Japanese army," "indiscriminate massacres and 'the Japanese people's responsibility,'" and "the necessity of keeping a record as perpetrators."[95] As Tsurumi observed at the time, like Ienaga, Honda's crucial intervention was to extend progressives' attention to Japanese aggression in Asia beyond (and prior to) the "fires of the Vietnam War."[96]

Notably, in mid-1972—on the eve of the anticipated normalization of Sino-Japanese relations—Honda traveled to the People's Republic of China, his self-declared mission to "shed light on the activities of the Japanese military in China during the war from *the perspective of China*" so as to "clearly understand the image of 'Japanese militarism' for the Chinese people who were subjected to invasion."[97] Specifically, Honda wanted to visit sites of Japanese military atrocities and meet with survivors to hear their stories. These travels resulted in two important, if controversial, 1972 books, *Chūgoku no tabi* (Travels in China) and *Chūgoku no Nihon gun* (The Japanese military in China).[98] Both volumes contained page after page of images and survivors' accounts of horrendous Japanese military barbarism in China: massacres at Pingdingshan, Shenyang, and Nanjing; inhumane forced labor and torture; and sickening accounts of medical experimentation.

In *Chūgoku no tabi*, first serialized in the *Asahi shinbun, Asahi jānaru,* and *Shūkan Asahi* in late 1971, Honda told his readers that genuine "normalization" of relations between Japan and the People's Republic of China would not be possible until the Japanese people faced their history of

95. For the essays see Honda, *Korosu-gawa*, 32, 307, 324.
96. Tsurumi Yoshiyuki, "Watashi no kanshin," 62.
97. Honda, *Chūgoku no tabi*, 13.
98. Honda, *Chūgoku no tabi* and *Chūgoku no Nihon gun*. I say "controversial" because, as Franziska Seraphim notes, "in the course of the debate it became clear, for example, that some of Honda's reports of killing competitions between soldiers in Nanjing in 1937 had no basis in fact (*War Memory*, 224). *Chūgoku no Nihon gun* contained descriptions of sword-killing competitions that Honda heard from survivors of the Nanjing massacre but that would later be questioned by centrist and right-wing critics. See Takashi Yoshida, "A Battle over History," 81.

aggression on the mainland.[99] His threefold aim in the book was to expose what the Japanese really did in China, in the process putting Japanese wartime suffering (such as that resulting from the atomic bombings) in perspective, and to foster an understanding of the Chinese people's suffering and their persistent distrust of Japan.[100] According to Honda, in the years after the war neither the government nor the mass media in Japan had engaged in any substantive attempt at facing the past head-on or fashioning a balanced popular memory of this past. As a result, the Japanese people knew only in a very "abstract" and "hearsay" fashion that "tens of millions of Chinese were murdered."[101] It was this potholed historical memory, he argued, that emboldened conservative leaders to venerate the Yasukuni Shrine and effectively "reverse the wheels of history."[102] While Honda recognized the desire and need to remember the firebombings of Tokyo and Osaka and the atomic bombings of Hiroshima and Nagasaki, he insisted that such victims' history be balanced by a recognition of Japan's past as a perpetrator that had invaded the countries of Asia. Honda said that through his writings on Japan's war in China, he wanted to help the Japanese people—activists in particular—understand why the Chinese were constantly worried about the revival of Japanese militarism in Asia. For the Chinese, he explained, Japanese militarism was neither "abstract" nor a set of "statistics."[103] On the contrary, it had a historical and psychological basis in memories of murdered loved ones and burned houses.[104] "Some people might ask 'why now,'" observed Honda, but the point was "precisely now" because a quarter of a century after the war, nothing had been solved.[105]

Honda's writings on both Vietnam and Asia had an indelible influence on progressives' attention to the past. The legal scholar Ōnuma Yasuaki (discussed in chapter 5) notes the significant impact of Honda's work in laying the ideational and empirical groundwork for the various "postwar responsibility" (*sengo sekinin*) initiatives among progressives

99.   Honda, *Chūgoku no tabi*, 13.
100. Takashi Yoshida, "Battle over History," 80.
101. Honda, *Chūgoku no tabi*, 14.
102. Honda, *Chūgoku no tabi*, 14.
103. Honda, *Chūgoku no tabi*, 14.
104. Honda, *Chūgoku no tabi*, 14–15.
105. Honda, *Chūgoku no tabi*, 15.

beginning in the 1980s.[106] Tsurumi used Honda's works in his pioneering Asia Study Group of the early 1970s, which became a kind of nursery for a new generation of Japanese activists involved in Asia. Moreover, the writers Ōe Kenzaburō and Inoue Hisashi are typical examples of leftist intellectuals—Iwanami-Asahi intellectuals—who began to reassess their earlier inattention to the war responsibility issue thanks to Honda's work.[107] As Ōnuma puts it, Honda's works compelled them to ask serious questions about how their fathers had "murdered," "pillaged," and "burned" their way through China.[108]

Ushio served as a venue for this progressive self-reflection and remorse about Japanese actions in Asia into the early 1970s, publishing numerous special reports on unresolved historical issues. Report titles throughout 1971 and 1972 speak for themselves: "Japanese atrocities and discrimination toward Koreans," "What were Chinese people forced to do in Japan?," "Alive yet hidden, A-bomb victims and racial prejudice," "Japanese racial discrimination: Koreans, Chinese," "Untried war crimes," and "Within the psychological makeup of the Japanese there exists an inexplicable and ghastly 'sense of superiority.'" The list of contributors also reads like a who's who of prominent progressives, including Tsurumi Shunsuke, Hani Gorō, Fujishima Udai, Ienaga Saburō, Kinoshita Junji, Kainō Michitaka, Hatada Takashi, and Yasuda Takeshi.[109] Their writings evidence the strongly repentant tone of the *Ushio* special reports. For example, writing of his childhood in the 1920s, the playwright Kinoshita recalled that "my first recollection of . . . society goes back to the Great Kantō Earthquake. In my third year of elementary school, I was walking along a road in the Koishikawa area when I witnessed a group of Japanese viciously beating a Korean with what looked like clubs. Thereafter I was constantly forced to watch at close proximity as Japanese like me committed untold acts of discrimination and abuse against Koreans."[110] Kinoshita likened the resident Korean issue to a log in the river of Japanese

106. Utsumi et al., *Sengo sekinin*, 124.

107. Iwanami Shoten is a publishing company known for its progressive-leaning publications.

108. Utsumi et al., *Sengo sekinin*, 125.

109. These special reports were included in the following volumes of *Ushio*: 144, 150, 153, 156, 157, and 168.

110. Kinoshita, "'Kawa no naka,'" 95.

history: regardless of how many years that river flowed, for the Japanese, resident Koreans remained unmoved. "The first requirement, then," he wrote, "is that we continue to recognize this as our original sin."[111]

In another essay for *Ushio*, like Irokawa, the historian Hani drew parallels between Nazi Germany and imperial Japan, observing that "as the wartime policy progressed, the number of Koreans forcibly brought to Japan to work increased dramatically in scale. The massacre and forced labor [of Koreans] corresponds startlingly to the Nazis' oppression of the Jews. Indeed, it is said that there is one Korean corpse for every railway sleeper on the Ōfunato train line in northern Honshū."[112] Nevertheless, Japanese remained blissfully insensitive to the anguish of Koreans: "The thousand-yen note we currently use in Japan contains the image of Itō Hirobumi. This is something unbearable for Koreans."[113]

In an essay titled "Jijitsu o mae ni shite omō koto" (Reflections on facing the facts), Tsurumi emphasized the negative outcomes of the Occupation for Japanese historical consciousness: "The fact that we have not adequately dealt with the significance and consequences of wartime Chinese forced labor overlaps with the inadequate interpretation of the Fifteen-Year War fashioned mainly by the Occupation forces just after defeat. Happening as it did in the Occupation era, people were induced to believe that [the war] was essentially a crime (*tsumi*) against the nations of Western civilization. Moreover, because the Western nations avoided difficult issues such as the dropping of the atomic bombs and the atrocities committed by Soviet troops as they entered Japanese towns, Japanese became skeptical about the pursuit of [their own] war responsibility."[114] But now, he said, the Japanese needed to "reconsider" interpretations of the war established by the Occupation and its Tokyo Tribunal. At his sardonic best, Tsurumi posed a thorny question to readers about the 1958 Liu Lianren case. After being found in Hokkaido, Liu was promptly arrested by the Japanese police. But Tsurumi wondered if Liu had been an American wartime escapee, would the Japanese police have handcuffed him? Here, of course, was the raw edge of discrimination for

111.   Kinoshita, "'Kawa no naka,'" 96.
112.   Hani, "Doitsu no Yudayajin," 150.
113.   Hani, "Doitsu no Yudayajin," 149.
114.   Tsurumi Shunsuke, "Jijitsu o mae," 93.

Tsurumi: "The Japanese lost to America but they believe they defeated China. This belief has been widespread among the Japanese, without any distinction among postwar Japanese ruling elites, intellectuals, and the masses. Moreover, the US Occupation reinforced this perspective."[115]

The important point to be emphasized in the interventions of Wada, Honda, Ienaga, Oda, and others in the period from the mid-1960s to early 1970s is the striking intensification of progressive self-reflexivity leading from Vietnam to America, Asia, Japan, and ultimately the self. The de-imperializing impulse was as much a journey inward as it was an external struggle for the truth. Moreover, because this self-transformation happened to those at the very forefront of civic movements, the ripple effects were felt by a great many other activists and civic groups. By the early 1970s, the result would be a new attention to Asia and Asian issues forged through the encounter with ethnic responsibility, the Vietnam War, and the draconian immigration system. What I wish to stress is how remarkably different this attention to the Asia problem was from the 1950s idealization of Asia—so much so that we might even say activists and intellectuals were now starting to speak a completely different language about Asia and beginning to see the region through remarkably different eyes.

Tsurumi Yoshiyuki's (1926–94) rejection of America, his attack on the parochialism of Japanese war memory, and his embrace of Southeast Asia is emblematic of this transformation, and it is all the more significant because of the leading role that he—along with Oda and Wada—would later play in directing Japanese civic groups and progressives back to Asia in the 1970s. Among all the progressives discussed above, Tsurumi also stands out for his pivotal role in connecting the Asia problem to concrete grassroots action in the region. Like other progressives, his intellectual journey began with a questioning of accepted and/or conservative versions of history. But he was not satisfied with historical inquiry and self-critique alone, and he went on to establish pioneering grassroots initiatives in Asia and contributed more than any other postwar intellectual-activist to the diffusion of knowledge about Southeast Asia among ordinary Japanese. I investigate Tsurumi's activism in Asia in chapter 5, but here I focus on his emerging criticism of Japanese war memory in the late 1960s and early 1970s.

115. Tsurumi Shunsuke, "Jijitsu o mae," 93.

The son of a Japanese diplomat, Tsurumi was born in the United States and as a youth lived in Los Angeles, Washington, and Portland, Oregon. During World War II, he spent one year as a student in an upper elementary school in Harbin, in the Japanese puppet state of Manchukuo—where, as he put it, his father served as a "representative of the colonial rulers."[116] Tsurumi had no memory of any Chinese people from this year in Manchukuo, only of an "impoverished White Russian émigré."[117] In the 1970s he could still recite the Manchukuo national anthem, which students at the Japanese elementary school sang in Mandarin "despite there being not one Chinese pupil" in the school.[118]

In 1949 he entered the prestigious Law Faculty of the University of Tokyo, where he participated in the progressive scholarly group Shisō no Kagaku Kenkyū Kai (Institute for the Science of Thought) headed by his cousin, Tsurumi Shunsuke, and deeply shaped by American pragmatism. After graduating in 1952, Tsurumi Yoshiyuki battled tuberculosis for some years and then took on full-time work in 1955 at the International House of Japan, at that point a haven for "U.S.-savvy" Japanese progressives eager to learn about (and relay) the "superior aspects" of American modernity to other Japanese.[119] In the early postwar years, at least, Tsurumi was completely submerged in all things American and, as he would soon realize, consequently blinded to Asia.

By the early 1960s Tsurumi was becoming increasingly "frustrated" by the elitism and American focus at the International House, and he began thinking more and more about making connections with "ordinary" people, especially those in the "Third World."[120] But he took no definitive action until the outbreak of the Vietnam War, which forced him and other progressives to directly interrogate the "modern" and "modernization" to which they had been so unquestioningly "devoted."[121] As Yoshimi Shun'ya explains, Tsurumi had to face the fact that he was but "one drop in the blood circulating between the two unequal bodies of

116. Tsurumi Yoshiyuki, "Ochita rekishi," 12.
117. Tsurumi Yoshiyuki, "Ochita rekishi," 14.
118. Tsurumi Yoshiyuki, "Ochita rekishi," 15.
119. Kano Masanao, "Kaisetsu," 408.
120. Tsurumi Yoshiyuki, *Tōnan Ajia,* 4.
121. Kano Masanao, "Kaisetsu," 408.

'America' and 'Japan.'"[122] But the Vietnam War made it impossible for Tsurumi to continue living safely within this cocoon of the "modern" and, as a result, also facilitated his discovery of Asia.[123]

Tsurumi participated in the first Beheiren demonstration in April 1965 with Oda and others, but his abandonment of America and embrace of Asia did not really begin until a life-altering experience months later in Saigon, which was followed by a study trip to America. The trip to the United States that began in July was to participate in Henry Kissinger's famed summer seminar at Harvard University for fifty young leaders from around the world. Along with Tsurumi, Ōe attended from Japan, joining an elite group of seminar alumni that included Nakasone Yasuhiro, later the country's prime minister. Tsurumi later recalled his viscerally negative reaction to "white professors" who were "theoretically opposed to the Vietnam War" yet continued to live their "elegant lifestyles" and drink their "French wine." "Thinking back now," he recalled in the 1990s, "that experience had a very big effect on me."[124] It was an experience made all the more disconcerting thanks to Tsurumi's traumatic encounter in Saigon just weeks before the seminar. On his way to Harvard, Tsurumi took the opportunity to stop in Southeast Asia and Europe. One morning while strolling the streets of Saigon he inadvertently witnessed the gruesome public execution of two Vietcong guerrillas captured by the newly installed and US-supported South Vietnamese regime of Nguyen Van Thieu. Tsurumi vividly recalled how the two had screamed "Long live Ho Chi Minh, overthrow American imperialism!" in the moments before they were shot dead.[125] "I will never forget the screams of those soldiers or the silence of the crowd," Tsurumi wrote. "It would be a lie to say that this experience in Saigon turned me against America, as I had already participated in Beheiren protests in April and May before leaving Japan. But there is no doubt that the experience in Saigon gave a certain direction to my stay in America. . . . You could say that the executed soldiers led me to 'Another America'—an America that discriminates

122.　Yoshimi Shun'ya, "Tsurumi Yoshiyuki," 208.
123.　Kano Masanao, "Kaisetsu," 408.
124.　Tsurumi Yoshiyuki, *Tōnan Ajia*, 7.
125.　Tsurumi Yoshiyuki, "Ajia o shiru," 246.

against black people and murders Asians."[126] The fact that the seminar at
Harvard came directly after this shocking experience in Vietnam was
critical in pushing Tsurumi away from America and toward Asia.

But just as importantly, the Vietnam War also directed Tsurumi's
attention to Japan and to himself as a "Japanese national." As the Vietnam quagmire deepened and the antiwar movement intensified in the late
1960s, Tsurumi supplemented his souring attitude to the United States
with a corresponding infuriation toward Japan. Influenced by Oda's
victim-perpetrator idea, he became more and more indignant about "belonging" to a nation complicit in the war, going so far as to write a provocative 1968 essay titled "Nihon kokumin toshite no dannen" (Renouncing my Japanese nationality).[127] Although he never did renounce his
nationality, Tsurumi's disgust with Japan's involvement served as his point
of entry into the country's unresolved historical transgressions in Asia and
its blinkered historical memory.

The titles of some of Tsurumi's essays published in the decade starting in 1965 offer a graphic insight into his evolving critique of popular
memory: "'Hachigatsu jūgonichi' fukken no tame ni" (How to rehabilitate 'August 15'; 1967), "Hachigatsu jūgonichi kara kieta Ajia" (The Asia
that disappeared from August 15; 1971), "Nihon to Ajia no hachigatsu
Jūgonichi" (August 15 for Japan and for Asia; 1972), and "Ochita rekishi
no yukue" (The whereabouts of omitted history; 1971–72).[128] As the titles reveal, Tsurumi's intellectual discovery of Asia emerged via an interrogation of the meaning of August 15, the day of Japan's surrender. As he
wrote in 1967, "when Japan's history as an aggressive imperialist nation
ended on August 15, 1945, and we attempted to revive ourselves as a peaceful nation, to what extent were we aware of the resolve and the means
necessary to follow through with this in the world? It is difficult to claim
that we settled our past aggression. Domestically attention was directed
toward pursuing the responsibility of the wartime leadership, and due
to the influence of powerful countries, the Japanese people found it very

126. Tsurumi Yoshiyuki, "Ajia o shiru," 246.
127. Tsurumi Yoshiyuki, "Nihon kokumin."
128. Tsurumi Yoshiyuki, "'Hachigatsu jūgonichi' fukken," "Hachigatsu jūgonichi
kara," "Nihon to Ajia," and "Ochita rekishi."

difficult to independently settle issues with China and the countries of
Southeast Asia who were the real victims of [Japanese] aggression."[129] Tsurumi argued that as the Japanese government "intentionally" moved
closer and closer to the United States, its approach to dealing with past
transgressions in Asia operated more and more within the acceptable limits determined by Washington—in other words, within the boundaries
of the US-erected "bamboo curtain" dividing Asia.[130]

As he elaborated in a series of essays published in the 1970s, because
Japan's defeat was explained principally through the lens of superior Western
technology, the country's "postwar blueprint" essentially "reconfirmed"
Japan's modernization trajectory from the mid-nineteenth century of "end-
lessly trying to catch up with the West."[131] Accordingly, August 15 was
less a disjuncture than a point of continuity in Japan's drive to abandon
Asia. The atomic bombings of Hiroshima and Nagasaki became the central
motifs of Japan's technological inferiority and, according to Tsurumi,
rendered the country's aggression in Asia more or less invisible in the
popular memory of the war: "That war was one against Asia inclusive of
China and it was a war involving Asia, yet the impact of the A-bombs
was so great that Asia completely disappeared from 'August 15.'"[132] "Stated
unsympathetically," Tsurumi provocatively concluded in 1972, "one
might speculate that August 15 commemorations" were no more than "self-
indulgent masturbation."[133]

Importantly too, from the perspective of progressive deimperialization, Tsurumi identified this same Asian blind spot in progressive thought
and civic movements in Japan. The attention that Beheiren activists—
including himself—paid to the United States revealed that even so-called
progressives had not entirely shed "the mentality of 'leaving Asia' written
into the very DNA of Japanese society from the Meiji period."[134] According to Tsurumi, "the way in which the side of the invader attempts to
forget the fact of invasion is a reflection of the structural framework of

129.   Tsurumi Yoshiyuki, "'Hachigatsu jūgonichi' fukken," 81.
130.   Tsurumi Yoshiyuki, "'Hachigatsu jūgonichi' fukken," 81.
131.   Tsurumi Yoshiyuki, "Ne toshite," 198–99.
132.   Tsurumi Yoshiyuki, "Hachigatsu jūgonichi kara," 209.
133.   Tsurumi Yoshiyuki, "Nihon to Ajia," 224.
134.   Tsurumi Yoshiyuki, "'Hankenryoku no shisō,'" 176.

that society."[135] Tsurumi admitted his own historical ignorance, which was laid bare during a visit to the Philippines for a conference in 1970. By coincidence his group arrived in Manila on the day (April 9) commemorating the fall of Bataan to the Japanese Imperial Army, yet not one member of his party realized that fact or even knew of this day. As Tsurumi put it, "the side of the perpetrator, Japan, lacked any conscious effort to remember that day."[136] What left him "feeling numb" was not only that the Japanese had "carried out the 'Bataan Death March,'" but that they "had absolutely no memory of this."[137] "If we really wanted to think seriously about August 15," he wrote, "we should be paying attention to April 9 in the Philippines and similar days in the People's Republic of China and other Asian countries."[138] But from the moment when the Japanese "failed to truly understand August 15" in this way "it became more and more distant" from them, and simultaneously it "no longer existed" in Asia.[139] "Put in my terms," Tsurumi explained, "the operation of 'omitting history' has been repeated again and again in postwar Japan, and to the extent [that] we do not deal with this, we will continue to do the same into the future."[140]

The message in all of this was clear. Rather than using America as a tool to understand Japan, what was crucial now was an approach in which Asia informed activists' critical scrutiny of their country. Activists needed to think about Japan and questions of "power on the Japanese mainland" from the "perspective of Vietnam, of Okinawa, of China, and of South Korea."[141] They needed to look within themselves for the "enemy of Asia."[142] Tsurumi and others' challenge here to the logic of postwar Japanese progressive thought, historical consciousness, and civic activism was immense. The Asia problem could no longer be ignored, nor could deimperialization be sidestepped.

135. Tsurumi Yoshiyuki, "Ochita rekishi," 19.
136. Tsurumi Yoshiyuki, "Nihon to Ajia," 224.
137. Tsurumi Yoshiyuki, "Ochita rekishi," 18.
138. Tsurumi Yoshiyuki, "Nihon to Ajia," 226.
139. Tsurumi Yoshiyuki, "Nihon to Ajia," 228.
140. Tsurumi Yoshiyuki, "Ochita rekishi," 19.
141. Tsurumi Yoshiyuki, "Hankenryoku no shisō,'" 176.
142. Tsurumi Yoshiyuki, "Ne toshite," 198.

The Immigration Control Struggle and the
Ōmura Detention Center

While revisionist histories and the Vietnam War stimulated Tsurumi, Honda, Ienaga, and others to challenge postwar Japanese popular memory, pacifism, and victim consciousness, developments at home in the mid- to late 1960s also pushed antiwar activists and, later, student groups in the direction of the Asia problem. The main spark here was Japan's immigration control system, which emerged as the quintessence of the discrimination and prejudice against Asia that were at the core of Japanese institutions and mentality. But this perspective was not immediately obvious to either war protesters or students. Like the assistance they provided to US military deserters, Beheiren activists' support for Koreans caught in the web of Japan's immigration control system began out of a sense of sympathy for antiwar comrades who had bravely accepted the labels of "traitors" and "unpatriotic persons" (*hikokumin*) in the name of shedding their complicity.[143] In a similar way, it took students some time to become sensitive to issues of ethnic responsibility lurking beneath their grandiose claims that all struggles—including those of resident Asians— would be solved in one fell swoop by an international proletarian revolution. Like the Beheiren activists, students realized quite belatedly that the problem was closer to home, submerged within themselves.

The first hints of an immigration control problem surfaced in 1967, when Beheiren activists were alerted to the case of Kim Dong-hee, a South Korean who had fled his homeland for Japan's Tsu Island after being drafted into the military for combat deployment to Vietnam.[144] After spending a year in a Japanese prison, in February 1967 Kim was transferred to the Ōmura Detention Center for illegal entrants in Nagasaki Prefecture to await deportation to South Korea. As a facility for scheduled deportees, Ōmura housed many resident Koreans who had been unable to prove their residency status that dated from the prewar period, a host of

143. Michiba, "Posuto-Betonamu," 104.
144. For more on this case, see Beheiren, "Chōsen shōnen" and "Kin Tō-ki." Kim Dong-hee also published a three-part series in the monthly *Tenbō*: "Watashi no kiroku (jō)," "Kankokugun shinpei," and "Kankokugun heishi."

other foreigners (predominantly Koreans, but also Chinese and other Asians) in breach of the Gaikokujin tōroku hō, illegal entrants, and military deserters seeking asylum. Kim claimed to fall under the latter category, but the Japanese government refused his claims for political asylum. When that happened, he began court proceedings to be granted political refugee status or, if this was not possible, to be deported to North Korea (he feared that he would be executed as a military deserter if he was returned to South Korea). Thanks in part to the wave of support for Kim in Japan, he was subsequently deported to North Korea in January 1968.

Primarily because of his involvement with resident Koreans and issues of ethnic responsibility, Fujishima Udai was among the first to bring attention to Kim's plight—which he did in a 1966 article for the monthly magazine *Gendai no me*.[145] But it was not until March 1967, after Kim's transfer to Ōmura, that Japanese progressive intellectuals and activists began to mobilize in support of his plea for asylum. Groups formed spontaneously in Kobe, Kyoto, Osaka, Nagoya, Tokyo, Nagano, and Sapporo.[146] Notably, on March 8, 1967, eleven activists and intellectuals (including Tsurumi Shunsuke, Oda, Hidaka Rokurō, Tamaki Motoi, and Suzuki Michihiko) released a public statement of support titled "Kin Tōki seinen no tame no uttae" (Appeal for the young Kim Dong-hee), while in April, Oda, Tsurumi, and Yoshikawa Yūichi of Beheiren delivered to the minister of justice a stack of signed petitions requesting that Kim be granted refugee status on humanitarian grounds.[147] As the names of those involved reveals, many of the same individuals who had earlier supported Lee Jin-wu and would later mobilize to advocate for Gwon Hui-ro joined this movement. During their work for Kim, Oda, Tsurumi, and around sixty other activists staged a small demonstration outside the Ōmura Detention Center, which was when most of them first learned of this facility's existence.

145. Fujishima, "Vietonamu sensō."
146. Some of these groups included the Association to Support and Protect Kim Dong-hee, in Fukuoka; the Association to Protect Kim Dong-hee, in Kyoto; the High School Students' Association to Protect Kim Dong-hee in the Keihin Industrial Area of Tokyo and Kanagawa Prefecture. See Tamaki, "Atarashii sedai," 256.
147. Beheiren, "Kin Tō-ki shōnen."

It seems that intellectuals and activists were drawn to Kim in 1967 primarily because of his opposition to the Vietnam War. For example, in that year Tsurumi explained that Kim had fled to Japan because of the symbolism of the "Japanese Constitution" and also because Japan was a "second homeland" for him, since three of his brothers lived in the country and he had gone to school in Japan until the third year of elementary school.[148] Kim confirmed such understandings, telling Beheiren activists from detention that he had deserted because he did "not want to murder Vietnamese" and had chosen Japan not due to its geographical proximity but because of the pacifist preamble and Article 9 (the war-renouncing clause) of the Japanese Constitution.[149]

However, especially after becoming aware of the Ōmura facility, perceptive observers soon realized that Kim was far more than just another case of conscientious objection, like the four US sailors who had deserted from the aircraft carrier *USS Intrepid* in October 1967. Kim's 1967 letter to activists hinting at human rights abuses at Ōmura—such as the arbitrary extensions of detention, beatings, violent suppression of dissent, and other inhumane treatment, some of which resulted in detainees' suicides—only added to this realization.[150] Beheiren's involvement with Kim thus fed into the process of recognizing Japan's "substantive linkages" to the "history of East Asia" that lurked "beneath the surface of the Vietnam War."[151] As Suzuki later opined, Kim represented a kind of emblem of empire for Beheiren, and his act of desertion was a "criticism" not only of the Vietnam War but also of the "history of Japanese-Korean relations from the prewar" era.[152] It is significant, too, that Kim appeared just as Oda, Ienaga, Wada, and others were facing off against the revisionism of Hayashi and the Meiji centennial.

Beheiren's involvement with Kim segued quite seamlessly into the brouhaha over Japan's immigration control system that erupted in February 1969. The immediate trigger was the Japanese government's move to convert the existing Shutsunyūkoku kanri rei (immigration control

---

148.　Tsurumi Shunsuke, "Kin Tō-ki," 109.
149.　Quoted in Beheiren, "Kin Tō-ki shōnen."
150.　The letter was later published as Kim Dong-hee, "Ōmura shūyōjo."
151.　Noh, "Beheiren," 83–84.
152.　Suzuki, *Ekkyō no toki*, 146.

ordinance)—one of the key sources of de-Asianization during the Occupation—into a more muscular Shutsunyūkoku kanri hō (immigration control law). Officials claimed that upgrading the ordinance to a law was needed to better manage criminal foreigners, simplify entry and departure procedures, and assist in investigations of foreigners who were harming the public interest. Of course, activists recognized the imminent risk of pushing the regulatory framework in a more antiforeign (read "anti-Asian") direction. By placing restrictions on the political activities of resident foreigners and enhancing state powers over entry, investigation, and deportation, the proposed law effectively empowered police to increase surveillance over resident members of South and North Korean communities, sanctioned state suppression of political activism by exchange students (from Vietnam, for example), and threatened to become a tool for blockading the expected inflow of Asians accompanying Japan's economic expansion into Asia.[153] In regulatory terms, the proposed law directly targeted Asians because most Western nations had visa (or visa waiver) agreements with Japan. For instance, the Status of Forces Agreement with the United States meant that American defense personnel and their family members were not subject to immigration, foreigner registration, or passport regulations.[154] Thanks to a robust opposition movement, the government ultimately abandoned the bill in August 1969, and despite three more attempts, it would not successfully amend the ordinance until 1982—and then only after removing the most controversial sections.[155]

Resident Korean and Chinese groups initiated the protest movement on learning of the proposed amendment. The Zainichi Kankoku Seinen Dōmei (Resident Korean Youth Alliance) was the first to mobilize, in March 1969; it was followed by numerous other groups of ordinary citizens and students nationwide.[156] In June, some five thousand opponents of the bill, led by the South Korean–affiliated Mindan association and

153. Beheiren, "'Shutsunyūkoku kanri rei' kaiaku ni hantai o."
154. Tsumura, *Warera no uchinaru*, 60.
155. Oguma, *1968 <ge>*, 236.
156. The other groups included the Anti-Immigration System Information Center, Northern Region Liaison Committee Opposing the Immigration System, Tokyo Relief Group, and the Citizens' Committee to Expose the Immigration System in Kyoto. For a more extensive list, see *Asahi jānaru*, "Risuto 3."

the Chūka Minkoku Ryūnichi Kakyō Rengō Sōkai (General Assembly of Overseas Taiwanese Residents in Japan), attended a protest rally in Tokyo. After police forcibly broke up the event, a number of activists began a hunger strike—the first of numerous similar displays of opposition in the coming months. The most shocking expression of dissent came in late April 1969, when Li Zhicheng, a resident Chinese medical student at Nara Medical University, committed suicide by swallowing poison to protest the proposed amendments. As I show below, this suicide caused some student activists to fundamentally question their commitment to the internationalist agenda of groups like Zenkyōtō (All-Campus Struggle Committee), especially their hitherto unquestioned fixation on the looming renewal of the US-Japan Security Treaty in 1970.

Fresh from their support for Kim, Beheiren activists dove headlong into the immigration control struggle. On March 31, 1969, around sixty Beheiren activists from across Japan staged a protest outside Ōmura, after which Oda, Tsurumi, and two others entered the facility to discuss matters with officials. Protesters waiting outside were deeply moved by the cries of *"arigato, arigato"* (thank you, thank you) coming from detainees on the other side of the wall. As Tsurumi observed in an essay in *Beheiren nyūsu*, "the massive wall in front of us is not only something imprisoning Koreans, it is also a wall obstructing the Japanese. Destroying this wall is necessary not only for the Koreans, but also for the Japanese people, for the Japanese antiwar movement, and for democracy."[157] Tsurumi pointed out that a great many detainees had actually been born in Japan and did not speak a word of Korean. Even worse, Westerners in violation of immigration regulations were detained at a separate facility in Yokohama—which for Tsurumi was a blatant display of racism and shameless cowering to the West. "Koreans have been discriminated against by the Japanese for almost one hundred years, since the Meiji Restoration," he observed, and "their separation into a different facility coupled with the nature of surveillance over them" was essentially "a continuation of this discrimination from the prewar era. Would it not be fairer for all [detainees] to be together in Yokohama or, even if it is inconvenient, to detain

---

157. Tsurumi Shunsuke, "Nihon no naka no kokkyō."

some offenders from the Netherlands, Sweden, and the United States together with Koreans at Ōmura?"[158]

As Sekiya Shigeru, another Beheiren member, observed, because antiwar activists' mobilizations in support of Koreans to date had been viewed only through the lens of opposition to the Vietnam War, these were only "partial victories": activists had failed to expand their vision to "the problems of Koreans" themselves.[159] Sekiya noted a similar trend in the opposition to the South Korea–Japan normalization treaty, which tended to focus on specifics rather than the wider predicament of Koreans in Japan. Only beginning in 1969, with movements against Ōmura and the new immigration bill, argued Sekiya, did Beheiren finally start to show an awareness of the Korean problem in the same way that white activists in the United States came to realize that the problems of Black Americans were their problems, too. For instance, some Beheiren activists were now thinking about the massacres after the 1923 Great Kantō Earthquake, forced relocations and labor during the 1930s and 1940s, and the Japanese government's clandestine decision to remove all Koreans from Japan that had been made on August 22, 1945, only days after the war's end.[160]

Some activists—such as Iinuma Jirō, a Kyoto University professor and activist in the Kyoto Beheiren group—began to redirect their activities toward support for Koreans in Japan. Iinuma became involved in a movement for Koreans detained by the Kobe Immigration Bureau, as well as in a mobilization supporting Im Seok-gyun, a political dissident who escaped to Japan in 1968 after being sentenced to death in absentia by the Park Chung-hee regime.[161] In mid-1969, Iinuma, together with Tsurumi, also began editing a grassroots newsletter titled *Chōsenjin* (Koreans), which focused on the conditions of resident Koreans and the political situation in South Korea—a new direction for Beheiren activists, who had previously focused primarily on the Vietnam War and the United

158. Tsurumi Shunsuke, "Nihon no naka no kokkyō."

159. Sekiya, "'Nihonjin mondai.'"

160. Sekiya, "'Nihonjin mondai.'"

161. Although initially detained in Ōmura, Im was subsequently granted provisional release on being diagnosed with tuberculosis of the liver in 1969. See Iinuma, "Nyūkan taisei," 105, and *Ashimoto no kokusaika*, 149.

States. By mid-1970 Iinuma was arguably the preeminent expert within activist circles on Japan's immigration system.

Coupled with growing sensitivity to historical transgressions against Asia thanks to the work of Ienaga, Tsurumi Yoshiyuki, Honda, and others, involvement in the immigration control struggle thus served as a critical catalyst toward deimperialization within Beheiren as the 1960s ended. Support for resident Asians was an opportunity to face the Asia within, interrogate the self as nothing more than a "resident Japanese" (*zainichi Nihonjin*), and, ultimately, open a path toward liberation of both the self and the Other.[162] As I show in chapter 4, such initiatives also became launchpads for a new array of grassroots initiatives throughout the 1970s.

Students, Asia, and the "Hitler Within"

Civic groups like Beheiren were not the only ones undergoing a reorientation toward Asia during this period, with student activists also experiencing their own Asia-focused moments of truth during the immigration control struggle. Along with Mindan and Beheiren, student groups were among the earliest to mobilize in opposition to the draft immigration control law, although not always with the same objectives as the other organizations. In March 1969, for instance, Southeast Asian exchange students joined with the Nihon Marukusu-Rēnin-shugisha Dōmei (Japan Alliance of Marxist-Leninists), the revolutionary Chūkaku-ha (Middle-Core Faction), the Choppari-kai (Friendship Group of Resident Koreans and Japanese), and the Kakyō Seinen Tōsō Iinkai (Overseas Chinese Youth Struggle Committee; KSTI) to form the Kokusai Seinen Kyōtō (Joint Struggle of International Students). Members of the Choppari-kai, Chūkaku-ha, Kokusai Seinen Kyōtō, and others also joined with Beheiren in the same month to establish the Shutsunyūkoku Kanri Hōan Funsai Tokyo Jikkō Iinkai (Tokyo Executive Committee for the Destruction of the Immigration Control Bill). In June, university students studying Asian languages

---

162. Noh, "Beheiren," 79. For some examples of this emerging mentality, see Nakayama, "Sakoku sakoku"; Tanaka Komako, "Nyūkan mondai."

mobilized, forming the Gogaku Kyōtō (Joint Struggle of Language Schools)—which began advocating for "ethnic responsibility" and "international solidarity."[163] Importantly, for ethnic minority student groups such as the KSTI, these mobilizations were about much more than a unified confrontation with the Japanese state. The mobilizations also offered ethnic minority students a golden opportunity to vent their dissatisfaction with Japanese-led student organizations, which they felt had ignored the critical issue of ethnic responsibility in their quest for internationalism. In the same way that Lee Jin-wu, Gwon Hui-ro, and Liu Lianren had forced progressive intellectuals and civic activists to face Asia, such castigations of resident Chinese and Korean students would compel their fellow Japanese youth to confront the discrimination within.

In a repeat of the 1967 Beheiren rally for Kim Dong-hee, in June 1969 a group of around eight hundred protesters—including members of the Choppari-kai and the Nyūkan Taisei Funsai Jikkō Iinkai (Executive Committee to Destroy the Immigration System)—demonstrated outside the Ōmura facility in Nagasaki.[164] In the following month, students gathered with Beheiren activists and others at the west entrance of Shinjuku train station in Tokyo in a so-called folk guerrilla teach-in denouncing the Vietnam War, the treatment of Gwon, and the immigration control bill. However, before the event could begin, police announced that the space had been reclassified as a passageway (*tsūro*) and, as such, could not be used for public gatherings. Any unauthorized rallies, the police warned, would be duly disbanded, by force if necessary.[165] The police proved true to their word. Early in the morning of July 2, riot squads forcefully expelled members of Beheiren, the KSTI, and other groups that had proceeded with the teach-in in contravention of official warnings. In the ensuing melee, around 150 protesters were injured, some quite seriously.[166] The police intervention was also marred by a strongly discriminatory undertone. As members of the riot squad attempted to expel resident Asian youths engaged in a hunger strike, they censured the students for "daring to defy the riot squad of His Majesty the Emperor" and threatened

163. Tsumura, *Warera no uchinaru*, 98–99.
164. Oguma, *1968 <ge>*, 236–37.
165. Suzuki, *Ekkyō no toki*, 223.
166. Tsumura, *Warera no uchinaru*, 105.

them with "deportation" should they be caught again.[167] Unperturbed, KSTI students persisted with their hunger strike for a further three weeks, until it was finally broken by another police offensive in late July.[168] In the course of their protest, the students issued a statement that left no ambiguity about the direct connections they drew between the immigration control issue and Japan's historical transgressions in Asia: "We want you to remember what the Japanese government and Japanese people did to Chinese, Korean, and other Asian people in the name of the emperor."[169] Similarly, in another statement, the Kokusai Seinen Kyōtō characterized the hunger strike as "a struggle that views the problem of Korea and resident Koreans as the moments of original sin (*genzaiten*) within Japanese history and for the Japanese people."[170]

It is important to emphasize, however, that this attention to Asia and the past was by no means prevalent within the wider Japanese student movement of the late 1960s, and thus these statements by minority student groups were aimed as much at Japanese student activists as they were at state officials or politicians. New Left activists trained in postwar Japanese social science did not make an automatic or strong connection between their "own liberation" and that of resident Koreans and Asian peoples.[171] According to Oguma, certain factors tended to exacerbate this mentality. To begin with, Marxist theory led most students to the conclusion that issues of discrimination need not be directly addressed in the present because they would be swept away in the coming socialist revolution. But more prosaically, students' "single-minded" focus on "self-negation" and the looming renewal of the security treaty in 1970 essentially blinded them to issues of discrimination against resident Asians.[172] Oguma gives the example of some five thousand posters and pamphlets issued by students during the upheavals at the University of Tokyo in 1968 and 1969, only one of which mentioned the "problems of resident Koreans."[173] The comments of one Chūkaku-ha leader about the KSTI

---

167. Quoted in Tsumura, *Warera no uchinaru*, 104 and 106.
168. Tsumura, *Warera no uchinaru*, 106.
169. The statement is reproduced in Tsumura, *Warera no uchinaru*, 106.
170. Tsumura, *Warera no uchinaru*, 106.
171. Yoon, "Sengo shisō," 161.
172. Oguma, "Japan's 1968," 18. See also Oguma, *1968 <ge>*, 237.
173. Oguma, *1968 <ge>*, 229.

protest and hunger strike is typical of this dismissive and patronizing attitude toward minority groups. "Let them be," he said. "We need people participating from a humanitarian perspective."[174]

Nonetheless, although many in the mainstream of the student movement remained indifferent to or even contemptuous of the Asia problem, the winds of change had begun to swirl as early as 1968, and by mid-1970 they would be striking student activists with gale force. This new energy grew out of a gradual awakening to ethnic responsibility among certain influential student activists, none more so than Tsumura Takashi (1948–2020)—who was then a student at Waseda University and an active participant in Zenkyōtō. Suga Hidemi has described Tsumura as the "principal ideologue" of "1968" and the activist most responsible for initiating a debate on "discrimination" among students at a time of high "Maoism" and calls for "cultural revolution" in the late 1960s.[175] Tsumura spoke and published prolifically in these years, with his 1970 book, *Warera no uchinaru sabetsu* (The discrimination within us), a compilation of essays written throughout 1969 and 1970, being particularly influential.[176] Oguma explains how this book emerged out of the so-called "within" craze (as in, for example, the "Vietnam within") among idealistic youth intent on turning their critical gaze inward in search of genuine identity.[177] In terms of processes of deimperialization and attention to the Asia problem, Tsumura played a catalytic role in the student movement similar to that of Oda and Tsurumi in Beheiren; Ienaga, Wada, and Honda among historians; and Fujishima and Tamaki in the ethnic responsibility debate of the early 1960s.

The son of a high-ranking official in the Nihon Rōdō Kumiai Sōhyō Kaigi (General Council of Trade Unions of Japan, or Sōhyō), Tsumura was able to travel to China with his father in 1964 (while still a high school student) and 1967. He was deeply impressed by Mao Zedong and the achievements of the CCP and simultaneously disturbed by Japan's tarnished history in the country.[178] It was during a tour of Nanjing that

174.   Quoted in Oguma, *1968 <ge>*, 237–38.
175.   Suga, "Kaisetsu," 381 and 385.
176.   Tsumura, *Warera no uchinaru sabetsu*.
177.   Oguma, *1968 <ge>*, 238.
178.   Suga, "Kaisetsu," 385.

Tsumura underwent an epiphany of sorts, awakening to the unresolved problem of Japan's ethnic responsibility in Asia. As Tsumura explained, his striking realization in Nanjing was that the term "anti-Japanese" (*kōnichi*) included none other than "himself" (*jibun*), and that in fact he was the "direct object" (*mokutekikaku*) of a word he had used "so nonchalantly hundreds of times" in the past.[179] Tsumura likened this epiphany to "running headlong into 'something' beyond ordinary experience" yet "unavoidable to the extent he was a Japanese person."[180] He vividly recalled the chilling response of his Chinese interpreter when asked about his family: "his expression darkened," and "he quietly said that the 'Japanese army killed them all, every one of them.' "[181] Until then, this interpreter had seemed like a "brother" to Tsumura, but the revelation of such horror exposed the "fallacy" of their seemingly "uncomplicated" relationship. For the first time Tsumura saw his interpreter "as a Chinese person qualitatively different" from "himself." Thereafter he began to refer to this "sense of having lost his virginity" in China as "ethnic responsibility" (*minzokuteki sekinin*), drawing on Tamaki's 1969 volume *Minzokuteki sekinin to shisō*—which helped bring into focus his own vague feelings about "original sin."[182]

Tsumura's contribution to deimperialization in the student movement began in May 1968, when he and fellow activists from the Waseda Wadatsumi-kai (Memorial Society for the Student-Soldiers Killed in the War), Beheiren, and other groups released a declaration titled "7–7 (Rokōkyō 'Jiken') 31 Shūnen Sōdai Sengen" (The Waseda University declaration on the 31st anniversary of 7–7 (Marco Polo Bridge "incident"); hereafter the Waseda Declaration).[183] Authored by Tsumura and his colleague Katō Tsuneo, the Waseda Declaration took aim at the triumphant mood surrounding the Meiji centennial celebrations of 1968, denouncing the postwar generation for having ignored their "original sin" and "responsibility" for militarism in China—epitomized by the Marco Polo Bridge

179. Tsumura, "Nihonjin no minzokuteki sekinin," 110.

180. Tsumura, "Nihonjin no minzokuteki sekinin," 109.

181. Tsumura, "Nihonjin no minzokuteki sekinin," 109.

182. Tsumura, "Nihonjin no minzokuteki sekinin," 108 and 110. Tsumura advised readers to read this book alongside his *Warera no uchinaru sabetsu* (231).

183. For the complete statement and a list of the signatories, see 7–7 (Rokōkyō "Jiken"), "7–7 (Rokōkyō 'Jiken')."

Incident of 1937.[184] The declaration lambasted progressives for "relaxing in
the warmth" of postwar peace and democracy while avoiding their responsibility for not having prevented the war against China or the postwar
divorce of Japan from its Asian neighbor. Because the established Left was
unable to "question itself about the 'meaning' of history," it would be
"constantly susceptible to becoming an 'accomplice' of power."[185] Without
facing this "Hitler within ourselves" (*wareware jishin no naka no Hitorā*),
the declaration reasoned, the Japanese people were essentially abandoning
the pursuit of "responsibility" for having "supported Japanese imperialism
from within." Youth simply could not be content with the "war experience" discourse of a "handful of intellectuals" who had "reduced war responsibility to nothing more than victim consciousness."[186] "Without
shouldering the shadow of history we cannot move history forward," and
"without accepting responsibility for the crimes committed in the name of
the 'Japanese people' and continuing to annihilate this [crime] within ourselves," the statement concluded, "we will not be able to transcend the fact
that we are Japanese!"[187]

Against the rising tide of revisionist history, Tsumura envisioned the
statement as a "declaration of war" against "Japanese nationalism," while
Niijima Atsuyoshi, a Chinese literature specialist at Waseda University,
championed it as "the first declaration of Japan's cultural revolution."[188]
These are exaggerations to be sure, but the declaration was undoubtedly
more provocative than similar tracts of the time such as Tsurumi Shunsuke's 1968 speech about "original crime" discussed in chapter 2.[189] Such
positive appraisals aside, however, Tsumura could only lament the declaration's lack of traction at the time, with issues about war responsibility
and minorities barely figuring in the massive campus disputes of 1968.
Despite the declaration's raising critical issues of "war responsibility, discriminatory consciousness, and the historical rupture between Japan and
China," apart from an "enlightened few" it was all but ignored.[190]

184. Tsumura, "Nihonjin no minzokuteki sekinin," 112.
185. 7–7 (Rokōkyō "Jiken"), "7–7 (Rokōkyō 'jiken'), 204.
186. 7–7 (Rokōkyō "Jiken"), "7–7 (Rokōkyō 'jiken'), 205.
187. 7–7 (Rokōkyō "Jiken"), "7–7 (Rokōkyō 'jiken'), 205.
188. Quoted in 7–7 (Rokōkyō "Jiken"), "7–7 (Rokōkyō 'jiken')," 203.
189. Oguma, *1968* <ge>, 244.
190. Tsumura, *Warera no uchinaru*, 16; Oguma, *1968* <ge>, 248.

Although Tsumura does not say as much, it seems that in 1968 he too remained only partially committed to this new Asian agenda, still viewing it within the wider revolutionary struggle. Indeed, after the Waseda Declaration, Tsumura and his fellow students dove headlong into the campus radicalism of 1968. But things changed dramatically with the appearance of the immigration control issue in early 1969 and, most shockingly, the protest suicide of medical student Li Zhicheng in April, which brought the revolutionary fervor of Tsumura and others to a screeching halt. For Tsumura, this death was a devastating "condemnation" of their revolutionary struggle and Zenkyōtō, and it undermined their resolve by exposing the disgraceful ease with which they had "overlooked" their "ethnic responsibility."[191] Li's act was especially consequential for Tsumura, who thereafter lost all "passion for the Waseda struggle," devoting himself instead to the plight of "foreigners."[192] In contrast to the death of the student activist Yamazaki Hiroaki, which Tsumura experienced as a kind of "amputation," Li's suicide—a "death" at the "extremities" of the "nation"—disrupted his preoccupation with current issues, forcing him back "once again" to "July 7" (that is, the Marco Polo Bridge Incident of 1937) and "historical reality."[193] Just as the petty criminal Jean Genet triggered a penitent self-reflection in Jean-Paul Sartre, Li compelled Tsumura to interrogate "himself" and the content of his world.[194] What resulted was Tsumura's stunning and merciless denunciation of everything that revolutionary students had come to believe.

In a pamphlet titled "Aru 'Ihōjin' no shi" (The death of a certain foreigner), which circulated just two days after Li's suicide, Tsumura characterized the death as "a condemnation of we Japanese." The government's "brazen advocacy" of the proposed bill was "built on the discriminatory attitude toward 'non-Japanese'" by "each and every" Japanese person. And because this was "such an unconscious attitude," it was "all the more pernicious, consistently fashioning the deepest structure of 'postwar democracy.'"

191. Tsumura, *Warera no uchinaru*, 17.

192. Tsumura, *Warera no uchinaru* , 17 and 19.

193. Tsumura, "Aru 'Ihōjin,'" 249. Yamazaki Hiroaki, a student radical from Kyoto University, was killed in clashes with riot police as the student protesters attempted to storm Tokyo's Haneda Airport to prevent Prime Minister Satō Eisaku from departing for an official visit to South Vietnam on October 8, 1967.

194. Tsumura, *Warera no uchinaru*, 121.

The older consciousness of 'chinks' (*chankoro*)" had been "transformed, surviving within a structure of 'oppressive tolerance' (*yokuatsuteki kan'yō*)" born of "fear" and "apathy."[195] To progressives' claims that democracy had "taken root," resident Chinese and Koreans demanded "evidence." For Tsumura, this was the "invisible question mark deeply engraved" in the "void" left behind by Li.[196]

Closer to home, Li's suicide fueled Tsumura's assault on the façade of "internationalism," which he believed obscured the dark underbelly of "nationalism" within revolutionary student activism. "Since the first Bund there have been repeated cries for internationalism, world revolution, and the overthrow of Japanese imperialism," Tsumura explained, "but who has actually realized an alliance with the peoples of Asia and resident Asians in Japan who are the 'external proletariat' of Japanese imperialism?!"[197] For Tsumura, internationalist calls for "border-crossing revolution" demanded great caution because historically "all that had 'crossed borders' from Japan to Asia in the modern period" were the "imperialist bourgeoisie and their stooges."[198] Student radicals claimed to "hate being Japanese," but simply adopting the "un-'complicated'" rhetoric of "internationalism" could not negate the reality that they were "living in Japan and daily devouring the things secreted by the 'structure'" of the country with "the second largest GNP [gross national product]." They were but "parts of this socioeconomic configuration."[199] "Behind" the "theoretical façade" of their "internationalism," "nationality" remained engrained in the "daily lives" of students, laying bare for Tsumura the "gap" between "words and reality" in the "student New Left."[200]

195. Tsumura, "Aru 'Ihōjin,'" 250.

196. Tsumura, *Warera no uchinaru*, 15.

197. Tsumura, "Nyūkan taisei," 264. The Bund, also known as the Communist League, was an anti-JCP Marxist student organization established in 1958. After dividing into numerous sects following the US-Japan Security Treaty protests in 1960, the league (also called the second Bund) reunited in 1966, thereafter becoming involved in student protests of the late 1960s and early 1970s. See Kapur, *Japan at the Crossroads*, 146–53.

198. Tsumura, "Radikarizumu to nashonarizumu," 178–79.

199. Tsumura, "Radikarizumu to nashonarizumu," 174.

200. Go and Tsumura, "Taidan 'zainichi Nihonjin,'" 75.

As Tsumura wrote in 1970, the postwar project to liberate Japan from "ultranationalism" paradoxically resulted in the struggle against the "national" being "driven from consciousness." The result was a "distinct configuration" characterized by "internationalism on the surface" and "nationalism underneath." "Latent" though it may have been, this "subterranean nationalism" was, in the end, a form of "aggression." In fact, here was the disheartening terminus of "postwar thought": a condition of advocating internationalism and pacifism while remaining oblivious to the "actual structure of discrimination and oppression" in which activists were embedded.[201] In this sense, the immigration control struggle represented the first step by Japanese people in the direction of "transcending borders," forming "concrete ties with resident Koreans and Asians," and developing a sense of "ethnic responsibility" through an "internal critique of daily life."[202] In the process, some activists had finally recognized that the problems of resident Asians and the immigration system were actually "problems of the Japanese people."[203] Although the university struggles certainly signaled "the end of the postwar [period] in terms of ideals," for Tsumura the immigration control struggle "revealed the existence of an even deeper postwar fiction."[204] Lurking beneath the "façade of the supposedly new cultural order" was the "ghost of the emperor system" embedded within the "everyday consciousness" of the Japanese.[205] As one resident Korean had trenchantly observed, "put three Japanese together and you'll see the emperor system."[206] For Tsumura and his colleagues, here lay the crux of the problem and the task at hand: now was the time for "resident Japanese" to extirpate the "Hitler within."[207]

Tsumura's conclusion here marked a striking revision of the revolutionary internationalism that had permeated student activism until that point. Together with Oda's provocative notion of "perpetration," in the years following the renewal of the US-Japan Security Treaty in 1970 it

201. Go and Tsumura, "Taidan 'zainichi Nihonjin,'" 75.
202. Tsumura, *Warera no uchinaru*, 34–35.
203. Tsumura, *Warera no uchinaru*, 121.
204. Tsumura, "'Tasha' toshite," 48.
205. Go and Tsumura, "Taidan 'zainichi Nihonjin,'" 72.
206. Quoted in Go and Tsumura, "Taidan 'zainichi Nihonjin,'" 72.
207. Tsumura, *Warera no uchinaru*, 121.

would serve as an important ideological framework for student involvement in grassroots initiatives focused on Asia and resident Asians.

The final act in the awakening of Tsumura and his fellow students
to the Asia problem came in mid-1970. At the request of the KSTI and
Gogaku Kyōtō, the Fujin Jinmin Kurabu (Women's Democratic Club),
Beheiren, and other groups established a joint committee to prepare for
a rally on July 7, 1970, to mark the thirty-third anniversary of the Marco
Polo Bridge Incident.[208] Although the organizing committee envisioned
broad-based participation in the event, student groups such as Chūkaku-ha
viewed it as a prime opportunity to advance their revolutionary agenda.
As a result, tensions between the organizing committee and radical student groups continued to fester until, in early July, Chūkaku-ha and other
student groups forced Beheiren and the other committee members to resign, after which they assumed control. The KSTI renounced its observer status on the committee in protest, issuing a scathing denunciation of Japanese student groups for their "ethnocentrism" and for distorting
the original objective of the event.[209] Adding fuel to an already volatile
situation, Yamamori Shigeo, the secretary-general of Chūkaku-ha, was
accused of using "discriminatory language" after blithely stating that the
"KSTI left of their own accord, so what's the problem?"[210] In the face of
a fierce backlash, Yamamori subsequently issued an apology, admitting
that his remarks had been "discriminatory," he and colleagues had been
"hostile" to the KSTI since its formation, and they had not properly
grasped the significance of "7–7."[211] But for students like Tsumura and
the members of minority youth groups, the damage had already been
done and their rejection of revolutionary internationalism more or less
settled. As Tsumura observed during the struggle, the KSTI and other
ethnic minority student groups were essentially treated as "decoration"
by Japanese students: "We raised [the] KSTI and other resident Asians
onto our altar and made them symbols of our 'unity,'" but the "KSTI

---

208. Tsumura, "'Sengo' no kokufuku," 59–60.
209. Suga, *1968*, 3. See Tsumura, "'Sengo' no kokufuku," 61–62, for details of the
denunciation.
210. Tsumura, "'Sengo' no kokufuku," 62.
211. Tsumura, "'Sengo' no kokufuku," 62.

exited in protest over their forced objectivation." Indeed, they were made into the "ornamental guests" at a "rhetorical banquet."[212] The KSTI's declaration of disassociation of July 1970 encapsulated this sense of betrayal and pent-up frustration that minority groups felt toward Japanese student groups:

> To those Japanese who participated in today's rally as oppressors!
>
> On the 33rd anniversary of the Marco Polo Bridge Incident we must recognize that the struggle of resident Chinese and Koreans is a denunciation of the Japanese class struggle. The Japanese people must recognize that the issues surrounding the 33rd anniversary of the Marco Polo Bridge Incident and the problems of resident Koreans and Chinese are fundamentally connected. You comrades must realize that you are being denounced as oppressors. . . .
>
> We want to point out that in the prewar and postwar [periods] the Japanese people, after succumbing to authority, brutally suppressed us. We can no longer trust your words. There has been no praxis and, to the extent there is no praxis, any talk of solidarity is simple nonsense. We want you to thoroughly consider your position as oppressors.
>
> We will struggle from our standpoint to the bitter end.
>
> We declare these matters, and make this our declaration of disassociation.[213]

According to Suga, the KSTI's declaration was "one of the most important incidents" in Japan's "postwar intellectual history" because only with this denunciation in 1970 was the "substance" of the "1968" struggle finally realized.[214] At the heart of the KSTI's denunciation was the trenchant criticism that New Left groups were simply "playing

212. Tsumura, "Nyūkan tōsō," 288.

213. Kakyō Seinen, "Nana." The fact that this declaration was reproduced in the Chūkaku-ha newsletter, *Zenshin*, on July 13, 1970, suggests that students in that group were by then at least cognizant of the seriousness of the matter. See also Lee, *"Nikkan rentai,"* 93 and 142 (n. 16). The KSTI's statement days earlier on July 7—the anniversary of the Marco Polo Bridge Incident—also dealt with this tension between internationalism and ethnic discrimination within the student movement, although still in a spirit of collaboration at that point. See Kakyō Seinen, "Nyūkan tōsō."

214. Suga, "Kaisetsu," 381.

revolution"—in other words, that their movements were not really hit-
ting at the heart of the problems but were instead mired in juvenile
romanticism.[215] This condition became patently obvious after the US-
Japan Security Treaty was extended with relative quiet in June 1970.
Zenkyōtō and the various student sects were left deflated, with many
members wondering what to do next.[216] For students like Tsumura, however, there was never any doubt: the movement needed to shift its focus
from overarching problems like monopoly capitalism and the US-Japan
alliance to more concrete issues of discrimination embedded in daily
life.[217] While he did not reject "flying flags" of protest outside Ōmura,
Tsumura saw more value now in pursuing more "mundane" forms of
resistance, such as providing support for the visa struggles of Vietnamese exchange students or conducting research on the discrimination
faced by resident Asians and relevant court decisions.[218] In contrast to
the Waseda Declaration in 1968, after mid-1970 and the KSTI denunciation, Tsumura's approach gained real traction among students. Many
became involved in more concrete, localized issues with visible human
faces—issues like industrial pollution; immigration detainees; women;
local antidevelopment struggles; and minorities like Koreans, Okinawans, Ainu, and Burakumin. Suga characterizes the change as a "tac-
tical shift," while Oguma is more superlative, describing nothing short
of a "paradigm shift."[219] Descriptions aside, there is no doubt that during the period from around 1968 to mid-1970 there was significant
movement toward deimperialization within the student movement and,
by consequence, recognition of the Asia problem as one demanding
concerted action. Though Tsumura and his colleagues would be criticized
for abandoning revolution in favor of tepid gradualism, the reality is
that in the space of a few short years they, together with minority student
groups, had succeeded in making visible a serious problem that had
previously been obscured by students' naïve and largely self-indulgent
revolutionary fantasies.

215. Suga, *1968*, 10.
216. Oguma, *1968 <ge>*, 256.
217. Tsumura, "'Sengo' no kokufuku," 64.
218. Tsumura, "'Sengo' no kokufuku," 70–71.
219. Suga, *1968*, 3; Oguma, *1968 <ge>*, 254 and 262.

Into the 1970s: Legacies for
Deimperialization and Activism

What conclusions can we draw about processes of deimperialization and attention to the Asia problem from the mid-1960s through the early 1970s? First, it is important to recognize the role of Koreans and Chinese in forcing their predicaments into the consciousness of Japanese intellectuals, civic activists, and students. In the case of Liu Lianren, this happened quite unintentionally after his "arrest," but groups like the KSTI set out to intentionally provoke their Japanese student counterparts. Li Zhicheng's protest suicide by poisoning was without doubt the most graphic and tragic instance of this campaign, undermining many students' almost mechanical attachment to internationalism. Ōmura detainees like Kim Dong-hee also helped Beheiren activists connect their antiwar movement to questions of ethnic responsibility. Without such interventions, the awakening of Oda, Tsurumi, Tsumura, and others to the Asia problem might have taken far longer or not even happened at all.

Second, by formulating notions of perpetration in Vietnam, Beheiren activists—Oda especially, but also both Tsurumi Shunsuke and Tsurumi Yoshiyuki, as well as Wada—helped shift progressives' attention from criticism of America to Japanese complicity in Indochina. Tsurumi Yoshiyuki and Honda subsequently redirected this self-reflexive critique backward onto the history of Japanese imperialism and militarism in Asia. As we saw, this process culminated in Tsurumi Yoshiyuki's denunciation of August 15 and the victim consciousness that blinded postwar progressives to Asia. Activists like Iinuma then connected perpetration to resident Koreans, immigration detainees, and political dissidents from South Korea. In 1970 Iinuma and his colleagues established the Sabetsu Yokuatsu Kenkyūkai (Discrimination and Oppression Study Group) to address these issues. The group declared in its founding statement that "as much as we are perpetrators in the Vietnamese atrocity, we are discriminating even more against resident Koreans and Burakumin. Exposing the discrimination within ourselves and liberating the discriminated and oppressed in Japan is the way to a genuine alliance with Asian people."[220]

220. Kurokawa, "Betonamu hansen," 359.

In 1971 the group renamed itself Mukuge no Kai (Hibiscus Association) and thereafter focused closely on Korean language, culture, history, and political economy, as well as nationality issues and Korean atomic bomb victims.[221]

Third, we should also acknowledge the role of historians like Pak, Ienaga, and Irokawa, who took the Pacific War view of history to task through their gut-wrenching histories of colonial and military aggression. The disturbingly unsanitized accounts of murder, brutality, and horrifying acts of violence in their works were very much a response to the rise of conservative revisionism in the 1960s. Historians like Wada also chimed in with caustic denunciations of so-called progressive historians, whose works lacked any self-reflexive impulse toward deimperialization.

Fourth, toward the end of the 1960s, students like Tsumura and members of the KSTI brought the Asia problem and deimperialization into the student movement. The attention of Tsumura and others to July 7, 1937; their involvement in the immigration control struggle; and their denunciations of groups like Chūkaku-ha not only exposed the fallacies of internationalism but also laid the foundations for a new movement praxis, anchored at the grass roots in concrete initiatives for previously invisible groups. Tsumura's notion of the "Hitler within" offered a self-reflexive mechanism for ensuring that these initiatives would not deteriorate into a kind of patronizing sense of noblesse oblige toward pitiful Asians.

But although the movements and intellectual breakthroughs of the late 1950s through the early 1970s opened a pathway for genuine remorse and introspection, problems remained. Even enlightened student activists like Tsumura conflated notions of ethnicity and nationality, making it impossible for them to reimagine Japan beyond its monoethnic boundaries. To be fair, the legacy of enforced Japanization under Japanese imperialism made them wary of discourses of assimilation, but their continued use of the prefix "resident" reinforced the assumption that Koreans, Chinese, and indeed any other nonethnic Japanese did not really belong. As we will see, this problem of ethnicity remained unresolved, resurfacing in the 1990s in debates about ways of mourning and Asian regionalism.[222]

221. Kurokawa, "Betonamu hansen," 363 and 367.
222. Oguma similarly identifies this weakness in the thought of Tsumura. See Oguma, *1968 <ge>*, 253.

Moreover, the ties between activists and both internal and external Asians remained somewhat abstract and included paternalistic displays of compassion that often did more damage than good. Beheiren, as I explained above, was certainly a movement for fellow Asians (Vietnamese and later Koreans) but hardly a movement with Asians. Only in the latter stages of Beheiren did the voices of Asian activists begin to appear in movement publications, and even then they appeared only intermittently. As Yoshioka Shinobu, a Beheiren member, later recalled, activists had no real sense of the "daily lives" and "thinking" of the Vietnamese people, and the same was true for people in Thailand, Malaysia, Singapore, Indonesia, and the Philippines.[223] Likewise, the ties between Japanese students and Asians (within and without) were also fraught, and only some Japanese, like Tsumura, forged genuine solidarities—which furthermore tended to be short-lived. It would be to this task of genuinely knowing, allying with, and learning from fellow Asians that activists would turn in the 1970s and beyond.

223. Yoshioka, "Kaneko Mitsuharu," 183.

CHAPTER 4

Grassroots Regionalization and Asian Solidarity in the 1970s

In the 1970s the Japanese proletariat will face the people of Asia
"once again." They will have no choice but to face them.

—Tsumura Takashi, *Warera no uchinaru sabetsu*

Tsumura Takashi's 1970 observation about facing Asia appears almost prophetic in hindsight, because it presaged the paradigmatic
transformations that would unfold within progressive Japanese thought
and activism in the 1970s thanks to an all-embracing encounter with the
region. Building on the earlier efforts of antiwar activists, journalists, historians, and university students, in the 1970s many more progressives
began to place Asia, Asian problems, and Japan-Asia relations at the core
of their intellectual and political agendas. Asia also figured far more prominently than it had in the pages of progressive publications like *Sekai* and
the *Asahi jānaru* as well as in national newspapers, prompting some people
to speak of an "Asia boom" in the country.[1] Through these publications
and at a variety of Asia-focused events, progressives began to audibly and
distinctly lament their lack of knowledge about Asia, their essentially nonexistent connections with people in the region, and their desire to forge
substantive solidarities and exchanges.

Historically speaking, the rise of this discourse about not knowing and needing to know Asia signposts a critical moment of progressive
reconnection to the region in the 1970s. To be sure, throughout the
late 1950s and 1960s some civic activists, intellectuals, and students
had diligently continued to pursue the Asia problem and to strive—

---

1. Yamazaki, "Ajia josei kōryū," 441.

self-consciously or not—for deimperialization, but their focus remained largely on the internal Asia, whether on an intellectual level or in actual mobilizations in support of Asians or Asian causes (for example, Lee Jin-wu or the immigration detainees). However, their knowledge about conditions in other Asian countries was scant at best, and their connections with activists and intellectuals in other Asian countries were weak. Even the anti–Vietnam War movement focused more on denouncing America than on reaching out to the Vietnamese. But from the 1970s onward, progressives began to connect the Asia problem ever more directly to an urgent program for understanding the region and building ties with other Asian people, so much so that there was arguably the genesis of a grassroots regionalization of progressive mentalities and activism in Japan.

But why did this happen in the 1970s? What sparked this increased desire to know and connect with Asia among Japanese activists and intellectuals? Part of the answer lies in the growing number of linkages between a resplendent Japanese economy and the countries of East Asia. The 1970s was the first intensive phase of Japanese economic penetration into the region in the postwar era. This Japanese return to Asia—what the Filipino intellectual Renato Constantino acerbically branded Japan's "second invasion"—raised a host of thorny political, environmental, economic, and social problems that simply could not be ignored.[2] Faced with these issues, intellectuals and activists (some of whom came from the student movement and Beheiren, but many others of whom had no prior interest in Asia) mobilized in response to these problems, often in transnational solidarity movements with activists in other Asian countries. As Michiba Chikanobu explains, in contrast to the movements of the 1960s, these Asian solidarity movements focused on the links between Japanese high-speed economic growth and authoritarian regimes in Asia through issues relating to human rights, democratization, the environment, and peace. In the process, the 1970s movements developed an "expansive shared space" that would continue to mature within Japanese civil society over the coming decades.[3]

Another notable difference between the 1970s movements and the Asia-focused initiatives of the 1960s was a novel emphasis on activism not

2. Constantino, *Second Invasion*.
3. Michiba, "Posuto-Betonamu," 97.

only for Asia or fellow Asians (such as that in the immigration control struggles) but also with fellow Asians in the pursuit of diverse yet shared objectives. Japanese activists realized that mobilizations with other Asians were not simply or only about developments "over there" but were connected at the deepest levels to questions of democracy and rights within Japan. This was an important realization indeed, because it opened the door to new forms of engagement with Asia that undermined earlier tendencies to abandon the region and learn from the West. Through these new grassroots connections, Japanese activists and intellectuals realized that there were many things for Japanese to learn from Asian ideas and struggles that could be injected back into initiatives at home. Not the least of these things was the realization that Asian struggles and solidarities could provide critical insights into the shortcomings of both Japanese democracy and the condition of progressive thought and activism in the country.

Japan's Triumphant Return to Asia in the 1970s

The spread of Japanese political and economic influence throughout East Asia beginning around the late 1960s set the stage for intensive progressive reengagement in the region. The Japanese government had already begun the process of mending broken diplomatic fences, most conspicuously with South Korea in 1965 and the People's Republic of China in 1972. Along with formal treaties and diplomatic niceties, government elites dangled weighty financial enticements in front of Asian leaders. Statistics show that in 1970 a startling 94.4 percent of Japanese official development assistance (ODA) flowed into Asia.[4] Like earlier war reparations payments, this assistance was very much "with strings attached."[5] Government officials strategically deployed ODA as a tool to foster markets for the Japanese heavy and chemical industries.[6] Moreover, as Ishida

---

4. Gaimushō, *2012-nenban*, 50.
5. Nishikawa, "70-nendai Ajia," 37.
6. In fact, reparations had never been purely about compensation—at least not in the minds of Japan's leaders. As Yoshida Shigeru recalled after stepping down as prime

Takeshi astutely observes, the shift from "reparations" to "ODA" also had symbolic utility, simultaneously relegating the issue of war responsibility to the past while rehabilitating prewar notions of Japanese superiority and leadership in Asian modernization.[7]

Japanese business had its own reasons for returning to Asia at this time. With a rising yen after the floating of the US dollar in 1971—the so-called Nixon shock—Japanese businesses turned to Asian countries for cheap labor, abundant natural resources, and often lax regulatory environments. In fact 1972 was touted as the "New Era of [Foreign] Investment" (*tōshi gannen*), much of which headed to Asia.[8] From 1965 to 1970, for example, total Japanese foreign direct investment (FDI) was around $160 million, but in 1972 alone it jumped to a massive $2.3 billion, increasing to $3.5 billion the following year.[9] Some 30 percent of FDI went to Asian countries, slightly exceeding the share that went to North America. Japanese FDI in South Korea is the most eye-opening in this context. In 1971 Japanese companies invested only $26 million in South Korea. But in 1972 this amount increased threefold, to $78 million, representing a stunning 70 percent of all FDI received by South Korea.[10] For the six years leading up to 1973, Japanese FDI in South Korea totaled $159 million, but in the first six months of 1973 alone it exceeded $169 million.[11]

To be sure, this 1970s Asian investment boom was minuscule compared to the Japanese FDI tsunami that would engulf East Asia in the wake of the Plaza Accord in 1985, but it had significant ramifications nonetheless.[12] Most visible for people in Asian countries was the infiltration of the phrase "made in Japan" into every nook and cranny of their daily lives. In a 1973 article for the labor union publication *Gekkan sōhyō* aptly titled

---

minister, "they [Asian countries] didn't want us to use the term investment, so to keep them happy we called it compensation, but from our perspective it was investment" (quoted in Nishikawa, "70-nendai Ajia," 37).

7.   Ishida, *Shakai kagaku*, 59.

8.   Kobayashi Hideo, *Sengo Ajia to Nihon*, 68.

9.   Kobayashi Hideo, *Sengo Ajia to Nihon*, 68.

10.   See Nagai Michio et al., "Genchi Nikkei kigyō," 192.

11.   Koyama Mutsumi, "Kisen kankō," 17.

12.   The official name of the accord is "Announcement of the Ministers of Finance and Central Bank Governors of France, Germany, Japan, the United Kingdom, and the United States."

"Ajia no nikumaremono *Nippon*" (*Nippon* the villain of Asia), Kajitani Yo-shihisa described Asian capital cities inundated with "neon advertising" for Japanese products: "Over 50 percent of the cars driving around the city are made in Japan," people "brush their teeth in the morning with Japanese toothpaste," they "put on clothes made with Japanese fabric," "they travel to work on buses made in Japan," and their "company buildings are made with cement imported from Japan. . . . On returning home they turn on the TV, get some water from the fridge, and eat instant ramen for dinner. All of these are imported from Japan. In fact, it's said that the only things not made in Japan are their wives."[13]

But Japanese industry brought with it more than an all-embracing culture of consumption. The dark underbelly of Japanese FDI became apparent in industrial pollution, labor and resource exploitation, and a flood of Japanese corporate warriors and their families in numbers not seen since the days of empire and the co-prosperity sphere. The backlash from Asian countries was swift and sometimes savage. Beginning in the late 1960s, the Japanese were startled to learn of a series of violent acts against Japanese businessmen throughout Asia. In late 1969, for example, a disgruntled former hostess at a Bangkok nightclub was fired after a Japanese trading company executive accused her of infecting him with a venereal disease. In a fit of rage the woman shot the man dead at the Sunny Chateau Bar, taking her own life thereafter.[14] In 1971, three shots were fired into the Noguchi Gymnasium in Bangkok, which was run by a Japanese entrepreneur who had stoked the ire of Thai youth by referring to the traditional national sport of Muay Thai as "kick boxing."[15] Later in the same year, three Japanese employees of the Sumitomo Trading Company were attacked in broad daylight in Manila on their way home from playing golf, with the branch manager being killed.[16] As an essay in *Sekai* observed, such incidents were a "warning about the un-ethical business dealings" of Japanese companies, which approached local business "like bulldozers leveling the ground."[17]

13.   Kajitani, "Ajia no nikumaremono," 62–63.
14.   Tokuoka, *Ierō Yankī*, 14.
15.   Ishii Yoneo, "Kaisetsu," 210.
16.   Sekai Henshūbu, "Takamaru Firipin," 160.
17.   Sekai Henshūbu, "Takamaru Firipin," 160.

But the Asian backlash against Japan went much further than isolated incidents of violence. In the early 1970s anti-Japanese sentiment began to take on a worryingly more political character that threatened to undermine Japan's smooth return to the region. Local populations drew a direct connection between Japanese economic penetration and structural corruption in their countries, and they displayed a brave willingness to oppose this situation. For instance, Thailand became an unlikely hotbed of anti-Japanese sentiment in Asia, with even government officials joining the barrage of criticism. In a series of speeches before journalists and Japanese business and government elites in 1969 and 1970, the Thai minister of commerce, Boonchana Attakorn, bluntly criticized Japanese business practices in Asia. Attakorn took aim at Japanese tourists who he said flew to Thailand on "Japan Airlines," "traveled in Japanese buses to their Japanese hotels," went "sightseeing in Japanese cars," "ate at Japanese restaurants," and "went to nightclubs run by Japanese." "Even the guides" are "Japanese," Attakorn complained. "Why then are we Thais expected to welcome Japanese tourists who leave no money in the hands of Thais?"[18]

Thai university students also spearheaded the anti-Japan wave in Asia. In 1972 the National Student Center of Thailand led a nationwide boycott of Japanese products, beginning with a demonstration outside the Daimaru department store (a Japanese business) in Bangkok.[19] In a handbill the students distributed at their protest, they accused Japan of "dominating the domestic market" to such an extent that Thailand had become an "economic slave of Japan."[20] The students identified three causes of anti-Japanese sentiment. First, there was a widespread sense among students and others that Japanese corporations and investment did not contribute to "independence of the Thai economy and its development": Japanese corporations were seemingly only interested in making "quick profits" and taking these back to Japan. Second, students pointed to discriminatory practices within Japanese companies operating in Southeast Asia, including the fact that those companies paid local people far lower wages on average than those paid by American or European companies.

18. Quoted in Tokuoka, *Ierō Yankī*, 53. Also see Ishii Isamu, "'Ajia no Nihonjin," 239.
19. Ishii Yoneo, "Kaisetsu," 210.
20. Reproduced in Namatto and Bunyottyana, "'Tai' Gō ni haite," 63.

And finally, the torrent of Japanese products made Thais fearful that "at this rate" the Thai economy would end up "wholly subordinate to Japan."[21] In a similar vein, days later members of the National Student Center of Thailand presented the Japanese embassy with a letter addressed to Prime Minister Tanaka Kakuei, criticizing the Japanese government for not "seriously attempting to improve the situation." If investment in Thailand and the undesirable behavior of Japanese businessmen in the country did not improve, the letter warned, there would be damage to Japanese assets.[22]

The students were true to their word. Anti-Japanese sentiment reached its peak in January 1974, when Tanaka set out on an ill-fated tour of East Asian nations. After a smooth visit to the Philippines, where the dictator President Ferdinand Marcos ensured public order with an iron fist, Tanaka was confronted by riots in Indonesia and Thailand. In Jakarta, anti-Japanese protesters destroyed Japanese-made automobiles and set fire to the headquarters of the Toyota Astra International Building. Outside the Japanese embassy angry mobs threw stones and confiscated the Japanese flag, prompting the regime of President Suharto to impose a temporary curfew. Trapped in the president's residence, Tanaka was forced to board a helicopter that took him to the airport for a hasty retreat from the country. In Thailand around five thousand demonstrators (nowhere near as violent as those in Indonesia) surrounded Tanaka's hotel, where they denounced "Japanese economic invasion" and demanded that the Japanese "economic animal" "go to hell" and that Tanaka "get out."[23]

Government, Business, and Media Responses

The eruption of such vehement anti-Japanese sentiment caught most Japanese by surprise and, just as Tsumura had predicted in 1970, forced a hurried reconsideration of the country's reckless pursuit of cheap resources and new markets in the region. Political and business elites were among the earliest to respond. As an immediate measure, in cooperation with

21.   Nagai Michio, "Genchi Nikkei kigyō," 194.
22.   Ishii Yoneo, "Kaisetsu," 210.
23.   Halloran, "Violent Crowds."

other groups, the Japan Business Federation (Nihon Keizai Dantai Rengōkai, or Keidanren) set up several outreach organizations, including the Japan-Thai Cooperation Committee (1972) and the Japan Overseas Enterprises Association (1974). Reeling from the violence in Indonesia, in 1974 the Toyota Corporation established a grant-giving organization, the Toyota Foundation, which supported grassroots initiatives in Asia. In mid-1973 the East West Seminar, a conservative think tank, sponsored a conference of Japanese and Asian intellectuals and officials at Chulalongkorn University in Thailand, at which Japan's image in the region was scrutinized.[24] Southeast Asian participants did not mince their words at the event, with one Thai economist accusing Japan of waging a "warm war" in Asia: a war that was neither "hot" nor "cold" but was based on economic exploitation. He said that this war was "extremely destructive" for Southeast Asian economies because it "crept up" on them unawares, just like trickling water.[25]

The Japanese government also responded with several diplomatic initiatives, such as the establishment of the Japan Foundation in 1972 to serve as an official instrument for fostering understanding and cooperation between Japan and the outside world—particularly Asia. Following Tanaka's disastrous visit in 1974, "pro-Asia" Prime Minister Fukuda Takeo finally got diplomatic relations back on track in 1977 with a six-nation tour of Southeast Asia. The highlight of the tour was the prime minister's Manila speech in which he articulated the so-called Fukuda Doctrine, promising fellow Asians that Japan would "pursue peace and never become a military superpower." Japan would develop a "relationship of mutual trust" with the people of Southeast Asia based on "heart-to-heart understanding as genuine friends," not only politically but also economically, culturally, and socially.[26] Overall, Fukuda's overture was received positively throughout Asia, and Japan's seeming commitment to the region was reinforced the following year with the signing of the Treaty of Peace and Friendship between Japan and the People's Republic of China.

Of course, political and business leaders could quite easily generate Asian goodwill through material promises about investment, loans, and

24. For the proceedings of this conference, see Shibusawa and Saitō, *Tōnan Ajia*.
25. Quoted in Kawamura, "Kōdo seichō," 313.
26. For the speech see Fukuda, "Fukuda sōri daijin."

other largesse. Moreover, these leaders could rely on support from Asian dictators like Park Chung-hee and Marcos, who were more than willing to brutally suppress dissent at home in return for a share of Japanese riches. It also helped that regional leaders like Malaysia's Mahathir bin Mohamad and Singapore's Lew Kuan Yew had become so enamored of the Japanese economic miracle that by the 1980s they would even attempt to import the Japanese model wholesale in policy initiatives like "Look East" and "Learn from Japan."[27]

By fomenting regional dissent and resuscitating some of the ugly residues of co-prosperity, government and business elites also unwittingly encouraged progressives' reorientation to Asia. Of course, responding to Japan's haughty return to the region and the fiery backlash of locals would not be easy for progressives because, unlike their political and business counterparts, they possessed no treasures to use to fabricate amity with Asians or to deceive themselves about the homecoming of Asia's prodigal son. Rather, what progressives faced in the early 1970s was a Japan once again spreading its nefarious tentacles throughout the region, this time under the guise of ODA and FDI and often in collusion with dictatorial regimes.

Yet distressing though this reality was, in the context of deimperialization, it proved to provide an important opportunity. The encounter with Japan in Asia by a wider spectrum of activists and intellectuals than ever before meant that deimperialization and regional consciousness began to permeate distant corners of Japan's civic landscape, stimulating diverse spheres of activism, making possible new visions of Japan in Asia, and underwriting novel transnational solidarities.

We can trace the origins of this progressive attention to the region to a discussion about anti-Japanese sentiment in Asia that unfolded in various weekly and monthly publications and books beginning around the late 1960s. *Ekonomisuto*, a business-oriented weekly magazine, first identified Japan's image problem in the region in a December 1969 special issue titled "Ajia de kirawareru Nihonjin, 'Ierō Yankī,' 'shinryakusha'" (The Japanese despised in Asia, "yellow Yankees," "invaders") that included articles from correspondents across the region. The reporter in South Korea lamented that Japanese male tourists were thronging to the country to

27. Avenell, "Beyond Mimesis."

"purchase" Korean women for "$200 a night"—known as "kisaeng" sex tourism, using a term for traditional Korean courtesans.[28] Further south, the report from Indonesia observed that "50 percent of the cars driving around Jakarta" were "made in Japan" and that Japanese products had penetrated "even the most out-of-the-way places." One Indonesian weekly even likened Japanese to "devils," observing that when "they leave Japan" they "do as they please," overfishing, cutting down forests, and "taking all of this back home with them."[29] As the reporter from Bangkok despondently concluded, "it used to be ugly Americans" in Asia, but "now" it was "ugly Japanese," who looked a lot like the "American GIs" who had blithely swaggered into Japanese houses "with their shoes on" during the Occupation years.[30] As Renato Constantino wrote in a March 1972 article for the *Manila Times*—a translation was published in *Sekai* in the same year— the Japanese had "not once" "acted like Asians," and "never" had they "thought themselves to be Asians." Indeed, Constantino said that the Japanese considered themselves to be "the little Americans of Asia," who disparaged peoples of the region with their "patronizing" attitude.[31]

The *Ekonomisuto* articles were just the tip of an iceberg of attention to anti-Japanese sentiment in the Japanese media in the early 1970s. The titles of other articles offer a vivid portrait of the tone of this discourse: "Are the Japanese in Asia ugly?" (1970), "Offensive Japanese are an enormous nuisance" (1970), "Asians and Japanese—Asia's villain" (1970), "The 'ugly Japanese' in Southeast Asia" (1970), "The advance of an economic superpower into Southeast Asia and what follows after that" (1970), "What the Japanese must not do in Asia" (1974), and "Why does Asia hate the Japanese?" (1974).[32] So prominent did this discourse become that in 1970 Tokuoka Takao, a reporter for the *Mainichi shinbun*, authored a thick volume titled *Ierō Yankī* (Yellow Yankee). The book combined reportage and prophecy, with chapters on the murder in Thailand, Asian distrust of Japanese ODA, fears about Asia becoming a "yen colony," and the possibility that the Japanese

---

28. Ishikawa, "Sōru," 148.
29. Ishikawa, "Sōru," 148.
30. Tokuoka, "Bankoku," 154.
31. Quoted in Sekai Henshūbu, "Takamaru Firipin," 163.
32. Ishii Isamu, "'Ajia no Nihonjin"; Yamashita et al., "Tōnan Ajia"; Kyū, "Ajiajin to Nihonjin"; Morii, "Tōnan Ajia"; Yoshinaga, "Keizai Taikoku"; Yano Tōru, "Kindai Nihon"; *Asahi Jānaru*, "Ajia wa Naze."

"economic animal" would become a "military" one.[33] Above all, Tokuoka felt compelled to warn Japanese about the coming Asian backlash if they "continued their single-minded pursuit of wealth ignorant of the situation of Asians."[34] In an uncannily accurate prediction, given the subsequent Thai protests (1972) and Tanaka riots (1974), Tokuoka expressed his anxiety that a Japanese embassy might be set on fire somewhere in Southeast Asia before the end of the 1970s. "The day will definitely come," he said, when an External Trade Organization office would be "pelted with stones" or a tourist information desk run by the Ministry of Transport "trashed by rioters."[35] He warned that "someday an economic Vietnam War will occur, and we will be repelled like Yankee soldiers at the hands of forces attempting to liberate Southeast Asia."[36] "Having seen the intensification of 'anti-Japanese' [sentiment]," he concluded, "I can predict this with a degree of certainty."[37]

Giving Voice to Asians

One immediate response by activists, authors, and publications was to reach out to fellow Asians to understand their grievances toward Japan and then faithfully present their voices to the Japanese, often in the form of meticulous translations. Compared to the somewhat sporadic and ad hoc attempts to give voice to Asians described in previous chapters, this 1970s response was a far more methodical one, opening the way for substantive transnational solidarities while simultaneously inviting reflexive scrutiny within progressive communities.

Beheiren was among the earliest groups to respond through the ten-part series "Ajia kara no Shisen" (The gaze from Asia) published in the movement's monthly newsletter, *Beheiren nyūsu*, starting in November 1971.[38] Early items in the series included translations from mainstream

33.   Tokuoka, *Ierō Yankī*, 61, 228.
34.   Tokuoka, *Ierō Yankī*, 2.
35.   Tokuoka, *Ierō Yankī*, 236.
36.   Tokuoka, *Ierō Yankī*, 2.
37.   Tokuoka, *Ierō Yankī*, 236.
38.   See Beheiren, *"Beheiren Nyūsu,"* 464, 473, 483, 491, 499, 507, 515, 523, 535, 547.

newspapers like the *Sin chew jit poh* in Singapore and the *Manila Chronicle* in the Philippines, but later the series expanded to include extracts from the leading progressive Thai academic journal *Sangkhomsat parithat* (Social science review), writings by Asian intellectuals and political dissidents such as the South Korean poet Kim Chi-ha and Constantino, and radical political tracts drawn from publications like the *National Liberation Fortnightly* of the Movement for a Democratic Philippines. In one way or another, all of these translations dealt with Asian condemnations of Japanese political and corporate indiscretions in the region.

Japanese scholars and activists also edited several influential volumes in response to Asian criticisms of Japan in these years. In 1971, for example, the political scientist Mushakōji Kinhide and colleagues edited the amusingly titled volume *Futotta Nihonjin* (The fat Japanese), containing perspectives on Japan from 321 Asian observers on topics as diverse as Japan and nuclear weapons, the Japanese as "polite egoists," Japan's "Caucasian complex," "nationalistic" Japanese newspapers, and the "lie" of the Japanese Constitution's war-renouncing Article 9. Like Constantino, Mushakōji and his coauthors could only conclude that the Japanese were "Asians who do not know Asia."[39] The following year Tanaka Hiroshi (see chapter 5), an economist and advocate for foreigners and exchange students in Japan, published *Nihon o mitsumeru Ajiajin no me* (Asian eyes focused on Japan), containing translations from the *Sin chew jit poh*, the *Manila Times*, and other Asian newspapers. In the preface Tanaka expressed his frustrations over Japanese journalists' seeming obliviousness to the vernacular presses of the region and his hope that the book would begin the important task of communicating some of these ignored perspectives on Japan to a domestic audience.[40] Behind Tanaka's endeavor lay his belief that Japan's attitude toward Asia had remained largely unreconstructed in the postwar era. As he explained, "the issue we needed to most earnestly address in 1945 was not reconciliation with . . . America and Britain but with the people of Asia and the Asian world. We have placed too much emphasis on the historical 'change of course' contained in the narrative of Pearl Harbor—Midway sea battles—the dropping of the atomic bombs—the Peace Treaty—[and] the US-Japan Security

39. Mushakōji and Ajia Seinen, "Hajime ni," 4.
40. Tanaka Hiroshi, "Ajia ni koso," 9–10.

Treaty."[41] Finally, in 1974 Tsurumi Yoshiyuki edited *Ajia kara no choku-gen* (Candid opinions from Asia), which contained a collection of newspaper articles by Asian intellectuals previously serialized in the *Tokyo shinbun*.[42] In addition to translating all the articles into Japanese, Tsurumi organized a conference for these Asian intellectuals at the International House in Tokyo in the hope of further raising their profile among progressives in Japan. Like Mushakōji and Tanaka, Tsurumi was gravely concerned about Japanese corporate transgressions and the resulting anti-Japanese ethnic nationalist sentiment throughout Asia. As he observed, the common view among Asian intellectuals and students was that the Japanese were "accomplishing with economic power what they had not been able to with military power."[43] Yet according to Tsurumi the Japanese did not see this continuity because "for a century" they had "lived a history of abandoning Asia and joining the West."[44] By ending this history of ignorance through his book, Tsurumi wanted to show the Japanese that the "imagination of Japan in Europe and America" was remarkably different from that in Asia. Doing so, he felt, would open a new pathway toward understanding Japan.[45]

Mainstream centrist and left-leaning publications also began to set aside space for Asian perspectives and voices in the 1970s, marking an important break from their earlier emphasis on the lofty views of Japanese and Western experts. The high-circulation publisher Chūō Kōronsha is a case in point. In *Chūō kōron* (February 1973) and *Chūō kōron keiei mondai* (June 1974) the company published extensive translations from *Sangkhomsat parithat*, which had run two special reports on Japan as the new "Yellow Peril" in Asia in April 1972 and March 1974.[46] In the introduction to the first translation in 1973, *Chūō kōron* advised readers that they "should view the discussion unfolding [in this journal] as one more or less shared with other Asian nations. In the term 'Yellow Peril' we can see the complicated relationship between Japan and Asia in the 1970s. In

41. Tanaka Hiroshi, "Ajia ni koso," 9.
42. Tsurumi Yoshiyuki, *Ajia kara no chokugen*.
43. Tsurumi Yoshiyuki, *Ajia kara no chokugen*, 11.
44. Tsurumi Yoshiyuki, *Ajia kara no chokugen*, 202.
45. Tsurumi Yoshiyuki, *Ajia kara no chokugen*, 202.
46. "Nihon kōka tokushū"; "Tai yūryokushi."

this sense, we feel this [material] is essential reading for Japanese, so here we offer an almost complete translation."[47] Articles translated from *Sangkhomsat parithat* for *Chūō kōron* in 1973 included (translated into English) "Thai Concerns about Japan's New Economic Posture," "A Message from Japan: Japanese Militarism," "The Japanese Military-Industrial Complex," and "The Expansion of an Economic Animal and Its Consequences." The 1974 translations in *Chūō kōron keiei mondai* had similar themes but took on an even more ominous tone, coming in the wake of Tanaka's disastrous 1974 visit and the earlier Thai popular uprising in October 1973, which resulted in the ousting of the pro-Japan Thanom Kittikachorn regime. The editors noted that the sense of "warmheartedness" toward Japan still evident in the 1972 "Yellow Peril" publication was now absent, with Japan and Thanom's (now defunct) military dictatorship portrayed as jointly constituting the new "Yellow Peril."[48] Translated articles reflected this tone with titles (translated into English) like "Your Excellency, Negotiating with the Japanese Government is Worthless," "Is Japan or China the Model for Thailand?," "The Japanese Military Industrial Complex—The Fearsome Yellow Peril," and "Japan's New Export: Pollution." The issue also included extracts from the novella *Yūkoku* (Patriotism) by the fanatical right-wing novelist Mishima Yukio, who had committed ritual suicide by disembowelment in spectacular fashion in 1970.[49] Adding to the threatening tone, these extracts were accompanied by an image of the muscular Mishima wearing only a loincloth and headband while clasping a samurai sword.[50] As the editors concluded, "we must thoroughly understand this discourse and adopt a new approach."[51]

Left-leaning publications like *Ushio*, *Asahi jānaru*, and *Sekai* also began to devote space to Asian voices and perspectives. In June 1973 *Ushio* included a special section exploring what the Japanese were "doing in Asia," featuring short essays by journalists, academics, students, activists, workers, and entertainers from Southeast Asia, Taiwan, and Hong Kong.[52]

47. Ishii Yoneo, "Kaisetsu," 209.
48. Yoshizawa Toshiharu and Akagi, "Kaisetsu," 313.
49. Yoshizawa Toshiharu and Akagi, "Kaisetsu," 313.
50. "Tai yūryokushi," 318.
51. Yoshizawa Toshiharu and Akagi, "Kaisetsu," 313.
52. Ushio, "Tokubetsu kikaku."

Topics were diverse, including discrimination and prejudice against local employees in Japanese companies, "bogus" Japanese "kick boxing," unethical Japanese tour companies, rambunctious Japanese tourists, and reminiscences from the days of Japanese colonization.[53] Not all the reports in *Ushio* were negative, but the overall tone was of a Japan once again extending its influence throughout Asia with little consideration for local sentiment.

The monthly publication *Sekai* demands special attention in the context of this trend to listen to Asian voices in the progressive media. Throughout the 1970s *Sekai* became a crucial medium for the transmission of information about Asian grassroots struggles, particularly democratization movements in South Korea through series such as Chi Myong-kwan's "Kankoku kara no tsūshin" (Correspondence from South Korea, published under the pseudonym of T. K. Sei).[54] Like the other publications discussed above, this attention to Asia marked an important shift in emphasis for *Sekai*. Although the publication had previously been attentive to Asian problems, it had primarily focused on the region through the lens of American power and Cold War politics, particularly the Vietnam War. The turning point came with the return of Yasue Ryōsuke to *Sekai* in 1971 and his elevation to editor in chief the following year.

Yasue began his career at Iwanami Shoten, the publisher of *Sekai*, in the late 1950s, where he developed close ties with leading progressive intellectuals and facilitated the publication of their work in books and monthly magazines such as *Sekai*. In the late 1960s he served as a personal secretary to Minobe Ryōkichi, the progressive governor of Tokyo, during which time he was instrumental in gaining official authorization for ethnic Korean schools in Tokyo. On returning to Iwanami in 1971, Yasue spearheaded a far-reaching reorientation to Asia in the pages of *Sekai*, beginning in 1972 with a series titled "Ajia kara no ronchō: Nihon wa dō mirareteiru?" (Opinions from Asia: how is Japan viewed?).[55] In contrast to the translations in *Chūō kōron* and the opinion pieces by Asians in *Ushio*, the *Sekai* series consisted of a monthly article authored by the editorial board that contained

---

53. Ushio, "Tokubetsu kikaku," 108.
54. The correspondence was later published in four volumes. See T. K. Sei and "Sekai" Henshūbu, *Dai-San Kankoku kara*, *Gunsei to junan*, *Kankoku kara no tsūshin*, and *Kankoku kara no tsūshin zoku*.
55. This series ran in eight issues (314–16, 318, 321, and 323–25) of *Sekai* during 1972.

lengthy translations from publications, reports, and work by intellectuals and other influential Asian commentators. Again, topics were extremely diverse, including ownership of the Diaoyu or Senkaku Islands, Japanese economic expansion into the Philippines, democracy and anti-Japanese sentiment in Hong Kong, and Taiwanese reactions to the normalization of Sino-Japanese relations in 1972. The first article of the series noted that although Japan had become "the target of criticism from Asian peoples" due to its "inability to settle the mistake of World War II" and its "economic expansion lacking any concern for others," the reality was that few Japanese had attempted to "genuinely and carefully listen to this criticism." As the editors wrote, "the reason we want to introduce anew the views and criticisms of Japan from the peoples of Asia is because we fear that Japan will be left behind as an 'isolated superpower' in Asia. Moreover, it is also because we deeply desire the pursuit of a new way to build friendship and solidarity with the peoples of Asia."[56] As the articles in the series revealed, achieving this objective depended greatly on Japanese finally recognizing, for example, that Filipinos deeply feared "economic invasion" and the "revival of Japanese militarism" and that they detested the "intense discrimination and contempt" that many Japanese felt toward them.[57] *Sekai* showcased the perspective of one Filipino commentator, who observed that "the Japanese 'economic animal' looks at Filipinos with contempt. In other words, Japanese people despise us, and the perceptive Filipino people are very aware of the Japanese attitude that, absent commercial necessity, they would certainly not be in such a country."[58]

"We Don't Know Asia": Overcoming Progressives' Ignorance

Listening to and transmitting these voices from Asia in the early 1970s resonated closely with the processes of introspection and self-critique that we saw developing among antiwar activists, students, and intellectuals

56. Sekai Henshūbu, "Nihon shihon ni keikai," 219.
57. Sekai Henshūbu, "Takamaru Firipin," 154 and 155.
58. Quoted in Sekai Henshūbu, "Takamaru Firipin," 160.

throughout the 1960s and into the new decade. But now, in the face of widespread anti-Japanese sentiment, facing Asia took on an ever more urgent tenor. In addition to the thorny challenges of ethnic responsibility and original sin toward Asia, progressives now had to confront their woeful ignorance about the region and Japan's involvement in it, not to mention their essentially nonexistent connections with other Asian people.

Stimulated by their earlier support for South Korean antiwar deserters, in the early 1970s Beheiren activists were among the first to directly address the predicament of not knowing Asia. On the suggestion of Oda Makoto, in 1972 the weekly magazine *Asahi jānaru* ran a special issue titled "Tokushū: Watashitachi wa Ajia o shiranai" (Special report: We don't know Asia) that included essays by Oda, Wada Haruki, Tsurumi, and others.[59] The sociologist Takeuchi Ikurō wrote on anti-Japanese sentiment in the Asian media, Wada discussed Japan's "hyena corporations," and the economist Nishikawa Jun denounced the "division of Asia" by "US and Japanese capital" in his essay.[60] Oda's and Tsurumi's contributions homed in on the root of the problem: why did the Japanese know so little about Asia and, more important, what was to be done? With customary bluntness, Oda declared to readers that the Japanese "had no choice" but to admit they "knew nothing about Asia." "In other words," he said, "both me writing this essay and you reading it know nothing. And to add another fact: we have not even attempted to know anything in the past, nor are we trying to know anything now."[61] This was the "raw truth" Japanese needed to "affix" to themselves if they ever hoped to "genuinely know" their region. By way of illustration, Oda quizzed readers on their knowledge of Cambodia. At best, they might have heard about the US bombing there, but probably they knew no more. While most Japanese could confidently list American presidents like "Nixon," "Johnson," and "Kennedy," how many could name "Sihanouk"?[62] Moreover, although the average Japanese could imagine the names of American soldiers like "Smith" or "Jackson" fighting in the jungles of Cambodia, most would be hard pressed to think of a Cambodian soldier's name.

59. *Asahi Jānaru*, "Tokushū."
60. Nishikawa, "Ajia bundan e," 20.
61. Oda, "'Domin' to 'Nihon kōhei,'" 5.
62. Oda, "'Domin' to 'Nihon kōhei,'" 5.

Writing a couple of years later, Oda made a similar observation about Vietnam. While he and many other Japanese could visualize people in "Belfast" eating bacon and eggs for breakfast, most had not the faintest idea of what the Vietnamese might be eating, despite the "struggle of the Vietnamese people" supposedly becoming "deeply embedded" in their "hearts." And the fact that Japanese lacked such basic knowledge about the lives of fellow Asians, argued Oda, represented the "fundamental barrier" preventing Japanese from making the Vietnam issue or any other Asian issue "their own problem." Worse than ignorance, it was an "ignorance of ignorance" erected upon a history of abandoning backward Asia for the glittering West.[63] As Oda observed, although Japanese thinkers could write about Japan with great profundity through the lens of "Paris" or "London," apart from the occasional maverick author like Hotta Yoshie, few ever contemplated their country from the perspective of "Bangkok" or "Singapore" because the map of Asia had receded from the geographical imaginary of their intellectual consciousness.[64]

Oda's traumatic awakening to his own ignorance of Asia came during the Beheiren protest outside the Ōmura Detention Center in 1969 discussed in chapter 3: "As I was calling out through the megaphone one single fact became obvious, and that fact was an indescribable shame which quickly spread throughout my body, weighing me down. I wondered to myself, why wasn't I calling out in Korean? The answer was simple—I can't speak Korean. But the answer isn't that simple—why is it that I can speak English but not the Korean of our neighboring country? Moreover, since I knew I couldn't [speak Korean], why had I not invited a Korean speaker to come along with us?"[65] Oda compared this protest to his actions against the arrival of the US nuclear-powered aircraft carrier, the *USS Intrepid*, in Sasebo City sometime earlier. Before the protest he had prepared a cassette tape with his appeals recorded in English. Moreover, while circling the *Intrepid* in a small boat, he had shouted out in English, primarily "because the American soldiers did not understand Japanese." Why, then, had he shouted out in Japanese at Ōmura? On one

63.   Oda, "Ajiajin no kome," 204.

64.   Oda, "Ajiajin no kome," 202. Hotta, the exception to this generalization, traveled to and wrote about India in the mid- to late 1950s in *Indo de kangaeta koto*.

65.   Oda, "'Domin' to 'Nihon kōhei,'" 6.

level it was certainly because he did not speak Korean. But it was also because the Koreans in the detention center understood Japanese. Or rather "more accurately," it was because he "arbitrarily assumed they did." And for Oda, this assumption that other Asians—Koreans in particular—spoke Japanese laid bare the problematic nature of his and other progressives' contempt-filled consciousness of Korea and Asia more generally.[66]

For Oda, then, the Japanese, especially progressives, simply had to come to terms with the new reality of the relationship between their country and Asia in the 1970s. In the 1950s, it had been relatively easy for the Left to imagine Japan in brotherhood with the new nations of Asia and Africa, reduced as it was to a "pawn of American imperialism."[67] For the JCP and other leftist groups at the time, "small" Japan clearly belonged to the "A-A" (Africa and Asia) club because it was both a "direct victim" of America and "far from being a superpower."[68] But now Japan was "no longer a victim," it was an economic "superpower"—and if the Japanese people failed to "act," if they did not "resolutely oppose the direction of the mainstream," "before realizing it" they would become but "one part" of the Japanese economic juggernaut "weighing down on Asia."[69] The bottom line, explained Oda, was that theatrical expressions of "self-accusation" and "denunciation" and catchy slogans like "the Asian aggressor within us" or "we, the yellow Caucasians" ironically spoke more to youths' self-absorption than to any sincere concerns for the people of the region.[70] What such youths failed to recognize was that "Asia" and the "Japan weighing down on" it had become embedded in their own daily lives.[71]

Only through an excruciating "remapping" of the region could students and other progressives begin the journey toward genuine knowledge of Asia. For Oda's generation, this remapping would involve a courageous reconstruction of their fathers' "Asian invasion." It would mean superimposing these individual cartographies of transgression one on top of the other to reveal "for the first time" that it was not "Japan" that had

66. Oda, "'Domin' to 'Nihon kōhei,'" 6.
67. Oda, "'Domin' to 'Nihon kōhei,'" 7.
68. Oda, "'Domin' to 'Nihon kōhei,'" 8.
69. Oda, "'Domin' to 'Nihon kōhei,'" 10.
70. Oda, "'Domin' to 'Nihon kōhei,'" 10–11.
71. Oda, "'Domin' to 'Nihon kōhei,'" 10.

"invaded Asia" but *"Japanese people"* just like themselves.[72] Youths, on the other hand, faced a remarkably different challenge because their maps of Asia were "absolutely blank." They had "no clear idea" where countries such as Laos or Cambodia were located, nor could they describe the "characteristics of individual Laotians or Cambodians" such as the ways they "walked" or the issues of great concern to them. "Put frankly," Oda lamented, "I have the feeling that most youths haven't even realized they possess such a blank map."[73] In Oda's 1972 call for a remapping of Asia in the progressive mind, then, we begin to see a fusion of the earlier drive for ethnic responsibility with a newer aspiration to genuinely know Asia.

Like Oda, Tsurumi also began to articulate his own methodology for knowing Asia (his way of "mapping" the region), which he outlined in a discussion with Katō Yūzō in the same 1972 issue of the *Asahi jānaru*. Far more than Oda, for Tsurumi, visiting the region would be paramount. Only by meeting with local people in their living spaces, eating their food, and seeing their lifeways would it be possible to genuinely understand the regions of Asia in all their nuances. Tsurumi called this method "thinking while walking through Asia" (*Ajia o arukinagara kangaeru*).[74] For example, as much as possible, Tsurumi tried to "meet with local Chinese" when traveling in the Malay peninsula, or to consult with Asian youths who would be the future leaders of the region.[75] Early on he had even adopted a strict policy of absolute "immersion" (*genchishugi*)—"not meeting with Japanese" and making every effort to act just like the locals.[76] Only through such immersion did he feel that it was possible to understand Asia in all its nuances. In Tsurumi's experience, attitudes toward Japanese "militarism" and "economic invasion," for example, differed greatly among the nations of Southeast Asia thanks to their respective wartime experiences.[77] Yet such nuances became visible only with the use of methods of active immersion and interaction. Moreover, together with immersion, Tsurumi cautioned his readers that understanding

72. Oda, "'Domin' to 'Nihon kōhei,'" 12.
73. Oda, "'Domin' to 'Nihon kōhei,'" 12.
74. Tsurumi and Katō, "Ajia o arukinagara," 13.
75. Tsurumi and Katō, "Ajia o arukinagara," 14.
76. Tsurumi and Katō, "Ajia o arukinagara," 18.
77. Tsurumi and Katō, "Ajia o arukinagara," 16.

would depend greatly on Japanese abandoning their conceited attitude of "teaching things to Asians" and instead recognizing their "need to learn" from the region.[78] As Oda put it, rather than "merely thinking about" Asia or, worse, trying to influence its people, the time had come to truly know Asia through a new lens of humble receptivity.[79]

Tsurumi, Oda, and their fellow anti–Vietnam War activists wasted no time in developing concrete initiatives to know Asia and connect with fellow Asians in the early 1970s. In 1971, for instance, Tsurumi and a group of university students established the Ajia Benkyō Kai (Asia Study Group), whose members met regularly to discuss Asian issues and read works by influential Asia observers like Honda Katsuichi. In 1972, Tsurumi and the first cohort of students in the group went on a study tour of Hong Kong, Thailand, Malaysia, and Singapore. Inoue Sumio, a young Behei-ren activist and a member of the study group for two years, later recalled that he was "revitalized" by Tsurumi's Asia initiative after prolonged participation in the anti–Vietnam War movement. It was through the study group that Inoue finally awoke to the reality of a Japan "located in Asia" while simultaneously being its "enemy."[80] Thanks to this awakening, Inoue shifted his activist agenda, eventually spearheading transnational mobilizations against Japanese industrial pollution in South Korea and Southeast Asia.[81] While Inoue had been well aware of the nefarious ties between Japan, the United States, and Vietnam, Tsurumi's group effec-tively expanded and magnified his and others' perspective on the region, planting the seeds for their subsequent Asia-focused activism.[82]

As we have seen, Tsurumi also strove at this time to give voice to Asians through publications and events. Beheiren did the same in *Be-heiren nyūsu*, which now carried articles on issues like South Korean democratization movements and Japanese industrial pollution in Thai-land. As Michiba explains, such activities reveal how a generation of anti–Vietnam War activists were beginning to connect their notions of

78.   Tsurumi and Katō, "Ajia o arukinagara," 18.
79.   Oda, "Ajiajin no kome," 217.
80.   Inoue Sumio, "Undō no naka," 31.
81.   See Avenell, *Transnational Japan*, 122–32.
82.   Inoue Sumio, "Undō no naka," 31.

invasion and perpetration to Japanese corporate expansion into the region and the resulting consequences for the environment, human health, and political freedom. Attention to Asia in these ways was a new and important development for the Japanese New Left (and, in fact, the Left more generally).

But Beheiren activists were not content to simply enlighten fellow progressives about the realities of Japan in Asia: they also began to foster initiatives to reach out to fellow Asians at this time. In 1969, for example, Beheiren started a new English-language publication, *AMPO: A Report on the Japanese People's Movements*, with "AMPO" in the title referring to the much-maligned security treaty between Japan and the United States. Until 1973 *AMPO* focused primarily on issues relating to conservative rule in Japan, the Vietnam War, and US influence in Japan, but when the Pacific-Asia Resources Center (PARC) took over editorial duties after its establishment in 1973, the publication's focus changed noticeably. The periodical was retitled *AMPO: Japan-Asia Quarterly Review*, and both its content and authors took on a conspicuously Asian flavor with topics such as Japan-Indonesia corruption, crackdowns in Singapore, Filipino political prisoners, Bangkok slum dwellers, repression in Malaysia, and Park Chung-hee versus the South Korean people. Contributors now came from across Asia, including Kim Chi-ha of South Korea, Ngiam Peng Teck of Singapore, Datuk The Lim of Malaysia, Linda Guilatco of the Philippines, and Phuu Phaakphuum of Thailand. Prominent Japanese civic activists and intellectuals such as Oda, Wada, Hidaka Rokurō, Inoue Kiyoshi, Honda Katsuichi, Tsurumi Yoshiyuki, and Ui Jun offered intellectual guidance for both PARC and *AMPO* from within Japan, while American scholars like Douglass Lummis and Mark Selden, both of whom were involved in the Committee of Concerned Asian Scholars, offered a North American perspective. Drawing on this large pool of Asian knowledge, from June 1974 Oda and his colleagues began a seminar series titled "Yoyogi Ajia Daigakkō" (The Yoyogi Asia University) aimed at "genuinely understanding Asia inclusive of Japan" and "strengthening Japan's ties [with Asia] at the level of the people through studying about Asia."[83] Oda started the series with a lecture titled "how Asians boil rice," delivered in a

83. "'Ajia daigakkō' hiraku," 10.

packed lecture hall before an audience of six hundred, and Tsurumi gave the second lecture, on "how to know Asia."[84] Through this strategy of connecting with activists and movements in the region via *AMPO* and of fostering knowledge and interest in Asia at home through *Beheiren nyūsu* and the seminar series, PARC's leaders strove to peel back the corrosive de-Asianization of their country begun so many years before.

The Conference of Asians held in mid-1974 represented perhaps the most ambitious attempt by former Beheiren activists to begin the process of forging genuine understanding of, and grassroots ties with, fellow Asians at this time. Proposed by Oda in 1973 and organized by former Beheiren members, antipollution activists, and members of Christian groups, the conference focused on three key issues: the state of Japan's economic invasion of Asia, pollution by Japanese industry in the region, and political repression under Asian authoritarian regimes. Around forty Asian participants from Thailand, Malaysia, Singapore, the Philippines, and elsewhere joined 180 Japanese participants and a small number of American and European observers. Civic activists, university students, and academics comprised the majority of the conference participants, but there were also labor union leaders, blue-collar workers, journalists, Christians, and environmentalists.

After visiting sites of pollution and protest such as Sanrizuka (near the controversial New Tokyo International Airport) and the Tokyo-Chiba industrial zone on the first two days, participants engaged in an overnight teach-in at the Yugyōji Buddhist temple in Fujisawa City, where they were joined by the progressive local mayor, Hayama Shun. Here participants divided into subgroups, discussing issues such as pollution in South Korea (both industrial and "moral"), Singapore's "police state," the "FDI paradise" of Malaysia, martial law in the Philippines, and—at the last-minute request of female participants, who had felt that their interests were slighted by the program—women's issues in Asia. Thereafter participants traveled to Hachiōji for the main conference, stopping on the way to inspect a US munitions supply facility in Sagamihara and the Mitsubishi Caterpillar factory. The final day of the event was a gathering open to the public at Meguro Ward Hall in central Tokyo, during which participants ratified the *Joint Declaration of Asian People*, a list of commitments,

84. "Ajia o shiru zemi," 12. For Oda's lecture, see Oda, "Ajiajin no kome."

and numerous resolutions relating to the Korea problem, the treatment of political prisoners, and women's issues.[85]

Above all, conference organizers wanted the event to be about increasing grassroots knowledge of Asia and building connections among Asians. As the conference invitation announced, "this will be a conference of Asians, not a conference on Asia. In other words, it will be a gathering of Asian people—people who were born there, people who live there, and people who struggle there. . . . Why are we holding this gathering? It is because Japan, undeniably a part of Asia, is attempting to dominate [the region] once again." The conference would thus be an opportunity to "tease out in concrete detail the nature of [Japan's] economic penetration" and, "through solidarity with the peoples of Asia" whose "daily lives" had been "stolen," build a "network of struggle to reclaim these daily lives."[86] In a repeat of his 1972 article in the *Asahi jānaru*, at the Fujisawa teach-in Oda suggested that the first step in this direction would be to increase mutual understanding: "One of the reasons this teach-in came about is because, even though we are Asians, we know nothing about Asia. . . . We Japanese know almost nothing about South Korea, and nor do we know about Thailand or Singapore."[87]

For Oda and other participants, the key thus lay in constructing an Asia different from that of Tanaka, Park, Marcos, and Suharto, who trumpeted "Asia is One" while colluding for their own benefit.[88] As the *Joint Declaration of Asian People* emphasized, "We are not power holders, nor are we rulers. . . . We must struggle against those people who possess power and money. Through this struggle our connections will take root. Indeed, it is solidarity that will bring about our ultimate victory. In this we are common, we are one. In this Asian people are one."[89]

For Japanese participants the conference was at once mortifying and galvanizing, as they faced the distressing realities of Japan in Asia while attempting to join hands with people from the region for perhaps the first

85. For the conference proceedings, see Oda, *Ajia o kangaeru*. For a condensed version of the proceedings in English, see *AMPO*, "Special Issue."

86. Oda, *Ajia o kangaeru*, 3.

87. Oda, *Ajia o kangaeru*, 16.

88. Oda, *Ajia o kangaeru*, 134.

89. Oda, *Ajia o kangaeru*, 279.

time in the postwar era. Hirayama Takasada, an activist fighting the exportation of pollution, was scathing in his evaluation of Japan after the conference, accusing the Japanese of "leading daily lives stained by the blood and sweat of Asian people." "Today Asia is integrated into Japan's industrial structure like a rubbish heap of contradictions," he said. "We (*latent*) *victims of Japanese pollution* must recognize our position as *joint perpetrators and beneficiaries of Japanese imperialism*, and we must engage in the struggle to slice into [its] innards. . . . Failing to do so, we will not be able to form strong bonds with the people of Asia and all those countries dominated by Japanese imperialism."[90] For Hirayama, this struggle had to be underwritten by Japanese "regret for a hundred years of incessant invasion of Asia from the Meiji era on" and the "*responsibility of all Japanese* for their direct and indirect complicity in this violence."[91] As Muto Ichiyo observed, blindly championing a "democracy" and "affluence" divorced from the "context of Asia" invited co-optation by government and business elites whose members also trumpeted the "defense of Japanese democracy and affluence"—even if this meant sacrificing fellow Asians and propping up despotic regimes in the region. The reality was that conditions in Japan could not be viewed as somehow "detached" from Asia, and to the extent that progressives continued to think that they could be, they risked being drawn ever more deeply into the orbit of those they claimed to oppose.[92]

Muto's and Hirayama's musings on the conference were somber indeed, but in retrospect they tell us much about the more concrete understandings of Asia emerging among certain activists and intellectuals at the time. For such individuals, the region could no longer be understood quite simply as somewhere "over there" or even as the site of past transgressions. Just as Japanese capital had spread into every corner of the region, Asia had permeated all aspects of Japan, including its peaceful and affluent daily life and its beloved democracy. Indeed, as Tsumura had predicted, "once again" Asia had become the historic site on which Japan's fate depended, so the region could no longer be ignored, nor could it be pitied or romanticized.

90. Oda, *Ajia o kangaeru*, 327.
91. Oda, *Ajia o kangaeru*, 328.
92. Muto, *Konkyochi to bunka*, 200.

Historically speaking, this 1970s awakening to Japan in Asia marked a striking evolution of the progressive views of Asia that we witnessed in 1950s Asian idealism—and even in the tortured confrontation with ethnic responsibility of the 1950s and 1960s—because it emerged on top of a growing knowledge about Japan's 1970s penetration of Asia. As I noted above, progressives were both mortified and galvanized. Activists like Muto, although deeply ashamed of postwar Japan, also saw the birth of "something new" within Japanese popular movements that he articulated as a "sense of being Asian" (*Ajiajin toshite no ishiki*).[93] The conference thus marked a pivotal moment of awakening to the reality of Japanese material affluence and political freedom built on the sacrifice of other Asian people. In turn, the combination of self-reproach and moral obligation for this situation helped fuel a variety of new movements that mobilized in response.

Resisting Japan in Asia: The New Solidarity Movements

If listening to fellow Asians and addressing their ignorance of the region were the first two notable responses of Japanese progressives to the Asia problem in the 1970s, then the third—and perhaps most impressive of all—was an assemblage of new civic movements mobilized in solidarity with fellow Asians. This vibrant realm of civic activism addressed overlapping issues relating to environmental pollution, gender, human rights, and democratization. The activists involved reached out both domestically to other movements at home and overseas to counterparts throughout Asia. As the decade progressed, the number of groups and participants proliferated along with the range of issues, producing an expansive shared space of Asian solidarity movements and activism unseen previously.

Within this space, three streams of activism were particularly influential due to their innovative involvements in Asia and their critical role in shifting the mentalities of Japanese civic activists from their largely

93. Muto, *Konkyochi to bunka*, 188.

domestic, victim-centered focus to a new vision of the region informed by a sense of complicity and perpetration. The first stream of activism grew out of the domestic Japanese environmental movement, developing in opposition to Japanese exportation of pollution to Asia. The second emerged from the women's movement, unfolding as a mobilization against Japanese sex tourism. And the third traced its roots to the intellectual and activist initiatives to address ethnic responsibility of the late 1950s and 1960s, now reborn in a series of mobilizations supporting the South Korean democratization movement and its intrepid protagonists. For clarity we will look at each stream separately, but in reality, there was a great deal of overlap among the issues and the activists. It is important to keep this notion of communality and cross-fertilization in mind because it was the sum total of this sphere of activism—combined with the intellectual initiatives discussed above—that helped regionalize progressives' mentalities throughout the 1970s.

POLLUTION EXPORT AND THE AWAKENING TO ASIA IN ENVIRONMENTAL MOVEMENTS

Environmental activists' awakening to Asia in the 1970s traced its roots to the historic successes of their earlier struggle against pollution at home. Thanks to Japan's amazing spurt of industrial development and economic growth that began in the mid-1950s, by the late 1960s the country's economy was the third most productive in the world, behind only those of the United States and the Soviet Union. However, the underside of this economic miracle was a pollution nightmare, devastating to both the natural environment and human health. So bad was the situation in the 1960s that Japan earned the unenviable international reputation of a polluters' paradise. After a period of suffering in silence that began in the 1960s and stretched into the early 1970s, pollution victims, opponents of development, and a cadre of lawyers and scientists mobilized in protest movements and used lawsuits that resulted in significant regulatory reform, watershed legal victories, and an overall improvement in the natural environment. But these achievements were not without consequences. Environmental groups soon learned that certain Japanese companies were planning to relocate the most polluting components of their production abroad—specifically, to Asian countries where regulations were lax or nonexistent and authoritarian regimes were willing to brutally suppress dissent. The revelation of this so-called pollution export came as a rude shock to Japanese environmental activists, who until then had believed that they had orchestrated a miraculous pollution cleanup. But faced with the march of polluting industries to Asia, this victory now began to look disturbingly hollow, a distressing process of Japan's outsourcing its negative externalities to the region. Infuriated by this corporate misconduct, in 1975 Inoue Sumio, a campaigner against pollution export and a Beheiren activist, accused Japan of playing an unscrupulous game of old maid, duping Asian countries into accepting the pollution joker with inducements of employment and economic development.

As I have discussed elsewhere, the revelation of pollution export coincided with numerous initiatives by antipollution groups, scientific experts, and victims to communicate the horrific story of Japanese industrial pollution to the world in the hope of preventing similar tragedies elsewhere.[94] As the attention of environmental activists expanded outward in this way, some of them began to consider more carefully the operations of Japanese industry abroad, particularly in Asia. Media reports on the rising wave of anti-Japanese sentiment in the region only added to this attentiveness. In 1972, for instance, Hirayama started an "Asia group" (*Ajia gurūpu*) within the influential antipollution network Jishu Kōza.[95] In a sharp break with the earlier domestic focus of that network, Hirayama and his group began a column titled "Ajia no Mado" (Window on Asia) in the movement's monthly newsletter, *Jishu kōza*, providing detailed reports and statistics on Japanese FDI and industrial activity across the region.[96] Some members of the group even traveled to Asian countries. For example, in November 1972 Matsuoka Nobuo visited Thailand, where he met with student activists and delivered a presentation on Japanese pollution.[97] Others, like Inoue, gravitated toward

94. See Avenell, *Transnational Japan.*
95. On Jishu Kōza, see Avenell, *Making Japanese Citizens*, 162–66, and *Transnational Japan*, 39–42.
96. For example see Matsuoka, "Mō hitotsu."
97. Matsuoka, "Mō Hitotsu."

the movement against pollution export thanks to his earlier involvement in Beheiren and Tsurumi's Asia Study Group. As we have seen above, in the late 1960s and early 1970s Beheiren activists were focusing more attention on Japanese industry, first in terms of Japanese munitions and logistical support for the US military and later through scrutiny of Japan's "hyena corporations" in Asia.

Thus, when the first instances of pollution export surfaced in the early 1970s, a handful of Japanese environmental activists with an interest in, and rudimentary knowledge of, Asia were ready to face the challenge. It would be a historical inaccuracy to argue that the resulting movements somehow came to dominate the attention and activism of the Japanese environmental movement thereafter. They certainly did not. Nevertheless, the movements made Asia visible and a matter of pressing concern in environmental circles as it had not been before. Like the women's movement discussed below, the regionalization of environmentalist mentalities and activism unfolded as a discovery of perpetration against Asia by Japanese industry, the Japanese state, and ordinary Japanese. Just as antiwar pacifists were forced to face their position as perpetrators vis-à-vis the Vietnamese people, environmental activists faced a similar conundrum as citizens and consumers benefiting from the destruction of Asian environments and damage to the health of fellow Asians. Once victims of industrial pollution and excessive development at home, they had become complicit in hideous transgressions against Asia.

The first mobilization against pollution export came in response to a Japanese industrial operation in Thailand in 1973, soon after the anti-Japanese demonstrations of the previous year in that country. During an August visit to Bangkok to meet student activists, Hirayama learned that the Thai Asahi Caustic Soda Company, a subsidiary of the Japanese Asahi Glass Company of the Mitsubishi Group, was responsible for dumping effluent into Bangkok's Chao Phraya River, resulting in massive fish kills and digestive disorders among people who consumed the fish. Subsequent tests of the effluent revealed traces of mercury and other toxic compounds. In response, Inoue, Hirayama, and others quickly established the Nichi-Tai Seinen Yūkō Undō (Japan-Thailand Youth Friendship Movement), which thereafter conducted numerous demonstrations outside Asahi Glass's headquarters in Tokyo—some of which were planned to coincide with protests in Thailand.[98] A highlight of this transnational Thai-Japanese collaboration was an exhibition on Japanese pollution held at Thammasat University in September 1974. The exhibit was attended by over 15,000 people, including activists from Japan who supplied photographs, slides, and other materials.[99] For Japanese activists, the Thai Asahi Caustic Soda Company contamination incident was a wake-up call to both pollution export and their individual complicity as Japanese citizens. Okuda Takaharu, who was in Bangkok at the time of the exhibition, succinctly articulated this new sense of perpetration among fellow activists in an article published in the English-language *KOGAI* in 1975:

> We Japanese have been too indifferent to the existing exploitation system which we and the Asian people around us are caught in. Surely we are now living in an expanding "empire." We have not been aware of the economic relations between Asia and Japan, in which the present "prosperity" of Japan stands on the sacrifice of Asian people. The more Japanese (or more exactly, the more a small number of Japanese) become wealthy, the poorer the other Asian people become. And what is more important, we haven't realized that Asian people are developing their own movements seeking their own socio-economic development and independence. Now we must gain the perspective not of what we can do for them, but what we must not do to them.[100]

More Asia-focused movements against pollution export ensued. In 1974 Inoue and Hirayama learned that the Toyama Chemical Company planned to relocate its polluting mercurochrome operations by subcontracting production to a South Korean operator and importing the finished product back into Japan. Incensed, Inoue and Hirayama immediately established the Toyama Kagaku no Kōgai Yushutsu o Yamesaseru Jikkō Iinkai (Executive Committee to Stop Toyama Chemical from Exporting Pollution), which thereafter became the hub for activism against

98. This group published a newsletter, *Nichitai seinen yūkō undō nyūsu* (Newsletter of the Japan-Thailand Youth Friendship Movement), starting in 1973.
99. For more on the exhibition, see Okuda Takaharu, "Documents."
100. Okuda Takaharu, "Documents," 11.

pollution export in Japan through its long-lived newsletter *Kōgai o no-gasu na!* (Don't let the pollution escape!).[101] Participants on the Japanese side were both moved and humbled to learn from their Christian colleagues that members of the Incheon Young Women's Christian Association (YWCA) had appealed to the Incheon mayor to stop Sanwa Chemical Company (the subcontractor) from starting operations at the mercuro-chrome plant. In Japan activists could protest freely, but these women had risked their lives by appealing to local authorities under the thumb of Park, who was then actively encouraging polluting Japanese industries to relocate to South Korea. As the Japanese activists keenly recognized, this was a lesson in commitment and fearlessness: a case of fellow Asians teaching Japanese the real meaning of struggle. As the leaders of the Toyama movement put it, "probably, the sisters in Korea had more difficulties and were placed under worse conditions than us. . . . But they were brave, and we must learn from their anti-pollution movement. On our part though, we have changed gradually through our movement. We have really come to think seriously that we must change the present Korea-Japan relationship from its foundation. [This] relationship is serving only the interests of the LDP . . . and Park regimes."[102]

In the following years, Inoue and Hirayama's group and various other local movements escalated their campaign against Japanese companies exporting pollution to Asia. In 1974, for instance, after forcing Toyama Chemical to abandon its South Korean plan, activists turned their attention to the Nippon Chemical Company, which had established a joint venture in the Ulsan industrial region of South Korea to manufacture sodium bichromate and mirabilite anhydride—both known for their toxic by-products like hexavalent chromium.[103] Alongside this struggle, starting in 1975 activists confronted Kawasaki Steel, which had announced plans to relocate a highly polluting sintering plant to Mindanao in the Philippines. Similar to Park's patronage of Japanese business in South Korea, Marcos actively supported this project: he speedily ratified the long-dormant Japan-Philippines Treaty and created a special free-trade

---

101.   On this movement, see Avenell, *Transnational Japan*, chapter 4.

102.   Executive Committee, "Cut Off the Path," 7.

103.   This issue was reported on in detail in *Kōgai o nogasu na!*, starting in its third issue (August 1974).

zone inside which foreign companies paid no tax or duties and had free rein over their use of resources and labor, as well as their discharge of pollution.[104] Making matters worse, executives of Kawasaki Steel openly acknowledged the company's pollution export to the Philippines. Speaking under oath at a court case brought by Chiba Prefecture residents against the company in 1975, an executive acknowledged that "in the entire iron and steel manufacturing process the sintering plant [was] inevitably responsible for discharging the largest quantities of air polluting waste materials." Hence the company had "made the decision to construct the new sintering plant . . . not at the Chiba Steelworks site but at a site overseas."[105]

Significantly, as activists became more deeply involved in these mobilizations, they slowly began to ask questions about the longer history of Japanese corporate involvement in Asia. Delving into the past of Nippon Chemical, for example, they discovered a tainted history of collaboration with the prewar Japanese state and its policies for expansion throughout the region. Issues of *Kōgai o nogasu na!* throughout the 1970s carried article after article documenting Nippon Chemical's prewar involvement in the production and supply of armaments and military equipment, as well as its merciless treatment of forced Korean laborers.[106] In July 1976, for example, the newsletter ran a full translation of an article from the South Korean weekly *Jugan kyunghyang*, documenting the cruel treatment of Korean laborers at the company's chromium mine in Hokkaido. Along with grueling twelve-hour workdays, the article described malnutrition, torture, and countless deaths among the Korean workers.[107] Such revelations of what Japanese companies were doing in the present and what they had done in the past in Asia precipitated a fundamental reconsideration among environmental activists, including even those not directly involved in opposing pollution export. For instance, a group of Tokyo residents struggling against pollution from a nearby Nippon Chemical factory drew a direct connection between their struggle and

104. See Yoshiwara, "Kawasaki Steel."
105. Quoted in Yoshiwara, "Kawasaki Steel," 15.
106. See, for example, articles in the issues of *Kōgai o nogasuna!* of December 1974, January 1975, and July 1976.
107. "Hokkaidō tankomura."

pollution export. At a June 1975 demonstration, the residents declared that "there could be nothing more disrespectful to South Korea and its people than to impose" pollution on them "simply because" it was "not possible in Japan." They argued that "Japan Chemical must not be allowed to replicate the same 'imperialist mentality' from the war when it forcibly brought Koreans to Japan and imposed abusive labor on them. We will fight until pollution export is stopped so that normal ties of friendship and goodwill that will last for a hundred years, two hundred years, or forever can be constructed between South Korea and Japan."[108]

This process of awakening to Asia in the environmental movement attained its fullest expression in April 1976 at a highly publicized event called the "People's Rally against Pollution Export to Asia."[109] Attended by members of some forty-five civic groups from across Japan, this was the first high-profile rally at which antipollution groups focused entirely on pollution export and economic aggression. Participants candidly acknowledged that breaking the system of oppression and exploitation within Japan would not be possible without "frontal attacks upon the structure of Japan's pollution export and economic invasion of Asia."[110] As the declaration delivered at the rally observed, Japan's postwar economy had "been greatly enlarged through secondary participation in the Korean War and the Vietnam War." Although Japanese leaders called this "prosperity," the declaration called on Japanese people to "reject" this affluence, "maintained at the expense of our friends in Asia and the rest of the Third World." Activists had no choice but "to radically remake the structure of Japan's economy which in its present form" could not "survive without an economic invasion upon the countries and people of the Third World."[111]

Such sentiments marked a radical shift from the national, victim-centered focus that was common among environmental activists of just a few years earlier. The pollution export problem made these activists face Asia for the first time and, in the process, tackle thorny questions about their individual complicity in matters both past and present. More

---

108.   Quoted in "Damatte wa irarenai."
109.   "'Kōgai yushutsu.'"
110.   Yoshiwara, "Kawasaki Steel," 21.
111.   Yoshiwara, "Kawasaki Steel," 21.

practically, thereafter Asia and the problem of Japan in Asia became an important element of Japanese environmental activism. The Han-Kōgai Yushutsu Tsūhō Sentā (Anti–Pollution Export Information Center) established at the 1976 rally became the connective tissue between Japanese activists and their counterparts abroad. Moreover, as I show in chapter 5, during the 1980s activists like Tsurumi expanded their vision from pollution export to wider questions of inequity emerging from Japanese economic activity in the region. Finally, we should also keep in mind that environmental activists' struggle against pollution export unfolded within the shared space of progressive Asian rediscovery in the early 1970s. As a result, its influence stretched beyond the confines of environmental circles, feeding into the wider grassroots regionalization among civic groups.

KISAENG SEX TOURISM AND THE AWAKENING
TO ASIA IN THE WOMEN'S MOVEMENT

Industrial pollution export forced environmental activists to face Asia for the first time, but it was another variety of pollution that galvanized Japanese women activists. Following in the footsteps of industry, in the 1970s Japanese tourists with pockets full of yen began flocking overseas to East Asia and elsewhere. In 1972, total outbound tourism from Japan increased by around 50 percent from the previous year, while for South Korea alone the increase was an astounding 200 percent. Around 500,000 Japanese were visiting South Korea per year—mostly men, many of whom were traveling on packaged sex or "kisaeng" tours.[112] Reports of the time paint an ugly picture of this dark trade. Recounting her 1973 visit to Seoul in the pages of *Sekai*, Takahashi Kikue, an anti-kisaeng activist, expressed her "instinctive repulsion" at the "large groups of almost totally male Japanese tourists, looking like an army of black, marauding ants."[113] In the evenings she described seeing "men propositioning girls in Japanese, and the 'go-betweens' slipping money into their purses," while in the mornings she witnessed "successions of pretty and stylish young women parading out of the rear entrances" of hotels.[114] A 1973 article on the issue in *Time* noted

---

112. Takahashi's *Sekai* article was later published in English in the *Japan Interpreter* from which I quote here. Takahashi, "Kisaeng Tourism"; Matsui, "Intabyū."

113. Takahashi, "Kisaeng Tourism," 214.

114. Takahashi, "Kisaeng Tourism," 214.

the "equivocal response" of South Koreans to the "newest Japanese invasion": "On the one hand, the money is welcome: hotels and flights are jammed, and at least a dozen new hotels are now under construction in Seoul to provide more rooms."[115] But "some South Koreans" were "disturbed" by the fact that "their country" was becoming "Japan's bordello." As one American tourist asked after being "shoved around at Kimpo Airport by a mass of eager arrivals from Tokyo," "Does the U.S. have to post 40,000 G.I.s in Korea to defend these guys' right to have a good time?"[116]

Making matters worse, kisaeng tourism enjoyed official blessing.[117] Although prostitution was illegal in the country, in 1973 the Korean Tourism Association issued special permits to around twenty-four hundred women to work as registered kisaeng. Private restaurants also certified women, taking the number involved to a massive forty thousand.[118] Japanese officialdom also offered its stamp of approval to the practice. A 1974 report by the Kaigai Gijutsu Kyōryoku Jigyōdan (Overseas Technical Cooperation Agency) on the development of tourism on South Korea's Jeju Island listed "kisaeng parties" as one of the "attractive" nightlife options available to visitors, along with "casinos" and "nightclubs."[119] If these "unique" and "outstanding" aspects of Jeju became the core of tourism planning on the island, the report suggested, the industry had a "bright future" indeed.[120]

Similar to environmental activists' discovery of pollution export, then, the officially sanctioned kisaeng trade served as a critical stimulus for Japanese women activists' awakening to Asia and their sense of perpetration and complicity toward Asian women. However, somewhat in contrast to the environmental movement—which had been largely oblivious to Asia before pollution export—opposition to kisaeng tourism grew out of and, indeed, drew on an emerging attention to Asia and to prostitution within Japan among a small number of women activists. As with the trajectories of other activists and intellectuals of the time, this was a

115.   "Seoul of Hospitality."
116.   "Seoul of Hospitality."
117.   "Seoul of Hospitality."
118.   Itō Takiko, "Kīsen kankō," 327.
119.   Kaigai Gijutsu, *Cheju tō*, 27.
120.   Kaigai Gijutsu, *Cheju tō*, 27.

deeply reflexive process for women activists: their pervasive sense of victimization was complicated by the revelation of their perpetration.

Two pioneering groups were particularly important in laying the groundwork for this reflexive mentality in the movement opposing kisaeng tourism: the writer Yamazaki Tomoko's Ajia Josei Kōryū Shi Kenkyūkai (Research Group on the History of Asian Women's Interactions; AJKK), established in 1966; and the activist and former Marxist revolutionary Iijima Aiko's Shinryaku = Sabetsu to Tatakau Ajia Fujin Kaigi (Asian Women's Conference Opposing Invasion = Discrimination; SSAFK), formed in 1970. Both groups helped bring Asia onto the agenda of the women's movement, where it had been largely absent before.

The AJKK owed much to Yamazaki's (1932–2018) personal trajectory. Yamazaki was raised by her mother after the untimely death of her father, a low-ranking navy officer, in her third year of elementary school. In the 1950s Yamazaki moved to Tokyo with dreams of a career in acting, and she became involved with a Korean graduate student at the University of Tokyo who was active in the pro-North Korean Sōren association. As Yamazaki recalled, "together we lived a life of penury, and moreover, because I was discriminated against by Japanese, I could see that there was something in common" between the position of women and Asians in Japan.[121] The relationship was short-lived, thanks to opposition from within Sōren, and in 1959 Yamazaki met and married Kami Shōichirō, an author of children's books. Her interest in women's history developed in the early 1960s. Frustrated with the prospect of being "confined to homemaking and child rearing," in 1966 Yamazaki, Kami, and three others established the AJKK as a reading group whose members met twice monthly to explore the broad themes of "women" and "Asia."[122]

Yamazaki's earlier relationship with the Korean student certainly influenced this Asia focus in the AJKK, but it also emerged from her rejection of what she saw as a Western bias in Japanese women's history writing.[123] As Yamazaki explained, after World War II, women's histories covering all periods of Japan's past flourished, but most focused on the

---

121. Yamazaki, *Ai to senketsu*, 17.
122. Yamazaki, "Ajia josei kōryū shi kenkyūkai no kaisan."
123. Park Sunmi, "70-nendai Nihon," 123.

lives of "elite women" and "were constructed using Western perspectives and values."[124] Absent were the lives of those who "lived as ordinary people" at the "base of society"—prostitutes, waitresses, housemaids, women factory workers, and the wives of farmers and fishermen.[125] As Park Sunmi observes, the real breakthrough of Yamazaki's AJKK was to extend these histories across borders by looking at interactions between Japanese women and Asia.[126] For Yamazaki, investigating the stories of countless women at the grassroots level revealed how "deeply connected" many were to Asia. Moreover, in contrast to "intellectual women" linked to the West "through culture or thought," the connection of these lowly women to Asia unfolded as a physical "entanglement of the flesh."[127] Yamazaki pointed to the so-called *karayuki-san*, the young women from poor rural villages who went to China and elsewhere in Asia in the late nineteenth and early twentieth centuries "offering their flesh to locals and white [men] who had come to manage the colonies."[128] Then there were the wives who accompanied their husbands to Manchukuo and the women who married "Korean laborers" under the policy of so-called Japanese-Korean Marriage.[129] Worlds apart from the elevated relationship of elite women to the West, the entanglement of these women to Asia was "far more demanding and severe."[130]

As its membership increased, in November 1967 the AJKK began publishing a semiregular magazine titled *Ajia josei kōryū shi kenkyū* (Research on the history of Asian women's interactions) that dealt with the lives of these ordinary women and Asia.[131] Despite its humble beginnings, the publication soon attracted an impressive array of contributors. Luminaries from the Japanese women's movement like Yamakawa Kikue and Hiratsuka Raichō penned lengthy essays on the Asian women they had

124.   Yamazaki, *Ai to senketsu*, 15.
125.   Yamazaki, *Ai to senketsu*, 17 and 18.
126.   Park Sunmi, "70-nendai Nihon," 122.
127.   Yamazaki, *Ai to senketsu*, 19.
128.   *Karayuki-san* roughly means "miss gone-to-China" but, as noted, these women went to many other countries throughout Asia and the Pacific.
129.   Yamazaki, *Ai to senketsu*, 19.
130.   Yamazaki, *Ai to senketsu*, 20.
131.   Yamazaki and Kami, *Ajia josei kōryū*.

known, while others like the sinologist Takeuchi Yoshimi encouraged readers to study Korean.[132] Later issues contained articles on the kisaeng tourism problem.[133] Yamazaki was also surprised when the renowned writer Morisaki Kazue asked to become a member of the group and soon afterward submitted a poem titled *Chōsen kaikyō* (The straits of Joseon) for publication in the magazine's second issue.[134] Morisaki, born in Korea in 1927, was active in grassroots movements among mining communities in northern Kyūshū, publishing the literary journal *Sākuru mura* (Circle village) with the poet Tanigawa Gan and the historian Ueno Eishin.[135] Her concern for women and oppressed groups such as resident Koreans and blue-collar workers undoubtedly drew Morisaki to the AJKK, and she subsequently established a chapter of the group in the Chikuhō region of northern Kyūshū, contributing a column titled "Kyūshū kara no tayori" (Correspondence from Kyūshū) beginning in the fifth issue of the AJKK's journal.[136]

The first issue of *Ajia josei kōryū shi kenkyū* conveyed the AJKK's strong desire to study the history of Asian women's interactions through the lens of members' remorse for Japan's transgressions in Asia:

> In the past, China and the countries of Asia were Japan's teachers and the places we felt closest to. But with the beginning of modernization at the Meiji Restoration, in its haste to catch up with the West, Japan donned military boots and trampled over Asian countries without the slightest sense of shame. . . . Japan's defeat in World War II proved that pursuit of the West was a mistake and signaled the dawn of Japan's return to Asia. But the Japanese nation, which could not change its character of old, came under the influence of the West even more than before and intentionally shifted its gaze away from Asia. . . . In order to make amends for the

132. For Yamakawa's and Hiratsuka's essays, see Yamazaki and Kami, *Ajia josei kōryū*, 44–48, 73–78, 115–20, 148–51, 190–92, and 216–17.

133. See, for example, Yamaguchi, "Kankoku no josei-tachi," 557.

134. Yamazaki, "'Ajia josei kōryū shi kenkyū' no omoide," 13.

135. See Sasaki-Uemura, "Tanigawa Gan's Politics"; Fuji Shuppan, *Sākuru mura*; Matsubara, *Gen'ei no kommyūn*.

136. Yamazaki, "'Ajia josei kōryū shi kenkyū' no omoide," 15. Some of Morisaki's related publications include *Makkura*, *Dai-san no sei*, and *Karayuki-san*.

indiscretions of our countrymen in their military boots, we must transcend the idea of the Japanese nation and join hands with the peoples of Asian nations.[137]

Most important of all in the AJKK's and Yamazaki's thought was the rudimentary attempt to tackle deimperialization—in other words, the thorny issue of women's complicity in Japan's aggression toward, and invasion of, Asia. As Yamazaki wrote in 1970, "it is obvious that the diplomacy of the state in international politics was based on a policy of pursuing Japanese interests through the sacrifice of Asian nations. But the economic expansion and academic and cultural exchanges carried out by private individuals, while weaving their own patterns, also fundamentally followed that same line." Indeed, "the connections Japanese women forged with Asian countries, from an overall perspective, were nothing more than one link in the Japanese state's Asian aggression."[138] "The *karayuki-san*, mainland settlers' wives, and the women who married Koreans became the arms and legs of state policy as they moved around," Yamazaki observed, and "from the perspective of Asian countries, they were elements of Japanese imperialism" (*Nihon teikokushugi no ichiin*).[139] Yet unlike "elite women who had freedom to choose their own paths," those at the base did not elect to become prostitutes or settlers' wives. "Rather, from lives of absolute poverty—of not knowing how they would live from day to day"—they were left with "no choice."[140] Thus, although "on one level these women undoubtedly served on the extremities of the modern Japanese state's invasion of Asia," for Yamazaki they were "in essence" ultimately "victims of the Japanese state," which put them in a relationship of "mutual alliance" and not "antagonism" with the "peoples of invaded Asian nations."[141]

Together with the important accomplishment of putting Asia on the agenda of the Japanese women's movement, Yamazaki and the AJKK—by simply intimating, even if in a qualified way, that Japanese women may

---

137. Reproduced in Yamazaki and Kami, *Ajia josei kōryū*, 43.
138. Yamazaki, *Ai to senketsu*, 22.
139. Yamazaki, *Ai to senketsu*, 22.
140. Yamazaki, *Ai to senketsu*, 23.
141. Yamazaki, *Ai to senketsu*, 24.

have been somehow implicated in Japan's imperial project—opened an intellectual pathway to the provocative idea that any discussion about discrimination against women within Japan could not unfold in isolation from an examination of Japanese aggression toward Asia and women's complicity therein. On this point Yamazaki's logic resonated with Oda's notion of the Japanese as both victims and perpetrators in the context of the Vietnam War.

The task of pushing this latter perspective into the foreground fell to Iijima Aiko (1932–2005) and her group, the SSAFK. Iijima was a leading figure in the Japanese women's liberation movement of the late 1960s, and some credit her with "igniting" second-wave feminism in the country.[142] In 1952 Iijima, a self-described "pure-bred Marxist-Leninist girl," married Ōta Ryū, the founder of Japanese Trotskyism, after which she plunged headlong into the maelstrom of 1950s and 1960s protests.[143] After the abortive 1960 Anpo protests, in 1962 Iijima established the Nihon Fujin Kaigi (Japan Women's Conference) within the JSP, where she fostered connections with the Fujin Minshu Kurabu (Women's Democratic Club) of the JCP and the pacifist Haha Oya Taikai (Mothers' Conference). During these years Iijima also became involved in women's wage struggles in the annual labor "spring offensives" (*shuntō*), as well as participating in constitutional study groups.[144]

It was the rise of the New Left, however, that "forcibly awoke" Iijima to the "emptiness" of ideas like "protecting peace and democracy" that had animated much postwar women's activism.[145] Faced with the Vietnam War, the discriminatory immigration control system, and denunciations from minority student groups like the resident Chinese KSTI (discussed in chapter 3), Iijima and fellow women's liberation activists felt compelled to confront the perpetration in and prejudice toward Asia previously disregarded in the women's movement, much in the same way that Oda and Beheiren had earlier dissected one-country antiwar pacifism. Beginning in the late 1960s Iijima mounted a scathing attack on

142. Kanō, "Shinryaku = sabetsu," 153.
143. Iijima, *Shinryaku = sabetsu*, 139.
144. Iijima, *Shinryaku = sabetsu*, 104. For more on Iijima, see Shigematsu, *Scream from the Shadows*, 11–17.
145. Iijima, *Shinryaku = sabetsu*, 140.

the Haha Oya Taikai for its focus on mothers as "peace-loving"; "innately maternal"; and, significantly, historic "victims" of the Japanese state.[146] In a 1975 essay she openly lambasted the organization for advocating a pacifism based on "victim consciousness," with no sense of perpetration or complicity.[147] As Iijima put it in 1975, "the Haha Oya Taikai was based on the victim consciousness of not wanting to become involved in another war due to the experience of defeat in war. Hence, 'peace' took on the passive meaning of not being in a state of war. And mothers, being the agents responsible for protecting that peace, became largely classless and genderless entities who cherished peace precisely because they were mothers."[148] Missing from this mind-set for Iijima was any recognition of women's wartime role on the home front as individuals who actively supported the invasion of Asia.[149] Absent too was any recognition of women's contemporary responsibility as accomplices in the Vietnam War or as wives and mothers producing the Japanese men "purchasing sex from Asian women."[150] In fact, by the late 1960s, Iijima had concluded that "silently accepting" Japan's complicity in Indochina as the Haha Oya Taikai was doing made women into "frightening accomplices in the massacre of the Vietnamese people."[151]

The denunciation by Iijima and other activists of "victim consciousness" in the Haha Oya Taikai was thus critical in pushing the Asia problem and deimperialization onto the agenda of the women's liberation movement. For Yamazaki and the AJKK, women's perpetration was very

146.   Quoted in Park Sunmi, "Nikkan josei," 3.

147.   Iijima, "Watashitachi wa doko," 299.

148.   Iijima, "Watashitachi wa doko," 300. Ueno Chizuko makes a similar point, noting that "a commonality in postwar women's movements up to the 1960s was that 'women' were not problematized. Peace was the 'hope of women,' and behind this was the sentiment that [this hope] was 'natural for mothers'" ("Sengo josei," 173).

149.   The historian Kanō Mikiyo, who participated in the SSAFK for a time, would—together with others in the Onna-tachi no Genzai o Tō Kai (Association to Scrutinize Women's Present)—conduct pathbreaking research into Japanese women on the home front during World War II, exploring troubling questions of women's historical responsibility. See Onna-tachi, *Jūgoshi nōto*. The group then turned its attention to the postwar era. See Onna-tachi, *Jūgoshi nōto sengohen*.

150.   Quoted in Park Sunmi, "Nikkan josei," 3. Iijima's critical essays of 1969–70 are reproduced in Iijima, *Shinryaku = sabetsu*.

151.   Iijima, "Donoyō ni tatakau," 172.

much a function of their unavoidable victimization and disempowerment vis-à-vis men and the state. In contrast, for Iijima and the SSAFK, women were assumed to have had agency in their perpetration toward Asia—that is, they were responsible for the ways they willingly supported the state and capitalism in the past and the present. The SSAFK served as the organizational vehicle for nurturing this critical reflexivity among women activists eager to confront the "deep connection" between "gender discrimination" and "Japan's imperialist invasion of Asia and its xenophobia toward other [Asian] peoples."[152] As the historian Kanō Mikiyo incisively observes, the use of "invasion = discrimination" (*shinryaku = sabetsu*) in the group's name pointed directly to this ambiguous position of Japanese women. "They were certainly victims of discrimination," but with the "reorganization of Japanese imperialism," they were also complicit as perpetrators "supporting the system from within."[153] According to Ueno Chizuko, this was a kind of "self-reflexive questioning" previously absent in the Japanese women's movement.[154] Like anti–Vietnam War activists, students, intellectuals, and environmentalists, this questioning reveals a recognition by some women's liberation activists that aspects of the women's movement to date that were based on the simplistic desire to "be at peace" (or "not be at war") had ignored "perpetration" in the "past war of aggression" and the current era of "high-speed growth."[155]

In this context, the revelation of the kisaeng tourism issue in 1973 served as a kind of litmus test for women activists' nascent sense of perpetration against Asia. The issue first came to the attention of the Japanese side following a meeting of South Korean and Japanese Christians in Seoul in July 1973, at which the Women's League of the Christian

152. Iijima, "Watashitachi wa doko," 314.

153. Kanō, "Shinryaku = Sabetsu," 154.

154. Ueno Chizuko, "Sengo josei," 172.

155. Iijima, "Hoi 1," 145. Both Ueno Chizuko ("Sengo josei," 175) and Setsu Shigematsu (*Scream from the Shadows*, 18) also point to the famous women's liberation manifesto "Benjo kara no kaihō" (Liberation from the toilet) by the activist Tanaka Mitsu—which, by "connect[ing] the 'chaste' status of the Japanese wife to the violation of those euphemistically referred to as the 'comfort women,'" caused what Ueno describes as a "rupture in the discourse on peace" due to its "multilayering of perpetration and victimization" ("Sengo Josei," 175). There were numerous versions of Tanaka's "Benjo kara no kaihō." For one version, see Tanaka Mitsu, "Benjo kara."

Church of South Korea submitted a statement lambasting Japanese men for "making South Korean women into sexual slaves" on the basis of Japan's "economic superiority."[156] Back in Japan this statement was translated and circulated among women's groups, which immediately began to organize in opposition. Two Christian organizations and an antiprostitution group took the lead: the Nihon Kirisutokyō Kyōgikai Fujin Iinkai (Women's Committee of the National Christian Council in Japan; WCNCC), the Nihon Kirisutokyō Kyōfūkai (Japan Christian Women's Organization; JCWO), and the Baishun Mondai to Torikumu Kai (Association Concerned with the Prostitution Problem). Yamaguchi Akiko of the WCNCC and Takahashi of the JCWO and the Baishun Mondai to Torikumu Kai were among the first to take up the issue, but they were soon joined by others, including Yamazaki; Iijima; Yuasa Rei of the JCP's Fujin Minshu Kurabu; and Matsui Yayori, an influential *Asahi shinbun* journalist.[157]

Their movement adopted an impressive array of strategies, beginning in September 1973 when the WCNCC issued a statement authored by Yamaguchi that drew a direct connection between kisaeng tourism and Japan's sullied past.[158] "The indecent activity of Japanese male tourists in South Korea stems from their lack of individual self-awareness and the shallowness of their consciousness of respecting human rights," the statement explained, "but, at the same time, it is also a product of the lack of remorse for the mistaken perpetration of the past."[159] Meanwhile, Takahashi of the JCWO began collecting background information on the issue with assistance from Naganuma Setsuo of the Jiji Press and Chi Myong-kwan (T. K. Sei), the South Korean democracy activist who translated relevant South Korean newspaper articles into Japanese.[160] With encouragement from Matsui, Takahashi and colleagues assembled all of this information—including the results of "an investigation of travel agencies and their modes of operation"—into a publication that they

156. Quoted in Takahashi, "Kankoku kirisutosha," 19. For a timeline of the Kisaeng tourism opposition movement see Kīsen kankō, "Kai no hossoku to katsudō," 54–56.
157. Yamaguchi, "Kankō baishun," 337.
158. Yamaguchi, "Kankō baishun," 336.
159. Nihon Kirisutokyō, "Nihon Kirisutokyō Kyōgikai," 64.
160. Takahashi, "Baibaishun," 21, and "Kankoku kirisutosha," 19.

sent to "women Diet members, women's groups, news agencies, and other potentially interested organizations in an effort to mount a publicity campaign."[161] Women also lobbied business associations, government officials, and politicians. For example, in October 1973 with support from the Zenkoku Kankō Rōdō Kumiai Renmei (National Alliance of Tourism Labor Unions), they lobbied officials at the Nihon Ryokōgyō Kyōkai (Japan Association of Travel Agents), and in November 1973 they held discussions with bureaucrats responsible for tourism at the Ministry of Transport. These lobbying efforts paid off when both JCP and JSP Diet members in the influential Lower House Budget Subcommittee raised questions about tour operators, noting criticisms from South Korea of Japanese tourists as "sex animals."[162] Opposition Diet members also questioned the government about the report on Jeju tourism development, in which the growth of "kisaeng parties" was encouraged.[163] In addition to these efforts at home, in November Takahashi and Yamaguchi set off on a fact-finding mission to South Korea, where they observed kisaeng tourism firsthand with much "repulsion" and forged solidarity with South Korean Christian women's groups opposing the practice.[164] Yamaguchi and Takahashi left South Korea both enraged and emboldened. As Takahashi recalled, "the effect of this exchange of views [with South Korean Christian women], and our mutually beneficial cooperative action, was to instill a greater sense of responsibility in the Japanese and a consciousness of common goals, and to strengthen a solidarity that transcends national boundaries."[165]

Reflecting this transnational solidarity, on Christmas Day, 1973, around fifty women activists gathered in a demonstration at Tokyo's Haneda International Airport under the banner of the Kīsen Kankō ni Hantai suru Onna-tachi no Kai (Women's Group Opposing Kisaeng Tourism), which had been formed thanks to the organizing efforts of Matsui in collaboration with Iijima of the SSAFK, women from the Lib

161. Takahashi, "Kisaeng Tourism," 211.

162. Quoted in Kitazawa, "Kīsen kankō," 14.

163. For a record of this debate in the Japanese Diet, see Kokkai shūgiin, "Dai-71-kai," especially 7–10.

164. Takahashi, "Kisaeng Tourism," 214.

165. Takahashi, "Kisaeng Tourism," 217.

Shinjuku Center, and student groups from women's universities.[166] The demonstration was planned as a direct display of support for, and allegiance with, women's groups in South Korea that were struggling against kisaeng tourism. Most notably, in October 1973, members of the student association at Ehwa Woman's University and other Christian women boldly issued a public appeal to the Park regime calling for an immediate ban on kisaeng tourism.[167] "Our homeland must never again become a colony of Japan," their statement declared, "but thanks to an astronomic national debt of fifty-five billion [US] dollars countless women are being sold as the playthings of an economic animal under the pretext of 'tourism policy.' ... The Japanese are once again taking control of our land as rulers, and the burning desire of fifty million people for a pathway to peaceful and autonomous reunification is moving farther and farther out of reach."[168] Ehwa students followed up on December 19, 1973, with a demonstration at Gimpo Airport that, importantly, received press coverage in Japan, leading to the Haneda demonstration in the following week.[169]

Japanese demonstrators at the Haneda protest focused their attention on passengers traveling to South Korea. Their handbill, titled "Haji o shire! Baishun meate no kankōdan—Ikari o komete uttaeru (Shame on you! Sex tour groups—we appeal to you in anger), pointed out that as "in the past," when Japanese had "hunted out countless young girls to become military comfort women," again "today" Japanese men were "forming tour groups to dishonor the women" of South Korea, "simply" because they had "money." Worse yet, the Park regime was using the "foreign income from these young girls" to service a yearly deficit of "$700 million," while Japanese FDI capitalized on this economic weakness to extend its control "over 70 percent of South Korea's major industries." Given this situation, the handbill asked, "can we still let our husbands and partners, our brothers, and our male work colleagues travel to South

---

166. Park Sunmi, "70-nendai no Kankoku," 333.
167. Park Sunmi, "70-nendai no Kankoku," 331.
168. This statement was also translated into Japanese and circulated among women's groups in Japan. See Ifa Joshi Daigakkō, "Ifa joshi dai."
169. Shigematsu, *Scream from the Shadows*, 94.

Korea?" Sex tours had to be stopped "immediately," but so did "the economic 'assistance' bankrupting the South Korean economy," "the ministerial meetings between Japan and South Korea," and the revival of Japanese "colonization."[170]

Thanks to input from Matsui, the handbill coined two new and influential terms: *"sei shinryaku"* (sexual invasion), to accompany the existing idea of *"keizai shinryaku"* (economic invasion), and *"baishun"* (literally, buying spring). The latter term retained the same pronunciation as the Japanese word for prostitution (*baishun*; literally, selling spring) but exchanged the Chinese character for selling to that for buying to shift emphasis to Japanese men as the perpetrators purchasing sex.

How did the kisaeng tourism problem and related activism feed into the processes of Asian awakening and deimperialization that we have been tracing in the 1970s? The various public statements and appeals by activists certainly reveal a growing sensitivity to the dual problems of war responsibility toward Asia and the current transgressions of Japanese capital and tourists in the region. But closer to home, kisaeng tourism also motivated the Japanese women activists involved to embark on a more reflexive scrutiny of their own aggression, perpetration, and complicity that were constructed on top of the ethnic discrimination and contempt woven deep into the fabric of Japanese mentalities toward Asia. As Park Sunmi incisively observes, these women began to realize that because they "stood in the position of defending" Japanese soldiers in the past and "corporate warriors" in the present, and because they had internalized this "division of labor by gender" without the slightest reservation, they had unwittingly become "embodiments" of "imperialism."[171]

It is important to emphasize that this intellectual transformation was by no means ubiquitous in Japanese women's activism of the time (or thereafter): most attention was focused on the struggle for gender equality at home. Nevertheless, it was important as an integral part of the broader 1970s Asian awakening that we have been charting among progressive thinkers and movements, as well as in terms of planting seeds for later mobilizations concerning wartime sexual violence and military

170.   Kīsen Kankō, "Haji o shire!"
171.   Park Sunmi, "70-nendai no Kankoku," 334.

prostitution.[172] Yamaguchi of the WCNCC, for instance, argued vociferously that kisaeng tourism was not simply a question of personal morality but was connected at the deepest level to the Japanese people's historical attitudes and behavior toward Korea. It was an "expression of the contempt toward Asia deeply rooted within the Japanese people," a "concentrated reflection" of their "deformed view of humanity and other nations."[173] In an essay penned for the kisaeng opposition movement, Matsuoka, an activist in the movement against pollution export, emphasized that "the use of these women as objects of pleasure emerges as a problem of character (*seishitsu*), transcending the dimension of simple individual morality or individual likes and dislikes."[174] Critical for Matsuoka was the recognition that "the system producing countless kisaeng among South Korean girls" was "not of their own making" but something "we" (the Japanese) had "created" by allowing "countless" Japanese men to "cross the sea to spend an evening with these girls."[175] And, importantly, for Matsuoka, this was a "we" that included progressive activists.

Like Matsuoka, Yamaguchi adopted this self-critical stance despite being the epitome of sensitivity and remorse toward Asia, having married a second-generation resident Korean and having devoted boundless energy to forging grassroots transnational connections between Japan and the region. The weight of her past as a "colonizer" and her present as a "perpetrator" under the new Japanese "empire" made Yamaguchi feel "unbearably miserable" when engaging with people from Asian countries. She could only conclude that this must be the "consciousness of a perpetrator."[176]

Yamaguchi was not alone in her feelings. In 1974, Amano Michimi, an artist and women's liberation activist, observed that a "unique aspect

172. Both Matsui (Kitazawa, Matsui, and Yunomae, "The Women's Movement," 30) and Yamaguchi ("Kankō baishun," 339) noted that the kisaeng issue served as a stepping-stone to later activism surrounding the comfort women issue, but this latter movement would not fully develop until the 1990s, after a survivor came forward. According to Matsui, part of the reason for this two-decade delay was Japanese activists' attention to the democratization struggle in South Korea, which occupied most of their energies.
173. Yamaguchi, "Kankoku no kirisutosha."
174. Matsuoka, "Chōsen josei," 35.
175. Matsuoka, "Chōsen josei," 35.
176. Yamaguchi, "Watashi to Ajia," 335.

of kisaeng prostitution (*baibaishun*)" was how "for a very long time gender discrimination" had been "buttressed by ethnic discrimination." Japanese women simply had to recognize the "self-deception" that, just because this horrid trade was "happening in another country," they personally "were not being violated." She asked "just what is the existence of we Japanese women who keep company with Japanese men whose pitifully filthy Eros is simply 'if we can't do it here then we'll go over there'? What is the women's liberation of we who offer tacit consent to those men? This problem is not at all one of saving the women of an impoverished neighboring country, it is a problem that brings into question our very own liberation."[177] Amano certainly agreed that Japanese women were a "violated sex" at home, but out in the world "as Japanese" they became gruesome "perpetrators."[178]

Matsui Yayori (1934–2002) joined this chorus of self-critique, noting the troubling connection between kisaeng tourism and ethnic discrimination. She recalled her sense of being "stabbed" in the heart on learning of the South Korean women's protests against kisaeng tourism in a Christian newspaper in 1973.[179] What "flashed through" her mind was the realization that "the Japanese had forgotten their disgraceful history of having trampled on and subordinated neighboring Korea, and now they were repeating their barbaric acts."[180] Moreover, Matsui identified "something fundamentally different" in kisaeng tourism compared to, say, "Japanese men buying a prostitute in Rome or New York, or going to a Turkish [bathhouse] in Japan. It was not something that could be resolved [as a] simple question of morals."[181] Like her fellow activists, Matsui identified an intertwining of "gender discrimination" and "ethnic prejudice" within "the mentalities" of the Japanese men "flocking in groups" to South Korea for sex.[182] In kisaeng tourism, the present was superimposed on the past, forming an unbroken history of perpetration. As Matsui explained, "the Japanese men making commodities of South Korean women based on their economic supremacy" were grotesque reembodiments of the "former

177.   Amano, "Watashi ni totte," 39.
178.   Amano, "Watashi ni totte," 39.
179.   Matsui, "Watashi wa naze," 88.
180.   Matsui, "Kokka kenryoku."
181.   Matsui, "Watashi wa naze," 88.
182.   Matsui, "Kokka kenryoku."

criminals (*zenkasha*) who hunted out Korean women for 'women's volunteer corps' and sent them to the battlefields in China and Southeast Asia as military comfort women for Japanese soldiers."[183]

What we witness, then, in the thought and activism of all of these women activists stretching from the mid-1960s through to the kisaeng problem is a gradual awakening to Asia coupled with an intensifying commitment to deimperialization through a confrontation with their internalized perpetration and complicity. In terms of concrete outcomes, their transnational movement with South Korean women had some encouraging successes—what Chi Myong-kwan (T. K. Sei) described as a "small victory" (*chiisana shōri*).[184] In response to nationwide protests throughout Japan in 1974, the Japan Association of Travel Agents prohibited the advertising and promotion of kisaeng tours by its members.[185] In South Korea, government authorities ordered tour operators to immediately cease any "undesirable activities" or face "severe punishment," while tour companies implemented a voluntary "purification movement" in their industry, promising to "refrain from arranging kisaeng parties."[186] Important too were the transnational connections forged between Japanese and South Korean women involved in the kisaeng opposition movement. Similar to the border-crossing connections that environmental and antiwar activists were forging at the time, these ties helped women activists address their self-diagnosed ailment of "not knowing" Asia or fellow Asians, not to mention fostering a consciousness of learning from the region.

Furthermore, this process of coming to know Asia in a consciously reflexive way flowered in the coming years, most notably in Matsui's Ajia Onnatachi no Kai (Asian Women's Association; AWA), purposely established on March 1, 1977—the anniversary of the March 1 Movement against the Japanese colonization of Korea in 1919.[187] The AWA originated from the hastily convened women's session at the Conference of Asians in 1974 organized by Matsui, the artist Tomiyama Taeko, and the translator

183. Matsui, "Watashi wa naze," 93.
184. Sei, "Chiisana shōri."
185. Shigematsu, *Scream from the Shadows*, 94.
186. Sei, "Chiisana shōri."
187. In 1994 the organization's name was changed to the Ajia josei shiryō sentā (Asia-Japan Women's Resource Center), a body that still operates today. See http://ajwrc.org/jp/index.php.

and PARC member Kaji Etsuko. As noted above, the three were infuriated that the kisaeng issue was not taken up at the conference, pointing out to Oda and other male activists that Japan's "sexual invasion" of Asia was just as serious as its economic invasion and that knowing Asia also meant knowing about Asian women.[188] Determined to develop this agenda in activist circles, after the conference the three formed an Asian women's study group that held a regular monthly seminar (the Onna daigaku [Women's University]) at which presenters spoke about women's issues in Thailand, Vietnam, South Korea, Indonesia, Taiwan, and elsewhere.[189] Speakers included a mixture of notable Asia experts like Tsurumi, Asian exchange students, and Japanese women with experiences in the region. On its formation the AWA began publishing a newsletter titled *Ajia to josei kaihō* (Asia and women's liberation), which ran special issues on sex tourism, Japanese cultural invasion, and war responsibility in addition to articles on diverse issues such as women's and human rights, the Kokuseki hō (the nationality law), and the history of women on the home front.[190] As the founding declaration in the first newsletter noted, although people joined the AWA with diverse concerns, their "shared departure point" was a recognition of their "war responsibility" and their desire to "never again stand in the position of oppressor toward the peoples of Asia."[191] The first issue of the newsletter succinctly encapsulated this nascent reflexivity in the women's movement, noting that "Japan's 'modernization' from the Meiji era onward" was "nothing but a history of Asian aggression," and that "the women" who had "lived these hundred years" were "perpetrators," "contributing" to the "aggression."[192] After all, "just how different" were the "lives" of postwar women to those of their "grandmothers and mothers"? Was the postwar era of "revival" and "high-speed economic growth" not "built upon on spilled blood in Korea and Vietnam"? And given that Japanese women had "part of the

188. Matsui, "Intabyū," 353.

189. Matsui, "Intabyū," 353.

190. The full run of this newsletter is available online at the National Women's Education Center of Japan Repository. See https://nwec.repo.nii.ac.jp/.

191. The declaration was signed by Tomiyama Taeko, Yuasa Rei, Matsui Yayori, Yamaguchi Akiko, Andō Misako, Gotō Shōko, and Kaji Etsuko. See Tomiyama et al., "Ajia to josei kaihō."

192. Tomiyama et al., "Ajia to josei kaihō," 1.

responsibility for economic aggression toward Asia," just how was the "condition of women today substantively different from the situation of women before the war?" It was only thanks to "women struggling throughout Asia" that Japanese women were, "at long last," awakening to this reality. As the statement observed, "today, women in the Third World such as Southeast Asia and South Korea are rising up in the combined struggle for ethnic liberation and women's liberation. They are directly showing us that these two [struggles] cannot be separated."[193]

Nowhere did Asian activists more frankly communicate the necessity for this kind of struggle to Japanese women activists than at the World Conference on Women, held in Mexico in 1975. At an event rife with divisions between delegates from the global North and those from the global South, Matsui and her Japanese colleagues were left red-faced and dumbfounded when Asian delegates accused them of being "white bananas"—"yellow-skinned" on the outside, no doubt, but "Caucasian" within.[194] Even more than "economic invader" or "sex animal," the term "white banana" was a stark reminder for women activists that truly knowing and genuinely connecting with fellow Asian women rested ultimately on the combination of external struggle with internal deimperialization.

THE JAPAN–SOUTH KOREA
SOLIDARITY MOVEMENT

Along with pollution export and sex tourism, the South Korean struggle for democratization was critical in both refocusing Japanese activists' attention toward Asia and nurturing a grassroots community committed to Asian activism in the 1970s. The key movement here—actually, it was more like a network of movements—was the imposingly named Nihon no Taikan Seisaku o Tadashi, Kankoku Minshuka Tōsō ni Rentai suru Nihon Renraku Kaigi (Japan Liaison Committee to Remedy Japanese Policy toward South Korea and Ally with the South Korean Democratization Struggle) or, more simply, Nikkanren, established in April 1974. The initial stimulus for this movement was the kidnapping of Kim Dae-jung, a South Korean politician and dissident, by Korean Central

193.   Tomiyama et al., "Ajia to josei kaihō," 1.
194.   Yoshitake, "Heiwa to kokusai," 229.

Intelligence Agency (KCIA) agents at a Tokyo hotel in August 1973. Facing rigorous surveillance and suppression under the Park regime, especially after the declaration of martial law and promulgation of the Yushin Constitution in 1972, Kim took his struggle to the United States and Japan, where he mistakenly assumed it would be safe to criticize Park's Yushin agenda. Days after his abduction in Tokyo, Kim resurfaced in Seoul, deposited outside his residence by a criminal gang and promptly placed under house arrest. Subsequent Japanese police investigations revealed the fingerprints of a South Korean diplomat (and KCIA agent) in Kim's Tokyo hotel room, leaving no doubt that the Park regime—if not Park himself—had orchestrated the affair. Kim narrowly avoided murder at the hands of the KCIA thanks to the last-minute intervention of US officials.[195]

The Kim kidnapping was critical in directing progressive attention and energies toward Korea in the wake of an eight-year struggle against the Vietnam War. Sales of the August issue of the progressive publication *Sekai*—released by coincidence on the day of the abduction—soared, as people rushed to read a discussion on the "path to South Korean democratization" between Kim and Yasue Ryōsuke, the head of Iwanami Shoten publishers.[196] Later in the month, Beheiren members and other concerned progressives including Oda, Wada, Tsurumi Shunsuke, Ōe Kenzaburō, Ōoka Shōhei, and Fujishima Udai released a statement titled "Seimei: Kimu Dejun-shi jiken ni kanshite ryōkoku seifu ni yōkyū suru" (Declaration: Demands to both governments concerning the Kim Dae-jung incident), insisting that the police release details about the incident, the Japanese government prohibit KCIA activities in the country, the South Korean government guarantee the safety of Kim and his family, and both governments facilitate Kim's immediate return to Japan.[197] In November and December Japanese intellectuals and activists organized rallies, again pressing for Kim's release and return to Japan.[198]

Like the mobilizations against pollution export and kisaeng tourism, the Nikkanren movement had dual motivations: a reflexive moment of deimperialization and a desire for transnational solidarity through

195. Wada, "Chishikijin—shimin," 166.
196. Kim Dae-jung and Yasue, "Kankoku minshuka."
197. The statement is reproduced in Aochi et al., "Seimei."
198. Wada, "Materials Related," 37.

support for South Korean democratization. Universalist notions of liberty and human rights were repeatedly and intentionally couched in the discourse of responsibility for what Japan had done to Korea in the past, what it was doing in the present, and what progressives must do to end their complicity as perpetrators. By pushing the "South" into the foreground, the Kim abduction challenged leftists of all persuasions—socialists, communists, and members of labor unions and New Left student groups—to reconsider their naïve lionization of Kim Il-sung's North Korea and patronizing disregard for democratization movements under Park.

The fact that Kim Dae-jung had been kidnapped on Japanese soil also proved to be an important factor behind the formation of Nikkan-ren. Japanese critics on both the Left and the Right had been quick to mount vehement condemnations of the Park regime for its blatant violation of Japanese sovereignty. But as perceptive activists and intellectuals rightly recognized, such claims reeked of a hypocrisy born of historical amnesia. After all, what greater violation of sovereignty had there been than the Japanese colonization of Korea—for which Japan had not once apologized? And given this past, did the Japanese not first need to scrutinize and atone for their own history of violation before assuming the moral high ground vis-à-vis President Park?

Japanese Christians led the way here, linking their campaign for South Korean democratization to the unresolved transgressions of Japanese Christians against Asia. In early 1974, members of the WCNCC and the Nihon Kirisuto Kyōdan (United Church of Christ in Japan) established the Kankoku Mondai Kirisutosha Kinkyū Kaigi (Emergency Christian Conference on Korean Problems).[199] Rehearsing a historical narrative that became increasingly common in the progressive discourse of the late 1960s and early 1970s, the Kankoku Mondai Kirisutosha Kinkyū Kaigi's founding statement lambasted the Japanese for "advancing modernization" and achieving "high-speed growth" through the "sacrifice of Asian people, beginning with the South Koreans."[200] According to the statement, "thirty-six years of colonial rule" had paved the way for political oppression under Park, while the Korean War had "revitalized"

199.   Wada, "Materials Related," 38.
200.   Kankoku mondai, "Kankoku mondai," 77.

the Japanese economy and the 1965 treaty made possible an "economic invasion" under the "pretext" of "assistance and cooperation."[201] Critically, the statement emphasized the complicity of Japanese Christians in this process, calling on them to "take responsibility before God."[202] After all, during the war many Christians had "ridden the wave" of "the Greater East Asia Co-Prosperity Sphere," naïvely believing that this invasion of Asia might benefit the "expansion of the church."[203] Worse yet, many Christians had "still not genuinely acknowledged" or "harshly questioned" their "war responsibility" some thirty years later, laying bare "the absence of an Asian perspective" that was absolutely vital if they ever hoped to "build solidarity" with the South Korean democratization movement.[204]

Nikkanren adopted a similar stance in its founding declaration of April 1974, accusing Japanese industry of lining its pockets "by sucking the blood and sweat of the South Korean people."[205] With "lobbyists" such as former Prime Minister Kishi Nobusuke "furtively working as go-betweens," Japanese industry was "using the Park regime" to "pollute the South Korean countryside" and "exploit" its people—all for the good of what elites called the Japanese "mainland" (*naichi*), a term harking back to the "good old days" of empire. Moreover, ordinary Japanese men "travelling on kisaeng tours" to "violate South Korean women through the power of their wallets" had become grotesque "accomplices with the Japanese and South Korean governments" in this reprehensible architecture of "assault."[206] The solutions were crystal clear: Japanese industry must "stop" its "economic invasion," "pollution export," and "exploitative wages"; Japanese tourists and travel agents must abandon their "shameful kisaeng tourism and group sex tours"; media organizations must resist "intimidation and courageously continue to report on South Korea"; and ordinary citizens in Japan must "eradicate ethnic discrimination against resident North and South Koreans."[207] Only through such a multipronged response could

201. Kankoku mondai, "Kankoku mondai," 77–78.
202. Kankoku mondai, "Kankoku mondai," 77.
203. Kankoku mondai, "Kankoku mondai," 78.
204. Kankoku mondai, "Kankoku mondai," 79.
205. Nihon no Taikan Seisaku, "Nikkan rentai renraku," 122.
206. Nihon no Taikan Seisaku, "Nikkan rentai renraku," 122.
207. Nihon no Taikan Seisaku, "Nikkan rentai renraku," 122.

the Japanese people genuinely support the democratic struggle of South Koreans.

In its function as a network, Nikkanren used its publications and events to create a critical discursive space for intellectuals to debate Japan–South Korea issues, and the organization also served as a hub for a range of activists involved in various movements connected to South Korea. Actors included women's liberation advocates, Christians, resident Koreans, journalists, students, and academics. The issues addressed ranged from kisaeng tourism to pollution export, political dissidents, discrimination against resident Koreans, war compensation, and political corruption. Most of the environmental and women's groups discussed above maintained a connection with Nikkanren, often through the movement's newsletter *Nikkan rentai nyūsu* (Japan-Korea solidarity news), founded in June 1974. Wada served as Nikkanren's general secretary, and the journalist Aochi Shin assumed the role of chairman. Aochi brought a strong track record of progressive dissidence and advocacy to the movement. In 1944, while serving as deputy editor of the monthly *Chūō kōron*, Aochi was arrested along with other journalists under the Chian Iji Hō (peace preservation law) and tortured into giving a false confession as part of the Yokohama Incident. During his time in prison, Aochi was deeply impressed by a Korean youth who refused to admit having committed alleged crimes despite prolonged and brutal mistreatment by Japan's notorious Special Higher Police. After the war, Aochi devoted his journalistic energies to combating the practice of forced confessions, which persisted despite Japan's democratic revolution. His bitter experience with violent repression, his admiration for the bravery of fellow Asians, and his commitment to justice made Aochi almost the perfect choice to lead Nikkanren when it was established in 1974.

Along with its activities on behalf of Kim Dae-jung, Nikkanren's support for Kim Chi-ha (b. 1941), a dissident South Korean poet, offers an illuminating insight into the Asian awakening and growing reflexivity among Japanese progressives facilitated by caustic denunciations from the mouths of fellow Asian progressives. Like Constantino in the Philippines and university students in Thailand, Kim Chi-ha used his profile not only to advocate for the democratization struggle at home, but also to interrogate claims of Asian solidarity among Japanese progressives against the backdrop of their unwitting entanglement in a mechanism of perpetration. Kim initially came into conflict with the Park regime in 1965 while he was a student at the prestigious Seoul National University, being arrested (the first of many arrests) for protesting the Japan–South Korea normalization treaty. In May 1970 he was detained again on charges of abetting North Korea after publishing a poem titled *Ojeok* (Five bandits) in the intellectual journal *Sasanggye*. This poem ostensibly dealt with the five Korean ministers of state who signed the notorious Japan-Korea Treaty of November 1905, making their country a protectorate of Japan. In reality, Kim used the poem as thinly veiled camouflage for mounting a critique of South Korea's five contemporary traitors: big business, members of the National Assembly, senior officials, generals (including Park), and cabinet ministers. Kim's 1970 arrest for the poem was reported in the Japanese media, and in response, eighteen Japanese intellectuals issued a statement denouncing the arrest as an assault on free speech.[208] This statement marked the beginning of prolonged support for Kim among Japanese progressives, who found themselves drawn not only to his courageous democratic struggle but also to his relentless criticism of the Japanese. Knowledge about Kim within Japan spread thereafter, particularly after Chūō Kōronsha published a collection of Kim's works titled *Nagai kurayami no kanata ni* (Far away in the extended darkness) in late 1971.[209]

The first sustained Japanese mobilizations for Kim were organized in 1972 (two years before the formation of Nikkanren), when the poet was arrested yet again under the Anti-Communist Act for his work *Piŏ* (Groundless rumors), a scathing satire of corruption within the Park regime. In April 1972 Tomiyama, together with members of Amnesty International Japan and others, formed the Kimu Ji-ha o Kyūen suru Iinkai (Committee to Save Kim Chi-ha), while in May Oda, Tsurumi Shunsuke, and others close to Beheiren established another group with the same name. As we have seen, Tomiyama was a close associate of Matsui, forming the women's subcommittee at the 1974 Conference of Asians and subsequently helping Matsui build the AWA.[210] Like other Japanese activists discussed in this chapter, Tomiyama (b. 1921) was also a child of

---

208. Lee, *"Nikkan rentai,"* 96.
209. Kim Chi-ha, *Nagai kurayami.*
210. Hein, "Postcolonial Conscience," 10.

empire, having grown up in Harbin, Manchuria, and also experiencing Korea under Japanese colonial rule.[211] Until the late 1960s, Tomiyama focused on producing art that depicted life in and around coal mines— much like Morisaki—but in an effort to completely "refresh" herself, in late 1970 she traveled to South Korea, where she first came into contact with Kim.[212] Tomiyama's activism for Kim focused primarily on spreading knowledge of the dissident through cultural activities such as performances and exhibitions, including a series of lithographs on Kim's works and a traveling slide show with music and narration.[213]

While Tomiyama used her art, activists in the group centered on Beheiren conducted a signature campaign for the poet's release, culminating in a historic meeting with Kim in late 1972. After Oda was refused a visa by the South Korean government, Tsurumi, the novelist Matsugi Nobuhiko, and the translator Kanai Kazuko traveled to South Korea hoping to submit their petition to representatives of the Park regime. During their visit the three journeyed to Masan, where they were allowed to meet with Kim, who had been transferred to a prison hospital to undergo treatment for tuberculosis.[214] As Tsurumi later recounted, when they showed Kim the petition and signatures from around the world, he calmly replied in English, "Your movement cannot help me. But I will add my voice to it to help your movement."[215] As Wada later recalled, "these words" became the "spirit" of the Nikkanren movement, particularly after Tsurumi wrote about the fateful encounter in the July 1974 issue of *Nikkan rentai nyūsu*.[216] Here, said Wada, was Kim's "unequivocal rejection" of Japanese activists' "simplistic movement of support and solidarity."[217] For Wada, Kim's words implied that their movement had to become one

---

211. For more on Tomiyama's life, see Tomiyama, "Hidane to naru."
212. Tomiyama, "Gakuen funsō," 305.
213. Throughout the 1970s Tomiyama screened her slide show in Japan, the United States, and Mexico. She was assisted in producing the show (including versions in English, Spanish, and French) by the United Church of Christ in Japan, PARC, the documentary director Tsuchimoto Noriaki (famous for his films on Minamata disease), musicians, and a director from Nippon Television. See Tomiyama, "Hidane to naru mono," 351–54.
214. Wada, "Nikkan rentai," 54.
215. Quoted in Tsurumi, Ueno, and Oguma, *Sensō ga nokoshita*, 336.
216. Wada, "Chishikijin—shimin," 173.
217. Wada, "Nikkan rentai," 54.

to rescue the Japanese from the "frightening situation" in which their country "was assisting the Park regime" to "drive Kim Chi-ha into a corner."[218] The humbling realization for Nikkanren activists after hearing these words was that it was the Japanese who were being "assisted" by Kim even as "he stood at the precipice of life and death."[219] As Wada opined in 1975, "being moved by the suffering of our neighbor was built upon our causing suffering for that neighbor; it was at that moment we discovered how we ourselves were inside a repressive mechanism and we ran into the structural logic that it was about saving ourselves from this [mechanism]."[220]

Although Kim was subsequently released, his situation worsened dramatically in 1974 after the promulgation of a series of emergency decrees by the Park regime in the face of persistent social unrest. One spark for these crackdowns came in April, when the Jeongug Minju Cheongnyeon Hagsaeng Chon Yeonmaeng Sageon (National Alliance of Democratic Youth and Students) called for a demonstration in Seoul.[221] Kim was arrested on charges of having authored the long-form poem *Minjung-ui soli* (Voices of the people), which expressed frustration at the hardships of daily life and called for immediate political reform. In fact, the author was not Kim but Jang Gipyo, a Seoul National University law student and activist.[222] Nevertheless, Kim was detained together with some 180 suspects for allegedly colluding to establish a communist regime in South Korea. After a short trial in July, Kim and several others received death sentences for their involvement. Ultimately, the sentences against Kim and many others were commuted to lengthy prison terms, although eight members of the Inmin Hyeongmyeong Dang (People's Revolutionary Party) were executed in April 1975, a mere eighteen hours after being sentenced.

In July 1974, however, the fate of Kim and his fellow arrestees appeared grim, thus leading Nikkanren to enter its most vigorous phase of activism for the South Korean democracy movement. Along with the fraudulent death sentence, Japanese intellectuals and activists were

218. Wada, "Nikkan rentai," 54–55.
219. Wada, "Nikkan rentai," 55.
220. Wada, "Nikkan rentai," 55.
221. The group's name in Japanese is Zenkoku Minshu Seinen Gakusei Sōrenmei.
222. Wada, "Chishikijin—shimin," 172.

particularly moved by *Minjung-ui soli* which—although erroneously attributed to Kim—was published in Japanese in 1974 under the title *Minshū no koe* (Voices of the people) along with other works by the poet.[223] Oda, Tsurumi, Wada, Ōe, Hidaka, and others quickly organized the *Kimu Ji-ha-ra o Tasukeru Kai* (Association to Assist Kim Chi-ha and Colleagues) on July 10, 1974, releasing a statement on that day expressing their respect for Kim's literary work, calling for his release, and demanding that the Park regime listen to the "voices of the people." Thanks to Oda and other Beheiren members' international connections, signatories included Howard Zinn, Noam Chomsky, Edwin Reischauer, Jean-Paul Sartre, and Simone de Beauvoir, who collectively formed the International Committee of the Association to Assist Kim Chi-ha and Colleagues.[224] Following the handing down of death sentences on July 13, Japanese members of the committee also engaged in a series of protest events. On July 16, for instance, Matsugi and two resident Korean writers (Kim Sukbum and Kim Si-jong) began a hunger strike in Tokyo's Sukiyabashi Park, followed by yet another on July 27 that involved Tsurumi and the writers Kim Tal-su and Hario Ichirō.[225] Both hunger strikes attracted media attention, the second managing to raise around a million yen in donations in less than a week.[226] The group also held two rallies on July 19 and 25 (which drew modest crowds of one thousand and fifteen hundred people, respectively), followed by a massive rally of around thirty thousand in Tokyo's Meiji Park in September that was organized by Nikkanren, the JSP, the JCP, and the Kōmeitō (Clean Government Party).[227] Late in 1974, Hidaka, the Nobel laureate zoologist George Wald, and three others traveled to Seoul carrying a petition with seventeen thousand signatures calling for the release of Kim and the other arrestees.[228]

Just as he had done from his hospital bed in 1972, Kim used the attention from Japan to once again force his Japanese advocates to cast their critical gaze inward. Soon after his short-lived release from jail in February

223. Kim Chi-ha, *Minshū no koe.*
224. Kimu Ji Ha ra o Tasukeru Kai, "Uttae," 131–32.
225. Wada, "Chishikijin—shimin," 173–74.
226. Nikkan Rentai, "Watashitachi wa nani o."
227. Wada, "Materials Related," 40.
228. Nikkan Rentai, "Watashitachi wa nani o"; Lee, *"Nikkan Rentai,"* 111.

1975 (in March he was arrested yet again on charges of communism), Kim released a provocative statement titled "Sengen 1975-3-1: Nihon minshū e no teian" (Declaration March 1, 1975: a proposal to the Japanese) timed to coincide with the annual anniversary of the March 1 Uprising of 1919. As Kim explained in the declaration, "March 1 fifty-six years ago is a day that both we, the South Korean people, and you, the Japanese people, must together remember with humanity and deep anguish. . . . You, the Japanese people, self-indulgently invaded, oppressed, and exploited our people. But on that day we not only attempted to seek revenge on you as our bitter enemies. By proclaiming our sovereignty and independence in the form of a nonviolent and peaceful movement, at the same time we hoped to save you, the Japanese people, the cruel and inhuman perpetrators, as well as our people who were the victims."[229] Despite this history, Kim accused the Japanese of once again "attempting to eliminate" Koreans "from the world by trampling [their] dignity and rights as human beings."[230] For instance, not only were Japanese companies "exploiting the labor of young women factory workers in the duty-free export zone of Masan," Japanese men were also exploiting Korean women through "so-called kisaeng parties."[231] And in a warning reminiscent of that by Thai university students in 1972, Kim declared that "if the rage and hatred our people feel toward you, the Japanese people today, regardless of its expression, is not resolved through humane and rational efforts, it will ultimately explode as an unconscionable [display] of violent revenge. And it is clear the outcome will be that both you and we will once again experience an era of inhumane hell like those thirty-six years in the past."[232]

Like kisaeng tourism and pollution export, Kim's scathing criticism hit at the heart of the Asia problem and progressive deimperialization. Its potency emerged from Kim's defiant insistence that both historically and in the present the Koreans had persistently tried to "save" the Japanese, but the Japanese had not been able to recognize this because of their contemptuous imperial attitude toward Koreans. To be sure, Kim's interpretation here was probably overstated, but it was critically important

229. Kim Chi-ha, "Sengen 1975-3-1," 202.
230. Kim Chi-ha, "Sengen 1975-3-1," 203.
231. Kim Chi-ha, "Sengen 1975-3-1," 203.
232. Kim Chi-ha, "Sengen 1975-3-1," 204.

in terms of its implications for, and impact on, Wada and other members of Nikkanren. From their perspective, Kim's words applied just as much to Japanese progressives as they did to conservatives or even the Japanese more generally. Kim's criticism exposed the progressive mentality that still seemed to believe that help moved only in one direction—from Japan to pitiful Asia—and that it was the role of the Japanese to assist rather than to learn from or be "saved" by fellow Asians.

As their movement progressed, Nikkanren members increasingly acknowledged the ways in which engagement with South Korean activists like Kim and their struggles had engendered a process of self-transformation and learning from fellow Asians. For instance, on the first anniversary of Kim's March 1975 declaration, Nikkanren organized an open forum titled Nihonjin to 3-1 Dokuritsu Undō (The Japanese and the 3-1 Independence Movement), at which Wada called on the Japanese to develop a new understanding of the March 1 Declaration of Independence of 1919 and presented Nikkanren as the "third chance" for Japan to make amends with Korea.[233] As we have seen, Wada believed that Japan had squandered two earlier opportunities for reconciliation: the first right after its defeat in World War II and the second before the signing of the Japan–South Korea normalization treaty in 1965. But with the advent of pollution export, kisaeng tourism, and the suppression of democratization activists like Kim Dae-jung and Kim Chi-ha, the Japanese had a third chance. "We were slow to wake up," Wada explained, but with the kidnapping of Kim Dae-jung, the "veil concealing the reality of the Japan–South Korea Treaty for eight years was swept away, and it appeared before our eyes. . . . Considering the deep and problematic ties between Japanese and Koreans over history, we cannot avoid the criticism that this departure [of ours] came far too late. And, looking back, we feel deeply ashamed."[234] But thanks to individuals like Kim Dae-jung, Kim Chi-ha, and Chi Myong-kwan (T. K. Sei), they now had a "clearer sight" of the Korean people, and through these "teachers" they had learned "what needed to be done" in the "pursuit of human rights" and "democracy."[235] Thanks to them, Wada and his colleagues had finally recognized that genuine solidarity grew out of "learning

233. Wada, "Chishikijin—shimin," 180.
234. Wada, "Nikkan rentai," 52–53.
235. Wada, "Nikkan rentai," 54.

from the struggle of the South Koreans" and, through this knowledge, "changing the character" of Japan to bring about an internal "transformation." To be sure, their "comprehension" was still "shallow," "confused," and prone to "error," but "by carefully watching the South Korean people and listening to their voices," this "comprehension" was "gradually improving."[236] And in a powerful statement evidencing how progressives' commitment to learning from Asia was, in turn, fashioning a consciousness of "Asian solidarity" remarkably different from that of the 1950s, Wada observed that "now more than ever solidarity between the peoples of Japan and Korea is needed. This is not about Japanese from an advanced democratic nation assisting the Koreans from a backward dictatorship. It is not at all a 'solidarity for the purpose of progress.' More than anything else, it is a solidarity for the purpose of our rebirth through seeing the Korean people, engaging with them as human beings, and learning from their claims and struggles."[237] As one contributor to the final edition of *Nikkan rentai nyūsu* in 1978 wrote, "I want to express my gratitude to all of the South Korean people engaged in the democratization struggle. They have been my 'life teachers.' Whether famous or nameless, again and again, I have been energized by their words, their struggle, and their cries. How desolate my life would be had I not encountered them."[238] To be sure, not all or even most Japanese progressive activists and intellectuals had reached this point by the late 1970s, but the fact that some had must certainly distinguish this period as one of the more important moments of deimperialization in the postwar era.

Aochi, Nikkanren's inimitable chairman, keenly recognized the important self-transformative aspect of the new Asian solidarity movements. On one level, Aochi could not help recognizing the movement's shortcomings: "Was our movement—our futile three-year journey—no more than a footprint in the sand carried away by the wind?" After all, despite the hunger strikes, protests, and petitions, Kim Dae-jung and others were still incarcerated, and the "lesion" of "dark collusion" between Japan and South Korea remained untreated.[239] But, given the "hundred

236. Wada, "Kankoku no minshū," 63.
237. Wada, "Kankoku no minshū," 65.
238. Kurosaki, "Watashi no ketsui."
239. Aochi, "Ima made."

years of Japanese encroachment on the Korean peninsula," Aochi admitted that it was perhaps unrealistic to have expected a disentanglement in "three short years."[240] Moreover, although "on the surface the horrible situation" in which they were "enmeshed" had "not changed," "beneath the solid ice" he believed that something was "coming to life" and something was "beginning to move." As Aochi put it, the demands of Nikkanren and others for change in South Korea and Japanese–South Korean relations were "also demands for our own self-transformation and a denunciation of we ourselves. The fact that we have almost painfully come to realize this fact through our movement over three years is a step forward."[241] Indeed, for Aochi and many others involved in Asian solidarity movements of the 1970s, these "emotional connections" born of a genuine desire to know and learn from the Other were "more important than anything else."[242]

Conclusion

Beginning with the criticisms of Japanese economic expansion into East Asia in the late 1960s, the period until around 1978 witnessed an intensified level of Japanese progressives' engagement with Asia both intellectually and in the realm of civic activism. Japanese activists and intellectuals awakening to their lack of knowledge about the people and countries of the region contributed to a new and proactive commitment to genuinely knowing Asia and to listening and learning from its people. This new mentality was accompanied by an assemblage of Asia-focused movements whose agenda was as much about mobilizing together with fellow Asians and addressing Japanese problems as it was about assisting fellow Asians in their struggles.

This sense of solidarity among equals and shared learning, not to mention an openness to denunciations from Asian Others, marked a new phase of progressives' interaction with, and understanding of, Asia in the postwar era. Although Asia occupied the full attention of only a small

240. Aochi, "Watashitachi."
241. Aochi, "Watashitachi."
242. Aochi, "Ima made."

number of activists and intellectuals, by the late 1970s their influence was extending into diverse spheres of progressive concern such as the environment, gender, human rights, antiwar pacifism, and democratization. Activists who had previously not considered Asia now felt obliged to do so, opening the way to an uncomfortable encounter with their complicity in aggression in the past and present. At the same time, this sense of guilt and complicity was accompanied by new visions of Japan in Asia and Asia in Japan that would, in turn, feed into new streams of civic activism and help grow Japanese civil society into the 1980s and 1990s. The Asia problem certainly remained an ongoing issue for progressives, resurfacing in divisive historical controversies and questions about how to engage at the grassroots level in the coming decades. But in contrast to the situation in the 1950s and 1960s, by the late 1970s there was a cadre of intellectuals and activists equipped with a more distinct—if still rudimentary—mental map of the region and, importantly, a commitment to sustained activism in solidarity with other Asian people. Thanks to this 1970s moment of criticism from Asia and progressive response from within Japan, we might say that de-Asianization was slowly giving way to the grassroots regionalization of progressives' consciousness and activism. Many more intellectuals and activists were able to see Asia and how the region reflected back on to themselves and Japan.

CHAPTER 5

Another Internationalization

Postwar Responsibility, Inter-People
Diplomacy, and Bananas

A mong all the catchwords in Japan in the 1970s and 1980s, "internationalization" (*kokusaika*), as one observer put it, was probably the "most overworked."[1] On one level, the idea encapsulated the advent of a brash, brand-driven consumerism at home fueled by the proliferation of things made in Japan to every corner of the globe. As an ideological construct, internationalization also simultaneously embodied an emerging cultural and economic nationalism in which the country assumed its rightful position as a full member of the group of economic superpowers. A search for "*kokusaika*" in the *Asahi shinbun*, Japan's newspaper of record, reveals only 49 occurrences of the term in the 1960s, but in the 1970s and 1980s this number swells to 523 and 553, respectively. Conservative political leaders embraced the triumphant symbolism of *kokusaika*. Most conspicuous of these was Nakasone Yasuhiro, an LDP heavyweight who waxed lyrical about "Japan, the international state" (*kokusai kokka Nippon*) during his tenure as prime minister (1982–87). For Nakasone and many other conservatives, internationalization was the critical mechanism that Japan could use to project its economic power to the world, and conservative calls for Japanese to develop an "international awareness" (*kokusai kankaku*) were almost always underwritten by a cultural essentialism derived from the supposedly unique traits fueling Japan's amazing postwar revival. The so-called *Nihonjinron* (theories on Japan and the Japanese

1.   Dower, "Peace and Democracy," 31.

people) that were so prevalent from the 1970s onward were an overt expression of this mind-set.[2] So too was the government's establishment of the International Center for the Study of Japanese Culture in 1988 and, in the previous year, its doubling of the budget for the Japan Foundation—an essential instrument in the country's cultural diplomacy.

Like the earlier idea of modernization, the discourse on internationalization in these decades unfolded mostly as a validation of Japanese culture based on Western (now primarily American) standards of economic development. From such validation could be extracted a virtuous circle of the cultural vitalizing the economic, which in turn vitalized the cultural, and so on. As an ideological tool for national validation and prowess, internationalization thus conformed to a time-honored process of separation from, and abandonment of, Asia—what Carol Gluck calls the "triangulation of the West, Japan, and Asia"—only now Japan's liminality could be fruitfully deployed to explain its success.[3] The fact that government-led internationalization harbored a fundamentally chauvinistic impulse was never in doubt. In 1985, Nakasone confirmed this, becoming the first postwar prime minister to make an official visit to the controversial Yasukuni Shrine for the war dead. This was the hard edge of internationalization, and its significance, along with moves to whitewash history textbooks in 1982, was not lost on Japan's East Asian neighbors.

Critics, many of whom had one eye on Asia or Asian minorities, were not fooled by the cosmopolitan veneer of top-down internationalization. In 1985, Yoon Keun-cha, a political scientist and second-generation resident Korean, identified internationalization as yet another form of camouflage for Japanese nationalism. For Yoon, the term encapsulated Japan's time-honored practice of "abandoning Asia and joining the West," just as ideas like "Westernization" and "modernization" had in the past. The more Japan "internationalized," Yoon argued, the more it charted a path of "national essentialism" away from Asia.[4] Hatsuse Ryūhei, a scholar of international relations, agreed, observing that "internationalization" was "premised on a thoroughly Western model" and had roots in the prewar

2. See Befu, *Hegemony of Homogeneity*; Dale, *Myth of Japanese.*
3. Gluck, "Call for a New Asian," 3.
4. Yoon, *Ishitsu to kyōzon*, 16.

mentality of "abandoning Asia" that ultimately precipitated Japan's "invasion" of the region. Although this earlier phase of "abandoning" (and invading) Asia ended in 1945, Hatsuse said that "internationalization" potentially heralded a new kind of Japanese incursion into the region based on Japan's haughty attitude as an entitled, wealthy "Northern" country.[5] As we saw in chapter 4, many Asians felt the same way about Japan— Asia's "Yellow Yankee"—and expressed their anxieties most explosively in Thailand and Indonesia in the mid-1970s.

In spite of such valid criticisms, it would be a mistake to reduce Japanese internationalization in the 1970s and 1980s to nothing more than an exercise in cultural self-indulgence and puffery. In fact, I suggest that doing so risks overlooking the ways internationalization—understood as a wider process of border-crossing relationships and engagements inclusive of Asia—was genuinely transforming Japan at the grassroots level. Concealed beneath internationalization driven from above by political and business elites was another internationalization spearheaded by activists and intellectuals who began to introduce the potent perspectives of human rights and social and economic justice into the issue of war responsibility, the meaning of Asia for Japan, and the process of forging genuine relations of equality and reciprocity with people of the region. The legal scholar and war responsibility advocate Ōnuma Yasuaki recalls that in the 1970s, he and others became increasingly aware of, and began to research and advocate for, "the human rights" of "foreigners," "particularly Asians who had suffered great harm due to Japan's war of aggression and colonial rule."[6] "The idea of realizing human rights," Ōnuma and others realized, was not only something "in the heads of intellectuals" but also an ethical imperative connected to the "concrete realities of everyday life." For instance, it meant comprehending the "deeply ingrained discrimination and prejudice" against resident Koreans as a deplorable "violation" of their "human rights," as well as reconsidering mundane commodities like bananas or fried shrimp as ironic emblems of the economic exploitation and social injustices connecting affluent Japanese consumers to plantation laborers in the Philippines or factory workers in Thailand.[7]

5. Hatsuse, "Majikku mirā," 6.
6. Utsumi et al., *Sengo sekinin*, 105.
7. Utsumi et al., *Sengo sekinin*, 105.

In fact, this internationalization from below based on human rights and social justice evidences how, in the late 1970s and even more so in the 1980s, engagement with Asian activists and Asian issues was increasingly woven into the fabric of progressive thought and activism in Japan. Complementing the grassroots regionalization of Japanese thought and activism that we saw unfolding starting in the early 1970s, Asia-focused activism and engagement in this period cultivated a process of "grassroots globalization" in Japanese civil society in which the norms and practices of an emerging global civil society (like human rights, gender equity, environmental and social justice, local economic empowerment, and humanitarianism) began to flow back into progressive circles in Japan. The critical point is that activism and involvements in Asia—Japan's region—served as critical media for this flow of norms and practices. As one activist put it, Asia was fast becoming a "teacher" for Japan: to know the region was to know the self, certainly as a member of Asia but also, and more concretely, as a consumer, citizen, and human being imbued with inalienable rights and responsibilities toward others across the globe.

In this chapter I examine four historical phenomena that clearly show this process of grassroots globalization through involvement in Asia: first, 1980s initiatives to reconceptualize war responsibility (*sensō sekinin*) as postwar responsibility (*sengo sekinin*); second, the movement for inter-people diplomacy (*minsai gaikō*) in local government; third, Tsurumi Yoshiyuki's project to rethink postwar Japan through the lenses of Southeast Asia and commodities like bananas; and fourth, the new generation of Japanese NGOs active in Asia from the late 1970s onward. Together, these phenomena reveal the growing importance of Asia for a new generation of activists and intellectuals, not only as a performative space for the pursuit of progressive initiatives, but also as a conduit for reimagining and refashioning postwar Japanese identity, democratic praxis, and external relations. Refracted through the overlapping lenses of grassroots regionalization and grassroots globalization, the developments of this period tell a very different history of Japanese internationalization in the 1970s and 1980s that would have significant implications not only for progressives' approaches to the Asia problem and deimperialization, but also for Japanese politics, civil society, and imaginations of the region and Japan's place therein in the coming decades.

Postwar Responsibility

The movement for postwar responsibility typifies this emerging synthesis of deimperialization, human rights consciousness, and historical sensitivity in the 1980s. Although intellectuals had taken up the issue of war responsibility immediately after the war, as we have seen, policies of de-Asianization, the impact of the Tokyo Tribunal, and their own ideological and idealistic idiosyncrasies regarding Asia meant that explicit attention to Japan's responsibility toward the region did not emerge until around the 1960s. Tsurumi Shunsuke's "Fifteen-Year War" concept in 1956 was an early and important intervention, opening the way to 1960s conceptualizations of original sin and ethnic responsibility. The 1980s idea of postwar responsibility traced its lineage to these earlier developments but also grew out of the particular historical milieu of the late 1970s and 1980s—especially the emerging norms and discourse of human rights worldwide. As Akiko Hashimoto notes, it was during the 1980s and 1990s that "a global memory culture began to coalesce around emerging human rights and transitional justice movements that focused on redressing past wrongs."[8] In essence, the notion of postwar responsibility pointed to the necessity for the current generation to make amends (that is, take responsibility) for the deeds of earlier generations.

Japan's ratification of several international legal instruments concerning human rights and refugees was critical in fostering a consciousness of postwar responsibility. With the country's rising prominence as an economic superpower, Japan came under increasing pressure to meet its responsibilities as a conscientious member of the international community. In response, in 1979 Japan ratified and passed two human rights covenants: the International Covenant on Economic, Social and Cultural Rights and the International Covenant on Civil and Political Rights. And in 1982 it ratified and passed the Convention Relating to the Status of Refugees. Numerous laws limiting the rights of permanent residents were subsequently revised, resulting in significant improvements in the official treatment of foreign residents. With the signing of the refugee convention, for example, many laws directly impacting resident Koreans were

8. Hashimoto, *Long Defeat*, 17.

amended. The Shutsunyūkoku kanri rei that had caused such an uproar in 1969 was amended to the Shutsunyūkoku kanri oyobi nanmin ninshō hō (immigration control and refugee recognition act), opening a pathway to special residency status for permanent residents from countries lacking diplomatic relations with Japan, such as North Korea. Citizenship prerequisites were also removed from the Kokumin nenkin hō (national pension act) and the Jidō teate hō (child allowance act). The generally positive outcomes of these international instruments for domestic minorities had the added effect of reminding many Japanese—especially progressive intellectuals and activists—about unresolved issues stemming from Japan's Asian war. In other words, addressing responsibilities of the present through the lens of human rights raised questions about so-called postwar responsibility.[9]

Historical anniversaries and controversies also fed into attentiveness to postwar responsibility. The year 1980, of course, was the thirty-fifth anniversary of war's end, while 1983 marked thirty-five years since the adjournment of the Tokyo Tribunal, which had so deeply shaped subsequent understandings of the war and Japanese responsibility. As if to throw fuel on the fire at this moment of historical remembrance, in 1982 a controversy erupted over apparent attempts by national education bureaucrats to force alterations in the language and descriptions of Japanese militarism in school history textbooks. Much to the consternation of China, Korea, and Southeast Asian nations, descriptions of Japan's "invasion" of Asia were euphemistically reworded as an "advance."[10] Groups like the Emergency Christian Conference on Korean Problems, mentioned in chapter 4, demanded immediate revisions. Moreover, as discussed in chapter 6, Wada Haruki and other Japanese activists established what would become a sustained campaign to have the Japanese government and Diet issue a genuine apology to Japan's wartime victims in Asia. Miyazawa Kiichi, the chief cabinet secretary at the time, eventually issued a statement recognizing the "extreme suffering and damage" of the peoples of Asia caused by the Japanese military, and he also agreed to

9.   Tanaka Hiroshi, "Ajia ni taisuru," 49.

10.   For recent treatments of the history controversies involving Japan and Asia, see Saito, *History Problem*; Hitomi Koyama, *On the Persistence*.

252 Another Internationalization

textbook revisions.[11] Notwithstanding such damage control, the outcome was to harden attitudes toward Japan in both China and South Korea, which increased the sense of suspicion among Japan's neighbors thereafter.[12]

The textbook controversy was also important for those who began to advance the idea of postwar responsibility. Ōnuma (1946–2018) recalled his "embarrassment" that China and South Korea had criticized the textbook revisions before supposedly "responsible" Japanese like him had done so, and he felt compelled to carefully rethink the notion of war responsibility—a term toward which he personally harbored a degree of ambivalence, as he had been born in 1946.[13] More directly, thereafter Ōnuma began to publish copiously about the textbook controversy in the mainstream media, while intensifying his studies of the Tokyo Tribunal and its impact on historical memory and reconciliation in postwar Japan.[14]

Together with Ōnuma, Tanaka Hiroshi and Utsumi Aiko took the lead in propagating the notion of postwar responsibility in the early 1980s, each approaching the issue from their own remarkably different backgrounds and perspectives. Ōnuma's specialization in international jurisprudence and his earlier research into the Tokyo Tribunal, the legalities of war responsibility, and the status of resident Koreans, almost inevitably led him to the issue of postwar responsibility. His experiences during the 1960s as a student also appear to have been important. He recalled his "sense of disillusionment with socialist systems and mistrust of 'progressive intellectuals' and the mass media, which did not attempt any criticism of oppression under the Soviet regime," his disappointment over the failure of movements on behalf of South Korean political prisoners, and his growing concern about how his "mentality and actions might look from the perspective of South Koreans."[15]

Tanaka (b. 1937) arrived at the postwar responsibility issue via his lengthy engagement with exchange students from 1962 to 1972, while he

---

11. Miyazawa, "Rekishi kyōkasho."
12. Wakamiya, Sengo 70-nen, 248.
13. Utsumi et al., Sengo sekinin, 165–66.
14. See, for example, his August 3, 1982, article on the textbook approval process in the *Mainichi shinbun* newspaper, reproduced in Ōnuma, *Tokyo saiban*, 210–16.
15. Utsumi et al., Sengo sekinin, 96.

was working at the Asian Students' Cultural Association.[16] He recalled a particularly confronting experience in November 1963 soon after the release of the new thousand-yen note. A South Korean exchange student living in the association's dormitory asked Tanaka "what the Japanese were thinking" when they decided to use the image of Itō Hirobumi—the "ringleader of the suppression of the Korean race"—on the new note. Most alarming for this student was the fact that "not one Japanese had raised this issue," despite the apparent "freedom of expression in Japan."[17] "Schooled in postwar democratic education," Tanaka said that he was "left speechless" by the encounter.[18] Until then his memory of the war had been confined to the Pacific War view of history, beginning with the Japanese attack on Pearl Harbor, the defeat at the Battle of Midway, the atomic bombings at Hiroshima and Nagasaki, the emperor's surrender broadcast, and the American-led Occupation. "Within this synthesis there was no touchpoint with Asia," which explained his "'speechlessness' after the encounter with that exchange student."[19] Tanaka's blind faith in postwar Peace and Democracy seems to have come crashing down with this. As he explained in 1983, "the main enemy in the war may have been the 'West' but the war was completely about the conquest of Asia. Historicizing and conceptualizing this 'synchronic experience' with Asia must become the linchpin of any synthesis [of the past]. It is here that postwar responsibility toward Asia is to be found."[20]

The historian Utsumi Aiko (b. 1941) was the third important proponent of postwar responsibility starting in the early 1980s. Utsumi's awakening to war responsibility appears to have begun when she read Fujishima Udai's pioneering 1965 volume *Dokyumento Chōsenjin: Nihon gendai shi no kurai kage* (discussed in chapter 2). Utsumi recalls her shock at having graduated from Waseda University totally ignorant about the existence of this history.[21] With a fire in her belly, thereafter Utsumi dove headlong into a range of movements and initiatives relating to Asia and Asians. In

16. Tanaka Hiroshi, "Yakusha no atogaki," 204.
17. Tanaka Hiroshi, "Ajia ni taisuru," 41–42.
18. Tanaka Hiroshi, "Ajia ni taisuru," 42.
19. Tanaka Hiroshi, "Ajia ni taisuru," 42.
20. Tanaka Hiroshi, "Ajia ni taisuru," 43.
21. Utsumi et al., *Sengo sekinin*, 7.

the late 1960s, for example, she was swept up in the movement against amendments to the immigration control ordinance, while beginning in the 1970s she participated in the NCK and the cultural circle Mukuge no Kai (Korean rose association), conducting interviews with resident Korean women while she was a graduate student.[22] From 1975 to 1977 Utsumi taught Japanese at Padjadjaran University in Bandung, Indonesia, after which she returned to Japan to take up another academic position. It was at this time that she joined the AWA that was led, as we saw in chapter 4, by Matsui Yayori, Tomiyama Taeko, and others.[23] Thereafter Utsumi published prolifically on all things Asian. Most relevant in the context of postwar responsibility was her 1982 *Chōsenjin BC-kyū senpan no kiroku* (Record of B- and C-class Korean war criminals), which detailed the traumatic experience of Koreans imprisoned or executed for their activities as members of the Japanese military. The volume described the twofold discrimination experienced by these individuals and their families: first through their conscription into Japan's military and later via the Japanese government's refusal to offer them veterans' compensation on account of their not holding Japanese citizenship. The fourth chapter of the volume, titled "Sensō sekinin to sengo sekinin" (War responsibility and postwar responsibility), was among the first publications to use the term "postwar responsibility."[24]

How, then, did Ōnuma, Tanaka, Utsumi, and others conceptualize and deploy this new formulation of responsibility, and what does this tell us about the intersection of deimperialization and human rights discourse in the 1980s? Although the term "postwar responsibility" had been used in the 1950s by Japanese Christians and intellectuals like Yoshimoto Takaaki in debates about the war responsibility of the literati, the understanding of Ōnuma and his colleagues of postwar responsibility grew directly out of—and in reaction to—the evolving progressive consciousness of responsibility toward Asia that started in the mid- to late 1950s. A key watershed on the path toward a consciousness of postwar responsibility was the logic of perpetration and aggression developed in Beheiren and the Zenkyōtō movement. According to Ōnuma, at this

22. Utsumi et al., *Sengo sekinin*, 8.
23. Utsumi et al., *Sengo sekinin*, 168.
24. Utsumi, *Chōsenjin BC-kyū*.

time a new perspective emerged that problematized not only "past actions" but also the "actual significance of inaction" in the present: for example, the responsibility of ordinary Japanese for their lack of opposition to US military special procurements in the Vietnam War or to structural discrimination against resident Koreans, making them "perpetrators" against Asia. This awakening, as we have already seen, led to a reexamination of the problems inherent in the "structure" of "modern Japan."[25] Here Ōnuma emphasized Tamaki Motoi's 1967 *Minzokuteki sekinin no shisō* (The philosophy of ethnic responsibility) as a particularly important influence in his awakening to the notion of postwar responsibility.[26] Although the focus on acts of perpetration toward resident Koreans in the present was not directly connected to responsibility for the war, Ōnuma said that Tamaki's work represented a critical intellectual breakthrough because "ethnic responsibility" highlighted the "abandoning Asia and joining the West" attitude of modern Japan toward Asian peoples—a structure that remained unchanged in the present and, hence, became a problem of postwar responsibility.[27]

Initially the idea of postwar responsibility had very little traction, and Ōnuma recalled that copy editors—assuming a typographical error—often changed his use of "postwar responsibility" to "war responsibility."[28] For Ōnuma, however, the idea of postwar responsibility finally made it possible to connect two areas of concern he had been researching in relative isolation: the problems of war responsibility, war crimes, the Tokyo Tribunal, and the Nuremburg Tribunal, on the one hand, and problems relating to the legal status of resident Koreans, on the other hand. Through the concept of postwar responsibility, he had a theoretical apparatus to connect these issues as two aspects of a single continuum of human rights violations, encapsulated in the "problem of 'abandoning Asia and joining the West' pursued by modern Japan," which continued to "dominate Japanese society to the present as a deep-seated belief."[29]

25. Ōnuma, "Tokyo saiban, sensō sekinin," 92.
26. Tamaki, *Minzokuteki sekinin no shisō*. See chapter 2 for a discussion of Tamaki's thought.
27. Ōnuma, "Tokyo saiban, sensō sekinin," 92.
28. Utsumi et al., *Sengo sekinin*, 118.
29. Ōnuma, "Atogaki," 237.

These various intellectual and movement trajectories leading to a consciousness of postwar responsibility coalesced in 1983 when Ōnuma, Utsumi, Tanaka, and like-minded intellectuals and lawyers established the Ajia ni taisuru Sengo Sekinin o Kangaeru Kai (Association to Consider Postwar Responsibility toward Asia; ASSK).[30] Although the group was active only until around 1987, through high-profile symposia, writings in the mass media and activist publications, and mobilizations for Japan's Asian war victims, its members succeeded in revitalizing and refashioning the notion of war responsibility for a new age of human rights—and, moreover, for a postwar generation that bore no direct responsibility for the deeds of their forebears in Asia.

Ōnuma articulated the most thorough exegesis of postwar responsibility in the first issue of the association's short-lived publication, *Sengo sekinin* (Postwar responsibility), released in 1983.[31] "Postwar responsibility," he explained, was a "way of thinking" about Japan's situation "in the present." It shed light on the various unresolved problems of Japan's "Fifteen-Year War," such as the Koreans left behind on Sakhalin Island and the Taiwanese and Koreans in the Japanese military—whose families had never received compensation and some of whom had been executed as war criminals.[32] The time had come for Japanese of the present to "reinvestigate" their conceited assumption that the postwar period "was over" simply because they were ignoring these unresolved issues.[33] Ōnuma told his readers that postwar responsibility required the Japanese to comprehend "the war from 1941 to 1945 not as an extraordinary, one-off historical incident, but as one phase of a movement to 'catch up with and overtake the West' based on the creed of abandoning Asia and joining the West."[34] The "remaining work and challenge" for the "postwar" generation lay in methodically "dismantling" such consciousness through direct engagement with each of the unresolved problems of the "postwar settlement." Doing so, concluded Ōnuma, would liberate the Japanese to finally "construct a sincere relationship" in which they could

30. "Sengo sekinin kangaeru," 22.
31. The last of the publication's four issues appeared in 1987.
32. Ōnuma, "'Sengo sekinin'," 198–99.
33. Ōnuma, "'Sengo sekinin'," 199.
34. Ōnuma, "'Sengo sekinin'," 199.

confidently talk about right and wrong in the same way to Koreans and Chinese as they could to Americans. "Postwar responsibility" was "precisely the thinking aimed at this kind of freedom, this kind of liberation."[35] As Ōnuma wrote in *Shisō* in 1984, "postwar responsibility" toward Asia was "not simply an abstract intellectual problem." It was "the accumulated result of inaction on the part of each and every person in postwar Japanese society."[36] Although such inaction may have been "unavoidable for most Japanese immediately after the war as they lived cheek by jowl with starvation," the continuation of such inaction "thirty-nine years" later in an affluent Japan was simply inexcusable. Today it was necessary for the Japanese people to reconsider the "postwar mentality" producing this outcome; it was about them "expelling" (*eguridasu*) a mentality that had "ruled" their "daily actions."[37] In contrast to the term "war responsibility," which remained ambiguous and open to various interpretations, Ōnuma and his colleagues saw great value in the "philosophy and movement" for "postwar responsibility" because it always involved people acting ethically in the present on behalf of "specific victims" (*gutaitekina higaisha*) and "wounded people" (*kizutsuitamono*).[38]

Indeed, it is precisely in this sense that postwar responsibility intersected with the ethics and dictates of human rights prominent in Japan from the late 1970s onward. The postwar responsibility initiative found expression in numerous concrete initiatives for and with fellow Asians. In 1984 Ōnuma and his colleagues organized an international symposium on the Tokyo Tribunal at the Sunshine City building in northern Tokyo—built on top of the former Sugamo Prison, home to political detainees during the war and Tokyo Tribunal defendants after Japan's defeat. With around a thousand attendees, the symposium brought together scholars from the Netherlands, the United Kingdom, and elsewhere who were responsible for a new wave of research on the tribunal; one of the original tribunal judges; and Japanese intellectuals such as Tsurumi and Kinoshita Junji.[39] Importantly, the

35. Ōnuma, "'Sengo sekinin'," 203.
36. Ōnuma, "Tokyo saiban, sensō sekinin," 95.
37. Ōnuma, "Tokyo saiban, sensō sekinin," 95–96.
38. Utsumi et al., *Sengo sekinin*, 204.
39. For more on the symposium proceedings and related material, see Hosoya, Andō, and Ōnuma, *Kokusai shinpojiumu*.

organizers made sure to include Asian perspectives and participants (since these had largely been lacking in the tribunal), among whom were an international law specialist from South Korea and historians from China and Myanmar.[40] In his speech at the event, Ōnuma rehearsed some of the major criticisms of the tribunal: its victors' justice, retrospective application of the law, and exemption of Emperor Hirohito and the Japanese people from scrutiny.[41] But above all, Ōnuma lambasted the tribunal for failing to treat transgressions and crimes against Asia as the central issues for adjudication, a failure most evident in the fact that only three of the eleven judges were Asian (one each from China, the Philippines, and British India). Nor was there any representation of Korea or Indonesia (the latter was apparently represented by its colonizer, the Netherlands).[42] The breakthrough of the 1984 symposium, then, was to foreground Asia in discussion of the Tokyo Tribunal where research had largely been silent before and, through this, move beyond debates over victors' justice to a new perspective on Japan's unresolved responsibility to the region.

Ōnuma and other members of the ASSK also developed the project of postwar responsibility in support for Koreans deserted on the Soviet-controlled Sakhalin Island. This problem traced its origins to the war years, when thousands of Koreans were forcibly taken to work in coal mines on Sakhalin, then under Japanese control.[43] At the war's end there were estimated to be around forty thousand Koreans and Japanese on the island. The Japanese government subsequently negotiated with the US and Soviet governments for the repatriation of Japanese citizens, but the Koreans on Sakhalin were abandoned on the pretext that the "Greater Japanese Empire" of which they had been subjects was now defunct.[44] Only Japanese (and their Korean spouses) were repatriated on the basis of postwar nationality or existing familial ties.[45] Resident Koreans pointed out the double standards of the Japanese, who showed "great sympathy" for the plight of Japanese children left behind in China yet at the

---

40. Ōnuma, "'Tokyo saiban' shinpojiumu," 71–72.
41. Ōnuma, "Tokyo saiban."
42. Ōnuma, "Tokyo saiban," 47.
43. For more on this issue, see Ōnuma, *Saharin kimin.*
44. Utsumi et al., *Sengo sekinin,* 143.
45. Akimoto et al., "Ajia ni taisuru," 80.

same time were "disinterested" in the Koreans they were responsible for abandoning in Sakhalin.[46] The plight of these Koreans had also been largely ignored by the Japanese Left because engaging in such a movement could easily have been associated with "anti-Soviet" and "anticommunist" stances.[47]

A resident Korean who had returned to Japan from Sakhalin with his Japanese wife later began a movement for the repatriation of these abandoned people to South Korea. With assistance from a young activist lawyer named Takaki Ken'ichi, in 1975 the group began legal proceedings for official compensation for the Sakhalin Koreans. They also approached Ōnuma for support, due to his involvement in legal issues involving resident Koreans. This networking eventually resulted in the formation of the ASSK in 1983.[48] Importantly, in 1986 Igarashi Kōzō, a nonaligned JSP Diet member, began his decade-long involvement in the movement. Deeply influenced by the notion of postwar responsibility, while later serving as chief cabinet secretary in the JSP-led Murayama government of the mid-1990s, Igarashi was instrumental in establishing the Japan Center for Asian Historical Records and the Asian Women's Fund for former so-called comfort women, as well as helping partially resolve the Sakhalin issue.[49]

Hence, by the 1990s, the processes of deimperialization that I have been tracing thus far (inclusive of the postwar responsibility movement) were beginning to find a voice in national politics. In this connection, it is also important to mention the movement for an official government apology to Asia begun by Wada and others following the textbook controversy in 1982. Such initiatives toward the acceptance of postwar responsibility provided at least part of the impetus for watershed statements of apology by Japanese political leaders like Hosokawa Morihiro and Kōno Yōhei in 1993 and Murayama Tomiichi in 1995. Finally, driven by their sense of postwar responsibility and human rights, in the early 1980s Japanese activists joined resident Koreans in opposing mandatory fingerprinting of

---

46. Akimoto et al., "Ajia ni taisuru," 82.

47. Utsumi et al., *Sengo sekinin*, 143.

48. Utsumi et al., *Sengo sekinin*, 145.

49. The Murayama government financed construction of a facility (providing medical services and apartments) for returnees from Sakhalin in South Korea, which opened in 2000. See Utsumi et al., *Sengo sekinin*, 177.

foreign residents. Here again war responsibility, postwar responsibility, and human rights converged into a concrete movement for social justice.

Tsurumi Yoshiyuki: Rethinking Japan through Asia

For Ōnuma and his colleagues, internationalization was about injecting the normative framework of international human rights into the country's Asia problem to produce an ethics and praxis of postwar responsibility. For others, however, internationalization unfolded as a project to rethink Japan in the world both within and through Asia. While champions of mainstream internationalization remained in the thrall of the West as the solitary global standard to scrutinize, position, and rank Japan (even while celebrating native culture), proponents of this alternative vision of internationalization focused on excavating detailed, local knowledge about the region and Japan's place therein as a tool for self-critique and a source of inspiration for imagining an alternative, more regionally grounded, Japan beyond the fanfare of economic sensationalism. This was a provocative intellectual endeavor indeed because it rejected Japan's postwar miracle as nothing more than an iteration of the age-old mentality of "abandoning Asia and joining the West," while simultaneously advocating for an alternative internationalization premised on Japan in Asia and Asia in Japan.

Historically speaking, this endeavor resonated with and built upon the earlier efforts of Oda Makoto and others in the 1970s to know an unknown Asia, but it did so in far more grounded ways, focusing on concrete (if obscured) social, economic, and political entanglements with the region. Moreover, it did so with an eye to self-critique: a Japan made visible through the looking glass of Asia. In 1985, Hatsuse Ryūhei spoke of a "magic mirror" in which Asians could clearly see Japan, yet the Japanese were blinded to their region. This magic mirror was a product of both the past and the present. It emerged from a modern history in which Japan was the "invading nation" and Asian countries the "victims," but it was also a consequence of "North-South relations" in the present. Much in the way that bright areas are visible from the shadows, the poor could see the wealthy, but the reverse was not the case.[50] For Hatsuse, this mentality—this blindness—of wealthy Northern nations was the present-day manifestation of Japan's "abandoning Asia" mentality, and it would not be overcome until the Japanese had purged the prejudices informing it.[51]

The great irony of this magic mirror that engendered a blindness toward Asia was that Japanese were literally enveloped and permeated by things Asian: bananas from the Philippines; liquid natural gas from Indonesia, Brunei, and Malaysia; rubber and chicken from Thailand; and the *Japayuki*, so-called female entertainers from Thailand and the Philippines.[52] Because Asia was literally so close, Hatsuse said Japanese need not become "high-flying cosmopolitans" in the age of internationalization: rather, they could pursue "international relations in the nearby spaces of daily life"—an "internationalization within" (*uchinaru kokusaika*)—and by discovering Asia in this way, uncover the mechanism of "abandoning Asia" that powered this magic mirror.[53]

The late 1970s and 1980s witnessed a flurry of publications on politics, daily life, and Japanese entanglements in Asia, especially Southeast Asia. In contrast to publications in the early 1970s that addressed anti-Japanese sentiment in the region—the "ugly Japanese" (*minikui Nihonjin*)—the newer works had a different focus, concentrating on realities on the ground. In 1978, for example, the Nihon Ajia-Afurika Sakka Kaigi (Japan Conference of Afro-Asia writers) published *Ajia o aruku: Tōnan Ajia hen* (Walking through Asia: Southeast Asia edition), containing essays by Oda, Utsumi, Hario Ichirō, and others who wrote about life in the Philippines, Thailand, Vietnam, Singapore, Malaysia, and Indonesia.[54] In January 1983, the *Asahi jānaru* contained a special section on students in Asia, featuring Korean students' reactions to the textbook controversy, student movements in Thailand, and the new post–Cultural Revolution generation in Communist China.[55] The following year a team

50. Hatsuse, "Majikku mirā," 6 and 18.
51. Hatsuse, "Majikku mirā," 6.
52. Hatsuse, "Majikku mirā," 12–16.
53. Hatsuse, "Majikku mirā," 24.
54. Nihon Ajia-Afurika, *Ajia o aruku*.
55. *Asahi Jānaru*, "Ajia o hiraku." This special section also contained a list of Japanese civic groups involved with Asia (124–25).

of reporters from Nippon Hōsō Kyōkai (NHK) published *Ajia to no taiwa* (Dialogue with Asia), containing articles on Japanese ODA to Indonesia, attitudes toward Japan in South Korea, the Japan boom in Singapore, and a series of translated opinion pieces on Japan by Asian writers.[56] Matsui, who served as foreign correspondent for the *Asahi shinbun* newspaper in Southeast Asia in the early 1980s, produced a veritable torrent of articles and books on Asia during this decade. For instance, her 1985 *Tamashii ni fureru Ajia* (Asia pulsating with spirit) spotlighted women, children, and the poverty-stricken people of the region. In India, Matsui met with the inspiring women of the Chipko environmental movement, while in Nepal, Laos, Myanmar, Singapore, and elsewhere she investigated Buddhism, child labor, environmental destruction, and Asian reactions to the textbook controversy.[57] Matsui followed up with the 1987 *Ajia— onna—minshū (Ajia ga mietekuru 1)* (Asia—women—the people (Asia comes into view 1)), which examined the situation of women in farming communities, slums, and the sex industry. Early in this book, Matsui asked the same critical question that Hatsuse had posed: "Why can't the Japanese see Asia?"[58]

The growing attention to Asian realities also had a domestic focus. In 1985, Tanaka's *Nihon no naka no Ajia* (The Asia in Japan) described the difficulties faced by Asian exchange students and resident Koreans in Japan.[59] The book marked the beginning of Tanaka's sustained public advocacy for the human rights of foreigners in Japan, evidenced by subsequent publications like *Zainichi gaikokujin: Hō no kabe, kokoro no mizo* (Foreign residents in Japan: The barrier of law and the spiritual divide), *Kyomō no kokusai kokka: Nihon Ajia no shiten kara* (The fictitious international state: Japan from the perspective of Asia), and *"Kokusaika" no wasuremono: Rinjin toshite no gaikokujin o kangaeru* (The forgotten people of "internationalization": Thinking about foreigners as our neighbors).[60] Together with Ōnuma, Utsumi, and others, in these years Tanaka also collaborated

---

56.   Yano and Isomura, *Ajia to no taiwa.*
57.   Matsui, *Tamashii ni fureru.*
58.   Matsui, *Ajia—onna—minshū,* 9.
59.   Tanaka Hiroshi, *Nihon no naka.*
60.   Tanaka Hiroshi, *Zainichi gaikokujin* and *Kyomō no kokusai*; Tanaka Hiroshi et al., *"Kokusaika" no wasuremono.*

in numerous projects on the history of forced Chinese wartime laborers.[61] Finally, the progressive journal *Shisō no kagaku*, which had for many years been captive to American philosophy and social science theory, began to devote more attention to Asia. In 1985, for example, the publication ran a special issue titled "Ajia no tabi: 15-nen shudai" (Journey in Asia: A fifteen-year motif), with topics such as "the Asia on our dinner plates" and "Thailand, Japan, and chicken nuggets."[62] In 1988 the journal contained yet another special section titled "Nihon no naka no Ajia" (The Asia in Japan), which included articles on the lives of Asian residents and workers in downtown Tokyo such as the *Japayuki*.[63] The fact that a publication so permeated by Western (mainly American) theories and perspectives was devoting attention to a tangible Asia is testament to just how far progressives' consciousness regarding Asia had come by this time.

Within this upsurge in attention to the region among progressives starting in the late 1970s and continuing throughout the 1980s, Tsurumi Yoshiyuki emerged as perhaps the most influential activist writing on and advocating for Asia and Asian peoples in Japan. As I discussed in chapter 4, against the backdrop of Oda's "We don't know Asia" critique of the early 1970s, Tsurumi offered several thought-provoking ways forward: "thinking while walking through Asia," every person drawing their own "map" of the region, and the practice of absolute "immersion" when traveling in Asia.[64] These ideas became the core of the approach that Tsurumi and his cadre of youthful researchers took to fieldwork in the region and profoundly shaped the study of Asia in Japan thereafter, although Tsurumi would not be involved in mainstream academia until very late in life. With his focus on grounded fieldwork in the spaces of everyday life in Southeast Asia, along with his attention to the relationships of inequity between Japan and its Asian neighbors, Tsurumi exemplified the alternative internationalization from below that was unfolding among progressive activists and intellectuals at this time. Even more significantly, for Tsurumi Southeast Asia became far more than an object of research to be observed and analyzed. It also served as a model—a "teacher"—for

61. See, for example, Tanaka, Utsumi, and Niimi, *Shiryō*.
62. Kitahara, "Osara no mukō"; Tai, "Tai to chikin."
63. *Shisō no Kagaku*, ed., "Nihon no naka."
64. See below for a discussion of these ideas.

him to use in criticizing the state of Japan and proposing an alternative for a country that, in 1967, he had even proposed abandoning. The Filipino sociologist Randolf David, Tsurumi's close colleague and research collaborator, described Tsurumi as "first and foremost, a keen observer and critic of the contemporary Japanese way of life" for whom Southeast Asia "serve[d] as a kind of mirror for his readers, notably the young Japanese, so they could look at themselves in a reflective way."[65]

To be sure, Tsurumi's presentation of Southeast Asia was often romanticized, and his interpretations were open to criticism, but the notion of using Southeast Asia and its flexible cultures (*yawarakai bunka*) as models for the transformation of Japan was strikingly new because it flipped the logic of abandoning Asia on its head and challenged the seeming "certainty" of "Japan" and "Japanese culture" so lauded by *Nihonjinron* ideologues. As Tsurumi put it in 1977, "the act of observing is also a process of being observed. By observing we make new discoveries, yet we ourselves are also transformed. Hence the relationship of observer and observed is necessarily a relationship of mutual transformation."[66] Tsurumi's studies of Southeast Asia pointed to the minute and far-reaching ways in which Japanese people were connected to impoverished communities in the Philippines, Indonesia, Thailand, and elsewhere through mundane commodities like automobiles, bananas, shrimp, palm oil, tuna fish, and timber. Mainstream internationalization was mostly about the triumphant march of goods made in Japan throughout the world, but Tsurumi's alternative view of internationalization raised troubling questions about the social, economic, political, and environmental costs for fellow Asians of an endless supply of inexpensive fried shrimp and cavendish bananas. The contribution of Tsurumi and his colleagues was to demand self-reflection and action on the part of ordinary Japanese as consumers and citizens through their troubling encounter with Southeast Asia.

LEARNING FROM ASIA

Consider first the ways Tsurumi used Southeast Asia to reconsider and reimagine Japan. As we have seen, Tsurumi's trajectory toward Asia grew out

65. David, "Philippine Society Today," 12.
66. Tsurumi Yoshiyuki, "Nihon-gata," 331.

of, first, his desire to break away from the intellectual orbit of the Shisō no Kagaku Kenkyūkai (Institute for the Science of Thought) spearheaded by his cousin Tsurumi Shunsuke and, second, his distress over Japan's entanglements in the Vietnam War. Tsurumi Yoshiyuki's interest in Southeast Asia intensified from the late 1960s, beginning with his fifty-day tour of the region in 1968.[67] Around the same time, he established the Ajia to no Bunka Kōryū Keikaku (Project for Cultural Exchange with Asia) at the International House in Tokyo, which further facilitated his travels and connections in the region and, as discussed in chapter 4, resulted in the 1974 volume *Ajia kara no chokugen*.[68] In 1971 Tsurumi first convened his legendary Ajia Benkyō Kai (Asia Study Group), which had three cohorts until 1980—with each cohort containing around twenty youths who read and discussed books on the region, conducted field research, and produced pioneering reports on topics such as banana exports to Japan.[69] Moreover, after leaving full-time employment at the International House in 1973, Tsurumi helped establish PARC, which served as the organizational and spiritual base for his activities in Southeast Asia and Japan thereafter.

Throughout the 1970s and 1980s Tsurumi produced an astounding number of publications on Asia in the form of books, newspaper articles, and essays for both highbrow and mainstream journals, weeklies, and monthlies. His books from the time include *Ajiajin to Nihonjin* (Asians and Japanese; 1980), *Ajia o shiru tame ni* (for the purpose of knowing Asia) (1981), *Ajia wa naze mazushiinoka* (Why is Asia poor?; 1982), and the bestselling *Banana to Nihonjin: Firipin nōen to shokutaku no aida* (Bananas and the Japanese: Between Philippine plantations and the dining table; 1982).[70]

Despite his faithful commitment to the Japanese New Left and Beheiren in particular, over time Tsurumi became increasingly frustrated with activists' ignorance of Asia. As early as 1970, he criticized the excessive attention activists paid to the US-Japan relationship while knowing next to nothing about Asia. This condition revealed to him how even the

67. Tsurumi Yoshiyuki, "Shinraikan no ketsujo," 102.
68. Tsurumi Yoshiyuki, "Watashi no kanshin," 62. See also Tsurumi Yoshiyuki, *Ajia kara no chokugen*.
69. For more on the Ajia Benkyōkai, see Murai, "Tsurumi Yoshiyuki," 300.
70. Tsurumi Yoshiyuki, *Ajiajin to Nihonjin*, *Ajia wa naze*, and *Banana to Nihonjin*.

"anti-American" Beheiren had been unable to completely discard the mentality of "abandoning Asia" that had been written into the DNA of Japanese society since the Meiji period.[71] In response, Tsurumi began to publicly advocate for the "design of a movement" to scrutinize Japan "using Asia" and not America as a "guidepost."[72] This perspective was nothing short of avant-garde in the early 1970s, and it looked to some like the fantasies of a well-intentioned eccentric. After Tsurumi delivered a speech on learning from Asia to the Shisō no Kagaku Kenkyū Kai in 1974, the group's younger members ridiculed him as a "romantic," saying his ideas were an Asianist reincarnation of the 1910s White Birch Society (*shirakaba-ha*)—which had quixotically advocated for the unencumbered embrace of Western art, literature, and ideas in Japan.[73] Tsurumi, they felt, had merely substituted romanticism about Asia for romanticism about the West. To be sure, as the sociologist Miyauchi Taisuke (one of Tsurumi's acolytes) admitted, part of the attraction of Southeast Asia was a kind of nostalgia for a lost Japan that Tsurumi and his colleagues believed they had rediscovered there.[74]

But Tsurumi was by no means advocating a revamped Asianism. Nor was he calling on the Japanese to look through the lens of an abstract, idealized Asia, as 1950s proponents of the nonaligned movement had. On the contrary, for Tsurumi the point was to look at Japan through the confronting reality of Asia and the Third World.[75] It was about abandoning "study of the visible" (*omote-gaku*) for "study of the backwaters" (*ura-gaku*), switching attention from the busy Straits of Malacca to the "backwater thoroughfare" of the Makassar Strait.[76] Far from championing some mythical Asians, Tsurumi's project was about seeing specific people like the Batak, Minangkabau, Hakka, Bugis, Maguindanao, and Manabo—who, while collectively being "Asian," all "maintained subtly different identities."[77]

71. Tsurumi Yoshiyuki, "'Hankenryoku,'" 176.
72. Tsurumi Yoshiyuki, "'Hankenryoku,'" 176.
73. Hanasaki, "Tsurumi Yoshiyuki," 7–8.
74. Miyauchi, "Chizu no egakikata," 393.
75. Tsurumi Yoshiyuki, *Tōnan Ajia*, 8.
76. Tsurumi Yoshiyuki, "Minkangaku ni tsuite," 386.
77. Tsurumi Yoshiyuki, *Ajia wa naze*, 187.

Indeed, it was through such Southeast Asian diversity that Tsurumi identified the way forward for what he saw as a hopelessly standardized Japan. As he argued, the Japanese had consistently used rigid cultures (*katai bunka*) like the West and China as comparative yardsticks. In "classic modernization" theories, the West became a touchstone against which Japanese history was comprehended and critiqued.[78] While Takeuchi Yoshimi had certainly presented an alternative in his depiction of Japanese modernity as Western mimicry and of Chinese modernity as born of internal fortitude and resistance to the West, Tsurumi said that the comparison still resembled modernization theory inasmuch as Takeuchi viewed China, like the West, as a "universally great culture, superior to Japan." The question thus inevitably became whether Japan had attained that cultural level—and if not, why not? It was about comparing Japan to an Other assumed a priori to be "superior."[79]

But Tsurumi wondered how Japan might look through the lens of Southeast Asia, where many countries lacked strong traditions as nations, and groups had existed on the "peripheries" or even totally "outside" of the influence of great civilizations like China and India.[80] Tsurumi viewed such peripheries as "flexible cultures," to which he believed both Japan and Korea belonged.[81] In Southeast Asia, the prototype of a flexible culture was to be found in societies of the coastal mangrove swamplands, whose mode of production and daily life was both "dispersed" and "migratory."[82] If life became difficult in one region or if a headman became too overbearing, villagers would simply pack up and move elsewhere. Such a culture, Tsurumi argued, meant that nationalism remained relatively underdeveloped in Southeast Asia—or, as he put it, that "the mechanisms of the ethnic nation and the nation state" were "not absolutely necessary," and hence the people of Southeast Asia (Indonesia, the Philippines, and Malaysia in particular) continued to happily exist "without the need for nations or unified states" until they were regrettably

78. Tsurumi Yoshiyuki, "Firipin shi kara," 311.
79. Tsurumi Yoshiyuki, "Ajia wa naze mazushiika," 203.
80. Tsurumi Yoshiyuki, "Firipin shi kara," 311, and "Atarashii Ajia," 335.
81. Tsurumi Yoshiyuki, "Ajia o shiru," 250.
82. Tsurumi Yoshiyuki, *Mangurōbu no numachi*, 4.

"devoured by the Western powers."[83] In turn, no "Gandhi," "Lu Xun," or "Mao Zedong" was born from the culture of coastal swamplands, not because the people there were somehow less intellectually sophisticated than those in societies of settled cultivation, but because they were able to "live peacefully" without provoking "revolutions" or producing "great ideologies."[84] And here was the critical insight for Tsurumi: if people "could live equitably" without the need to establish a nation and all its associated ideological regalia, then it would be wrong to accuse them of backwardness and "incoherence" compared to "advanced" nation-states.[85] Indeed, this model might even remind the Japanese that their own nation (seemingly so certain and unified) had once been a scattered conglomeration of peoples too.[86]

Tsurumi's interest in the Philippines and the work of the Filipino historian Renato Constantino (1919–99) provided the intellectual stimulus for his advocacy of flexible culture. He first learned about Constantino from Filipino students while attending the Asia Is One conference for journalists in Manila in 1970. Tsurumi met the historian soon afterward and in 1977 published a translated collection of Constantino's essays under the title *Firipin nashonarizumu ron* (On Filipino nationalism).[87] As I discussed in chapter 4, Constantino was a vocal critic of Japan's postwar return to Asia in the 1970s and 1980s, accusing the country of engaging in a "second invasion" as "the little Americans of Asia," "the beachheads of Western imperialism," and "the un-Asian Asians."[88] Constantino also wrote prolifically on Filipino history, national identity, and nationalism, and he joined the movement opposing the brutal dictatorship of Ferdinand Marcos.

Tsurumi found the greatest inspiration in Constantino's conceptualization of Filipino nationalism as an "emergent formation" (*tōjō keisei*), encapsulated in the latter's 1969 *The Making of a Filipino: A Story of Philippine Colonial Politics* on the nationalist leader Claro M. Recto.[89] Astonishing for Tsurumi was that "the ethnic concept of 'Filipino'" was

83. Tsurumi Yoshiyuki, *Mangurōbu no numachi*, 4.
84. Tsurumi Yoshiyuki, *Mangurōbu no numachi*, 271.
85. Tsurumi Yoshiyuki, *Mangurōbu no numachi*, 5.
86. Tsurumi Yoshiyuki, *Mangurōbu no numachi*, 4.
87. Constantino, *Firipin nashonarizumu*.
88. Quoted in Sekai Henshūbu, "Takamaru Firipin," 162–3.
89. Constantino, *Making of a Filipino*.

"only about a century old, dating from around the time of [Japan's] Meiji Restoration," when it had referred to Spaniards born in the Philippine archipelago. In other words, "when Spain colonized this land in the early sixteenth century there was no such concept of 'We Filipinos.'" The same was true for "Malaysians" and "Indonesians," terms that were also relatively new.[90] According to Tsurumi, Philippine nationalism for Constantino became an "emergent formation" and the identity of the "Filipino" a "developing concept" (*hatten gainen*).[91] Constantino's "aim in rewriting Philippine history" was to show that "before the Filipino people had a chance to develop a sense of 'nation' they were overcome by Spanish intervention followed by American cultural imperialism," meaning that "Filipino national consciousness remained undeveloped" and was still in the process of developing.[92] "Accordingly, the only task for the Filipino people was a future history": theirs was a nationalism assigned to the future.[93] Tsurumi contrasted this condition with the staid concept of "Japan." As the notion of "being born a Japanese" implied, almost no one in Japan viewed "being Japanese" as a "developing concept," since people were simply considered "Japanese by birth." Pitifully, no one seemed to think about "reinventing 'being a Japanese'" or "becoming this or that kind of Japanese in the future."[94]

Tsurumi thus contrasted a living and dynamic history in Southeast Asia with the encumbered and static history of Japan—or in his terms, "history as willpower" (*nenryoku toshite no rekishi*) versus "history as relic" (*kaseki toshite no rekishi*; literally "history as fossil"). As he explained, "history as relic" was history "written on the basis of objective facts," whereas "history as willpower" was "an attitude in which one feels that history will not live unless it is subjectively constituted and reconstituted."[95] This was history "as the energy of subject formation that had to be conceptualized when the people of any society attempted to sketch out the shape of tomorrow. This might be called willpower" or "the energy of being exhorted

90. Tsurumi Yoshiyuki, "Atarashii Ajia," 336.
91. Tsurumi and Tsuno, "Taidan," 73. See also Constantino, *Making of a Filipino*, 4–5.
92. Tsurumi Yoshiyuki, "Firipin shi kara," 312.
93. Tsurumi Yoshiyuki, "Firipin shi kara," 313.
94. Tsurumi and Tsuno, "Taidan," 73.
95. Tsurumi Yoshiyuki, "Chizu wa ugoku," 352.

by history."[96] "I am not making the simplistic comparison that in Southeast Asia . . . there is history as willpower, while in Japan there is only history as relic," he explained. "Rather, my observation is that there is a
greater sense of urgency about having to make history among Asians."
"For the people of Southeast Asia," he noted, "history is a problem of harsh
reality, whereas for us it is merely a task of filling in the gaps in high school
world history texts."[97]

Tsurumi saw multiple benefits for Japan in learning such things from
Southeast Asia. To begin with, an awareness of the diversity in Southeast
Asian societies could help the Japanese "unravel" the "insular," "honor student" mentality written into their culture, opening the way for a "re-
excavation" of the "diversity" within Japan.[98] Rethinking Japan through
this future-focused "history as willpower" could help Japanese question the
very "certainty" of being "Japanese."[99] After all, for a great many years
Japan—like the Philippines—had been "no more than a collection of tribes
living side by side."[100] The lesson from Southeast Asia, then, was that Japanese culture could be rethought by discarding mythologies of "uniformity."
Doing so had the potential to "open up Japanese history to world history
and make possible an equal relationship between Japanese people and
peoples' of the Third World."[101] Although "being Japanese" appeared to be
an "immovable, self-evident truth," through Constantino's notion of "Filipino," Tsurumi believed that it was still possible to treat "Japan" and "the
Japanese" as "developing concepts," ideas that could be transformed.[102]

WHY IS ASIA POOR? THE POLITICAL ECONOMY
OF BANANAS

While Tsurumi worked to recast Southeast Asian culture as a model for
postwar Japan, together with colleagues he also strove just as conscientiously to expose Japan's complicity in the cycle of poverty ravaging and

96. Tsurumi Yoshiyuki, "Chizu wa ugoku," 352.
97. Tsurumi Yoshiyuki, "Chizu wa ugoku," 358.
98. Tsurumi Yoshiyuki, "Ajia o shiru," 264, and "Atarashii Ajia," 337.
99. Tsurumi Yoshiyuki, "Firipin shi kara," 313.
100. Tsurumi Yoshiyuki, "Atarashii Ajia," 337.
101. Tsurumi Yoshiyuki, "Atarashii Ajia," 337.
102. Tsurumi Yoshiyuki, "Chizu wa ugoku" 362.

incapacitating communities throughout the region. As he explained in the 1992 *Ajia wa naze mazushiinoka*, "the more people in Asia work, the poorer they become"—not because of their inefficiency or "backwardness," but because their "liberty" and "wealth" were being systematically "stolen" by multinational corporations and domestic elites who collaborated to produce products for consumption by wealthy consumers in Japan and elsewhere.[103] Tapping into the emerging international discourse on human rights, global inequity, and dependency, Tsurumi lambasted derisive accusations from advanced capitalist nations of the "immaturity of democracy" in the developing world. As he said, "make no mistake, in the nineteenth century and still today, our democracy, liberty, and affluence is to a large extent due to the poverty and violation of human rights in the societies of the Third World."[104] The structural poverty that people in countries like the Philippines faced represented not the "remnants" of an earlier colonialism but its "reproduction" in new and more invasive forms in the present.[105]

Even more distressing for Tsurumi was the fact that people in wealthy countries like Japan were seemingly oblivious to the ways such poverty supported their affluence, despite the fact that Japan had become "mired" in things Asian—Hatsuse's so-called magic mirror syndrome.[106] Japanese people had "no awareness" of the ways "supposedly beneficial" projects like the construction of dams with ODA actually "robbed" local people of their autonomy and forced them into relations of dependency. "Dams, factories, and plantations" were "foisted on the locals without any consultation," as though they had "descended from the heavens." Once impoverished communities were "drawn into this system," there was "little means of escape."[107]

Thus, the problem was not only that Japanese did not know about Asia, but also that they were blind to their complicity in its social and economic devastation—disabled by the insidious "magic mirror" in which light eclipsed the shadows. Addressing this myopia of the affluent formed

103. Tsurumi Yoshiyuki, *Ajia wa naze*, 187.
104. Tsurumi Yoshiyuki, *Ajia wa naze*, 189.
105. Tsurumi Yoshiyuki, *Ajia wa naze*, 187.
106. Tsurumi Yoshiyuki, "Chizu o egaku," 352.
107. Tsurumi Yoshiyuki, *Ajia wa naze*, 189.

the backbone of Tsurumi's writings and activism throughout the 1970s and 1980s. He first set out to understand the political economy of poverty in Asia, stretching from the plantation to the Japanese dining table, and then, armed with this knowledge, he sought to enlighten the Japanese people about their complicity in the "reproduction of poverty" and the "suppression of democracy" in Asia and the developing world.[108]

Historically speaking, Tsurumi's ideas here are evidence of yet another important evolution in postwar progressives' attention to the Asia problem, this time through the injection of concerns about justice and rights in the present. Moreover, connecting as they did to actual grassroots responses and value change among ordinary Japanese as consumers and global citizens (*chikyū shimin*), Tsurumi's public advocacy for human rights and social justice in Asia fed directly into the nascent process of grassroots globalization in Japanese civil society, albeit that process was obscured in the shadows of a resplendent internationalization.

Tsurumi's introduction to the political economy of exploitation in Asia began, once again, through his involvement in the Philippines. During his attendance at the Asia Is One conference, Tsurumi learned of an export processing zone established by order of President Marcos in the city of Mariveles on the Bataan peninsula. Marcos borrowed the idea from the Park regime in South Korea, which had created these areas to lure foreign capital through tax exemptions and other incentives.[109] As I explained in chapter 4, Japanese corporations subsequently leaped at the opportunity to relocate their most polluting manufacturing processes to South Korea. Together with Ford, the American automotive giant, corporations from Japan, Hong Kong, and Australia similarly invested in the Bataan zone in the Philippines, which exported products ranging from toys, shoes, watches, and clothing to automotive parts—many of which were labeled as being made in the investing company's country of origin. Tsurumi's fieldwork in Mariveles in the early 1970s revealed large-scale environmental destruction and social disruption. Owners of the land now occupied by the zone had been forced to relocate and, with the commencement of martial law in September 1972, essentially lost their right of appeal and protest. In their place came luxury hotels, highways,

---

108.   Tsurumi Yoshiyuki, *Ajia wa naze*, 190.
109.   David, "Philippine Society," 8.

exclusive housing estates for foreigners, and a host of other infrastructure projects that completely transformed the local environment and society. Although promoted as a new source of employment, the reality of low wages coupled with the rising cost of living meant that locals were actually worse off than before. With the support of the Marcos regime, corporations in the zone stifled union organizing by promptly dismissing militant workers. The Bataan export processing zone thus revealed to Tsurumi the reality of a neo-imperialism buttressed by the force of a ruthless dictatorship and corrupt local elites. The cruel historical irony was that this neo-imperialism was unfolding in the very same location as the Japanese army's murderous Bataan death march of 1942. How many Japanese knew of that past or this present?

Tsurumi wrote several articles on the Bataan export zone for the PARC publication *AMPO* under the pen name "Ohara Ken," but he was not convinced that discussions about far-flung "export processing zones" could ignite a response among ordinary people.[110] Necessary was something closer to daily life, something far more tangible and immediate. At first, Tsurumi turned to tuna fish, tracing where it "was being caught in the Philippines, by whom, under what circumstances, and on what terms it was exported to Japan."[111] But thanks to his involvement with David and the Third World Studies Center in Mindanao, his attention soon turned to another mundane commodity: the banana. As David later recalled, Tsurumi "was looking for the points of connection and found them in the products that were traded, in the investments that were promoted, and in the forms of official development assistance that flowed from Japan into the region. Bananas and tuna from the Philippines, shrimps and sea cucumber from Indonesia, and, from Japan, highly-polluting industries like the Kawasaki Sintering Plant in Mindanao and so-called official development assistance (ODA)—all these became for Tsurumi important signifiers of a new kind of Japanese presence in a region that was just beginning to recover from the painful memories of Japanese military aggression during the Second World War."[112] Through

110.   Murai, "Tsurumi Yoshiyuki," 298. See also Ohara, "Philippines" and "Strategies for the Asian."

111.   David, "Philippine Society," 9.

112.   David, "Philippine Society," 2.

the commonplace banana so nonchalantly consumed by Japanese people, Tsurumi realized that he could tell an important story about the "exploitive, destructive, and predatory conditions" under which plantation laborers toiled.[113] Moreover, exposing the political economy of the banana could show how the money Japanese were using to repay their "home loans" or cover their "groceries" was partially earned through the exploitation of people in Asia.[114]

Tsurumi and members of his Asia Study Group began to investigate Philippine bananas in earnest in the late 1970s, visiting plantations on Mindanao Island numerous times from 1978 to 1980. Together with David and the Third World Studies Center, in 1981 Tsurumi and his group coauthored *Transnational Corporations and the Philippine Banana Export Industry* along with an *AMPO* article titled "TNE Control of the Philippine Banana Industry."[115] To communicate their message in Japan, with the support of PARC, Tsurumi and his group put together a thirty-minute slide show provocatively titled *Hito o kū banana* (The bananas that eat people), which was thereafter widely screened by a range of civic groups, schools, and universities.[116] Tsurumi reached an even wider audience with his Hamlet-inspired 1982 essay "Banana: kūbekika, kuwazubekika" (Bananas: To eat or not to eat) for the high-circulation weekly *Asahi gurafu*.[117]

But it was Tsurumi's best-selling *Banana to Nihonjin*, published in affordable pocketbook format in 1982 that generated most interest at the grassroots level, opening the way to numerous innovative civic responses.[118] Thanks to the book, Tsurumi became something of a citizen celebrity, invited to deliver presentations for civic groups and in classrooms nationwide. Part of the book's wide-reaching appeal related to the way it scrutinized relations of inequity between Japan and the Philippines through the seemingly innocuous materiality of the banana.[119] Many readers were attracted because of their sense of unease over the ubiquitous

113. Tsurumi Yoshiyuki, "Mienai banana," 155.

114. Tsurumi Yoshiyuki, "Mienai banana," 155.

115. David et al., *Transnational Corporations*; Third World Studies Center, "TNE Control."

116. Ajia Taiheiyō, *Hito o kū*.

117. Tsurumi Yoshiyuki, "Banana."

118. Tsurumi Yoshiyuki, *Banana to Nihonjin*.

119. Tsurumi Yoshiyuki, *Banana to Nihonjin*, 133.

celebration of internationalization by politicians, business elites, and the media. *Banana to Nihonjin* became for them a kind of alternative, if not an antidote, to Prime Minister Nakasone's catchphrase "Japan, the international state," which was first enunciated in the same year the book was published.

Selling over fifty thousand copies in its first print run and written in accessible language, the book laid out the background history of Spanish and American colonialism in the Philippines, the situation of laborers working on banana plantations in Mindanao, the corporations and governments bankrolling and controlling the banana business, and the Japanese banana distribution system.[120] As Tsurumi explained, "today bananas are available year-round even in the remotest of rural areas. Given their low cost, they are now among the cheapest of fruits. As they have no seeds and are easy to peel, they are the perfect snack for children."[121] Yet this had not always been the case. Until the late 1960s most bananas were imported from Taiwan and countries in South America, like Ecuador. They were much rarer and far more expensive then.[122] But by the mid-1970s Philippine bananas—mostly from Mindanao—had come to dominate the Japanese market, increasing their share from 65 percent in 1965 to 91 percent by 1981.[123] Philippine bananas were preferred by suppliers and retailers in Japan because of their cheapness and year-round supply—made possible due to the shameful practice of ocean and river dumping of banana harvests in periods of lower consumption.[124]

Indeed, behind this story of the banana's meteoric rise in the Japanese diet lay a more sinister tale of monopolization, exploitation, and devastation. Tsurumi described "absolutely massive" banana plantations containing "hundreds and thousands of hectares" on Mindanao, 80 percent of which were owned or wholly subcontracted by multinational agribusinesses like Del Monte, Castle and Cooke (Dole), United Brands (Chiquita), and Sumitomo Trading (Bananbo).[125] As he put it, "we Japanese

---

120. Tsurumi Yoshiyuki, *Banana to Nihonjin*, 17.
121. Tsurumi Yoshiyuki, *Banana to Nihonjin*, 3.
122. Tsurumi Yoshiyuki, *Banana to Nihonjin*, 3.
123. Tsurumi Yoshiyuki, *Banana to Nihonjin*, 7.
124. Tsurumi Yoshiyuki, *Banana to Nihonjin*, 7, and "Banana," 138.
125. Tsurumi Yoshiyuki, *Banana to Nihonjin*, 10 and 12.

are eating the fruits of Filipinos' work. But it is actually the shareholders of American companies who are reaping the greatest benefits of this exchange relationship."[126] Although bananas were considered "cheap" in Japan, their selling price was eighty times the cost of their production and transport— meaning that great profits were being siphoned off by these multinational giants.

And it was the Filipino laborers of Mindanao who were paying the price with their bodies and daily lives: "When we Japanese see bananas at fruit stores or supermarkets we are inclined to think that they have been exported due to increased production in tropical regions. But . . . this is not the case." In fact, the laborers cultivating cavendish bananas on Mindanao rarely even ate them. As an introduced species, the cavendish did not suit the tastes of locals. Moreover, laborers knew firsthand about the intensive use of pesticides in banana production. In the tropical heat, few laborers used protective clothing when spraying, resulting in skin diseases and other maladies. The laborers told Tsurumi that the "strongest pesticides" were "hidden away" when buyers visited the plantations.[127] Little wonder they refused to consume the fruits of their labors. Nevertheless, divested of their traditional farming culture, Mindanao laborers had now become absolutely dependent on banana exports to Japan. Tsurumi noted the ironic juxtaposition of bananas carefully packed and transported to Japan from these remote regions versus the plantation laborers being forced to purchase canned fish from Japan because they could not afford to travel to nearby waters to fish.[128]

As Tsurumi opined in the 1982 essay for *Asahi gurafu*, "thinking about the poverty of the farmers and the pesticides, I feel like Hamlet: to eat or not to eat bananas. This 'torment of the banana' is being foisted upon the very first laborer and the final consumer."[129] Yet despite this fateful connection, Tsurumi could only lament the simultaneous "separation" between Mindanao laborers and Japanese consumers. Ultimately, Japanese consumers were interested only in questions of "price," "nutrition," and

126. Tsurumi Yoshiyuki, *Banana to Nihonjin*, 16.
127. Tsurumi Yoshiyuki, *Banana to Nihonjin*, 11; "Mienai banana," 158; and "Banana," 142.
128. Tsurumi Yoshiyuki, "Banana," 139.
129. Tsurumi Yoshiyuki, "Banana," 142.

"safety."[130] Issues of social justice and human rights did not arise. To be sure, "liberation and the restoration of independence" were certainly issues that "those involved" needed to solve by themselves. But as Tsurumi observed, "those involved" also included the Japanese people who were the ones "importing and eating" the bananas. Hence, "the most decent approach as consumers" would be "to give at least some thought to the hardships of those people growing this food."[131] Tsurumi told his readers that knowing the reality of those laborers' lives through an investigation of the banana, that most mundane of foods, could become the "the impetus for the citizens of Japan and the Philippines to join hands on equal terms" for perhaps the first time ever.[132] Although no immediate "solutions" were apparent, Tsurumi called on consumers to at least begin thinking about their "connection" to the "lives" and "production" of laborers in the Philippines.[133] The critical first step lay in analyzing the socioeconomic structure in which one was embedded, and especially how this structure crossed borders, connecting Japanese consumers to exploited, poverty-stricken laborers on Mindanao through the humble banana. This is what Tsurumi meant by each and every Japanese drawing their own map of Asia. It was about Asia becoming the wellspring for a fundamental transformation of the self, society, and Japan, the international state.

Another Internationalization: Grassroots Globalization and Asia

Building on their investigations into Philippine bananas, in subsequent years Tsurumi and his colleagues produced fascinating studies of other Asian commodities like shrimp, palm oil, bonito fish, and sea cucumber.[134] Moreover, their project to rethink Japan through Asia and to reconfigure

130. Tsurumi Yoshiyuki, *Banana to Nihonjin*, 130.
131. Tsurumi Yoshiyuki, *Banana to Nihonjin*, 131.
132. Tsurumi Yoshiyuki, *Banana to Nihonjin*, 131.
133. Tsurumi Yoshiyuki, "Mienai banana," 160.
134. See, for example, Murai, *Ebi to Nihonjin*; Tsurumi Yoshiyuki, *Namako no me*; Tsurumi Yoshiyuki and Miyauchi, *Yashi no mi*; Miyauchi and Fujibayashi, *Katsuobushi*.

the country's unequal relationship with the region dovetailed with a wider movement among NGOs and local governments, which also began to turn their attention and energies to Asia in the 1970s and 1980s. Although these entities' areas of engagement with the region were broad— including support for refugees, cultural exchange, medical assistance, grassroots infrastructure development, education, technical training, and fair trade—they shared a cluster of values and perspectives that would prove crucial in the subsequent growth of Japanese civil society. Most of all, they understood their activism as an ethical alternative, if not a direct challenge, to the West-centric internationalization propagated by big business and the Japanese government. In contrast to the state, which used hardheaded international diplomacy (*kokusai gaikō*), they advocated a softer, more empathetic, people-to-people or inter-people diplomacy founded on equitable relations between Japanese citizens and the people of Asia, as well as those in other developing regions of the world. As Matsui Yayori (herself deeply involved in Asia through the AWA) observed in 1990, the new NGOs active in Asia represented an "alternative internationalization" (*mōhitotsu no kokusaika*) at the level of ordinary "citizens" and "based on human rights and social justice."[135]

This desire to connect with fellow Asians based on equality and mutual respect resonated strongly with the postwar responsibility movement and the activities of Tsurumi. Moreover, it is evidence of the greater self-reflexivity with which progressive activists were approaching Asia by this time. Far more than the activists involved in the movements explored in chapters 3 and 4, the activists in these NGOs and local governments were at pains to emphasize the aspect of their activism in alliance with fellow Asians in relations of reciprocity. Like Tsurumi, they argued that they and all Japanese needed Asia, not as a source of natural resources, a market, or a strategic bulwark, but as a source of knowledge (a teacher) to help Japan regain a humanity lost in the process of growth and increasing affluence. In a recurrent theme among progressives at this time, knowing and engaging with Asia for these NGOs and local governments was directly linked to fundamental self-transformation within the individual, civil society, and Japan as a whole.

135. Matsui, *Shimin to enjo*, 251.

INTER-PEOPLE VERSUS
INTERNATIONAL DIPLOMACY

The Marxian economist Nagasu Kazuji (1919–99) and his policies while
governor of Kanagawa Prefecture (1975–95) led the way in defining an alternative internationalization grounded in Asia, most distinctly in his idea
(and later policy) of inter-people diplomacy. Nagasu studied economics at
the Tokyo College of Commerce (renamed Hitotsubashi University in
1949), graduating in 1944. In 1947 he joined the Department of Economics
at Yokohama National University. At that time he became involved in the
JCP, but he abandoned the party in the early 1960s in the wake of the
failed struggle against the US-Japan Security Treaty. Thereafter Nagasu
was a proponent of the so-called structural reform faction in leftist circles,
becoming a founding member of the journal *Gendai no riron*, which
served as a mouthpiece for this faction beginning in 1964. As Nick Kapur
explains, "the structural reformers were essentially realists" who "sought a
way forward to achieve socialist ends but were willing to sacrifice certain
aspects of Marxist dogma to do so. In particular, they recognized that a
party based, in theory, only on the working class . . . would be doomed to
permanent minority status in the Diet, and thus they sought a program
that would broaden their base of support to other parts of Japanese
society."[136] Such realism was a critically important factor behind Nagasu's
successful run for the governorship of Kanagawa Prefecture in 1975.

Once elected, Nagasu built his policy agenda around three ideas that
he and colleagues had been refining since the early 1970s: "the age of localism" (*chihō no jidai*), "citizen participation" (*shimin sanka*), and inter-
people diplomacy.[137] Each idea was related to the desire of Nagasu and
his colleagues to wrest power back from the powerful postwar Japanese
state, putting it in the hands of ordinary citizens who could begin the
reform of Japan from below. In 1979, Nagasu argued that the slogan "the
age of localism" had historical significance not only as an expression of
the "stance and interests of local government" but also as a tool to reem-
power ordinary citizens. "Local government," he loftily declared, was to
be a space for "nurturing, constructing, producing, and demonstrating a

136.   Kapur, *Japan at the Crossroads*, 122–23.
137.   On "citizen participation," see Avenell, *Making Japanese Citizens*, 178–91.

new democracy"—it was the "pasture" and "workshop" of democracy.[138] An integral part of this "workshop" would be the practice of inter-people diplomacy, in which ordinary citizens would construct their own connections and relationships with foreigners both outside and within Japan and that would be quite distinct from the "state diplomacy" (*kokka gaikō*) controlled by bureaucratic and political elites. Most significant for our discussion, inter-people diplomacy was, first and foremost, aimed at building grassroots relationships of equity and reciprocity between Japanese people and fellow Asians.

Nagasu had developed an interest in Asia years before entering political office, especially after a month-long tour of East Asia in 1970 with the novelist Hotta Yoshie sponsored by the magazine *Ekonomisuto*. On his return, Nagasu penned the ominously titled *Nanshin suru Nihon shihonshugi* (The southern advance of Japanese capitalism), which deftly portrayed anxieties about Japan's corporate infiltration into the region among Asian and Japanese commentators alike. As Nagasu observed, the Japanese had a "common view" of being "close" yet "far" from Asia, encapsulated in historical phases of "abandoning" and "joining" the region. Although these phases seemed "antithetical," Nagasu described them as "two sides of the same, noncontradictory, coin." The country "joined Asia" precisely because it abandoned the region: its "return" to Asia as a colonizer was nothing other than a "manifestation of the Japanese people's self-identity as an exceptional and outstanding people who were the only ones to have successfully modernized within the great sea of Asian premodernity."[139] The Japanese "energetically climbed the ladder of a hierarchically ranked world and, on reaching a fairly lofty level, cast their eyes downward as leaders and guardians of a premodern Asia" with catastrophic results.[140] Considering the penetration of the region by Japanese corporations in the present, Nagasu wondered if the country was not "once again" in danger of "repeating this earlier cycle" of "abandoning" and "returning." What guarantee was there that Japan would not "fall into the trap" that it had been caught in previously—that it would not

138.   Nagasu, *Gendai shihonshugi*, 2 and 4. On the "age of localism," see Nagasu, *Chihō no jidai*.

139.   Nagasu, *Nanshin suru Nihon*, 297.

140.   Nagasu, *Nanshin suru Nihon*, 298.

"reproduce the cycle of mistakes and tragedy?"[141] Just as Japan's first modernization had come at the expense of a "monumental failure in Asia," the country's current penetration of Asia as a "GNP superpower" risked yet another "bitter defeat and failure."[142]

Yet nothing would be changed through "pessimistic criticisms." Necessary now, Nagasu argued, was for Japan to "abandon" the "great power arrogance" of trying to be a "bridge between East and West" or an "intermediary between the North and South" and instead position itself "on the side" of "small and medium-size Asian nations, their people, and their desires for transformation."[143] Regardless of how "agonizing" it might be, Nagasu told readers that ordinary Japanese needed to "dissect" their "view of Asia" and their "ignorance" of the region as a first step toward building a new "Japan in Asia."[144] In 1975 Nagasu would elaborate this perspective in the idea and policy program of inter-people diplomacy.

Nagasu was neither the first nor the only politician—local or national, conservative or progressive—to focus on Asia in the 1970s. As I noted in chapter 4, facing criticism and sometimes violent protest in Southeast Asia, the national government also began to develop its cultural diplomacy with the region more carefully in these decades. The two key developments of the 1970s in this connection were the establishment of the Japan Foundation in 1972 and the so-called Fukuda Doctrine of 1977, in which the prime minister vowed to build heart-to-heart relationships between Japan and countries in the Association of Southeast Asian Nations (ASEAN). Into the 1980s Prime Minister Nakasone and his successor, Takeshita Noboru, both supported increased cultural exchanges with the region. After meeting with former exchange students during a visit to Southeast Asia in 1983, Nakasone directed the minister of education to establish a private panel to formulate a "plan for one hundred thousand exchange students."[145] Four years later Takeshita doubled the budget of the Japan Foundation, after learning of the lack of progress in cultural exchanges with Southeast Asia during his visit there. The foundation was

141. Nagasu, *Nanshin suru Nihon*, 305.
142. Nagasu, *Nanshin suru Nihon*, 1.
143. Nagasu, *Nanshin suru Nihon*, 373.
144. Nagasu, *Nanshin suru Nihon*, 1.
145. Hirano and Sengo Nihon, *Sengo Nihon*, 8–9.

overjoyed by its newly brimming coffers, and in a 1989 report it christened 1987 "year one of the international cultural exchange era" (*kokusai bunka kōryū gannen*).[146] With a mandate to build cultural relations throughout Asia, in 1990 the foundation established the ASEAN Culture Center—which in 1996, under the Murayama government, further expanded its remit and was renamed the Asia Center.

Throughout the 1970s and increasingly in the 1980s, local governments around Japan also began to pay more attention to building ties with the region as well as Asian communities within Japan.[147] One of the earliest people to act was Minobe Ryōkichi, the progressive governor of Tokyo from 1967 to 1979, who implemented favorable policies for resident Koreans in the capital and made high-profile visits to Communist China and North Korea. Fukuoka City also became a hub for Asian art and culture in Japan through the city's art museum, which collected and displayed Asian art from the time of its establishment in 1979.[148] Bucking the West-centric overtones of internationalist discourse in these decades, city officials purposely designed their international policy around Fukuoka City as a "base for human exchange in the Asian region."[149] In 1987 the city's *Sixth Basic Policy Plan* described Fukuoka as an "Asian hub" (*Ajia no kyoten toshi*), and after organizing the Asia-Pacific Exposition in 1989, the city began having an annual "Asia month" and an "Asia-Focused Fukuoka Film Festival," along with awarding the Fukuoka Asian Culture Prize (later the Fukuoka Prize) to people who made significant contributions to academia, the arts, and culture in the region.[150]

Nagasu's inter-people diplomacy unfolded at the cutting edge of these developments in cultural policy in the 1970s and 1980s. In his inaugural gubernatorial address, Nagasu declared that "the only way for Japan to survive in a transforming Asia" would be "to seek a new international order and mode of international exchange based on shared rights, equality,

---

146. Kokusai Kōryū Kikin, *Kokusai bunka*.
147. Hirano and Sengo Nihon, *Sengo Nihon*, 15.
148. Hirano and Sengo Nihon, *Sengo Nihon*, 9.
149. Hirano and Sengo Nihon, *Sengo Nihon*, 172.
150. See http://fukuoka-prize.org/en/. Interestingly, in 2019 the prize was awarded to Randolf David who, as I explained above, was Tsurumi's primary contact and research partner in the Philippines in the early 1980s.

self-determination, and reciprocity with other peoples."[151] To this end, Kanagawa Prefecture would adopt an "inter-people diplomacy," accompanying the "international diplomacy of the nation" and "connecting citizens of different countries."[152] Under Nagasu's leadership, Kanagawa was among the first prefectures in Japan to establish a *kokusai kōryū ka* (international exchange office), which became a prototype for other prefectures and municipalities.[153] In keeping with his notion of local government as the "back office" (*jimukyoku*) for civil society, in 1977 Nagasu set up the Kanagawa-ken Kokusai Kōryū Kai (Kanagawa Prefecture International Exchange Association) to foster ties among civic groups involved in intercultural exchange.[154] In 1982 the prefecture began funding inter-people diplomacy initiatives, creating the Kokusai Kōryū Renraku Kai (International Exchange Liaison Committee) in 1984 to promote grassroots networking and, in 1987, providing a physical space for civic groups known as the Kanagawa Information Station.[155] As a result, the number of groups in Kanagawa that were involved in international exchange with Asia proliferated.[156] In an era before systematic governmental support for international NGOs and volunteer organizations in Japan, Nagasu's inter-people diplomacy policies undoubtedly nurtured the growing social awareness in Japan during the 1980s of the need for, and value of, NGOs and civil society more generally. Nagasu developed a particularly strong relationship with the Japan Volunteer Center (JVC), a pioneering international NGO, after visiting members of the group at a refugee camp in Thailand to deliver twenty-six million yen in donations collected from Kanagawa residents after the Indochina refugee crisis in 1980 (discussed below). Thereafter the prefecture supported JVC operations in far-off Ethiopia and engaged the organization to run an international forum on inter-people diplomacy in the late 1980s.[157]

---

151.   Quoted in Hirano and Sengo Nihon, *Sengo Nihon*, 20.

152.   Kanagawa Ken Shōgai Bu, *Minsai gaikō*, 5.

153.   In 1980 only 7 prefectures had international exchange offices, but this number rose to 21 in 1986, 211 in 1987, and 417 in 1995. See Tanami, "Sengo Nihon," 41.

154.   Nagasu, *Chihō no jidai*, 177.

155.   Hirano and Sengo Nihon, *Sengo Nihon*, 93.

156.   Hirano and Sengo Nihon, *Sengo Nihon*, 92.

157.   Kanagawa Ken, *Minsai gaikō*, 18.

The Nagasu administration's involvement with the JVC also reveals another extremely important aspect of the inter-people idea: namely, its sensitivity to the Asia within. The Indochina refugee crisis of the late 1970s and early 1980s and subsequent arrival of so-called boat people in Japan was an important stimulus here. In 1980 Kanagawa Prefecture agreed to a request from the central government to establish the Yamato Nanmin Teijū Sokushin Sentā (Yamato Refugee Settlement Promotion Center), run by the Ajia Fukushi Kyōiku Zaidan (Asian Welfare and Education Foundation), to provide temporary housing and support for the new arrivals.[158] At a public gathering called the Indoshina Nanmin Mondai o Kangaeru Tsudoi (Gathering to Consider the Indochina Refugee Problem) in that year, prefectural officials pointed out the "distress" of refugees forced to live away from their home country and, accordingly, the need to build a local society in which people from different nations could live with dignity. To this end, Kanagawa Prefecture began to offer subsidies to civic groups that provided volunteer services for refugees, and it facilitated newcomers' access to public housing.[159] In the late 1980s the prefecture engaged the JVC to conduct a survey of Indochinese refugees, examining their daily lives, access to education and employment, and overall adaptation to and acceptance in Japan.[160] So-called oldcomers like resident Koreans were not forgotten either, and indeed the policy of inter-people diplomacy within the prefecture was in great part a response to the international human rights covenants signed and ratified around this time.[161] In 1980 the prefecture initiated its "inter-people diplomacy within" policy by sponsoring a lecture by Tanaka on the "status and challenges of resident foreigners," and in 1984 it published the results of an extensive survey of resident Koreans living in the prefecture under the title *Kanagawa no Kankoku-Chōsenjin: Jichitai genba kara no teigen* (South and North Koreans in Kanagawa prefecture: recommendations from the seat of local government).[162]

158.　For more on this center, see Ajia Fukushi Kyōiku, *Yamato teijū.*

159.　Kanagawa Ken Shōgai Bu, *Minsai gaikō 20-nen*, 8.

160.　See Kanagawa Kennai Gaikokujin, *Kanagawa kennai zaijū.*

161.　Kanagawa Ken Shōgai Bu, *Minsai gaikō*, 80.

162.　Kanagawa Ken Shōgai Bu, *Minsai gaikō 20-nen*, 7; Kanagawa Ken Jichi, *Kanagawa no Kankoku.*

Whether or not such initiatives resulted in substantive improvements for resident Koreans is debatable, as is the overall impact of Nagasu's inter-people initiative in the long run. As Hirano and his colleagues note, inter-people diplomacy was hampered by its implicit structure of "proactive" Japanese providing assistance to "vulnerable" and "passive" foreigners, who were "excluded" from playing an active role in the creation of their future in Japan—albeit unintentionally and in the context of good intentions.[163] "Reciprocity" and "equality" looked fine on paper and in political speeches but proved far more difficult to attain in practice.

Nevertheless, to the extent that the welfare and human rights of both newcomer and oldcomer Asians had entered the consciousness of local officials by the late 1980s, Nagasu's inter-people diplomacy can be considered to have made progress, particularly in laying a foundation for future endeavors. In the 1990s more and more local governments around Japan took up the challenge of integrating foreign residents—especially those from Asia—into local society, but they replaced Nagasu's idea of inter-people diplomacy with a new discourse on multicultural coexistence (*tabunka kyōsei*). Thereafter such local initiatives would continue to develop alongside—and often in tension with—starkly divergent approaches to Asia at the national level.

INTERNATIONAL NGOS AND ASIA

As we saw in chapter 4, Japanese grassroots transnational activism in Asia began to expand and diversify from around the early 1970s, with new movements focused on Japanese pollution export, political dictatorships, and sex tourism. This trend continued throughout the decade and intensified during the 1980s. In the context of the Asia problem and deimperialization, the new NGOs of the 1980s were important in at least three ways. First, although many were initially motivated by a somewhat unsophisticated sense of charity, as their involvement deepened, the development of relationships based on reciprocity, equity, and mutual respect with other Asians became a core value of their activism. Second, reflexivity also animated these new NGOs: in other words, the process of helping fellow Asians was also about reconsidering and transforming their

163. Hirano and Sengo Nihon, *Sengo Nihon*, 96–97.

own attitudes and daily lives and, if possible, effecting fundamental change in Japan. And third, the new NGOs' involvement in Asia contributed to the alternative internationalization (what I am calling grassroots globalization) that began to unfold in Japanese civil society around the 1980s. Journeying into Asia served as a conduit for activists to be socialized in a host of new norms and practices relating to social justice, human rights, the environment, and grassroots development. Such learning in Asia fed back into the development of civil society within Japan in the 1980s and beyond.

In fact, a handful of faith-based Japanese NGOs had been active in Asia since the 1960s, their activities motivated primarily by notions of religious charity. One example is the Asian Rural Institute (Ajia Gakuin; ARI), a Christian group established in Tokyo in 1960 and run by the Reverend Takami Toshihirō. The ARI's activities have involved bringing students from Asia and Africa to Japan for ten months at a time to study methods for improving agricultural productivity and rural standards of living. The movement originated in a request for Japanese churches to train Asian rural pastors made during the inaugural meeting of the Christian Council of Asia in Malaysia in 1959.[164] Also in 1960, the Japan Overseas Christian Medical Service (Nihon Kirisutokyō Kaigai Iryō Kyōryokukai; JOCS) was established to facilitate the provision of medical services by Japanese doctors in Asia—similar to Médecins Sans Frontières, which was established over a decade later. Finally, in 1961, the conservative, nationalist-leaning Organization for Industrial, Spiritual, and Cultural Advancement (OISCA) was established as an outgrowth of a new Shinto-based religion for the promotion of rural development in areas of Asia.[165] In addition to their Christian orientation, both the ARI and the JOCS brought a strong sense of war remorse and responsibility into their activism. As the founding statement of the JOCS pronounced, "Accompanying our great sense of responsibility for the war our country waged on brethren in nearby countries, in the presence of God, we express remorse for the error of militarist aggression and, in a spirit of

164. See http://www.ari-edu.org/.

165. See http://www.oisca.org/. For more on this complicated and fascinating movement, see Chika Watanabe, *Becoming One*.

repentance, we have accepted the appeal from our Asian brethren as a call from God."[166] In fact, the JOCS could trace it roots back to 1938, when a young Christian pastor in Kyoto organized Christian medical students into a field treatment unit that traveled to China to treat Chinese victims of the war with Japan that had begun in 1937. As hostilities worsened, the group was forced to return to Japan, and its efforts in Asia did not resume until the establishment of the JOCS in 1960.[167]

But except for a few pioneering NGOs like PARC, the watershed in terms of the establishment of new international NGOs was the Indochinese refugee crisis in 1978–80, following the commencement of Vietnamese military incursions into Cambodia. The ending of the Vietnam War and the existence of the so-called killing fields of the Khmer Rouge in Cambodia also played a role. As a result, in the late 1970s thousands of Vietnamese, Laotian, and Cambodian refugees began to pour into makeshift camps in Thailand. The first boat people from Indochina had already arrived in Japan in 1975, but it was not until 1978 that the Japanese media began extensively reporting on Southeast Asian refugees. Shocked to learn of the absence of any Japanese groups involved in the humanitarian effort to help these people, which was led mainly by Western NGOs, Japanese individuals and groups motivated by a strong sense of civic consciousness mobilized in support. The result was an upsurge—an "explosive increase," in one telling—in new NGO formations, prompting some to designate 1979 "Year One of the NGO Era" (*NGO gannen*).[168] In 1978–80 forty-three new NGOs were established—a number that seems small but is impressive nonetheless, given that a 1980 directory of Japanese international NGOs indicated a total of only fifty-nine in the country.[169] Importantly, some of Japan's most influential NGOs, both domestically and internationally, were established during this crisis in Asia, including the JVC (1980), Shanti Volunteer Association (SVA) (1981), Association for Aid and Relief Japan (AAR) (1979), Nippon International Cooperation for Community Development (NICCO) (1979), and Caring for

166. Nihon Kirisutokyō Kaigai, "Kihon hōshin."
167. Itō Michio, "NGO no kokusai," 93.
168. Gaimushō, *Nihon NGO renkei*, 1; Hirano and Sengo Nihon, *Sengo Nihon*, 81.
169. Hirata, *Civil Society*, 34.

Young Refugees (CYR) (1980).[170] As Keiko Hirata observes, "these NGOs maintained high visibility and stimulated people either to join them or organize similar groups." While the crisis did not precipitate a "full-scale NGO movement in Japan . . . it did serve as a catalyst for later NGO activism."[171]

Furthermore, other issues such as poverty, human rights, health, fair trade, and the environment in Asia also encouraged NGO formation in Japan during these decades, represented by pioneering groups like Shapla Neer = Citizens Committee in Japan for Overseas Support (1972), PARC (1973), the Japan Silver Volunteers (1977), the PHD (for Peace, Health, and human Development) Association (1981), the Japan Committee for Negros Campaign (JCNC; 1986), and the Japan Rainforest Action Network (JATAN) (1987).[172] Asia-focused NGOs also began to form networks like the People's Forum on Cambodia, the Mekong Watch Network Japan, the Japan NGO Network on Indonesia, the Nippon NGO Forum for Nepal, and the Burma People's Forum.[173] Network hubs like the Japan NGO Center for International Cooperation (JANIC) (1987), the Kansai NGO Council (1987), and the Nagoya NGO Center (1988) also served as vocal mouthpieces for these NGOs within Japan, with JANIC playing a particularly important role in the movement for regulatory reform in the nonprofit sector in the 1990s.[174] In short, Japanese NGOs active in Asia and their networks formed at this time served as a critical foundation for the development of the country's civil society thereafter.

But as I have suggested, these new NGOs were also important in the context of the Asia problem and deimperialization. Like Ōnuma, Tsurumi, and others, they challenged the mentality of "abandoning Asia and joining the West" through their commitment to relationships of equality and reciprocity. Moreover, they recognized the value of Asia as

170. I use the current names of these organizations here. See https://www.ngo-jvc .net/, https://sva.or.jp/english/, https://www.aarjapan.gr.jp/, https://kyoto-nicco.org/, and http://www.cyr.or.jp/.

171. Hirata, *Civil Society*, 32.

172. See https://www.shaplaneer.org/, http://parc-jp.org/index.html, http://www .jsv.or.jp/, http://www.phd-kobe.org/, https://www.apla.jp/aboutus/jcnc, and http:// www.jatan.org/.

173. Hirata, *Civil Society*, 45.

174. See https://www.janic.org/, http://kansaingo.net/, and http://nangoc.org/.

a teacher—a reflexive vehicle—through which to critique, reimagine, and transform themselves and Japan. We can see evidence of this mentality in the activities of any number of NGOs of the time. JVC activists, for instance, were acutely aware of the link between the devastation they discovered in Thai refugee camps and Japanese affluence. A JVC activist described the organization's view that the "problems of so-called 'developing' regions are deeply connected to Japanese policies and society, hence solutions to these problems demand a transformation in our lifestyles. Thus, we seek 'self-transformation accompanied by toil' from the Japanese people. In other words, we say 'please support our activities and, moreover, change your own lifestyle.'"[175] Along with providing "sympathy" for and "goodwill" toward those in distress, the JVC aimed to "raise questions about contemporary Japanese society," interrogating "the political and economic structure supporting . . . Japanese affluence."[176] Key to this self-reflexivity was the ability to go further than providing charity or aid to a poor Asia. The goal was to see the human face of Asia. As one JVC activist named Hoshino Shōko wrote in 1990, what she found most "different" about the Japanese volunteering in the refugee camps compared to those at home was that they treated "Asians other than Japanese" as "human beings" just "like themselves."[177]

This desire to truly know fellow Asians (and hence the self) rather than simply helping faceless Asians is a common theme among NGOs of the time, although it was something learned through trial and error. Shapla Neer is a case in point. The organization was established by Christian youths in the early 1970s who had traveled to Bangladesh to provide emergency volunteer assistance in the wake of the country's civil war of 1971. On returning to Japan they established the Help Bangladesh Committee to raise funds to purchase pencils and other educational materials for impoverished children in Bangladesh. To their dismay, after sending the materials the youths learned that these children were quickly exchanging the items for food. Thereafter the group slowly became attuned to the limits of one-sided charity and the need to develop equal relationships based on mutual communication. Instead of simply sending resources,

175. Nakano Emi, "Shimin o dō tsunagaruka," 188–89.
176. JVC, "Hajime ni," 3.
177. JVC, "Hajime ni," 6.

Shapla Neer activists shifted their focus to helping local communities empower themselves—for instance, by selling in Japan handicrafts produced by Bangladeshi women. Moreover, the NGO decided that local operations should be in the hands of locals with Japanese serving merely in a supporting role, a process it called participatory development. In the course of forging this more equitable and reciprocal relationship with Bangladeshis in the 1970s and 1980s, Shapla Neer activists (like those in the JVC) came to appreciate the value of the movement for themselves: it caused a gradual shift in consciousness from knowing and helping Bangladesh to knowing and helping Japan. As a 1989 movement publication noted, "we have no intention of changing Bangladesh, nor are we trying to fulfill governmental responsibilities. Our impact is very limited, but in reality, what we want to change is our society and the nature of Japan's involvement internationally. In other words, it is about the attitudes of Japanese toward cooperation and assistance, and toward the downtrodden."[178]

Kusachi Ken'ichi (1941–2000) of the PHD Association articulated the reflexively driven agenda of the new NGOs perhaps better than anyone else, couching his ideas in a critique of both charity and the West-centric overtones of international exchange. The association was established in 1981 with seed funding from its founder, Iwamura Noboru (1927–2005), who had served as a field doctor in Nepal for the JOCS from 1962 to 1980. Iwamura wanted the PHD Association, like other Japanese international NGOs established at this time, to transcend the supplying of temporary aid in the form of providing money and resources in favor of people-to-people exchange and education at the grassroots level. Critically, for Iwamura this was to be a bidirectional process. As he put it, "offering 10 percent [of our income] for people at the grassroots [level] in Asia and the South Pacific, the PHD movement is about producing new human relationships within Japan around both you and me."[179] Specifically, the organization hosts youths from Asia and the South Pacific in Japan for training in various fields like agriculture, nursing, dressmaking, hygiene, and sanitation.[180]

178. Shapura Nīru, *Shapura Nīru*, 16.
179. http://www.phd-kobe.org/about/.
180. Jichitai Kokusaika Fōramu, "Kurōzu appu NGO-NPO," 43.

Kusachi, a Christian pastor and leader in the YMCA, joined the association in 1984. He traced his commitment to the situation of Asia and the Third World to two formative factors. The first was his activism in movements for children in the coal-mining Chikuhō region of Kyūshū during his student days. Here, Kusachi encountered Koreans, Burakumin, and other poverty-stricken people who were discriminated against and forced to work in oppressive industries for low wages: "This structure of oppression and oppressed is present in the Third World today, and quite inevitably the condition of the Third World [is] connected to my activism while a student."[181]

The second factor was Kusachi's sense of war responsibility as a Japanese Christian. He explained that, based on his church's declaration of "war responsibility" in 1967, in 1973 he traveled to Asia to engage in relief work as part of the process of atonement.[182] This sense of responsibility underwrote Kusachi's approach to the association. Like Iwamura, Kusachi rejected one-sided charity, which he viewed as hierarchical and producing only division and dependency among recipients. Although the PHD Association had begun by providing medical assistance, activists learned that "no matter how much assistance" they offered, "the number of patients failed to decrease because, ultimately, people did not have sufficient food." Kusachi says that the activists realized that "it would be critical for people to solve and overcome" the problem of "food supply and equitable distribution" through "their own efforts." The association thus committed itself to complementing its relief work with cooperative work based on mutual learning, communication, and solidarity.[183]

Kusachi contrasted this approach with mainstream "international exchange," "international cooperation," and "cultural understanding," fashionable terms frequently "bandied about" but lacking in clarity.[184] More to the point, he observed that "exchange" could easily degenerate into "serving tea, arranging flowers, and introducing traditional Japanese culture to blond-haired, blue-eyed (Caucasian) foreigners," while international

181. Kusachi, *Ajia kusanone*, 205.
182. Kusachi, *Ajia kusanone*, 206.
183. Kusachi, *Ajia kusanone*, 207.
184. Kusachi, *Ajia kusanone*, 208.

"cooperation" became nothing more than "collecting money and materials to help 'poor, starving, backward' Asians out of our sense of charity."[185] Moreover, he could not help but sense the "Hinomaru" (Japanese flag) and "Kimigayo" (Japanese national anthem) floating behind the Japanese government's emphasis on "international understanding." The PHD Association, in contrast, was not at all about "justifying" the Japanese way of life but about "pursuing a major transformation in lifestyle through exchange with the villagers of grassroots Asia who have an abundance of spirit over material wealth." "Exchange" needed to be "for the benefit of both sides, and not only for the benefit of one."[186] It was important for Kusachi that activists develop an appreciation of the global injustice fueling poverty and their complicity therein. When people recognized that "affluence" was "concentrated in the Northern countries and enjoyed by them alone," they began to approach the mentality of "global citizens" cognizant of the fact that "assistance" and "cooperation" were not about "charity" but rather about "transcending 'injustice.'"[187] The goal was to move from a consciousness of "poor Asia" to one of "Asia being made poor."[188]

Here again we can see the self-reflexive moment of activism evident in other NGOs. As Kusachi put it, "through such interaction with Asia, our own lifestyles have come into question, we have learned many things, and this learning has outweighed [what we have given]. It is not at all a question of doing something for backward, pitiful, filthy, poor, ignorant, and indolent Asia. Daily we are taught that it is we who must change."[189]

Thanks to the writings and advocacy of Tsurumi and PARC, and drawing on the mandate articulated by Kusachi and others, in the 1980s several innovative new NGOs turned their attention to bananas in an attempt to forge relations of equity and reciprocity with fellow Asians as well as to reform their daily lives. A small-scale, yet emblematic, example was the Firipin Banana to Watashitachi Nagoya Gurūpu (Philippine Bananas and Us Nagoya group), which was established in late 1980 after

185. Kusachi, *Ajia kusanone*, 183.
186. Kusachi, *Ajia kusanone*, 203.
187. Kusachi, *Ajia kusanone*, 23.
188. Kusachi, *Ajia kusanone*, 184.
189. Kusachi, *Ajia kusanone*, 206.

activists heard a talk on the dire situation of Filipino banana plantation laborers by a visiting representative known as Dodon Santos (a pseudonym). Over the ensuing three years the group's activities evolved from simple self-study on the Philippine banana issue to public advocacy and activism. In 1982, for instance, the group began showing PARC's slide show "bananas eating people" together with a homemade storyboard presentation titled *Banana monogatari* (Banana story). The following year the group established the Firipin Jōhō Sentā Nagoya (Nagoya Center for Philippine Concerns), which communicated information from the Philippines otherwise ignored in the Japanese print and electronic media. To better understand realities on the ground, the group studied the regional distribution of Philippine bananas at the Hiwajima wholesale market in Nagoya, and in late 1983 representatives traveled to Mindanao to observe the operations of banana plantations firsthand. In terms of public advocacy, the group sent an open letter to the Sumitomo Trading Company asking for details of its dealings in Philippine bananas and its understanding of the working conditions of laborers on plantations.[190]

Most significant about the Nagoya group was the way activists couched their movement in terms of social justice and the human rights of Asian workers. As the movement's leaders explained, the Philippine banana problem was not only about the "rights and wrongs" of consumption, nor was it simply a problem of "reducing pesticides" to make the bananas "safer." On the contrary, it was about the "human rights of those producing or, rather, those forced to produce bananas."[191] Considering the problem only from the perspective of "consumers" resulted in a myopic, self-interested, concern with "pesticide residues, price, shape, size, and freshness" and left no room to consider the "pain and suffering" of the plantation laborers. But when laborers' perspectives were considered, the Philippine banana issue was transformed into questions about whether people were being "respected as human beings in society" and "whether their basic right to survival and fundamental human rights" were "present and guaranteed."[192]

190. On the activism of this group, see Ikezumi, Sugimoto, and Nakamura, *Banana kara jinken*, 16, 23, 30, and 38–39.

191. Ikezumi, Sugimoto, and Nakamura, *Banana kara jinken*, 185–86.

192. Ikezumi, Sugimoto, and Nakamura, *Banana kara jinken*, 186.

Moreover, as was the case with the other NGOs discussed above, leaders of the Nagoya group recognized that their encounter with the inequities of banana production in the Philippines simultaneously raised questions about their daily lives in Japan. As Ikezumi Yoshinori and fellow members explained in 1988, Japan certainly "needed Asia," but not for the predictable reasons relating to "growth and affluence in the Japanese economy." Instead, in a "dehumanized" Japan of "excessive consumption," Asia was absolutely necessary for the rediscovery and recovery of a lost humanity. Their movement was just as much about "learning from Asia" as it was about helping plantation laborers. "Asia," they declared, was "Japan's teacher."[193]

The JCNC went even further than the Nagoya group in constructing an alternative relationship with fellow Asians. The original spark for the movement came when people learned of widespread malnutrition on Negros Island in the southern Philippines, due to unemployment and poverty among tenant sugarcane farmers following the 1970s collapse in global sugar prices.[194] The JCNC initially provided emergency relief in the form of food supplies and medicine however, like many other Japanese international NGOs of the time, soon switched to initiatives for the restoration of Negros farmers' daily lives and livelihoods.[195] The JCNC pursued to the utmost what one of its leaders called "international cooperation with a human face." This meant fashioning its support in dialogue with the people of Negros—who, in the words of one local activist, needed "fishing nets," not "fish."[196] In response, the JCNC initiated a range of livelihood restoration programs such as agricultural training seminars and the provision of agricultural tools, seeds, and even buffalos.[197]

Among the most innovative of the JCNC's projects was the so-called Alter-Trade initiative, which involved Japanese consumer groups and Negros farmers starting in the late 1980s. The idea for the initiative was hatched during the famed Banana Boat cruise by members of Japanese

---

193. Ikezumi, Sugimoto, and Nakamura, *Banana kara jinken*, 175.
194. Hotta Masahiko, "Munōyaku banana . . . (jō)," 153; Akiyama Naoe, "Banana minshū," 13.
195. Hotta Masahiko, "Munōyaku banana . . . (jō)," 153.
196. Quoted in Akiyama Naoe, "Banana minshū," 16.
197. Akiyama Naoe, "Banana minshū," 16.

civic groups from Kobe to Ishigakijima in late 1986.[198] Among the passengers were two guests from the Philippines, who asked the Japanese activists to consider direct imports of agricultural products from Negros. After an initial experiment with Mascobado sugar, in 1989 the Green Coop alliance of consumer cooperatives agreed to purchase and distribute pesticide-free Balangon bananas imported from Negros.[199] The Green Coop's interest in this project stemmed from coop members' concerns (informed by Tsurumi's 1982 best seller) about food safety and the violation of laborers' human rights inherent in the globalized banana agribusiness.[200] Above all, activists portrayed the Alter-Trade initiative as a method for Japanese consumers to appreciate bananas as both "commodities" and "learning resources"—in other words, as a way to uncover the mechanisms operating beneath everyday commodities and the effects of these mechanisms on their own lives and the lives of the people producing the commodities.[201] As JCNC leader Hotta Masahiko explained in 1990, activists realized that "to think about the independence of the Negros people was also to think about the independence of the Japanese people."[202] Through grassroots people-to-people trade (*minshū kōeki*), the JCNC and its collaborators believed that the "Japanese kitchen" would be "opened up to Asia," and people could "experience the joy of collaborating together" and "building the future" with their "own hands."[203] Such collaboration and reciprocity transcended the somewhat "simplistic" notion of the Japanese making amends for their role as "perpetrators" on the one hand, and the people of Negros receiving assistance as the "victims" on the other hand.[204] Indeed, thanks to the people of Negros, Japanese activists and consumers had been presented with the gift of being empowered to reconsider their own daily lives.

As Hirano and his colleagues explained, one unintended consequence of this NGO activity in Asia in the 1970s and 1980s was the emergence among Japanese activists of a consciousness of the "self as Asian." As their

198.   On this cruise, see Avenell, *Making Japanese Citizens*, 228–29.
199.   Andō, *Nyūrefuto undō*, 193.
200.   Hotta Masahiko, "Munōyaku banana . . . (ge)," 153.
201.   Hotta Masahiko, "Munōyaku banana . . . (ge)," 153.
202.   Quoted in Takayanagi, "7," 225.
203.   Hotta Masahiko, "Munōyaku banana . . . (ge)," 163.
204.   Andō, *Nyūrefuto undō*, 196–97.

networks grew and strengthened, activists began to see the connections between their international activities in Asia and problems back at home, like the situation of resident Koreans. They began to imagine civil society as a community that transcended borders in both directions—Japan in Asia and Asia in Japan. For some observers, this mentality spoke to the emergence of a New Asianism within Japanese progressives' thinking and activism. The historian Uemura Kimio described these new movements of "anonymous citizens" focused on Asia as the harbingers of a new "grassroots Asianism" in the postwar era, aimed at addressing the entanglements between Japanese daily life and Asia such as "chicken yakitori" from Thailand or "cup ramen shrimp" from India.[205] Hatsuse agreed. In contrast to prewar versions of Asianism focused on Asian nation-states, he said that the Asianism of the 1980s was about "people to people" ties at the level of everyday life. Their Asianism was a philosophy focused on respect for human rights and the pursuit of international coexistence, especially coexistence within Asia.[206] To be sure, very few—if any—of the new Japanese NGOs characterized their activism in the region as "Asianism," but they were undoubtedly moving beyond earlier notions of Asia as Other and toward an imagination of Japan as part of a collective Asian community—in other words, the "self as Asian."[207]

Conclusion

The discourse on postwar responsibility, the thought and activism of Tsurumi, the initiatives of local governments like Kanagawa Prefecture, and the new international NGOs of the 1970s and 1980s were connected by a shared attention to Japan's relationship with Asia, refracted through the lens of human rights and questions of historical, social, and economic justice. These phenomena demonstrate just how important discussions about, and attention to, Asia were becoming in the evolution of Japanese civil society and the public sphere by the late 1980s. Throughout the 1970s

---

205.   Uemura Kimio, "Sengo shi," 52.
206.   Hatsuse, "Ajiashugi," 24.
207.   Hirano and Sengo Nihon, *Sengo Nihon*, 12.

and 1980s, Asia emerged as a critical space for self-reflexive learning and transformation among Japanese progressive intellectuals and activists in ways not evidenced earlier. In debates over postwar responsibility, the ideas of Asian intellectuals like Constantino, mundane commodities like bananas, and concrete humanitarian efforts and fair-trade initiatives, Asian issues and Asian people forced Japanese progressives and conscientious consumers alike to reconsider the foundations of postwar growth and affluence. At the same time, the region also served as a space for Japanese activists to absorb and put into practice the norms of an emerging global civil society, especially notions of human rights and social justice. This alternative internationalization or grassroots globalization rooted in Asia challenged—without dismantling—the potent and self-congratulatory discourse of internationalization that was championed by corporations and conservative leaders in the period. It also hinted at a new future of Asian community. With the end of the Cold War and the apparent waning of "Japan, the international state" in the 1990s, ideas about regional community building and multicultural coexistence would come to dominate progressive discourse on Asia.

CHAPTER 6

The Breakthrough

Asian Community and Identity
in a Time of Change

In 1995, the Japanese literary critic Katō Norihiro (1948–2019) ignited a storm of criticism with the publication of a provocative essay titled "Haisengoron" (After defeat) published in the highbrow monthly publication *Gunzō*.[1] Katō's essay asserted that for the Japanese people to express genuine remorse to the twenty million Asian war dead, they first needed to fashion a national subject capable of mourning the country's own three million lost souls.[2] Although hardly the stuff of far-right historical denialism, as Harry Harootunian observes, by privileging national mourning—indeed, making it a precondition for any apology to Asia—"even in commemoration" Katō managed to reproduce "the structure of colonialism among the dead."[3] Moreover, by presenting the nation as a homogeneous ethnic body, Katō implicitly excluded those not sharing a "certain mystical relationship to 'Japan's' war dead," in effect obliterating the Asia within while replicating the country's time-honored logic of separation from the region—even as he claimed to be offering a "realistic" method for reconciliation.[4] In one fell swoop, Katō rendered impossible both Japan in Asia and Asia in Japan, which, as we will see, put him somewhat at odds with a

---

1. Some passages in this chapter were published earlier in Avenell, "What Is Asia for Us and Can We Be Asians?"
2. Katō, "Haisengoron," 5–93.
3. Harootunian, "Japan's Long Postwar," 109.
4. Koschmann, "National Subjectivity," 131–32.

great many pundits who were calling in the 1990s for a return to the region.

Ethical and epistemological problems aside, Katō's essay revealed how integrally important Asia would become in rightist stratagems to restore national prestige and regain social cohesion at this time, whether in the fabrication of historical heroism through denial, the championing of Asian exceptionalism, or (as with Katō) the reification of the ethnic nation via the ruse of mourning and apology. By raising the question of national subjectivity and the appropriate subject of apology, Katō unwittingly became part of a wider reconsideration of the problem of Japanese identity and Asia through his logic of separation. As both Yumiko Iida and J. Victor Koschmann point out, Katō's and other nationalist tracts of the 1990s emerged out of a deep sense of conservative anxiety over the decline of power and prestige stemming from Japan's prolonged recession and a society seemingly on the "verge of collapse."[5] As previously suppressed antipathies and unresolved historical issues battered popular consciousness and troubling new dilemmas began to appear on the horizon, pundits and commentators of all political hues struggled to find stable footing on the rocky terrain of Japan after its economic miracle. The problem was not only that the short-lived economic bubble had burst, but also that a society and polity very recently lauded as number one now seemed to be afflicted with all manner of social and moral maladies. How could a Japan that had been successful for so long stumble so quickly to the precipice of decay and degeneration? And, more urgently, what could be done to halt this internal decline and deflect ever-intensifying demands from without? The demands included those from supposed allies like the United States, which was now forcefully insisting that Japan open up its closed markets and fulfill its responsibilities by supporting American wars.

Significantly, Asia figured prominently in this quest for remedies, redirections, and the reinvigoration of identity as Japan transitioned from decades of unprecedented economic growth and relative political and social stability to a new, post–Cold War era of festering decline at home and uncertainty abroad. The 1990s witnessed nothing short of an explosion in public discussion and debates about Asian regionalism and the

5. Iida, *Rethinking Identity*, 250–51. See also Koschmann, "National Subjectivity," 122–23.

East Asian community among a hodgepodge of hard-line Asianists, civilizational warriors, moderate instrumentalists, Asia-Pacific fusionists, and progressive visionaries. For hard-line Asianists, concerned primarily about Japan's domestic decline and subservience to the United States, so-called Asian values emerged as the solution to unbridled global capitalism and the ravages of decadent Western culture. Some chauvinists even brazenly presented East Asian regionalism as a tool to resurrect the corpse of co-prosperity. For those of a more moderate persuasion, the specter of national decline also figured prominently, although the problem and its solution were not articulated in the language of resistance but in terms of "fusion," "third openings," national "collapse," and "grand strategies for a new Asia." Whereas the West—most recently the United States—had previously determined the rules of the game, an affluent Asia could now confidently broadcast its agenda to the world, while combining the best of both civilizations into a new Pan-Pacific order. Many moderates even envisioned salvation for recessionary Japan in Asia—the country revitalized by the so-called Asian Tigers, a burgeoning ASEAN, and the awakening colossus of China.

As I show in this chapter, it is impossible to properly understand the transformations in progressive thinking about the Asia problem and the process of deimperialization in the 1990s and beyond without taking these new visions into account. After close to fifty years of addressing the Asia problem largely beyond the public spotlight, progressives now found themselves in a crowded field of New Asianists who were positing an array of fantastic scenarios about the revival of Asia, the rise of Confucian capitalism, and Japan's re-Asianization in a resplendent East Asian community capable of restraining—if not supplanting—an America arguably responsible for Japan's Asian estrangement and wounded identity. For progressives who had long grappled with the Asia problem, the emergence of this New Asianism represented both a threat and an opportunity. Ominously, the entry of far-right hard-liners and utilitarian centrists into discussions of Asian community threatened to bury the Asia problem under a veil of Asian values, regional strategies, and anti-Western rhetoric. There was a real risk that the problem might be diluted or even transformed into an Asian solution before it had been resolved.

But the New Asianism also offered progressives a unique opportunity to reengage—ever so carefully—with the loaded symbolism of Asian

community. As we have seen, from the 1960s to the 1980s activists and
intellectuals interested in the region had striven to expose Japanese identity and consciousness to the gaze of Asia—both the Asia within and the
Asia without. But under the shadow of co-prosperity and the weight of
postwar responsibility, like Katō (but for different reasons), they had been
able to present Japan and Asia only in separation. Indeed, for many, this
self-imposed separation from the region exemplified the very highest expression of the Japanese people's ethical imperative toward fellow Asians.

However, the critical conceptual breakthrough came in the context of
the New Asianism and the release of energies accompanying the end
of the Cold War, the death of Emperor Hirohito, and the bursting of the
economic bubble. Like the new NGOs and civic movements of the 1970s
and 1980s, some progressives began to feel confident enough to position
their ethical imperative of apology and reconciliation on a trajectory not
away from but toward Asian community. In other words, they reached
the conclusion that solving the Asia problem and accomplishing the ca-
tharsis of deimperialization might not necessarily be at odds with the pursuit of Asian community, if that pursuit proceeded through a sentiment
and praxis of remorse. Most prominent here were Wada Haruki and Kang
Sang-jung, a resident Korean intellectual, both of whom began to call for
a common house of Northeast Asia. Although Japan had abused the idea
of Asia in the past and had yet to address lingering issues of postwar responsibility in the present, Wada and Kang argued that these problems
need not prevent sincere initiatives for regional community building from
within Japan. Wada and Kang's Asian communitarianism was supported
by a new generation of historians like Hamashita Takeshi and Amino
Yoshihiko, who used their studies of Asia to disrupt internalist national
imaginaries and recast Japan within a history of intraregional fluidity, exchange, and entanglements. Japan, they argued, was a hybrid construction that simply could not be separated from the region, despite a modern history underwritten by the logic of abandonment.

To be sure, the challenge of recalibrating Japanese identity for a new
age was hardly resolved in progressive or any other visions of Asian community at this time. Nor was the Asia problem solved. In fact, in many
ways, the problem was made all the more complicated by the ragtag collection of New Asianists with their nationalistic and utilitarian designs
for Asia, as well as the intensifying chorus of demands for apologies and

redress from Japan's wartime victims and their advocates. But it was in
the midst of this intellectual and political maelstrom that progressives
found the confidence and vocabulary to reimagine Japan as part of an
Asian community after decades of self-imposed prohibition. This was a
significant intellectual breakthrough, made even more noteworthy by the
internal Others who stood at the forefront of its articulation. Their presence hinted at a hybridized solution to the Asia problem, in which the
journey back to region and toward deimperialization unfolded as a reflexive recognition of the Other as an inseparable and constitutive element of the self.

The Asia Boom in Post-Bubble Japan: Building an East Asian Community

The progressive breakthrough to Asian community owed much to a
broader 1990s rediscovery of Asia in Japan among public commentators
and pundits, journalists, political and business elites, and ordinary Japanese. In the same year that Katō's "Haisengoron" appeared, the journalist Funabashi Yōichi (b. 1944) went so far as to speak of an "Asian fever"
that was "enveloping Japan." Not only was the region "the essence of economic vitality," but for many Japanese now it was "also something chic
and trendy." "The Asia boom," Funabashi declared, "is becoming Japan's
boon."[6] Throughout the decade, others also noted this Asia craze in the
country, fueled by the massive influx of Japanese investment in East Asia;
the greater numbers of Japanese students, tourists, and expatriates in the
region; and the increased cultural, intellectual, and scholarly exchanges.[7]
Nor did the upsurge go only one way: while Japanese flocked to Asia,
members of the rising middle classes of the region were indulging in all
manner of Japanese cultural products like animation, television dramas,
cuisine, and popular music. Notably, after having banned Japanese popular
culture for around a half-century, in 1998 South Korea eased restrictions,

---

6.   Funabashi, *Ajia Taiheiyō fyūjon*, 334.
7.   Hein and Hammond, "Homing in on Asia," 3; Hiraishi, "The Asia Boom."

opening a veritable cultural deluge.[8] Government organizations and political leaders were quick to respond. As I noted in chapter 5, in 1990 the
Japan Foundation established its ASEAN Culture Center, which was expanded and renamed the Asia Center in 1996 as part of Prime Minister
Murayama Tomiichi's "Peace, Friendship, and Exchange Initiative,"
commemorating the fiftieth anniversary of the end of World War II. As
Hirano Ken'ichirō and his colleagues explain, the center's name change
had to do not only with expanding its purview: the change was also an
integral element of Murayama's desire to construct a new history with
Asian nations, which was also evident in his support for the establishment of the Japan Center for Asian Historical Records in 1994.[9]

As figure 1 shows, there was a literal explosion in attention to Asia in
the *Asahi shinbun* (a typical representative of mainstream Japanese newspapers and other publications) from around the late 1980s, which continued unabated into the new century. A relentless stream of multivolume
scholarly collections appeared with titles such as *Kōza tōyō shisō* (Lectures
in Oriental thought, 16 vols., 1988–91), *Kōza Tōnan Ajia gaku* (Lectures on
Southeast Asian studies, 10 vols., 1990–92), *Ajia no naka no Nihon shi*
(A history of Japan in Asia, 6 vols., 1992), *Ajia kara kangaeru* (Thinking
from Asia, 7 vols., 1993–94), *Kōza gendai Ajia* (Lectures on contemporary
Asia, 4 vols., 1994), *Gendai Ajia no shōzō* (Portraits of contemporary Asia,
15 vols., 1996), *Umi no Ajia* (Maritime Asia, 6 vols., 2000–2001), *Ajia shin
seiki* (The Asian new century, 8 vols., 2002–3), *Gendai Minami Ajia* (Contemporary South Asia, 6 vols., 2002–3), *Ajiagaku no susume* (Advancing
Asian studies, 3 vols., 2010), and *Iwanami kōza: Higasahi Ajia kingendai
tsūshi* (Iwanami lectures: A comprehensive modern and contemporary history of East Asia, 11 vols., 2010–11).[10] In 1994, Hiraishi Naoaki, a University of Tokyo historian, attributed this boom in Asian publishing to the
simultaneous rise of East Asia's Newly Industrialized Economies (NIEs:

8.　Hirano and Sengo Nihon, *Sengo Nihon*, 26.
9.　See https://www.jacar.go.jp/english/index.html.
10.　Nagao et al., *Kōza Tōyō shisō*; Yano Noboru et al., *Kōza Tōnan Ajia gaku*;
Arano et al., *Ajia no naka no Nihon shi*; Mizoguchi et al., *Ajia kara kangaeru*; Tsuchiya
et al., *Kōza gendai Ajia*; Yokoyama et al., *Gendai Ajia*; Ōmoto et al., *Umi no Ajia*; Aoki
et al., *Ajia shin seiki*; Nagasaki et al., *Gendai Minami Ajia*; Terada, et al., *Ajiagaku no
susume*; Wada et al., *Iwanami kōza*.

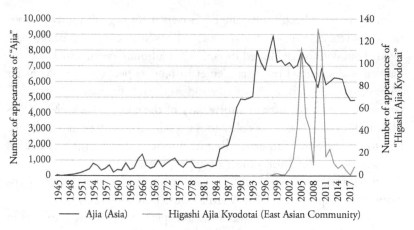

FIGURE I. Appearances of "Asia" and "East Asian Community" in the *Asahi Shinbun*, 1945–2018. *Source*: Asahi Shinbun, *Kikuzo II Visual*, accessed September 9, 2020, https://database.asahi.com/index.shtml.

Hong Kong, South Korea, Singapore, and Taiwan) and Japan's growing trade frictions with the United States.[11]

Others—such as the writer Asuna Mizuho (b. 1973) in her 2004 *"Ajian" no seiki: Shin sedai ga tsukuru ekkyō bunka* (The "Asian" century: The new generation building a border-crossing culture)—connected the boom to the emergence of a new "third approach" to Asia among Japanese, replacing the old dichotomy of "optimism" (Pan Asianism) or "pessimism" (abandoning Asia) with a new "cultural perspective." In the 1960s and 1970s involvement with Asia had been about rather serious activism, but now it was about young office workers patronizing Taiwanese teahouses, Chinese fruit wines being on the menus of local bars, and housewives gossiping about the latest television soap opera from South Korea. This was the new "Asian" (*Ajian*) style, and it differed fundamentally from the earlier, ideologically charged "Asia."[12] To be sure, the "Asian boom," which included initiatives to "rediscover" the authentic Japan, could be somewhat superficial, but it demonstrated to Asuna that, for the current generation, Asia no longer signified "poverty" and "stagnation"

11. Hiraishi, "Asia Boom," 27.
12. Asuna, *"Ajian" no seiki*, 5.

but something "strong" and "fascinating."[13] While earlier Asianism was formulated to resist the West and later became a ghastly tool for Japanese expansionism, the new "Asian orientation" was "developing as a quiet resistance to the excessive standardization of globalization," and it was not intended to support a Japanese "advance onto the world stage."[14] Moreover, superficial though the new Asian orientation and culture may have been, in them Asuna identified "solutions" to the "big three challenges of the twenty-first century": environmental destruction, devastation of the human spirit, and ethnic coexistence. The "formation of local cultural spheres," she argued, were serving as "power spots," "interlacing" Asian countries together into a regional formation known as the "East Asian Community."[15] Fearful of being "swallowed up by globalization," within these Asian spheres people were engaged in a process of "creative self-realization" and the search for a "new legitimacy" that was beyond "economic benefit" and embedded in the "expression" of "the ethnic."[16] "Given the despair of these times and the extreme situation," Asuna concluded, "I pray for a vigorous self-recovery from within Asia. I end this book with a prayer in my heart: 'Asia, Rise Up.'"[17]

A constellation of domestic and international factors fed into this Asia boom: the end of the Cold War in Europe, the rise and then demise of the Japanese bubble economy, the emergence of new East Asian powers and their growing economic interdependence, regionalist responses to globalization in other parts of the world, and ongoing trade conflicts with the United States. The immediate catalyst for Japan's Asia boom was the mid-1980s reconfiguration of the global monetary system. With the 40 percent appreciation of the yen against the US dollar after the 1985 Plaza Accord, many Japanese businesses were forced to relocate their production facilities offshore, resulting in a massive influx of Japanese investment in the NIEs and ASEAN countries that dwarfed Japan's earlier industrial forays into the region in the 1970s.[18] As Edith Terry notes, in

13. Asuna, *"Ajian" no seiki,* 12.
14. Asuna, *"Ajian" no seiki,* 245.
15. Asuna, *"Ajian" no seiki,* 265–66.
16. Asuna, *"Ajian" no seiki,* 245 and 254.
17. Asuna, *"Ajian" no seiki,* 267.
18. For statistics on this surge in FDI, see Munakata, *Transforming East Asia,* 38–39.

1991 Japanese exports to Asia exceeded those to America, and in 1995, Japanese trade with Asia was 50 percent greater than that with the United States. By the end of the decade Japan was exporting 16 percent more to Asia than America, and in 2000 the country imported more from Asia than from the United States and the European Union combined.[19]

The regional impact of Japan's economic shift to East Asia was profound, contributing to an overall spurt in economic growth and development among many countries throughout the region. In its influential 1993 book aptly titled *The East Asian Miracle*, the World Bank lauded East Asian countries for their "appropriate" use of "macroeconomic policy," "active export promotion," and "selective" market "interventions"—all of which were drawn from the Japanese model, a miracle in its own right.[20] Indeed, both Japanese and fellow Asians accepted the view that industrial development in East Asia after 1985 had unfolded by way of a "flying geese pattern," in which Japan as the "lead goose" (via its investment in the region and relocation of production facilities to it) was "effectively pulling East Asia together economically through the 'power of the market.'"[21]

The collapse of Japan's bubble economy in the early 1990s against the backdrop of continued stunning growth in neighboring countries certainly dented Japan's image as East Asia's "lead goose," but it only further convinced many Japanese of the necessity for their country's regional integration, a view that was articulated increasingly frequently in discussions of the notion of an East Asian Community (EAC) to rival the European Union and the North American Free Trade Agreement. Mahathir bin Mohamad, the prime minister of Malaysia, was among the earliest advocates of an EAC, proposing the formation of the East Asian Economic Group during a meeting with Li Peng, the Chinese premier in 1990.[22] Interestingly, one of Mahathir's goals for the group (later converted into an East Asian Economic Caucus) was for it to be a counterbalance against both America and Japan, as well as economic blocs elsewhere. Nonetheless, the proposal garnered a degree of support among Japanese elites—

19.   Terry, *How Asia Got Rich*, 107.
20.   World Bank, *East Asian Miracle*, iv, 23, 205.
21.   Shiraishi, "Higashi Ajia chiiki," 93.
22.   Tanaka Akihiko, *Ajia no naka*, 110.

especially younger bureaucrats in the Ministries of Foreign Affairs, Finance (MOF), and International Trade and Industry who hoped to give institutional form to the economic regionalization unfolding throughout the region.[23]

Quite by happenstance, Japan was presented with an opportunity to take the lead in region building in 1997, when East Asian countries faced a monetary crisis of historic proportions. Beginning with the Thai baht and thereafter spreading to the currencies of Hong Kong, South Korea, and other ASEAN countries, the Asian Financial Crisis (AFC) involved a widespread currency collapse following a massive outflow of Western capital that had previously been pouring into the region. In an attempt to resuscitate flailing Asian economies, in 1998 Miyazawa Kiichi, Japan's prime minister, launched his thirty-billion-dollar "New Miyazawa Initiative," while leading Japanese bureaucrats such as Sakakibara Eisuke of the MOF—known as "Mr. Yen"—floated the idea of an Asian Monetary Fund (AMF). Despite their best efforts, this initiative was eventually abandoned due to strident opposition from the United States (which feared the formation of a yen bloc in Asia). It was replaced in 2000 by the Chiang Mai Initiative, which established a system of Asian currency swap agreements for times of economic crisis. Nonetheless, the AFC led many policy makers and EAC pundits in Japan and across the region to conclude that East Asia needed an institutional framework that was independent of the United States and capable of responding to financial crises. According to Ōba Mie, the resistance of the Americans to the AMF proposal, coupled with the intraregional mutual support led by Japan during the crisis, produced a stronger "sense of us" among policy makers and intellectuals in the region and further stimulated moves toward an EAC.[24] Important for this discussion, American opposition to proactive Japanese initiatives for East Asian region building in the late 1990s also encouraged prominent Japanese progressives to begin seriously rethinking the Japan-America–East Asia nexus.

In the new millennium, Japan became an active, if cautious, participant in initiatives for East Asian region building. It was both sensitive to attitudes in Washington and wary of a rising China. Notably, in 2002,

23. Tanaka Akihiko, *Ajia no naka*, 113.
24. Ōba, "'Higashi Ajia," 446.

the populist prime minister, Koizumi Jun'ichirō, proposed the formation of an EAC in a speech while visiting Singapore. However, Koizumi's "community" came with a small "c," meaning that it would be an "open," nonexclusive entity that included countries like Australia and New Zealand and that it would recognize the "indispensable" "role to be played by the United States."[25] Here Koizumi's vision diverged dramatically from Mahathir's exclusivist idea of an East Asian Economic Caucus (which was criticized as a "caucus without Caucasians") as well as the later "ASEAN Plus Three" meetings, which many Japanese feared would become slave to the overwhelming influence of China.[26] In spite of its limitations, Koizumi's speech provided yet another stimulus to the Asia boom in Japan, with related publications and media reportage on an EAC skyrocketing at the time (see figure 1).

Attention to building an EAC peaked again in 2009, when the newly minted Prime Minister Hatoyama Yukio, of the Democratic Party of Japan, similarly proposed the construction of an EAC in a summit with Hu Jintao, the Chinese president. In contrast to Koizumi's proposal, Hatoyama's was less about appeasing the United States than about building trust among the big three powers of Northeast Asia: China, Japan, and South Korea. Hatoyama's vision revolved around the notion of building "fraternity" (*yūai*) among these countries, and according to Takashi Inoguchi, its inspiration came from Hatoyama's grandfather, Hatoyama Ichirō (the prime minister in 1955–57), who had similarly been dissatisfied with American influence over Japan and wished to "inculcate . . . good neighborly relations with Korea and China."[27] Hatoyama Yukio's vision was short-lived, however, as he was forced to resign the prime ministership in mid-2010 after reneging on a promise to close a US military base on Okinawa under pressure from the administration of President Barack Obama. Soon thereafter tensions over territorial issues with both China and South Korea began to escalate, which in turn precipitated a steady decline in attention to the idea of an EAC. Nonetheless, processes

    25. For the speech, see https://www.mofa.go.jp/region/asia-paci/pmv0201/speech .html.
    26. Munakata, *Transforming East Asia*, 75. The "plus three" are China, South Korea, and Japan.
    27. Inoguchi, "Japanese Ideas," 239.

of regionalization (economic integration) and regionalism (EAC) in the period from the late 1980s to the early 2010s were critical in stimulating the widespread debate about Asia within Japan, offering progressive Asia advocates a unique historical opportunity to begin rethinking regional community and the Asia problem.

The Return of the Past: Movements for Compensation and Reconciliation

However, the progressive breakthrough to a new regional imaginary was not only a response to growing economic regionalization and regionalist initiatives among elites. It also arose at a critical juncture in the evolution of collective memory in postwar Japan. At the same time that pundits began championing the country's rosy future in the region, others more attuned to the past were pursuing a very different agenda with fellow Asians in movements and campaigns for war compensation, reconciliation, and apologies. Although somewhat at odds, both processes grew out of the "fortuitous overlap" of occurrences at the time, including the rise and demise of Japan's bubble economy and the stunning growth of its East Asian neighbors, the death of Emperor Hirohito in 1989, the end of the Cold War, the anniversaries of the beginning (1991) and end (1995) of the Asia-Pacific War, the collapse (if only fleeting) of postwar conservative rule, and "the return of Asia to Japan's geopolitical agenda."[28]

These developments set free a plethora of previously suppressed issues and initiatives relating to Japan's colored past in the region, prominent among which were numerous actions to achieve substantive redress for Japan's wartime transgressions. Many of the activists and intellectuals discussed in previous chapters spearheaded these movements. In 1989, for instance, a group of Chinese sent to perform forced labor at the

28.   Gluck, "Operations of Memory," 64. Use of the term "Asia-Pacific War" (*Ajia Taiheiyō Sensō*) instead of "Pacific War" became more widespread in Japan during the 1990s in response to greater attention to the unresolved issues between Japan and its former colonies and victims of Japanese militarism. See Gluck, "Operations of Memory," 64.

Hanaoka Mine in northern Japan in 1944 issued an open letter to the mine's former operator, the Kajima Corporation, demanding an apology, the establishment of memorial museums, and compensation for the victims. Taking up their cause, Tanaka Hiroshi, together with activist lawyers, began negotiations with the company for compensation and, after these broke down, assisted the victims in launching a lawsuit in the Tokyo District Court.[29] Building on the postwar responsibility movements discussed in chapter 5, in the mid-1990, Koreans who had been abandoned on Sakhalin Island after Japan's withdrawal in 1945 began litigation for compensation with their families, and soon thereafter there were cases involving former Korean B and C class war criminals and actions by the so-called comfort women who had been mobilized into Japan's system of wartime sexual exploitation.[30]

Among these initiatives, the plight of the former comfort women received considerable media attention in Japan and elsewhere and deeply shaped subsequent diplomatic relations between Japan and its regional neighbors while bringing its own unique—and troublingly grim—valence to the discourse on Japan's 1990s Asian revival. As we saw in chapter 4, Matsui Yayori and other activists involved in the kisaeng sex tourism problem of the 1970s were aware of the comfort women issue at that time, although they did not begin to engage with the problem until around the mid- to late 1980s. In 1986, for instance, the artist Tomiyama Taeko had an exhibit of paintings and drawings that evoked the unfathomable agony of the Korean comfort women.[31] Tomiyama had decided to concentrate more intensively on the issue after meeting a Korean intellectual who made her aware of the taboo surrounding the problem and the need to give voice to these neglected wartime victims.[32]

Attention to the comfort women among the broader public in Japan grew after a former soldier in the Japanese Imperial Army confessed to

29. Tanaka Hiroshi, "Hanron," 267–68.
30. On the Sakhalin Koreans' movement, see Arai, *Saharin no kankokujin*. B and C class war criminals were those found guilty of violations of international law and established war crimes such as the murder and rape of civilians, maltreatment of prisoners of war under the Geneva Convention, and the use of prohibited chemical weapons. On the Korean B and C class war criminals' lawsuit, see Kawakami, "Rensai tokushū."
31. Gluck, "Operations of Memory," 67.
32. Hein, "Postcolonial Conscience," 20.

having been involved in the forced recruitment of women. This confession was subsequently transmitted to South Korea in a 1990 television documentary, prompting a South Korean woman, Kim Hak-sun, to publicly announce in 1991 that she had been a comfort woman.[33] Thereafter other women publicly identified themselves as victims, and they began to demand apologies and mobilize resources for legal proceedings.[34] Liberal media outlets and grassroots activists within Japan supported these moves, and the *Asahi shinbun* newspaper caused a stir in early 1992 when it reported on the historian Yoshimi Yoshiaki's discovery in the Japanese Defense Agency Archive of documents showing evidence of the involvement of the Japanese military in administering military brothels.[35]

Like Tomiyama, Matsui became a leading advocate for the former comfort women over these decades. As part of her reportage while serving as special correspondent for the *Asahi shinbun* in Singapore in the early 1980s, Matsui traveled to the border of southern Thailand to interview a Korean woman who had been forced into prostitution during the war and, faced with severe social stigma if she returned home, had chosen to remain in the region. Deeply moved by the encounter, thereafter Matsui began to build connections with Korean and Japanese researchers on the issue. In 1997, emboldened by the rising global attention to violence against women and the public identification and court cases of former victims in the 1990s, Matsui organized the International Conference on Violence against Women in War and Armed Conflict Situations in Tokyo. And in the following year she established the Violence Against Women in War—Network Japan (VA WW—Net Japan). Building on these initiatives, in late 2000 Matsui, the VA WW—Net Japan, and activists and victims from across Asia organized the Women's International War Crimes Tribunal for the Trial of Japan's Military Sexual Slavery in Tokyo. Although its decision lacked legal enforceability, the widely publicized and reported tribunal found Emperor Hirohito and nine other Japanese leaders criminally liable for "rape and sexual slavery as crimes against humanity," stemming from Japan's war in Asia in the 1930s and 1940s. In its judgment, the tribunal called on the Japanese government

33.   Tanaka Akihiko, *Ajia no naka*, 165.
34.   Koyama Hitomi, *On the Persistence*, 104–5.
35.   Koyama Hitomi, *On the Persistence*, 104–5.

to acknowledge its responsibility, offer an apology, and provide appropriate compensation to the victims.[36]

While Matsui, Tomiyama, and others addressed Japanese responsibility through the comfort women issue, others like Wada spearheaded a sustained campaign for a Diet resolution recognizing Japan's crimes against Asia during the war. Although the final resolution would be far from satisfying for Wada and his colleagues, their efforts led directly to several historic statements by Japanese political leaders throughout the 1990s. As we saw in chapter 5, the Diet resolution campaign traced its roots to the school history textbook controversy of the early 1980s and contemporaneous movements for postwar responsibility. In 1984 and again in 1985, Wada—together with a group of familiar characters including Aochi Shin, Ienaga Saburō, Tsurumi Shunsuke, Hidaka Rokurō, Yasue Ryōsuke, Iinuma Jirō, Utsumi Aiko, Tomiyama, and others—issued statements calling for a Diet resolution and governmental commitments to provide substantive compensation.[37] Largely ignored at first, their movement began to gain political traction thanks to the election of Doi Takako to the chairmanship of the JSP in 1986, after which the party worked toward achieving a historical reconciliation with the Koreas. The demise of Emperor Hirohito and the looming anniversaries of the war served as launchpads for a series of rallies, symposia, and signature campaigns in 1989 and 1990 that finally alerted the Japanese public to the need for an official resolution on Japan's past at this important historical juncture.[38]

The campaign of Wada and his colleagues began to bear political fruit in the early 1990s, just as the New Asianism was taking off. In January 1992, for example, Prime Minister Miyazawa Kiichi expressed his "apologies" and "remorse" to South Korean President Roh Tae Woo during a visit to South Korea and promised to conduct investigations into the comfort women issue, which had risen to domestic and international

36. For documentation on the case and the original verdicts, see http://www.internationalcrimesdatabase.org/Case/981/The-Prosecutors-and-the-Peoples-of-the-Asia-Pacific-Region/.

37. For these statements, see Wada and Ishizaka, *Nihon wa shokuminchi*, 17–23 and 25–28.

38. Wada and Ishizaka, *Nihon wa shokuminchi*, 13.

prominence in 1991.[39] On receipt of the second of these reports in August 1993, Chief Cabinet Secretary Kōno Yōhei issued a historic statement—known as the Kōno danwa (Kōno statement)—acknowledging either the direct or indirect involvement of the Japanese military in the hiring of brokers who "cajoled" or "pressured" women to become comfort women against their wishes and in the establishment and management of "comfort stations."[40] Following the collapse of LDP rule in 1993, Hosokawa Morihiro, the coalition prime minister, expressed his personal view at an August press conference that the war had been one of "aggression" and ultimately a "mistake," which made him the first prime minister to unambiguously describe Japan's actions as a "war of aggression" (*shinryaku sensō*).[41] Hosokawa followed up with further expressions of remorse and regret for colonial rule and aggression during his first speech to the Diet later in the same month and again during a meeting with the South Korean president toward the end of 1993.

Prime Minister Murayama continued this process of apology after assuming leadership at the head of an unsteady coalition of the JSP, LDP, and Sakigake in 1994. On August 15, 1995 (the fiftieth anniversary of the war's end), Murayama issued the Murayama danwa (Murayama statement), in which he expressed "deep remorse" and a "heartfelt apology" for the "colonial rule and aggression" that had "caused tremendous damage and suffering to the people of many countries, particularly to those of Asian nations."[42] Moreover, in a Pyrrhic victory for Wada and his fellow activists, in June the Diet had finally passed a resolution on the war, but due to opposition from within the brittle coalition and from conservative civic groups, all mention of "aggression" and "apology" was removed, leaving only the ambiguous statement that the country should "humbly learn from past mistakes."[43]

Murayama and supportive progressives' efforts at reconciliation were further hindered by the largely unsuccessful Asian Women's Fund (AWF;

---

39. Quoted in Tanaka Akihiko, *Ajia no naka*, 165.

40. Kōno, "Ianfu kankei chōsa." See also Tanaka Akihiko, *Ajia no naka*, 166.

41. Quoted in Wakamiya, *Sengo 70-nen*, 23.

42. For the statement, see https://www.mofa.go.jp/mofaj/press/danwa/07/dmu_0815.html.

43. For the statement, see http://www.awf.or.jp/6/statement-06.html.

Josei no tame no Ajia heiwa kokumin kikin), which was set up as a non-governmental body with mostly public monies in July 1995 to provide compensation to former comfort women. Ōnuma Yasuaki, Wada, and the JSP politician Igarashi Kōzō (then chief cabinet secretary) master-minded the initiative, which they saw as the most realistic and a "once in a lifetime" method to provide speedy compensation to the aging victims.[44] As Ōnuma wrote in the *Yomiuri shinbun* newspaper at the time, "criticizing the government proposal is easy. But if we reject this proposal then [by] what cabinet and by what method will we be able to provide compensation to former comfort women? To the extent [that] there is no concrete, realistic alternative, rejecting this proposal amounts to a rejection of compensation for the former comfort women."[45] Such pleas were ultimately in vain, with the AWF coming in for scathing criticism from both Japan and South Korea for deflecting responsibility away from the Japanese government, where it truly lay.[46] For their efforts Ōnuma and Wada were labeled "traitors" by progressive critics—a rather callous and uninformed vilification, regardless of the problematic political optics of the fund, and woefully ignorant of these individuals' tireless advocacy for Japan's Asian victims over the years.[47]

Making matters worse, progressives' efforts toward apology, reconciliation, and compensation for fellow Asians in the 1990s and early 2000s

44. For a trenchant comparison of the fund to Katō's essay, see Koschmann, "National Subjectivity," 135.

45. Murayama appears to have supported the idea of a nongovernmental fund due to the 1965 Japan–South Korea normalization treaty, which declared the full and final settlement of all claims for compensation and property rights between the two states, while Ōnuma and Wada believed that LDP opposition would make it impossible to pass any special legislation authorizing compensation. Ōnuma and Wada also feared that legal action to provide compensation would be so protracted that many victims would not live to see the verdicts and receive any help. Some 285 former comfort women in the Netherlands and Philippines ultimately accepted compensation, together with a letter of apology from the prime minister. The fund was not implemented in China, Taiwan, or South Korea, and it was quietly disestablished in 2007 after the construction of an aged-care facility for former comfort women in Indonesia. See Wada, "Kichō hōkoku," 8.

46. For critiques of the AWF, see Kang, "Musubi ni kaete," 198; Ueno, *Ikinobiru no tame*, 209–28.

47. Wakamiya, *Sengo 70-nen*, 265.

were constantly confounded by conservative politicians—often cabinet ministers—who responded to official apologies by Kōno, Hosokawa, Murayama, and others with brazen claims that the use of comfort women and the Rape of Nanjing were fabrications, the Greater East Asia Co-Prosperity Sphere had been "legal," the war had not been one of "aggression," and Japan would do best to discard its peace constitution.[48] Incensed by the humiliation of apology, groups of conservative scholars, politicians, and others also began to mobilize into revisionist groups aimed at generating a more affirmative view of Japan and Japanese history among youth, supposedly remedying their masochism (*jigyaku*) and Japan-hating.[49] For Katō, such radical disjunctures between the Left and Right reflected the fundamental "split personality" affecting postwar Japanese consciousness—a "Jekyll and Hyde" syndrome in which apology was always met by denial, and the only exit (for Katō, at least) a reconstructed national expression of grief for Japan's war dead.[50]

To be sure, some individuals like Koizumi Jun'ichirō appeared to embody this split personality: for example, on the one hand Koizumi made repeated visits to the controversial Yasukuni Shrine for Japan's war dead (including war criminals), while on the other hand he called for an EAC and brokered a historic deal with North Korea. This was undeniably the stuff of conflicted messaging. But if we zoom out to take in the wider historical terrain of this moment, the limits of Katō's metaphor, which stemmed from his problematic homogenization of the nation, become all too apparent. The fact that there could be two—actually three, if we count right-wing denialists—very different approaches to Asia at this time speaks less to the rupture of some imagined national psyche than it does to the reality of politics, a public sphere, and a popular mentality increasingly sculpted by the country's multidimensional connections to the Asia within and the Asia without. This was the economic and political context in which progressives' breakthrough to Asian community unfolded.

48. Wakamiya, *Sengo 70-nen*, 32–33; Koyama Hitomi, *On the Persistence*, 118.

49. The formation of the Jiyūshugi Shikan Kenkyūkai (Liberal View of History Group) in 1996 is a case in point. On these revisionist groups see Saaler, *Politics, Memory, and Public Opinion*.

50. Katō, "Haisengoron," 46–53.

Indeed, it was precisely because of this complex intertwining of Japan and its region at this juncture that questions of history could not be divorced from those of community.

The New Asianism: Resistance, Revival, or a New Common House?

As noted above, until around the 1990s, progressives were able to ruminate on Asia and questions of historical responsibility in a relatively unencumbered discursive space. Although geopolitical and geoeconomic discussions of Asia had proliferated, attention to Asia was generally subdued except during periodic crises, and progressives faced little pressure from other pundits eager to advance their own visions of Asia and Japan's role and place therein. But this situation changed dramatically with the transformations of the 1990s and the rise of the New Asianism—which, by propagating new and compelling Asian questions and solutions, encouraged progressives to reconsider the taboo on Asian community that had so haunted their postwar reengagement with the region. To this extent, the evolution of the Asia problem from this time on is best understood in the context of a tense yet productive dialogue with the New Asianism.

Both cultural and economic nationalism undoubtedly dominated the discourse on Asia in the early to mid-1990s, but as the range of participants widened over time, the discourse diversified and became far richer. As they had in the past, progressives continued to be flag bearers for the Asia problem and deimperialization, but now they competed for space with others who proposed more utilitarian, geopolitical, and culturally essentialist agendas. Moreover, as these competing ideas and aspirations interacted and sometimes collided with one another, the very notion of an Asia problem began to morph as pundits—including progressives—attempted to reconceptualize historical encumbrances within affirmative visions of Asian community. It was not that the past disappeared (although it certainly did in some versions of the New Asianism). Rather, as I have argued, the past became an element of the project to open up a new future for Japan in and with Asia. Except for a few who rejected regionalism and an EAC altogether, most agreed on this strategy. Where they differed, however, was in the philosophy informing their advocacy and the methods they believed had to be used in Japan's return to the region. Here pundits tended to gravitate around one of three broad perspectives: those of the hard-line Asianists and civilizational warriors, who were motivated by their nationalism and anti-American sentiment and/or a desire to rehabilitate the world through Asia; the moderate instrumentalists and fusionists, who saw in Asia a momentous economic and cultural transformation of which Japan had to be a part; and the progressive visionaries, for whom Asian regionalism became a blueprint for solving the Asia problem and securing a prosperous and peaceful future in a regional common house.[51] Investigating their respective positions reveals how integral Asia was becoming in reimaginations of national identity in 1990s Japan.

HARD-LINE ASIANISTS AND CIVILIZATIONAL WARRIORS

For the Asianist hard-liners of the early 1990s, Asia mostly served as a subterfuge for justifying Japanese leadership and preeminence in the region, while reinforcing a nationalist rhetoric of resistance to American-led globalism and the evils of Western civilization. Echoing wartime Pan-Asianist rhetoric, hard-line Asianists like Ishihara Shintarō and Ogura Kazuo appealed to Asian values, practices, and other supposed commonalities of a cultural sphere in which Japan stood at the apex as a benevolent benefactor and exemplar. Others, like Hara Yōnosuke, invoked a "clash of civilizations" in which Japanese and fellow Asians—an "alliance of the weak"—waged a life-and-death battle against the ravages of globalization.[52] Less stridently, the sinologist Nakayashiki Hiroshi promoted the view that a symbiotic and regenerative Asian civilization was the antidote for the ills of the West, similar in many ways to Asuna's notion of Asian "power spots."[53] And as Japan's economic woes dragged on beyond the so-called lost decade of the 1990s, others like Shindō Eiichi offered fantastic

---

51. This taxonomy was more porous in practice, and, as we will see, some individuals and groups fell into more than one category. Nevertheless, I believe it faithfully captures the broad contours of the discourse.

52. Miyadai, "Ajiashugi no kanōsei."

53. Asuna, *"Ajian" no seiki*, 12.

narratives about Japan's historic and repeated martyrdom for Asia in the face of relentless Western military and economic penetration. Almost totally lacking from such propositions was any recognition of Japan's unresolved past with Asia or the existence of a diverse Asia within Japan.

Ogura (b. 1938), a diplomat and later president of the Japan Foundation, was among the most outspoken of the early hard-liners with his calls for an "Asian revival" and the "creation of a new Asia" throughout the 1990s. He attracted considerable attention and criticism from American observers at the time.[54] In a widely read 1993 essay titled "A Call for a New Concept of Asia," Ogura complained that "Asia" was an idea that had been "abused, distorted, and worn out" by Westerners who had "manufactured" it "to suit themselves" throughout the modern period.[55] But "in the past few years" (that is, after 1985), this image had begun to change. The "negative" values long "associated with Asia" were finally receding and being replaced by "positive ones," and Asians were now searching for "common directions and a common destiny." Indeed, a "new Asia" was rising up, but this time it was "something with a real presence instead of . . . an empty concept created by people in the West."[56] Ogura pointed to Asian culture and values as the backbone of Japan's economic miracle, which had now become a "model for the world." He invoked the words of Mahathir—who, in the controversial 1970 *The Malay Dilemma*, identified the "work ethic of the Japanese and Koreans," based on "discipline, loyalty, and diligence," and the prioritizing of the "group" and "nation" over the "individual" as the key dynamics fueling such countries' "economic and social development."[57] For Ogura, this commendation from Asian leaders was evidence not only of a new Asian pride but also that the region was looking to Japan as the font of Asian values.

More controversially, Ogura envisaged a historic role for Asia in which the united region would gradually "Asianize" the world. In a clever reinvocation of Takeuchi Yoshimi's ideas of the 1960s, Ogura urged Asians to "thoroughly absorb what the West has offered" and "develop a new set

54. See, for example, Gluck, "Call for a New Asian"; Hein and Hammond, "Homing in on Asia," 10–16; Duus, "The 'New Asianism,'" 250.
55. Ogura, "Call for a New Concept," 37–38.
56. Ogura, "Call for a New Concept," 39–40.
57. Quoted in Ogura, "Call for a New Concept," 39–40.

of values" that they could "transmit to the world." He pointed to the supposed Asian love of nature, the natural group harmony of Asians, and the sophisticated arts of the Japanese tea ceremony as potentially useful exports to a world crippled and degraded by "mechanical civilization."[58] By the "world," of course, Ogura meant the United States, which he said must "Asianize itself" just as Asia had been "Americanized." The United States, he insisted, must "understand" and "learn" from Asia and "accept some Asian values."[59] And, as he clarified in an essay some years later, Japan would have to "shoulder" a "large part of the leadership" in the creation of this new Asia and the subsequent Asianization of the world.[60]

In hindsight, particularly given the subsequent rise of China, Ogura's designs for global Asianization led by Japan seem almost delusional, but in the context of Japanese success they made perfect sense. Until around the mid-1990s it was still possible for hard-line Asianists to conceive of an economically powerful Japan elevating Asia (and its values) to an unprecedented historical level. Countless others also shared Ogura's prognostications in the 1990s, if in more moderate terms. In 1995, for instance, Sakakibara Eisuke, MOF bureaucrat and architect of the later AMF idea, waxed lyrical about Japan's "non-capitalistic market economy" and the broader Asian "respect" for "nature and the environment," as well as the region's traditions of "peaceful coexistence between civilizations"— all of which he posited as solutions for the destructive anthropocentrism of the West.[61] A few years earlier, Kobayashi Yōtarō, president of the Fuji-Xerox Corporation, a US-Japan joint venture, caused a stir when he called on the Japanese to "re-Asianize" (*sai-Ajiaka*) themselves after having strayed from their emotional and cultural roots in the pursuit of Western modernity. Strikingly at odds with his cosmopolitan background and Wharton Business School education, Kobayashi suggested that Japan should "share leadership" in Asia not with the United States but with China, which would become a "co-chair" and trusted partner.[62] According to Kobayashi, Japanese and fellow Asians like the Chinese shared a

---

58. Ogura, "Call for a New Concept," 41.
59. Ogura, "Call for a New Concept," 44.
60. Ogura, "Creating a New Asia," 12.
61. Sakakibara, "End of Progressivism," 14.
62. Kobayashi, "Sai-Ajiaka no susume," 45.

natural affinity for cooperation because of their "emotional orientation," which differed from the "logical orientation" of Americans.[63]

But the most resplendent articulation of hard-line Asianism in the early 1990s came from the mercurial novelist and politician Ishihara Shintarō (b. 1932), who became the self-appointed mouthpiece for a Japan and Asia that would resolutely say no to the West. Ishihara expressed this sentiment most vehemently in a series of relay essays with Mahathir published in the 1994 *"NO" to ieru Ajia: Tai-Ōbei no hōsaku* (The Asia that can say no: A plan for dealing with the West), which expanded to the whole of Asia Ishihara's earlier nationalist tract, *The Japan That Can Say No: Why Japan Will Be First among Equals.*[64] Writing in the 1994 volume, Ishihara declared that in the twenty-first century the region would "revive" and the world would "enter an Asian era."[65] Although some, like Funabashi Yōichi (discussed below), imagined a fusion between the East and West, Ishihara proclaimed that the time had come for Japan to declare once and for all that it was "a member of Asia" and had "returned [to] the 'East.'" Of course, Japan's relationship with America could not "be ignored" and would continue to be "indispensable," but from a historical perspective, Ishihara said that it was only "natural" that Japan should pivot toward a rising Asia.[66] In spite of its "return," to Asia the nationalist Ishihara situated Japan as the leading actor in this historic drama. Instead of continuing its shameless and continuous acquiescence to American demands, the time had come for Japan to clearly say "YES" or "NO." This was the kind of leadership that the countries of Asia expected from a Japan that shouldered the "aspirations of Asians."[67]

Demonstrating his confidence in the centrality and supremacy of Japanese civilization in the region, Ishihara emphasized the popularity in Asia of Japanese dramas such as *Oshin* and the animation *Doraemon*, supposedly evidence of the "invisible yet distinct commonalities" flowing in

63. Kobayashi, "Sai-Ajiaka no susume," 46.
64. Mahathir and Ishihara, *"NO" to ieru Ajia.* The English version was published in 1995 under the title *The Voice of Asia: Two Leaders Discuss the Coming Century.* Also see Ishihara, *The Japan That Can Say No.*
65. Mahathir and Ishihara, *"NO" to ieru Ajia,* 29.
66. Mahathir and Ishihara, *"NO" to ieru Ajia,* 45.
67. Mahathir and Ishihara, *"NO" to ieru Ajia,* 87.

the "blood of Asians."[68] In the drama *Oshin*—a tale of one Japanese woman's perseverance in an age of tribulation—Ishihara identified the Asian tendency for hard work. Westerners, he argued, wanted to live by avoiding working if they could, but this was not the case for Asians. While Westerners "hated" those "who did nothing but eat and drink," they also secretly "envied" them. Asians, however, felt a great sense of sympathy for those who did not work, regardless of their wealth.[69] According to Ishihara, underlying this commitment to work and perseverance lay a "tolerant spiritual foundation that recognized and accepted difference" and a spirit of harmony (*wa*).[70] Lamentably, these were values that the Japanese had abandoned in their determination "to import Western civilization," leading them to "forget" that they were "Asians."[71] Now, however, was the historic moment for Japan to shed this Westernized self-deceit.

Invoking disturbingly controversial language of the past, Ishihara called for the creation of a new "Co-Prosperity Sphere" (*kyōeiken*) in Asia, supposedly different from the Greater East Asia Co-Prosperity Sphere of the war because of the "decline of the West and the relative rising affluence of Asia." Unlike the wartime version of co-prosperity, which had been tainted by Western logic, this "new history of Asian co-prosperity" would arguably be free of "Western-style maladies" and infused with the unadulterated spirit of Asia.[72] Japan needed to supply as much funding and technology to Asia as possible, and in doing so, the country would make up for the transgressions of the past while helping realize the "genuine ideals" of its earlier projects in the region. The point was not to have Japan "managing" Asia but rather playing its "role" as a "member of Asia" in a context of "solidarity" with fellow Asians.[73] As Ishihara concluded, "the Japanese" were, "after all, an Asian people."[74]

68. Mahathir and Ishihara, *"NO" to ieru Ajia*, 129.
69. Mahathir and Ishihara, *"NO" to ieru Ajia*, 129–30.
70. Mahathir and Ishihara, *"NO" to ieru Ajia*, 135 and 155–56.
71. Mahathir and Ishihara, *"NO" to ieru Ajia*, 130.
72. Mahathir and Ishihara, *"NO" to ieru Ajia*, 11 and 208.
73. Mahathir and Ishihara, *"NO" to ieru Ajia*, 208.
74. Mahathir and Ishihara, *"NO" to ieru Ajia*, 237. Ishihara's professed affinity for Asia came into question later, with his use of derogatory language to describe immigrants (primarily Asian) in 2000 and his declaration in 2012 that the Tokyo Municipal

Ishihara's audacious blustering offered low-hanging fruit to critics of the New Asianism, essentially confirming their suspicions of it as a dressed-up version of Japanese cultural nationalism that underpinned designs for regional domination. But as Japan's economic woes worsened and the fortunes of other Asian nations grew, the early hard-line Asianism underwent creative modification. In place of Asian revival, re-Asianization, or an Asian era, some began to exhume older ideas of Asian resistance, feeding these into new discourses about the clash of civilizations and Asia's mission as an authentic life-world capable of transcending Western decadence and leading humanity out of a global modernity gone awry. Others, still wedded to the idea of Japanese leadership in Asia yet unable to deny the onset of national decline, concocted incredible narratives of the country's repeated martyrdom for the region on the altar of Western greed. Despite this change in tone, however, there was no hint of an Asia problem in need of solving.

In a provocatively titled 2002 book, *Shin-Tōaron* (A new treatise on East Asia), the economist Hara Yōnosuke encapsulated this growing anxiety of an "Asia" (read "Japan") under siege from globalization and the hope among some New Asianists that if Japan could no longer lead Asia economically, it might still play a leading role in the civilizational struggle between the global and the regional.[75] Contrary to the political scientist Francis Fukuyama's declaration of the "end of history," in his book Hara argued that the end of the Cold War and the terrorist attacks on the United States in September 2001 marked not the end of history, but its "revival."[76] According to Hara, "all the modern West produced was a concrete-filled, puny, self-absorbed ego."[77] The progressivism of the Western age was about exclusion: it tried to create the future by destroying the past or by absorbing the past into the present. But this world had ended, and now nobody—especially those in the non-Western world—

Government planned to purchase the disputed Diaoyu or Senkaku Islands. See "Ishihara Slammed for Racist Remarks."

75. I say the work was provocatively titled because Hara intentionally used the Chinese character compound *Tōa* for Asia that was common in wartime and prewar Japan, instead of the now-standard syllabarized *Ajia*. See Hara, *Shin-Tōaron*.

76. Hara, *Shin-Tōaron*, 12.

77. Hara, *Shin-Tōaron*, 21.

could envision their future as an "extension of Western society."[78] In Hara's telling, the secularism and political ideology of the previous century was being challenged by a "completely different" and "richer" concept of the ego firmly embedded in community. Likewise, globalization faced opposition from regional formations constructed around "interpretive, lifeworld civilizations" (like East Asia) that accepted multiple worldviews, superimposing them one on top of the other.[79] Drawing on Samuel Huntington's "clash of civilizations" theory, popular in the 1990s, in the midst of this "clash" between the global and the regional, Hara urged the Japanese to seriously reconsider their position and role in Asia. The taboo about discussing Asianism in the country for the past half-century had made it all too easy for the Japanese to rely on globalism (that is, Americanism), but with the collapse of the Cold War order, Japan and East Asia had begun a "silent fusion."[80] Japan now had to play its part in the construction of this new civilization, a "polymorphic" world order in which Western liberalism was no longer the default principle of organization.[81]

While Hara and others proffered a rhetoric of collision and struggle in the early 2000s, still others presented a somewhat milder civilizational perspective in which Asia would assist in humanity's regeneration after the devastation of globalization. In the 2004 *Ajia no fukken: Seichō no bunmei ka kyōsei no bunmei ka* (Asia's revival: A civilization of economic growth or a civilization of symbiosis), the sinologist Nakayashiki Hiroshi (b. 1935) called for an "Asian revival" based on his conviction that "the civilization and era known as the 'modern'" had "reached the end of its life," as was evident in "complicated problems like environmental degradation and terrorism."[82] As he explained, the book was an attempt to show how Asian civilization could become a "positive" force for "the transformation and regeneration" of this wounded modernity through its unique approach to "nature, humanity, ethics, and daily life."[83] "The pathway to the regeneration of contemporary lifestyle and culture,"

78. Hara, *Shin-Tōaron*, 12.
79. Hara, *Shin-Tōaron*, 24.
80. Hara, *Shin-Tōaron*, 32–33.
81. Hara, *Shin-Tōaron*, 31.
82. Nakayashiki, *Ajia no fukken*, 1.
83. Nakayashiki, *Ajia no fukken*, 3–4.

according to Nakayashiki, lay in "nothing other than a revival of the principles of 'coexistence' (*kyōzon*) and 'symbiosis' (*kyōsei*) in Asian civilization." It was not a matter of simply reviving the Asia of "yesterday" just "as it had been" but instead one of "uncovering the method and contours of Asian civilizational principles from within contemporary conditions."[84] The first step would be for Asians to "rescue themselves," starting with Asian political leaders' recognizing the "illusion of economic growth" and "reviving" the Asia "within their own mentalities."[85] Moreover, Japan would command a special place in the Asian revival because the country "stood closest to uncovering the profile of this future civilization." Having "most profoundly experienced both Asian and modern civilizations," Japan supposedly had the "deepest understanding of their substance" of any country in the world. Thus, if the Japanese could "uncover a method for sublating 'modern civilization' into the 'Asia' within" themselves, the potential existed for orchestrating a breakthrough of "enormous significance for the world into the future."[86]

The pinnacle of these civilizational Asianist discourses came from Shindō Eiichi, the international relations scholar who in a 2007 publication presented Japan as a Christ-like figure, sacrificing its financial vitality and existence for the economic liberation of the region. According to Shindō, the region was undergoing nothing less than a "Confucian Asian Renaissance" powered by "civic Confucian capitalism"—the antithesis of "American-led casino capitalism."[87] Drawing on the work of the political scientist Robert Putnam and other Western theorists of social capital, Shindō pointed to the crisis in Western civilization—especially Anglo-American neoliberalism—where competition and individualism had supposedly eroded social ties and trust and fatally wounded the institutions of marriage and the extended family.[88] In contrast, Shindō posited Confucian capitalism as the embodiment of a burgeoning and mature Asia. No longer a tool of feudal business conglomerates or despotic rulers, Confucian capitalism belonged to the people and had become a "civic" device

84. Nakayashiki, *Ajia no fukken*, 4.
85. Nakayashiki, *Ajia no fukken*, 4–5.
86. Nakayashiki, *Ajia no fukken*, 194.
87. Shindō, *Higashi Ajia*, 241.
88. Shindō, *Higashi Ajia*, 244.

for their empowerment. Echoing Takeuchi's logic, Shindō suggested that civic Confucianism enriched (that is, "repackaged") the social capital idea by infusing it with the very best of Confucian ethics. For instance, when filtered through a modern civic lens, Mencius's four fundamental principles of benevolence, virtue, propriety, and wisdom spontaneously flowered into modern East Asian expressions of trust, civility, value for education, self-discipline, and peaceful socioeconomic development.[89]

Yet as overstated and fanciful as this vision appears, it pales in comparison to Shindō's explanation of Japan's leading role in the rise of civic Confucianism, which he attributed to two instances of national sacrifice for Asia in 1945 and 1985. According to Shindō, as an Asian forerunner, Japan had repeatedly fallen prey to the "spell of alliances" with Western powers—first with Germany and later with the United States—which in both cases had resulted in national destruction but also, and importantly for him, the liberation of Asia. Here Shindō echoed a very old refrain in the history of Japanese far-right thought: namely, that the "Japanese people," conceived of as a unitary ethnic nation (*minzoku*), had been repeatedly victimized by government and business elites and an international system controlled by the West. Shindō described the Asia-Pacific War—which ended in the country's initial or "first defeat in war" (*daiichi no haisen*)—as essentially a battle for ethnic liberation from the Western colonial powers. Japan, he said, facilitated "the eruption of Asian ethnic nationalism" by "assisting" revolutionary Asians in their "struggle for ethnic self-determination," even while the Japanese set about "oppressing these same people."[90] Japan's "second defeat in war" happened with the Plaza Accord, when an appreciated yen gutted Japanese manufacturing competitiveness. But just as the doomed Japanese wartime empire resulted in the burgeoning of movements for decolonialization (that is, East Asian civil society), Japanese corporate expansion into Asia after the Plaza Accord, argued Shindō, both nurtured capitalism in East Asia and reignited civil society, this time as civic Confucianism. As he explained, "if one disregards the presence or absence of physical destruction, what becomes clear from the first defeat in a military war and the second defeat in an economic war is that in both defeats Japan not only

89. Shindō, *Higashi Ajia*, 243.
90. Shindō, *Higashi Ajia*, 57.

surrendered to the hegemonic American enemy but it also catalyzed East Asian Liberation."[91]

Viewed in wide angle, the "Asian values" of Ishihara and Ogura and the civilizational discourses of Hara, Nakayashiki, and Shindō show how intensively conservatives began to deploy Asia in their writings and public discourse in the 1990s and beyond. Although hard-liners started out with crudely hierarchical imaginaries about Japan leading the flock of Asian geese, as Japan's fortunes changed, others concocted more sophisticated narratives based on civilizational conflict, Japan's selfless sacrifice for the region, and Asia as the harbinger of global revitalization. Regardless of the perspective, however, in the hands of hard-line Asianists and civilizational warriors, the Asia problem took on a decidedly different tenor than it had in its earlier manifestations in progressive thought and activism. Although conservative pundits ostensibly identified the problem as Japan's lost Asian roots or the destructive impact of the West on the region, such assertions served primarily as a camouflage for their real concern about Japan's steady decline and its interminable subservience to America. Yet, as much as this nationalist manipulation of Asia threatened to replace the Asia problem with a fraudulent solution, it also simultaneously opened a conduit for progressives to legitimately reenter the symbolic territory of Asian community—if only to defend against rightist strategies to obliterate or revise the past.

MODERATE INSTRUMENTALISTS AND FUSIONISTS

Alongside the hard-liners and civilizational warriors emerged a more moderate group of instrumentalists and fusionists whose perception of the Asia problem grew out of a sense of opportunity, urgency, and on occasion crisis. Rather than a staunchly chauvinistic or Asianist ideology, most subscribed to a kind of patriotic realism based on the growing interdependence among countries of the region, particularly in East Asia. For many moderates, this regionalization underwrote their support of a formalized regional infrastructure like an EAC that would embed so-called universal values—the rule of law, the free market, and political freedom—

91. Shindō, *Higashi Ajia*, 63.

in regional interactions, while maintaining openness to the outside world. Illustrative of this perspective was the political scientist Shiraishi Takashi, who called on Japan to leave behind the chauvinistic Asianism of old for a new, realistic, and pragmatic regionalist outlook based on the reality of Asia's stunning economic performance. Some moderates, like the economist Morishima Michio, framed the problem in terms of a national crisis: faced with dire domestic decline, Japan simply had no choice but to commit to East Asia, or the country would "collapse."[92] As we will see, progressives drew liberally on the ideas of such moderates as they crafted their own visions of Asian community—particularly the notion of recalibrating Japan's relations with America by moving closer to the country's Asian neighbors. But although moderates certainly recognized the unresolved historical issues between Japan and Asia and the need for reconciliation, for the most part theirs was a forward-looking perspective that differed fundamentally from that of progressives, for whom overcoming ethical and historical encumbrances outweighed geopolitical or economic concerns. For this reason, it was easier for moderates to advocate a vision of Asian community in which everyone could be a winner.

The moderate New Asianism of the early 1990s grew out of the "flying geese" analogies of the 1970s and 1980s, which positioned Japan as the leading goose in an East Asian miracle. In 1993, for example, Okazaki Hisahiko, a bureaucrat in the Ministry of Foreign Affairs and later ambassador to Thailand, outlined his "grand strategy for a new Asia," in which Japanese-led economic development would strengthen the economic base of the Asia-Pacific region.[93] Unlike assistance from the International Monetary Fund or World Bank, Japanese investment, explained Okazaki, came "interest free" and would produce an "overall improvement in economic and technological standards." Investment in Asia would also help Japan solve the problems of a shrinking labor force and limited land. More strategically, exporting the Japanese model to Asia would create "captive" markets that would empower the Japanese economy to expand globally. In short, Japanese economic penetration of East Asia was "all good" for both Japan and the region.[94]

92.   Morishima, *Naze Nihon*, v.
93.   Okazaki, *Atarashii Ajia*.
94.   Okazaki, *Atarashii Ajia*, 77 and 86.

But as Japan's domestic recession continued through the 1990s, scenarios of a Japanese economic takeover of East Asia gave way to more urgent appeals for Japan to engage with the region as a matter of national survival: Asia was seen not as a problem but as a solution. The Okuda Report of 1999, commissioned by the cabinet of Prime Minister Obuchi Keizō and headed by Okuda Hiroshi—then chairman of the Toyota Motor Corporation and the Japan Business Federation—encapsulated this growing sense of Asia as a solution among many moderate academics, business elites, and high-level diplomats in the late 1990s. Coming on the heels of the 1997 AFC and ongoing Japanese economic stagnation, the report appealed to a "common destiny" among Asian countries and proposed a "third opening" (*daisan kaikoku*) of Japan, after the first opening of the Meiji Restoration and the second opening of 1945.[95] In what Edith Terry characterizes as a "blistering attack on the government's Asia policy," Okuda—through his shadow author, the diplomat and Asia specialist Kohara Masahiro—accused officials of intentionally restricting Asian imports and inflows of Asian workers. He called for free-trade agreements with Asian countries and demanded that Japanese visa requirements be eased for Asian workers, especially those with skills in caring for the aged. The sense of Asia as the only solution to a national crisis is palpable throughout the report.

Moderates propagating this "Japanese-crisis, Asian-solution" thesis inspired a virtual cottage industry of publications from around the mid- to late 1990s, with most authors predicting economic ruin if the country failed to engage with Asia and open up to Asian workers. Morishima Michio (1923–2004) was among the most outspoken here, and the titles of his books from the mid-1990s on reveal an intensifying sense of crisis: *Nihon no sentaku: Atarashii kunizukuri ni mukete* (Choices for Japan: Toward the construction of a new nation) in 1995, *Naze Nihon wa botsuraku suru ka* (Why Japan will collapse) in 1999, and *Nihon ni dekiru koto wa nanika: Higashi Ajia kyōdōtai o teian suru* (What can Japan do? Propose an EAC) in 2001.[96] His ideas read very much like the tracts on

95. Okuda Hiroshi, *Ajia keizai saisei*.
96. Morishima, *Nihon no sentaku*, *Naze Nihon*, and *Nihon ni dekiru*. In English, see Morishima, *Collaborative Development*. Morishima was telling a different story in the early 1980s. See Morishima, *Why Has Japan "Succeeded"?*

national survival written by patriotic samurai of the era before the Meiji Restoration, and in fact, Morishima saw many parallels between Japan's contemporary condition and the national crisis of the mid-nineteenth century. But in stark contrast to the Restoration patriots, Morishima's program for survival revolved around Japan joining, not leaving, Asia. Indeed, if the Japanese failed to embrace an EAC, he believed that only ruin awaited—in the form of "spiritual," "financial," "industrial," and "educational" "devastation."[97] Yet the Japanese people were "not attracted to this kind of proposal," he lamented, because "even Japanese today think they are the best in Asia."[98]

Among all the Asian solutions put forward by moderates in these years, Morishima's was among the most idealistic (some might even say quixotic), but it offered progressives a valuable blueprint as they responded to hard-liners with their own visions of Asian community. To begin with, Morishima took great care to distinguish his concept of an Asian Economic Community (AEC) from the bankrupt Greater East Asia Co-Prosperity Sphere because the new vision was not about Japanese "monopolization" of power but about "independent decision making on the part of participating states."[99] Consisting of the nations of Northeast Asia, the AEC would be divided into twelve "blocs": six for China, two for Korea, two for Japan, one for Taiwan, and one for an independent Okinawa, which would serve as the political and administrative headquarters of the community as Brussels does in the European Union.[100] According to Morishima, this bloc system would be necessary to prevent China from dominating the future "Asian Parliament" and, in turn, undermining the stability of the whole community.[101] Before the AEC developed

97. These characterizations of devastation correspond to chapter titles in Morishima's 1999 *Naze Nihon*.

98. Morishima, *Naze Nihon*, viii.

99. Morishima, *Nihon no sentaku*, 268.

100. Morishima, *Nihon no sentaku*, 269, and *Naze Nihon*, 155. In earlier versions of his AEC, Morishima posited only ten blocs, based on five blocs for China. No doubt the rising power of China encouraged him to want to further dilute that country's influence in any future community. In addition, Morishima excluded Southeast Asia because of ethnic and cultural differences between it and the rest of Asia in terms of such things as writing systems, types of Buddhism, and religions. See Morishima, *Naze Nihon*, 159–60.

101. Morishima, *Nihon no sentaku*, 269.

into a formalized political community, Morishima posited a phase of economic and developmental cooperation when it would avoid political and cultural matters, operating more as a "construction community."[102] This phase would involve joint projects for dams, canals, leisure facilities, a bullet train network, and a shipping community linking the region across multiple sectors.[103] The AEC would accept different "customs" and "etiquette," and countries would be free to follow their own models. Nonetheless, as happened during the evolution of the European Economic Community into the European Union, Morishima predicted that over time common "customs and manners" would develop among members through interaction.[104]

Grassroots, people-to-people interactions would also promote community. Because the peoples of Northeast Asia were "not so physically different," Morishima predicted that the number of "mixed race" people would proliferate, thanks to more "international marriages." In turn, such blood connections would "deepen mutual understanding of different lifestyles and manners," and the "barriers of ethnic consciousness" would begin to "break down." In this way, the "economic community of the AEC" would "pave the way for a communal society (*gemeinschaft*) of East Asian people (*Tōa minzoku*)."[105] At this stage, the AEC would evolve into an Asian Union, with member countries cooperating across all sectors and gradually relinquishing independent state functions like policing and defense.[106] Morishima imagined a regional identity analogous to the United Kingdom, in which the English, Scots, and Welsh all considered themselves to be "British."[107] Ultimately, the "age of ethnic nations" would "come to an end" in the region, with the countries of Northeast Asia crystalizing into a "new broad-reaching state" that Morishima called—quite curiously—the "United States of Asia" (*Ajia gasshū koku*).[108] Attracted by Morishima's utopian vision of East Asian interconnection, in the coming

102.   Morishima, *Nihon ni dekiru*, 179.
103.   Morishima, *Nihon no sentaku*, 271 and 276, and *Naze Nihon*, 155.
104.   Morishima, *Nihon no sentaku*, 277.
105.   Morishima, *Nihon no sentaku*, 279–80.
106.   Morishima, *Nihon no sentaku*, 281.
107.   Morishima, *Nihon no sentaku*, 281.
108.   Morishima, *Nihon no sentaku*, 284. Morishima also later used the term "United States of East Asia" (*higashi Ajia gasshū koku*). See Morishima, *Nihon ni dekiru*, 189.

years progressives like Kang Sang-jung subsequently adopted many of these ideas into their own visions of Asian community.

Although approaching the region from a somewhat different perspective, another group of moderates offered an analogous discourse of Asia as a solution for Japan, in this case relating not so much to the country's domestic woes but to its influence as an international power and its relationship with the United States. Some, for instance, advocated a critical new role for Japan as an "honest broker" between Asia and the West, "taking advantage of Japan's Asian cultural tradition on the one hand and its modern experiences of Westernization on the other."[109] In 1995, Takenaka Heizō, an economist who became finance minister in Koizumi's cabinet (2001–6), called on Japan to become a "kind of glue" that would bind together "the European Union, the North American Free Trade Agreement, and APEC [the Asia-Pacific Economic Cooperation]," helping foster "creative tension" as opposed to "rigid blocs."[110] Funabashi Yōichi voiced a similar mantra throughout the 1990s with his ideas about an "Asia-Pacific fusion." As he asserted in an influential 1993 essay in *Foreign Affairs*, Asia had "at long last started to define itself," and "Asian consciousness and identity" were "coming vigorously to life."[111] Rejecting the "Asianist sentiments and excessive calculations" of Mahathir, Ishihara, and other hardliners, Funabashi suggested that the "spirit of the times" was "predominantly affirmative and forward-thinking, not reactionary and nostalgic."[112] He identified a contemporary Asian consciousness "animated by workday pragmatism," the rise of "a flourishing middle class," and the "moxie of technocrats," all tied together by the "power of electronic communications technology."[113] Flatly rejecting Huntington's "clash of civilizations" hypothesis, Funabashi argued in his 1995 *Ajia Taiheiyō fyūjon: APEC to Nihon* (Asia-Pacific fusion: APEC and Japan) that the "economic and cultural dynamics of the Asia-Pacific" were conversely "promoting economic mutual interdependence and civilizational cross-fertilization" that, in

---

109.   Yamakage, "Japan's National Security," 301.
110.   Takenaka Heizō, "Can Japan Glue," 18.
111.   Funabashi, "Asianization of Asia," 75.
112.   Funabashi, "Asianization of Asia," 77. See also Funabashi, *Ajia Taiheiyō*, 376.
113.   Funabashi, "Asianization of Asia," 75 and 78.

turn, had the potential to "temper" and even "overcome" divisions of "race and ideology."[114] In this "massive civilizational experiment happening in the Asia-Pacific," an "intellectual fusion" was underway: "the work ethic, focus on education, and social cohesion of East Asia" was "joining with the free market and democracy of Western society . . . stimulating the countries of North America and Oceania and, in turn, energizing the Asia-Pacific."[115] For Japan, the issue was no longer one of choosing either America or Asia but one of choosing both—"joining Asia and joining the West." Moreover—and importantly—Japan could "not be content with its role as a mediator between the West (Europe and America) and the East (Asia)." Its mission was nothing short of helping catalyze the "fusion" of a historic "Asia-Pacific Civilization."[116]

At first glance, Funabashi's fusionism appears to be a movement away from the New Asianist agenda in the direction of the West, but as observers noted, such Pan-Pacific perspectives also implied a Japanese movement away from the United States by placing a greater distance between the two nations and, more generally, "restoring the balance" between Asia and the West.[117] Indeed, for Funabashi, the New Asianism emerged from a "spiritual aspiration" to create more distance from America: "the days when the United States sneezed and Asia caught a cold" were "over," and thus Japan needed to recalibrate its relations with countries on both sides of the Pacific.[118] American observers of Japan concurred. In 1997 the American political scientist T. J. Pempel concluded that "the most fitting image of Japan's proper role is the *torii*, the large wooden gate that stands at key points outside a Shinto shrine and which consists of two large columns joined by an equally strong lintel. For many Japanese, their country is the ideal lintel—the top beam or crossbar uniting the otherwise isolated columns, which represent Asia and the West. Japan is ideally positioned economically and culturally to be the 'bridge between East and West.'"[119]

114. Funabashi, *Ajia Taiheiyō*, 22–23.
115. Funabashi, *Ajia Taiheiyō*, 21–22.
116. Funabashi, *Ajia Taiheiyō*, 84–85 and 417.
117. Morris-Suzuki, "Invisible Countries," 11.
118. Funabashi, "Asianization of Asia," 78, and *Ajia Taiheiyō*, 337.
119. Pempel, "Transpacific Torii," 51.

Shiraishi Takashi (b. 1950) was among the most outspoken supporters of such realist and instrumentalist regionalism, taking aim at those
proposing an exclusivist community based on shared culture and identity. As he argued in 2000, it would be an "act of madness" to abandon
the West for Asianism: "The aims" should be to "harmonize internationalism and Asianism" and to create "a stable Asian regional order," along
with "expanding and deepening exchange" through "economic cooperation, cultural cooperation, intellectual cooperation, [and] technological
cooperation."[120] Taking aim at hard-line Asianist ideologues, Shiraishi asserted that "Japan is not the light of Asia," "and however much Japanese
chauvinists such as Shintarō Ishihara would love to see it become such,
that is a role that Japan cannot pull off. To make this point two ghosts
must be put to rest: the wartime Co-Prosperity Sphere and the postwar
developmental state."[121] "Today's Asia is not the same as the Asia of the
past," argued Shiraishi and coauthor Caroline Sy Hau in a 2009 essay.
The region was no longer associated with "humiliation, poverty, and despotism" but with affluence, democratization, and development.[122] In
short, "the Eurocentric order that the Asianism of the past criticized" was
"long gone," and Asianism was "of no use in explaining the project to
construct an East Asian Community."[123]

While Shiraishi's fervent endeavors to dissociate the idea of an East
Asian Community from the Asianism of the hard-liners and the shadow
of co-prosperity were genuine enough, like most other moderate instrumentalists, he still presented Asia largely in terms of its utility for Japan's
economic well-being and survival. In other words, there was no overt recognition of an Asia problem in need of resolution, as there was in progressive thought and activism. On the contrary, the message of moderates was mostly about a burgeoning Asia becoming the solution to Japan's
domestic problems. It would be up to progressives to join the dots between the unresolved past, on the one hand, and moderates' generally rosy
vision of Asian community, on the other hand.

120. Shiraishi, "Ajia o dō kangaeru," 71.
121. Shiraishi, "Japan and Southeast Asia," 170.
122. Shiraishi and Hau, "Beyond the Spell," 35.
123. Shiraishi and Hau, "Beyond the Spell," 35; Shiraishi, "Higashi Ajia chiiki," 88.

PROGRESSIVE VISIONARIES

In contrast to both the hard-liners and the moderates who entered this debate in the 1990s with a strongly instrumentalist agenda—in other words, using the region as a vehicle for national strength, enrichment, or survival—progressives charted a trajectory that was strongly shaped by decades of unremitting and often agonizing encounters with the historical legacies and contemporary complications of the Asia problem. Accordingly, while drawing on the energy of the New Asianism, their blueprints for Japan's return to the region most often began from the standpoints of history and responsibility. Asian community, they argued, must serve as a mechanism for reining in the excesses of nationalism in the region, especially the troubling stranglehold of ethnocentrism on Japanese identity and historical consciousness. At the same time, most progressives accepted the ongoing role of nation-states in the region, with none prophesying a future "United States of Asia," as Morishima had in the mid-1990s. Few if any progressives envisaged a complete abandonment of Japan for some future Asian identity. Instead, their intellectual efforts unfolded as a fascinating synthesis of historical awareness, attention to diversity and hybridity, and receptiveness to the New Asianist discourses on Asian community.

The historian Arano Yasunori and colleagues were among the earliest to begin rethinking Japan in its region, with trailblazing publications like the 1988 _Kinsei Nihon to Higashi Ajia_ (Early modern Japan and East Asia) and the 1992 multivolume _Ajia no naka no Nihon shi_ (Japanese history in East Asia).[124] Thereafter the historian Amino Yoshihiko and colleagues produced important studies on the impact of East Asian maritime exchanges on Japanese cultural diversity, while other groups published collections on "modern Japan and colonialism," "thinking from Asia," and "Maritime Asia."[125] As the political scientist Yoon Keun-cha observed in the mid-1990s, all of this research was slowly breaking down the "closed country" mentality so prominent in Japanese historiography and other disciplines.[126]

---

124. Arano, _Kinsei Nihon_; Arano et al., _Ajia no naka_.
125. Amino et al., _Umi kara mita Nihon bunka_; Ōe Shinobu et al., _Iwanami kōza_; Mizoguchi et al., _Ajia kara kangaeru_; Ōmoto et al., _Umi no Ajia_.
126. Yoon, _Nihon kokumin_, 210.

To be sure, these scholars were not starting with a blank slate. As early as 1963 the historians Ishimoda Shō, Tōma Seita, Tōyama Shigeki, Matsumoto Shinpachirō and others had proposed the idea of "East Asian history" (*Higashi Ajia shi*) at a meeting of Rekiken (Historical Science Society of Japan) in an attempt to challenge the dominance of so-called world history based on general principles.[127] Thereafter, Tōma conducted pioneering research on exchanges between Korea, China, and Japan in the ancient period as he searched for the roots of an "East Asian world."[128] Around the same time, both Uehara Senroku and Tōyama began to speak of the "East Asian region" (*Higashi Ajia chiiki*), with Uehara positing Japan, Korea, China, and Vietnam as its constituent members. Tōyama also published several important articles on East Asian history in the mid-1960s, including "Kindai shi kara mita Higashi Ajia" (East Asia from the perspective of modern history) and "Sekai shi ni okeru chiiki shi no mondaiten" (The question of regional history in world history).[129]

But as Sonoda Shigeto explains, academic studies of Asia failed to proliferate thereafter, partly because of the close connection of wartime Asian studies to Japan's military aggression, but also because of the difficulties Japanese researchers faced in securing Asian collaborators due to lingering anti-Japanese sentiment.[130] Intellectual biases also inhibited attention to Asia within the Japanese academy. Sonoda gives the example of sociology, where the supremacy of American theories resulted in the relegation of studies on Asia to the "niche" or "specialty" field of "area studies," thus largely sidelining them from mainstream sociological research.[131] Furthermore, as we saw in chapter 1, the focus on modernization among Japanese academics in the early postwar years and again in the 1960s produced a mentality—a "psychological mechanism," according to Sonoda—that Japan was (or should be) fundamentally "different" from Asia. This mentality of separation was only further "confirmed" by Japan's astounding economic transformation in the ensuing years.[132]

---

127. See Tōyama, "Higashi Ajia."
128. Tōma, *Higashi Ajia sekai*.
129. Tōyama, "Kindai shi" and "Sekai shi."
130. Sonoda, "Fīrudo toshite," 23.
131. Sonoda, "Fīrudo toshite," 23.
132. Sonoda, "Fīrudo toshite," 24.

Nonetheless, the 1970s and 1980s were hardly barren ground in the study of Asia in Japan, albeit much important work in that period unfolded beyond the traditional institutions of knowledge production. As we saw in chapter 5, Tsurumi Yoshiyuki's pioneering fieldwork and writings on Southeast Asia in the 1970s and 1980s laid important foundations for the 1990s boom in attention to Asia. Not only activists but also a new generation of Asia-focused academics were awakened to the region through works such as Tsurumi's best-selling 1982 *Banana to Nihonjin* and his ensuing studies of shrimp, sea slugs, and coastal Asia.

However, the economic transformations of the late 1980s and early 1990s propelled Asia to the forefront of progressives' consciousness as never before, almost demanding new imaginations of the region—especially as Japan's miraculous "distinctiveness" gradually evaporated and the countries of Asia prospered. Moreover, the rise of hard-line Asianists and moderate fusionists who threatened to push the discussion of Asia in a wholly instrumentalist direction gave the issue even greater urgency. A seminal publication at this moment was the seven-volume work titled *Ajia kara kangaeru* (Thinking from Asia) published by the University of Tokyo Press in 1993–94 and edited by the historians Mizoguchi Yūzō (China), Hamashita Takeshi (East Asia), Hiraishi Naoaki (Japan), and Miyajima Hiroshi (Korea). According to Sun Ge, "most remarkable" in the multivolume work was the "collaboration between Mizoguchi Yūzō and Hamashita Takeshi," a symbolic "joining of intellectual history and regional studies" not witnessed since the dialogue between Takeuchi Yoshimi and Umesao Tadao in 1961 (see chapter 1).[133]

Writing in the preface of the multivolume work, Mizoguchi and his fellow editors observed that to date, Asia had mostly been understood in comparison to Europe or Japan, with these serving as the "standard" or "primary axes." But the task the editors wished to pursue was to reconceptualize Asia as a "space of self-recognition"—in other words, an "imagination of Asia from within."[134] With respect to Japan, moreover, the editors said the aim of the work was to "situate" the country "in the context of Asia," "scrutinizing" how "Japan's self-recognition" had "unfolded historically in connection with" the region. Was it possible, they asked, to "relativize"

133. Sun, "How Does Asia Mean?," 43.
134. Mizoguchi et al., "Kankō ni atatte," ii.

Japan's "historical position" not on the basis of "centripetal forces" (that is, abandoning Asia) but instead on the basis of "centrifugal forces" (that is, through Japan's "connections with the various regions of Asia")?[135]

Hamashita Takeshi (b. 1943) led the way in this project with his pioneering efforts to uncover a history of regional maritime engagements that had long been obscured by the powerful and rigidly internalist narratives of national history. As Dick Stegewerns notes, Hamashita's proposal of an "Asian trade network" (*Ajia kōekiken*) was "greeted as [a] ground-breaking effort in the early 1990s."[136] Indeed, over time, Hamashita emerged as the leader of a new intellectual project to present Asia as an "integrated historical system" unified by "a single regional economy" and a "region-wide tribute trade relationship" centered on China.[137] As Hamashita explained, "East Asian history in modern times" had to be analyzed on "its own terms, with special attention to how its internal dynamism led to its transformation and how it accommodated the 'impact' of the coming of European powers and the rise of a new international system."[138]

Like Kang Sang-jung and other progressive advocates of Asian regionalism, Hamashita criticized the myopia in Japanese identity formation, which he viewed as a persistent process of differentiation from superficially imagined Others: first China and later the West. He argued that the overwhelming emphasis on the nation-state from the beginning of modernization in Japan served to obliterate consciousness of the Japanese archipelago as part of a regional system. Instead, the region was continuously reframed as—or, as Hamashita put it, "condensed" into—national identity.[139] Although Japanese civilization was itself a hybrid construction of imported regional and domestic forces, Hamashita said that the Japanese had purposely "detached" and decoupled the aspects of their civilization that had been borrowed from peripheral regions, making no attempt to understand them from within the "negotiations and exchanges" with cultures of the adjoining seas of Okhotsk, Japan, and East and South China. Such regional aspects of Japanese civilization were disassociated

---

135. Mizoguchi et al., "Kankō ni atatte," iii.
136. Stegewerns, "Forgotten Leaders," 101.
137. Hye Jeong Park, "East Asian Odyssey towards One Region," 891.
138. Hamashita, "Intra-Regional System," 113.
139. Hamashita, "Ajia kenkyū," 6.

from the region and inserted into the "center" so that they appeared to be distinctively "Japanese."[140] The negative outcome, for Hamashita, was the disappearance of the region from Japanese consciousness and identity, and this left only the nation, which served as a poor substitute for the country's historical embeddedness in the region.[141] Absent this consciousness of region, Hamashita concluded that it would be extremely difficult for the Japanese to "relativize" (*sōtaika*; that is, regionally contextualize) their nation, which had long served as the cozy (if fictitious) surrogate for the country's East Asian roots.

In spite of such conceptual barriers, Hamashita strove assiduously in the 1990s to "position Japan within an Asian context," detaching the study of Asia from its strongly Euro- and Japan-centric biases and demonstrating that the country had indeed constructed its identity through historical engagements "within" the region.[142] He stressed the historical existence of several maritime areas, including Northeast, East, and Southeast Asia: "Within this vast area, countries, regions, and trading centers and subcenters interacted with one another." The "region," he argued, was "not one large expanse of water like the Indian and Pacific Oceans," but "a series of seas connected by straits."[143] In this maritime conceptualization of East Asia—deeply influenced by Ferdinand Braudel's notion of the Mediterranean world—Japan emerged not as an isolated archipelago on the fringes of continental Asia but as an integral part of an organically intertwined system of regional networks.[144] Japan, in Hamashita's model, was unequivocally positioned within Asia.

Hamashita's colleague in this regional project, Hiraishi Naoaki (b. 1945), pursued a similar regionalization of Japan in the ideational realm through a provocative reconsideration of prewar Pan-Asianist thought in the country. Hiraishi attempted to detach this prewar Asianism from its

140. Hamashita, "Ajia kenkyū," 6.

141. Hamashita, "Ajia kenkyū," 7.

142. Hamashita, "Ajia kenkyū," 1–2. See also, for example, Hamashita, *Higashi Ajia sekai* and "Intra-Regional System."

143. Hamashita, "Intra-Regional System," 115.

144. In the mid-1990s Hamashita, Amino, and other Japanese academics joined with the American sociologist Immanuel Wallerstein to produce a collection of essays on Braudel's *The Mediterranean and the Mediterranean World in the Age of Philip II*. See Amino et al., *Umi kara mita.*

sullied association with colonialism and imperialism, resituating the Japanese discourse within the broader Pan-Asianist movement for liberation. He unambiguously distanced his project from Takeuchi—who, he argued, approached Asianism primarily from the perspective of Japan's wartime responsibility. Takeuchi's study of Asianism, according to Hiraishi, was a method for understanding why a movement for "solidarity" resulted in "aggression," and in this sense it conformed to the progressive postwar project to identify and root out the pathology of modern Japanese history and thus was a fundamentally national perspective.[145]

But according to Hiraishi, to properly understand war responsibility and the Japan-Asia connection, it was also necessary to examine how the various strains of Japanese Pan Asianism were molded by external ideas, political events, and economic developments in Asia.[146] Hiraishi pointed to a number of prewar Japanese Asianists who he said must be understood within such a regional intellectual history. One example was the Meiji political activist Tarui Tōkichi (1850–1922)—who, in his 1893 "Daitō gappō ron" (Treatise on a greater East Asian union), called for a confederation of Asian states based on "independence" and "equality."[147] Similar was the politician Konoe Atsumaro (1863–1904)—who, in an influential 1898 essay titled "Dō jinshu dōmei tsuketari Shina mondai no kenkyū no hitsuyō" (A same-race alliance and on the necessity of studying the Chinese question) advocated "Eastern solidarity" and proposed an "Asian Monroe Doctrine" that caught the eye of the Chinese political thinker and reformer Kang Youwei (1858–1927).[148] For Hiraishi, Konoe's call for this doctrine was a significant early expression of "the East for the East," and the reach of Konoe's ideas beyond Japan proved for him the regional interconnectedness and wider influence of Japanese Pan-Asianist thought at the time.[149] Hiraishi also identified a similar panregional perspective in the thought of Okakura Tenshin (1862–1913), whose negative reaction to modern Western civilization as the "destroyer

---

145. Hiraishi, "Kindai Nihon," 266.
146. Hiraishi, "Kindai Nihon," 266.
147. Tarui, "Daitō gappō ron."
148. Hiraishi, "Kindai Nihon," 275–76 and 278. For an English translation of Konoe's essay see Zachmann, "Konoe Atsumaro," 89–92.
149. Hiraishi, "Kindai Nihon," 278.

of Asian tradition" and identification of spiritual and civilizational commonalities in China and India were an "indication" of "revitalized confidence" among Asian intellectuals.[150] Hiraishi said that in contrast to Konoe's "Asian Monroe Doctrine," Okakura was less interested in a pan-Asian political alliance against the West than he was in an Asian "self-renewal deeply rooted in tradition" and focused on the "ethnic awakening of individual nations." Hiraishi explained Okakura's "positive" and "offensive" (*kōseiteki*; in contrast to "defensive") Asianism as a product of his encounter with the anti-British liberation movement in India in the early twentieth century, especially his interactions with Indian intellectuals like Rabindranath Tagore.[151]

Taken together, the maritime and intellectual histories represented by Hamashita and Hiraishi show that progressive scholarship on Asia in the 1990s drew considerable energy from the growing economic interdependence in East Asia and the related burgeoning of ideas about an EAC. But in contrast to hard-line Asianists (who, in the face of regionalization, attempted to buttress national history through stories of Japan's Asian leadership or national sacrifice) and even moderates (who found national salvation in Asia), Hamashita, Hiraishi, and other progressives skillfully mobilized the energy of regionalization to undermine the internalist mythologies underwriting Japanese national history and identity and, from this standpoint, propose a new future built on histories of interconnection and shared destiny.

Other progressives—rightly termed "progressive visionaries"—injected this discourse on historical interconnection and shared destiny into their blueprints for Japan's future in the region. They drew on the ideas and movements for Asian reconnection that we have seen developing in progressive thought and activism from the 1970s onward, but now they made the intellectual breakthrough of stepping into the previously taboo territory of an Asian communal imaginary. Strikingly at odds with the visions of other New Asianists who called for community, their proposals were firmly rooted in the unbendable requirement that past aggressors must, first and foremost, offer a "meaningful apology and compensation" to victims, particularly with Japan making such offers to China

150. Hiraishi, "Kindai Nihon," 281.
151. Hiraishi, "Kindai Nihon," 281.

and Korea.[152] As we have seen, activist intellectuals like Wada Haruki, Tanaka Hiroshi, and Matsui Yayori backed up this stance in a diverse range of grassroots movements and public advocacy.

The University of Tokyo professor (1998–2013) and high-profile public intellectual Kang Sang-jung (b. 1950) was among the most trenchant and influential progressive visionaries here, joined by the stalwart Asia advocate Wada; the Kyoto University historian Yamamuro Shin'ichi; and Sakamoto Yoshikazu, a proponent of "inter-people diplomacy." Although Kang was still very much a voice in the wilderness, the fact that a resident Korean could exert such influence in discussions about Asia at this time speaks volumes about the substantive progress that had been made toward deimperialization in progressive circles. Genuinely committed though they had been to the situation of Asian minorities in Japan and the status of Japan in Asia, progressives had unquestioningly assumed throughout the postwar era that it was their responsibility and moral duty to speak on behalf of voiceless fellow Asians and "Asia" more generally. However, Kang's emergence symbolized a significant recalibration of this imperialistic specter that still haunted the progressive psyche.

A second-generation resident Korean, Kang's thinking about Asian community grew out of his experience as a member of an ethnic minority group that was discriminated against, as well as from his intense concern about relations between Japan and the two Koreas. Kang's father had served as a high-ranking official in Japan's feared wartime military police (*kenpei*), making him a rarity among members of minority groups in Japan at the time. As Kang explained to a Diet subcommittee in 2001, "thanks to this strange twist of fate, I flatter myself on being someone who knows, most of all, about the physiology of Japanese society. Put frankly, on this point I have a positive opinion about being *made in Japan*."[153] That said, Kang's writings and speeches were hardly Panglossian, taking aim at the pervasive discrimination against Asian minorities in Japan as one root cause of the country's deeply distorted understanding of the region. From the late 1980s into the 1990s, Kang focused intensively on what he termed a "Japanese-style Orientalism," according to which resident Koreans, Chinese, and Taiwanese were forced to subsist in a subservient realm as "internal

152. Selden and Selden, "Wada Haruki," 373.
153. Kang, *Tōhoku Ajia*, 19. Kang used the English phrase "made in Japan."

others" (*uchinaru tasha*), burdened with representing "backward Asia" in an "advanced Japan."[154] It was within this "cultural hegemony" that the Japanese clarified their identity. By "laying an uncrossable boundary" between Asia and themselves, the Japanese constructed a "stereotyped" Asian "space" at the very "extremity" of an "extremely intimate space" reserved "only" for the Japanese—a prototype for which could be found in Japan's relations with Korea.[155] And for Kang, this cultural hegemony resulted in Asia's constant relegation to the level of an instrument or "means" for some Japanese "objective," whether that be related to resources, markets, or manpower.[156] "Not once" in the country's modern history had "Asia itself" become the "aim" for Japan.[157] Indeed, in the most emotional language, Kang described Japan as a "changeling born of the East Asian world": by "biting into its [mother's] womb this changeling had dismantled East Asia" and, in the process, secured its triumphant entry onto the "modern world" stage.[158] Given this self-destructive nature, Kang could only speculate whether it would ever be "possible" for the Japanese to "construct a relationship" with Asia "in which both sides mutually became the objective of the other." If not, he feared that Asia might be doomed to become yet again "a national policy" or "a foothold for some specific national objective" in Japan.[159]

Kang appears to have arrived at the "common house of Asia" idea as a kind of solution—or, more accurately, therapy—for the scathing critique of modern Japan that he and others articulated in the early 1990s, particularly in the wake of Emperor Hirohito's demise (1989) and the looming anniversaries of the Asia-Pacific War (1991 and 1995). It was a critique premised on Japan's postwar neglect of Asia and the horrific costs of its modernity for the region. According to Kang, historical contingencies (some intellectual, others institutional) had intervened to shut regional consciousness out from the Japanese psyche in the postwar era, undermining the historic opportunity offered by defeat in war to fundamentally

---

154. Kang, "'Nihonteki orientarizumu,'" 134.
155. Kang, "'Nihonteki orientarizumu,'" 134.
156. Kang, *Ajia kara Nihon*, 27.
157. Kang, *Ajia kara Nihon*, 3.
158. Kang, "Nihon no Ajiakan," 77.
159. Kang, *Ajia kara Nihon*, 3.

transform the country's relationship with Asia. Kang pointed to the shortcomings of Marxist and modernist thought in Japan (such as the ideas of Maruyama Masao and Ōtsuka Hisao), which, as we saw in chapter 1, tended to reinforce visions of a backward Asia. Moreover, as discussed above, until at least the mid-1950s many intellectuals were loath to touch the contaminated notion of regionalism, which became taboo. As Wada explained, the "bankruptcy" of the Greater East Asia Co-Prosperity Sphere meant that any proposal of a regionalism inclusive of Japan "became something wicked," leaving many progressives convinced that the Japanese were wholly "unqualified to think about such things."[160]

In addition to such intellectual obstacles, Kang recognized the role of political and institutional factors in progressives' alienation from Asia and regionalist thought. Thanks to America, the relatively painless dismantling of Japan's empire had made defeat into a one-dimensional process of demilitarization that lacked any consciousness of decolonization (that is, deimperialization), which was very different from the traumatic experiences of France and other former colonial powers.[161] For most Japanese, including returnees from the Korean and Taiwanese colonies, the sense was one of having been victimized, and there was "no opportunity to face decolonization as their own problem."[162] Some government officials actually believed that Japan might retain some of its Northeast Asian territories.[163] Together with the Tokyo Tribunal, which "shelved" the "issue of the colonies" because it cut too close to the bone for the British, Dutch, and French, the hub-and-spokes unilateralism of the US-Japan alliance only exacerbated this alienation from Asia and the incomplete nature of the postwar settlement.[164] For Kang, the "one-sided" peace settlement (*tandoku kōwa*) and the signing of the US-Japan Security Treaty in 1951 short-circuited Japan's historic opportunity for reconciliation and reconfiguration of the country's relationship with Asia.[165] The Asia policy of the United States stymied any possibility of a community

160. Wada, *Tōhoku Ajia kyōdō*, 10.
161. Kang, *Ajia kara Nihon*, 12.
162. Kang, *Ajia kara Nihon*, 13.
163. Kang, *Ajia kara Nihon*, 13.
164. Kang, *Ajia kara Nihon*, 17.
165. Kang, *Ajia kara Nihon*, 10.

similar to the European Union's emerging in the region, making it "structurally impossible for . . . bilateral friendships to develop."[166] Furthermore, the subsequent redirection of nationalism from the past toward a "forward looking" ideology of "productivity"—what Kang called Japan's "second abandoning of Asia and joining the West"—resulted in a new "narrative of modernity" in which the country emerged as a "successful example of 'uniquely' employing the Western pattern," while simultaneously pushing it even further away from Asia than in the prewar period.[167] Indeed, Kang controversially suggested that though it was certainly "distorted," the prewar consciousness of Asia within Japan was far richer and contained many "treasures" that were either "cleared out" or "put in storage" after defeat.[168]

As a result, Kang said that the Japanese (progressives included) had come to understand their nation and the nature of its "internationalization" in the postwar era primarily as "Americanization." The country's foreign policy was essentially driven by efforts not to aggravate policy makers and political heavyweights in Washington, half a world away.[169] Consequently, Japan's relations with Asia and its consciousness of the region had atrophied. This "Asia-less postwar" era facilitated a "historical amnesia" or "memoricide" (*kiokugoroshi*) in which the problems of war and postwar responsibility "vanished into the hazy mist."[170] This "lack of a 'synchronic experience' with Asia" also underwrote the "structural distortion" in Japanese politics: the more "divorced" Japan became from the region, the more it was "forced to rely on America," becoming a pathetically "quasi-incompetent entity" (*jun-kinchisansha*) in international matters.[171] Moreover, the "Asia-less postwar" in Kang's telling was a paradoxical story inasmuch as exclusion and obliteration existed alongside historical continuity. Although Japan's "internal Others" were "excluded as heterogeneous elements potentially endangering the 'imagined community,'" they "simultaneously—and paradoxically—"also played the part of a "decrepit

166. Kang, *Ajia kara Nihon*, 26.
167. Kang, "Rekishi to no tatakai," 135 and 137.
168. Mōri et al., "Ajia gaku," 6.
169. Kang, *Ajia kara Nihon*, 27.
170. Kang, "Sengo paradaimu," 111; "Rekishi to no tatakai," 137; and "Musubi ni kaete," 194.
171. Kang, "Ajia to no danzetsu," 158.

Asia against which the Japanese collectively authenticated their sense of unity as Japanese within a 'dignified space.'" Here, said Kang, was a "stark manifestation of an 'Asia-less postwar' with its accumulation of postcolonial problems left intact."[172]

It was from within this strikingly bleak assessment of postwar Japanese history and identity that both Kang and Wada made the groundbreaking leap to their concept of a "common house of Northeast Asia." As I have argued, political, economic, and intellectual developments of the time greatly facilitated this breakthrough. For Kang in particular, the end of both the Cold War and the Shōwa era (1926–89) exposed the fiction of Japan's "monoethnic," "insider narrative," challenging him and other progressives to develop a "multidimensional" history and future.[173] If the Japanese could unequivocally recognize their war responsibility toward Asia, resolve the unresolved postwar settlement, and leave behind their mentality of a "second abandoning Asia and joining the West," Kang envisaged dazzling futures in which the country might even become a "good-willed partner" and "mediator" in initiatives for peace and unification on the Korean peninsula. So interconnected might the region become that even the American treaty system in Asia might fade away, forcing the United States to adopt an altogether different posture in Asia.[174] It is important to note that Kang's vision of responsibility, remorse, and apology opening a pathway toward Asian community was an explicit reaction to Katō's call for the Japanese to fashion a "subject of apology" through the rehabilitation of national community built on self-mourning and separation from Asia. As Kang wrote in response to Katō's screed in late 1995,

> the project to rouse historical memory and a subject of responsibility through the cohesive power of "national illusion" will not alleviate the tragedy of Okinawa and former colonies. . . . Launching the "national" again is akin to driving the wedge of an "internal border" into the heart of each and every "Japanese person," using historical settlement as the lever. What will be produced as a result? The war victims and their memory will again be clearly divided into that inside and that outside the nation, and the

172. Kang, "Shōwa no owari," 20.
173. Kang, "Hajime ni futatsu," 11.
174. Kang, "Sengo paradaimu," 126–27.

boundary between those who belong to "the Japanese" and those who do
not will become patently obvious. . . . But this will only be a new form of
violence . . . because the dead from those former colonies who had previously been Japanese—[the ones] who had tried so desperately to become
"first-rate Japanese" by clinging to the "national illusion" but were ultimately forgotten as "traitors"—will continue to wander [the earth] without belonging behind any national border.[175]

But a regional "common house" promised a way out of this national
illusion through the nurturing of a therapeutic community. Wada Haruki,
the initial architect of the concept, said that he began conceptualizing and
advocating for this idea in the early 1990s, drawing originally on Mikhail
Gorbachev's call for the creation of a "European Common House" after
the collapse of the Soviet Union.[176] Wada continued to refine the concept
throughout the 1990s, moving from a "Northeast Asian house of human
symbiosis" (*Tōhoku Ajia jinrui kyōsei no ie*) in 1990 to a "shared house of
East Asia" (*Higashi Ajia kyōtsū no ie*) that included Vietnam in 1994 and
ultimately to a "common house of Northeast Asia" in 1995.[177] Although
both Wada and Kang were interested in Asia more generally, they viewed
Northeast Asia (especially the Korean peninsula) as the central axis for
designing regional stability and peace. Wada even reserved a special role
for Koreans in the construction of this common house. "As a result of an
unfortunate history," he explained, the Korean diaspora extended to "far-
flung" areas including Japan, China, Sakhalin, and the United States and,
for this reason, the Koreans were perfectly placed to be the leading architects in the project.[178] Interestingly too, Wada's "common house of Northeast Asia" was not exclusively Asian in membership, as it included both
the United States and Russia. He felt that the exclusion of North Korea, the
United States, and Russia was a weakness in many formulations of an
EAC, since all three would be crucial actors in any regional framework
alongside Japan and China.[179] Kang likewise called for a Northeast Asian

175. Kang, "Musubi ni Kaete," 197.
176. Wada, *Tōhoku Ajia kyōdō*, 16.
177. Wada, *Tōhoku Ajia kyōdō*, 14, 17, 23, and 27.
178. Selden and Selden, "Wada Haruki," 376. See also Wada, *Tōhoku Ajia kyōdō*, 28.
179. Wada, *Tōhoku Ajia kyōdō*, 28.

common house that included America.[180] Moreover, reflecting their shared attentiveness to history, both recognized that the main obstacle to this common house was deep-seated "distrust of Japan" among Koreans, Chinese, and Taiwanese due to the country's past transgressions—hence the requirement that the Japanese engage in genuine soul searching, apology, and reparations as the basic preconditions for a new future of community.[181] Indeed, as I have suggested above, the connection of remorse to community marked a critical breakthrough for progressives.

Kang set out his concrete proposal for this common house in a historic speech before the Research Commission on the Constitution (Kenpō Chōsakai) of the Japanese House of Representatives in March 2001. The fact that Kang was invited to address this commission testifies to his high public profile and legitimacy as a respected commentator on Japan and Asia. But both the invitation and the speech also had a larger symbolic significance, indicative of the inroads Japan's internal Others were making into both elite and mainstream consciousness at the time—limited and short-lived though this may have been. In 2003, Wada described Kang's speech as an "epoch-making" (*kakkiteki*) "incident" (*jiken*). After all, there was no dismissing the historic symbolism of a "resident-Korean intellectual" arriving at the halls of Japanese power and calling on the nation's leaders to consider a "common house of Northeast Asia" as the most desirable "vision" for Japan's future in the region.[182]

Kang's proposals were as visionary as the speech was historic, resonating with Morishima's contemporaneous advocacy of an AEC (although not going as far as the latter's "United States of Asia"). Kang argued that Japan, with its great wealth and vibrant consumer culture, might replace the United States as the "absorbing" and "importing superpower" (*yunyū taikoku*) of Asia if it could first overcome the challenges of domestic reform.[183] While the "1955 System" was primarily a politics of the "plus sum" (that is, wrangling over the "distribution" of wealth), recessionary Japan now confronted a "minus sum" situation that demanded a "nimble" and

180. Kang, *Tōhoku Ajia*, 25.
181. Wada, *Tōhoku Ajia kyōdō*, 140.
182. Wada, *Tōhoku Ajia kyōdō*, 37.
183. Kang, *Tōhoku Ajia*, 32–33.

"imaginative" politics alert to the region.[184] Faced with new needs in welfare provision, care for the aged, and intellectual technology support, Japan could no longer remain closed to the growing population of mobile workers who were enthusiastically circulating in the region.[185] The time had come for the country to open its borders to fellow Asians. To help facilitate this human circulation, Kang (like Morishima and others) proposed the construction of a massive transportation network in Northeast Asia, for instance, in the form of an undersea tunnel for a bullet train that would link South Korea and Japan as the Channel Tunnel between France and the United Kingdom does. This common house would also be tied together through enhanced satellite broadcasting and an information highway that crossed regional seas. Along with the dynamic circulation of popular culture, Kang also proposed increased student exchanges through a system of course accreditation among regional universities. To address the history textbook problem, he suggested that texts be translated into Chinese, Korean, and Japanese and then used alongside domestically produced texts in classrooms as a point of comparison for students. In this way the "common house" could help lower the "voltage" of nationalism in the region.[186] Echoing the ideas of moderate New Asianists like Funabashi, Kang also believed that a common house could rectify the "distortion in US-Japan relations" by recalibrating this relationship to suit a new "multilateral security framework in Northeast Asia" based on Japan's "robust partnerships" with its neighbors—including North Korea, which Kang said should be "dragged into" this community.[187] Ultimately, if Japan and its Northeast Asian neighbors could cooperate in the design and construction of this common house, Kang believed that the dangerous rise of patriotism and nationalism could be restrained and the region cushioned from the turmoil of American-led globalization.[188]

Idealistic aspirations aside, Kang was careful to note that he had arrived at this proposal with his eyes wide open. His vision of a "common house" was conceived with the "full knowledge that Japan, half a century

184.	Kang, *Tōhoku Ajia*, 21.
185.	Kang, *Tōhoku Ajia*, 37.
186.	Kang, *Tōhoku Ajia*, 36 and 51.
187.	Kang, *Tōhoku Ajia*, 43 and 48.
188.	Kang, *Tōhoku Ajia*, 14.

after the war, had yet to come to terms with its negative history."[189] Wada thought similarly, positing a staged approach to Northeast Asian community through, first and foremost, Japanese apology and reparation, followed by cooperation in environmental, economic, and (ultimately) security matters.[190] As Wada explained in 2008, "the people of this region that was at war for eighty years aspire to total reconciliation. Only when everyone begins to walk in this direction will progress toward a common house for Northeast Asia be possible. The passion for reconciliation is an identity that unites this area."[191]

Resonating with Wada's and Kang's "common house" idea, the voices of other progressives began to emphasize the potential of nonstate actors and civil society in the realization of Asian community. In a speech delivered to a Korean audience in 2010, Sakamoto Yoshikazu called for the "creation of a transregional civil society" in East Asia, a "community of civic solidarity" aimed at "producing a new 'humane' way of living." Rather than an internalist region-building project, Sakamoto envisioned civic initiatives for East Asian identity and community contributing to the larger endeavor of "creating a world of strengthened humanity." Boosting civil society across Asia would certainly benefit the region, but in Sakamoto's telling, it could also "transcend" East Asia, contributing to the development of civil society globally.[192]

The historian Yamamuro Shin'ichi (b. 1951) advocated a similar role for civil society in East Asia, proposing a "complementary" or "para" diplomacy based on processes of "inter-local" networking outside of traditional state diplomacy. Like Sakamoto's, Yamamuro's vision traced a lineage from the "inter-people diplomacy" proposed in the 1970s and 1980s by Nagasu Kazuji, the governor of Kanagawa Prefecture (see chapter 5). But it also grew out of Yamamuro's intriguing intellectual project to detach much-maligned "Asian values" from the static essentialism of conservative Asianist hard-liners, reimagining these values as a collection of progressive possibilities capable of contributing to humanity. As Yamamuro explained, his advocacy of Asian values was not aimed at

189. Kang, *Tōhoku Ajia*, 14.
190. Wada, *Tōhoku Ajia kyōdō*, 234.
191. Selden and Selden, "Wada Haruki," 376.
192. Sakamoto, "Higashi Ajia," 180.

"resisting," "rejecting," or overcoming "the West and Western civilization" based on Asia's "unique existential significance" but rather at promoting those values, practices, and tendencies in Asia that might have some relevance or "validity" as "universals" in spaces beyond the region. Admittedly, the very concept of "Asian values" took Yamamuro into very treacherous and ambiguous territory, but unlike the hard-line Asianists and civilizational warriors, who largely arrived at resistance, Yamamuro's journey led to a progressive vision of Asian community based on the acceptance of diversity—or "hybridity," in his terminology—beyond the nation-state and in the hands of ordinary people.[193]

Yamamuro first outlined his concept of Asian values in an essay titled "'Ta ni shite ichi' no chitsujo genri to Nihon no sentaku" (The principle of "many as one" and Japan's choice) for the 1998 volume *"Ajiateki kachi" to wa nanika* (What are "Asian values"?). Here he put forward hybridity (*konsei*) as the core value of East Asia and argued that its disappearance in modern Japan was the cause of the country's malaise. Yamamuro called for a more complex and dynamic understanding of Asian values than the static categories of familism, groupism, and benevolent dictatorship that had earlier been trumpeted by Ishihara, Lee Kuan Yew, and Mahathir. Instead, he described Asian values as no more than "working hypotheses" that pointed toward "issues for the coming century" and hinted at "new principles of order and modes of individual existence."[194] For example, according to Yamamuro, the seeming lack of structure throughout Asia—evident in the chaos of many Asian cities—was not an indication of disorder but a manifestation of the Asian ability to seamlessly resolve opposites. A stretch of railroad tracks by day may at night metamorphose into a food-stall market only to revert to a railroad in the morning. Although such arrangements were "anti-structural" (*han-kōzō*), for Yamamuro this did not equate to "anti-order" (*han-chitsujo*). On the contrary, behind the fluidity and lack of stability a "concealed principle of order" was at work that constantly knit together disparate elements into a diverse, yet harmonious, chorus.[195] Pointing to Chuang Tzu's concept of "double walking" or "walking two paths" (*liangxing; ryōkō*), Yamamuro suggested that when

193. Yamamuro, "Higashi Ajia," 199.
194. Yamamuro, "'Ta ni shite ichi,'" 48.
195. Yamamuro, "'Ta ni shite ichi,'" 58.

faced with opposition, the Asian solution was to create a new condition by equally incorporating the opposites. Asian culture resembled the phenomenon of a "hybrid system" in nature that was capable of incorporating more and more subsystems within its structure.[196] As contemporary examples of such dynamic and flexible hybridity in Asia, Yamamuro (not unproblematically, in retrospect) noted China's "one-country two-systems" policy in Hong Kong and the ASEAN principle of mutual non-interference and nonuse of military force among member states.[197]

Indeed, for Yamamuro, the loss of hybridity became the leitmotif for contemporary Japanese stagnation and psychological discontent. His argument—which resonated with the ruminations of Asuna Mizuho— was that the growing interest in Asia among Japanese had to do with a longing or nostalgia for a Japan lost to hypermodernity. Wartime standardization and regulation, followed by occupation and reconstruction, high-speed economic growth, and the belt tightening of the 1970s, had standardized and homogenized daily life in Japan, stifling diversity to the point where ordinary people began to long for a return of "chaos" and "disorder."[198] Yamamuro argued that the bursting of the economic bubble in 1990 provided an opportunity for the Japanese people to look at Asia in an authentic way for perhaps the first time in history. What they discovered was a space replete with hybridity. On the one hand, Asia had clearly become a space of "economic dynamism" and the emerging center of the world economy for the coming century. Yet on the other hand, it was also a place where the deep strata of human culture and nature lost to both Japan and the West seemed to have been preserved.[199] In Japan after the economic miracle, Yamamuro suggested, this vibrant Asia exposed the Japanese loss of self-confidence and sense of restriction—it presented a vision of both what the country had once been and what it had degenerated into. As he lamented, there was even a view that "these days Asia has everything Japan has, and the things Japan does not have, Asia has." Yamamuro imagined Asia as a fantastic mixture of the "premodern," the "modern," and the "hypermodern," all of which reacted,

196. Yamamuro, "'Ta ni shite ichi,'" 58.
197. Yamamuro, "'Ta ni shite ichi,'" 59.
198. Yamamuro, "'Ta ni shite ichi,'" 57.
199. Yamamuro, "'Ta ni shite ichi,'" 55.

"giving off sparks" to produce the "fascination" of a "wonderland" far more authentic than the ordered monotony of urban life in contemporary Japan.[200]

Yamamuro's Asian values undoubtedly contained the same vulnerabilities and ambiguities inherent in other more chauvinistic versions of the time and, like Tsurumi's earlier idealization of coastal Southeast Asia, incorporated a healthy dose of romanticism. But the interesting point is how Yamamuro's attention to so-called Asian hybridity led him toward movements and initiatives for an EAC beyond the nation-state. In 2008, he observed that although an EAC already existed thanks to the increasing economic ties among nations in the region, as yet there was no shared "blueprint" among countries outlining a "vision" for the internal dynamics of this community and the means for constructing it.[201] This was not necessarily a negative thing for Yamamuro, who argued that connecting ideas like "Asianism" or "Asia is One" to discussions of an EAC might do "more harm than good."[202] Such discussions also risked being drawn into geostrategic concerns over the rise of Chinese influence. Prime Minister Koizumi's call for an EAC "that acts together and advances together" in Singapore in 2002, Yamamuro observed, was just such an example of Japanese "alarm" over possibly being overtaken by China in the game of region building.[203]

Although most invocations of an EAC were focused on an economic or strategic community, Yamamuro emphasized instead the importance of other hybrid formulations such as antiwar communities or "communities for environmental protection and ecological preservation."[204] In this sense, it was "not necessarily meaningless" to think about an EAC beyond the "common sense" approach of imagining it narrowly in terms of connections at the state level.[205] Here Yamamuro pointed to the involvement of local governments in "border-crossing" initiatives in recent years, through sister city arrangements, technical support, and training in

200. Yamamuro, "'Ta ni shite ichi,'" 56.
201. Yamamuro, "Higashi Ajia," 192.
202. Yamamuro, "Higashi Ajia," 191.
203. Yamamuro, "Higashi Ajia," 193.
204. Yamamuro, "Higashi Ajia," 193.
205. Yamamuro, "Higashi Ajia," 193.

areas such as environmental preservation and pollution abatement.[206] Groups like the Association of Northeast Asian Regional Governments were working at the subnational level to create a peaceful region through meetings and exchanges, with a particular focus on the environment. Similar were groups like the Acid Deposition Monitoring Network in East Asia.[207] Such local linkages, he explained, could be understood as a kind of "para" or "complementary" diplomacy. Although they had no "legal" or "institutional" force, these "inter-local" connections had the potential to "make political boundaries meaningless" through the creation of "joint communities" (*yūgō kyōdōtai*) produced "functionally" by "people living their daily lives."[208]

Going further than even Kang or Wada, Yamamuro argued that if the idea of an EAC had any "conceptual" contribution to make to the twenty-first century, then it certainly must be in the way such an organization could challenge the primacy of sovereign states. In keeping with his vision of Asian hybridity, he noted that "at the very least, the value of considering East Asian Community or Asianism" was that it presented "an opportunity to think about community based on multiple spaces." Moreover, rather than "demarcating a unique space called Asia" and "laying a fault line between this and other spaces," through the concept of hybridity Yamamuro believed it was possible to discover within the "regional" new "universals" that had validity far beyond Asia.[209] Reawakened to their region, Japanese had a key role to play in meeting this historic new challenge for Asia.

To be sure, progressive visions of a hybrid Asian "common house" and a new world-historic role for Asia proved elusive, even unrealistic, in the rough-and-tumble of international politics. But in the context of postwar progressive thought and activism, they were evidence that a critical intellectual transformation was underway. As late as the 1980s, progressives had not dared imagine an Asian community lest they exacerbate the

---

206. Yamamuro, "Higashi Ajia," 194.
207. Yamamuro, "Higashi Ajia," 195. See also http://www.neargov.org/en/and https://www.eanet.asia/.
208. Yamamuro, "Higashi Ajia," 196 and 198.
209. Yamamuro, "Higashi Ajia," 197.

still-festering wounds Japan had inflicted on its regional neighbors. The
critical task for them was to address Japan's Asia problem both in the past
and in the present. But with the historic changes of the 1990s and the
provocation of New Asianisms and nationalist overtures for mourning,
it became possible for progressives—for the first time in Japan's postwar
period—to connect the Asia problem and the process of deimperialization to a new vision of community.

Conclusion

Stimulated by the dynamic growth in East Asia after 1985 and the historic transformations both within Japan and globally in the early 1990s,
Japanese diplomats, politicians, academics, intellectuals, and business
elites began to debate and advocate for the creation of an EAC and regional integration with an intensity unseen since wartime discussions of
the Greater East Asia Co-Prosperity Sphere. The Asia problem—the domain of progressives alone for so many years—now came into sharp relief alongside rival discourses on Asian miracles, opportunities, and solutions and against the backdrop of intensifying demands from victims
across Asia. This 1990s Asia boom emerged as both a threat and an opportunity for progressives, particularly in terms of tackling the task of
deimperialization into the future. On the one hand, as a largely upbeat,
Japan-centric discourse, the New Asianism threatened to sideline and
even obfuscate Japan's unresolved issues with its neighbors in the name
of future-oriented designs for Asian community. But on the other hand,
the discourse also proved to be an important catalyst, creating a progressive breakthrough to Asian community that had long been hampered by
the country's tainted history in the region and its de-Asianization under
the Allied Occupation.

As if responding to the hard-liners and instrumentalists who (largely
ignoring history) began to champion the region as a method for national
empowerment or salvation, some progressives took the bold step of entering the forbidden territory of an Asian communal imaginary—a common house under whose roof Japan might once again reside with the
blessing of its regional neighbors. However, they did so on a platform of

historically informed humility and with a forthright rejection of Japan's somehow being the wellspring of Asian values or the trailblazing goose leading a backward gaggle of goslings to a resplendent future of abundance. Above all, progressive visions of Asian community emphasized Japan's multidimensional and historically entangled relations with the region, fraught and troubled though these may have been. In striking contrast to pundits like Katō, whose mechanism of self-mourning enabling apology masked a deeper logic of separation, progressives (through their activism and ideas) made apology the critical element in their projects for reconnection.

To be sure, there was a tension in this strategy because apology assumed the existence of an apologizing subject—a Japan that must first disconnect from Asia in the name of contrition before it could humbly return, fully deimperialized. For progressives who recognized the need for apology yet desperately wanted to relativize the grip of national identity through a reconnection to region, this was a tricky endeavor indeed. The dilemmas of belonging, community, and identity hit at the heart of the Asia problem and the viscera of what deimperialization was all about. It is hardly surprising, then, that no categorical solution was forthcoming either at the time or thereafter. But the fact that progressives could now talk about Asian community in the same breath as responsibility, apology, and remorse marked a historic intellectual breakthrough that was previously unimaginable under the weight of an unresolved Asia problem and the long shadow of co-prosperity.

Moreover, the symbolism of an internal Other like Kang Sang-jung emerging as a leading progressive voice on Japan's future in Asia made it possible to imagine—if only for a fleeting moment—a route to Asian community premised not on apology through separation into homogeneous ethnic collectivities but on contrition through recognition of the Other within the self. This was exactly the kind of hybridity, entanglement, and fluidity in Japanese identity that Hamashita, Yamamuro, and others had been pointing to. Indeed, if there was to be an answer to Katō, deimperialization, the question of identity, and the Asia problem more generally, then it was probably to be found in the reflexive implications and possibilities implicit in this hybrid symbolism.

CONCLUSION

Japan's Postwar Odyssey with Asia

> Areas are not facts but artifacts of our interests and our fantasies
> as well as of our needs to know, to remember, and to forget.
> —Arjun Appadurai, "Grassroots Globalization and the
> Research Imagination"

In a thought-provoking essay the historian Hye Jeong Park asks what the regional history of East Asia would look like if we removed "the teleology of regionalism": "Would it still testify to the history of regionalization as it is assumed, or would it rather encompass a history of an odyssey-like process without an ultimate destination and without the telos of 'one' region?"[1] Rejecting "congruity," "continuity," and civilizational similarity, Park suggests that we approach the region as an "open space where trans-local and trans-cultural dynamics have overwhelmed civilizational borders" in a "process of ceaseless and dynamic regionalization."[2] Others propose a similar "alternative architecture" for understanding regions. Arjun Appadurai, for instance, conceptualizes regions as "process geographies" shaped by multifarious kinds of "action, interaction, and motion," while Tessa Morris-Suzuki imagines a "*liquid area studies*" in which "an area is *brought into being only by human activity*—travel, trade, and communication."[3] The Northeast Asian region, Morris-Suzuki argues, "is thus forever being reconstructed and reinvented."[4] Important for this study, such ideas apply as much to the nation-states within regions (for example, Japan in Asia) as they do to the

---

1. Hye Jeong Park, "East Asian Odyssey," 891.
2. Hye Jeong Park, "East Asian Odyssey," 896.
3. Appadurai, "Grassroots Globalization," 7; Morris-Suzuki, "Japan and Its Region," 124, and "Liquid Area Studies," 217.
4. Morris-Suzuki, "Liquid Area Studies," 218.

regions themselves. As I have argued elsewhere, similar to "liquid area studies," one methodological way of expanding our understanding of so-called postwar Japanese history may be through a conceptual "liquification" of national borders, not to (erroneously) deny the reality of such boundaries but to recognize their fundamental permeability, ambiguity, and conductivity.[5] Indeed, the question I have grappled with in this study is what we might learn about postwar Japan by expanding our spatial purview beyond an archipelagic history or a history of Japan in America's embrace, in favor of a regionally embedded and regionally focused narrative—in other words, the history of Japan in a dynamic conversation and negotiation with the physical and symbolic geography of Asia.[6] Doing so, I argue, can help us understand the ways progressive intellectuals' and activists' awakening to and engagement with Asia has influenced understandings and debates on war responsibility, the evolution of civic activism, and the struggle over national identity in postwar Japan.

Park's notion of East Asia as an odyssey or open-ended journey rather than an objective or *telos* is extremely useful when considering this dynamic interrelationship and entanglement of Asia and postwar Japan. The imagery of an odyssey encourages us to pull back from the specific historical artifacts—in this case, thought and activism—and inquire as to their broader historical implications and significance for contemporary Japan.[7] For instance, how different might so-called Japanese thought and activism in the postwar era look when reconsidered through the lens of Asia? Might these domains not take on remarkably different hues, becoming far more decentered, fluid, and mobile phenomena than the national, cultural, and geographical modifier "Japanese" would have us believe? Moreover, might not the discovery of this fluidity and interconnectedness encourage us to reconsider the formative forces of Japan's postwar era, if not "Japanese" identity itself?

A central aim of this study has been to reveal how progressives' encounter with the Asia problem and the agony of their deimperialization serve as evidence of the country's ongoing and inexorable entanglement

5. Avenell, "Japan's Environmental Injustice," 219.
6. See Choi, "Guest Editor's Introduction," 9.
7. Appadurai, "Grassroots Globalization," 8.

with the region, extending to the core of identity and the fundamental motivations shaping progressive praxis. In the preceding chapters I have attempted to provide a new perspective on our understanding of the evolution of postwar Japanese progressive thought and activism by anchoring these in processes of deimperialization, discourses on Asia and East Asia and grassroots engagements throughout Northeast, Southeast, and even South Asia. Scholars of East Asian politics and international relations have long been sensitive to the role of the region in contemporary Japanese political, economic, and social development.[8] More recently, humanities scholars—some from an area studies perspective and others from transnational, cultural studies, and historical perspectives—have also begun to pay more attention to the country's contemporary history in the context of Asia, East Asia, and Northeast Asia.[9] Their work shows that, similar to the inspirational yardsticks of Europe, the United States, and the West, Asian regional imaginaries and interactions have been critical lenses in and through which postwar intellectuals and political actors have grappled with questions of identity, political action, and history. We might say that region—meaning Asia, its various subregions, or both— has been the wider community of fate in which postwar Japanese intellectuals and activists operated, whether self-consciously or not. Oguma Eiji goes so far as to argue that "more than a true representation of the actual circumstances of Asian nations," postwar "constructions [of Asia] reflected a Japanese national identity that changed amidst shifts in domestic political and economic conditions."[10] This observation certainly holds until around the mid- to late 1950s, but the nature of progressive engagement with Asia changed thereafter as historians and others delved into Japan's colored regional past and a new generation of activists like Oda Makoto and Tsurumi Yoshiyuki began visiting and studying Asian countries. The awareness of region thus came to combine a "social and cognitive" symbolism "rooted in political practice" with a concrete perception of a physical geography in the world (albeit loosely and variously

---

8. Hatch, *Asia's Flying Geese*; Katzenstein and Shiraishi, *Network Power*.

9. Hoppens, *China Problem*; Kushner and Muminov, *Dismantling of Japan's Empire*; Esselstrom, *That Distant Country*; Morris-Suzuki, *Borderline Japan* and *Exodus to North Korea*; Choi, "Guest Editor's Introduction."

10. Oguma, "Postwar Intellectuals," 211.

demarcated) based on the "flow of goods and people across physical space."[11]

I believe that this multilayered and fluid notion of region best encapsulates the ways postwar progressives came to approach Asia, how they were transformed in the process, and how this transformation fed into broader approaches to the past, civic activism, and national identity. Asia was at once an imagined geography for the production of ideas, aspirations, and ethical foundations in the wake of empire and co-prosperity; a physical place, both internal and external to Japan, in which a new and ethical political praxis became possible; and, to use Manuel Castells's terminology, a "space of flows" revealing the corporeality of motion, connection, and exchange that undermined the internalist and exclusivist pretensions of so-called national identity.[12]

In Japan immediately after defeat, Asia undoubtedly served as a convenient tool—a scapegoat—in the reformulation of national identity among progressive intellectuals, but the discovery of lived experiences, conflicts, suffering, and struggles for territory in the region folded back on progressives forcing a self-reflexive reconsideration of theory and praxis from the inside out. We cannot understand the ideational shifts in postwar progressive thought and activism in Japan without taking into account the impact of this traumatizing encounter with the realities of Japan in Asia and Asia in Japan, both from the past and in the present. Moreover, we cannot completely explain the transformations in civic activism or the influx of the new norms of global civil society into the country without recognizing the critical mediating role of grassroots involvement in the region. Borrowing Takeuchi Yoshimi's metaphor, we might say that Asia served as a "method" for postwar Japanese progressives on multiple levels: in facing the aporias of national identity, addressing the task of deimperialization, reformulating civic movement praxis, and imagining new visions of Japan's embeddedness in a regional community and geography.

As Morris-Suzuki observes, "discussions of Japan in its region" or of the country's "regional role" tend to focus on "the grand narratives of inter-state relations or of regional institution building." Often disregarded,

---

11. Katzenstein, "Regionalism and Asia," 354.
12. Castells, *Rise of the Network Society*, xxxii.

however, are the "the mass of fine intertwined threads that bind particular Japanese localities across national frontiers to places throughout Asia and beyond."[13] Along with such local interconnections in Asia, I suggest that progressive thought and activism have also served as critical "intertwined threads" that bind Japan to its region. The fact that empire largely disappeared from progressive (and popular) memory for a time after defeat in war, as well as the fact that Asia remerged primarily as a postwar and postimperial problem for them, should not blind us to this shared and ongoing odyssey of Japan with its region. The vagaries of politics certainly make it difficult to determine where this odyssey is headed: whether or not Japan will eventually solve its Asia problem and finally make its peace with former colonies and victimized people throughout East Asia. History provides no predictive guidance here, just as it offers no answer as to when or if deimperialization will ever be a completed odyssey. Yet important as these questions are for the Japanese as they negotiate their present and future in Asia, as I have suggested, focusing narrowly on the historical artifacts risks overlooking the more palpable historical fact—or searching for the "wrong address," as Park puts it.[14] The critical implication of this postwar history is the inseparability of Japan from its region and the centrality of the symbolic geography of Asia in Japanese reimaginations of the self after empire and co-prosperity. In terms of forging a new politics of hope, I feel that the recognition of this inseparability—of the Other within the self and the self within the Other—may be the most important legacy of this history for the future.

Rethinking Postwar Japan in, through, and with Asia

How, then, might we rethink postwar Japanese history as inseparable from region—a postwar historical odyssey in, through, and with Asia? And how might this historical odyssey be mapped onto existing chronological and interpretive topographies of the postwar era? As I have noted

13. Morris-Suzuki, "Japan and Its Region," 124.
14. Hye Jeong Park, "East Asian Odyssey," 893.

above, the postwar regional odyssey for progressives unfolded as a gradual awakening and response to a complicated Asia problem, containing
elements of prejudice, transgression, forgetting, and reconciliation. At the
base was a complication from the deepest past: an encumbrance of ingrained attitudes and mentalities stretching back to the origins of industrial modernity in Japan and encapsulated in Fukuzawa Yukichi's 1885
call for the Japanese to "abandon Asia."[15] This prejudice of abandonment and separation was written deeply into the mentality of modern
Japanese, including progressives, and it proved remarkably resilient and
resistant to eradication despite the cataclysmic disjuncture of defeat in
war and the collapse of colonial empire. Yet the problem went further.
Coupled with this prejudice from the deep past was the more recent legacy of Japan's colonial empire and militarism in Asia, expressed (or, for a
time, disregarded) in the evolving discourse on responsibility. As I discuss below, while the idea of war responsibility captured progressives' attention early on and persisted throughout the postwar era, across the
same years notions of ethnic and postwar responsibility forced a shift in
emphasis and focus from the issue of the responsibility of who and for
what to the issue of responsibility to whom. Further complicating engagement with issues of prejudice and responsibility was the immediate postwar process of de-Asianization under the Occupation, which induced a
form of forgetting. This forgetting underwrote, at first, the persistence of
an ideological denunciation of everything Asiatic but, thereafter, a stunning idealization of revolutionary Asia in the late 1940s and 1950s. As progressives struggled through the tangled historical backwoods of this Asia
problem, they slowly unearthed its roots, awakening eventually to the ob-
ligations of reconciliation and reconnection. The problem revealed itself
to them as one of erecting a new community on the ruins of empire and
the morbid wound of transgression, as well as one of reconstructing their
own identities beyond the strictures of ethnos. Here the sheer historical
weight of the Asia problem connected to a politics of possibility and hope.

The ways in which progressive intellectuals and civic activists
responded—or failed to respond—to these challenges encapsulated in
the Asia problem, I suggest, offers a novel insight into the chronological
contours and undulations of Japan's postwar era, especially previously

15. Fukuzawa, "Datsu A ron."

obscured and unacknowledged moments of intellectual breakthrough. Throughout this book I have explored what I believe were the six critical historical moments of transformation in progressives' thought and activism in response to the Asia problem from 1945 to the present. On one level, these transformations occurred as progressives responded to Japan's fraught past and present in the region, but they also grew out of a troubling encounter with the internal Asia and thus struck at the core of identity, stimulating a self-reflexive process of deimperialization.

The first transformation transpired in the years from 1945 to around 1958, as progressives partially overcame the problem of abandonment and superiority and the obstacles of de-Asianization. As we saw in chapter 1, notions of Asian stagnation and backwardness were pervasive in both Marxist and modernist discourses of the late 1940s, as intellectuals struggled to explain the mechanisms behind Japan's pathological descent into barbaric militarism. Eradicating these Asiatic remnants became a critical element of progressive visions of peace and democracy. But with the momentous events in China, the onset of the Cold War (which was hot on the Korean peninsula), and the rise of Asian nationalism, the ideology of the early postwar period was tempered by a new Asian idealism that undermined notions of Asiatic stagnation. To be sure, the view of Asia was still a blinkered one, mobilized primarily in the name of an anti-American ethnic nationalism among progressives. But the break from ideologies of stagnation and backwardness was significant. Moreover, Asian idealism, precisely because of its self-interested and myopic ethnocentrism, provoked a critique from observers like Umesao Tadao and Nakane Chie that there was still no comprehension of the region in its concrete realities. "Asia," Umesao and others intimated, was merely an empty signifier filled by a progressive ethnic and national agenda.

The second transformation, from 1958 to 1965, involved a more historically sensitive engagement with issues of abandonment and superiority and colonial empire and militarism. For all its success in transcending deeply embedded prejudices against Asia, the Asian idealism of the early to mid-1950s barely recognized Japan's former status as a regional colonizer and aggressor. But with the arrest, conviction, and execution of the resident Korean youth Lee Jin-wu in 1958, the commencement of the project of repatriating resident Koreans to North Korea in 1959, and the ongoing treaty negotiations between Japan and South Korea, we witness a critical intellectual transformation from the left ethnic nationalism (*minzokushugi*), which had been born of the nonaligned movement and anti-Americanism of the early to mid-1950s, to a growing sense of ethnic responsibility (*minzokuteki sekinin*). Informed by this troublingly self-reflexive awakening, some progressives began to ask questions about the condition of Japan's internal Asia and, moreover, the issue of responsibility to whom, which had been left largely unresolved in early postwar discussions of war responsibility.

The third transformation, from around 1965 to 1972, unfolded against the backdrop of the Vietnam War, the history debates of the 1960s, protests over Japan's immigration detention system, and the rise of Asian voices in the Japanese student movement. The significance of this transformation lay in its breadth (the diversity of intellectuals and activists involved) and its depth (the comprehensiveness of its attention to the problem of Japan's colonial empire and militarism in Asia). Japanese opposition to the Vietnam War began as an awakening to the country's complicity with the United States in its transgressions against Vietnam. However, this awakening to perpetration in the present stimulated intensive and detailed investigations of perpetration in the past, which were far more extensive than earlier progressive forays into ethnic responsibility. Honda Katsuichi, Ienaga Saburō, and others' investigations into Japan's transgressions in China, Korea, and Southeast Asia were spurred by contemporaneous moves among conservatives such as Hayashi Fusao to affirm Japan's Greater East Asian War, along with the arrival of American modernization theory—which more or less affirmed Japan's modern trajectory. The subsequent involvement of students and civic activists in protests over Japan's immigration control system in the late 1960s helped connect this past of prejudice and transgression to a present still contaminated by the scourge of discrimination toward Asians. Thanks to the visibility of internal Others like the medical student Li Zhicheng, the Korean military deserter Kim Dong-Hee, and the KSTI, the complex substance of the Asia problem came into sharp relief within progressive circles for perhaps the first time in the postwar era.

Yet despite their genuine commitment to the Vietnamese and to addressing the plight of Asians within Japan, both students and civic activists of the 1960s still lacked solid and substantial ties with fellow Asians, a point neatly encapsulated in the *Asahi jānaru*'s provocative 1972 special report on not knowing Asia. Indeed, the fourth critical transformation, throughout the 1970s, witnessed the rise of a wave of new progressive movements active in Asia, which precipitated a kind of grassroots regionalization in Japanese civic activism. Stimulated in part by the return of Japanese industry to the region and the resulting backlash from Asian countries, in these years Japanese activists mobilized into a variety of pioneering transnational solidarity movements that addressed industrial pollution, sex tourism, and democratization initiatives in the region. In a remarkable contrast to earlier mobilizations in which Japanese activists largely spoke and acted on behalf of fellow Asians, these border-crossing solidarity movements pursued repertoires of cooperation with Asian activists. Moreover, Japanese progressives drew lessons and inspiration from other Asian activists for their struggles at home. This flowering of transnational Asian solidarity movements in the 1970s marked an important evolution for Japanese civic activism in the postwar era—a "grassroots regionalization" in which activists from multiple spheres of concern became attuned to Asia and Asian issues.

The fifth transformation, beginning in the late 1970s and continuing into the 1990s, witnessed both a broadening and an enhancing of the Asian solidarity movements of the 1970s. Against the backdrop of a resplendent Japanese miracle and the rhetoric of internationalization, a kind of alternative internationalization was unfolding in grassroots action and interactions in Asia. While official versions of internationalization championed a brash cultural nationalism based on economic prowess vis-à-vis the West, the alternative grassroots internationalism drew on an emerging language and practice of human rights and was steadfastly focused on Asia. It found expression in movements for postwar responsibility such as the mobilization for Koreans deserted on Sakhalin at the end of World War II and the inter-people diplomacy of Nagasu Kazuji in Kanagawa Prefecture, as well as in the advocacy of individuals like Tsurumi Yoshiyuki and a new generation of NGO activists who pointed to the economies of exploitation operating between Japan and the region and involving mundane commodities like bananas. The transformation of this period lay not only in the ways activism and exchanges in Asia transcended or addressed prejudice, transgression, and forgetting, but also in how they served as a platform for the norms of global civil society to begin flowing back into Japan in a process of grassroots globalization.

The sixth transformation began around the mid-1990s and continued into the new century, most notably in visions of a common house of
Northeast Asia. The great breakthrough of this moment lay in the way
progressives connected ongoing processes of remorse, responsibility, reconciliation, and reconnection to novel regional imaginaries. Throughout
most of the postwar era, the idea of Asian community had been forbidden territory for progressives under the long, dark shadow of the Greater
East Asia Co-Prosperity Sphere. But the rise of initiatives for regional integration throughout East Asia and the challenge of instrumentalist and
often chauvinistic New Asianisms from within Japan stimulated some
progressives to begin delineating their ideas for a new Asian community
based on recognition of the past, mutual respect and trust, and a desire
for the construction of regional peace. The participation of individuals
like Kang Sang-jung from Japan's internal Asia made this breakthrough
all the more potent, evidencing the significant movement toward deimperialization among progressive intellectuals and activists, while offering
the glimpse of another Japan in which the "*habitus* of homogeneity" receded for the reality of multeity.[16] This moment was hardly a point of
arrival and, in fact, might best be understood as the faint indication of a
possible new beginning as Japan entered an uncertain age within its region. Moreover, we must also candidly recognize how this promising
breakthrough to Asia on the Left was accompanied by the rise of a haughty
new nationalism on the Right embodied in what Nakano Koichi has
called the "New Right transformation of Japanese politics."[17]

Mapping Asia onto Postwar Japan

How, then, might the above moments of transformation be mapped onto
existing chronologies and histories of Japan's postwar period, and what
new understandings might be possible? As Deokhyo Choi has noted, since
at least the 1980s historians of postwar Japan have been challenging both
the temporal and spatial frameworks of this era, conventionally starting

16. Befu, "Foreword," xxiv.
17. Nakano, "Contemporary Political Dynamics."

with Emperor Hirohito's surrender speech on August 15, 1945.[18] These historians call attention to a wealth of institutional, intellectual, political, cultural, and other transwar continuities that undermine the notion of an all-encompassing temporal disjuncture in 1945.[19] Moreover, recently scholars have also begun to challenge the spatial boundaries of historiography on postwar Japan, centered on what Choi calls "island histories" and using the nation as their basic "unit of analysis."[20] Of course, the aim in such spatializations of the historical terrain is to rethink postwar Japan within regional, transnational, transcultural, or global narratives, destabilizing "Japan" from both the inside and the outside.[21] These interventions resonate with critiques of and initiatives to rethink area studies proposed by Appadurai, Naoki Sakai, Morris-Suzuki, and others.[22] In proposing the "trans-Pacific" as a new context, for instance, Sakai and Hyon Joo Yoo hope to "radically overcome the way in which 'the nation' and 'the region' are understood and used in Asian Studies and Area Studies, as well as in National Studies of separate nation-states."[23] They offer the example of how the study of national literatures of East Asian countries "precludes a conversation that places these nations and literatures in a regional context."[24] The same kind of conversational preclusion is arguably present in national history writing on East Asian nations like Japan. Some scholars go even further. For example, Gavin Walker argues that "area studies cannot be *overcome*, but must be bisected by a subtractive strategy of exodus, a removal of its basic element, which is ourselves."[25]

Although I cannot claim to have comprehensively adopted such self-reflexive and postnational methodologies in this book or to have engaged in self-exodus (and, in certain ways, I remain trapped within the

18. Choi, "Guest Editor's Introduction," 3.

19. Dower, "Useful War"; Yamanouchi, "Total War"; Garon, *State and Labor*; Johnson, *MITI*.

20. Choi, "Guest Editor's Introduction," 3.

21. See, for example, Avenell, *Transnational Japan* and "Asia and the Development of Civic Activism"; Iacobelli, Leary, and Takahashi, *Transnational Japan as History*.

22. For an important collection of essays critiquing and rethinking area studies, see the special edition of *positions* 27, no. 1 (2019).

23. Sakai and Yoo, preface, x.

24. Sakai and Yoo, preface, x.

25. Walker, "Accumulation of Difference," 93.

paradigm), I believe that the history of thought and activism analyzed in the preceding chapters offers clues as to how we might expand the postwar period both temporally and spatially. In temporal terms, this history confirms both continuity and disjuncture. As I discussed above, the continuity was not only from the 1930s and 1940s or even the genesis of colonial empire. Rather, it dated back to the beginning of Japanese industrial modernization in the mid-nineteenth century, in notions of abandonment of and superiority vis-à-vis Asia. Such attitudes survived the moment of defeat, becoming a core focus of deimperialization. Yet along with such transwar continuity, this history also paradoxically speaks to considerable discontinuity between the prewar and wartime period, on the one hand, and the postwar era, on the other hand, inasmuch as defeat and the collapse of colonial empire in 1945 undoubtedly opened the way for the subsequent transformations in progressives' thought and activism. The one qualification, however, is that the temporal disjuncture did not elicit a productive response until after the phase of de-Asianization in the early postwar era.

What about the spatial implications of this history for our comprehension of Japan's postwar period? How did growing interaction with and attention to the people, political economy, history, and symbolic geography of Asia shape progressives' thought and activism in Japan? Here I would highlight the trajectories of three postwar phenomena that clearly illustrate this impact of the region: the first relating to the evolving idea and politics of responsibility, the second to the development of civic activism and civil society more generally, and the third to the shifting contours of identity.

ASIA AND RESPONSIBILITY

Consider first the notion of responsibility (*sekinin*).[26] In its earliest formulation as war responsibility (*sensō sekinin*), this idea connected directly to questions about who had been responsible for leading Japan into war, who had commanded the war effort, and ultimately who was responsible for Japan's defeat and the nature of its surrender. Here attention focused primarily on the military and wartime leadership—what Hiro Saito calls

---

26. For an important discussion of responsibility, see Gluck, *"Sekinin."*

a "government-centered view" of war responsibility, deeply shaped by the Allied Occupation and the Tokyo Tribunal, as discussed in chapter 1.[27] Of course, the Japanese were not oblivious to the complicity of ordinary Japanese people for having "permitted the ascension" of the wartime leaders.[28] Moreover, progressives weighed into the war responsibility issue through self-critique: why had they not been able to prevent the war, and more "painfully," why had some even used their "intellectual energy" in support of it?[29] These latter self-critiques by Ōkuma Nobuyuki, Tsurumi Shunsuke, and others undoubtedly shifted the focus of responsibility from the state to the individual. Yet as we have seen above, for some years after the war the problem of responsibility toward the victims of colonial empire and militarism remained largely unexamined.

At least two moments of attention to Asia helped widen the spatial dimensions of how responsibility was comprehended. The first occurred following the arrest and execution of Lee Jin-wu, a resident Korean youth; the repatriation project to North Korea; and the Japan–South Korea Treaty dialogues of the late 1950s and early 1960s. Through their involvement in related movements, progressive intellectuals gradually became sensitive to the problem of their own ethnic responsibility toward Asian Others in the country. In his influential 1960 *Nihon no minzoku undō* (Ethnic movements in Japan), Fujishima Udai first articulated the notion of Japanese original sin (*genzai*) toward Asia, while Suzuki Michihiko deployed the idea of ethnic responsibility to shift part of the responsibility for Lee's crimes back onto the Japanese and their discriminatory society. Later in the 1960s Tamaki Motoi consolidated these ideas into his influential 1967 *Minzokuteki sekinin to shisō* (Ethnic responsibility and thought). With the rising opposition to the Vietnam War and immigration control system, in the late 1960s the student activist Tsumura Takashi pushed the concept of ethnic responsibility even further in his lamentations over the suicide of the medical student Li Zhicheng, while Tsurumi Shunsuke and others began to explore original sin in the context of Japanese colonization and militarism in Asia. As a result, the issue of responsibility to whom began to rise to the surface of responsibility thinking and politics.

27. Saito, *History Problem*, 146; Gluck, *"Sekinin,"* 95.
28. Gluck, *"Sekinin,"* 95.
29. Barshay, "Postwar Social and Political Thought," 283.

Yet another moment of attention to Asia that began in 1983 opened the way for further spatialization and a generational transposition of the concept of responsibility—this time as postwar responsibility. The key development here was the formation of the ASSK by Ōnuma Yasuaki, Tanaka Hiroshi, Utsumi Aiko, and others. The three distinguished postwar responsibility (*sengo sekinin*) from war responsibility based on the former's relevance for the current generation. As Ōnuma explained, postwar responsibility was far more than an "abstract intellectual problem" for the postwar generation, since the hands of its members were unstained by wartime involvement. Instead, postwar responsibility represented the totality of "inaction on the part of each and every person in postwar Japanese society" vis-à-vis the country's past in Asia as well as its discriminatory treatment of Asian minorities in the present. The critical point is that through both iterations of responsibility ("ethnic" and "postwar"), attention to Asia connected to a spatial magnification of progressives' comprehensions of responsibility that, in turn, spurred both ideational transformation and concrete political action. The various official apologies and movements for redress in the 1990s, while certainly flawed and relentlessly undermined, owed part of their genesis and development to these earlier processes among progressives in which responsibility was reconceptualized as a problem spanning both past and present and, critically, stretching across borders to Japan's former Asian victims and internally to the Asia within.

ASIA AND CIVIL SOCIETY

Engagements in Asia also shaped and enhanced the evolution of postwar civic activism in Japan. In an earlier study I described the years from around 1975 to 1990 as a "transformative" phase in the development of civic activism in postwar Japan.[30] The transformation I perceived was a transition from an earlier era of contentious protest to a new era of so-called constructive or proposal-style citizen activities. At the heart of the new civic agenda was a desire to formulate solutions to social, economic, and political problems from the grassroots level up, using the resources

30. Avenell, *Making Japanese Citizens*, 240–45.

and ingenuity of ordinary citizens. At the time, my attention was solely on domestic developments, but as this study reveals, the transformation of civic activism in these years went much further. With the anti–Vietnam War movement and immigration control protests as key points of departure, throughout the 1970s a new sphere of Asian solidarity movements involving Japanese and fellow activists from Asia mobilized around issues such as the environment, gender, human rights, and democratization. This attention to the region was largely absent among most civic movements in the early 1970s (which explains the lamentations about not knowing Asia), but by the decade's end Asia was an issue that almost no activist could ignore. In keeping with the constructive, bottom-up mentality of the moment, Japanese civic activists expanded their agendas to include grassroots responses to Asian issues—especially those growing out of Japan's contemporary economic and political entanglements in the region.

I suggest that such activism from the early 1970s onward represented the genesis of a wide-ranging grassroots regionalization within postwar Japanese civic activism, during which Asia attracted an increasing amount of attention from many more activists and became more and more prominent in their programs of activism. Specifically, I think that these new Asian solidarity movements were significant in at least four ways. First and most obviously, they stimulated attention to the region within a broader range of civic groups whose focus had been largely domestic before. Second, they encouraged new groups to build transnational interconnections with fellow Asian activists at the grassroots level through networking abroad and advocacy at home. Third, they compelled civic activists to begin reflecting not only on Japan's problematic activities in Asia in the present but also on its colored past in the region, in this way introducing the Asia problem and the project of deimperialization to a new postwar generation of grassroots actors. And fourth, looking forward, these Asian solidarity movements—by becoming progenitors of transnational activism in Asia—paved the way for a subsequent flourishing of Japanese international NGOs with agendas and activities firmly rooted in the region.

But the impact of activism in Asia arguably went further, connecting to a "grassroots globalization" and a new "social expectation" that

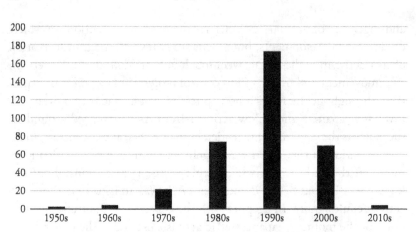

FIGURE 2. Numbers of Japanese International NGOs Formed, 1950s–2010s. *Source*: Kokusai Kyōryoku NGO Sentā (JANIC), *NGO dētabukku 2016: Sūji de miru Nihon no NGO* (Tokyo: Gaimushō Kokusai Kyōryoku Kyoku Minkan Enjo Renkei Shitsu, 2016), 15.

unfolded within Japanese civil society (and Japan more generally) during the 1980s and especially throughout the 1990s.[31] As figure 2 reveals, there was a boom in the establishment of internationally active NGOs in Japan in the 1980s, 1990s, and 2000s. Significantly, close to 70 percent of these organizations listed Asia as their primary or only area of activity.[32] These NGOs played an important role in expanding the regionalizing agenda of the earlier Asian solidarity movements of the 1970s, but they also served a critical mediating role in communicating the norms of an emerging global civil society back to Japan—in other words, facilitating the grassroots globalization of Japanese civil society. What matters in the context of this study is that NGO learning and action related to the norms of human rights, humanitarianism, health, gender, economic self-empowerment, and local community building developed in important ways through such NGOs' involvements in the region. Moreover, these norms found a voice in activism for Japan's internal Asia—for example, in movements for foreign workers and entertainers, most of whom were from

31. "Grassroots globalization" is Appadurai's term, although his use of it and mine differ. See Appadurai, "Grassroots Globalization," 3.

32. Kokusai Kyōryoku NGO, *NGO dētabukku*, 23.

Asia; established minority communities (for instance, in antifingerprint-
ing movements); and Asian exchange students. The human rights agenda
also fueled mobilizations seeking redress for victims of Japanese colonialism and militarism like the Koreans deserted on Sakhalin and the former
so-called comfort women. In these mobilizations for redress advocates and
victims tapped into the language and principles of human rights and restorative justice.

Going one step further, I also suggest that these processes of grassroots regionalization and globalization born of civic activism with, in, and
for other Asians came at a critical moment in the development of civil
society in postwar Japan. Culminating with the passing of the Tokutei
hieiri katsudō sokushin hō (the law to promote specified nonprofit activities), or simply the NPO Law, in 1998, this decade witnessed the flowering and maturation of civil society in Japan. Numerous factors facilitated
this process: the influence of civic models from the United States and Europe, the end of the Cold War, the onset of economic decline, the (brief)
collapse of conservative rule, and the gradual loss of faith in state institutions. But civic groups and advocates also played a role in fostering civil
society at this time, especially in their efforts to promote the sector as
necessary for Japanese social, political, and economic well-being in the
future. In this connection, Koichi Hasegawa, Chika Shinohara, and Jeffrey Broadbent argue that NGO leaders, academic experts, liberal politicians, journalists, and others played a critical role in creating a "social expectation" of a stronger civil society in the country through their public
advocacy.[33] It is no coincidence that Japanese NGOs active in Asia—those
responsible for fostering grassroots globalization—were leading actors in
this process of expectation building. As groups with strong international
connections and agendas, they exemplified the kind of independent and
proactive civil society that advocates hoped to create in Japan. In an influential 1994 report from the Sōgō Kenkyū Kaihatsu Kikō (Japanese National Institute for Research Advancement; NIRA) on civic activism in
Japan, the JVC, PARC, and Shapla Neer (all deeply involved in Asia) were
featured alongside other leading groups as exemplars of the new activism.[34] Here again, I argue, we witness the concrete ways that grassroots

---

33. Hasegawa, Shinohara, and Broadbent, "Effects of 'Social Expectation.'"
34. Sōgō Kenkyū, *Shimin kōeki katsudō*, 64.

involvements in Asia were reflected back to Japan, helping shape the contemporary development of civil society in the country.

ASIA AND NATIONAL IDENTITY

Finally, I believe that attention to the Asia factor can open our eyes to important developments in progressives' understandings of, and contributions to, constructions of identity across the postwar era. As I have shown above, in the early postwar period progressives tapped into a pejorative vision of Asia in the form of Asiatic backwardness and stagnation as they attempted to reconstruct Japanese identity for a new age of peace and democracy. Asiaticness was certainly understood as something internalized by the Japanese that made them Asians, but it was internalized in a very negative way, as if it were a pathogen or genetic defect in need of urgent therapy. To this extent, Asia still served as a tool for othering in the process of identity formation. Progressives' captivation with Asian nationalism of the 1950s certainly helped undermine the pejorative vision of Asia, but lurking behind the brittle language of unity with Asia and the Third World was an ethnic nationalism that also continued to imagine an ethnically homogeneous Japan distinct from its regional neighbors—albeit alongside them in a brotherhood of the weak.

However, the transformations in progressives' thought and activism from the late 1950s onward precipitated a gradual reconsideration of Japan separated from the region, as the realities of Japan in Asia and Asia in Japan forced their way into progressives' consciousness. Indeed, things regional, progressives discovered, were everywhere: from the back streets of Tokyo to the operations of the US-Japan Security Treaty on Okinawa and behind the padlocked bars of the Ōmura Detention Center in Nagasaki. Moreover, Japan could not be extracted from the region, whether this be in sex tourism in South Korea, exploitative banana plantations on Mindanao, or toxic effluent contaminating the Chao Phraya River. Japan was in Asia and Asia was in Japan, regardless of whether one chose to look or not.

The sum total of these internal and external entanglements with Asia elicited a visceral response in the form of protests and civic mobilizations, but by the 1990s, it also connected to novel initiatives to reconsider

Japan and Japanese identity within a regional imaginary. Here progressives stood at the cusp of an identity breakthrough that promised to shatter the logic of separation and othering that was so deeply entrenched in Japanese imaginations of Asia and national identity. Indeed, as minority voices became more prominent in progressive discourse, the structure of so-called Japanese progressives speaking about Asia as the Other also began to look more uncertain—although the increasing uncertainty was in an affirmative and hopeful direction. The new possibility here was about more than the multicultural symbiosis concurrently being championed by government officials and a great many civic groups in the wake of internationalization because it promised something more than banal consumption of an exotic Asia—in food, festivals, and fashion—or the artifice of naturalized ethnic groups nestled together in comfortable cultural isolation. On the contrary, the postwar progressive trajectory toward Asia in Japan and Japan in Asia was arguably also leading toward a recognition of the inherent multiplicity of Japan itself.[35] It was a movement toward "a new definition of 'Japan'" in which "hybridity" became "part of the legitimate landscape."[36] This "transcultural" potentiality born of progressives' encounter with the Asia problem and their struggle for deimperialization promised to transcend the banality of multiculturalism by releasing the ethnic territory of "Japan" to an "internally plural 'praxis of culture'" in which the self-other dichotomy began to collapse.[37]

The odyssey, in this sense, was not about abandoning the West for Asia in a reversal of history but recognizing how reconciliation with the Other was also simultaneously the discovery of another hybrid self. As much as it was a restorative odyssey, then, the encounter with the Asia problem and deimperialization also unfolded as a productive and transformative journey (a method, perhaps) pointing beyond the *telos* of one region and national redemption toward a new language and a new self-understanding. To borrow from Sakai and Yoo, the odyssey presaged the possibility of a "'heterolingual' forum in which, by being humiliated for their colonial past, [the Japanese] allow themselves to re-inscribe new

35. Morris-Suzuki, *Reinventing Japan*, 140.
36. Befu, "Foreword," xxv.
37. Willis and Murphy-Shigematsu, "Transcultural Japan," 9.

channels for their identification, and to create different and new social relations with themselves and non-Japanese."[38] We might understand this as the promise of a new intellectual "space" born of the "borderlands," where "inside and outside" could no longer be determined by "the conventional definition of Japan."[39] As the longtime activist Muto Ichiyo observed in 2010, "if Asia meaningfully matters in the present historical conjuncture . . . let me say it does so only as inter-Asia, as dynamic processes. The inter-Asia we envisage is not a state-level affair but people's level processes of interaction, cross-fertilization and formation taking place amongst hundreds of millions of different people, living, speaking, and dreaming differently. And the point here is that, of necessity, inter-Asia can and will emerge beyond the horizons of modernization and modernity."[40]

In late 2016 Japan's prime minister, Abe Shinzō, made a historic visit to Pearl Harbor, Hawaii, the site of the Japanese military attack in December 1941 that precipitated the Pacific War. Although the event was a carefully orchestrated political spectacle, the historical symbolism of the leader of the former enemy visiting the location of his country's aggression was significant, just as President Barack Obama's visit to Hiroshima some months earlier had been. Yet for all the historic significance, perhaps most striking (or strikingly absent) about Abe's visit to Pearl Harbor was its message—albeit an implicit one—about the sites of wartime misery that the Japanese leader would not be visiting. Will the day ever come when a Japanese prime minister or emperor performs a *kniefall* in the style of German Chancellor Willy Brandt at a site of Japanese atrocity or transgression in Asia or bows their head in remorse before a former Asian victim or their family? In the heated political rivalries of Northeast Asia, at least at this writing, such an outcome seems highly unlikely.

Nonetheless, although history can fill us with despair, it can also inspire a "politics of hope" based on potentialities, visions, and "lived realities."[41] As Anne Allison reminds us in her study of precarity in

38. Sakai and Yoo, "Introduction," 19.
39. Befu, "Foreword," xxiv–xxv.
40. Muto, "Asia, Inter-Asia, and Movement," 181.
41. Lindroth and Sinevaara-Niskanen, "Politics of Hope," 644. For discussions of hope in Japan, see Allison, *Precarious Japan*; Leheny, *Empire of Hope*.

contemporary Japan, "hope shouldn't be topdown—or pronounced in the name of a collective Japan that exerts pressures and exclusions all its own. Rather, it should come from going to the scene itself and hearing from those victimized."[42] The history of Japanese progressives' thought and activism in and with Asia during the postwar era speaks powerfully to this process of "going to the scene itself" and facing the victims. It attests to the capacity for recognition of the Other; for transformation through discovery of the Other within the self; and above all, the ability to imagine visions of a variegated yet interlaced future.

42. Allison, *Precarious Japan*, 199.

Bibliography

7-7 (Rokōkyō "Jiken") 31 Shūnen Sōdai Shūkai Jikkō Iinkai. "7–7 (Rokōkyō 'Jiken') 31 shūnen Sōdai sengen." In Tsumura Takashi, *Tamashii ni fureru kakumei*, 203–6. Tokyo: Rain Shuppan, 1970.

"Agreement between the Republic of India and the People's Republic of China on Trade and Intercourse between the Tibet Region of China and India." April 29, 1954. https://www.mea.gov.in/bilateral-documents.htm?dtl/7807/Agreement+on+Trade+and+Intercourse+with+Tibet+Region.

"'Ajia daigakkō' hiraku: Asu, Oda Makoto-ra no te de." *Mainichi shinbun*, June 24, 1974, evening edition, 10.

Ajia Fukushi Kyōiku Zaidan Nanmin Jigyō Honbu, ed. *Yamato teijū sokushin sentā 18-nen shi: Indoshina nanmin no Nihon teijū shien sentā no kiseki*. Tokyo: Ajia Fukushi Kyōiku Zaidan Nanmin Jigyō Honbu, 1998.

"Ajia o shiru zemi kon'ya kōkai Oda Makoto-shi-ra." *Asahi shinbun*, June 25, 1974, evening edition, 12.

Ajia Taiheiyō Shiryō Sentā. *Hito o kū banana*. Tokyo: Ajia Taiheiyō Shiryō Sentā, 1980. Slide show.

Akimoto Hideo, Ōnuma Yasuaki, and Tsurumi Shunsuke. "Ajia ni taisuru sensō sekinin." *Kikan sanzenri* 41 (1985): 80–90.

Akimoto Yukio. "Ajia no jinmin wa naze tandoku kōwa ni hantai shiteiruka." *Zen'ei* 62 (1951): 17–20.

Akiyama. "Shokuminchishugi no hitei: Ajia-Afurika kaigi no seika." *Kankō rōdō* 9, no. 6 (1955): 30–31.

Akiyama Naoe. "Banana minshū kōeki ga hajimaru made." Lecture at Banana Tantōsha Kaigi, February 20, 2009. http://www.altertrade.co.jp/ATJ20anniversary/topic/images/090604.pdf.

Allison, Anne. *Precarious Japan*. Durham, NC: Duke University Press, 2013.

Amano Michio. "Watashi ni totte no kīsen mondai." In *Shiryo—sei shinryaku o koku-hatsu suru: Kīsen kankō*, edited by Kīsen Kankō ni Hantai suru Onna-tachi no Kai, 38–39. Tokyo: Kīsen Kankō ni Hantai suru Onna-tachi no Kai, 1974.

Amino Yoshihiko, Tanigawa Ken'ichi, Mori Kōichi, Ōbayashi Taryō, and Miyata Noboru. *Umi kara mita Nihon bunka*. Tokyo: Shogakkan, 1992.

AMPO, ed. "Special Issue on the Conference of Asians." *AMPO* 21–22 (1974).

Andō Hikotarō, Terao Gorō, Miyata Setsuko, and Yoshioka Yoshinori. *Nichi-Chō-Chū sangoku jinmin rentai no rekishi to rentai*. In *Nihon Chōsen kenkyūjo shoki shiryō*, vol. 3, edited by Inoue Manabu and Higuchi Yūichi, 141–336. Tokyo: Ryokuin Shobō, 2017.

Andō Takemasa. *Nyūrefuto undō to shimin shakai: "Rokujū-nendai" no shisō no yukue*, Tokyo: Sekaishisōsha, 2013.

"Announcement the Ministers of Finance and Central Bank Governors of France, Germany, Japan, the United Kingdom, and the United States (Plaza Accord)," September 22, 1985. http://www.g7.utoronto.ca/finance/fm850922.htm.

Aochi Shin. "Ima made to kore kara." *Nikkan rentai nyūsu* 44 (1978): 1.

———. "Watashitachi wa aseranai." *Nikkan rentai nyūsu* 31 (1977): 3.

Aochi Shin et al. "Seimei." *Sekai* 335 (1973): 108–9.

Aochi Shin and Wada Haruki, eds. *Nikkan rentai no shisō to kōdō*. Tokyo: Gendai Hyōronsha, 1977.

Aoki Tamotsu et al., eds. *Ajia shin seiki*. 8 vols. Tokyo: Iwanami Shoten, 2002–3.

Appadurai, Arjun. "Grassroots Globalization and the Research Imagination." *Public Culture* 12, no. 1 (2000): 1–19.

Ara Matsuo. "Ajia no ninshiki to Ajia no kenkyū." *Sekai* 192 (1961): 185–92.

Arai Sawako. *Saharin no Kankokujin wa naze kaerenakatta no ka: Kikan undō ni kaketa aru fūfu no 40-nen*. Tokyo: Sōshisha, 1997.

Arano Yasunori. *Kinsei Nihon to Higashi Ajia*. Tokyo: Tokyo Daigaku Shuppankai, 1988.

Arano Yasunori et al., eds. *Ajia no naka no Nihon shi*. 6 vols. Tokyo: Tokyo Daigaku Shuppankai, 1992.

Arase Yutaka. "Minshū to sekinin no mondai." In *Gendai 11: Gendai no minshū*, 223–38. Tokyo: Iwanami Shoten, 1964.

Asahi Jānaru, ed. "Ajia o hiraku wakamono-tachi." *Asahi jānaru*, January 7, 1983, 10–125.

———. "Ajia wa naze Nihonjin o kirauka." *Asahi jānaru*, July 5, 1974, 18–22.

———. "Risuto 3: Nyūkan, Zainichi gaikokujin shien." *Asahi jānaru*, April 23, 1971, 60–61.

———, ed. "Tokushū: Watashitachi wa Ajia o shiranai." *Asahi jānaru*, January 14, 1972, 4–45, 97–107.

Asahi Shinbun. *Kikuzo II Visual*. https://database.asahi.com/index.shtml.

Asuna Mizuho. *"Ajian" no seiki: Shin sedai ga tsukuru ekkyō bunka*. Tokyo: Chūō Kōron Shinsha, 2004.

Avenell, Simon. "Asia and the Development of Civic Activism in Post-War Japan." In *Social Movements and Political Activism in Contemporary Japan: Re-Emerging from Invisibility*, edited by David Chiavacci and Julia Obinger, 51–70. New York: Routledge, 2018.

———. "Beyond Mimesis: Japan and the Uses of Political Ideology in Singapore." In *Imagining Japan in Postwar East Asia: Identity Politics, Schooling, and Popular Culture*, edited by Paul Morris, Edward Vickers, and Naoko Shimazu, 29–48. London: Routledge, 2013.

———. "Japan's Environmental Injustice Paradigm and Transnational Activism." In *New Frontiers in Japanese Studies*, edited by Philip Seaton and Akihiro Ogawa, 209–20. London: Routledge, 2020.

———. *Making Japanese Citizens: Civil Society and the Mythology of the Shimin in Postwar Japan*. Berkeley: University of California Press, 2010.

———. *Transnational Japan in the Global Environmental Movement*. Honolulu: University of Hawai'i Press, 2017.

———. "What Is Asia for Us and Can We Be Asians? The New Asianism in Contemporary Japan." *Modern Asian Studies* 44, no. 6 (2014): 1594–636.

Aydin, Cemil. *The Politics of Anti-Westernism in Asia: Visions of World Order in Pan-Islamic and Pan-Asian Thought*. New York: Columbia University Press, 2007.

Babicz, Lionel. "Japan–Korea, France–Algeria: Colonialism and Post-Colonialism." *Japanese Studies* 33, no. 2 (2013): 201–11.

Barber, Stephen. *Jean Genet*. London: Reaktion, 2004.

Barshay, Andrew. "Postwar Social and Political Thought." In *Modern Japanese Thought*, edited by Bob Tadashi Wakabayashi, 273–355. Cambridge: Cambridge University Press, 1998.

Befu, Harumi. "Foreword: Toward Zones of Hybridity in Japan." In *Transcultural Japan: At the Borderlands of Race, Gender, and Identity*, edited by David Blake Willis and Stephen Murphy-Shigematsu, xxii–xxv. London: Routledge, 2008.

———. *Hegemony of Homogeneity: An Anthropological Analysis of Nihonjinron*. Melbourne, Australia: TransPacific Press, 2001.

Beheiren: "Betonamu ni Heiwa o!" Shimin Rengō, ed. *"Beheiren nyūsu" gappon shukusatsuban 1965–1974*. Tokyo: Beheiren: "Betonamu ni Heiwa o!" Shimin Rengō, 1974.

———. "Chōsen shōnen Kin Tō-ki shi o mamorō." In *Shiryō "Beheiren" undō*, vol. 1, edited by Betonamu ni Heiwa o! Shimin Rengō, 194–95. Tokyo: Kawade Shobō Shinsha, 1974.

———. "Haena kigyō o kokuhatsu suru! Betonamu o oshitsubusu watashitachi no Nihon." In *"Beheiren nyūsu" gappon shukusatsuban 1965–1974*, edited by Beheiren: "Betonamu ni Heiwa o!" Shimin Rengō, 528. Tokyo: Beheiren: "Betonamu ni Heiwa o!" Shimin Rengō, 1974.

———. "Kin Tō-ki shōnen o mamorō: Watashi wa Betonamujin o koroshitakunai—dassō shita Kankoku gunpeichō no uttae." In *"Beheiren nyūsu" gappon shukusatsuban 1965–1974*, edited by Beheiren: "Betonamu ni Heiwa o!" Shimin Rengō, 49. Tokyo: Beheiren: "Betonamu ni Heiwa o!" Shimin Rengō, 1974.

———. "Nihon no naka no kokkyō: Ōmura shūyōjo no kabe no naka e." In *"Beheiren nyūsu" gappon shukusatsuban 1965–1974*, edited by Beheiren: "Betonamu ni Heiwa o!" Shimin Rengō, 228. Tokyo: Beheiren: "Betonamu ni Heiwa o!" Shimin Rengō, 1974.

———. "Saidai no 'kōgai' seizōgyōsha. Shi no shōnin, daigunju sangyō o kyūdan shiyō—Mitsubishi jūkōgyō no hitokabunushi undō o susume. In *"Beheiren nyūsu" gappon shukusatsuban 1965–1974*, edited by Beheiren: "Betonamu ni Heiwa o!" Shimin Rengō, 363. Tokyo: Beheiren: "Betonamu ni Heiwa o!" Shimin Rengō, 1974.

———. "'Shutsunyūkoku kanri rei' kaiaku ni hantai o." In *"Beheiren nyūsu" gappon shukusatsuban 1965–1974*, edited by Beheiren: "Betonamu ni Heiwa o!" Shimin Rengō, 210. Tokyo: Beheiren: "Betonamu ni Heiwa o!" Shimin Rengō, 1974.

Benedict, Ruth. *The Chrysanthemum and the Sword*. Boston: Houghton Mifflin, 1946.

Bronson, Adam. *One Hundred Million Philosophers: Science of Thought and the Culture of Democracy in Postwar Japan*. Honolulu: University of Hawai'i Press, 2016.

Buettner, Elizabeth. *Europe after Empire: Decolonization, Society, and Culture*. Cambridge: Cambridge University Press, 2016.

Burkett, Jodi. *Constructing Post-Imperial Britain: Britishness, "Race" and the Radical Left in the 1960s*. Basingstoke, UK: Palgrave Macmillan, 2013.

Castells, Manuel. *The Rise of the Network Society*. West Sussex, UK: Wiley Blackwell, 2010.

Chen, Kuan-Hsing. *Asia as Method: Toward Deimperialization*. Durham, NC: Duke University Press, 2010.

Choi, Deokhyo. "Guest Editor's Introduction: Writing the 'Empire' Back into the History of Postwar Japan." *International Journal of Korean History* 22, no. 1 (2017): 1–10.

Chūgokujin Junansha Meibo Kyōdō Sakusei Jikkō Iinkai. *Chūgokujin kyōsei renkō jiken ni kansuru hōkokusho*. 3 vols. Tokyo: Chūgokujin Junansha Meibo Kyōdō Sakusei Jikkō Iinkai, 1960–61.

———. *Yonmannin Chūgokujin kyōsei renkō no kiroku*. Tokyo: Chūgokujin Junansha Meibo Kyōdō Sakusei Jikkō Iinkai, 1961.

Chūgokujin Kyōsei Renkō Jiken Shiryō Hensan Iinkai. *Kusa no bohyō: Chūgokujin kyōsei renkō jiken no kiroku*. Tokyo: Shinnihon Shuppansha, 1964.

Confino, Alon. "Remembering the Second World War, 1945–1965: Narratives of Victimhood and Genocide." *Cultural Analysis* 4 (2005): 46–75.

Conrad, Sebastian. "'The Colonial Ties Are Liquidated': Modernization Theory, Post-War Japan and the Global Cold War." *Past and Present* 216 (2012): 181–214.

———. *The Quest for the Lost Nation: Writing History in Germany and Japan in the American Century*. Translated by Alan Nothnagle. Berkeley: University of California Press, 2010.

Conrad, Sebastian, and Prasenjit Duara. *Viewing Regionalisms from East Asia*. Washington: American Historical Association, 2003.

Constantino, Renato. *Firipin nashonarizumu ron*. Translated by Tsurumi Yoshiyuki. Tokyo: Imura Bunka Jigyōsha, 1977.

———. *The Making of a Filipino: A Story of Philippine Colonial Politics*. Quezon City, Philippines: Malaya Books, 1969.

———. *The Second Invasion: Japan and the Philippines*. Quezon City, Philippines: Karrel, 1989.

Dale, Peter. *The Myth of Japanese Uniqueness*. London: Routledge, 2012.

"'Damatte wa irarenai' jimoto higaisha ga dantai o kessei: Nippon Kagaku dai-8-kai kōgi demo ni hatsu sanka." Reprinted in *Kōgai o nogasu na!*, July 10, 1975, 31.

David, Randolf S. "Philippine Society Today: Yoshiyuki Tsurumi as an Anchoring Point." July 3, 2015. Research Center for Cooperative Civil Societies, Rikkyo University. http://hdl.handle.net/11008/1334.

David, Randolf S., Temario C. Rivera, Patricio N. Abinales, Oliver G. Teves, and Procopio S. Resabal Jr., in collaboration with Yoshiyuki Tsurumi, Kiyomi Higuchi, Shigeru Hikichi, and Takako Yamamoto. *Transnational Corporations and the Philippine Banana Export Industry*. Quezon City, Philippines: Third World Studies Center, University of the Philippines, 1981.

Dennehy, Kristine. "Overcoming Colonialism at Bandung, 1955." In *Pan-Asianism in Modern Japanese History: Colonialism, Regionalism and Borders*, edited by Sven Saaler and J. Victor Koschmann, 213–25. New York: Routledge, 2007.

Doi Masaoki. "Iwai no hanran." In *Sekai shi ni okeru Ajia: 1953-nendo rekishigaku kenkyūkai taikai hōkoku*, edited by Rekishigaku Kenkyūkai, 2–5. Tokyo: Iwanami Shoten, 1953.

Dower, John. "Peace and Democracy in Two Systems: External Policy and Internal Conflict." In *Postwar Japan as History*, edited by Andrew Gordon, 3-33. Berkeley: University of California Press, 1993.

————. "The Useful War." In John Dower, *Japan in War and Peace*, 9–32. New York: New Press, 1993.

Duara, Prasenjit. "Asia Redux: Conceptualizing a Region for Our Times." *Journal of Asian Studies* 69, no. 4 (2010): 963–83.

————. "The Discourse of Civilization and Pan-Asianism." *Journal of World History* 12, no. 1 (Spring 2001): 99–130.

————. *Sovereignty and Authenticity: Manchukuo and the East Asian Moderns*. Lanham, MD: Rowman and Littlefield, 2003.

Duus, Peter. "The 'New Asianism.'" In *Can Japan Globalize: Studies on Japan's Changing Political Economy and the Process of Globalization in Honor of Sung-Jo Park*, edited by Arne Holzhausen, 245–56. Heidelberg, Germany: Physica-Verlag, 2001.

Eguchi Bokurō. "Joron: Sekai shi ni okeru Ajia." *Chūō kōron* 68, no. 8 (1953): 264–66.

Esselstrom, Erik. *That Distant Country Next Door: Popular Japanese Perceptions of Mao's China*. Honolulu: University of Hawai'i Press, 2019.

Executive Committee to Stop the Toyama Chemical Co. from Exporting Pollution. "Cut Off the Path of Retreat for Pollution!! The Beginning of Anti-'Pollution Exporting' Movements by Combined Forces of Japanese and Korean Citizens." *KOGAI*, Spring 1975, 2–7.

Ferguson, Niall, Charles S. Maier, Erez Manela, and Daniel J. Sargent, eds. *The Shock of the Global: The 1970s in Perspective*. Cambridge, MA: Belknap Press of Harvard University Press, 2011.

"Final Communique of the Asian-African Conference, Held at Bandung from 18–24 April 1955." *Interventions: International Journal of Postcolonial Studies* 11, no. 1 (2009): 94–102.

Fogel, Joshua A. *The Nanjing Massacre in History and Historiography*. Berkeley: University of California Press, 2000.

Fuji Shuppan, ed. *Sākuru mura.* 5 vols. Tokyo: Fuji Shuppan, 2006.

Fujishima Udai. "Chōsenjin kikoku to Nihonjin no mōten." *Sekai* 166 (1959): 190–95.

———. "Jo." In *Dokyumento Chōsenjin: Nihon gendai shi no kurai kage,* edited by Fujishima Udai et al., 1–4. Tokyo: Nihon Dokusho Shinbun Shuppanbu, 1965.

———. "Kankoku no taishū hōki." *Chūō kōron* 870 (1960): 182–92.

———. "'Manshū' daigyakusatsu no genkei: Nisshin sensō." *Ushio* 159 (1972): 146–57.

———. *Nihon no minzoku undō.* Tokyo: Kōbundō, 1960.

———. "Nihon no naka no Chōsenjin: Sabetsu no jittai to haikei." *Ekonomisuto,* December 3, 1963, 40–44.

———. "Tonari no kuni, Daikanminkoku." *Chūō kōron* 856 (1959): 88–102.

———. "Vietonamu sensō kara dassō shita Kankokuhei." *Gendai no me* 7, no. 5 (1966): 188–96.

Fujishima Udai et al. *Dokyumento Chōsenjin: Nihon gendai shi no kurai kage.* Tokyo: Nihon Dokusho Shinbun Shuppanbu, 1965.

Fujishima Udai, Maruyama Kunio, and Murakami Hyōei. "Chōsenjin rokujūmannin no genjitsu." *Chūō kōron* 73, no. 13 (1958): 175–96.

Fukuda Takeo. "Fukuda sōri daijin no Manira niokeru supīchi (waga kuni no Tōnan Ajia seisaku) (Fukuda dokutorin enzetsu)." August 18, 1977. Contained in the Nihonseiji—Kokusai Kankei Database of the National Graduate Institute for Policy Studies and Institute of Advanced studies for Asia, University of Tokyo. https://worldjpn.grips.ac.jp/documents/texts/docs/19770818.S1J.html.

Fukuzawa Yukichi. "Datsu A ron." In Fukuzawa Yukichi, *Fukuzawa Yukichi chosakushū,* vol. 8: *Jijikogoto tsūzoku gaikō ron,* edited by Iwatani Jūrō and Nishikawa Shunsaku, 261–65. Tokyo: Keiō Gijuku Daigaku Shuppankai, 2003.

Funabashi Yōichi. *Ajia Taiheiyō fyūjon: APEC to Nihon.* Tokyo: Chūō Kōronsha, 1995.

———. "The Asianization of Asia." *Foreign Affairs* 72, no. 5 (1993): 75–85.

Gaimushō, ed. *2012-nenban seifu kaihatsu enjo (ODA) hakusho: Nihon no kokusai kyōryoku.* Tokyo: Bunka Kōbō, 2013.

———. *Nihon NGO renkei mushō shikin kyōryoku no hyōka (daisansha hyōka).* Tokyo: Japanese Ministry of Foreign Affairs, 2011. https://www.mofa.go.jp/mofaj/gaiko/oda /shiryo/hyouka/kunibetu/gai/cambodia/nsk10_01_index.html/.

Garon, Sheldon. *The State and Labor in Modern Japan.* Berkeley: University of California Press, 1987.

Gayle, Curtis Anderson. *Marxist History and Postwar Japanese Nationalism.* London: RoutledgeCurzon, 2003.

———. "Progressive Representations of the Nation: Early Postwar Japan and Beyond." *Social Science Japan Journal* 4, no. 1 (2001): 1–19.

General Headquarters Supreme Commander for the Allied Powers. "Definition of United, Neutral, Enemy, Special Status and Undetermined Status Nations." SCAPIN 1757. August 4, 1947. National Diet Library of Japan "Birth of the Constitution of Japan" collection. https://dl.ndl.go.jp/info:ndljp/pid/9887025.

Gluck, Carol. "The Call for a New Asian Identity: An Examination of the Cultural Arguments and Their Implications." *Carnegie Council on International Affairs: Japan Programs Occasional Papers* 5 (1994): 3–6.

————. "Operations of Memory: 'Comfort Women' and the World." In *Ruptured Histories: War, Memory, and the Post-Cold War in Asia*, edited by Sheila Miyoshi Jager and Rana Mitter, 47–77. Cambridge, MA: Harvard University Press, 2007.

————. "The Past in the Present." In *Postwar Japan as History*, edited by Andrew Gordon, 64–95. Berkeley: University of California Press, 1993.

————. "*Sekinin*: Responsibility in Modern Japan." In *Words in Motion: Toward a Global Lexicon*, edited by Carol Gluck and Anna Lowenhaupt Tsing, 83–106. Durham, NC: Duke University Press, 2009.

Go Rin-shun and Tsumura Takashi. "Taidan 'Zainichi Nihonjin' to Zainichi Chōsenjin: Taiken no saisoshiki no tame ni." *Shin Nihon bungaku* 25, no. 11 (1970): 64–77.

"Gokajō goseimon o tai shi, zen sekai to kyōzon kyōei, shushō kyūdenka no gokeirin," *Asahi shinbun*, August 30, 1945, morning edition, 1.

Gordon, Andrew. Conclusion to *Postwar Japan as History*, edited by Andrew Gordon, 449–64. Berkeley: University of California Press, 1993.

————. "Society and Politics from Transwar through Postwar Japan." In *Historical Perspectives on Contemporary East Asia*, edited by Merle Goldman and Andrew Gordon, 277–96. Cambridge, MA: Harvard University Press, 2000.

Hall, Ian. *Dilemmas of Decline: British Intellectuals and World Politics, 1945–1975*. Berkeley: University of California Press, 2012.

Halloran, Richard. "Violent Crowds in Jakarta Protest the Visit by Tanaka." *New York Times*, January 16, 1974, late city edition, 3.

Hamanishi Kenjirō. "Ajia no minzokushugi undō to Nihon." *Nihon oyobi Nihonjin* 7, no. 2 (1956): 16–24.

Hamashita Takeshi, ed. *Higashi Ajia sekai no chiiki nettowāku*, vol. 3. Tokyo: Kokusai Bunka Kōryū Suishin Kyōkai, 1999.

————. "The Intra-Regional System in East Asia in Modern Times." In *Network Power: Japan and Asia*, edited by Peter J. Katzenstein and Takashi Shiraishi, 113–35. Ithaca, NY: Cornell University Press, 1997.

Hanasaki Kōhei. "Decolonization and Assumption of War Responsibility." In *The Inter-Asia Cultural Studies Reader*, edited by Kuan-Hsing Chen and Chua Beng Huat, 178–90. London: Routledge: 2007.

————. "Tsurumi Yoshiyuki no kokkyō no koekata." In *Tsurumi Yoshiyuki no kokkyō no koekata*, edited by Ajia Taiheiyō Shiryō Sentā, 6–20. Tokyo: Ajia Taiheiyō Shiryō Sentā (PARC), 1999.

Handō Kazutoshi. *Shōwashi sengohen 1945–1989*. Tokyo: Heibonsha, 2009.

Hani Gorō. "Doitsu no Yudayajin dan'atsu to kokuji." *Ushio* 144 (1971): 149–50.

Hara Yōnosuke. *Shin-Tōaron*. Tokyo: NTT Shuppan, 2002.

Harootunian, Harry. "Japan's Long Postwar: The Trick of Memory and the Ruse of History." In *Japan After Japan: Social and Cultural Life from the Recessionary 1990s to the Present*, edited by Tomiko Yoda and Harry Harootunian, 98–121. Durham, NC: Duke University Press, 2006.

————. "Postcoloniality's Unconscious / Area Studies' Desire." In *Learning Places: The Afterlives of Area Studies*, edited by Masao Miyoshi and H. D. Harootunian, 150–74. Durham, NC: Duke University Press, 2002.

Hasegawa, Koichi, Chika Shinohara, and Jeffrey P. Broadbent. "The Effects of 'Social Expectation' on the Development of Civil Society in Japan." *Journal of Civil Society* 3, no. 28 (2007): 179–203.

Hashimoto, Akiko. *The Long Defeat: Cultural Trauma, Memory, and Identity in Japan.* New York: Oxford University Press, 2015.

Hatada Takashi. "Nihonjin no Chōsenjinkan." *Sekai* 274 (1968): 64–72.

———. *Nihonjin no Chōsenkan.* Tokyo: Keisō Shobō, 1969.

———. "Nikkan mondai wa owatte-inai: Shokuminchishugi hitei kara no shuppatsu." In Hatada Takashi, *Nihonjin no Chōsenkan*, 122–24. Tokyo: Keisō Shobō, 1969.

Hatch, Walter F. *Asia's Flying Geese: How Regionalization Shapes Japan.* Ithaca, NY: Cornell University Press, 2010.

Hatsuse Ryūhei. "Ajiashugi no tenkan: Genjiten." *Kōbe hōgaku zasshi* 39, no. 1 (1989): 11–33.

———. "Majikku mirā no uragawa." In *Uchinaru kokusaika*, edited by Hatsuse Ryūhei, 5–25. Tokyo: Mitsumine Shobō, 1985.

Hayashi Fusao. *Dai Tōa sensō kōtei ron.* Tokyo: Chūō Kōron Shinsha, 2014.

He, Yinan. "National Mythmaking and the Problems of History in Sino-Japanese Relations." In *Japan's Relations with China: Facing a Rising Power*, edited by Lam Peng Er, 69–91. London: Routledge, 2006.

Hein, Laura. "Postcolonial Conscience: Making Moral Sense of Japan's Modern World." In *Imagination without Borders: Feminist Artist Tomiyama Taeko and Social Responsibility*, edited by Laura Hein and Rebecca Jennison, 1–28. Ann Arbor: Center for Japanese Studies, University of Michigan, 2010.

Hein, Laura, and Ellen H. Hammond. "Homing in on Asia: Identity in Contemporary Japan." *Bulletin of Concerned Asian Scholars* 27, no. 3 (1995): 3–17.

Heiwa Mondai Danwakai. "Mitatabi heiwa ni tsuite." *Sekai* 60 (1950): 21–52.

Hidaka Rokurō et al. "Kokumin bunka kaigi shinpojiumu 'Nikkan mondai to Nihon no chishikijin.'" *Gendai no Me* 7, no. 2 (1966): 42–87.

Higuchi Yūichi. "Kaisetsu 1." In *Nihon Chōsen kenkyūjo shoki shiryō*, vol. 3, edited by Inoue Manabu and Higuchi Yūichi, 411–20. Tokyo: Ryokuin Shobō, 2017.

Hiraishi Naoaki. "The Asia Boom in Japanese Publishing." *Social Science Japan*, July 1994, 27–28.

———. "Kindai Nihon no Ajiashugi: Meijiki no shorinen o chūshin ni." In *Ajia kara kangaeru*, vol. 5: *Kindaikazō*, edited by Mizoguchi Yūzō, Hamashita Takeshi, Hiraishi Naoaki, and Miyajima Hiroshi, 265–91. Tokyo: Tokyo Daigaku Shuppankai, 1994.

Hirano Ken'ichirō and Sengo Nihon Kokusai Bunka Kōryū Kenkyū Kai. *Sengo Nihon kokusai bunka kōryū.* Keisō Shobō, 2005.

Hirata, Keiko. *Civil Society in Japan: The Growing Role of NGOs in Tokyo's Aid Development Policy.* New York: Palgrave Macmillan, 2002.

"Hokkaidō tankomura: Ikijigoku no naka no Chōsenjintachi." Translated from Korean by Fujisawa Yutaka. *Kōgai o nogasu na!*, July 1976, 41–45.

Honda Katsuichi. *America Gasshūkoku.* Tokyo: Asahi Shinbunsha, 1970.

———. *Chūgoku no Nihon gun.* Tokyo: Sōjusha, 1972.

———. *Chūgoku no tabi.* Tokyo: Suzusawa Shoten, 1972.

———. *Korosu-gawa no ronri*. Tokyo: Susuzawa Shoten, 1972.

———. *Senjō no mura*. Tokyo: Asahi Shinbunsha, 1968.

———. *Soshite waga sokoku Nihon*. Tokyo: Suzusawa Shoten, 1976.

———. *Vietnam War: A Report through Asian Eyes*. Translated by Koyoshi Miulla. Tokyo: Miraisha, 1972.

Hoppens, Robert. *The China Problem in Postwar Japan: Japanese National Identity and Sino-Japanese Relations*. London: Bloomsbury Academic, 2015.

Hosoya Chihiro, Andō Nisuke, and Ōnuma Yasuaki, eds. *Kokusai shinpojiumu Tokyo saiban o tō*. Tokyo: Kōdansha, 1984.

Hotta, Eri. *Pan-Asianism and Japan's War 1931–1945*. New York: Palgrave Macmillan, 2008.

Hotta Masahiko. "Munōyaku banana no kusanone yunyū: Mōhitotsu no kakawari o motomete (ge)." *Kōmei* 334 (1989): 148–63.

———. "Munōyaku banana no kusanone yunyū: Mōhitotsu no kakawari o motomete (jō)." *Kōmei* 333 (1989): 148–57.

Hotta Yoshie. *Indo de kangaeta koto*. Tokyo: Iwanami Shoten, 1957.

Iacobelli, Pedro, Danton Leary, and Shinnosuke Takahashi, eds. *Transnational Japan as History: Empire, Migration, and Social Movements*. New York: Palgrave Macmillan, 2015.

Ienaga Saburō. *Japan's Last War: World War II and the Japanese, 1931–1945*. Translated by Frank Baldwin. Canberra: Australian National University Press, 1979.

———. *Taiheiyō sensō*. Tokyo: Iwanami Shoten, 1968.

Iida, Yumiko. *Rethinking Identity in Modern Japan: Nationalism as Aesthetics*. London: Routledge, 2002.

Ifa Joshi Daigakkō Gakusei Kai. "Ifa Joshi Dai no seimeibun." In *Shiryo—sei shinryaku o kokuhatsu-suru: Kīsen kankō*, edited by Kīsen Kankō ni Hantai suru Onna-tachi no Kai, 62. Tokyo: Kīsen Kankō ni Hantai suru Onna-tachi no Kai, 1974.

Iijima Aiko. "Donoyō ni tatakau koto ga hitsuyō to sareteiruka. In Iijima Aiko, *Shinryaku = sabetsu no kanata e: Aru feminisuto no hansei*, 172–82. Tokyo: Inpakuto Shuppankai, 2006.

———. "Hoi 1: Naze 'shinryaku = sabetsu to tatakau Ajia fujin kaigi' datta no ka." In Iijima Aiko, *Shinryaku = sabetsu no kanata e: Aru feminisuto no hansei*, 138–57. Tokyo: Inpakuto Shuppankai, 2006.

———. "Watashitachi wa doko e mukaō to shiteiruka." In Iijima Aiko, *Shinryaku = sabetsu no kanata e: Aru feminisuto no hansei*, 293–316. Tokyo: Inpakuto Shuppankai, 2006.

Iinuma Jirō, ed. *Ashimoto no kokusaika: Zainichi Kankokujin—Chōsenjin no rekishi to genjō*. Osaka: Kaifūsha, 1993.

———. "Nyūkan taisei no yokuatsu kōzō." *Gendai no me* 11, no. 6 (1970): 104–13.

Iizuka Kenji. "Ajia no kakumei to nashonarizumu." *Kaizō* 32, no. 3 (1951): 10–19.

Ikezumi Yoshinori, Sugimoto Teruko, and Nakamura Yōko. *Banana kara jinken e: Firipin banana o meguru shimin undō*. Tokyo: Dōbunkan Shuppan, 1988.

Inoguchi, Takashi. "Japanese Ideas of Asian Regionalism." *Japanese Journal of Political Science* 12, no. 2 (2011): 233–49.

Inoue Kiyoshi. "Nihon teikokushugi to Ajia." In *Sekai shi ni okeru Ajia: 1953-nendo rek-ishigaku kenkyūkai taikai hōkoku*, edited by Rekishigaku Kenkyūkai, 120–32. Tokyo: Iwanami Shoten, 1953.

Inoue Sumio. "Undō no naka de kanjita 70-nendai." In Inoue Sumio, *Arukitsuzukeru to iu ryūgi*, 27–38. Tokyo: Shōbunsha, 1982.

Iokibe Kaoru, Komiya Kazuo, and Hosoya Yuichi, eds. *History, Memory, and Politics in Postwar Japan*. Boulder, CO: Lynne Rienner, 2020.

Irokawa Daikichi. "Kindai Nihon to Ajia kaihō." *Ushio* 79 (1967): 115–23.

Ishida Takeshi. *Shakai kagaku saikō: Haisen kara hanseiki no dōjidaishi*. Tokyo: Tokyo Daigaku Shuppankai, 1995.

Ishihara, Shintarō. *The Japan That Can Say No: Why Japan Will Be First among Equals*. Translated by Frank Baldwin. New York: Simon and Schuster, 1991.

"Ishihara Slammed for Racist Remarks." *Japan Times*, March 10, 2001. https://www.japantimes.co.jp/news/2001/03/10/national/ishihara-slammed-for-racist-remarks/.

Ishii Isamu. "'Ajia no Nihonjin wa minikui' ka." *Bungei shunjū*, August 1970, 236–44.

Ishii Yoneo. "Kaisetsu: Nihon kōka tokushū no haikei." *Chūō kōron* 88, no. 2 (1973): 210–15.

Ishikawa Akira. "Sōru." In "Tokuhain hōkoku: Ajia de kirawareru Nihonjin 'ierō Yankī,' 'shinryakusha,'" special issue, *Ekonomisuto*, December 20, 1969, 145–48.

Ishimoda Shō. "Chūsei seiritsu shi no nisan no mondai." In *Nihon shakai no shiteki kyūmei*, edited by Rekishigaku Kenkyūkai, 33–71. Tokyo: Iwanami Shoten, 1949.

———. "Chūsei shi kenkyū no kiten." In Ishimoda Shō, *Chūseiteki sekai no keisei*, 398–433. Tokyo: Itō Shoten, 1950.

———. "Kindai shigaku no hitsuyō ni tsuite." In Ishimoda Shō, *Sengo rekishigaku no shisō*, 226–43. Tokyo: Hōsei Daigaku Shuppankyoku, 1977.

———. "Rekishikan ni tsuite." In Ishimoda Shō, *Sengo rekishigaku no shisō*, 207–25. Tokyo: Hōsei Daigaku Shuppankyoku, 1977.

———. *Rekishi to minzoku no hakken: Rekishigaku no kadai to hōhō*. Tokyo: Tokyo Daigaku Shuppankai.

Itō Michio. "NGO no kokusai kyōryoku katsudō." In *Kusanone no kokusai kōryū to kokusai kyōryoku*, edited by Menju Toshihiro, 92–113. Tokyo: Akashi Shoten, 2003.

Itō Takiko. "Kīsen kankō ni shōchō sareru nanboku mondai." In *Zenkyōtō kara ribu e: jūgoshi nōto sengohen*, edited by Onnatachi no Ima o Tō Kai, 325–34. Tokyo: Inpakuto Shuppankai, 1996.

Iwabuchi, Koichi. *Recentering Globalization: Popular Culture and Japanese Transnationalism*. Durham, NC: Duke University Press, 2002.

Izumi Seiichi. "Nihonjin no jinshuteki henken: Chōsen mondai to kanren shite," *Sekai* 207 (1963): 80–89.

Jichitai Kokusaika Fōramu. "Kurōzu appu NGO-NPO: Zaidan hōjin PHD kyōkai (Peace, Health, and Human Development) heiwa to kenkō o ninau hitozukuri." *Jichitai kokusaika fōramu* 244 (2010): 42–43.

Johnson, Chalmers. *MITI and the Japanese Miracle*. Stanford, CA: Stanford University Press, 1982.

Joint Chiefs of Staff. "Basic Directive for Post-Surrender Military Government in Japan Proper." J.C.S. Directive 1380/15. November 3, 1945. National Diet Library of Japan "Birth of the Constitution of Japan" collection. https://www.ndl.go.jp/constitution/e /shiryo/01/036/036tx.html.

JVC "NGO no Chōsen" Henshū Iinkai. "Hajime ni." In *NGO no chōsen (jō): Nihon kokusai borantia sentā (JVC) 10-nen no kiroku*, edited by JVC "NGO no Chōsen" Henshū Iinkai, 3–5. Tokyo: Mekon, 1990.

Kaigai Gijutsu Kyōryoku Jigyōdan. *Cheju tō kankō kaihatsu keikaku chōsa hōkokusho*. Tokyo: Kaigai Gijutsu Kyōryoku Jigyōdan, 1972.

Kajitani Yoshihisa. "Ajia no nikumaremono *Nippon*." *Gekkan sōhyō*, January 1973, 60–65.

Kakyō Seinen Tōsō Iinkai. "Nana—nana shūkai ni okeru kaseitō daihyō no hatsugen." *Zenshin*, July 13, 1970, 3.

———. "Nyūkan tōsō o tatakau naka kara minzoku no tamashii no fukken o." In *Shin sayoku riron zenshi*, edited by Hensha Shin Sayoku Riron Zen Shi Henshū Iinkai, 505–12. Tokyo: Ryūdō Shuppan, 1979.

Kamachi, Noriko. "Japanese Writings on Post-1945 Japan—China Relations." In *Japan's Relations with China: Facing a Rising Power*, edited by Lam Peng Er, 50–68. London: Routledge, 2006.

Kanagawa Ken Jichi Sōgō Kenkyū Sentā "kokusaika ni taiō shita chiiki shakai no arikata" Kenkyū Chīmu. *Kanagawa no Kankoku-Chōsenjin: Jichitai genba kara no teigen*. Tokyo: Kōjinsha, 1984.

Kanagawa Ken Shōgai Bu. *Minsai gaikō 20-nen: Sekai ni hirakareta kanagawa ken o mezashite*. Kanagawa, Japan: Kanagawa Ken Shōgai Bu Sōmu Shitsu, 1995.

Kanagawa Kennai Gaikokujin Jittai Chōsa Iinkai. *Kanagawa kennai zaijū Indoshina nanmin jittai chōsa hōkokusho*. Kanagawa, Japan: Kanagawa Kennai Gaikokujin Jittai Chōsa Iinkai, 1988.

Kang Sang-jung. *Ajia kara Nihon o tō*. Tokyo: Iwanami Shoten, 1994.

———. "Ajia to no danzetsu, rekishi to no danzetsu: 'Ajia to no wakai naki heiwa' no fusai." *Sekai* 573 (1992): 152–61.

———. "Hajime ni futatsu no shinpojiumu o tsūjite." In Kang Sang-jung, *Futatsu no sengo to Nihon: Ajia kara tō sengo 50-nen*, 7–16. Tokyo: San'ichi Shobō, 1995.

———. "The Imaginary Geography of a Nation and Denationalized Narrative." In *Contemporary Japanese Thought*, edited by Richard F. Calichman, 71–83. New York: Columbia University Press, 2005.

———. "Musubi ni kaete: 'Sengo—go' ni mukete." In Kang Sang-jung, *Futatsu no sengo to Nihon: Ajia kara tō sengo 50-nen*, 184–99. Tokyo: San'ichi Shobō, 1995.

———. "Nihon no Ajiakan no tenkan ni mukete." In *Nihon wa doko e ikunoka*, by Carol Gluck, Kang Sang-jung, Tessa Morris-Suzuki, Hiyane Teruo, Iwasaki Naoko, Takashi Fujitani, and Harry Harootunian, 64–100. Tokyo: Kōdansha, 2003.

———. "'Nihonteki orientarizumu' no genzai: Kokusaika ni hisomu hizumi," *Sekai* 522 (1988): 133–39.

———. "Rekishi to no tatakai wa owatta ka." In Kang Sang-jung, *Futatsu no sengo to Nihon: Ajia kara tō sengo 50-nen*, 130–48. Tokyo: San'ichi Shobō, 1995.

———. "Sengo paradaimu wa yomigaeru ka." In Kang Sang-jung, *Futatsu no sengo to Nihon: Ajia kara tō sengo 50-nen*, 103–28. Tokyo: San'ichi Shobō, 1995.

———. "Shōwa no owari to Nihon no Ajia kan o tō." In Kang Sang-jung, *Futatsu no sengo to Nihon: Ajia kara tō sengo 50-nen*, 18–67. Tokyo: San'ichi Shobō, 1995.

———. *Tōhoku Ajia no kyōdō no ie o mezashite*. Tokyo: Heibonsha, 2001.

Kankoku Mondai Kirisutosha Kinkyū Kaigi. "Kankoku mondai kirisutosha kinkyū kaigi seimei." In *Kankoku minshuka tōsō shiryō shū*, edited by Kankoku Mondai Kirisutosha Kinkyū Kaigi, 76–82. Tokyo: Shinkyō Shuppansha, 1976.

Kano Masanao. "Kaisetsu: Betonamu hansen kara Ajiagaku e." In *Tsurumi Yoshiyuki chosakushū*, vol. 3: *Ajia to no deai*, edited by Yoshikawa Yūichi, 405–19. Tokyo: Misuzu Shobō, 2002.

Kanō Mikiyo. "Shinryaku = sabetsu to tatakau Ajia fujin kaigi to dai-2-ha feminizumu." *Joseigaku kenkyū* 18 (2011): 149–65.

Kapur, Nick. "The Empire Strikes Back? The 1968 Meiji Centennial Celebrations and the Revival of Japanese Nationalism." *Japanese Studies* 38, no. 3 (2018): 305–28.

———. *Japan at the Crossroads: Conflict and Compromise after Anpo*. Cambridge, MA: Harvard University Press, 2018.

Katō Norihiro. "Haisengoron." In Katō Norihiro, *Haisengoron*, 5–93. Tokyo: Kōdansha, 1997.

Katzenstein, Peter, J. "Regionalism and Asia." *New Political Economy* 5, no. 3 (2000): 353–68.

Katzenstein, Peter J., and Takashi Shiraishi, eds. *Network Power: Japan and Asia*. Ithaca, NY: Cornell University Press, 1997.

Kawakami Eiichi. "Rensai tokushū hōtei de sabakareru Nihon no sensō sekinin (41): Kankoku-Chōsenjin BC kyū senpan kōshiki chinsha seikyū soshō—jindō ni han suru minzoku-sabetsu hanketsu." *Gunshuku mondai shiryō* 337 (2008): 64–73.

Kawamura Masami. "Kōdo seichō to Tōnan Ajia: 'Kaihatsu' to iu reisen—'Betonamu sensō' to iu nessen no naka de," in *Kōdo seichō no jidai*, vol. 2: *Kanetsu to yuragi*, edited by Ōkado Masakatsu et al., 303–48. Tokyo: Ōtsuki Shoten, 2010.

Kawashima Takeyoshi. "Nihon hōkensei no Ajiateki seishitsu." *Chūō kōron* 62, no. 5 (1947): 6–19.

Keizai Kikakuchō. *Shōwa 31nen: Nenji keizai hōkoku*. https://www5.cao.go.jp/keizai3/keizaiwp/wp-je56/wp-je56-00001i.html.

Kim Chi-ha. *Minshū no koe*. Edited and translated by Kim Chi-ha Sakuhinshū Kankō Iinkai. Tokyo: Simul Shuppankai 1974.

———. *Nagai kurayami no kanata ni*. Translated by Shibuya Sentarō. Tokyo: Chūō Kōronsha, 1971.

———. "Sengen 1975-3-1: Nihon minshū e no teian." In *Nikkan rentai no shisō to kōdō*, edited by Aochi Shin and Wada Haruki, 202–8. Tokyo: Gendai Hyōronsha, 1977.

Kim Dae-jung and Yasue Ryōsuke. "Kankoku minshuka e no michi: Paku seiken no mujun wa kakudai shiteiru." *Sekai* 334 (1973): 102–22.

Kim Dong-hee. "Kankokugun heishi gunzō—Watashi no kiroku daisanbu." *Tenbō* 124 (1969): 93–119.

———. "Kankokugun shinpei kunrenjo—Watashi no kiroku dainibu." *Tenbō* 123 (1969): 88–119.

————. "Ōmura shūyōjo kara no tegami." *Tenbō* 110 (1968): 55–59.

————. "Watashi no kiroku (jō)." *Tenbō* 122 (1969): 114–45.

Kimu Ji Ha ra o Tasukeru Kai. "Uttae." In *Nikkan rentai no shisō to kōdō*, edited by Aochi Shin and Wada Haruki, 131–2. Tokyo: Gendai Hyōronsha, 1977.

Kim Tal-su. "Kin Hi-ro to wa nanika." *Chūō kōron* 80, no. 10 (1969): 320–29.

————. "Komatsugawa jiken no uchi to soto." In *Nihon no naka no Chōsen*, edited by Usami Shō et al., 143–209. Tokyo: Taihei Shuppansha, 1966.

Kinoshita Junji. "Aru bungakuteki jiken: Kin Hi-ro ga uttaeru mono." In Kinoshita Junji, *Kinoshita Junji shū*, vol. 10, 317–21. Tokyo: Iwanami Shoten, 1988.

————. "'Kawa no naka no kui' toshite." *Ushio* 144 (1971): 95–97.

Kīsen Kankō ni Hantai suru Onna-tachi no Kai. "Haji o shire! Kaishun meate no kankōdan: ikari o komete uttaeru." In *Nikkan rentai no shisō to kōdō*, edited by Aochi Shin and Wada Haruki, 96–98. Tokyo: Gendai Hyōronsha, 1977.

————. "Kai no hossoku to katsudō." In *Shiryō—sei shinryaku o kokuhatsu-suru: Kīsen kankō*, edited by Kīsen Kankō ni Hantai suru Onna-tachi no Kai, 54–56. Tokyo: Kīsen Kankō ni Hantai suru Onna-tachi no Kai, 1974.

Kitahara Taeko. "Osara no mukō no Ajia." *Shisō no kagaku* 65 (1985): 42–49.

Kitazawa Yōko. "Kīsen kankō no seijigaku." In *Shiryo—sei shinryaku o kokuhatsu-suru: Kīsen kankō*, edited by Kīsen Kankō ni Hantai suru Onna-tachi no Kai, 13–16. Tokyo: Kīsen Kankō ni Hantai suru Onna-tachi no Kai, 1974.

Kitazawa Yōko, Matsui Yayori, and Yunomae Tomoko. "The Women's Movement: Progress and Obstacles: Dialogue with Kitazawa Yoko, Matsui Yayori, and Yunomae Tomoko." In *Voices from the Japanese Women's Movement*, edited by AMPO, 23–37. New York: M. E. Sharpe, 1996.

Kobayashi Hideo. *Sengo Ajia to Nihon kigyō*. Tokyo: Iwanami Shoten, 2001.

Kobayashi Yōtarō. "'Sai-Ajiaka' no susume," *Foresight*, April 1991, 44–46.

"'Kōgai yushutsu wa yurusanu': Jūmin dantai tsūhō sentā o secchi." *Asahi shinbun*, April 9, 1976, morning edition, 22.

Kokkai Shūgiin Kessan Iinkai. "Dai-71-kai kokkai shūgiin, kessan iinkai giroku dai-28-gō (heikaichū shinsa)." November 13, 1973, 1–22. https://kokkai.ndl.go.jp/txt /107104103X02819731113.

Kokusai Kōryū Kikin. *Kokusai bunka kōryū gannen e no kitai: Shinbun hōdō 1985–1988*. Tokyo: Kokusai Kōryū Kikin, 1988.

Kokusai Kyōryoku NGO Sentā (JANIC). *NGO dētabukku 2016: Sūji de miru Nihon no NGO*. Tokyo: Gaimushō Kokusai Kyōryoku Kyoku Minkan Enjo Renkei Shitsu, 2016.

Komatsu Shigeo. "Watashi no taiken ni okeru Chōsen mondai." *Tenbō* 83 (1965): 14–33.

Kōno Yōhei. "Ianfu kankei chōsa kekka happyō ni kansuru Kōno naikaku kanbō chōkan danwa." August 4, 1993. https://www.mofa.go.jp/mofaj/area/taisen/kono.html.

Koschmann, J. Victor. "Asianism's Ambivalent Legacy." In *Network Power: Japan and Asia*, edited by Peter J. Katzenstein and Takashi Shiraishi, 83–110. Ithaca, NY: Cornell University Press, 1997.

————. "National Subjectivity and the Uses of Atonement in the Age of Recession." In *Japan after Japan: Social and Cultural Life from the Recessionary 1990s to the Present*, edited by Tomiko Yoda and Harry Harootunian, 121–41. Durham, NC: Duke University Press, 2006.

———. *Revolution and Subjectivity in Postwar Japan*. Chicago: University of Chicago Press, 1996.

Koyama, Hitomi. *On the Persistence of the Japanese "History Problem": Historicism and the International Politics of History*. Oxford: Routledge, 2018.

Koyama Mutsumi. "Kīsen kankō no keizaiteki haikei." In *Shiryō—sei shinryaku o kokuhatsu suru: Kīsen kankō*, edited by Kīsen Kankō ni Hantai suru Onnatachi no Kai, 16–19. Tokyo: Kīsen Kankō ni Hantai suru Onnatachi no Kai, 1974.

Kumagai, Naoko. *The Comfort Women: Historical, Political, Legal and Moral Perspectives*. Translated by David Noble. Tokyo: International House of Japan, 2016.

Kurokawa Iori. "Betonamu hansen kara uchinaru Ajia e: Beheiren Kōbe no kiseki." In *Sengo Nihon shisō to chishikijin no yakuwari*, edited by Izuhara Masao, 351–71. Kyoto: Hōritsu Bunka Sha, 2015.

Kurosaki Jun'ichi. "Watashi no ketsui." *Nikkan rentai nyūsu* 44 (1978): 2.

Kusachi Ken'ichi. *Ajia kusanone kokusai kōryū: PHD kyōkai no jissen*. Tokyo: Akashi Shoten, 1993.

Kushner, Barak. *Men to Devils, Devils to Men: Japanese War Crimes and Chinese Justice*. Cambridge, MA: Harvard University Press, 2015.

Kushner, Barak, and Sherzod Muminov, eds. *The Dismantling of Japan's Empire in East Asia: Deimperialization, Postwar Legitimation and Imperial Afterlife*. London: Routledge, 2017.

Kyū Eikan. "Ajiajin to Nihonjin: Ajia no nikumareyaku." *Jiyū* 12, no. 9 (1970): 69–76.

Lee Misook. *"Nikkan rentai undō" no jidai: 1970–80 nendai no toranzunashonaru na kōkyōken to media*. Tokyo: Tokyo Daigaku Shuppankai, 2018.

Leheny, David. *Empire of Hope: The Sentimental Politics of Japanese Decline*. Ithaca, NY: Cornell University Press, 2018.

Lie, John. Introduction to *The Impoverished Spirit in Contemporary Japan: Selected Essays of Honda Katsuichi*, edited by John Lie, 9–42. New York: Monthly Review Press, 1993.

———. *Zainichi (Koreans in Japan): Diasporic Nationalism and Postcolonial Identity*. Berkeley: University of California Press, 2008.

Lindroth, Marjo, and Heidi Sinevaara-Niskanen. "Politics of Hope." *Globalizations* 16, no. 5 (2019): 644–48.

Mahathir, bin Mohamad, and Ishihara Shintarō. *"NO" to ieru Ajia: Tai-Ōbei e no hōsaku*. Tokyo: Kōbunsha, 1994.

———. *The Voice of Asia: Two Leaders Discuss the Coming Century*. Translated by Frank Baldwin. Tokyo: Kodansha International, 1995.

Maruyama Masao. "Kindai Nihon no chishikijin." In *Maruyama Masao shū*, vol. 10, edited by Matsuzawa Hiroaki and Uete Michiari, 223–68. Tokyo: Iwanami Shoten, 1996.

———. *Nihon seiji shisō kenkyū*. Tokyo: Tokyo Daigaku Shuppankai, 1952.

———. "'Nihon seiji shisō kenkyū' atogaki." In *Maruyama Masao shū*, vol. 5, edited by Matsuzawa Hiroaki and Uete Michiari, 283–94. Tokyo: Iwanami Shoten, 1995.

———. "Sengo Nihon no nashonarizumu no ippanteki kōsatsu." In *Ajia no minzokushugi: Rakunō kaigi no seika to kadai*, edited by Nihon Taiheiyō Mondai Chōsakai, 168–87. Tokyo: Iwanami Shoten, 1951.

———. *Studies in the Intellectual History of Tokugawa Japan*. Translated by Mikiso Hane. Princeton, NJ: Princeton University Press, 1974.

———. "Theory and Psychology of Ultra-Nationalism." Translated by Ivan Morris. In *Thought and Behavior in Modern Japanese Politics*, edited by Ivan Morris, 1–24. Tokyo: Oxford University Press, 1969.

Marx, Karl. "Preface: A Contribution to the Critique of Political Economy." In *Karl Marx: Selected Writings*, edited by Lawrence H. Simon, 209–12. Indianapolis: Hackett Publishing, 1994.

Masubuchi Tatsuo. "Rekishi ishiki to kokusai kankaku: Nihon no kindai shigaku shi ni okeru Chūgoku to Nihon 1." *Shisō* 464 (1963): 161–78.

Matsubara Shinichi. *Gen'ei no kommyūn: "Sākuru mura" o kenshō suru*. Fukuoka, Japan: Sōgensha, 2001.

Matsui Yayori. *Ajia—onna—minshū (Ajia ga mietekuru 1)*. Tokyo: Shinkansha, 1987.

———. "Intabyū: Gurōbaru feminizumu no kanōsei." In *Zenkyōtō kara ribu e: Jūgoshi nōto sengohen*, edited by Onnatachi no Ima o Tō Kai, 346–61. Tokyo: Inpakuto Shuppankai, 1996.

———. "Kokka kenryoku to sei." In *Shiryo—sei shinryaku o kokuhatsu-suru: Kīsen kankō*, edited by Kīsen Kankō ni Hantai suru Onna-tachi no Kai, 41. Tokyo: Kīsen Kankō ni Hantai suru Onna-tachi no Kai, 1974.

———. *Shimin to enjo: Ima nani ga dekiru ka*. Tokyo: Iwanami Shoten, 1990.

———. *Tamashii ni fureru Ajia*. Tokyo: Asahi Shinbunsha, 1985.

———. "Watashi wa naze kīsen kankō ni hantai suru no ka: Keizai shinryaku to seishinryaku no kōzō o abaku." In *Matsui Yayori, Josei kaihō to wa nani ka*, 87–100. Tokyo: Miraisha, 1975.

Matsumoto Jiichirō. "Ajiajin no Ajia ni: Shūgiin ni okeru daihyō shitsumon sakkiroku kara." *Buraku* 43 (1953): 4–8.

Matsuoka Nobuo. "Chōsen josei no rekishi ni omō." In *Shiryō—sei shinryaku o kokuhatsu-suru: kīsen kankō*, edited by Kīsen kankō ni hantai suru onna-tachi no Kai, 34–35. Tokyo: Kīsen Kankō ni Hantai suru Onna-tachi no Kai, 1974.

———. "Mō hitotsu no omoni o seō kakugo o: Higashi Ajia no tabi kara (3)." In *Ui Jun shūshū kōgai mondai shiryō 1 fukkoku "jishu kōza" dai-4-kan*, edited by Saitama Daigaku Kyōsei Shakai Kenkyū Sentā, 103–6. Tokyo: Suirensha, 2005.

Michiba Chikanobu. "Posuto-Betonamu sensōki ni okeru Ajia rentai undō: 'Uchinaru Ajia' to 'Ajia no naka no Nihon' no aida de." In *Iwanami kōza Higashi Ajia kingendai tsūshi*, vol. 8: *Betonamu sensō no jidai 1960–1975nen*, edited by Wada Haruki et al., 97–127. Tokyo: Iwanami Shoten, 2011.

———. *Senryō to heiwa: Sengo to iu keiken*. Tokyo: Seidosha, 2005.

Mihashi Osamu. *Sabetsu ron nōto*. Tokyo: Shinsensha, 1973.

Minobe Ryōkichi. "Ajia to Nihon." *Tenchijin* 4 (1953): 34–37.

Mitani Taichirō. *Kindai Nihon no sensō to seiji.* Tokyo: Iwanami Shoten, 1995.

Miyadai Shinji. "Ajiashugi no kanōsei," *Asahi shinbun,* August 18, 2003, evening edition, 16.

Miyauchi Taisuke. "Chizu no egakikata, ajitēshon no shikata." In *Tsurumi Yoshiyuki chosakushū,* vol. 4: *Shūdatsu no kōzō,* edited by Nakamura Hisashi, 385–94. Tokyo: Misuzu Shobō, 1999.

Miyauchi Taisuke and Fujibayashi Yasushi. *Katsuobushi to Nihonjin.* Tokyo: Iwanami Shoten, 2013.

Miyazawa Kiichi. "'Rekishi kyōkasho' ni kansuru Miyazawa naikaku kanbō chōkan danwa." https://www.mofa.go.jp/mofaj/area/taisen/miyazawa.html.

Mizoguchi Yūzō, Hamashita Takeshi, Hiraishi Naoaki, and Miyajima Hiroshi, eds. *Ajia kara kangaeru.* 7 vols. Tokyo: Tokyo Daigaku Shuppankai, 1993–94.

———. "Kankō ni atatte." In *Ajia kara kangaeru,* vol 1: *Kōsaku suru Ajia,* edited by Mizoguchi Yūzō, Hamashita Takeshi, Hiraishi Naoaki, and Miyajima Hiroshi, i–iv. Tokyo: Tokyo Daigaku Shuppankai, 1993.

Moeller, Robert G. "Response." *Cultural Analysis* 4 (2005): 66–72.

Mōri Kazuko et al. "Ajia gaku no tsukurikata, Ajia no tsukurikata: 'Tōyō' kara 'Ajia shin-seiki' e no kakyō o mezashite." In *Kōsō: Ajia shin seiki e,* edited by Aoki Tamotsu et al., 1–40. Tokyo: Iwanami Shoten, 2003.

Morii Kiyoshi. "Tōnan Ajia no 'minikui Nihonjin.'" *Bungei shunjū,* special issue, March 1970, 298–304.

Morisaki Kazue. *Dai-san no sei: Harukanaru erosu.* Tokyo: San'ichi Shobō, 1965.

———. *Karayuki-san.* Tokyo: Asahi Shinbunsha, 1976.

———. *Makkura: Onnakōfu kara no kikigaki.* Tokyo: Rironsha, 1961.

Morishima, Michio. *Collaborative Development in Northeast Asia.* New York: Palgrave, 2001.

———. *Naze Nihon wa botsuraku suru ka.* Tokyo: Iwanami Shoten, 1999.

———. *Nihon ni dekiru koto wa nanika: Higashi Ajia kyōdōtai o teian suru.* Tokyo: Iwanami Shoten, 2001.

———. *Nihon no sentaku: Atarashii kunizukuri ni mukete.* Tokyo: Iwanami Shoten, 1995.

———. *Why Has Japan "Succeeded"? Western Technology and the Japanese Ethos.* Cambridge: Cambridge University Press, 1984.

Morris-Suzuki, Tessa. *Borderline Japan: Foreigners and Frontier Controls in the Postwar Era.* Cambridge: Cambridge University Press, 2010.

———. *Exodus to North Korea: Shadows from Japan's Cold War.* Lanham, MD: Rowman and Littlefield, 2007.

———. "Invisible Countries: Japan and the Asian Dream." *Asian Studies Review* 22, no. 1 (1998): 5–22.

———. "Japan and Its Region: Changing Historical Perceptions." *Sungkyun Journal of East Asian Studies* 11, no. 2 (2011): 123–42.

———. "Liquid Area Studies: Northeast Asia in Motion as Viewed from Mount Geum-gang." *positions* 27, no. 1 (2019): 209–39.

———. *Reinventing Japan: Time, Space, Nation.* London: Routledge, 1998.

Moses, A. Dirk. *German Intellectuals and the Nazi Past.* Cambridge: Cambridge University Press, 2007.

Munakata, Naoko. *Transforming East Asia: The Evolution of Regional Economic Integration*. Washington: Brookings Institution Press, 2006.

Murai Yoshinori. *Ebi to Nihonjin*. Tokyo: Iwanami Shoten, 1988.

———. "Tsurumi Yoshiyuki banana kenkyū to sono shūhen." In *Tsurumi Yoshiyuki Chosakushū*, vol. 6: *Banana*, edited by Murai Yoshinori, 295–304. Tokyo: Misuzu Shobō, 1998.

Mushakōji Kinhide and Ajia Seinen Renraku Kaigi. "Hajime ni." In *Futotta Nihonjin: Atsumerareta 321-nin no nikusei*, edited by Mushakōji Kinhide and Ajia Seinen Renraku Kaigi, 1–4. Tokyo: Daiyamondosha, 1971.

Muto Ichiyo. "Asia, Inter-Asia, and Movement: Decolonization into the Future." *Inter-Asia Cultural Studies* 11, no. 2 (2010): 178–83.

———. *Konkyochi to bunka: Daisan sekai to no gōryū o motomete*. Tokyo: Tabata Shoten, 1975.

Nagahara Keiji. "Sengo Nihon shigaku no tenkai to shochōryū." In *Iwanami kōza Nihon rekishi*, vol. 24: *Bekkan 1 sengo Nihon shigaku no tenkai*, edited by Asao Naohiro et al., 1–58. Tokyo: Iwanami Shoten, 1977.

Nagai Kazu. "Sengo Marukusushugi shigaku to Ajia ninshiki: 'Ajiateki teitaiseiron' no aporia." In *Kindai Nihon no Ajia ninshiki*, edited by Furuya Tetsuo, 641–704. Tokyo: Tokyo Daigaku Shuppankai, 1994.

Nagai Michio et al. "Genchi Nikkei kigyō no kono genjitsu (shinpojiumu)." *Chūō kōron* 89, no. 1 (1974): 192–211.

Nagao Masato et al., eds. *Kōza tōyō shisō*. 16 vols. Tokyo: Iwanami Shoten, 1988–91.

Nagasaki Nobuko et al., eds. *Gendai Minami Ajia*. 6 vols. Tokyo Daigaku Shuppankai, 2002–3.

Nagasu Kazuji. *Chihō no jidai to jichitai kakushin*. Tokyo: Nihon Hyōronsha, 1980.

———. *Gendai shihonshugi to tagen shakai*. Tokyo: Nihon Hyōronsha, 1979.

———. *Nanshin suru Nihon shihonshugi*. Tokyo: Mainichi Shinbunsha, 1971.

Nakane Chie. "Koji Nihon no ninshiki." *Chūō kōron* 73, no. 10 (1958): 32–45.

Nakano Emi. "Shimin o dō tsunagaruka." In *NGO no jidai: Heiwa—kyōsei—jiritsu*, edited by Nihon Kokusai Borantia Sentā, 186–92. Tokyo: Mekon, 2000.

Nakano Koichi. "Contemporary Political Dynamics of Japanese Nationalism." *Asia-Pacific Journal* 14, no. 20 (2016). https://apjjf.org/2016/20/Nakano.html.

Nakano Toshio, Takahashi Tetsuya, Nakanishi Shintarō, and So Kyong-sik. "Tettei tōron 'sengo saikō': 'Sengo' to wa nan dattanoka." *Zen'ya* 3 (Spring 2005): 18–60.

Nakayama. "Sakoku sakoku: Sakoku o koeru mono toshite." In *"Beheiren nyūsu" gappon shukusatsuban 1965–1974*, edited by Beheiren: "Betonamu ni Heiwa o!" Shimin Rengō, 328. Tokyo: Beheiren: "Betonamu ni Heiwa o!" Shimin Rengō, 1974.

Nakayashiki Hiroshi. *Ajia no fukken: Seichō no bunmei ka kyōsei no bunmei ka*. Tokyo: Nōsangyoson Bunka Kyōkai, 2004.

Namatto, Anfon, and Bunsanon Bunyottyana. "'Tai' gō ni haite gō ni shitagawanu Nihonjin: Keizai teikokushugi no jittai." *Jiyū* 15, no. 6 (1973): 62–69.

Nehru, Pandit Jawaharlal. "Opening Address." In *Asian Nationalism and Western Policies: Preliminary Report of the Eleventh Conference of the Institute of Pacific Relations*,

Lucknow, India, October 3–15, 1950, 1–8. New York: International Secretariat, Institute of Pacific Relations, 1951.

Nicolaïdis, Kalypso, Berny Sebe, and Gabrielle Maas, eds. *Echoes of Empire: Memory, Identity and Colonial Legacies*. London: I. B. Tauris, 2015.

Nihon Ajia-Afurika Sakka Kaigi. *Ajia o aruku: Tōnan Ajia-hen*. Tokyo: Bun'yūsha, 1978.

Nihon Chōsen Kenkyūjo. "Setsuritsu shuisho." In *Nihon Chōsen kenkyūjo shoki shiryō 1961–69*, vol. 1, edited by Inoue Manabu and Higuchi Yūichi, 3–11. Tokyo: Ryokuin Shobō, 2017.

Nihon Kirisutokyō Kaigai Iryō Kyōryokukai, "Kihon hōshin." https://www.jocs.or.jp/wp-content/uploads/kihon_houshin.pdf.

Nihon Kirisutokyō Kyōgikai Fujin Iinkai. "Nihon Kirisutokyō kyōgikai fujin iinkai seimei." In *Shiryo—sei shinryaku o kokuhatsu-suru: Kīsen kankō*, edited by Kīsen Kankō ni Hantai suru Onna-tachi no Kai, 64–65. Tokyo: Kīsen Kankō ni Hantai suru Onna-tachi no Kai, 1974.

"Nihon kōka tokushū: Taikoku no daihyōteki zasshi 'shakai kagaku hyōron' no Nihon hihan ikkyo teisai." *Chūō kōron* 88, no. 2 (1973): 209–69.

Nihon no Taikan Seisaku o Tadasu Kokumin Shūkai. "Nikkan rentai renraku kaigi kessei sengen." In *Nikkan rentai no shisō to kōdō*, edited by Aochi Shin and Wada Haruki, 121–3. Tokyo: Gendai Hyōronsha, 1977.

"'Nikkan jōyaku no hantai suru rekishika no tsudoi' hirakaru." *Rekishigaku kenkyū* 305 (1965): 59–63.

Nikkan Rentai Nyūsu Henshūbu. "Watashitachi wa nani o donoyō ni tatakattekita no ka." *Nikkan rentai nyūsu*, September 19, 1974, extra edition, 2.

Nishikawa Jun. "70-nendai Ajia to Nihon no sentaku." *Nihon no shōrai* 1 (1972): 28–47.

———. "Ajia bundan e susumu Nichibei shihon." *Asahi jānaru*, January 14, 1972, 20–25.

Noh Eunmyoung. "Beheiren no han 'nyūkan taisei' undō: Sono ronri to undō no tenkai." *Seiji kenkyū* 57 (2010): 59–93.

Nozawa Rokusuke. *Ri Chin'u nōto: Shikei ni sareta Chōsenjin*. Tokyo: San'ichi Shobō, 1994.

Ōba Mie. "'Higashi Ajia kyōdōtai' ron no tenkai: Sono haikei, genjō, tenbō." In *Higashi Ajia kenkyū*, vol. 1: *Ekkyō*, edited by Takahara Akio, Tamura Keiko, and Satō Yukihito, 443–68. Tokyo: Keiō Gijuku Daigaku Shuppankai, 2008.

Oda Makoto, ed. *Ajia o kangaeru: Ajiajin kaigi no zenkiroku*. Tokyo: Ushio Shuppansha, 1976.

———. "Ajiajin no kome no takikata." *Chūō kōron* 89, no. 7 (1974): 201–17.

———. "'Domin' to 'Nihon kōhei.'" *Asahi jānaru*, January 14, 1972, 5–12.

———. "Heiwa e no gutaiteki teigen: Nichibei shimin kaigi de no bōtō enzetsu." In *Shiryō "Beheiren" undō*, vol. 1, edited by Betonamu ni Heiwa o! Shimin Rengō, 104–18. Tokyo: Kawade Shobō Shinsha, 1974.

———. "Heiwa o tsukuru." In Oda Makoto, *Oda Makoto zenshigoto*, vol. 9: *Hyōron 3 / ningen kara ningen e*, 113–31. Tokyo: Kawade Shobō Shinsha, 1970.

———. "Kanbi na nigekōjō." In Oda Makoto, *Oda Makoto zenshigoto*, vol. 7: *Hyōron / koko kara shuppatsu shite*, 263–65. Tokyo: Kawade Shobō Shinsha, 1970.

————. *Nandemo mite yarō.* In Oda Makoto, *Oda Makoto zenshigoto,* vol. 6: *Nandemo mite yarō / shūketsu no naka no hattan,* 5–254. Tokyo: Kawade Shobō Shinsha, 1971.

————. "Rekishi ni chokushi suru." In Oda Makoto, *Oda Makoto zenshigoto,* vol. 9: *Hyōron 3 / ningen kara ningen e,* 259–66. Tokyo: Kawade Shobō Shinsha, 1970.

————. "Sore o sakete tōru koto wa dekinai." In Oda Makoto, *Oda Makoto zenshigoto,* vol. 7: *Hyōron / koko kara shuppatsu shite,* 223–42. Tokyo: Kawade Shobō Shinsha, 1970.

Ōe Kenzaburō. "Portrait of the Postwar Generation." In *Sources of Japanese Tradition,* vol. 2: *1600–2000,* edited by Wm. Theodore de Bary, Carol Gluck, and Arthur E. Tiedemann, 1250–53. New York: Columbia University Press, 2005.

————. *Sakebigoe.* Tokyo: Kōdansha, 1963.

————. "Seijiteki sōzōryoku to satsujinsha no sōzōryoku: Wareware ni totte Kin Hi-ro to wa nanika." *Gunzō,* April 1968, 154–69.

Ōe Shinobu et al. *Iwanami kōza kindai Nihon to shokuminchi.* 8 vols. Tokyo: Iwanami Shoten, 1992–93.

Ogasawara Kazuhiko. *Ri Chin'u no nazo: Naze hankō o mitometanoka.* Tokyo: San'ichi Shobō, 1987.

Oguma Eiji. *1968 <ge>: Hanran no shūen to sono isan.* Tokyo: Shin'yōsha, 2009.

————. *1968 <jō>: Wakamonotachi no hanran to sono haikei.* Tokyo: Shin'yōsha, 2009.

————. *A Genealogy of Japanese Self-Images.* Melbourne: Trans Pacific Press, 2002.

————. "Japan's 1968: A Collective Reaction to Rapid Economic Growth in an Age of Turmoil." Translated by Nick Kapur with Samuel Malissa and Stephen Poland. *Asia-Pacific Journal* 13, no. 2 (2015): 1-27. https://apjjf.org/2015/13/11/Oguma-Eiji/4300.html.

————. *Minshu to aikoku: Sengo nashonarizumu to kōkyōsei.* Tokyo: Shin'yōsha, 2002.

————. "The Postwar Intellectuals' View of 'Asia.'" In *Pan-Asianism in Modern Japanese History: Colonialism, Regionalism and Borders,* edited by Sven Saaler and J. Victor Koschmann, 200–12. New York: Routledge, 2007.

Ogura Kazuo. "A Call for a New Concept of Asia." *Japan Echo* 20, no. 3 (1993): 37–44.

————. "Creating a New Asia." *Japan Echo* 26, no. 3 (1999): 12–16.

Ohara Ken [Tsurumi Yoshiyuki]. "Philippines: Bataan Export Processing Zone: Its Development and Social Implications." *AMPO* 8, no. 4, and 9, nos. 1–2 (1977): 92–119.

————. "Strategies for the Asian Regionalism—World Auto-Industries and National Governments." *AMPO* 8, no. 4, and 9, nos. 1–2 (1977): 168–97.

Okakura, Kakuzō. *The Ideals of the East with Special Reference to the Art of Japan.* London: J. Murray, 1903.

Okamoto Saburō. "Ajiateki seisan yōshiki ni tsuite." *Shisō* 287 (1948): 305–20.

Okazaki Hisahiko. *Atarashii Ajia e no daisenryaku.* Tokyo: Yomiuri Shinbunsha, 1993.

Okuda Hiroshi. *Ajia keizai saisei misshon' hōkokusho: 21 seiki no Ajia to kyōsei suru Nippon o mezashite.* Tokyo: Ministry of Foreign Affairs, 1999. http://www.mofa.go.jp/mofaj/area/asiakeizai/saisei/index.html.

Okuda Takaharu. "Documents of the First Co-operation between Japanese Citizens and Thai People Acting Simultaneously to Stop the Exporting Pollution." *KOGAI* 7 (1975): 8–11.

Ōkuma Nobuyuki. *Kokkaaku: Jinrui ni mirai wa aruka.* Tokyo: Ushio Shuppan, 1969.

————. *Sensō sekinin ron: Sengo shichō no tenbō.* Tokyo: Yuijinsha, 1948.

Okura Yayoi. "Promoting Prostitution." In *Voices from the Japanese Women's Movement*, edited by *AMPO*, 111–14. New York: M. E. Sharpe, 1996.

Olson, Lawrence. *Dimensions of Japan: A Collection of Reports Written for the American Universities Field Staff*. New York: American Universities Field Staff, 1963.

Ōmoto Keiichi et al., eds. *Umi no Ajia*. 6 vols. Tokyo: Iwanami Shoten, 2000–2001.

Onabe Teruhiko et al. *Sekai shi kōza*. 8 vols. Tokyo: Tōyō Keizai Shinpōsha, 1955–56.

Onna-tachi no Genzai o Tō Kai. *Jūgoshi nōto*. Tokyo: Onna-tachi no Genzai o Tō Kai, 1980.

———. *Jūgoshi nōto sengohen*. 8 vols. Tokyo: Inpakuto Shuppankai, 1986–96.

Ōnuma Yasuaki. "Atogaki." In Ōnuma Yasuaki, *Tokyo saiban kara sengo sekinin no shisō e*, 236–240. Tokyo: Yūshindō Kōbunsha, 1985.

———. *Saharin kimin: Sensō sekinin no tenkei*. Tokyo: Chūkō Shinsho, 1992.

———. "'Sengo sekinin' to iu kangaekata." In Ōnuma Yasuaki, *Tokyo saiban kara sengo sekinin no shisō e*, 198–203. Tokyo: Yūshindō Kōbunsha, 1985.

———. "Tokyo saiban: Hō to seiji no hazama." In *Kokusai shinpojiumu Tokyo saiban o tō*, edited by Hosoya Chihiro, Andō Nisuke, and Ōnuma Yasuaki, 45–58. Tokyo: Kōdansha, 1984.

———. "Tokyo saiban, sensō sekinin, sengo sekinin." *Shisō* 719 (1984): 70–100.

———. *Tokyo saiban kara sengo sekinin no shisō e*. Tokyo: Yūshindō Kōbunsha, 1985.

———. "'Tokyo saiban' shinpojiumu no yume to makoto." In Ōnuma Yasuaki, *Tokyo saiban kara sengo sekinin no shisō e*, 68–72. Tokyo: Yūshindō Kōbunsha, 1985.

Orr, James J. *The Victim as Hero: Ideologies of Peace and National Identity in Postwar Japan*. Honolulu: University of Hawai'i Press, 2001.

Ōta Masakuni. "Minzoku—shokuminchi mondai e no kakusei: Paku Sunamu 'Chōsenjin kyōsei renkō no kiroku' ni furete." In *Sengoron zongi: Revijon (saishin) dai-1-shū*, edited by Kurihara Yukio, 184–89. Tokyo: Shakai Hyōronsha, 1998.

Ōtsuka Hisao. "Kindaiteki ningen ruikei no sōshutsu: Seijiteki shutai no minshūteki kiban no mondai." In *Gendai Nihon shisō taikei*, vol. 34: *Kindaishugi*, edited by Hidaka Rokurō, 93–98. Tokyo: Chikuma Shobō, 1964.

Ouyang Wenbin. *Ana ni kakurete 14-nen: Chūgokujin furyo Ryū Renjin no kiroku*. Tokyo: Shindokushosha Shuppanbu, 1959.

Pak Kyong-sik. *Chōsenjin kyōsei renkō no kiroku*. Tokyo: Miraisha, 1965.

Pak Sunam, ed. *Ri Chin'u zenshokanshū*. Tokyo: Shinjinbutsu Ōraisha, 1979.

———, ed. *Tsumi to shi to ai to*. Tokyo: San'ichi Shinsho, 1984.

Park, Hye Jeong. "East Asian Odyssey towards One Region: The Problem of East Asia as a Historiographical Category." *History Compass* 12, no. 12 (2014): 889–900.

Park Sunmi. "70-nendai Nihon josei no Ajia ninshiki." *Gendai no riron* 25 (2010): 120–31.

———. "70-nendai no Kankoku to Nihon ni okeru kīsen kankō hantai undō: Kannichi josei undō shi ni okeru '70-nendai' no igi." *Nihon kenkyū* 16 (2011): 325–49.

———. "Nikkan josei no kōryū to sōgo ninshiki: 1960-nendai—70-nendai o chūshin ni." Report: Kagaku Kenkyūhi Josei Jigyō [Kagaku Kenkyūhi Hojokin] Kenkyū Seika Hōkokusho, 2013.

Pempel, T. J. "Transpacific Torii: Japan and the Emerging Asian Regionalism." In *Network Power: Japan and Asia*, edited by Peter J. Katzenstein and Takashi Shiraishi, 47–82. Ithaca, NY: Cornell University Press, 1997.

Reischauer, Edwin O., and Nakayama Ichirō. "Nihon no kindaika no rekishiteki hyōka (taidan)." *Chūō kōron* 76, no. 9 (1961): 84–97.

Rekishigaku Kenkyūkai, ed. *Sekai shi ni okeru Ajia: 1953-nendo rekishigaku kenkyūkai taikai hōkoku.* Tokyo: Iwanami Shoten, 1953.

Rothermund, Dietmar. "Memories of Post-imperial Nations: Silences and Concerns." *India Quarterly* 70, no. 1 (2014): 59–70.

———, ed. *Memories of Post-Imperial Nations: The Aftermath of Decolonization, 1945–2013.* Cambridge: Cambridge University Press, 2015.

Saaler, Sven. "Pan-Asianism in Modern Japanese History: Overcoming the Nation, Creating a Region, Forging an Empire." In *Pan-Asianism in Modern Japanese History: Colonialism, Regionalism and Borders*, edited by Sven Saaler and J. Victor Koschmann, 1–18. New York: Routledge, 2007.

———. *Politics, Memory, and Public Opinion: The History Textbook Controversy and Japanese Society.* München: Iudicium, 2005.

Saaler, Sven, and J. Victor Koschmann, eds. *Pan-Asianism in Modern Japanese History: Colonialism, Regionalism, and Borders.* New York: Routledge, 2007.

Saaler, Sven, and Christopher W. A. Szpilman, eds. *Pan Asianism: A Documentary History*, vol. 1: *1850–1920.* Lanham, MD: Rowman and Littlefield, 2011.

———. *Pan Asianism: A Documentary History*, vol. 2: *1920–Present.* Lanham, MD: Rowman and Littlefield, 2011.

Saito, Hiro. *The History Problem: The Politics of War Commemoration in East Asia.* Honolulu: University of Hawai'i Press, 2017.

Sakai, Naoki. "From Area Studies toward Transnational Studies." *Inter-Asia Cultural Studies* 11, no. 2 (2010): 265–74.

———. "Trans-Pacific Studies and the US-Japan Complicity." In *The Trans-Pacific Imagination—Rethinking Boundary, Culture, and Society*, edited by Naoki Sakai and Hyon Joo Yoo, 279–315. Singapore: World Scientific Press, 2012.

Sakai, Naoki, and Hyon Joo Yoo. "Introduction: The Trans-Pacific Imagination—Rethinking Boundary, Culture, and Society." In *The Trans-Pacific Imagination—Rethinking Boundary, Culture, and Society*, edited by Naoki Sakai and Hyon Joo Yoo, 1–44. Singapore: World Scientific Press, 2012.

———. Preface to *The Trans-Pacific Imagination—Rethinking Boundary, Culture, and Society*, edited by Naoki Sakai and Hyon Joo Yoo, v–xi. Singapore: World Scientific Press, 2012.

Sakakibara, Eisuke. "The End of Progressivism: A Search for New Goals." *Foreign Affairs* 74, no. 5 (1995): 8–14.

Sakamoto Yoshikazu. "Higashi Ajia o koeta 'Higashi Ajia kyōdōtai' no kōsō o: Hyūmaniti to tabunka sekai." *Sekai* 800 (2010): 169–80.

Sasaki-Uemura, Wesley. *Organizing the Spontaneous: Citizen Protest in Postwar Japan.* Honolulu: University of Hawai'i Press, 2001.

———. "Tanigawa Gan's Politics of the Margins in Kyushu and Nagano." *positions* 7, no. 1 (1999): 129–63.

Schwarz, Bill. "Actually Existing Postcolonialism." *Radical Philosophy* 104 (2000): 16–24.

Sei, T. K. "Chiisana shōri." In *Shiryo—sei shinryaku o kokuhatsu-suru: Kīsen kankō*, edited by Kīsen Kankō ni Hantai suru Onna-tachi no Kai, 31. Tokyo: Kīsen Kankō ni Hantai suru Onna-tachi no Kai, 1974.

Sei, T. K., and "Sekai" Henshūbu, eds. *Dai-san Kankoku kara no tsūshin 1975–7–1977–8.* Tokyo: Iwanami Shoten: 1977.

———. *Gunsei to junan: Dai-yon Kankoku kara no tsūshin.* Tokyo: Iwanami Shoten: 1980.

———. *Kankoku kara no tsūshin 1972–11–1974–6.* Tokyo: Iwanami Shoten: 1974.

———. *Kankoku kara no tsūshin zoku 1974–7–1975–6.* Tokyo: Iwanami Shoten: 1975.

Sekai Henshūbu. "Nihon shihon ni keikai o fukameru Kankoku." *Sekai* 314 (1972): 219–27.

———. "Takamaru Firipin no Tainichi keikaishin: 'Nisshōki no Fukki—Teikoku Guntai no shippai ni Kawatte.'" *Sekai* 321 (1972): 153–63.

Sekiya Shigeru. "'Nihonjin mondai' toshite no 'Kankokujin mondai.'" In *"Beheiren nyūsu" gappon shukusatsuban 1965–1974*, edited by Beheiren: "Betonamu ni Heiwa o!" Shimin Rengō, 273. Tokyo: Beheiren: "Betonamu ni Heiwa o!" Shimin Rengō, 1974.

Selden, Kyoko, and Mark Selden. "Wada Haruki: 'Maritime Asia and the Future of a Northeast Asia Community,' 2008." In *Pan Asianism: A Documentary History*, vol. 2: *1920–Present*, edited by Sven Saaler and Christopher W. A. Szpilman, 371–77. Lanham, MD: Rowman and Littlefield, 2011.

"Sengo sekinin kangaeru kai: Bunkajin-ra setsuritsu sōkai." *Asahi shinbun*, April 18, 1983, morning edition, 22.

"Senjichū ni okeru Chūgokujin kyōsei renkō no kiroku." *Sekai* 173 (1960): 131–71.

"The Seoul of Hospitality." *Time*, June 4, 1973, 47.

Seraphim, Franziska. *War Memory and Social Politics in Japan, 1945–2005.* Cambridge, MA: Harvard University Asia Center, 2006.

Shapura Nīru Katsudō Kiroku Henshū Bu. *Shapura Nīru no atsui kaze.* Tokyo: Mekon, 1989.

Shibahara Takuji. "Meiji ishin to Ajia no henkaku." *Chūō kōron* 77, no. 5 (1962): 270–78.

Shibusawa Masahide and Saitō Shirō, eds. *Tōnan Ajia no Nihon hihan: "Shinpojiumu" Ajia kyōdōtai o kangaeru.* Tokyo: Simul Shuppankai, 1974.

Shigematsu, Setsu. *Scream from the Shadows: The Women's Liberation Movement in Japan.* Minneapolis: University of Minnesota Press, 2012.

Shimizu Ikutarō. "Nihonjin." *Chūō kōron* 66, no. 1 (1951): 4–16.

Shindō Eiichi. *Higashi Ajia kyōdōtai o dō tsukuru ka.* Tokyo: Chikuma Shobō, 2007.

Shiraishi Takashi. "Ajia o dō kangaeru ka: (Rensai) umi no teikoku—saishūkai." *Chūō kōron* 115, no. 5 (2000): 58–71.

———. "Higashi Ajia chiiki shisutemu o dō kangaeru ka." In *Ajia wa kawaru no ka: kaiteiban*, edited by Matsui Takafumi and Matsumoto Ken'ichi, 87–106. Tokyo: Uejji, 2009.

———. "Japan and Southeast Asia." In *Network Power: Japan and Asia*, edited by Peter J. Katzenstein and Takashi Shiraishi, 169–94. Ithaca, NY: Cornell University Press, 1997.

Shiraishi, Takashi, and Caroline Sy Hau. "Beyond the Spell of Asianism." *Japan Echo* 36, no. 3 (2009): 32–37.

Shisō no Kagaku, ed. "Nihon no naka no Ajia." *Shisō no kagaku* 106 (1988): 4–117.

Shōji Jun'ichirō. "Sengo Nihon ni okeru rekishi ninshiki: Taiheiyō sensō o chūshin toshite." *Bōei kenkyūji kiyō* 4, no. 3 (2002): 100–19.

Sodei Rinjirō, ed. and trans. *Yoshida = Makkāsā ōfuku shokanshū 1945–1951*. Tokyo: Hōsei Daigaku Shuppankyoku, 2000.

Sōgō Kenkyū Kaihatsu Kikō (NIRA). *Shimin kōeki katsudō kihon seibi ni kansuru chōsa kenkyū*. Tokyo: Sōgō Kenkyū Kaihatasu Kikō, 1994.

Sonoda Shigeto. "Fīrudo toshite no Ajia." In *Ajia kara kangaeru*, vol 1: *Kōsaku suru Ajia*, edited by Mizoguchi Yūzō, Hamashita Takeshi, Hiraishi Naoaki, and Miyajima Hiroshi, 13–32. Tokyo: Tokyo Daigaku Shuppankai, 1993.

Stam, Robert, and Ella Shohat. "French Intellectuals and the Postcolonial." *Interventions* 14, no. 1 (2012): 83–119.

Stegewerns, Dick. "Forgotten Leaders of the Interwar Debate on Regional Integration: Introducing Sugimori Kōjirō." In *Pan-Asianism in Modern Japanese History: Colonialism, Regionalism, and Borders*, edited by Sven Saaler and J. Victor Koschmann, 101–14. New York: Routledge, 2007.

Stockwin, J. A. A. *Collected Writings of J. A. A. Stockwin: Part 1: The Politics and Political Environment of Japan*. London: Routledge, 2004.

Suga Hidemi. *1968—Shisō dokuhon [11]*. Tokyo: Sakuhinsha, 2005.

———. "Kaisetsu: '1968-nen' to 3–11 ikō o tsunagu shikō." In *Tsumura Takashi seisen hyōronshū—<1968>-nen igo*, edited by Suga Hidemi, 381–92. Tokyo: Ronsōsha, 2012.

Sun Ge. "How Does Asia Mean?" In *The Inter-Asia Cultural Studies Reader*, edited by Kuan-Hsing Chen and Chua Beng Huat, 9–65. London: Routledge: 2007.

Suzuki Michihiko. "Aku no sentaku." In Suzuki Michihiko, *Ekkyō no toki: 1960-nendai to zainichi*, 77–97. Tokyo: Shūeisha, 2007.

———. *Ekkyō no toki: 1960-nendai to zainichi*. Tokyo: Shūeisha, 2007.

———. "Hitei no minzokushugi." In *Gendai Nihon shisō taikei*, vol. 4: *Nashonarizumu*, edited by Yoshimoto Takaaki, 3–5. Tokyo: Chikuma Shobō, 1964.

———. "Minzokuteki sekinin ni tsuite." *Ajia-Afurika tsūshin* 19–20 (1963): 1–5 and 11.

Tai Kazu. "Tai to chikin nagetto no misshingu rinku." *Shisō no kagaku* 65 (1985): 16–24.

"Tai yūryokushi no Nihon kōka tokushū: Nihon sōgō shōsha to kōgai e no kokuhatsu," *Chūō kōron keiei mondai* 13, no. 2 (1974): 312–36.

Taihei Shuppansha. "Atogaki." In *Nihon no naka no Chōsen*, edited by Usami Shō et al., 283–84. Tokyo: Taihei Shuppansha, 1966.

Takahashi Kikue. "Baibaishun: 'Ianfu' mondai o chūshin ni." *Onna-tachi no 21 seiki* 34 (2003): 21–22.

———. "Kankoku Kirisutosha josei to rentai shite." In *Shiryo—sei shinryaku o kokuhatsu-suru: Kīsen kankō*, edited by Kīsen Kankō ni Hantai suru Onna-tachi no Kai, 19–21. Tokyo: Kīsen Kankō ni Hantai suru Onna-tachi no Kai, 1974.

———. "Kisaeng Tourism." *Japan Interpreter* 9 (1974): 210–18.

Takayanagi Akio. "7: Kyōsei no tame no ODA to NGO." In *Ajia no kusanone nettowākingu*, edited by Ajia Shimin Fōramu, 213–27. Tokyo: Gakuyō Shobō, 1990.

Takeda Kiyoko. "Atarashiki Ajia no sedai." *Asahi hyōron*, April 1949, 58–63.

Takenaka, Akiko. *Yasukuni Shrine: History, Memory, and Japan's Unending Postwar.* Honolulu: University of Hawai'i Press, 2015.

Takenaka Heizō. "Can Japan Glue Together Asia and the Pacific?" *Japan Echo* 22, no. 4 (1995): 18–22.

Takeuchi Yoshimi. "Ajia no nashonarizumu." In Takeuchi Yoshimi, *Nihon to Ajia*, 125–8. Tokyo: Chikuma Shobō, 1993.

———. "Ajia no nashonarizumu ni tsuite." In Takeuchi Yoshimi, *Nihon to Ajia*, 112–15. Tokyo: Chikuma Shobō, 1993.

———. "Asia as Method." In Takeuchi Yoshimi, *What Is Modernity? Writings of Takeuchi Yoshimi,* 149–65. Edited and translated by Richard F. Calichman. New York: Columbia University Press, 2005.

———. "Chūgoku no kindai to Nihon no kindai." In Takeuchi Yoshimi, *Nihon to Ajia*, 11–57. Tokyo: Chikuma Shobō, 1993.

———, ed. *Gendai Nihon shisō taikei*, vol. 9: *Ajiashugi*. Tokyo: Chikuma Shobō, 1963.

———. "Nihonjin no Ajiakan." In Takeuchi Yoshimi, *Nihon to Ajia*, 92–111. Tokyo Chikuma Shobō, 1993.

———. "Nihonjin no Chūgokukan." In Takeuchi Yoshimi, *Nihon to Ajia*, 58–72. Tokyo: Chikuma Shobō, 1993.

———. "What Is Modernity (The Case of Japan and China)?" In Takeuchi Yoshimi, *What Is Modernity? Writings of Takeuchi Yoshimi,* 53–81. Edited and translated by Richard F. Calichman. New York: Columbia University Press, 2005.

Takeuchi Yoshimi, Ishida Takeshi, Hotta Yoshie, and Katō Shūichi. "Zadankai: Ajia no naka no Nihon." *Sekai* 149 (1958): 174–90.

Takeuchi Yoshimi and Umesao Tadao. "Ajia no rinen." *Shisō no kagaku* 34 (1961): 20–28.

Tamaki Motoi. "Atarashii sedai no tōjō: Ri Jin'u to Kin Tō-ki o megutte." In Tamaki Motoi, *Minzokuteki sekinin no shisō: Nihon minzoku no Chōsenjin taiken*, 237–60. Tokyo: Ochanomizu Shobō, 1967.

———. "Chōsen mondai no shisō." In Tamaki Motoi, *Minzokuteki sekinin no shisō: Nihon minzoku no Chōsenjin taiken*, 17–25. Tokyo: Ochanomizu Shobō, 1967.

———. "Gendai ni okeru Chōsenjin taiken." In Tamaki Motoi, *Minzokuteki sekinin no shisō: Nihon minzoku no Chōsenjin taiken*, 69–119. Tokyo: Ochanomizu Shobō, 1967.

———. *Minzokuteki sekinin no shisō: Nihon minzoku no Chōsenjin taiken.* Tokyo: Ochanomizu Shobō, 1967.

———. "Minzokuteki sekinin no shozai: Mondai seiri no tame no tenbō." In Tamaki Motoi, *Minzokuteki sekinin no shisō: Nihon minzoku no Chōsenjin taiken*, 27–44. Tokyo: Ochanomizu Shobō, 1967.

———. "Nihon Kyōsantō no zainichi Chōsenjin shidō." In Tamaki Motoi, *Minzokuteki sekinin no shisō: Nihon minzoku no Chōsenjin taiken*, 119–94. Tokyo: Ochanomizu Shobō, 1967.

Tanaka Akihiko. *Ajia no naka no Nihon.* Tokyo: NTT Shuppan, 2007.

Tanaka Hiroshi. "Ajia ni koso, wareware o tōte miyō." In *Nihon o mitsumeru Ajiajin no me*, edited and translated by Tanaka Hiroshi, 5–10. Tokyo: Tabata Shoten, 1972.

———. "Ajia ni taisuru sensō sekinin: Watashi no mitorizu." *Kikan sanzenri* 35 (1983): 41–50.

———. "Hanron: Hanaoka wakai no jijitsu to keika." *Sekai* 778 (2008): 267–78.

———. *Kyomō no kokusai kokka: Nihon Ajia no shiten kara.* Nagoya, Japan: Fūbaisha, 1990.

———. *Nihon no naka no Ajia.* Tokyo: Daiwa Shobō, 1980.

———. "Yakusha no atogaki." In Zhuo Nansheng, *Gendai no sakoku: Ajia kara Nihon no jitsuzō ga mieru,* 203–5. Translated by Tanaka Hiroshi and Kondō Masami. Tokyo: Mekon, 1985.

———. *Zainichi gaikokujin: Hō no kabe, kokoro no mizo.* Tokyo: Iwanami Shoten, 1991.

Tanaka Hiroshi, et al. *"Kokusaika" no wasuremono: Rinjin toshite no gaikokujin o kangaeru.* Osaka: Zainichi Kankoku-Chōsenjin Mondai Gakushū Sentā, 1990.

Tanaka Hiroshi, Utsumi Aiko, and Niimi Takashi. *Shiryō: Chūgokujin kyōsei renkō no kiroku.* Tokyo: Akaishi Shoten, 1990.

Tanaka Komako. "Nyūkan mondai to watashi." In *Fukkokuban Betonamu tsūshin: Kyoto Beheiren kikanshi—1969-11–1974-10,* 321–22. Tokyo: Fuji Shuppan, 1971.

Tanaka Mitsu. "Benjo kara no kaihō." In *Shiryō Nihon ūman ribu shi 1 zen 3-kan,* edited by Miki Sōko, Saeki Yōko, and Mizoguchi Akiyo, 201–7. Kyoto: Shōkōdō, 1992.

Tanaka, Stefan. *Japan's Orient: Rendering Pasts into History.* Berkeley: University of California Press, 1995.

Tanami Tatsuya. "Sengo Nihon no kokusai kōryū shi." In *Kokusai kōryū nyūmon,* edited by Enokida Katsutoshi, 32–48. Tokyo: Aruku, 1996.

Tarui Tōkichi. *Daitō gappō ron.* In *Gendai Nihon shisō taikei,* vol. 9: *Ajiashugi,* edited by Takeuchi Yoshimi, 106–29. Tokyo: Chikuma Shobō, 1963.

Terada Takashi et al., eds. *Ajiagaku no susume.* 3 vols. Tokyo: Kōbundō, 2010.

Terao Gorō, Kawagoe Keizō, Hatada Shigeo. *Nihon no shōrai to Nikkan kaidan: Porarisu dankai de no Nikkan no shomondai.* Tokyo: Gakushūnotomo, 1963.

Terao Gorō, Noguchi Hajime, and Hatada Shigo. *Watashitachi no seikatsu to Nikkan kaidan.* Tokyo: Nihon Chōsen Kenkyūjo, 1962.

Terry, Edith. *How Asia Got Rich: Japan, China, and the Asian Miracle.* New York: M. E. Sharpe, 2002.

Third World Studies Center, University of Philippines, in cooperation with the Pacific Asia Resources Center Research Team. "TNE Control of the Philippine Banana Industry." *AMPO* 13, no. 3 (1981): 2–61.

Tokuoka Takao. "Bankoku." In "Tokuhain hōkoku: Ajia de kirawareru Nihonjin 'ierō Yankī,' 'shinryakusha,'" special issue, *Ekonomisuto,* December 20, 1969, 153–55.

———. *Ierō Yankī: Ogoreru Nihonjin e no kokuhatsujō.* Tokyo: Ēru Shuppansha, 1970.

"Tokushū Nihon to Chōsen: Daishinsai Chōsenjin junan 40 shūnen ni yosete." *Rekishi hyōron* 157 (1963): 1–77.

Tōma Seita. *Higashi Ajia sekai no keisei.* Tokyo: Shunjūsha, 1966.

Tomiyama Taeko. "Gakuen funsō kara onna to bijutsu e no toi." In *Zenkyōtō kara ribu e: jūgoshi nōto sengohen,* edited by Onnatachi no ima o tō kai, 304–8. Tokyo: Inpakuto Shuppankai, 1996.

———. "Hidane to naru mono: 'Shibarareta te no inori' ni yosete." *Sekai* 350 (1978): 350–54.

Tomiyama Taeko, Yuasa Rei, Matsui Yayori, Yamaguchi Akiko, Andō Misako, Gotō Shōko, and Kaji Etsuko. "Ajia to josei kaihō: Watashitachi no sengen." *Ajia to josei kaihō* (preliminary founding issue) 1 (1977): 1–2.

Tōyama Shigeki. "Chōsen ni taisuru minzokuteki henken ni tsuite." *Rekishi hyōron* 152 (1963): 1–5.

———. "Higashi Ajia no rekishizō no kentō: Kingendai shi no tachiba kara." *Rekishigaku kenkyū* 281 (1963): 19–23.

———. "'Kindai' mondai teiki." In *Sekai shi ni okeru Ajia: 1953-nendo rekishigaku kenkyūkai taikai hōkoku*, edited by Rekishigaku Kenkyūkai, 118–19. Tokyo: Iwanami Shoten, 1953.

———. "Kindai shi kara mita Higashi Ajia." *Rekishigaku kenkyū* 276 (1963): 70–72.

———. "Sekai shi ni okeru chiiki shi no mondaiten." *Rekishigaku kenkyū* 301 (1965): 1–7.

———. *Sengo no rekishigaku to rekishi ninshiki*. Tokyo: Iwanami Shoten, 1968.

Tsuchiya Kenji et al., eds. *Kōza gendai Ajia*. 4 vols. Tokyo: Tokyo Daigaku Shuppankai, 1994.

Tsukiyama Toshiaki. *Mujitsu! Ri Chin'u: Komatsugawa jiken to makanaifugoroshi*. Tokyo: San'ichi Shobō, 1982.

Tsumura Takashi. "Aru 'Ihōjin' no shi." In Tsumura Takashi, *Tamashii ni fureru kakumei*, 249–52. Tokyo: Rain Shuppan, 1970.

———. "Nihonjin no minzokuteki sekinin." In Tsumura Takashi, *Rekishi no dakkan: Gendai nashonarizumu hihan no ronri*, 107–25. Tokyo: Serika Shobō, 1972.

———. "Nyūkan taisei funsai! Ajia jinmin to no gutaiteki rentai o!" In Tsumura Takashi, *Tamashii ni fureru kakumei*, 263–67. Tokyo: Rain Shuppan, 1970.

———. "Nyūkan tōsō ni okeru tokushusei to shukansei." In Tsumura Takashi, *Tamashii ni fureru kakumei*, 286–96. Tokyo: Rain Shuppan, 1970.

———. "Radikarizumu to nashonarizumu." In Tsumura Takashi, *Rekishi no dakkan: Gendai nashonarizumu hihan no ronri*, 173–94. Tokyo: Serika Shobō, 1972.

———. "'Sengo' no kokufuku to wa nani ka." In Tsumura Takashi, *Rekishi no dakkan: Gendai nashonarizumu hihan no ronri*, 57–73. Tokyo: Serika Shobō, 1972.

———. "'Tasha' toshite no Ajia." In Tsumura Takashi, *Rekishi no dakkan: Gendai nashonarizumu hihan no ronri*, 39–56. Tokyo: Serika Shobō, 1972.

———. *Warera no uchinaru sabetsu*. Tokyo: San'ichi Shobō, 1970.

Tsuneishi Keiichi. "Unit 731 and the Japanese Imperial Army's Biological Warfare Program." Translated by John Junkerman. *Asia-Pacific Journal—Japan Focus* 3, no. 11 (2005). https://apjjf.org/-Tsuneishi-Keiichi/2194/article.html.

Tsurumi Shunsuke. "Chishikijin no sensō sekinin." In Tsurumi Shunsuke, *Tsurumi Shunsuke chosakushū*, vol. 5: *Jiron, essei*, 9–16. Tokyo: Chikuma Shobō, 1976.

———. "Jijitsu o mae ni shite omō koto: 'Chūgokujin kyōsei renkō' no jijitsu o tsutae, sono imi o kangaeru koto ga kokka hihan no shiten ni natte iku." *Ushio* 153 (1972): 90–102.

———. "Kin Tō-ki ni totte Nihon wa dōiu kuni ka." In Tsurumi Shunsuke, *Tsurumi Shunsuke chosakushū*, vol. 5: *Jiron, essei*, 109–10. Tokyo: Chikuma Shobō, 1976.

———. "Nihon no naka no kokkyō: Ōmura shūyōjo no kabe no naka e." In *"Beheiren nyūsu" gappon shukusatsuban 1965–1974*, edited by Beheiren: "Betonamu ni Heiwa o!" Shimin Rengō, 228. Tokyo: Beheiren: "Betonamu ni Heiwa o!" Shimin Rengō, 1974.

———. "Sensō to Nihonjin." In Tsurumi Shunsuke, *Tsurumi Shunsuke chosakushū*, vol. 5: *Jiron, essei*, 134–42. Tokyo: Chikuma Shobō, 1976.

———. *Tsurumi Shunsuke shū*, vol. 4: *Tenkō kenkyū*. Tokyo: Chikuma Shobō, 1991.

Tsurumi Shunsuke et al. "Hansen e no ronri to kōdō (tōron)." *Bungei* 5, no. 10 (1966): 221–80.

Tsurumi Shunsuke, Ueno Chizuko, and Oguma Eiji. *Sensō ga nokoshita mono: Tsurumi Shunsuke ni sengo sedai ga kiku*. Tokyo: Shin'yōsha, 2004.

Tsurumi Yoshiyuki. "1970-nen to Beheiren: Tōitsu ni tsuite no shiteki oboegaki." In *Tsurumi Yoshiyuki chosakushū*, vol. 2: *Beheiren*, edited by Yoshikawa Yūichi, 156–68. Tokyo: Misuzu Shobō, 2002.

———, ed. *Ajia kara no chokugen*. Tokyo: Kōdansha, 1974.

———. *Ajia o shiru tame ni*. In *Tsurumi Yoshiyuki chosakushū*, vol. 4: *Shūdatsu no kōzu*, edited by Nakamura Hisashi, 245–65. Tokyo: Misuzu Shobō, 1999.

———. "Ajia wa naze mazushiika." In *Tsurumi Yoshiyuki chosakushū*, vol. 4: *Shūdatsu no kōzu*, edited by Nakamura Hisashi, 195–218. Tokyo: Misuzu Shobō, 1999.

———. *Ajia wa naze mazushiinoka*. In *Tsurumi Yoshiyuki chosakushū*, vol. 4: *Shūdatsu no kōzu*, edited by Nakamura Hisashi, 1–191. Tokyo: Misuzu Shobō, 1999.

———. *Ajiajin to Nihonjin*. Tokyo: Shōbunsha, 1980.

———. "Atarashii Ajia gaku no kokoromi." In *Tsurumi Yoshiyuki chosakushū*, vol. 3: *Ajia to no deai*, edited by Yoshikawa Yūichi, 335–38. Tokyo: Misuzu Shobō, 2002.

———. "Banana: Kūbekika kuwazubekika." In *Tsurumi Yoshiyuki chosakushū*, vol. 6: *Banana*, edited by Murai Yoshinori, 137–42. Tokyo: Misuzu Shobō, 1998.

———. *Banana to Nihonjin: Firipin nōen to shokutaku no aida*. In *Tsurumi Yoshiyuki chosakushū*, vol. 6: *Banana*, edited by Murai Yoshinori, 1–134. Tokyo: Misuzu Shobō, 1998.

———. "Betonamu sensō to Nihon tokuju sono hoka no mondai." In *"Beheiren nyūsu" gappon shukusatsuban 1965–1974*, edited by Beheiren: "Betonamu ni Heiwa o!" Shimin Rengō, 16. Tokyo: Beheiren: "Betonamu ni Heiwa o!" Shimin Rengō, 1974.

———. "Chizu o egaku." In *Tsurumi Yoshiyuki chosakushū*, vol. 4: *Shūdatsu no kōzu*, edited by Nakamura Hisashi, 345–81. Tokyo: Misuzu Shobō, 1999.

———. "Chizu wa ugoku." In *Tsurumi Yoshiyuki chosakushū*, vol. 3: *Ajia to no deai*, edited by Yoshikawa Yūichi, 352–62. Tokyo: Misuzu Shobō, 2002.

———. "Firipin shi kara Nihon shi o miru to." In *Tsurumi Yoshiyuki chosakushū*, vol. 3: *Ajia to no deai*, edited by Yoshikawa Yūichi, 311–13. Tokyo: Misuzu Shobō, 2002.

———. "'Hachigatsu jūgonichi' fukken no tame ni." In *Tsurumi Yoshiyuki chosakushū*, vol. 2: *Beheiren*, edited by Yoshikawa Yūichi, 80–82. Tokyo: Misuzu Shobō, 2002.

———. "Hachigatsu jūgonichi kara kieta Ajia." In *Tsurumi Yoshiyuki chosakushū*, vol. 2: *Beheiren*, edited by Yoshikawa Yūichi, 208–10. Tokyo: Misuzu Shobō, 2002.

———. "'Hankenryoku no shisō to kōdō' (Morita Shotenban) Atogaki." In *Tsurumi Yoshiyuki chosakushū*, vol. 2: *Beheiren*, edited by Yoshikawa Yūichi, 173–76. Tokyo: Misuzu Shobō, 2002.

———. *Mangurōbu no numachi de: Tōnan Ajia tōsho bunkaron e no sasoi*. In *Tsurumi Yoshiyuki chosakushū*, vol. 7: *Mangurōbu*, edited by Hanasaki Kōhei, 1–275. Tokyo: Misuzu Shobō, 1999.

———. "Mienai banana: Nihon to Firipin o musubu mono." In *Tsurumi Yoshiyuki chosakushū*, vol. 6: *Banana*, edited by Murai Yoshinori, 155–60. Tokyo: Misuzu Shobō, 1998.

————. "Minkangaku ni tsuite no danshō." In *Tsurumi Yoshiyuki chosakushū*, vol. 7: *Mangurōbu*, edited by Hanasaki Kōhei, 381–88. Tokyo: Misuzu Shobō, 1999.

————. *Namako no me*. Tokyo: Chikuma Shobō, 1993.

————. "Ne toshite no shimin shūdan: Totonoioeta tabidachi no tame ni." In *Tsurumi Yoshiyuki chosakushū*, vol. 2: *Beheiren*, edited by Yoshikawa Yūichi, 188–200. Tokyo: Misuzu Shobō, 2002.

————. "Nihon kokumin toshite no dannen: 'Kokka' no kokufuku o ika ni heiwa undō e kesshū suru ka." In *Tsurumi Yoshiyuki chosakushū*, vol. 2: *Beheiren*, edited by Yoshikawa Yūichi, 83–98. Tokyo: Misuzu Shobō, 2002.

————. "Nihon to Ajia no hachigatsu jūgonichi." In *Tsurumi Yoshiyuki chosakushū*, vol. 2: *Beheiren*, edited by Yoshikawa Yūichi, 222–28. Tokyo: Misuzu Shobō, 2002.

————. "Nihon-gata demo Chūgoku-gata demo naku." In *Tsurumi Yoshiyuki chosakushū*, vol. 3: *Ajia to no deai*, edited by Yoshikawa Yūichi, 331–34. Tokyo: Misuzu Shobō, 2002.

————. "Ochita rekishi no yukue." In *Tsurumi Yoshiyuki chosakushū*, vol. 3: *Ajia to no deai*, edited by Yoshikawa Yūichi, 12–23. Tokyo: Misuzu Shobō, 2002.

————. "Shinraikan no ketsujo o umeru tame ni." In *Tsurumi Yoshiyuki chosakushū*, vol. 2: *Beheiren*, edited by Yoshikawa Yūichi, 102–4. Tokyo: Misuzu Shobō, 2002.

————. *Tōnan Ajia o shiru: Watashi no hōhō*. Tokyo: Iwanami Shoten, 1995.

————. "Watashi no kanshin." In *Tsurumi Yoshiyuki chosakushū*, vol. 3: *Ajia to no deai*, edited by Yoshikawa Yūichi, 59–64. Tokyo: Misuzu Shobō, 2002.

Tsurumi Yoshiyuki and Katō Yūzō. "Ajia o arukinagara kangaeru." *Asahi jānaru*, January 14, 1972, 13–19.

Tsurumi Yoshiyuki and Miyauchi Ryōsuke. *Yashi no mi no Ajia gaku*. Tokyo: Komonzu, 1996.

Tsurumi Yoshiyuki and Tsuno Kaitarō. "Taidan: Ajia to Nihon 15-nen." *Shisō no kagaku* 65 (1985): 71–80.

Uehara Senroku. "Ajia no unmei." In Uehara Senroku, *Sekai shi ni okeru gendai Ajia—zōho kaitei ban*, 128–39. Tokyo: Miraisha, 1961.

————. "Ajia wa hitotsu ka." In Uehara Senroku, *Sekai shi ni okeru gendai Ajia—zōho kaitei ban*, 51–80. Tokyo: Miraisha, 1961.

————. "Gendai Ajia no rikai no tame ni." In Uehara Senroku, *Sekai shi ni okeru gendai Ajia—zōho kaitei ban*, 81–88. Tokyo: Miraisha, 1961.

————. "Sekai shi ni okeru gendai no Ajia." *Chūō kōron* 70, no. 1 (1955): 142–51.

————. "Sekai shi no kōzō to konnichi no Ajia." In Uehara Senroku, *Sekai shi ni okeru gendai Ajia—zōho kaitei ban*, 33–50. Tokyo: Miraisha, 1961.

Uehara Senroku et al. *Nihon kokumin no sekai shi*. Tokyo: Iwanami Shoten, 1960.

Uemura Kimio. "Sengo shi no naka no Ajiashugi." *Rekishigaku kenkyū* 561 (1986): 41–53.

Uemura Kunihiko. *Ajia wa "Ajiateki" ka*. Kyoto: Nakanishiya Shuppan, 2006.

Ueno Chizuko. *Ikinobiru no tame no shisō*. Tokyo: Iwanami Shoten, 2006.

————. "Sengo josei undō no chiseigaku: 'Heiwa' to 'josei' no aida." In *Sengo to iu chiseigaku*, edited by Nishikawa Yūko, 137–80. Tokyo: Tokyo Daigaku Shuppankai, 2006.

Umesao Tadao. "Bunmei no seitai shikan josetsu." *Chūō kōron* 72, no. 2 (1957): 32–49.

———. "Nihon wa Ajia no koji da." *Chisei* 3, no. 2 (1956): 174–89.

———. "Tōnan Ajia no tabi kara." *Chūō kōron* 73, no. 8 (1958): 32–48.

Usami Shō. "Ikaino no Chōsen shōnen wa watashi no Chōsenjin-kan o kaeta." In Usami Shō et al., *Nihon no naka no Chōsen*, 249–60. Tokyo: Taihei Shuppansha, 1966.

Usami Shō et al. *Nihon no naka no Chōsen*. Tokyo: Taihei Shuppansha, 1966.

Ushio, ed. "Tokubetsu kikaku: 'Dai-3 sekai' toshite no Ajia to Nihonjin—Ajia de Nihonjin wa nani o shiteiru ka. Genchi shuzai Tōnan-Ajia no hitobito 100-nin shōgen." *Ushio* 168 (1973): 84–187, 198–213, 226–34.

Utsumi Aiko. *Chōsenjin BC-kyū senpan no kiroku*. Tokyo: Keisō Shobō, 1982.

Utsumi Aiko, Ōnuma Yasuaki, Tanaka Hiroshi, and Katō Yōko. *Sengo sekinin: Ajia no manazashi ni kotaete*. Tokyo: Iwanami Shoten, 2014.

Wada Haruki. "Betonamu kaihō seiryoku no kōsei no naka de." In *"Beheiren nyūsu" gappon shukusatsuban 1965–1974*, edited by Beheiren: "Betonamu ni Heiwa o!" Shimin Rengō, 510. Tokyo: Beheiren: "Betonamu ni Heiwa o!" Shimin Rengō, 1974.

———. "Chishikijin—shimin no Nikkan rentai undō (1974–78)." In *Kin Dai-chū to Nikkan kankei: Minshushugi to heiwa no Nikkan gendai shi*, edited by Ryū Sōei, Wada Haruki, and Itō Naruhiko, 163–85. Seoul: Kim Dae-jung Presidential Library and Museum of Yonsei University, 2013.

———. "Dainiji Taisengo no Higashi Ajia: Nihon, Chōsen, Chūgoku no minshū." *Rekishigaku kenkyū* 312 (1966): 73–79.

———. "Kankoku no minshū o mitsumeru koto: Rekishi no naka kara no hansei." *Tenbō* 192 (1974): 52–65.

———. "Kichō hōkoku." In *Iwanami kōza Higashi Ajia kingendai tsūshi*, vol. 10: *Wakai to kyōryoku no mirai e 1990-nen ikō*, edited by Wada Haruki et al., 7–9. Tokyo: Iwanami Shoten, 2011.

———. "Materials Related with the Democratization Movement for Korea in Japan." In *Democratization Movement for Korea in Japan: Historical Documents and Korean Studies*, edited by Sang-young Rhyu, 35–49. Seoul: Yonsei University Press, 2007.

———. "Nikkan rentai undō no shisō to tenbō." *Sekai* 360 (1975): 52–58.

———. "Sengo no Nihonjin no hansei to rekishika." *Shisō no kagaku* 123 (1971): 97–103.

———. *Tōhoku Ajia kyōdō no ie: Shin chiikishugi sengen*. Tokyo: Heibonsha, 2003.

Wada Haruki et al., eds. *Iwanami kōza Higashi Ajia kingendai tsūshi*. 11 vols. Tokyo: Iwanami Shoten, 2010–2011.

Wada Haruki and Ishizaka Kōichi, eds. *Nihon wa shokuminchi shihai o dō kangaetekita ka: Kyōkasho ni kakarenakatta sensō, Part 26*. Tokyo: Nashinokisha, 1996.

Wada Haruki and Takasaki Sōji. *Kenshō: Nikkan kankei 60-nen shi*. Tokyo: Akaishi Shoten, 2005.

Wakamiya Yoshibumi. *Sengo 70-nen hoshu no Ajiakan*. Tokyo: Asahi Shinbun Shuppan, 2014.

Walker, Gavin. "The Accumulation of Difference and the Logic of Area." *positions* 27, no. 1 (2019): 67–98.

Watanabe, Chika. *Becoming One: Religion, Development, and Environmentalism in a Japanese NGO in Myanmar*. Honolulu: University of Hawai'i Press, 2019.

Watanabe Kazutami. <Tasha> toshite no Chōsen: Bungakuteki kōsatsu. Tokyo: Iwanami Shoten, 2003.

Weber, Torsten. Embracing "Asia" in China and Japan: Asianism Discourse and the Contest for Hegemony, 1912–1933. Cham, Switzerland: Palgrave Macmillan, 2018.

Willis, David Blake, and Stephen Murphy-Shigematsu. "Transcultural Japan: Metamorphosis in the Cultural Borderlands and Beyond." In Transcultural Japan: At the Borderlands of Race, Gender, and Identity, edited by David Blake Willis and Stephen Murphy-Shigematsu, 3–44. London: Routledge, 2008.

World Bank. The East Asian Miracle: Economic Growth and Public Policy. Oxford: Oxford University Press, 1993.

Yamaguchi Akiko. "Kankō baishun hantai undō o megutte." In Zenkyōtō kara ribu e: Jūgoshi nōto sengohen, edited by Onnatachi no Ima o Tō Kai, 336–39. Tokyo: Inpakuto Shuppankai, 1996.

———. "Kankoku no josei-tachi no uttae: Baishun kankō no sokuji chūshi o!" Ajia josei kōryūshi kenkyū 14 (1973): 557.

———. "Kankoku no kirisutosha to no majiwari no naka de." In Shiryo—sei shinryaku o kokuhatsu-suru: Kīsen kankō, edited by Kīsen Kankō ni Hantai suru Onna-tachi no Kai, 34. Tokyo: Kīsen Kankō ni Hantai suru Onna-tachi no Kai, 1974.

———. "Watashi to Ajia." Ajia josei kōryūshi kenkyū 9 (1971). In Ajia josei kōryū shi kenkyū zen-18-gō: 1967-nen 11-gatsu—1977-nen 2-gatsu, edited by Yamazaki Tomoko and Kami Shōichirō, 334–35. Kamakura, Japan: Minato no Hito, 2004.

Yamakage, Susumu. "Japan's National Security and Asia-Pacific's Regional Institutions in the Post-Cold War Era." In Network Power: Japan and Asia, edited by Peter J. Katzenstein and Takashi Shiraishi, 275–305. Ithaca, NY: Cornell University Press, 1997.

Yamamuro Shin'ichi. "Higashi Ajia ni okeru kyōdōtai to kūkan no isō." Kan: Rekishi—kankyō—bunmei 35 (2008): 189–201.

———. "'Ta ni shite ichi' no chitsujo genri to Nihon no sentaku." In "Ajiateki kachi" to wa nanika, edited by Aoki Tamotsu and Saeki Keishi, 43–63. Tokyo: TBS-Britannica, 1998.

Yamanouchi, Yasushi. "Total War and System Integration." In Total War and Modernization, edited by Yasushi Yamanouchi, J. Victor Koschmann, and Ryuichi Narita, 1–39. Ithaca, NY: Cornell University East Asia Program, 1998.

Yamashita Masao et al. "Tōnan Ajia no naka no Nihon: 'Iya na Nihonjin' to wa meiwaku senban." Sekai shūhō, April 21, 1970, 90–97.

Yamazaki Tomoko. Ai to senketsu: Ajia josei kōryū shi. Tokyo: Kōbunsha, 1985.

———. "Ajia josei kōryū shi kenkyū kai no kaisan to 'Ajia josei kōryū shi kenkyū' no seikaku kaihen ni tsuite." In Ajia josei kōryū shi kenkyū zen-18-gō: 1967-nen 11-gatsu—1977-nen 2-gatsu, edited by Yamazaki Tomoko and Kami Shōichirō, 441–42. Kamakura, Japan: Minato no Hito, 2004.

———. "'Ajia josei kōryū shi kenkyū' no omoide." In Ajia josei kōryū shi kenkyū zen-18-gō: 1967-nen 11-gatsu—1977-nen 2-gatsu, edited by Yamazaki Tomoko and Kami Shōichirō, 8–26. Kamakura, Japan: Minato no Hito, 2004.

Yamazaki Tomoko and Kami Shōichirō, eds. Ajia josei kōryū shi kenkyū zen-18-gō: 1967-nen 11-gatsu—1977-nen 2-gatsu. Kamakura, Japan: Minato no Hito, 2004.

Yano Noboru et al., eds. *Kōza Tōnan Ajia gaku.* 10 vols. Tokyo: Kōbundō, 1990–92.

Yano Tōru. "Kindai Nihon ni okeru nanshin no ronri." *Chūō kōron* 89, no. 1 (1974): 132–57.

Yano Tōru and Isomura Hisanori, eds. *Ajia to no taiwa.* Tokyo: Nihon Hōsō Shuppan Kyōkai, 1984.

Yokoyama Hiroaki et al., eds. *Gendai Ajia no shōzō.* 15 vols. Tokyo: Iwanami Shoten, 1996.

Yonetani Masafumi. *Ajia/Nihon: Shikō no furontia.* Tokyo: Iwanami Shoten, 2006.

Yoon Keun-cha. *Ishitsu to kyōzon: Sengo Nihon no kyōiku—shisō—minzokuron.* Tokyo: Iwanami Shoten, 1987.

———. *Nihon kokumin ron: Kindai Nihon no aidentiti.* Tokyo: Chikuma Shobō, 1997.

———. "Sengo shisō no shuppatsu to Ajiakan." In *Sengo Nihon senryō to kaikaku dai-3-kan: Sengo shisō to shakai ishiki,* edited by Nakamura Masanori, Amakawa Akira, Yoon Keun-Cha, and Igarashi Takeshi, 125–63. Tokyo: Iwanami Shoten, 1995.

Yoshida Shigeru. *Kaisō jūnen / Yoshida Shigeru.* Vol. 1. Tokyo: Shinchōsha, 1957.

Yoshida, Takashi. "A Battle over History in Japan." In *The Nanjing Massacre in History and Historiography,* edited by Joshua A. Fogel, 70–132. Berkeley: University of California Press, 2000.

———. *The Making of the "Rape of Nanking": History and Memory in Japan, China, and the United States.* New York: Oxford University Press, 2006.

Yoshimi Shun'ya. "Tsurumi Yoshiyuki to Amerika: Mōhitotsu no karuchuraru sutadīzu." *Shisō* 980 (2005): 201–23.

Yoshimi Yoshiaki. *Comfort Women: Sexual Slavery in the Japanese Military during World War II.* Translated by Suzanne O'Brien. New York: Columbia University Press, 2000.

Yoshinaga Tamegorō. "Keizai taikoku no Tōnan Ajia shinshutsu to sono ato ni kuru mono." *Shūkan anpo* 6 (1970): 18–21.

Yoshioka Shinobu. "Kaneko Mitsuharu no 'nan'yō' taiken." In *Sengo bungaku to Ajia,* edited by Nihon Ajia-Afurika Sakka Kaigi and Takasugi Haruo, 181–212. Tokyo: Mainichi Shinbunsha, 1978.

Yoshitake Teruko. "Heiwa to kokusai rentai." In *Kōdō suru onna-tachi ga hiraita michi: Mekushiko kara Nyūyōku e,* edited by Kōdō suru Kai Kirokushū Henshū Iinkai, 226–33. Tokyo: Miraisha, 1991.

Yoshiwara Toshiyuki. "The Kawasaki Steel Corporation: A Case Study of Japanese Pollution Export." *KOGAI,* Summer 1977, 12–24.

Yoshizawa Fumitoshi. *Sengo Nikkan kankei: Kokkō seijōka kōshō o megutte.* Tokyo: Kurein, 2015.

Yoshizawa Toshiharu and Akagi Osamu. "Kaisetsu." *Chūō kōron keiei mondai* 13, no. 2 (1974): 312–13.

Zachmann, Urs Matthias. "Konoe Atsumaro and the Idea of an Alliance of the Yellow Race, 1898." In *Pan Asianism: A Documentary History,* vol. 1: *1850–1920,* edited by Sven Saaler and Christopher W. A. Szpilman, 85–92. Lanham, MD: Rowman and Littlefield, 2011.

Index

Page numbers for figures are in italics.

victim consciousness, 15–17, 19, 75; 1970s movements and, 208; in environmental movement, 214; ethnic responsibility and, 103, 112; Honda Katsuichi's thinking on, 152; Oda Makoto's thinking on, 129, 131–32, 133; Vietnam War and, 134, 138; Waseda Declaration criticism of, 172; in West Germany, 11, 19, 81; women activists and, 217, 221–23. *See also* Oda Makoto
Vietnam War, 24, 25, 121–22, 163, 222, 364, 369, 371; Honda Katsuichi's writings on, 131, 150, 152; Japanese complicity in, 130–32, 179; Kim Dong-hee and, 161–63; opposition to, 124, 130–31, 133, 168; Tsurumi Yoshi-yuki and, 156–58; women activists and, 221, 222. *See also* Beheiren; Honda Katsuichi; Oda Makoto; Tsurumi Yoshiyuki; United States of America
Violence Against Women in War—Network Japan (VA WW—Net Japan), 311

Wada Haruki: anti-Vietnam War activism, 133; Asian Women's Fund involvement, 314; common house of Northeast Asia idea, 301, 345–46, 349; critique of progressive historiography, 145–46; on failed reconciliation with Asia, 146; on Kim Chi-ha, 238–39, 240; Kim Dae-jung support, 233; movement for official war apology, 251, 259, 312–13; Nikkanren involvement, 236
Wadatsumi-kai. *See* Memorial Society for the Soldiers Killed in the War
war, first Sino-Japanese (1894–95), 54, 96, 139, 147, 149
war crimes, 17, 35–36, 44, 150, 255–56, 315
war defeat, 1–2; by Asian countries, 9, 12, 35, 148; celebrated in Korea, 146; without deimperialization, 343
war responsibility, 2, 12, 19, 358, 362, 368–70; Asia and, 18, 19, 20, 27, 77;

colonial empire and, 91, 102, 110; common house of Northeast Asia idea and, 345; ethnic responsibility and, 84, 103, 111, 113; human rights and, 248, 260; *minzoku* discourse and, 47; postwar responsibility and, 249–50, 252, 253, 255, 256, 257; reparations agreements and, 38, 185; student activists attention to, 123, 172; women activists and, 227, 231. *See also* postwar responsibility; responsibility
Waseda University, 122, 170, 172, 253
Waseda University Declaration on the 31st Anniversary of 7-7 (Marco Polo Bridge "Incident"), 171, 173, 178
WCNCC. *See* Women's Committee of the National Christian Council in Japan
Wenbin Ouyang, 140
Western civilization: Asiatic stagnation and, 39; New Asianist criticism of, 317, 321, 324, 350
white bananas, Japanese women activists as, 232
women activists, sense of perpetration, 216–17, 221, 223, 227, 231. *See also* Iijima Aiko; Matsui Yayori; sex tourism; Takahashi Kikue; Yamazaki Tomoko
Women's Committee of the National Christian Council in Japan (WCNCC), 224, 228, 234
Women's Democratic Club, 176, 221
Women's Group Opposing Kisaeng Tourism, 225
Women's International War Crimes Tribunal for the Trial of Japan's Military Sexual Slavery in Tokyo, 311–12
Women's League of the Christian Church of South Korea, 223–24
women's liberation movement, 221, 222, 223, 229
Women's University (*Onna daigaku*), 231
World Bank, 306, 327

Harvard East Asian Monographs
(most recent titles)